RAGTIME

Its History, Composers, and Music

edited by
JOHN EDWARD HASSE

SMITHSONIAN INSTITUTION

M
MACMILLAN PRESS
LONDON

First published 1985

Published by
THE MACMILLAN PRESS LTD
Houndmills, Basingstoke, Hampshire RG21 2XS
and London
Companies and representatives
throughout the world

Printed in Hong Kong

Ragtime: its history, composers and music
1. Ragtime music
I. Hasse, John
781'.572   ML3530
ISBN 0-333-40516-1

Permission to reprint the following material is gratefully acknowledged:

Euday L. Bowman, *12th Street Rag*, Copyright 1914 Renewed by Shapiro, Bernstein & Co., Inc., and Jerry Vogel Music, New York. N.Y. Used by permission.
Zez Confrey, *Coaxing the Piano*, Copyright © 1922 Jack Mills, Inc. *Dizzy Fingers*, Copyright © 1923 Jack Mills, Inc. *Kitten on the Keys*, Copyright © 1921 Jack Mills, Inc. *My Pet*, Copyright © 1921 Jack Mills, Inc. Used by permission. All rights reserved.
T. S. Eliot, excerpts from "Fragment of an Agon," in *Collected Poems 1909–1962* by T. S. Eliot, Copyright 1936 by Harcourt Brace Jovanovich, Inc.; Copyright © 1963, 1964 by T. S. Eliot. Reprinted by permission of the publisher. Also reprinted by permission of Faber and Faber Ltd. from T. S. Eliot, *Collected Poems 1909–1962*.
Jesse Greer, *Flapperette*, Copyright © 1926 Mills Music, Inc. Used by permission. All rights reserved.
Scott Joplin, *Euphonic Sounds*, Copyright © 1909 by Mills Music Co. © renewed 1936. *Magnetic Rag*, Copyright © 1914 by Mills Music, Inc. © renewed 1938. Used by permission. All rights reserved.
Joseph Lamb, *Arctic Sunset*, Copyright © 1960 by Mills Music, Inc. *Cottontail Rag*, Copyright © 1959 by Mills Music, Inc. *Hot Cinders*, Copyright © 1959 by Mills Music, Inc. Used by permission. All rights reserved.
Joseph Lamb, *Top Liner Rag*, © 1916 Edwin H. Morris & Company, a division of MPL Communications, Inc. International Copyright secured. All rights reserved. Used by permission.
Vee Lawnhurst, *Keyboard Konversation*, Copyright 1923© by Jack Mills, Inc. Used by permission. All rights reserved.
Harold Potter, *Rippling Waters*, Copyright © 1923 by Jack Mills, Inc. Used by permission. All rights reserved.
James Scott, *Prosperity Rag*, © 1916 Edwin H. Morris & Company, a division of MPL Communications, Inc. © renewed 1944 Edwin H. Morris & Company, a division of MPL Communications, Inc. International Copyright secured. All rights reserved. Used by permission.

The piano figure ▐ᴅₓ is copyright © 1985 by John Edward Hasse. All rights reserved.

Contents

THE HISTORY OF RAGTIME

MAJOR RAGTIME FIGURES

THE MUSIC OF RAGTIME

Preface

When I began work on this book, *The Sting* — its soundtrack resonating with Scott Joplin rags — was helping to create the greatest boom in ragtime's popularity since the music's heyday in the early decades of the twentieth century. At the time of *The Sting,* only a few books on ragtime were available. I had been performing ragtime for about five years, and was overtaken by a desire to know more about this infectious music. As a bibliophile, I knew that a number of first-class articles on ragtime had been published in widely scattered sources. I decided to gather these articles together, in one volume, as a "ragtime reader."

I soon became aware, however, of gaps in existing scholarship on ragtime: such topics as ragtime songs and ragtime banjo had not been adequately covered. So I invited leading ragtime authorities to contribute chapters. I also determined to uncover new information for the book. To enhance its value as a reference tool, I traveled to libraries to unearth vintage photographs, old articles for the bibliography, and data for the other lists that support the text.

Since this project began, many new recordings and books on ragtime have appeared, including the noteworthy *Ragtime: A Musical and Cultural History* by Edward A. Berlin, *Scott Joplin* by James Haskins, *Rags and Ragtime* by David A. Jasen and Trebor Jay Tichenor, and *This Is Ragtime* by Terry Waldo. The present volume has been enriched by the continuing appearance of new material. I am heartened to witness the advances in ragtime scholarship.

This book is intended for both layman and specialist. The introduction and most of the chapters assume no technical knowledge of music on the part of the reader. Some chapters in part three, "The Music of Ragtime," however, will be made more accessible by such a knowledge.

The goals of this book are several. Its main purpose is to provide an overall introduction to the history, leading practitioners, and music of ragtime. Specifically, the book aims to summarize ragtime's history and revivals, profile its most significant composers, explore the heated debate ragtime engendered, and track ragtime's manifestations in other musical styles and genres. The book also undertakes to explain succinctly the musical elements of ragtime, especially its rhythms, and to survey the music of several of its top composers. To provide more historical context than is often supplied in ragtime studies, the introduction treats the relationship of ragtime and the piano, and furnishes a chronology of developments in politics, world affairs, the arts, and society during each year of the Ragtime Era.

A second aim is to fill in gaps in our knowledge of this important American style. Heretofore, ragtime songs, ragtime piano rolls, the role of women in ragtime, ragtime-derived novelty piano, band and orchestral ragtime, and the influence of ragtime on country music were little known. To fill the void, leading experts on these topics have written chapters expressly for this book.

A third aim is to broaden the current conceptions of ragtime. Ragtime was not just slumbound black "perfessers" beating out rhythms on tacky pianos in Saint Louis. Ragtime was not just the extraordinary appearance of a "black Chopin" like Scott Joplin. Ragtime was piano music, surely, but also songs, and music for banjo, band, and orchestra. Ragtime was produced by blacks and whites, but certainly most of the consumers were white, and most of the consumers of the sheet music were probably women. Ragtime was played as written and also used as the basis for improvisation. Ragtime was performed in the salon as well as the saloon, before royalty as well as Rough Riders. Ragtime spread throughout rural and urban America, and even to Europe and the Antipodes. It penetrated popular song, then-emerging jazz, novelty instrumental works, white country music, Western art ("classical") music, and even folk music.

A fourth aim is to assist the reader interested in further reading, listening, or performing. To that end, extensive lists of books, articles, recordings, and ragtime music folios are included in the back of the book.

I am pleased to restore to print and to bring to wider circulation some classic articles on ragtime, such as Guy Waterman's influential essays from the 1950s. These and the other reprinted chapters have withstood advances in ragtime scholarship surprisingly well. I am equally pleased that more than a dozen of today's leading ragtime experts have agreed to contribute new chapters to this book.

Each author expresses his own perspective, of course, and the reader will find no unanimity on such recurring issues as: What is ragtime? Does ragtime include songs? How should ragtime be performed? Is it valid to "jazz" a rag? A consensus of opinion could not be expected from twenty-one experts writing over a thirty-year period. I hope, however, that from the diversity of viewpoints, approaches, and subjects, the reader will gain a fuller understanding of the complex music we call ragtime. While each author is responsible for his text and musical examples, I am solely responsible for the selection and captioning of the photographs that appear throughout the book.

A single book cannot attempt to consider the complete range of topics in ragtime. Subjects awaiting future exploration include ragtime dancing, Ragtime-Era performance practice, black country ragtime, and ragtime abroad. If this book stimulates research into such topics, that would be ample reward for my work as editor.

JOHN EDWARD HASSE

Acknowledgments

Normally the editor of an anthology does not need to make many acknowledgments. This book is different because my own chapters and the reference lists entailed considerable original research, which was aided by many individuals. I undertook the research to provide scholarly under-pinnings in the form of the bibliography, the listing of folios, the list of rags by women composers, the checklist of compositions cited, and the photographs, as well as to gather materials for the introduction and the several chapters which carry my byline.

Special thanks go to two people. Frank J. Gillis, Director Emeritus of the Indiana University Archives of Traditional Music, gave freely and generously his time, counsel, library, and friendship. Judith McCulloh, editor at the University of Illinois Press, lent encouragement at the outset and provided sound advice throughout the project.

I wish to thank Max Morath, Michael Montgomery, Trebor Jay Tichenor, and especially Edward A. Berlin—all astute scholars of ragtime—for sharing unselfishly their remarkable knowledge and collections. Richard Zimmerman graciously supplied photographs and information from the archive of the Maple Leaf Club. Sam De Vincent offered hospitality and access to his astonishing collection of American popular sheet music. Rudi Blesh, the dean of ragtime historians, gave the project his blessing and welcomed me into his summer home for a series of interviews. In Washington, D.C., family friend Virginia Pinney graciously provided lodging and meals while I researched at the Library of Congress. At the Library, Gillian B. Anderson, Joseph C. Hickerson, Jon W. Newsom, William Parsons, and Wayne D. Shirley provided help. Also in Washington, Thornton Hagert opened his impressive private archives to my perusal.

I also traveled to use the holdings of: the Archive of Popular American Music at UCLA, the William Hogan Archive of New Orleans Jazz, the Newberry Library, the Missouri Historical Society, and the Missouri State Historical Society; the public libraries of Boston, Chicago, Cincinnati, Kansas City (Missouri), New York City, Saint Louis, and Sedalia; and the libraries of Columbia University, Harvard University, the University of Iowa, the University of Illinois, the University of Minnesota, the University of South Dakota, and Washington University in Saint Louis. I am grateful for the cooperation of the Archives of Traditional Music, the Lilly Library, and the Inter-Library Loan Office, all of Indiana University. The Carleton College Library, the Center for Research Libraries, the Cleveland Public Library, the Country Music Foundation Library and Media Center, the Ohio Historical Society, and the Kansas City, Kansas, Public Library provided assistance by mail.

During my travels, family members Ellen and John Buchanan, Paul and

Linda Hasse, Stanley R. and Ann Nelson, and Trudy Nepstad provided a "home away from home." My mother, the late Gladys Johnson Hasse, gave the project encouragement and shared her keen insights as a writer. Nancy E. Rallis supplied warm support.

In the early stages of my research, Richard B. Allen, William Long, W. K. McNeil, William Russell, Butch Thompson, and Martin T. Williams lent counsel. The offices of former United States Senators Birch Bayh and George McGovern helped in obtaining materials from the Library of Congress. Reba Berlin, Margaret Hasse, and H. James Stedronsky secured information from distant libraries. David N. Baker, Jr., Chairman of the Jazz Studies Department at the Indiana University School of Music, contributed a number of ideas as well as his genial backing. Anne S. Arenstein, Simon J. Bronner, John S. Lucas, Richard S. Sarason, Joseph R. Scotti, Richard K. Spottswood, and Gary Stanton kindly reviewed portions of the manuscript.

For their fine assistance, I wish to thank Karen Sherry and Walter Wager of ASCAP, Russell Sanjek of BMI, Daniel L. Gendasen of Belwin/Mills Publishing Corporation, and Bernard Kalban of Edward B. Marks Music Corporation, as well as to acknowledge the cooperation of CBS Records, Charles Hansen Publications, County Records, Folkways Records, and Stomp Off Records.

Thanks also go to the following for their kind help: Elliott Adams, William Albright, Andrew Balterman, Malcolm E. Bessom, Charles L. Boilés, Jr., William Bolcom, Erika Brady, Jared Carter, Dominique-René de Lerma, Lawrence Denton, the late Richard M. Dorson, Thomas Glastras, Solomon Goodman, Lawrence Gushee, Beverly A. Hamer, the late Alonzo Hayden, Frank L. Himpsl, David A. Jasen, Edythe Willard Johnson, Eva Johnson, Leslie Carole Johnson, Arthur LaBrew, Amelia Lamb, Paul Lasswell, Vera Brodsky Lawrence, Katherine M. Longyear, Joel Markowitz, Portia K. Maultsby, Frankie MacCormick, Turk Murphy, Bruno Nettl, Marilyn Niebergall, James and Elizabeth Nolan, John W. "Knocky" Parker, the late Abe Olman, Johannes Riedel, Patricia Riesenmann, Gertrude Robinson, Harvey N. Roehl, Samuel R. Rosen, Jake Siragusa, Eileen Southern, Louise S. Spear, John Steiner, Ruth M. Stone, George Temple, the late Joan Aufderheide Thompson, Terry Waldo, Guy Waterman, Richard Wentworth, Stephen Wild, Duke Woods, Tex Wyndham, and Nathan B. Young.

Several of the chapters have benefited from the keen editing skills of Caroline Card and Ann McMillan. Ronald Riddle, a meticulous editor and scholar's gentleman, volunteered to compile the index. The book itself would not have been possible without the faith of Ken Stuart, former Editorial Director of Schirmer Books. This book is much the better for the sound judgment of my editors at Schirmer, Abbie Meyer and especially Michael Sander, to whom I am also grateful for their flexibility and patience.

That so many people gave willingly of their time, knowledge, and materials was heartening to me, and served to maintain my faith in my fellow man. To those individuals cited above, to those I have forgotten to mention, to my resolute and talented contributors, and, most of all, to those gifted musicians who first created ragtime, goes my profound and eternal gratitude.

Ragtime: From the Top

John Edward Hasse

This chapter is intended to serve as both a general introduction to the book and an overview of ragtime. Topics include ragtime's origins, nature, appeal, repertory, and significance; the Ragtime Era; the piano and ragtime; and a thumbnail history of the style. Thirteen tables support the text.

Ragtime! The music that for two decades captivated a nation, set its toes to tapping, its feet to dancing, its fingers to playing, its blood to rushing. Ragtime! The name that has become a metaphor for an era. The very word evokes images of America at the dawn of the twentieth century. Images of dancers prancing to the syncopated stylings of saloon "ticklers." Of Sunday band concerts in the city square, featuring music of the "Red Back Book." Of hundreds of thousands of parlor pianists struggling to master the *Dill Pickles* and *Maple Leaf* rags.[1] Of pianolas pounding out ragged rhythms. Of charcoal-skinned "perfessors" playing in high-class hotels bedecked with potted palms and lazily turning ceiling fans.

Ragtime is one of the first truly American musics, and it is not quite like any other American style. It is a music of toe-tapping vitality, yet often of fragile beauty and subtle rhythmic complexity. Though based on orthodox harmonies, ragtime is never fully predictable. It has an immediate and direct appeal. Its charm and allure transcend the time and place of the Ragtime Era.

Ragtime is a music of diversity within similarity, of expressivity within a set of conventions, of apparent simplicity but often real complexity, of seeming ease of performance but actual difficulty.

1

The Nature of Ragtime

What is ragtime? Though it cannot be defined precisely, it can be described as a dance-based American vernacular music, featuring a syncopated melody against an even accompaniment. It arose in the 1890s and faded by the late 1910s.

There are four main types of ragtime: (1) instrumental rags, (2) ragtime songs, (3) ragtime or syncopated waltzes, and (4) "ragging" of classics and other preexisting pieces.

Instrumental Rag. While "ragtime" is a broad style, "rag" or "piano rag" is a much more specific term. A "rag" is an instrumental composition, usually for the piano, in duple meter, with a syncopated melody against a regular, *oom-pah* or march-style, bass. A rag comprises a number of self-contained sections or strains, usually sixteen measures each, which are often repeated. A typical formal structure of a piano rag is **AA BB A CC DD**, each letter indicating a separate strain with its own melody, rhythm, and harmony. Rags generally used conventional European harmonies. (The musical elements of rags are discussed in greater detail in Roland Nadeau's chapter in this book.)

Ragtime reached its highest musical development as an instrumental form. The public apparently liked ragtime songs better than piano rags, but the best piano rags have better stood the tests of time and modern critical judgment. The rags of Scott Joplin and his peers were frequently more syncopated and musically elaborate than ragtime songs. For these reasons, modern interest in ragtime has centered on instrumental rags.

It was rhythm that gave ragtime its musical distinctiveness and much of its appeal. (The syncopations of instrumental rags are explained in Frank J. Gillis's chapter in this book.) Rag rhythms underwent changes as the music developed. As Berlin shows, untied syncopations (Example 1) predominated through about 1900, after which tied syncopations (Example 2) came to dominate.[2]

Example 1. Untied syncopations.   **Example 2.** Tied syncopation.

Another change was the increasing use of a melodic motif sometimes called "secondary rag"[3] (Example 3). Table 1 lists a selection of rags incorporating this motif. Its use after 1906 was so frequent that it became a cliché.

Example 3. Charles L. Johnson, *Dill Pickles,* **A** strain, measures 1–2, melody line.

Table 1
Selected Piano Rags Containing "Secondary Rag" Motifs (1897–1917)

YEAR	TITLE	COMPOSER
1897	*Roustabout Rag*	Paul Sarebresole
1902	*Levee Rag*	Charles Mullen
1905	*The Cannon Ball*	Joseph Northrup, arr. Thomas Confare
	Peaches and Cream	Percy Wenrich
1906	*Dill Pickles*	Charles L. Johnson
1908	*Black and White Rag*	George Botsford
1909	*Pork and Beans*	Theron C. Bennett
1910	*Grizzly Bear Rag*	George Botsford
	Red Pepper: A Spicy Rag	Henry Lodge
	Spaghetti Rag	George Lyons and Bob Yosco
1910s	*Bees and Honey*	Les C. Copeland
1911	*Down Home Rag*	Wilbur Sweatman
	Honeysuckle Rag	George Botsford
1912	*Slippery Elm Rag*	Clarence Woods
1913	*Crazy Bone Rag*	Charles L. Johnson
	Hungarian Rag	Julius Lenzberg
	Incandescent Rag	George Botsford
	Lion Tamer Rag	Mark Janza
1914	*Hot House Rag*	Paul Pratt
	12th Street Rag	Euday L. Bowman
1916	*Shamrock Rag*	Euday L. Bowman
1917	*Shave 'em Dry*	Sam Wishnuff

To the Western ear, ragtime rhythms sound like syncopations or dislocations of the pulse, but they may also be perceived as on-beat, irregular rhythms, typical of much African music. West African music, a seminal root of Afro-American music, including ragtime, is characterized by alternate groups of two and three beats or pulses, sometimes referred to as "additive" rhythms, in contrast to the equal-beat structure of most European-American music. In this light, Joplin's *Original Rags* (1899) and *The Ragtime Dance* (1906) take on a different perspective:[4]

Example 4. Scott Joplin, *Original Rags,* **A** strain, measures 1–2.

Example 5. Scott Joplin, *The Ragtime Dance,* **A** strain, measures 1–2.

From this point of view, ragtime rhythms do not result from "playing with the time" of the melody; rather, they are fundamental to the very conception of the melody.

Ragtime Song. The second type of ragtime, the ragtime song, evolved from syncopated "coon songs" of the late 1890s. The word "ragtime" was, however, so marketable that it became widely applied to songs that were not syncopated or were only lightly syncopated. The label was also applied to songs whose only connection with ragtime was the mention of it in the lyrics. Edward Berlin notes in his chapter, "Ragtime Songs," that with the tremendous popularity of *Alexander's Ragtime Band* in the early 1910s the word "ragtime" came increasingly to mean a rhythmic, but not necessarily syncopated, popular song.

Ragtime Waltz. The ragtime or syncopated waltz has been heretofore overlooked by writers, probably because it was a minor genre. These waltzes are, like rags, multisectional pieces usually for piano solo, with a syncopated right hand played against a recurring left-hand pattern. The greatest difference, of course, is the meter: The waltzes are in $\frac{3}{4}$ meter, while most rags are written in $\frac{2}{4}$. Because of the metrical differences, the piano rag's forward propulsion is noticeably lacking in the waltzes. Consequently, ragtime waltzes never became widely popular.

Table 2 lists representative ragtime waltzes. The most enduring works of this type were written by Scott Joplin (*Pleasant Moments* and *Bethena*). The most prolific publishing center was Indianapolis, which produced several dozen syncopated waltzes of a decidedly commercial bent.[5]

"Ragging" Existing Music. A fourth type of ragtime was "ragging" of classics or other preexisting music. Mendelssohn's "Spring Song" and "Wedding March" and Rubinstein's "Melody in F" were among the favorite classics for "ragging."[6] To "rag" is to syncopate the melody of nonsyncopated work. This technique, which predates the first publication of rags by several decades, was a common performance practice of pianists. Most of this type of ragtime, like most modern jazz improvisations on existing popular songs, was probably never written down or recorded. However, some instructive examples of "ragging" survive, such as the piano rolls *Lucy's Sextette: Ragtime Travesty on the "Sextette" from "Lucia"* (by Harry L. Alford) and *Misery Rag: Ragtime on the "Miserere" from "Il Trovatore"* (by Carleton L. Colby).[7] Among the best-known examples in sheet music are George L. Cobb's *Russian Rag* (based on Rachmaninoff's Prelude in C-Sharp Minor) and Julius Lenzberg's Lizst-based *Hungarian Rag*. A good recorded example of "ragging" a march is Eubie Blake's rendition of Sousa's *The Stars and Stripes Forever*.[8]

Quantity of Publications. No one has made an exact count of how much ragtime sheet music was published during the Ragtime Era, but a good estimate is two to three thousand instrumental rags and a like number of ragtime songs. Perhaps fewer than a hundred ragtime waltzes were issued. It is difficult to estimate the number of publications that "ragged" existing music, for many such pieces were not issued separately, but rather were included in instruction manuals or in music magazines.

Table 2
Selected Ragtime Waltzes

TITLE	COMPOSER	RACE	YEAR	PUBLISHER AND CITY
Bethena: A Concert Waltz	Scott Joplin	black	1905	T. Bahnsen Piano Mfg. Co., Saint Louis
Covent Garden: Ragtime Waltz	Marcella A. Henry	white?	1917	Christensen School of Popular Music, Chicago
Daughters of Dahomey: Rag-Time Waltz	Harry P. Guy	black	1902	Harry P. Guy, Detroit
Day Dreams: Syncopated Waltz	Maxwell Gordon	white?	1912	Buck & Lowney, Saint Louis
Echoes from the Snowball Club: Ragtime Waltz	Harry P. Guy	black	1898	Willard Bryant, Detroit
Elaine: Syncopated Waltz	E. J. Stark	white	1913	Jos. W. Stern & Co., New York
Floreine: Syncopated Waltz	E. J. Schuster	white	1908	Warner C. Williams, Indianapolis
Il Trovatore: Syncopated Waltz	Warner C. Williams	white	1912	Warner C. Williams, Indianapolis
Love Dreams: Syncopated Waltz	Joseph F. Cohen	white	1915	Warner C. Williams, Indianapolis
Mandy's Ragtime Waltz	J. S. Zamecnik	white	1912	Sam Fox, Cleveland
Melody in F: (Syncopated) Waltzes	Will B. Morrison	white	1913	Warner C. Williams, Indianapolis
Pleasant Moments: Rag-Time Waltz	Scott Joplin	black	1909	Seminary Music Co., New York
Star and Garter Ragtime Waltz	Axel W. Christensen	white	1910	Christensen School of Popular Music, Chicago
Tobasco: Rag-Time Waltz	Charles L. Johnson	white	1909	Jerome H. Remick, New York
True Love: Syncopated Waltz	F. Henri Klickmann	white	1913	Frank K. Root, Chicago
Wiggle-Wag Ragtime Waltz	George W. Meyer	white	1913	Geo. W. Meyer Music Co., New York

5

It is important to note that most of what we know about ragtime is derived from *published* ragtime pieces. Undoubtedly, many compositions were never notated or published. This aurally transmitted ragtime is now lost forever to the winds of time.

Origins of Ragtime

"The origin of ragtime and coon songs," wrote a black theater critic in 1911, "has taken up as much space as the race problem. Every writer has a different view and backs it up with a good argument. The Negro has figured in them all."[9] More than seventy years later historians are still arguing about the origins of ragtime, though they agree it was originally an Afro-American idiom. The evidence is mounting that ragtime was in development some ten or twenty years before the first ragtime song, so labeled, was published in 1896. The practice of ragging an existing melody, though not under that name, dates back to at least the 1870s. The Georgia-born poet Sidney Lanier (1842–1881) wrote in 1876:

> *Syncopations . . . are characteristic of negro music. I have heard negroes change a well-known melody by adroitly syncopating it . . . so as to give it a* bizarre *effect scarcely imaginable; and nothing illustrates the negro's natural gifts in the way of keeping a difficult* tempo *more clearly than his perfect execution of airs thus transformed from simple to complex accentuation.*[10]

Lanier's perceptive remarks all but establish that the first and oldest type of ragtime was the ragging of an existing piece. Only later were new compositions—banjo and piano rags and ragtime songs—written in a "raggy" style, with the syncopations an inherent, not an "added-on," part of the music.

A few years after Lanier's account, an item appeared in print that strongly suggests that ragtime was in the air in Nebraska and other parts of the Midwest. In 1888 a Nebraska banjoist, probably white, wrote to a genteel banjo music magazine requesting some music with "broken time" like the "ear-players" played.[11] The magazine was unable to accommodate him, as this syncopated proto-ragtime, which he called "broken-time," was being performed at that time entirely in the aural tradition, *i.e.,* by musicians who played by ear, rather than from notation.

In 1886, George W. Cable described the *rhythm* of a black dance in New Orleans' Congo Square as "ragged."[12] Cable's term, and particularly the use in 1888 of the phrase "broken-time" in connection with aurally transmitted banjo music, give strong support to "ragged time" as the etymology of "rag-time."

As other commentators have noted, during the 1880s popular sheet music, such as Otto Gunnar's *New Coon in Town* (1884) and George Lansing's *Darkie's Dream* (1889), began to suggest the soon-to-emerge ragtime. The trend accelerated in the early and middle 1890s as more and more pieces labeled "characteristic," "patrol," "cakewalk," and "coon song" were published. Berlin argues that *The Darkies' Patrol* of E. A. Phelps, published without a "rag" appellation in 1892 but included in the 1899 folio *Brainard's Ragtime Collection*, "qualifies as one of the earliest, if not the earliest, published rag."[13]

The first substantiated use of the words "rag" and "rag-time" occurred in August, 1896. On August 3, Ernest Hogan's song *All Coons Look Alike to Me*, with an optional chorus labeled "Negro 'Rag' Accompaniment," was copyrighted. Two days later, a copyright was filed for Witmark's edition of Ben Harney's song *You've Been a Good Old Wagon But You've Done Broke Down.* The cover claimed that Harney was the "Original Introducer to the Stage of the Now Popular 'Rag Time' in Ethiopian Song."

The geographical origins of ragtime are uncertain. The limited evidence points to both Chicago and Saint Louis. Quite possibly, syncopated music coalesced into ragtime in several places at about the same time. The World's Fair of 1893 is said to have attracted a large number of itinerant pianists who played syncopated popular music. No one has yet located documentary

A bar at Market and Centre streets, near the notorious Chestnut Valley "sporting district" of Saint Louis, ca. 1907. Tom Turpin's famous Rosebud Bar was about seven blocks up Market Street. Black ragtime thrived in this area, which employed Scott Joplin, Tom Turpin, Artie Matthews, Louis Chauvin, Arthur Marshall, Charles Thompson, and white ragtime composer Charles H. Hunter. (*John Edward Hasse collection*)

proof of early ragtime performed at the fair, but evidence points to it. Only a few years after the fair, newspaper commentators were writing that ragtime music had come onto the public scene in Chicago at about the time of the fair.[14] The respected folk song collector and scholar Natalie Curtis (1875–1921) wrote in 1912 that "it has been said that 'rag-time' first appeared in our music-halls about the time of the Chicago World's Fair."[15]

Some Ragtime-Era commentators argued that ragtime came from Saint Louis. In the following account, laced with racial stereotyping typical of the time, a writer for the *Saint Louis Post-Dispatch* recounts what appears to be a local legend—with perhaps some basis in fact—that ragtime was heard as early as 1888 in the slums of Saint Louis.

A negro woman, whose name is unknown to fame, is declared to have invented ragtime in St. Louis in 1888, in a house, now fallen, at Broadway and Clark avenue. She was as glossy black as her forbears of the Dark Continent, tall and stalwart, and rich-voiced.

It was the day of Proctor Knott, a famous racehorse, and he was the theme of the epoch-making ballad which she sang. One stanza has been preserved: "I-za a-gwine tuh Little Rock, Tuh put mah money on-a Proctuh Knott."

There were hundreds of such verses, mostly as absurd with no regard for continuity of subject, and characterized by assonance rather than rhyme. But the new thing was the strangely alluring and exciting rhythm to which they were sung, a veritable call of the wild, which mightily stirred the pulses of city-bred people.

Syncopated time, as old as music, was the means of this effect. But it was syncopated time so exaggerated and emphasized as to reveal for the first time its capacity of powerful appeal to the flesh. It soon became a fad with young men to visit the slums to hear "Mammy," as she was called, sing her new music.

"That song sounds so ragged," was the comment of one who heard the conventional rhythms being torn to tatters. And the name "ragtime" was born.

One visitor was an Englishman, connected with a theatrical troupe. He studied ragtime until he had mastered its secret, and recrossed the ocean with his find.

Two years later an Irish comedy team was playing in St. Louis, and in the audience were several St. Louisans who had heard "Mammy" sing. What was their surprise to hear in the featured song the well-known strains of the negro composition. The music took the city by storm and swept across the country.[16]

Further support for Saint Louis as the birthplace for ragtime was given by Juli Jones, a black theater critic, who wrote in 1911 that "some claimed St. Louis as the father town for ragtime; some claimed Louisville, Ky. Anyway, St. Louis turned out the first and best players."[17] Whether the idiom sprang from Chicago, Saint Louis, or Louisville (one-time home of ragtime pioneer Ben Harney), the early commentators tend to agree that ragtime came from the Midwest.

Whatever its origins, it seems to have spread widely. By 1892, Charles Ives had heard ragtime in minstrel shows in his home town of Danbury, Connecticut.[18] After ragtime broke into print in 1896 it began to be published in a number of cities. The year 1897 saw at least twenty-three piano rags published in nine cities, mostly in the midwest, but also in New Orleans, Philadelphia, and New York (Table 3).

The Era

A Time of Change.   Ragtime came on the public scene at a time of great change in American society. Cities were growing rapidly—through migration from country to city, through natural population growth in the cities and through immigration from abroad. In 1890 only 22 percent of the U.S. population lived in a town or city (a place with twenty-five hundred or more people), but by the close of the Ragtime Era, the percentage had more than doubled. By 1920, 54 percent of Americans were urban dwellers.

Transportation was changing, as the railroad system was virtually completed, as a vast network of electric railways or "interurbans" linked many parts of the United States, as the motorcar began to displace the horseless carriage, and as manned flight began.

The Spanish-American War, a four-month conflict in 1898, turned the United States into a first-class world power, built an overseas empire, and helped to restore American optimism, which had suffered since the 1893 financial panic and resultant depression. Except for the Panic of 1907, the upbeat mood created by the War lasted until the First World War (1914–18).

Though some changes came too gradually to be identified with a specific year, many Ragtime-Era developments can be. Table 4 summarizes major events in American society and arts during this period.

Afro-American Life.   The Ragtime Era saw optimism generally in white America, but the period was a difficult one for blacks. In 1896, just as the era dawned, the United States Supreme Count ruled, in *Plessy* v. *Ferguson*, that racial discrimination was legal. The gains of Reconstruction were largely wiped out, and blacks were repeatedly set back in their efforts for equality and dignity. The next few years brought "Jim Crow" laws to many southern states, and by 1904 blacks had been disenfranchised in nearly the entire South. Since 90 percent of blacks still lived in the South in 1900, very few black men were able to vote (and of course, no women of any color).

The imperialism that the Spanish-American War both rode upon and fostered went hand in hand with racism. C. Vann Woodward writes that "at the very time that imperialism was sweeping the country, the doctrine of racism reached a crest of respectability and popularity among the respectable scholarly and intellectual circles." The late 1890s were such a bad time for Afro-Americans that Rayford W. Logan considers the period 1897 to 1901 as the nadir for blacks.[19] Not surprisingly, lynching was still common; in 1900 white mobs lynched 107 blacks.

Table 3
Piano Rags Published in 1897

CITY	TITLE	COMPOSER	PUBLISHER
Chicago	Alabama Rag Time: Cake Walk	J. E. Henning	Henning Music Co.
	Ben Harney's Rag Time Instructor	Ben Harney, arr. Theodore H. Northrup	Sol Bloom
	Louisiana Rag	Theodore H. Northrup	Thompson Music Co.
	Mississippi Rag	William H. Krell	S. Brainard's Sons*
	Night on the Levee	Theodore H. Northrup	Sol Bloom
	Plantation Echoes: Rag Two-Step	Theodore H. Northrup	Sol Bloom
	Rag Time March	Warren Beebe	Will Rossiter
	The Rag Time Patrol	R. J. Hamilton	National Music Co.
Cincinnati	A Bundle of Rags	Robert S. Roberts	Philip Kussel
	Pride of Bucktown	Robert S. Roberts	Philip Kussel
Kansas City	The Coons' Frolic (for band)	George Southwell	George Southwell
New Orleans	Roustabout Rag	Paul Sarabresole	Gruenewald
New York	At a Georgia Campmeeting	Kerry Mills	F. A. Mills
	De Captain of de Coontown Guards	Dave Reed, Jr.	M. Witmark & Sons
	Dinah's Jubilee: Characteristic March and Two Step	Jacob H. Ellis	Howley, Haviland
	Forest & Stream: Polka or Two-Step	William H. Tyers	F. A. Mills
	Rag Medley	Max Hoffmann	M. Witmark & Sons
	Walk Baby Walk or The Pickaninny Cake Walker	Theo C. Metz	Primrose & Rose
	Who'll Win de Cake Tonight? Ethiopian Schottische	Walter Hawley	George L. Spaulding
Philadelphia	Shifty Shuffles: Buck Dance	Eva Note Flennard	Welch & Wilsky
Saint Louis	Darktown Capers: An Original Southern Rag	Walter Starck	Shattinger Music Co.
	Harlem Rag	Tom Turpin	Robert De Yong & Co.
	Silver King Polka-March	Mamie A. Gunn	Thiebes-Stierlin
Saint Paul	Happy Little Nigs: Ragtime Two Step	George Elliott	George Elliott

*The S. Brainard's Sons imprint included both Chicago and New York.

As late as 1910 "coon songs" were still disseminating racially derogatory lyrics. The slanderous lyrics did not go unprotested by the black press. Complained the *Indianapolis Freeman* in 1905:

> *Song publishers will have to get their eyes open after awhile. Men who write words for songs can no longer write such mean rot as the words of "Whistling Coon" and expect respectable publishers to accept it no matter how good the music may be. Composers should not set music to a set of words that are a direct insult or indirect insinuation to the colored race. This style of literature is no longer appreciated.*[20]

It is one of the great ironies of the Ragtime Era that the lyrics of racially demeaning songs were frequently set to ragtime—a music created by the very people denigrated by the songs.

Compounding their other miseries, most blacks were forced to work in menial jobs. Only three professions were open to them in any numbers: those of preacher, teacher, and musician. Music was one field in which blacks could not only avoid menial labor, but achieve some success and upward mobility and make distinctive contributions to American culture.

Musical Culture. Drastic changes were also taking place in American musical culture during the Ragtime Era. This period saw the firm establishment of vaudeville throughout the United States; the opening of thousands of movie theaters and the creation of many accompanying jobs for musicians; the spread of organized labor among professional musicians; a quickening succession of dance crazes that swept the nation; the rise of music publishing as big business; the entrance of more blacks to popular song writing, arranging, and even publishing. The spread of the phonograph record and gramophone cylinder transformed musical life by bringing great music to the masses, greatly enhancing the dissemination of classical and popular music, and democratizing music by giving the public what it wanted—largely pop songs.[21]

For those who could afford them, player pianos and piano rolls also brought mechanized, repeatable music—classics and pops—into the home. Piano rolls could not bring you the voice of Arthur Collins or Sophie Tucker, as did recordings, but you could sing along and enjoy far greater fidelity from a resonant piano than from a tinny cylinder or Victrola horn.

The Piano and Ragtime

The role of the piano in the development and popularity of many types of music of the Ragtime Era, particularly ragtime itself, cannot be overestimated. The piano was a symbol of respectability—of arrival in the middle class. Before the advent of the automobile, the piano represented for many families the biggest single purchase, other than a house. The piano

Table 4
Societal Developments During the Ragtime Era, 1896–1920*

YEAR	U.S. AND WORLD AFFAIRS	THE ARTS	OTHER
1896	Supreme Court upholds segregation. Utah becomes forty-fifth state. Bryan, "Cross of Gold" speech.	McDowell, *Indian Suite.* American Fed'n of Musicians founded. Dunbar, *Lyrics of Lowly Life.*	Gold rush in Alaska. Olympic Games revived, Athens. First U.S. motion picture machines.
1897	McKinley inaugurated President. Queen Victoria's Diamond Jubilee.	Sousa, *The Stars and Stripes Forever.* Conrad, *The Nigger of the Narcissus.*	Mosquito discovered as malaria carrier. Thomson discovers the electron.
1898	Spanish-American War. U.S. annexes Hawaii.	James, *Turn of the Screw.* Wells, *War of the Worlds.*	Pierre and Marie Curie discover radium.
1899	U.S. "Open Door" policy for China. Boer War begins in South Africa.	Schoenberg, *Verklärte Nacht.* Sibelius, *Finlandia.*	Boll weevil begins destroying U.S. cotton. Veblen, *The Theory of the Leisure Class.*
1900	Boxer Rebellion in China. Hawaii becomes U.S. territory.	Philadelphia Orchestra founded. Dreiser, *Sister Carrie.*	Freud, *Traumdeutung.* U.S. population hits 75 million.
1901	McKinley shot, Roosevelt succeeds. Edward VII becomes King of England.	Mahler, Fourth Symphony. Mann, *Buddenbrooks.*	U.S. Steel, Victor Talking Machine Co. est'd. Max Planck develops quantum theory. First transatlantic radio broadcast.
1902	Five-month coal strike cripples U.S. Boer War ends.	Debussy, *Pelléas et Mélisande.* Caruso makes his first recording.	Rayon patented. Teddy Bear introduced.
1903	U.S. supports Panamanian revolution. Ida Tarbell exposes Standard Oil.	Shaw, *Man and Superman.* London, *Call of the Wild.*	Wright brothers, first airplane flight. First baseball world series.
1904	Russo-Japanese War. Roosevelt Corollary to Monroe Doc.	London Symphony founded. Puccini, *Madama Butterfly.*	Saint Louis World's Fair. Columbia introduces first flat records.
1905	First Russian Revolution. Roosevelt begins second term.	Strauss, *Salome.* Lehár, *The Merry Widow.*	Einstein, special relativity theory. First neon light signs. First motion picture theater.
1906	Pure Food and Drug Act in U.S. Troops quell Atlanta race riot.	Sinclair, *The Jungle.* Herbert, *The Red Mill.*	San Francisco earthquake and fire. Roosevelt helps coin term "muckraker."
1907	Oklahoma becomes forty-sixth state. Peace Conference at the Hague.	First Ziegfeld Follies, N.Y. Scriabin, *Poem of Ecstasy.*	Boy Scouts and Mother's Day founded. Financial panic causes run on banks.
1908	FBI established.	Bartok, String Quartet No. 1. Matisse coins term *cubism.*	Model "T" Ford produced. Jack Johnson becomes world heavyweight champ.

12

1909	Taft Inaugurated President. Congress sets high protective tariffs.	Wright, Robie house, Chicago. Schoenberg, Piano Pieces, Op. 11.	U.S. Copyright Law passed. Peary reaches North Pole.
1910	George V becomes King of England. NAACP organized in New York.	Stravinsky, *The Firebird*. Ravel, *Daphnis et Chloé*. Herbert, *Naughty Marietta*.	N.Y.'s Pennsylvania Station opens. Halley's Comet passes sun. Father's Day first celebrated in U.S.
1911	Chinese republic replaces dynasty. Supreme Court dissolves Standard Oil.	Mahler, *Das Lied von der Erde*. Strauss, *Der Rosenkavalier*.	Amundsen reaches South Pole. Carrier invents air conditioner.
1912	Arizona and New Mexico become states. Balkan Wars begin.	Schoenberg, *Pierrot Lunaire*. Flat records supersede cylinders.	Titanic sinking kills 1,513. F. W. Woolworth Co. founded.
1913	Wilson inaugurated President. U.S. income tax introduced. U.S. Dep't of Labor created.	Armory show brings modern art to U.S. Stravinsky, *Le Sacre du printemps*. Tango and dance craze sweeps U.S. Lawrence, *Sons and Lovers*.	Ford introduces moving assembly line. Indian head nickel introduced.
1914	World War begins in Europe. Panama Canal opens. U.S. intervenes in Mexico.	Handy, *St. Louis Blues*. ASCAP formed in New York. Joyce, *Dubliners*.	Teletype machine introduced. Elastic brassiere patented.
1915	World War intensifies. U.S. Coast Guard established.	Griffith, *Birth of a Nation*. Ives, *Concord sonata*. Maugham, *Of Human Bondage*.	Lusitania sinking kills 1,195. First U.S. transcontinental telephone.
1916	Battle of Verdun. Pershing chases Pancho Villa.	Ives, Fourth Symphony. Rockwell teams with *Saturday Evening Post*.	Einstein, general theory of relativity. First Rose Bowl football game.
1917	U.S. enters World War. Wilson inaugurated for second term. Russian Revolution overthrows czar.	First jazz recordings. Cohan, *Over There*.	Women's bobbed hair becomes fashionable. Jung, *The Psychology of the Unconscious*.
1918	Kaiser Wilhelm abdicates. Civil War grips Russia.	Stravinsky, *L'histoire du soldat*. Cather, *My Antonia*.	Worldwide influenza epidemic begins. Air mail begins in U.S.
1919	Treaty of Versailles ends World War. League of Nations formed.	Falla, *The Three-Cornered Hat*. Anderson, *Winesburg, Ohio*.	Prohibition ratified in U.S. First nonstop transatlantic flight.
1920	Harding elected President. "Red scare" grips U.S.	Holst, *The Planets*. Lewis, *Main Street*.	U.S. grants woman suffrage. First U.S. commercial radio stations.

*See also Table 12, A Chronology of Ragtime, 1896–1920.

provided a center for family and self-entertainment, it contributed to musical education, and it served to instill discipline and "culture" in the youth of America. It was the main instrument used for indoor public musical entertainment in saloons, restaurants, ball rooms, and theaters. Most published music was either composed for piano solo or for voice with piano accompaniment.

The piano played a fundamental role in ragtime, which reached its highest and most intricate development at the piano in the form of piano rags. Had it not been for the piano, ragtime doubtless would not have matured to the extent it did. The piano allowed for two hands (up to ten fingers) of melody, harmony, and rhythm. Furthermore, it allowed each hand to perform a separate musical role—the right to provide melody and some harmony, the left to execute an accompanying bass pattern (with harmony) in steady, equal-beat rhythm. The rhythmic juxtaposition of the two hands is what creates contrast and tension, making piano ragtime work.

Ragtime is essentially a percussive music, notwithstanding lyrical and singing rags such as *Heliotrope Bouquet* (by Scott Joplin and Louis Chauvin). Unlike other keyboard instruments—organ, harmonium, and accordion— the piano was perfectly suited to the percussive timbres that ragtime required. The piano's percussive capability was, I suspect, one of the reasons that the considerably more expensive piano succeeded in displacing the reed organ as the primary instrument of home music making. The piano better suited ragtime and the era's other lively popular styles, which, unlike sad ballads and solemn hymns, demanded crisp enunciation. As the primary instrument of ragtime, the piano was not without its disadvantages. Unlike the banjo, violin, or cornet, it was not portable and could not be used easily for parades, park concerts, and similar amusements. Also, the high cost of the instrument placed it beyond the reach of those without means.

Ragtime on the piano could not, of course, render the vocalisms traditional to Afro-American music—the swoops, slides, slurs, and *glissandi*—that can be imitated successfully on a guitar or trombone. But the piano was able to maintain the traditional percussive timbres and polyrhythms and, some would argue, even the polymeters that are a hallmark of Afro-American and West African music. And more than most instruments, the piano allowed for an open display of technical velocity and virtuosity.

During the Ragtime Era the piano was booming in popularity. As the graph on page 15 reveals, the piano reached its sales peak in 1909, roughly the midpoint of the Ragtime Era. It is significant that the number of published piano rags, according to my calculations, also reached a peak the very same year.[22] Ragtime and the piano were thus interdependent. The popularity of one spurred that of the other. The popularity of the piano and of music publishing in general were, in fact, mutually reinforcing. People purchasing pianos for their homes needed to have music to play; new songs

U.S. Piano and Player Piano Production, 1870-1940

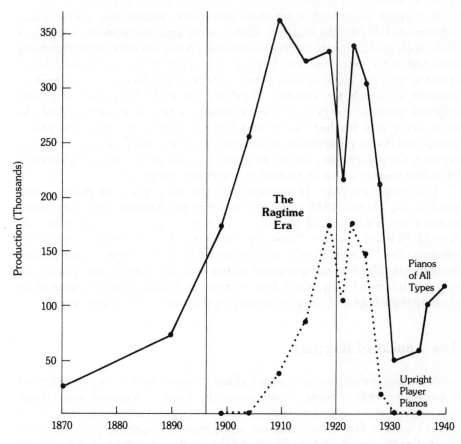

The
Ragtime
Era

Pianos
of All
Types

Upright
Player
Pianos

Production (Thousands)

Compiled from data included in Solomon Fabricant, *The Output of Manufacturing Industries, 1899-1937* (New York: National Bureau of Economic Research, 1940), pp. 597-99, and Cyril Ehrlich, *The Piano: A History* (London: J. M. Dent, 1976), p. 221.

and instrumentals were put before the public and marketed as never before; and people needed to have an instrument on which to play the current tunes.

Today, we have a hard time understanding how good ragtime piano sounded during its heyday. The pianos of the day were either grands or full uprights, capable of producing much more sound than the spinets of later years. Also, most homes were of solid wood construction. The sounding boards of the large pianos produced considerable volume, and buildings' wooden floors and walls amplified the sound to a full and rich resonance. The listener could actually *feel* the piano vibrations through his or her feet and bones. To the loudness and resonance were added the appealing and novel rag rhythms. It is no wonder that some people became intoxicated with ragtime.[23]

If ragtime played on a standard piano was compelling, player piano ragtime was downright exciting. Unlike most amateur pianists, the player piano rolls could execute the rags flawlessly. Also, the rolls were frequently enriched with extra octaves beyond the capacity of the human hand, creating an even fuller sound. Many rolls featured flashy effects, such as tremolo, to dazzle the listener. Watching the piano keys moving rapidly without human fingers was like witnessing a feat of wizardry. And the excitement was further heightened for the person pumping the player pedals, for the physical exertion also got the adrenaline pumping. For these reasons, the player piano played an important role in disseminating ragtime. (Ragtime on piano rolls is treated in a separate chapter.)

The graph on page 15 reveals that the peak years of player piano production, 1919 to 1923, came at the end of the Ragtime Era. This period marked the beginning of the piano novelty, a successor to ragtime (see Ronald Riddle's chapter, "Novelty Piano Music"). Another offshoot of ragtime, the "Harlem stride" jazz piano of James P. Johnson and Luckey Roberts was also becoming popular at this time (see the chapter "Conversations with James P. Johnson"). Stride pieces and piano novelties were often flashier than rags and were extremely well suited to the player piano.

The Appeal of Ragtime

Although some people couldn't abide ragtime, many others embraced it enthusiastically. Young people especially liked it. Ragtime was "their" music, just as several generations later teenagers took rock and roll as "their" music. For some, ragtime undoubtedly represented a rebellion against their parents. Ragtime echoed the restless energy and optimism of youth and of the American people in general during the late 1800s and early 1900s.

Above all, it was the rhythms of rag that created its allure. Today, after decades of syncopated jazz and other Afro-American idioms, we have difficulty appreciating how novel and exotic these rhythms must have been for Ragtime-Era listeners. White America had not heard such consistently syncopated music before. Verse-and-chorus waltz songs had dominated popular music; ragtime brought a refreshing contrast not only in rhythm, but also in tempo, formal structure, and mood. Rag was fresh and striking also because of its inherent percussiveness, emphasized by the timbres of the banjo, piano, or player piano.

During a visit in 1903 to the Georgia sea island of Jekyll, Dr. Gustav Kühl, a German musician, attended a masked ball at which music was provided by two black musicians. Kühl relates the jarring effect, at first negative and then positive, that these instrumental rag syncopations had upon him.

> *But my senses were captivated against my will by the music, which seemed to be produced by a little army of devils to my left. It seemed incredible to me for quite a while, how any person could dance a single step to such an irregular and noisy conglomeration of sounds; and it was even more difficult for me to understand how such complicated and to me unmusical noise was brought about. . . . Before a thoroughly dilapidated Grand Piano, . . . a muscular, short haired Negro . . . with his arms and elbows . . . belaboured the keys in sixteenths with such ease, and dexterity as many a pianist could wish for his wrists. In reality he produced all the music, as his colleague, with a Double Bass (minus one string) simply supported the bass notes, with vivacious and grunting strokes from his bow. . . . The continuous reappearance and succession of accentuations on the wrong parts of the bar and unnatural syncopations imparts somewhat of a* rhythmic compulsion *to the body which is nothing short of* irresistible *and which makes itself* felt *even before the ears have discerned the time or rhythmic value of the various parts of the bar.*[24]

Many other people found ragtime "irresistible" and "fascinating," as indicated in the titles of a number of instrumentals and songs, including *Irresistible Rag, Irresistible Fox Trot Rag, That Irresistible Rag, That Fascinating Rag, The Fascinator,* and *That Nifty Rag.*

As noted above, blacks suffered many setbacks during the ragtime years. Blacks struggled to survive economically, politically, socially, and spiritually. As the profession of musician was one of only three open in any numbers to blacks, music in general and ragtime in particular held promise of escape from poverty, anonymity, and powerlessness. Ragtime undoubtedly also appealed to black professional musicians by providing opportunity for masculine competitiveness, especially in the virtuosic "cutting contests." In addition, playing the piano brought a measure of respectability, especially compared with the banjo, which carried associations of plantations and minstrelsy. Thus, for black ragtime pianists, the music had deeper meaning and perhaps more profound appeal than it did for whites.

The People of Ragtime

Like any music, ragtime had two primary groups of participants: its producers and its consumers. The consumers—the people who comprised the audience—were diverse, including many young people, both black and

Table 5
Most Prolific Composers of Instrumental Rags

COMPOSER	LIFE SPAN	AGE WHEN FIRST RAG PUBLISHED	BIRTHPLACE	RACE	NUMBER OF RAGS*		
					SOLO	COLLABORATIVE	TOTAL
Aufderheide, May	1888–1972	19	Indianapolis, Indiana	white	7	0	7
Bennett, Theron	1879–1937	23	Pierce City, Missouri	white	8	0	8
Blake, Eubie	1883–1983	20	Baltimore, Maryland	black	13	1	14
Botsford, George	1874–1949	22	Sioux Falls, South Dakota	white	17	0	17
Campbell, Brun	1884–1952	†	Oberlin, Kansas	white	9	0	9
Christensen, Axel W.	1881–1955	27	Chicago, Illinois	white	7‡	0	7
Cobb, George L	1886–1942	22	Mexico, New York	white	16	0	16
Copeland, Les	1887–1942	21	Wichita, Kansas	white	9	1	10
Denney, Homer	1885–1975	20	NA	white	8	0	8
Giblin, Irene M.	1888–1974	16	Saint Louis, Missouri	white	10	0	10
Hunter, Charles H.	1876–1906	24	Columbia, Tennessee	white	8	0	8
Johnson, Charles L.	1876–1950	22	Kansas City, Kansas	white	32	0	32
Joplin, Scott	1868–1917	30	Bowie County, Texas	black	32	6	38
Jordan, Joe	1882–1971	19	Cincinnati, Ohio	black	6	0	6
Kortlander, Max	1890–1961	29	Grand Rapids, Michigan	white	8	0	8
Lamb, Joseph F.	1887–1960	19	Montclair, New Jersey	white	34	0	34

18

Composer	Birthplace	Dates	Age	Race			
Lodge, Henry	Providence, Rhode Island	1884–1933	25	white	0	15	15
Marshall, Arthur	Saline County, Missouri	1881–1968	18	black	1	9	10
Mentel, Louis H.	Covington, Kentucky	1880–1955	25	white	0	10	10
Olman, Abe	Cincinnati, Ohio	1888–1984	19	white	0	7	7
Pratt, Paul	New Salem, Indiana	1890–1948	18	white	0	15	15
Pryor, Arthur	Saint Joseph, Missouri	1870–1942	28	white	0	9	9
Roberts, Luckey	Philadelphia, Pennsylvania	1887–1968	25	black	0	7	7
Robinson, J. Russel	Indianapolis, Indiana	1892–1963	17	white	0	8	8
Stark, E. J.	Gosport, Indiana	1868–?	34	white	0	6	6
Straight, Charley	Chicago, Illinois	1891–1940	22	white	1	18	19
Scott, James	Neosho, Missouri	1886–1938	17	black	0	31	31
Tierney, Harry	Perth Amboy, New Jersey	1890–1965	19	white	0	15	15
Turpin, Tom	Savannah, Georgia	1873–1922	24	black	0	6	6
Wenrich, Percy	Joplin, Missouri	1880–1952	23	white	0	18	18
Woolsey, Calvin	Tinney's Point, Missouri	1884–1946	24	white	0	6	6

* Number of rags is approximate. Excludes "novelty piano." Includes works published in sheet music, issued on piano roll or recording, or which survive complete in manuscript.

† Since none of Campbell's rags were published, but exist only in recordings he made late in his life, it is impossible to ascertain his age at first composing rags.

‡ Excludes Christensen's ragtime instruction books and his numerous "ragtime arrangements of old favorite melodies" such as *Home! Sweet Home!*, *Old Black Joe*, and *Auld Lang Syne*.

NA = Not available.

Compiled from information in Rudi Blesh and Harriet Janis, *They All Played Ragtime*, 4th ed., rev., David A. Jasen and Trebor Jay Tichenor, *Rags and Ragtime: A Musical History*, and author's research.

white. The producers included ragtime's composers, arrangers, performers, and, by extension, publishers.

Instrumental rag composers. Although the two greatest ragtime composers—Scott Joplin and James Scott—were black, most of the published rag composers were white. As Table 5 demonstrates, only seven of the thirty-one most prolific, and largely the most representative, rag composers were black. This indicates that ragtime, originally an Afro-American idiom, was adopted by many white musicians. It also suggests, however, that some black composers of rags did not get published—by choice, because they lacked formal training in composing and notating music, or because of racial discrimination by publishers. It suggests, too, that many black ragtime pianists devoted their energies to *interpreting* existing pieces, rather than composing new ones, as have modern jazz performers such as Art Tatum and Oscar Peterson.

Table 6 also establishes that the major rag composers[25] generally became involved with ragtime in their youth.

Table 6
Age Composers First Wrote Rags

AGE	NUMBER OF COMPOSERS
16–19	10
20–22	7
23–25	8
26–28	2
29–31	2
32+	1

Most of the composers had their first rags published between the ages of 17 and 25. Ten of the most prolific were still teenagers at the time of their first publications. This data indicates clearly that ragtime was a music of youth, and it sheds light on the tremendous opposition ragtime engendered in many quarters. Youth was enjoying a new, somewhat irreverent music, and many adults resented it. (There were other reasons why ragtime met opposition, which are explored in Neil Leonard's chapter, "The Reactions to Ragtime.")

Rag Performers. Most ragtime was performed by amateur musicians, at home, for the amusement of themselves, their families, and friends. The majority of the amateur pianists were young white women who learned piano as an important part of their cultural upbringing. Since ragtime was frowned on by most piano teachers and some parents, playing the music must have been a furtive activity for many. Most of these amateurs played the music strictly as written, or to be more accurate, *strove* to play it as written, for pieces such as the *Maple Leaf Rag* were difficult to play.

These piano players bought the ragtime sheet music at music stores and at the music counters of department stores and dime stores. Many department store music sections had pianos on which the clerks (frequently young ladies) would obligingly demonstrate the latest ragtime and other popular music to any potential customer who wanted to know how it sounded.

The professionals formed a separate group. These were the "perfessors" and "ivory ticklers" who played in saloons, sporting houses, riverboats, restaurants, and theaters. This group, which included many blacks, formed the somewhat exotic rag fraternity engagingly described in *They All Played Ragtime*, the pioneering ragtime history by Rudi Blesh and Harriet Janis.[26] Jelly Roll Morton, James P. Johnson (see the chapter "Conversations with James P. Johnson"), Willie "the Lion" Smith, and Eubie Blake recorded their reminiscences of some of the most unusual and picturesque members of this fraternity.[27] Through them, the colorful, itinerant, struggling black ragtime pianist emerges a folk type—a recurring character in ragtime legend.

Of the many occasions on which rags were performed, one of the most sensational was the cutting contest. These were playing contests among professional ragtime pianists, to see who could best or "cut" the other players. These seem to have been held frequently on an informal basis during the era and occasionally on a formal basis with much public fanfare. Examples of the latter include the spectacular contest sponsored by *Police Gazette* magazine in New York City's Tammany Hall on January 23, 1900. The winner, Mike Bernard, received a handsome medal and the title of "Champion Rag Time Pianist of the World." During the early 1900s, Tom Turpin's Rosebud Bar in Saint Louis held annual piano playing contests and balls. The 1904 contest (held February 22) was won by Louis Chauvin, who is said to have won the giant contest at the Saint Louis World's Fair later that year. In January 1901, a black Indianapolis newspaper carried a large advertisement for a "Cake Walk" with "pie eating and piano playing contests," held at Tomlinson Hall. Chicago held a "Rag Time Piano Contest and Ball" on October 9, 1916, sponsored by the Piano Players Social Club. The black contestants came from throughout the Midwest and East.[28]

While the amateurs played—or struggled to play—the music as written, many of the professional rag pianists could and did "fake" or improvise on rags. Why else would Artie Matthews admonish pianists not to "fake" his *Pastime* rags? As Berlin astutely observes, ragtime rendered in a semi-improvisatory or improvisatory style constituted an early form of jazz in everything but name.[29]

Rag Publishers. For many of the ragtime composers, publication was all important, for it provided not only modest income, but also recognition and prestige. For Joseph Lamb, it was almost a goal in itself. Sheet music publication provided the primary means of disseminating and diffusing rags, since the recording industry was in its infancy, and since piano roll manufacturers normally depended upon prior sheet music publication for their arrangements. The publishers could not have existed, of course, without composers to write for them, but the reverse is nearly true. To the extent to which the composers depended on the publishers for earnings and for the dissemination of the music, we can say that the publishers were essential to the ragtime composers.

Without publishers and publication, ragtime might have remained an elusive, impermanent music in aural tradition, known primarily to itinerant and improvising musicians who learned by ear, not by note. Had it not been widely published, ragtime would not have had a pronounced influence on the American musical scene, nor would it have spread to Canada and Mexico or crossed the oceans to Europe and Australia with such ease and impact. The publication of ragtime gave the music a permanence which has made it available to millions of instrumentalists over the decades. Ragtime publication also provides us, seventy years later, the primary source documents, without which we could not reconstruct the history of this music.

Publication brought ragtime some respectability, and therefore entrée to settings where it would otherwise have been unknown or prohibited—the parlors of middle-class homes, where young ladies generally provided the family music. If ragtime had remained a shadowy, unnotated, unpublished music of the red-light districts and cultural "underground," few middle-class musicians, male or female, would have become involved with it.

Of the several hundred publishers of ragtime, no one did more to champion it than John Stark (1841–1927), a colorful, singularly independent pioneer. He was the primary publisher of Scott Joplin, James Scott, Joseph Lamb, Arthur Marshall, and Artie Matthews. Through articles in the musical press and numerous advertisements, Stark tirelessly promoted his

A rare photograph of publisher John Stark in his New York office, 1909. Note the labeled shelves of sheet music, the cluttered desk, and the rocking chair. (*John Edward Hasse collection*)

firm's catalogue of accomplished rags, which he called "classic rags." By publishing ragtime of artistic merit, Stark also helped set a high standard for others to emulate and helped ragtime achieve a modicum of respectability.[30]

With ragtime composer Charles N. Daniels (1878–1943) as its manager, the firm of Jerome H. Remick & Company became the largest publisher of instrumental rags, issuing more than twice as many rags as Stark. Remick was also perhaps the most prolific publisher of popular music from about 1900 to 1930. Table 7 presents key facts about Stark, Remick, and the other leading publishers of rags.

Rag Arrangers. The arrangers are a less important group than the publishers. Many rag composers didn't need arrangers. With few exceptions, Scott Joplin, James Scott, and Joseph Lamb apparently did all their own arranging.[31] According to Abe Olman and J. Russel Robinson, however, many composers submitted only a lead melody line to publishers, and staff arrangers filled in the harmony and bass.[32] These staff arrangers were often not identified on the sheet music. Those that were named include Artie Matthews, Paul Pratt, J. Russel Robinson, and Charles N. Daniels (see Table 8).

Ragtime Song Writers. The leading ragtime song writers were in most instances not the leading instrumental rag composers, as a comparison of Tables 4 and 9 makes clear. (Table 9 includes Scott Joplin among leading ragtime song writers, not because of a prolific output but because of the enduring quality of his ragtime songs.) Many composers of ragtime songs were Tin Pan Alley tune smiths, such as Harry Von Tilzer, Egbert Van Alstyne, and Lewis F. Muir. While they hailed from many parts of the United States, nearly all the successful ragtime songwriters lived in New York City. More instrumental rag composers achieved success in other cities, such as Saint Louis (Artie Matthews, Tom Turpin, Charles Hunter), Kansas City (Charles L. Johnson), Carthage, Missouri (James Scott), Chicago (Paul Pratt, Charley Straight), Indianapolis (May Aufderheide, J. Russel Robinson), and Boston (George L. Cobb). The success of ragtime and popular song writing was more dependent than instrumental writing on song plugging, vaudeville, and the entertainment complex based in New York City.

Although the leading instrumental rag writers did not devote their energies exclusively to ragtime, they seem to have been generally more committed to it than were the ragtime song composers. To the latter group, ragtime seems to have been a fad to exploit rather than a genre of enduring value to pursue.

Ragtime Song Performers. The best-known singers of ragtime songs were New Yorkers. Though no study of these individuals, mostly vaudevillians, has been carried out, we know that the leading ragtime singers included Sophie Tucker (1884–1966), Gene Greene (1877–1930), Arthur Collins (1864–1933), Dolly Connolly (Mrs. Percy Wenrich, 1888–1965), Bert Williams (1874–1922) and George Walker (1873–1911), Alex Rogers

Table 7
Leading Publishers of Piano Rags (in descending order of output)

FIRM	YEAR FOUNDED	PRINCIPAL CITIES	PROPRIETOR AND HIS LIFE SPAN	APPROX. NO. OF RAGS PUBLISHED
Jerome H. Remick & Co.	1905*	Detroit and New York	Jerome H. Remick (1868–1931)	ca. 300
Stark Music Co.	1892†	Sedalia, Missouri (1892–1900) Saint Louis (1900–1927) New York (1905–1910)	John Stillwell Stark (1841–1927)	115
Will Rossiter	1890	Chicago	Will Rossiter (1867–1954)	38
Jos. W. Stern	1894	New York	Joseph W. Stern (1870–1934)	37
Waterson, Berlin & Snyder	1912	New York	Henry Waterson Irving Berlin (b. 1888) Ted Snyder (1881–1965)	33
H. Kirkus Dugdale	ca. 1910	Washington, D.C.	H. Kirkus Dugdale	26
Vandersloot Music Co.	189–?	Williamsport, Pennsylvania, and New York	Frederick William Vandersloot (1866–) Caird Vandersloot (1869–)	23
J. H. Aufderheide & Co.	1908	Indianapolis	John H. Aufderheide (1865–1941)	21
Walter Jacobs	1894	Boston	Walter Jacobs (1872?–1945)	20
The S. Brainard's Sons Co.	1845	New York and Chicago	Silas Brainard (1814–1871) Henry M. Brainard	20
Axel W. Christensen	1903	Chicago	Axel W. Christensen (1881–1955)	19
Sam Fox	1906	Cleveland	Sam Fox (1882?–1971)	18
Jos. Morris	ca. 1895	Philadelphia	Jos. Morris	17
J. W. Jenkins Sons	1878	Kansas City, Missouri	John Woodward Jenkins (1827–1890) John Wesley Jenkins (1864?–1932)	15

*In 1898 Jerome H. Remick bought one-half interest in, and in 1900 whole control of, the Detroit music publishing firm of Whitney-Warner, whose name he maintained until 1904. In 1905, he changed the name to Jerome H. Remick & Company.
†John Stark & Son was founded by at least 1882 as a retail piano and music store, but did not begin music publishing until about 1892.

Table 8
Selected Piano Rag Arrangers and Representative Arrangements

ARRANGER	WORK	COMPOSER	YEAR
Alford, Harry L.	Frankfort Rag	Maude M. Thurston	1909
Campbell, Arthur	One More Rag	Minnie Berger	1909
Confare, Thomas R.	Cannon Ball	Joseph C. Northup	1905
Daniels, Charles N.	Original Rags	Scott Joplin	1899
DeLisle, D. S.	Bowery Buck	Tom Turpin	1899
	Harlem Rag	Tom Turpin	1897
	A Rag-Time Nightmare	Tom Turpin	1900
Epstein, Phil	That Texas Rag	Nell Wright Watson	1913
Fassbinder, William B.	Topsy Two Step	Libbie Erickson	1904
	Trixy Two Step	Libbie Erickson	1904
Frolich, Carl	Echoes of the Congo	Lylian M. Chapman	1903
Joplin, Scott	Sensation: A Rag	Joseph Lamb	1908
Matthews, Artie	Jinx Rag	Lucian P. Gibson	1911
	The Lily Rag	Charles Thompson	1914
Mooney, Arthur B.	Robardina Rag	E. Warren Furry	1902
Northrup, Theodore H.	Ben Harney's Rag Time Instructor	Ben Harney	1897
Pratt, Charles E.	Eli Green's Cake Walk	Sadie Koninsky	1898
Pratt, Paul	Nice and Easy: Rag Fox Trot	Cliff McKay	1916
Robinson, J. Russel	Kalamity Kid	Ferd Guttenberger	1909
	Log Cabin	Ferd Guttenberger	1908
Rosenbush, Julia	Checker: Rag Two Step	Bulah Arens	1908
Smith, Lee Orean	After the Cake Walk	Nathaniel Dett	1900
Tyers, Will	Harlem Rag	Tom Turpin	1899
	"Wiggy Waggy" Rag	Mattie Harl Burgess	1910

(1876–1930), Byron G. Harlan (1861–1936), Al Jolson (1886–1950), Billy Murray (1877–1954), Walter Van Brunt (b. 1892), and Ruth Roye (d. 1960). Many of their faces grace the sheet music covers of ragtime songs, and several made numerous recordings.

The Rag Repertory

With the revival of ragtime in the early 1970s, focus was placed upon the piano rags of Scott Joplin and a few others who also wrote "classic rags." This select group comprised Joseph Lamb and Missourians James Scott, Artie Matthews, Scott Hayden, and Arthur Marshall. Numerous recordings were made of Joplin's *The Entertainer, Pine Apple Rag, Easy Winners,* of Lamb's *Ragtime Nightingale,* and of Scott's *Ragtime Oriole.* Many people assumed that that was all there was to ragtime, at least, all there was of merit. Actually, Joplin and his peers represented only a small part of instrumental ragtime, and many other composers wrote praiseworthy rags.

Though commercial success does not guarantee quality and enduring value, it does indicate public taste. Commercial success, therefore, may be our best indicator of what was truly representative of ragtime as a whole. Although few sales records survive from that time and no "best seller" charts were compiled, the relative popularity of rags can be reconstructed from the number of sheet music copies and piano rolls which have survived; the number of sound recordings and piano rolls issued of each piece; and the quantity of advetising and publicity each work received in the musical press.

Table 9
Some Leading Composers of Ragtime Songs

COMPOSER	LIFE SPAN	BIRTHPLACE	RACE	REPRESENTATIVE RAGTIME SONGS
Berlin, Irving	1888–	Temun, Russia	white	Alexander's Ragtime Band The Ragtime Violin That Beautiful Rag That International Rag
Cannon, Hughie	1877–1912	Detroit	white	Bill Bailey, Won't You Please Come Home? He Done Me Wrong I Hates to Get Up Early in de Morn You Needn't Come Home
Harney, Ben	1871–1938	Middleboro, Kentucky	black?	The Cake-Walk in the Sky The Hat He Never Ate Mister Johnson Turn Me Loose You've Been a Good Old Wagon But You've Done Broke Down
Johnson, J. Rosamond	1873–1954	Jacksonville, Florida	black	Nobody's Looking but de Owl and de Moon Roll Them Cotton Bales St. Vitus Rag Under the Bamboo Tree
Jones, Irving	ca. 1874–1932	(unknown)	black	I Don't Understand Ragtime I'm Living Easy Rag-Time Queen Take Your Clothes and Go
Joplin, Scott	1868–1917	Bowie County, Texas	black	Maple Leaf Rag: Song Pine Apple Rag: Song The Rag Time Dance A Real Slow Drag

Name	Dates	Location	Race	Songs
Jordan, Joe	1882–1971	Cincinnati, Ohio	black	Dat's Ma Honey Sho's Yo' Born / Lovie Joe / That Raggedy Rag / That Teasin' Tag
Morse, Theodore	1873–1924	Washington, D.C.	white	Auntie Skinner's Chicken Dinners / Down In Jungle Town / That Good Old Irish Rag / Up in the Cocoanut Tree
Muir, Lewis F.	1883–1915	New York	white	Hitchy-Koo / Ragtime Cowboy Joe / Waiting for the Robert E. Lee / When Ragtime Rosie Ragged the Rosary
Smith, Chris	1879–1949	Charleston, South Carolina	black	All in Down and Out / Ballin' the Jack / Barnyard Rag / You're in the Right Church
Van Alstyne, Egbert	1882–1951	Chicago	white	Hold Up Rag / Honolulu Rag / Oh That Navajo Rag / That Devil Rag
Von Tilzer, Harry	1872–1946	Detroit	white	Alexander / Mr. Music Master / Under the Yum Yum Tree / What You Goin' To Do When the Rent Comes 'Round?
Wenrich, Percy	1887–1952	Joplin, Missouri	white	Alamo Rag / Ragtime Turkey Trot / Red Rose Rag / Skeleton Rag

Based on these criteria, Table 10 lists some of the rags most popular during the Ragtime Era. These would have been in the repertoire of most "perfessers," in addition to their own specialties, local favorites, a few "classic rags," perhaps, from the John Stark publishing firm, and some "ragging" of classics and old familiar songs.

As Table 10 reveals, few of the most successful rags were written by Scott Joplin and his peers. Most of the rags that became standards of the 1897–1920 repertory were written by composers more oriented towards popular appeal than were Joplin, Scott, and Lamb. However, Tin Pan Alley, which was amassing more and more conrol over music publishing, was not even close to having a monopoly on these hits. More than half came from musicians and publishers in other cities: Chicago, Indianapolis, Fort Worth, Oakland, Boston, and four towns in Missouri—Saint Louis, Kansas City, Sedalia, and Carthage.

Although sheet music, piano rolls, and live performance were the most important means of disseminating rags, cylinder and disc recordings also helped spread the syncopated sound. Because the sound quality of cylinder and disc recording and playback was poor in the first years of the twentieth century, these devices won acceptance by consumers only gradually. Nonetheless, hundreds of rags were recorded on 78 rpm discs during this era. Although the publication of new rags virtually ceased by 1920, the recording of rags did not. During the 1920s and succeeding decades many of the old rags were recorded anew. Two rags were particularly popular with recording artists, record companies, and the public. These were *12th Street Rag*, which by the end of the 78 rpm era in 1958 had almost one hundred-thirty recordings, and *Maple Leaf Rag*, which neared seventy. Table 11 lists other rags frequently recorded on 78 rpm records.[33]

A Thumbnail History

During its heyday, ragtime underwent a complete life cycle; it arose, developed, and faded. The life of ragtime is composed of many publications and events. Some of the most important of these are listed in Table 12. Some occurrences, of course, are not isolable to a specific year. Changes in the rhythms and the racial references happened gradually, as detailed by Berlin.[34] Thornton Hagert notes in his chapter, "Band and Orchestral Ragtime," that as ragtime gained popularity among small orchestras, publishers began issuing folios, and the functions of the instruments changed. The now-famous "Red Back Book" cannot yet be dated definitively; we know only that it was published sometime between 1910 and 1914. Other facets of ragtime that do not fall easily into a chronology are the reactions, pro and con, of the public and press, the gradual entrance of some ragtime hits into the aural tradition of folk and country music,[35] and the transformation of ragtime into jazz and into novelty piano music.

Ragtime originated and developed in the United States. Within a few

Table 10
Major Hits of the Rag Repertory, 1897–1920

RAG	COMPOSER	YEAR
At a Georgia Campmeeting	Kerry Mills	1897
Black and White Rag	George Botsford	1908
Cannon Ball	Joseph C. Northup	1905
Creole Belles	J. Bodewalt Lampe	1900
Dill Pickles	Charles L. Johnson	1906
Dusty Rag	May Aufderheide	1908
The Entertainer's Rag	Jay Roberts	1910
Frog Legs Rag	James Scott	1906
Grizzly Bear Rag	George Botsford	1911
Maple Leaf Rag	Scott Joplin	1899
Ragging the Scale	Edward B. Claypoole	1915
Red Pepper	Henry Lodge	1910
Russian Rag	George L. Cobb	1918
Smoky Mokes	Abe Holzmann	1898
St. Louis Tickle	Barney & Seymore	1904
Sunflower Slow Drag	Scott Joplin and Scott Hayden	1901
Temptation Rag	Henry Lodge	1909
That Eccentric Rag	J. Russel Robinson	1912
Tickled to Death	Charles H. Hunter	1901
Très Moutarde (Too Much Mustard)	Cecil Macklin	1911
Turkey in the Straw: A Rag-Time Fantasie	Otto Bonnell	1899
12th Street Rag	Euday L. Bowman	1914
Wild Cherries Rag	Ted Snyder	1908

years after it broke into print in the United States, it traveled abroad. One of those frequently credited with introducing live American ragtime to Europe was band leader John Philip Sousa. Although Sousa would not lead his band in recordings of ragtime (Assistant Conductor Arthur Pryor, himself a rag composer, often conducted these recordings), Sousa performed it before live audiences. His repertory included a number of early syncopated cakewalks, as well as some ragtime songs and ragtime arrangements of existing works. He made tours of Europe in 1900, 1901, 1903, and 1905. After his 1900 tour, in which he played ragtime for Kaiser Wilhelm of Germany, an American music magazine published a bit of untitled doggerel about Europe's reaction to Sousa's ragtime.

> To the Paris Exposition
> Went John Philip on a mission.
> To cut some Yankee capers,
> And take the town by storm.
> He played the latest rag-time
> All his marches, choicest jag-time,
> If it's true what's in the papers,
> His reception was quite warm.
>
> He played before the Kaiser,
> Whom they say is greatly wiser
> Than a thousand learned professors
> Of any land or clime.

(Continued on p. 32)

Table 11
Rags* Most Frequently Issued on 78 rpm Records, 1897–1958

NUMBER OF RECORDINGS	RAG	COMPOSER	YEAR PUBLISHED
128	12th Street Rag	Euday L. Bowman	1914
68	Maple Leaf Rag	Scott Joplin	1899
51	Temptation Rag	Henry Lodge	1909
48	Canadian Capers	Henry Cohen, Gus Chandler, and Bert White	1915
42	Whistling Rufus	Kerry Mills	1899
31	At a Georgia Campmeeting	Kerry Mills	1897
31	Dill Pickles	Charles L. Johnson	1906
27	Ragging the Scale	Edward B. Claypoole	1915
24	Red Pepper	Henry Lodge	1910
24	Smoky Mokes	Abe Holzmann	1898
23	Black and White Rag	George Botsford	1908
18	Russian Rag	George L. Cobb	1918
17	By Heck	S. R. Henry	1914
17	Coon Band Contest	Arthur Pryor	1899
15	Creole Belles	J. Bodewalt Lampe	1900
15	The Smiler	Percy Wenrich	1907
14	Gaby Glide	Louis Hirsch	1911
14	Grizzly Bear Rag	George Botsford	1911
11	The Colored Major	S. R. Henry	1900
10	Cotton Blossoms	Milton H. Hall	1898
10	Red Rose Rag	Percy Wenrich	1911
10	Spaghetti Rag	George Lyons and Bob Yosco	1910
10	Whitewash Rag	Jean Schwartz	1908
10	Très Moutarde (Too Much Mustard)	Cecil Macklin	1911

* Excludes rags composed after 1920. Includes syncopated cakewalks.

Compiled from data in David A. Jasen, Recorded Ragtime, 1897–1958 (Hamden, Connecticut: Archon Books, 1973).

30

Table 12
A Chronology of Ragtime, 1896–1920

YEAR	ACTIVITY
1896	First songs labeled ragtime published: *All Coons Look Alike to Me* (Ernest Hogan) and *My Coal Black Lady* (W. T. Jefferson).
1897	First instrumental rags published, including Mississippi Rag (W. H. Krell) and *Harlem Rag* (Tom Turpin).
	Ben Harney publishes his *Rag-Time Instructor.*
	First recordings of ragtime by banjo (Vess L. Ossman) and band (Metropolitan Orchestra).
	At a Georgia Campmeeting (Kerry Mills) issued; becomes cakewalk hit.
1898	A few more piano rags are published than in 1897, as rag idea spreads.
	Smoky Mokes (Abe Holzmann) published; becomes cakewalk hit.
1899	Scott Joplin's *Maple Leaf Rag* published; quickly becomes popular among public and influential among musicians.
	Rag publication more than triples from previous year.
	Eubie Blake creates *Charleston Rag,* though not copyrighted until 1917.
	Hello! Ma Baby (Joseph Howard and Ida Emerson) becomes ragtime song hit.
1900	Joplin and publisher Stark relocate from Sedalia to Saint Louis.
	Tom Turpin opens Rosebud Bar in Saint Louis; becomes a mecca for midwestern ragtime pianists.
	Sousa's Band (at Paris Exposition) and banjoist Vess L. Ossman (a tour of England) help introduce "live" ragtime to Europe.
	Creole Bells (J. Bodewalt Lampe) published, becomes popular.
1901	American Federation of Musicians votes to suppress ragtime.
	Tickled to Death (Charles H. Hunter) and *Sunflower Slow Drag* (Scott Joplin and Scott Hayden) issued, become hits.
1902	*Under the Bamboo Tree* (Cole and Johnson) becomes ragtime song hit.
	Joplin's The *"Rag Time Dance"* published as a folk ballet with lyrics.
	Charles Ives incorporates ragtime into *Set of Nine Ragtime Pieces.*
1903	Axel W. Christensen opens his first ragtime school, in Chicago.
	Joplin completes ragtime opera *A Guest of Honor,* tours Midwest with it.
	Sousa performs ragtime for royalty in England, Prussia, and Russia.
1904	Saint Louis World's Fair attracts many ragtime musicians; Joplin commemorates the Fair with *The Cascades.*
	St. Louis Tickle (Barney & Seymore) published, becomes popular.
	The first *Christensen's Rag-Time Instruction Book for Piano* issued.
	Rags' reference to blackness declines sharply.
1905	John Stark opens publishing office in New York City; Jerome H. Remick music publishing firm established in Detroit.
	Cannon Ball (Joseph C. Northup) issued, becomes favorite with public.
1906	*Dill Pickles* (Charles L. Johnson) published; becomes big hit in sheet music and rolls; popularizes "secondary rag" motif.
	James Scott's *Frog Legs Rag* issued; Joplin's *The Ragtime Dance* published as a piano rag.
	Claude Debussy incorporates ragtime into "Golliwog's Cakewalk."
1907	*Heliotrope Bouquet* (Scott Joplin and Louis Chauvin) issued.
	Joplin makes last move of his life, to New York City.
1908	Joplin's *Fig Leaf Rag, Pine Apple Rag,* and *School of Ragtime* issued.
	Black and White Rag (George Botsford), *Wild Cherries* (Ted Snyder), and *Dusty Rag* (May Aufderheide) published, become hits.
	Player piano makers adopt eighty-eight-note standard; industry takes off.
1909	U.S. piano production reaches all-time high and publication of piano rags peaks.
	Euphonic Sounds (Scott Joplin), *Grace and Beauty* (James Scott) published.
	Temptation Rag (Henry Lodge) issued, becomes hit.
1910	*The Entertainer's Rag* (Jay Roberts), *Red Pepper* (Henry Lodge) are hits.
	John Stark closes New York office, returns to Saint Louis.

(Continued)

Table 12 (*Continued*)
A Chronology of Ragtime, 1896–1920

YEAR	ACTIVITY
1911	Joplin completes, copyrights, and self-publishes his opera *Treemonisha*. Irving Berlin's *Alexander's Ragtime Band* becomes smash song hit. Other ragtime hits include *Très Moutarde* (Cecil Macklin), *Red Rose Rag* (song by Percy Wenrich and Edward Madden), and *Grizzly Bear Rag* (George Botsford). *Ragtime Oriole* (James Scott) published.
1912	First hand-played piano rolls issued. Mike Bernard becomes the first to regularly record ragtime piano.
1913	John Stark publishes the first of Artie Matthews' five *Pastime* rags. *American Beauty Rag* (Joseph Lamb), *Junk Man Rag* (Luckey Roberts) issued.
1914	*Magnetic Rag* (Joplin), *Cataract Rag* (Robert Hampton), *Hot House Rag* (Paul Pratt), *12th Street Rag* (Euday L. Bowman) issued. Axel Christensen begins publishing the monthly magazine *Rag Time Review*.
1915	*Ragtime Nightingale* (Lamb) published. Popular rag successes include *Ragging the Scale* (Edward B. Claypoole) and *Canadian Capers* (Cohen, Chandler, and White).
1916	*Top Liner Rag* (Lamb) published. Luckey Roberts becomes first black "stride" pianist to make records.
1917	Scott Joplin dies, his *Reflection Rag* published posthumously. *Rag Time Review* absorbed by *Melody* magazine. Erik Satie incorporates ragtime into *Parade*.
1918	*Russian Rag* (George Cobb) becomes one of the last rag hits during Ragtime Era. James P. Johnson makes piano roll of *Carolina Shout;* Jelly Roll Morton copyrights *Frog-I-More Rag*. Igor Stravinsky composes *Ragtime for Eleven Instruments* and "Rag-Music" from *L'histoire du soldat*.
1919	Player piano production reaches near-peak (peak is 1923).
1920	John Stark publishes the last of Artie Matthews' five *Pastime* rags. Igor Stravinsky composes *Piano Rag-Music*.

> And this great and only critic,
> Both didactic and analytic
> Said: "Es gibt nichts bessers.
> Ausgezeichnet ist 'rag-time'!"[36]

    American banjoists had brought ragtime to England even before 1900. Lowell Schreyer notes, in his chapter on "The Banjo in Ragtime," that Cadwallader L. Mays and Parke Hunter went to England in January 1897 to introduce ragtime to the British. In 1900 and again in 1903, American banjo virtuoso Vess L. Ossman carried ragtime to England. Ragtime also went to England by means of sheet music.[37] In some cases, American publishers sold ragtime (and other music) through their own branches in London. In other cases, they sold the British publishing rights to English firms.

    Back in the United States, ragtime publication continued strongly well into the 1910s, after which it all but ceased. By 1920, the Ragtime Era was decidedly over. Jazz recording was gathering momentum, after its beginning in 1917. Jelly Roll Morton and Eastern "stride" pianists were becoming major influences in Afro-American piano music. In 1921, novelty piano burst on

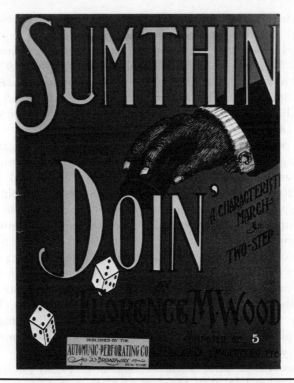

Florence M. Wood's rag *Sumthin' Doin'* (1904) illustrates the racial imagery common before about 1905. Racial stereotyping gradually gave way in succeeding years to genteel images. (*John Edward Hasse collection*)

the scene with the phenomenal success of Zez Confrey's *Kitten on the Keys*. Novelty piano, a flashy offshoot of ragtime, lasted throughout the 1920s.

It is incorrect, however, to say that ragtime died in the late 1910s. While the composition and publication of rags virtually ceased, the performance, recording, and enjoyment of ragtime did not. Millions upon millions of pieces of ragtime sheet music, ragtime piano rolls, and ragtime recordings were in the hands of the public, and it did not suddenly discard all this material. Ragtime remained in the repertory of countless pianists—amateur and professional—and other musicians. Rags continued to be heard on old piano rolls and old recordings. Some new recordings were made of rags. During the 1920s and 1930s, *12th Street Rag* was recorded forty-eight times and *Maple Leaf Rag* twenty-four times.[38]

The booming silent movie theaters provided a venue for ragtime as accompaniment to parts of films. And when talking pictures came in, ragtime was incorporated into their soundtracks.[39] Ragtime had, however, become old hat by the 1920s. In fact, it was frequently used in silent and talking pictures to evoke nostalgia. Think of all those old Western movies with the "perfesser" beating out rag rhythms on a battered saloon upright!

Another development of the 1920s was the continued use of ragtime by composers of Western art music ("classical" music). In the early 1900s, Charles Ives (1874–1954) pioneered in incorporating ragtime into "cultivated" works. Ives was followed by Claude Debussy (1862–1918) and, in the 1910s, by Henry F. Gilbert (1868–1928), Igor Stravinsky (1882–1971), and Erik Satie (1866–1925). The 1920s brought Darius Milhaud (1892–1974), Erwin Schulhoff (1894–1942), Paul Hindemith (1895–1963), and Louis Gruenberg (1884–1964) to ragtime.

A revival of interest in rag piano and traditional jazz began in the early 1940s. No single incident marks the beginning of renewed interest in piano ragtime. However, one of the first events of the revival took place in 1941, when Lu Watters' Yerba Buena Jazz Band began recording old rags, such as *Maple Leaf Rag, Black and White Rag, At a Georgia Campmeeting,* and *Smokey Mokes.* Watters' group was, in the words of Terry Waldo, "discontented with both the overarranged big bands and, at the other extreme, the unimaginative solo-after-solo small groups that had come to represent jazz music during the swing era of the 1930s,"[40] and turned to older ensemble styles of jazz. Through recordings, Watters' influence spread nationally and even internationally, albeit to a relatively small group of aficionados. This evidence reveals that the recording industry—and especially small, specialist companies—played a leading role in the revival of instrumental ragtime since the early 1940s.[41]

By the mid-1940s, jazz specialist magazines began publishing articles about Scott Joplin, Jelly Roll Morton, and other early figures. The event which had the most enduring impact was the publication in 1950 of the first history of ragtime, *They All Played Ragtime.* This now-classic book by Rudi Blesh and Harriet Janis rescued the ragtime story from otherwise likely oblivion, sparked the imagination of countless readers, and inspired a number of ragtime figures of later years to get involved with the music.

Despite the book's emphasis on "classic ragtime," however, the 1950s saw ragtime treated primarily as flashy, rinky-tinky "honky-tonk" music. Recording artists "Knuckles O'Toole," "Slugger Ryan," "Willie 'the Rock' Knox," and others featured pianos "doctored" to produce highly percussive sounds.[42]

Table 13 presents a number of other milestones in the revival of instrumental ragtime, concentrating on events that brought the sound of ragtime, directly or indirectly, to a large number of people. Two of these events, both concerning Scott Joplin, stand out as preeminent in spreading ragtime to a mass audience. In 1971, the New York Public Library issued the two-volume *Collected Works of Scott Joplin,* edited by the historian and concert pianist Vera Brodsky Lawrence. This handsome edition restored Joplin's work to print for the first time in sixty years and gathered nearly his entire oeuvre into one anthology. Joplin's music became readily available to professional and amateur pianists, and suddenly, all over America, pianos were resounding to Joplin's joyous syncopations. His rags began to be recorded and performed in public, including the concert stage. And the

Table 13
Milestones in the Revival of Ragtime

YEAR	EVENT
1941	Lu Watters' Yerba Buena Jazz Band begins recording old rags.
1942	Wally Rose makes his first piano rag recording.
1944	Brun Campbell and Roy Carew begin writing articles on ragtime for specialist magazines *Record Changer, Jazz Record, Jazz Journal.*
1946	Luckey Roberts and Brun Campbell make rag recordings.
1947	Jelly Roll Morton's Library of Congress recordings (recorded 1938) are issued by Rudi Blesh's Circle Records.
1948	Pee Wee Hunt's recording of *12th Street Rag* becomes smash hit.
1949	Pianists Marvin Ash, Don Ewell, Knocky Parker, Ralph Sutton, and Charley Thompson make their first rag recordings.
1940s	Professor Albert White forms Gaslight Orchestra, in San Francisco, to perform Ragtime-Era orchestrations of ragtime and popular music.
1950	*They All Played Ragtime* (Rudi Blesh and Harriet Janis) and *Mister Jelly Roll* (Alan Lomax) published, stimulate public interest.
	Lou Busch begins recording ragtime as "Joe 'Fingers' Carr."
1955	Bob Darch begins performing "classic ragtime" on the saloon circuit.
	Johnny Maddox has record hit with ragtime-oriented *Crazy Otto Medley.*
1956	Riverside issues LP of piano roll rags, as interest in rolls picks up and Aeolian manufacturers first U.S. player piano in nearly thirty years.
1959–60	Max Morath's *The Ragtime Era* series is broadcast on educational TV.
1960–62*	Knocky Parker becomes first to record complete piano rags of Scott Joplin and James Scott (Audiophile Records, two two-LP albums).
1961	Mills Music begins issuing piano rag folios, under Bernard Kalban.
1961–62	Max Morath's *Turn of the Century* series airs on educational TV.
1961	The *Ragtime Review* is founded by Trebor Tichenor and Russ Cassidy (publishes until 1966).
1962	The Ragtime Society is founded in Canada.
1963	Max Morath opens his ragtime act in New York City, at the Blue Angel.
1965	Saint Louis Ragtime Festival begins as annual event.
1967	Maple Leaf Club organized in Los Angeles by Dick Zimmerman.
1970	Joshua Rifkin's *Piano Rags by Scott Joplin* (Nonesuch Records) issued.
1971	*Collected Works of Scott Joplin* issued by New York Public Library.
	William Bolcom begins recording his own and classic rags (Nonesuch).
1972	Gunther Schuller founds New England Conservatory Ragtime Ensemble.
	Joplin's opera *Treemonisa* revived in Atlanta.
1973	Dover begins issuing piano rag anthologies, starting with *Classic Piano Rags* (Rudi Blesh, compiler).
	The Red Back Book LP of the New England Conservatory Ragtime Ensemble tops the classical record charts.
1974	Motion picture *The Sting*, featuring Joplin music, released.
	The Entertainer, from *The Sting* soundtrack, tops the pop record charts.
	National Public Radio broadcasts Terry Waldo's *This is Ragtime* series.
	Murray Hill issues Dick Zimmerman's five-LP complete Joplin piano works.
	Scott Joplin's grave finally receives a marker, courtesy ASCAP.
1975	Scott Joplin's opera *Treemonisa* opens on Broadway.
	RCA Red Seal issues Dick Hyman's five-LP complete Joplin piano works.
1976	Scott Joplin receives a special posthumous Pulitzer Prize in music.
1977	*Scott Joplin* movie released, starring Billy Dee Williams and Art Carney.
	Joplin home in Saint Louis is designated National Historic Landmark.
1970s	Folkways, Biograph, Herwin, and other small record companies issue many rag records, along with bigger CBS, RCA, MCA, Angel, and Nonesuch.
	Edward B. Marks, Belwin-Mills, Charles Hansen, *et al.* publish rag music folios.
1980	Edward A. Berlin's *Ragtime: A Musical and Cultural History* sets new standards in ragtime scholarship.
1982	The Smithsonian Institution issues Jelly Roll Morton's *Collected Piano Works* (James Dapogny, editor).
	Murray Hills issues Dick Zimmerman's five-LP *Collector's History of Ragtime.*
1983	Eubie Blake celebrates his one-hundredth birthday and, five days later, dies.
	U.S. Postal Service issues Scott Joplin commemorative postage stamp.

*Year approximate.

performance by professionals and dabblers alike is what truly made the Joplin revival.

The other far-reaching event was the adoption of Joplin rags into the soundtrack of *The Sting,* a movie hit of 1974. More than anything else, this film and its successful soundtrack recording spurred a Joplin and ragtime revival on records. Dozens of recording artists and record companies got into the act. By the late 1970s, more than two hundred LPs of ragtime had been issued. Once rags were on record, they were heard over the radio. "Classical" music stations, jazz stations, and even rock stations (while *The Sting* was hot) played rag records.

The Significance of Ragtime

Ragtime left its impact on American music and culture in a number of ways:

1. Combining African and European antecedents into a wholly new creation, ragtime was one of the first truly American musical genres.
2. Ragtime helped lead to jazz, which has had an enormous impact on music, and to novelty piano music, the popularity of which, though short lived, was pronounced. Ragtime's popularity spread throughout Canada, Europe, Australia, and elsewhere, paving the way for the later acceptance of American jazz abroad.
3. Ragtime allowed Afro-American rhythms to penetrate to the heart of the American musical culture, at a time when blacks were denied access to many avenues of American society. The popularity of ragtime provided entrée into commercial musical life for black musicians who might not otherwise have been accepted during an age of spreading "Jim Crow" laws and discrimination.
4. Ragtime, especially instrumental rags created by the most gifted composers, gave us a body of works of lasting merit.
5. The crisp rhythms of ragtime hurried the decline of the musically limited parlor organ and helped give rise to the more versatile piano as the primary instrument of home music making.
6. Ragtime helped spark public debate about popular music and American music, thereby raising awareness of America's musical achievements.

Thus, ragtime was significant in a number of ways. It may have created more impact than any previous type of American vernacular music.

Happily, ragtime appears to be with us to stay. I suspect that, having been nearly forgotten for sixty years, the work of Scott Joplin and some of his peers will be with us for a long time. While rags may never be in the forefront of the public stage, they will undoubtedly remain, like the marches of John Philip Sousa, a permanent part of America's musical consciousness, ever capable of stirring the listener.

Notes

1. Complete facts of publication for compositions mentioned in the text of this book can be found in the Checklist of Compositions.
2. Edward A. Berlin, *Ragtime: A Musical and Cultural History* (Berkeley and Los Angeles: University of California Press, 1980), pp. 128–30.
3. "Secondary rag" is discussed by Lowell Schreyer in footnote 29 to his chapter "The Banjo in Ragtime" in this book.
4. See Charles Hamm, *Music in the New World* (New York: Norton, 1983), pp. 393–94; and Samuel A. Floyd, Jr., and Marsha J. Reisser, "Social Dance Music of Black Composers in the Nineteenth Century and the Emergence of Classic Ragtime," *The Black Perspective in Music* 8, no. 2 (Fall 1980), pp. 172–73. This kind of analysis of rag rhythms first came to my attention through an ethnomusicology course taught by Professor Charles L. Boilés, at Indiana University in the spring of 1975.
5. John Edward Hasse, "The Creation and Dissemination of Indianapolis Ragtime, 1897–1930" (Ph.D. diss., Indiana University, 1981), pp. 233–37.
6. Berlin, *Ragtime*, pp. 66–71.
7. U.S. Music player piano rolls 6981 and 6963.
8. Included in Eubie Blake's LP record, *The Marches I Played on the Old Ragtime Piano*, 20th Century Fox 3009 [ca. 1958]. Reissued as RCA (France) T610.
9. Juli Jones, "Great Colored Song Writers and Their Songs," *The Freeman*, 23 December 1911, p. 6.
10. Sidney Lanier, *Florida: Its Scenery, Climate, and History . . . Being a Complete Hand-book and Guide* (Philadelphia: J. B. Lippincott, 1876), pp. 30–31. Quoted in Dena J. Epstein, *Sinful Tunes and Spirituals: Black Folk Music to the Civil War* (Urbana: University of Illinois Press), pp. 294–95.
11. Letter by unidentified correspondent in Beatrice, Nebraska, in "Correspondent's Column," *S. S. Stewart's Banjo and Guitar Journal* 5, no. 3 (August–September 1888): 2. Quoted by Lowell Schreyer in his chapter "The Banjo in Ragtime" in this book.
12. George W. Cable, "The Dance in Place Congo," *Century Magazine*, February 1886, p. 525. Quoted in Rudi Blesh and Harriet Janis, *They All Played Ragtime*, 4th ed., rev. (New York: Oak Publications, 1971), p. 83. Berlin (*Ragtime*, p. 26) points out that the musical example Cable includes does not reveal ragtime rhythms; however, this does not mean that the music performance was not syncopated. Cable, a novelist, might not have been accurate in transcribing the music to paper.
13. Berlin, *Ragtime*, pp. 81–2, 109. See also David A. Jasen and Trebor Jay Tichenor, *Rags and Ragtime: A Musical History* (New York: Seabury Press, 1978), pp. 10–11.
14. See untitled *Chicago Chronicle* article of 1897 quoted in Blesh and Janis, *They All Played Ragtime*, p. 150. In his discussion of the Chicago World's Fair, Berlin cites these sources: Isidore Witmark and Isaac Goldberg, *The Story of the House of Witmark* (New York: Lee Furman, 1939), pp. 169–70; "Questions and Answers," *Etude* 16 (December 1898): 349; and "'Coon Songs' on the Wane," *American Musician and Art Journal* 22 (12 June 1906): 26a.
15. Natalie Curtis, "The Negro's Contribution to the Music of America," *Craftsman* 23 (15 March 1913): 662.
16. "Ragtime (Invented in St. Louis) Is Dead," *Saint Louis Post-Dispatch*, 4 April 1909, p. 1.
17. Juli Jones, "Great Colored Song Writers."
18. Charles E. Ives, *Memos*, ed. John Kirkpatrick (New York: Norton, 1972), p. 56. Cited by Berlin, *Ragtime*, p. 16.
19. C. Vann Woodward, *The Strange Career of Jim Crow*, 2nd ed., rev. (New York: Oxford University Press, 1966), p. 74; Rayford W. Logan, *The Betrayal of the Negro: From Rutherford B. Hayes to Woodrow Wilson* (New York: Collier Books, 1965), p. 74.
20. Woodbine, "The Stage," *The Freeman*, 6 May 1905.
21. Daniel J. Boorstin, *The Americans: The Democratic Experience* (New York: Random House, 1973), p. 384.

22. My sample of 1,514 rags reveals a peak of 158 rags published in 1909. Using a smaller sample of 1,035 published piano rags, Berlin shows a publication peak of 124 rags in 1899. See Berlin, *Ragtime*, p. 73.

23. For a discussion of some physical effects of ragtime, see Neil Leonard's chapter "The Reaction to Ragtime," elsewhere in this book.

24. Gustav Kühl, "The Musical Possibilities of Rag-Time," trans. Gustav Saenger, *Metronome* 19 (March 1903): 11; (April 1903): 8. Emphasis added.

25. Scott Joplin, James Scott, Joseph Lamb, Brun Campbell, Jelly Roll Morton, and May Aufderheide are profiled in several chapters in this book. For further information on major rag composers, see especially Blesh and Janis, *They All Played Ragtime;* Jasen and Tichenor, *Rags and Ragtime;* and the Select Bibliography at the back of this book.

26. *They All Played Ragtime: The True Story of an American Music* by Rudi Blesh and Harriet Janis was first published by Alfred A. Knopf, New York, in 1950.

27. Eubie Blake tells about pianists Jesse Pickett, "Big Head" Wilbur, "One Leg" Willie Joseph, "Slew Foot" Nelson, Jack "the Bear" Wilson, "No Legs" Carey, Willie "the Lion" Smith, Sammy Ewell, Hughie Wolford, and others: Al Rose, *Eubie Blake* (New York: Schirmer Books, 1979), pp. 20, 40, 46, 148–50, 155. Jelly Roll Morton reminisced for Alan Lomax about Benny Frenchy, Alfred Wilson, Tony Jackson, Porter King, Artie Matthews, and other pianists: Alan Lomax, *Mister Jelly Roll,* 2nd ed. (Berkeley and Los Angeles: University of California Press, 1973), pp. 120–21, 137–40, and *passim.* See also Tom Davin, "Conversations with James P. Johnson" in this book; Willie "the Lion" Smith, *Music on My Mind: The Memoirs of an American Pianist,* with George Hoefer (Garden City, N.Y.: Doubleday, 1964). A ragtime piano contest held in Chicago in 1916 included the colorfully named "Sparrow," "Bert King, alias Black Diamond," and "Squirrel" (Harry Crosby): see advertisement for this contest reproduced in Blesh and Janis, *They All Played Ragtime,* 4th ed., rev., following p. 80.

28. Advertisement, *The Freeman,* 5 January 1901, p. 5.

29. Edward A. Berlin, "Ragtime and Improvised Piano: Another View," *Journal of Jazz Studies* 4, no. 2 (Spring/Summer 1977): 4–10.

30. Biographical information on Stark is included in Rudi Blesh and Harriet Janis, *They All Played Ragtime,* 4th ed., rev. (New York: Oak Publications, 1971), pp. 45–54 and *passim,* and David A. Jasen and Trebor Jay Tichenor, *Rags and Ragtime: A Musical History* (New York: Seabury Press, 1978), pp. 78–80.

31. The exceptions were Scott Joplin's first published rag, *Original Rags,* which was arranged by Charles N. Daniels (1899), and Joseph Lamb's *Sensation: A Rag* (1908), which carried Joplin's name as arranger.

32. Personal interview with Abe Olman, Rancho Mirage, California, 23 July 1980. Composer J. Russel Robinson said that the Stark Music Company "liked my work, because I was one of the few people who could write out the complete piano part." See J. Russel Robinson, "Dixieland Piano," as told to Ralph Auf der Heide, *Record Changer,* August 1947, p. 7.

33. LP recordings of rags are not included as there is, as yet, no thorough discography of rags on long-playing records.

34. Berlin, *Ragtime,* pp. 122–30.

35. For a treatment of rags in the aural tradition of white country music, see the chapter "Ragtime in Early Country Music," by Norm Cohen and David Cohen, in this book.

36. P. J. Meahl (untitled poem), *Brainard's Musical* 2, no. 2 (November 1900): 31.

37. Scott Joplin is alleged to have visited Germany, though no conclusive evidence has yet appeared. See James A. Haskins with Kathleen Benson, *Scott Joplin: The Man Who Made Ragtime* (New York: Doubleday, 1978), pp. 113, 151. See also Edward S. Walker, "Scott Joplin in England: An Investigation," *Storyville* no. 68 (December 1976–January 1977): 66–68.

38. See David A. Jasen, *Recorded Ragtime, 1897–1958* (Hamden, Conn.: Archon Books, 1973), pp. 63–65 and 99–102.

39. An early example is Walt Disney's 1932 cartoon *Whoopee Party,* which includes the *Maple Leaf Rag.* This recording is available on LP: Dick Schory, producer, *The Magical Music of Walt Disney: 50 Years of Original Motion Picture Sound Tracks,* (five-disc set), Ovation Records OV-5000, 1978, Vol. 1.

40. Terry Waldo, *This is Ragtime* (New York: Hawthorn Books, 1976), p. 133.

41. Ragtime songs have not yet undergone a full-scale revival. Perhaps this is because they are not as rhythmically interesting or as "jazzable" as piano rags. In some cases, too, the lyrics are offensive. Max Morath has revived some of the best ragtime songs in his stage shows, recordings, and writings. See, for example, *Max Morath's Songs of the Early 20th Century Entertainer* (New York: Edward B. Marks, 1977). Also useful in Ann Charters' collection, *The Ragtime Songbook* (New York: Oak Publications, 1963). Additional collections of ragtime songs are listed in "Ragtime Music Folios and Method Books," in the back of this book. In several of his recordings, singer Ian Whitcomb has brought back now-obscure ragtime songs. Examples include *Pianomelt,* Sierra Records SRS-8708, 1980; Ian Whitcomb and Dick Zimmerman, *"Don't Say Good-Bye, Miss Ragtime,"* Stomp Off Records S.O.S. 1017, 1981; and Ian Whitcomb and Dick Zimmerman, *My Wife is Dancing Mad!,* Stomp Off Records S.O.S. 1049, 1982.

42. These three names are all pseudonyms of pianist Dick Hyman. For further discussion of ragtime as honky-tonk music, see Waldo, *This is Ragtime,* pp. 156–63.

The
History
of
Ragtime

Ragtime

Guy Waterman

Guy Waterman wrote this influential article in 1959, at a time when very few people were exploring the subject. He draws a sharp distinction between ragtime, as a body of written compositions, and jazz, as an improvisatory art. Waterman limits ragtime to piano rags, and emphasizes the work of Scott Joplin and a few select peers.

Ragtime, as it will be discussed here, differs from perhaps all other jazz and related music in that it is a body of written compositions. Jazz, as we usually think of it, is an improvised or arranged music, the only permanent illustration of which take the form of recordings. Ragtime, in the context of this chapter, consists of printed music for piano.[1]

This difference is mentioned at the outset because it is more than a surface one. It reflects a difference in the orientation of the music. Jazz, whether written down in arrangements or improvised from the simplest resources (*e.g.*, a twelve-bar blues), starts with a melody and its supporting harmony. The creative process involves what is done with that melody and harmony. In ragtime, the creative process is in the writing of the whole piece in all its parts, horizontal and vertical. Ragtime lies more in the orientation of concert music than of jazz. Like all generalizations, this one obviously should be qualified; in its essential respect, however, it is valid.

It should be stressed that this distinction applies to ragtime "as it will be discussed here." It is well known that in the whole range of jazz there has been little final agreement on definitions and in many cases not even a consensus as to what is roughly meant by certain terms. For many people, including many authoritative people, the word ragtime means a particular style of playing which was used fully as much in early jazz piano as in the rag compositions. To some, ragtime is simply another name for early jazz. There is no special mandate for the definition used here, other than that which should presumably be the test for all definitions, namely, that it is *useful*—it facilitates analysis. We want to analyze this particular body of music and, in so doing, to shut off—or at least treat as different—other types of music. To do this requires that we use some terms for this music. If a term other than "ragtime" were desired, it could be substituted.

Briefly, the period of ragtime composition covers the first two decades of the twentieth century. While Roy J. Carew has traced the characteristic rhythm of ragtime (discussed below) back to an 1848 publication, it is customary to refer to the first ragtime publication as William Krell's *Mississippi Rag*, which appeared in 1897. In the same year, Tom Turpin's *Harlem Rag* appeared. In 1899 and 1900 a steady stream of published compositions bearing the title "rag" began to appear. For the first five years or so, the style was extremely simple and light. Toward the end of the first decade, more "serious" or "high-class" rags came out. The leading composers at this time were Scott Joplin, James Scott, and Joseph Lamb. Shortly after 1910, ragtime became a national fad, in a watered-down, ricky-ticky form suitable for mass audiences. This fad gave way to another, jazz, around the year 1920. The major composers published right on through the 'teens, and there were even a few rags in the early 1920s, but by 1925 ragtime composition had stopped altogether.

It will be convenient in this description of ragtime to center attention on the rags of the most important composers. These are Scott Joplin, James Scott, Joseph Lamb, Artie Matthews, Tom Turpin, and only occasionally others. This list may appear to select some and reject other composers arbitrarily, but the selection is actually based on the perusal which this writer has made of the field plus competent advice from those who have done more intensive research on the great flood of written material in the period.[2]

To the jazz audience, ragtime is a relatively little-known field. This is because the jazz audience is accustomed to dealing with recordings, not with the printed page. The number of rags which have been recorded "straight" is quite limited. It might be well to approach ragtime, therefore, by analyzing first the resources with which it works—the ragtime "orthodoxy," so to speak.

Rhythmically ragtime is most noted for its characteristic right-hand rhythmic phrases: ♫ ♩♪ and ♫♫♩♪ .

These characteristic phrases run through virtually all published rags. Pages of Joplin abound on little more rhythmically. A good illustration of these rhythms is to be found in Tom Turpin's *St. Louis Rag*, which fortunately is available in an excellent recording of ragtime piano rolls.[3] The first strain of this rag is almost wholly built on the phrase: ♫♫♩♫♫♩. The second strain then uses this phrase:♫♫♫. The third strain uses this phrase:♫♫♫.

In ragtime the sixteenth-note runs stopping on a syncopated beat are common. As one exaggerated example, take the sweeping line in Joplin's *Chrysanthemum*, first strain:

Example 6. Scott Joplin, *The Chrysanthemum*, **A** strain, right-hand part.

The left hand in ragtime is normally cast in a supporting role. The well-known oom-pah pattern of alternating single notes and chords is used. The left hand virtually never engages in syncopation. There are important exceptions, of course—*Cascades*, for example, third strain. When syncopation is used, however, it is usually more decorously done. James Scott's frequent left-hand syncopation always knows its place—that is, it is inserted in the eighth or sixteenth or perhaps seventh and eighth measures of a strain, where it will not interfere with the orthodox ragtime momentum.

This rhythmic phrasing is virtually never more complicated. It is of the essence of ragtime style that it can be trusted not to throw in less regular rhythmic patterns. One of the surest giveaways of Jelly's *jazz*, not ragtime, posture is his hitting the left hand a sixteenth note early. This can be seen in his "transformations" of *Maple Leaf Rag* and *Original Rags*. No rag writer would dream of such a blatant New Orleans crudity. Many of the revivalists fail to get an appropriate rag sound because of left-hand syncopation alone.

Ragtime's orthodoxy extends to the larger rhythmic scene—that is, to the organization of the whole strain. Virtually all rag strains are sixteen bars divided into four equal parts.[4] Many strains are organized as so many simple pieces in the classical period of Western art music (Haydn, Mozart, Beethoven): A, B, A, C, "B" being a semi-cadence, "C" a full cadence. This organization of tunes was carried over into jazz and became one of the essentials of jazz orthodoxy. In fact, while exceptions to the rule are rare in ragtime, they are still rarer in jazz, once the early New Orleans stage is over. The reason lies in the requirements of improvisation, the need to be able to assume without the slightest mental reservation that the chorus will be over exactly sixteen (or thirty-two or twelve) bars from now, not seventeen or fifteen.

We have noted the strict orthodoxy of ragtime in rhythmic phrasing and in the internal structure of the sixteen-bar strains. Moving to a still larger "rhythmic" dimension, the structure of the whole rag, we again find a remarkable degree of orthodoxy. A heavy majority of all rags are organized on the basis of four strains, either **ABCD** or **ABACD,** with a less common structure being **ABACDC.** In nearly all cases a repeat will be indicated for all strains except the return of a strain. There is remarkable agreement on this organization. For example, of thirty-nine Joplin rags (including collaborations), twenty-seven are built **ABACD.** Joplin's rags, as the archetype of the music, are unusually steadfast (until his late experimental period). In the whole Joplin literature only two rags, *Euphonic Sounds* and *Palm Leaf Rag,* have less than four themes and only two have more (coincidentally, the first and the last). Turpin generally used four strains. James Scott was willing to hold himself to three on occasion. Three of Artie Matthews' five *Pastimes* are organized **ABACD,** one **ABCD** and one **ABC.**

In developing the four-strain structure into a coherent whole, several approaches came into usage. The **A** theme will ordinarily be a straight-forward "statement" type of theme. It is a complete-in-itself type of home base, to which it will be possible to return after **B.** It is the theme which will be thought of as giving that rag its individuality. If asked to play *Fig Leaf Rag* or *St. Louis Rag,* one would play the first theme automatically. It is sometimes used as a special-effects type of theme, with the other strains being more typical two-beat (see *Maple Leaf Rag*).

The **B** theme will be a lighter, milder, less filled-in treatment. Often it will be prefaced by an unaccompanied right hand ♪ ♫ on the dominant. Often, though not always, the melodic line will have a tendency to soar, so that the effect of returning to **A** is a kind of coming back to the meat of things. As one device for achieving this type of effect, rag writers, quite unconsciously I am sure, saw fit to lead off theme **A** with a tonic chord but **B** with a dominant chord. This would certainly seem to be appropriate in light of the experience of tonal composers in legitimate, diatonic music. In some rags, the **B** strain modulates to the key of the dominant—Scott Joplin's *Chrysanthemum,* for example. In *The Strenuous Life,* Scott Joplin even modulates to the dominant chord of the dominant key, an awkward change. Perhaps the best way to point up the relationship between themes **A** and **B** in a rag is by analogy with the first and second themes of the standard sonata first movement. The contrast is precisely the same. The feeling of rising to the dominant key for the second theme is the effect which rag writers strove for without actually taking the plunge, except occasionally.

To note the relationship between the first and second themes, it would be useful to consult *Weeping Willow Rag* as very typical. Other typical illustrations include *Frog Legs Rag, Harlem Rag, Red Peppers Rag,* and *Pickles and Peppers.*

The function of the final two strains extends the development of the rag. Where strain **B** rises to a lighter vein than **A**, strain **C** instead sinks into a slightly darker color. Normally it modulates down a fifth; it will generally tend towards the lower register of the treble. In some rags it is analogous to the trio of a march—quiet, melodious, simple. It is more apt, however, to have a kind of rhythmic excitement—subdued, contained, waiting to burst out.

The release, of course, comes with strain **D**. This is ordinarily a blaze of triumph. Sometimes it comes back to the original tonic (in *Maple Leaf,* for example); this can produce a electrifying effect. But usually it remains in the new key, dispersing most, if not all, of its subdominant atmosphere, however.[5] Often it will have more of a riff quality than the other strains. It is, in general, certainly far more relaxed than **C**, perhaps more than all the other three. It gives the rag finality in a wholly positive vein.

For illustration of the relationship of these four themes to one another, Turpin's *St. Louis Rag* serves admirably, especially since it is available on LP. *St. Louis Rag* is atypical in the harmony which opens theme **A** and in the lack of a return to **A** after **B**; otherwise, however, it is a "perfect" rag. With reference to the tonal flavor of **C** and **D**, *St. Louis Rag* illustrates well how both themes use the same key, yet **C** is distinctly subdominant while in **D** no subdominant flavor is present.

Frog Legs Rag by James Scott is another in the mold, with one difference. The **A** strain is a straightforward detailed ragtime theme, followed by a soaring **B** theme (the kind of thing which brings out the best in Scott), followed by a return to **A**. The one departure from the norm is that the key of **C** and **D** then lies up a fifth rather than down. Strain **C**, however, serves the function previously suggested—that of being more subdued and suggestive, waiting for the final outburst. It is true that Scott's fury lies just under the surface in this kind of strain. The calm is threatened by the surge in bar six, but saved by the fact that seven and eight do not flare up as they do in equivalent passages of Scott's other rags (see *Grace and Beauty, Hilarity Rag,* etc.). Instead, bars seven and eight descend tamely in a sixteenth-note run. Theme **D** is then a typical blaze of triumph ignited by Scott's boundless energy.

It would be erroneous to suggest that this **ABACD** organization had anything like the universal acceptance of some of the other trappings of the ragtime orthodoxy. Plenty of departures may be found, especially in James Scott. Even old Tom Turpin's 1899 *Harlem Rag* is out of the cast, except that it does rise to the dominant for theme **B** and sinks with the final tonic.

Joplin in late years (from 1909 on) was moving towards considerably more varied and interesting structures, almost towards classical forms. This probably was *not* deliberate or conscious on his part. That is to say, he probably did not create within deliberately achieved classical forms as his objective; rather, he probably approached classical forms simply by developing ragtime as he saw it. For his creative mind this appeared to be the direction in which the music *had* to move after its tremendously productive years just before 1910. Both in ragtime orthodoxy as it had emerged then and in Joplin's new directions afterwards, form was the servant of substance, not vice versa.[6]

Magnetic Rag, it could be argued, points towards the sonata form essentially. The return to **A** has all the attributes of the classical recapitulation. The two preceding themes (**C** and **D**) resemble, as closely as ragtime could, a development section. **C** actually breaks through the sixteen-bar barrier, which, as has been mentioned, is a most rare incident. The **D** theme is in the tonic's own minor, in contrast to the normal use of the relative minor in ragtime and jazz. In keeping with the classical concept of key relationships significant to a development section, Joplin goes from B flat major into B flat minor. In the return, the classical method of "dominant preparation" (harping on and around the dominant of the key which is to be restored) is used fully. The key of theme **D**, it is especially worth noting, has been viciously exploded with the fourth beat of bar fourteen. The mere fact of destroying theme **D's** key within its own sixteen-bar framework suggests something like a development section.

Having examined the ragtime orthodoxy from the horizontal standpoint (rhythm and over-all structure), it may also be useful to note the well-known orthodoxy of ragtime harmony.

Much of ragtime harmony is based on standard tonic-dominant changes. There is extensive use of the common change: tonic to sub-mediant to super-tonic to dominant back to tonic. There is, of course, tonic to sub-dominant. Frequently the final four bars will run as follows: IV—IV minor—I—VI—II—V—I.

Frequently at the midpoint of a strain the harmony will move into the mediant minor, and then slide neatly into the dominant in preparation for return to the second half of the strain.

These harmonies, it is clear, are substantially identical to those used in early jazz. In fact, it is safe to say that from the standpoint of harmony alone, everything found in early jazz is found in ragtime, except that early jazz tended to place far more emphasis on the standard blues chorus and internal harmonies appropriate to that series of chord changes. It was well into the 1920's before jazz had need of more complex harmonic resources.

This is not to say that ragtime and early jazz have an identical concept of harmony. In the last-four transition from IV, for example, ragtime would typically use the VI minor, rather than the VI major seventh. More basic, harmonically, was the use of the cadential $^6_4$ chord in the middle of a tune where jazz always used the super-tonic, because of the preference in jazz for going up by fourths wherever possible. This is seen clearly in the tenth album of the Jelly Roll Morton Library of Congress series, in *My Gal Sal.* Here, in an old barbershop quartet, in so obvious a $^6_4$ situation, Jelly still substitutes the super-tonic, even the first time through, when he is ostensibly playing it straight. This makes the D the ninth of the super-tonic instead of the top $^6_4$ chord. What Jelly ever expected the whiskey tenor to do with that super-tonic is hard to guess. No orthodox tenor ever successfully got on top of a ninth chord.

Ragtime never had such an aversion for the $^6_4$ chord, particularly in the middle of a strain. The difference reflects the fundamental difference in orientation of ragtime itself. The foregoing description of the resources with which ragtime works is necessary to full appreciation of it. In every music there are these conventions which must develop before the music can become fully creative. For the listener to understand and fully absorb the profound experience of a really creative musical achievement, familiarity with the tools with which the music works is an essential first step.

But, having discussed the resources which the listener will need in approaching ragtime, it is perhaps appropriate to point out where the creative music within the field is to be found. Most of the significant names have already been mentioned. There is good ragtime to be found in the compositions of Tom Turpin, Charles Hunter, Charles L. Johnson, Henry Lodge, Paul Pratt, and some others. Arthur Marshall and Scott Hayden participated in some notable collaborations with Joplin. Every indiciation is that Louis Chauvin was one of the most creative musicians of the time. Unfortunately, however, there is precious little of Chauvin on the printed page. Of known stature are Joseph Lamb and Artie Matthews. Joseph Lamb entered ragtime publication between 1905 and 1910. Eight of his eleven published rags appeared after 1912. The style had already been staked out by Turpin, Joplin, and others. Lamb had no pioneering to do, but he did contribute some of the most powerful ragtime composition in the field. His *American Beauty Rag* is perhaps best known and is available on a recorded piano roll. It illustrates the imprint which is on every Lamb rag, the full, hard-hitting, rhythmically alive style. Lamb possibly made more use of the full range of the piano's register than any other significant rag writer. While his melodic invention was perhaps somewhat limited, he did not run out of ideas within the framework of classic ragtime.

Artie Matthews was quite a different composer from Lamb. Matthews came along well after the peak period of ragtime composition. He is known almost exclusively for five rags, all of which go under the title of *Pastime Rag*, No. 1, No. 2, etc.; and for the single composition, *Weary Blues*, which became widely used in jazz. The *Pastimes* are extraordinary little pieces of ragtime invention. They are not in the classic ragtime vein of Lamb, Joplin and Scott; nor do they follow the trend towards the stepped-up style of ragtime that is sometimes called "St. Louis." Moving against the trend of the times, Matthews chose a retiring, light style into which he poured one charming contrivance after another. It is not always heavy ragtime, neither in the sense of the sound which is achieved nor in the sense of the depth to which it aspires. But it is a major contribution to the field. Number 5 is very successful in grafting Spanish rhythms onto ragtime, just as Jelly Roll's "Spanish tinge" was applied to jazz.

With due respect to Lamb, Matthews, Turpin and the others, there is no question but that the most creative individuals to work within the framework of ragtime were Scott Joplin and James Scott.

Joplin is most well known for the rags which he produced prior to 1909. He was one of the first to enter ragtime composition, with *Original Rags* in 1899. His *Maple Leaf Rag* of the same year was the all-time best seller in the field, and remains the best-known rag today. Between 1901 and 1904, Joplin produced fourteen rags which, with the writing of Turpin, Hunter, and others, created the style. These early Joplin rags are almost incredible in their inexhaustible supply of musical expressiveness. They include such gems as *Sunflower Slow Drag, The Entertainer, Easy Winners* (said to be Joplin's favorite), *Elite Syncopations,* and *Weeping Willow Rag*—uniformly high-class and extremely characteristic rags. Two with a slight march-like flavor, but otherwise quite in the vein, are *Peacherine* and *The Strenuous Life. A Breeze from Alabama* and *Chrysanthemum* hint at an experimentalism which was to run riot in Joplin's later years. *The Cascades* is slightly patterned after *Maple Leaf* in form, but is otherwise quite different.

In 1907–08, Joplin produced nine rags, which represent a slightly different approach than that used in the earlier period. Here ragtime, the style having been established, was now capable of moving on to real artistic effort. Joplin was in the forefront, using the style which he had helped create to achieve a really "serious" music. To examine fully the nine 1907–08 rags would be a major job. They need only be listed here—and

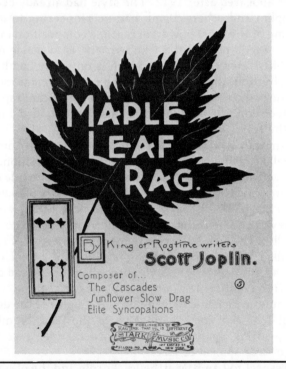

During the Ragtime Era, Scott Joplin's *Maple Leaf Rag* was the most successful, famous, and influential rag. (*John Edward Hasse collection*)

strongly recommended for those who can obtain the scores, recordings or rolls. They are: *The Non Pareil, Gladiolus Rag, Searchlight Rag, Heliotrope Bouquet, Rose Leaf Rag, Lily Queen, Fig Leaf Rag, Pine Apple Rag* and *Sugar Cane Rag*.

About this same time, James Scott emerged as a ragtime writer of major importance. Scott's *Frog Legs Rag* burst on the scene in 1906 (he had published three marches a few years earlier). This was followed by *Kansas City Rag* in 1907, and a flood from 1909 through 1911 which included *Sunburst Rag, The Ragtime Betty, Great Scott Rag, Grace and Beauty, Hilarity Rag, Quality Rag* and *Rag Time Oriole*—in short, a stream of creative ragtime comparable to Joplin's in quality, though different as night from day in personal approach.

Joplin's was a reflective spirit, seeking to control the essentially bouncy spirit of ragtime and direct it into longer phrases, sustained sixteenth-note runs, working towards four long phrases to the strain. Scott, on the other hand, used the established ragtime style to exploit its more dynamic qualities. Scott exploded in shorter and shorter phrases and splashes of color, with a furious energy that could not be controlled. There are few passages in Scott which sound truly in repose.

As has been indicated previously, Joplin ragtime is of interest not only because of the classical rags which he produced, along with Scott and Lamb, before 1910; but also because of the last period, which for Joplin begins with *Euphonic Sounds* and *Solace* in 1909. This last period of Joplin's is a curious one, representing a kind of mixture between throwbacks to the very early two-beat Turpin style (see especially the collaborations with Hayden, *Felicity Rag* and *Kismet Rag*) and the most ambitious musical efforts in the ragtime literature: *Euphonic Sounds, Magnetic Rag* and perhaps *Solace, Scott Joplin's New Rag, Reflection Rag*, and certainly the second Joplin opera, *Treemonisha*. In the final Joplin period there is growing preoccupation with form and structure, including experimentation with quasi-classical forms, such as the rondo in *Euphonic Sounds* and the sonata-like treatment in *Magnetic Rag*. As might be expected, his concern for structure was associated with interest in tonality. An additional quality of these late Joplin experiments was an attempt to abandon explicit rhythmic statement without losing the implicit momentum. It cannot be said that the final period was altogether successful. Nevertheless, it is a most fascinating chapter of the ragtime story and achieves some notable results in *Euphonic Sounds* (particularly the amazing second theme), *Magnetic Rag*, and widely scattered passages in *Treemonisha*.

The creative ragtime of Joplin, Scott, and the rest will probably enjoy an increasingly wide listening audience. The size of the audience has been narrowly constricted heretofore by two facts: the relatively limited number of good piano rolls which have been put on records, and the unfortunate failure of Revivalist jazz pianists to learn the approach necessary to ragtime (rather than jazz). While little more can be expected from recorded piano rolls, ragtime's tremendous musical potential would appear to make better-informed playing of rags inevitable before long. For a music whose actual creation stopped some thirty-five years ago, ragtime has a bright future from the listeners' standpoint.

Forty Selected Rags

Following is a list of forty rags. The selection is designed to isolate the most "significant" rags. Any such delineation is obviously somewhat arbitrary. It is felt, however, that this kind of listing may be interesting and, possibly, illuminating.

1897   *Harlem Rag* (Turpin); *Mississippi Rag* (Krell).
1899   *Maple Leaf Rag* (Joplin).
1901   *Possum and Taters* (Hunter); *Sunflower Slow Drag* (Hayden-Joplin).
1902   *The Entertainer* (Joplin).
1903   *St. Louis Rag* (Turpin).
1904   *Cascades* (Joplin); *St. Louis Tickle* (Barney-Seymore).
1905   *J.J.J. Rag* (Jordan).
1906   *Dill Pickles* (Johnson); *Frog Legs Rag* (Scott).
1907   *Fine and Dandy* (Johnson); *Heliotrope Bouquet* (Chauvin-Joplin).
1908   *Black and White Rag* (Botsford); *Fig Leaf Rag* (Joplin); *Sensation Rag* (Lamb).
1909   *Euphonic Sounds* (Joplin); *Ragtime Betty* (Scott); *Temptation Rag* (Lodge).
1910   *Dynamite Rag* (Robinson); *Grace and Beauty* (Scott); *Hilarity Rag* (Scott).
1911   *Ragtime Oriole* (Scott); *Sunflower Rag* (Wenrich).
1912   *Slippery Elm Rag* (Woods).
1913   *American Beauty Rag* (Lamb); *Billiken Rag* (Stark); *Pastime Rag No. 1* (Matthews); *Pastime Rag No. 2* (Matthews).
1914   *Climax Rag* (Scott); *Magnetic Rag* (Joplin).
1915   *Agitation Rag* (Hampton); *Ragtime Nightingale* (Lamb).
1916   *Pastime Rag No. 3* (Matthews); *Springtime Rag* (Pratt); *Top Liner Rag* (Lamb).
1917   *Reflection Rag* (Joplin).
1918   *Pastime Rag No. 5* (Matthews).
1920   *Pastime Rag No. 4* (Matthews).

Notes

1. The writer wishes to acknowledge his debt to Roy J. Carew, who made available both his extensive collection of printed music and his invaluable personal recollections concerning the years when the music first came out.

2. If perhaps an analogy may be drawn, it might be pointed out that, in regard to the classical period of concert-music composition, a similar sifting-out process is used. Typically we study Haydn, Mozart, and Beethoven and pay virtually no attention to any other composers in the period. It is generally felt that this selectivity is valid. Or, to use another analogy, future jazz historians may well select from the early bop period a handful of really creative musicians—Dizzy Gillespie, Charlie Parker, Thelonious Monk and maybe a few others. However, we are obviously too close to that period to make any such prediction with safety.

3. Riverside Records (RLP 12-126).

4. One minor departure from sixteen-bar and eight-bar structure involves the use of twenty-bar strains, a device which Tony Jackson was said to use and which is found in occasional rags.

5. It may legitimately be asked why the third and fourth themes may be in the same

key, yet the subdominant flavor present in **C** is virtually absent in **D**. The answer is not very subtle: the listener's ear has forgotten the original key. This fact about tonality has always been used. The classicists' establishment of a dominant key has always relied on sheer distance; not until the dominant had been harped on for some bars, usually in association with *its* dominant, would the ear forget the original tonic. But once it has been established, the listener becomes wholly attuned to the dominant as the new home base. Similarly, in ragtime the separation of **D** from **A** (or **B**) by **C** makes possible a triumphant flavor in **D**—distinctly not subdominant.

6. One writer observes: "It has become increasingly clear that 'form' need not be a confining mold into which tonal materials are poured, but rather that the forming process can be *directly* related to the musical material employed in a specific instance. In other words, form evolves *out* of the material itself and is not imposed upon it. We must learn to think of form as a verb rather than a noun." Gunther Schuller, "The Future of Form in Jazz," *Saturday Review*, 12 January 1957, p. 62. Schuller's comment has to do with the direction of modern jazz but applies to any music, including ragtime or concert music, or, for that matter, *all* of jazz. The healthy interest of today's jazz frontiersmen in the form is *not* in form for its own sake, but as one of the musical resources at their command.

The Banjo in Ragtime

Lowell H. Schreyer

The banjo played an important role in ragtime, but until now the topic has not been addressed. In this pioneering essay, written for this collection, banjoist Lowell Schreyer draws on documentary sources to explore banjo influences in the formation of ragtime. He also calls attention to rags composed expressly for the banjo, and considers the once-famous recording artists Vess Ossman, Fred Van Eps, and Harry Reser.

The banjo was used extensively in the early recording and performing of ragtime, but the instrument's role in the development of that music has not been well chronicled.[1] Nineteenth-century banjo writers and enthusiasts intent upon upgrading their instrument to legitimate status, in the European musical sense, preferred to diminish the importance of its ties to the plantation and Africa. Later, as the banjo became known as one of the principle instruments in aurally transmitted American folk music, the impression arose that the banjo had little if any literature through which its development could be traced.[2]

Music critic Rupert Hughes (1872–1956) noticed in 1899 that ragtime music contained what he called "banjo figurations,"[3] an observation echoed by a few writers since then. In 1956 musicologist Hans Nathan (b. 1910) analyzed minstrel banjo tunes of the 1840s and 1850s and concluded that some of them had enough rhythms of irregular accentuation to consider the banjo tunes a possible link between plantation music and ragtime.[4]

Further study leaves little doubt that the banjo was the middle passage through which rhythms of black music came to the piano. At the starting point of that passage was West Africa, where several banjolike stringed instruments existed, such as the *gunbri, bania, bandju,* and *cambreh* or *halam*.[5] Ethnomusicologist David Ames believes that the five-stringed *halam* of the Wolof of Senegal and Gambia may be the "grandfather" of the banjo.[6]

Following twenty-some years of research, Dena Epstein (b. 1916) has produced extensive documentation establishing that African musical instruments were transplanted to the New World, "some as remembered aspects of a lost life, and some as tangible objects carried aboard slaving ships."[7] She writes that "The *banza,* or banjo, seems to have been the most widely reported and longest lived of all the African instruments in the New World. Under a variety of names it can be documented throughout the British and French West Indies and in the southern mainland colonies before 1800. . . ."[8]

Early descriptions of blacks "thrumming," "beating," and "striking" the banjo indicate that blacks played it in a percussive and probably rhythmic style. Blacks frequently used the banjo as a rhythm instrument to accompany their dancing. A 1784 report states, "In America and on the [West Indies] islands they [Negroes] make use of this instrument greatly for the dance."[9] And an account in 1787 reports that the Virginia Negro kept "time and cadence, most exactly, with the music of the banjor" and an instrument resembling a drum.[10]

In the absence of written records by slaves, it is necessary to turn to those they influenced to continue the pre-ragtime banjo story. Aspects of black culture were already being borrowed by whites in the first half of the nineteenth century. By the 1820s, a number of white performers had donned blackface and were traveling the country performing "alleged Negro songs and dances in circuses and between the acts of plays." Not all of their material was derived from blacks, but a sizable part of it was. "Although blackface performers rarely credited specific material to blacks because they wanted to be known as creative artists as well as performers, many early minstrels claimed that they did 'field work' among Southern Negroes while they were traveling."[11]

An apparent borrower and important figure in blackface minstrelsy was Joel Sweeney (ca. 1810–1860), the Virginian sometimes credited with originating the five-stringed version of the banjo. The controversy over whether Sweeney was the one to add a fifth string to the banjo overshadows what may have been a more important contribution on his part—acting as a key figure in passing on the black way of playing the banjo to other whites on a significant scale. Born and raised on a plantation near Appomattox, Virginia, Sweeney was in a position to learn directly from blacks from boyhood on. Certainly other whites had similar experiences, but Sweeney's drive to entertain gave the banjo a public exposure it had not had before.

Sweeney's neighbor George W. Inge wrote in later years: "Several old and reliable farmers in Appomattox related to me how the negro slaves used to take large gourds and put on four strings made of horse hair, using a crooked handle gourd and putting in a stick for a staff and how Joe

Sweeney, then a lad, would hang around with the negroes at all times learning some of their rude songs and playing an accompaniment on a gourd banjo. . . ."[12] According to another neighbor, Judge R. B. Pore, Sweeney built his first five-stringed banjo when he was eighteen years old and was giving concerts by the time he was twenty-one.[13]

Another famous white banjoist credited with having studied black plantation music was Tom Briggs (1824–1854), who gained his reputation in the 1840s and early 1850s with companies such as Wood's Minstrels, Buckley's Serenaders and Christy's Minstrels. *Briggs' Banjo Instructor*, published in 1855, is identified as "A Collection of Pieces . . . Composed and arranged expressly for this work by Thomas F. Briggs." The publisher's preface claims, "This book contains many choice plantation melodies which the author learned when at the south from the negroes, which have never before been published."[14] While the publisher's claim may be exaggerated, the *Instructor* includes syncopations and irregular shifts of emphasis that hint strongly of influence other than European. In addition to illustrating obvious patterns of syncopation, ♫♫♩ and ♪♩ ♪, the Briggs book explains a more subtle means for inner rhythm—the banjo stroke technique. This style was common to minstrel banjo playing of the period. It produced shifts in emphasis, not always apparent in notation, by differences in timbre of notes within a phrase. They were sounded in rhythmic patterns by combinations of right hand index fingernail and soft flesh of the right-hand thumb, and slurs produced by hammering or snapping the strings with the left-hand fingers. A typical tune in this style is *Briggs' Jig* (Example 7).[15] In the first two measures of the third line, the notes produced by the striking of the index fingernail (marked "F") stand out as a regular onbeat melody (Example 8). Onto this is superimposed, in effect, a variant in irregular rhythm (see Example 9). In concept, this was not unlike West African drumming, which lay in the past, or ragtime, which was to come.

Example 7. Thomas F. Briggs [?], *Briggs' Jig*.

Example 8. *Briggs' Jig,* **B** strain, measures 1–2, notes struck by index fingernail.

Example 9. *Briggs' Jig,* **B** strain, measures 1–2, superimposed pattern of syncopation.

Another minstrel banjoist who acknowledged black influence was Frank Converse (1837–1903), who entered professional minstrelsy in the middle 1850s. Recognized by his peers as a very musical banjoist, Converse transcribed and thereby preserved a tune played by the first banjo player he had ever heard—a black man who entertained in Converse's boyhood hometown of Elmira, New York.

"The first banjo I ever heard was in the hands of a colored man—a bright mulatto—whose name I have forgotten," wrote Converse in later years. "He frequently visited Elmira and the neighboring villages, playing and singing and passing his hat for collections. . . . The following morceau, which I still recall, was his *piece de resistance.* . . ."16

Example 10. Frank Converse's transcription of black banjoist's tune.

Containing the syncopation characteristic of the later cakewalk, this is possibly the earliest piece of music that can be traced directly to a black banjoist. Converse was born in 1837 and probably heard this tune before 1850. A number of the early white banjoists who performed in minstrel shows, then, had had exposure, direct or indirect, to black music. They had some familiarity with the music they sought to imitate.

Now, what influence was the banjo having on players of the piano, the solo instrument on which ragtime was to reach its highest development? The piano already had its own tradition and growing literature, which were different from those developing for the banjo. The fact that pianists composed pieces based on their impressions of banjo playing suggests that they recognized it as a music distinct from piano music. The best-known piano composition in this vein is, of course, Gottschalk's showpiece of about 1854 to 1855, *The Banjo*. Another is *Imitation of the Banjo* composed by W. K. Batchelder in 1854 and dedicated on the cover to "T. F. Briggs, (The World Renowned Banjoist,) of Christy's Minstrels, N.Y." In 1883 *New Coon in Town* by J. S. Putnam was published with the subtitle, *Banjo Imitation*.[17] The notion of banjo imitation on piano was still around in 1893 with Charles Drumheller's *Banjo Twang*.

As pianos became available to blacks, some banjo transfer or imitation must have been occurring among them, as evidenced in Lafcadio Hearn's (1850-1904) comment in an 1881 letter to H. E. Krehbiel: "Did you ever hear negroes play the piano by ear? . . . They use the piano exactly like a banjo. It is good banjo-playing, but no piano-playing."[18]

"Banjo imitation" and using "the piano exactly like a banjo" obviously meant adopting characteristics of banjo playing—use of fill-in figures rising out of the banjo's inability to sustain long notes, irregular accentuation in these figures, and percussive attack. One of these fill-in devices consisted of playing a melody in broken-chord style; combined with a syncopated rhythm, this device became known as "ragging."[19] This technique of breaking up chords to create piano ragtime is explained in *Ben Harney's Rag Time Instructor* of 1897.[20]

In the same regard, it should not be overlooked that, according to Blesh and Janis, one of the pioneer ragtimers whom Scott Joplin (1868–1917) met at the World's Columbian Exposition in Chicago in 1893 was pianist "Plunk" Henry, "named for the banjo he had played earlier and from which he had derived his piano ragtime rhythms."[21]

Joplin's mother reportedly played the banjo and so Joplin may have had early exposure to the banjo at home. His first published rag, *Original Rags* (1899), seems to reflect banjo influence both in the music itself and in the credit, which reads "*picked* by Scott Joplin, arranged by Charles N. Daniels" (emphasis added). Broken-chord banjo-type figurations also appear in Joplin's most famous work, *Maple Leaf Rag*. *The Cascades* is "respectfully dedicated to Kimball and Donovan, banjoists," and *The Entertainer* is dedicated to practitioners of a related instrument—"James Brown and his Mandolin Club." Clearly, Joplin was acquainted with banjo and mandolin musicians, and evidently was influenced by their music.

The main thrust of ragtime development was apparently shifting to the piano. Meanwhile, back on the banjo, a new breed of performers was coming to the fore with a "guitar style" of playing the gut-strung five-stringed banjo. Aspiring to the level of the European masters, they left behind the boisterous jig music of the pre–Civil War minstrel days and turned to a more refined banjo music.

A central force in this movement was S. S. Stewart (1855–1898), a banjoist turned banjo manufacturer and writer whose efforts to elevate the banjo's status hovered somewhere between dedication and fanaticism. From 1882 to his death in 1898, Stewart campaigned vigorously for the banjo's new image through his *S. S. Stewart's Banjo and Guitar Journal.* Considering himself at the dawn of a new banjo era, he threw himself into technological improvements of the instrument, and at the same time became the leading publisher of music for the banjo. His catalog of publications consisted predominantly of European genres—polkas, schottisches, waltzes, mazurkas, and arrangements of the classics—all music that appealed to the high society of the day. With Stewart's drive for respectability for the banjo, it would have been out of place for him to publish many tunes with the irregular stress associated with early minstrel music.

Stewart summarized his attitude and position when he wrote in 1884, "The Banjo is now in what may be termed in intermediate state of development. It has partly risen from its standard as a 'negro minstrel instrument,' and got in a manner introduced among a better class of people. . . ."[23] In 1887 he wrote, "The banjo is becoming a recognized musical instrument and gradually finding its proper place in first class concerts as well as in the parlor and drawing room. The coming banjoist will be a musician; an artist; and will not have to 'black up' to make his salary. He will find his way to the concert stage and will be heard at musical entertainments where comic songs, gags and big shoes are not considered an attraction."[24]

Stewart and contributors to his journal tended to diminish plantation origins for the "elevated" banjo. By 1896 Stewart was saying, "It is quite a prevailing fallacy that the south is or rather was the home of the oldtime, so-called Plantation Banjo, but this is purely a fallacy and an exploded theory; even if there was any truth in it, as concerns the oldtime 'tub,' the modern banjo has very little, if any, relation to the 'tub' of years ago."[25]

As far as Stewart was concerned, the only good black banjo player was Horace Weston (1825–1890), and he was a free-born Connecticut Yankee. Ragtime? Just a careless way of playing an instrument, in Stewart's estimation. He exhibited very little comprehension of the new musical tide swelling up around him.

A subscriber in Nebraska wrote Stewart in 1888, saying that he was not satisfied with the music Stewart had sent him and that he wanted something with "broken time" like the "ear-players" played. Here was a banjoist hearing something he called "broken time" being played by improvising banjoists way out there in the Great Plains and Stewart couldn't give him any help in learning to play it. The best Stewart could do was scold him for his poor taste.[26]

When Stewart was confronted head on with the question of ragtime in 1898, he said

"Ragtime" evidently refers to the "rag baby" or stuffed "bull dog." It has no possible connection with a banjo, and was not originated with that instrument;

but it is, as everyone knows, about 10 times as hard to get rid of a bad habit as it is to acquire such a habit. It is also much easier to acquire slang terms and a slovenly system of execution upon an instrument than it is to acquire a finished style of playing.[27]

Although they were in the minority, some minstrel-type syncopated banjo solos did find their way into Stewart's music pages. They usually contained the cakewalk rhythm ♪♪♩ —which was an element of jigs in the 1840s and 1850s—but these pieces seldom became more complicated rhythmically. Within this limitation, some were little gems: *The Sick Indian* of 1886, the *Champion Wing Dance* of 1888, *Golden Rod Reel* of 1889, *Uncle Joe's Cake Dance* of 1890, and *Tiger Jig* of 1891.

Earlier, in 1884, Stewart had shown a rarely revealed talent for syncopating by using cakewalk variations in his own arrangement of *Old Folks at Home*. He called it *The Old Folks' Jig* (Example 11).

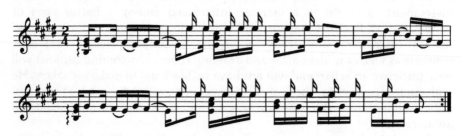

Example 11. S. S. Stewart, arr., *The Old Folks' Jig*, **A** strain.

Another early syncopated piece published by Stewart was E. H. Hulse's *Dakota Jig*, which appeared in Stewart's *The Minstrel Banjoist* book in 1881.[28] Notice the elementary "secondary rag"[29] in measure 4 (Example 12).

Example 12. Ed. H. Hulse, *Dakota Jig*, **A** strain.

In 1890 Stewart published *Mobile Persuasion*, complete with trombone-like slides, but with the warning, probably tongue-in-cheek, that it is "a newly concocted negroistic decoction" and that "the playing of such compositions frequently leads to unpleasant relations between neighbors."[30] Like most of the popular dance music of the period, *Mobile Persuasion* has a multisectional form, specifically **A BB C D EE.**

Meanwhile, the competition, *Gatcomb's Banjo and Guitar Gazette*, featured as its banjo musical supplement for December 1891 *The Mobile Buck*. Subtitled *The Famous Mississippi Steamboat Dance*, the arrangement by G. L. Lansing has cakewalk rhythms and an **AA BB CC D** format.

Cashing in on the "cakewalk" tag in titles of compositions for the banjo, mandolin, and guitar were William Huntley with his *Darkies' Cake Walk* in 1896, Stewart with *Flaxy Cunningham's Cakewalk* in 1897, and C. L. Partee advertising *De Coontown Jubilee Cakewalk* also in 1897. In 1892 banjoist Dan Emerson composed *Kullud Koons' Kake Walk*, which has a cakewalk title but not the syncopated rhythm associated with the term a few years later. *Cake Walk Reel* in Otto Langey's 1894 *Tutor for the Banjo* has both.[31]

After the first publication of a rag—Krell's *Mississippi Rag* in 1897—banjoists had available in published form both rag/cakewalks written especially for banjo and those arranged from piano rags. Probably the first composition written specifically for the banjo to bear a ragtime title was *Alabama Rag Time*, which appeared late in 1897 in *The Chicago Trio*, a magazine for banjoists, mandolinists, and guitarists. In the next few years the parade continued with Jos. W. Stern & Company advertising a Brooks and Denton banjo arrangement of *Eli Green's Cake Walk* in 1899, J. W. Jenkins' Sons Music Company of Kansas City, Missouri, publishing the Clarence L. Partee banjo arrangement of *Doc Brown's Cake Walk* in 1899, Stewart publishing the banjo duet *Raggy Rastus* in 1900, Feist and Frankenthaler promoting a "Hits That Hit" banjo solo arrangement of *Smoky Mokes* in 1901, and the vaudeville banjo team of Brooks and Denton (Ruby Brooks and Harry Denton) offering for sale their own banjo arrangement of George Rosey's *Ragtime Skedaddle* in 1902.[32]

During this time, many popular tunes—raggy or not—were published in multiple arrangements for banjo, mandolin, and guitar as solos, duos, trios, and with and without piano accompaniment. An 1897 advertisement from publisher Frederick Allen "Kerry" Mills indicates some of the instrumental combinations for which arrangements of *Whistling Rufus, At a Georgia Campmeeting*, and similar pieces were published.[33]

A surge of popularity of the mandolin between 1900 and 1910, in some respects surpassing that of the banjo, saw publishers bringing out numerous popular music arrangements and folios for combinations of two mandolins and guitar. In these ensembles, the mandolins played melody and harmony while the guitar was generally relegated to accompaniment parts.

Banjo clubs, eventually enlarged to include mandolins and guitars, had been gaining in popularity in colleges and small and large towns in the United States since the late 1880s. While polkas, waltzes, marches, and classical arrangements made up the bulk of their concerts, banjo clubs did perform numbers of a cakewalk flavor. To mention a few, the Haverford College Banjo Club of Philadelphia played *Dark Town Jubilee Patrol* in 1896, the Drexel Institute Banjo Club of West Philadelphia did *Rastus on Parade* in 1897, the Euterpe Club of Menomonie, Wisconsin, rendered a medley of *Mister Johnson, Turn Me Loose, My Gal Is a High Born Lady*, and *All Coons Look Alike*

An advertisement by publisher F. A. Mills lists numerous arrangements of cakewalks and other popular instrumentals, for banjo, mandolin, guitar, and combinations thereof. (*John Edward Hasse collection*)

to Me in 1898, and the Waldo Quintet Club of Saginaw, Michigan performed *Belle of the Cakewalk* in 1899.

Even banjo virtuoso Alfred A. Farland (1864–1954) left his classical persuasion long enough to include *Eli Green's Cake Walk, Smoky Mokes,* and *Whistling Rufus* among a group of phonograph records, mostly classical, that he made and advertised for sale.[34]

Ironically, banjo method books through this period included little instruction on how to play ragtime. Exceptions were *Howe's Figure Music for the Banjo,* 1899, which included a couple of ragtime songs, *My Gal is a High Born Lady* and *Mister Johnson, Turn Me Loose; James H. Jennings' Practical Banjo School,* 1902, which contained Jennings' own *At a Rag Time Ball* and *Sounds from the Cottonfields;* and J. E. Agnew's *The 20th Century Method for the Banjo,* 1901, with its *Hot Foot Ike Cake Walk.*[35]

Syncopation in rags and cakewalks written for the banjo and other fretted instruments rarely reached the rhythmic intricacies of the classic ragtime composed for piano. Even the work of Paul Eno (1869–1924), who is identified in banjo circles as a ragtime banjo composer, utilized little more than the simple cakewalk rhythm ♫♩ until after the advent of piano ragtime hits when his compositions more frequently included such rhythms as "secondary rag" and tied-note syncopations. Compare the mildly syncopated measures from Eno's *Alabama Echos* of 1894 (Example 13) to the second section of his more complex *Banjoisticus* of 1909 (Example 14).

Example 13. Paul Eno, *Alabama Echoes*, **B** strain, measures 1–8.

Example 14. Paul Eno, *Banjoisticus*, **B** strain, measures 1–6.

In 1913, in one of the more perceptive analyses of ragtime prior to World War I, Myron A. Bickford, prominent fretted instrument teacher and performer, traced this evolution of ragtime from the simple to the complex with similar examples.[36]

George L. Lansing (1860–1923) was another noted composer and arranger of banjo music who wrote syncopated pieces in the 1880s and 1890s. While much has been made of his *Darkie's Dream* (1887) as a syncopated pre-ragtime piece, an earlier Lansing banjo composition, *Oh! Swing Me, Honey* (1885), has much more of the feel of the cakewalk, with the characteristic rhythm occurring in the first strain in every measure but one (Example 15). The succeeding strains also contain syncopation.

Example 15. George L. Lansing, *Oh! Swing Me, Honey*, **A** strain.

For more advanced banjo syncopations in this period, one must turn to phonograph recordings, particularly those of Vess Ossman and Fred Van Eps. The percussive punch of the banjo caused it to record extremely well in the acoustic days of the phonograph, and it was the most popular solo instrument for recording ragtime. In that respect it far outdistanced the piano, which was rarely used for ragtime recordings before 1912.[37] Some of the earliest banjo recordings were made on Edison cylinders in 1889 by Will Lyle, who recorded pieces with such raggy-sounding titles as *Hunky Dory Darky* and *Rattle the Banjo*.[38]

As early as 1893, Vess L. Ossman (1868–1923), the banjoist who became an internationally famous figure, recorded the *Washington Post March* for North American,[39] and by 1897 was recording ragtime in the form of *Ragtime Medley* and *Hotfoot Sue*, both for Berliner. Ossman followed these renditions with a long line of ragtime and cakewalk recordings—some such as *Hot Corn* and *A Warm Reception*, for banjo, but others such as *St. Louis Rag*, *Buffalo Rag* and *Maple Leaf Rag* adapted from piano rags. One of his most popular recordings was *St. Louis Tickle*, made in 1906 by the Ossman-Dudley Trio (banjo, mandolin, and harp-guitar).

In addition to leaving his imprint on many American banjoists, Ossman carried his banjo ragtime to England in 1900 and 1903 and influenced British banjoists Charlie Rogers, Joe Morley, and others. Ossman's reception by the English in 1900 is described in an enthusiastic report from a London correspondent to Stewart's *Journal:* "London had never heard any ragtime music played on the banjo to amount to anything until Mr. Ossman put in an appearance. After his first selection of *A Bunch of Rags* one can well say that no banjoist ever received such an ovation, such bursts of applause, ever made such a hit as he, since the banjo first came to England."[40]

The banjo team of Cadwallader L. Mays (1873–ca. 1903) and Parke Hunter (1876–1912), however, apparently beat Ossman as the first Americans to bring banjo ragtime to the British. In an interview that took place upon the banjo duo's arrival in England in January 1897, Mays declared that they were going to introduce "what for lack of a better name, is called 'Rag Time.'"[41] It should be noted that the duo's introduction of "Rag Time" to England occurred the same month in which the first published piano rag, *Mississippi Rag*, appeared back in the United States. The compositional output of Parke Hunter, a banjoist at least as talented as Ossman, included *The Jungle Rag* and several cakewalk-like numbers with ragtime subtitles.

The man who eventually succeeded Ossman as America's dominant recording banjoist was Fred Van Eps (1878–1960), born in Somerville, New Jersey. Van Eps walked into the Edison Laboratory in 1897 with some homemade banjo cylinder recordings that started him on a recording career which lasted until 1926. Van Eps recorded a number of rags and he was not averse to tackling the intricacies of such James Scott piano rags as *Ragtime Oriole* and *Grace and Beauty*. Other selections in his recorded output of ragtime interest included *A Rag Time Episode, Chatterbox Rag, Rag Pickings, The*

Fred Van Eps, ca. 1900, who for several decades was America's premiere banjo recording artist. (*Courtesy Lowell Schreyer*)

Whitewash Man, Red Pepper, Black Diamond Rag, Florida Rag, Teasing the Cat, Down Home Rag and *Ragging the Scale*.

While their embellishments could give the impression of improvisation, both Ossman and Van Eps were literate musicians who could read and write music. Van Eps, particularly, was careful to plan his arrangements for maximum fingering efficiency and adaptability to the banjo.[42]

By the late 1890s, the banjo had evolved from the fretless instrument of early minstrel days to the fretted, five-stringed banjo as played by Ossman and Van Eps on their recordings. The fretless banjo survived in rural folk music, where it is still sometimes preferred.

New types of banjos were introduced in the first decade of the twentieth century. Mandolin-banjos and tenor banjos were tuned in fifths and played with picks on steel strings, rather than with bare fingers on gut strings like the old five-stringed banjos. Never identified as closely with ragtime as was the five-stringed banjo, these instruments had a part in pseudo-ragtime organizations such as James Reese Europe's (1881–1919) Clef Club orchestras just before World War I. The sound of a five-piece section of mandolin-banjos can be heard in Europe's Society Orchestra recordings of *Too Much Mustard* and *Down Home Rag*, both recorded for Victor on December

29, 1913. The mandolin-banjo gradually receded to amateur banjo club status while the tenor banjo went on to become the rhythmic force in jazz and fox trot dance bands of the 1920s.

The playing and composing of tenor banjoist Harry Reser (1896–1965) paralleled the Zez Confrey school of novelty piano in the 1920s. Often written at the virtuoso level, Reser's compositions incorporated high-speed technique, advanced harmonies, and split-stroke syncopations. Considered the ultimate challenge for tenor banjoists even today, his published solos were only a shadow of the rhythmic and imaginative variations Reser put into them on his own recordings. His most famous tenor banjo solo is *Lolly Pops*.[43] Reser also played the plectrum banjo, a pick-played four-stringed version of the five-stringer, but its showiest exponent was Eddie Peabody, whose use of ragtime rhythms was primarily in broken-chord variations on pop standards, his staple.

A lesser known but highly talented ragtime banjoist was William "Banjo Bill" Bowen (1880–1963), a soloist and composer on both five-stringed and plectrum banjos and occasional performing partner of Van Eps and Reser. He is best known among banjoists for compositions such as *A Ragtime Sneeze, Stepping Out, Nifty Notes,* and *Calico Rags*. The last is actually a medley of Bowen's improvisations based on sections of other rags including *African Pas'* and Joplin's *Peacherine Rag* and *The Entertainer*. Bowen did little recording in his heyday but a sample of his playing in his later years can be heard on the *Banjo-istics* LP compiled by banjo enthusiast Ted Shawnee in 1955.[44]

Although Fred Van Eps continued his recording career into the 1920s, the five-stringed banjo's eclipse in public popularity coincided roughly with the end of the Ragtime Era. By the close of World War I, ragtime was out and jazz was in. The five-stringed banjo was also out, while the tenor and plectrum banjos were in.

Did the 1920s bring an end to banjo ragtime? Hardly. Vestiges of it can be heard in country string band music and in the roll patterns of bluegrass banjo, though the connections are hazy. One possible link is pioneer country banjoist Charlie Poole (1892–1931). Influenced greatly by Fred Van Eps, he was a three-finger player who was familiar with the ragtime banjoist's records and played versions of some of Van Eps' recorded solos.[45]

The turn-of-the-century ragtime banjo style never disappeared entirely, although it has not been widely heard by the general public in the United States for a long time. In the 1950s Van Eps made a comeback and recorded two albums, both containing rags, on his own Five String Banjo label.[46] This accomplishment made Van Eps the only recording artist to span the wide gap from acoustic two-minute cylinders to high-fidelity microgroove LPs with his own work. His banjo style, known as "orthodox" or "classic," is perpetuated currently by a small group of banjoists, the American Banjo Fraternity, of which Van Eps, Bowen, Harry Denton, and Farland were members in their later years. The old banjo rags can still be heard at the Fraternity's semiannual rallies in Lewistown, Pennsylvania. In England this manner of playing the five-stringed banjo persisted more strongly than in the United States. An outstanding British soloist who played five-string banjo ragtime in the Van Eps tradition through the 1970s was Tom Edwards (1900–1979). More recently, young British ragtime banjoist Chris Sands became known as a strong exponent of the Vess Ossman style through his ragtime banjo LP, *A Bunch of Rags,* released on the Linden Sounds label in 1984. Some contemporary bluegrass banjoists expanding their repertoires have also turned in the direction of ragtime.

Many of the points rasied in this preliminary study beg further research, though a few conclusions can be drawn. Today the banjo is a long way from its African roots, yet the instrument emerges as the likely medium through which rhythmic fragments of West African music were transmitted to the melodic instruments of European background in the cultural interchange that became ragtime.

Banjo music also provided a means by which white musicians became aware of some of the rhythmic potential of black music early in the nineteenth century before pianist-composers showed what could be done at a more advanced level. Banjoists might wish that their instrument had been the one to carry ragtime all the way to its peak development. But the instrument's contrapuntal limitations and the nineteenth-century banjo publishers' meager interest in syncopation hindered the banjo. With the exception of early ragtime recordings where it was the leader, the banjo achieved no more than a secondary role in the new music. The two-handed capabilities of the keyboard were necessary to develop fully ideas the old banjo rhythms had suggested. If it weren't for the banjo, however, the piano might never have become the complete ragtime instrument.

Notes

1. This paper was supported in part by a Mankato State University research grant.

2. As recently as 1962, the following statement was made in an otherwise informative paper delivered at the annual meeting of the American Folklore Society at the Library of Congress: "Little is known about the playing styles of nineteenth-century banjoists; our knowledge goes back only to about 1900." The paper, by Lee Haring, was published as "Banjo Styles," *Country Dancer* (Summer 1963): 18–22; (Winter 1963–64): 4–8.

3. Rupert Hughes, "A Eulogy of Ragtime," *Musical Record,* no. 447 (1 April 1899), p. 158.

4. Hans Nathan, "Early Banjo Tunes and American Syncopation," *The Musical Quarterly* 42 (1956): 467–71. The article is reprinted as chapter 13 of Nathan's *Dan Emmett and the Rise of Early Negro Minstrelsy* (Norman: University of Oklahoma Press, 1962), pp. 189–213.

5. LeRoy Larson, "The Banjo: Pre-minstrelsy" (Three-quarter American Music paper in partial fulfillment of doctoral requirements, University of Minnesota, 1971), p. 84.

6. David Ames, notes accompanying *Wolof Music of Senegal and the Gambia,* Ethnic Folkways Album FE 4462, 1955, p. 4.

7. Dena J. Epstein, *Sinful Tunes and Spirituals: Black Folk Music to the Civil War* (Urbana: University of Illinois Press, 1977), p. 343.

8. Dena J. Epstein, "The Folk Banjo: A Documentary History," *Ethnomusicology* 19 (1975): 351–52.

9. Johann David Schoepf, *Travels in the Confederation (1783–1784)*, ed. and trans. Alfred J. Morrison (Philadelphia: W. J. Campbell, 1911), 2:261.

10. "Manner of Living of the Inhabitants of Virginia," *The American Museum* 1, no. 3 (March 1787), 2nd ed., pp. 214–16.

11. Robert C. Toll, *Blacking Up: The Minstrel Show in Nineteenth-Century America* (London, Oxford, and New York: Oxford University Press, 1974), pp. 27, 45.

12. Geo. Inge, Letter to J. E. Henning, 16 July 1890, *The Elite Banjoist* 1, no. 1 (October–November 1890): 3.

13. R. B. Pore, Letter to J. E. Henning, 25 July 1890, ibid.

14. Thomas F. Briggs, *Briggs' Banjo Instructor* (Boston: Ditson, 1855).

15. *Briggs' Jig* in Thomas F. Briggs, *Briggs' Banjo Instrutor* (Boston: Ditson, 1855), p. 24.

16. Frank B. Converse, "Banjo Reminiscences," *The Cadenza* 11, no. 7 (July 1901): 4.

17. Gilbert Chase, *America's Music: From the Pilgrims to the Present*, 2nd ed., rev. (New York: McGraw-Hill, 1966), p. 436.

18. Elizabeth Bisland, *The Life and Letters of Lafcadio Hearn*, 2 vols. (Boston and New York: Houghton, Mifflin, 1906), 1:232.

19. This observation was made by Joseph R. Scotti of Saint Louis, in a telephone interview by John Edward Hasse, 26 February 1978.

20. Ben Harney, *Ben Harney's Rag Time Instructor* (Chicago: Sol Bloom, 1897), Examples 1–3.

21. Rudi Blesh and Harriet Janis, *They All Played Ragtime*, 3rd ed., rev. (New York: Oak Publications, 1966), p. 41.

22. The guitar style of banjo playing, in which the notes are sounded with the bare thumb and fingers of the right hand, similar to classical guitar technique, largely replaced the more percussive and raucous stroke style of minstrel banjo playing to become the dominant banjo technique of the last quarter of the nineteenth century.

23. S. S. Stewart, "The Banjo vs. Guitar as a 'Ladies' Instrument'," *S. S. Stewart's Banjo and Guitar Journal* 3, no. 1 (December 1884–January 1885): 1.

24. S. S. Stewart, "The Banjo World," *S. S. Stewart's Banjo and Guitar Journal* 4, no. 1 (December 1886–January 1887): 3.

25. S. S. Stewart, "The Cotton States Exposition," *S. S. Stewart's Banjo and Guitar Journal* 12, no. 6 (February–March 1896): 3.

26. Letter by unidentified correspondent in Beatrice, Nebraska, and Stewart's reply in "Correspondent's Column," *S. S. Stewart's Banjo and Guitar Journal* 5, no. 3 (August–September 1888): 2.

27. S. S. Stewart's reply, untitled, to a correspondent's inquiry on what a "rag" is and to *Denver Times* article of Nov. 27, 1897, criticizing banjoist A. A. Farland's choice of classical music over ragtime for performance, *S. S. Stewart's Banjo and Guitar Journal* 14, no. 6 (February–March 1898): 5.

28. S. S. Stewart, *The Minstrel Banjoist* (Philadelphia: S. S. Stewart, 1881), p. 24.

29. Don Knowlton, writing on "The Anatomy of Jazz" in *Harper's Magazine* 152 (1926), p. 581, quotes a black guitar player as defining "primary rag" as simple syncopation and "secondary rag" and "the superimposition of *one*, two, three upon the basic one, two three, four." Some well-known pieces using secondary rag are Joseph Northrup's *The Cannon Ball*, Charles L. Johnson's *Dill Pickles Rag*, and George Botsford's *Black and White Rag*. The concept is discussed by Winthrop Sargeant, *Jazz: Hot and Hybrid*, 3rd enl. ed., (New York: Da Capo Press, 1975), pp. 58–59; Olly Wilson, "The Significance of the Relationship Between Afro-American Music and West African Music," *The Black Perspective in Music* 2 (Spring 1974): 7–9; and Edward A. Berlin, "Piano Ragtime: A Musical and Cultural Study" (Ph.D. diss., City University of New York, 1976), pp. 225–31, 234, 237–39, 246–47, 293, and 332.

30. S. S. Stewart, "The Banjo World," *S. S. Stewart's Banjo and Guitar Journal* 7, no. 3 (August–September 1890): 5.

31. Otto Langey, *Tutor for the Banjo* (Philadelphia: Harry Coleman, 1894), p. 73. *Cakewalk Reel* was one of a collection of pieces arranged for this tutor by Frank B. Converse.

32. The Jos. W. Stern & Company arrangement was advertised in *S. S. Stewart's Banjo, Guitar and Mandolin Journal* 17, no. 4 (October–November 1900): unnumbered advertising page. J. W. Jenkins' Sons Music Co. advertised *Doc Brown's Cake Walk* in *Cadenza* 5, no. 6 (July–August 1899): 45. Gatty Jones' *Raggy Rastus* banjo duet appeared in the music supplement section of *S. S. Stewart's Banjo, Guitar and Mandolin Journal* 18, no. 1 (December 1900). Feist and Frankenthaler advertised *Smoky Mokes* as a banjo solo in *Cadenza* 7, no. 8 (April 1901): 39. The Brooks and Denton *Ragtime Skedaddle* advertisement appeared in *Cadenza* 8, no. 12 (August 1902): 53.

33. Kerry Mills, *At a Georgia Campmeeting* (New York: F. A. Mills, 1897), front cover.

34. From an undated advertising sheet in the author's collection. Additional mention of Farland's recording activity, probably referring to these phonograph records, is made in "Trade Department," *Cadenza* 6, no. 6 (July–August 1900): 29.

35. A. O. Howe, *Howe's Figure Music for Banjo* (Chicago: A. O. and E. C. Howe, 1899), pages unnumbered; James H. Jennings, *James H. Jennings' Practical Banjo School* (Providence, R.I.: J. H. Jennings, 1902), pp. 64–67; and J. E. Agnew, *The 20th Century Method for the Banjo* (Des Moines: Agnew Publishing Co., 1901). In the Jennings method book, the 1893 composition *Sounds from the Cottonfields* is subtitled *A Ragtime Echo* but this was apparently added onto the 1902 reprint for commercial reasons. The subtitle is not included on the 1893 sheet music edition.

36. Myron A. Bickford, "Something About Ragtime," *The Cadenza* 20, no. 3 (September 1913): 13, and 20, no. 5 (November 1913): 10–11. Among other significant comments, Bickford was "in favor of restricting the word ragtime to its original definition, as meaning that time or rhythm in which the dominating and characteristic feature is syncopation."

37. David A. Jasen, *Recorded Ragtime 1897–1958* (Hamden, Conn.: Archon Books, 1973), p. 9.

38. *The First Book of Phonograph Records*, Edison Laboratory, 1889, as quoted in Allen Koenigsberg, *Edison Cylinder Records, 1889–1912* (New York: Stellar Productions, 1969), p. 123.

39. North American Phonograph Company brown wax cylinder no. 757, 1893, cited in Allen Koenigsberg, *Edison Cylinder Records, 1889–1912* (New York, Stellar Productions, 1969), p. 141. For discographical information on ragtime recordings by Vess Ossman and Fred Van Eps mentioned in this article and additional ragtime recordings, see Brian Rust, *Jazz Records 1897–1942*, 4th ed., rev., vol. 2 (New Rochelle, N.Y.: Arlington House, 1978), and David A. Jasen, *Recorded Ragtime 1897–1958* (Hamden, Conn.: Archon Books, 1973).

40. Report from an unidentified London correspondent in "The Soloists and Teachers," *S. S. Stewart's Banjo, Guitar, and Mandolin Journal* 18, no. 3 (August–September 1900): 9.

41. Elias and Madeleine Kaufman, "Parke Hunter," *The Five-Stringer*, no. 118 (Summer 1975), p. 2.

42. This assessment of Van Eps' arranging ability for the banjo is drawn from the author's conversations with banjoists who knew Van Eps and from Van Eps' unpublished manuscripts in private collections.

43. W. W. Triggs, *The Great Harry Reser* (London: Henry G. Waker, 1978), p. 34.

44. *Banjo-istics*, Americana Recording Company (Barneveld, N.Y.), A880. In this 1955 compilation of recordings by five banjoists, William Bowen does two solos, *Stepping Out* and *Old Stone House*.

45. Tony Trischka, *Banjo Song Book* (New York: Oak Publications, 1977), p. 25.

46. *Van Eps Five String Banjo*, 78 rpm three-record album, Fred Van Eps, banjo, Robert Van Eps, piano, Van Eps Lab (Plainfield, N.J.), released 1952; ragtime selections include *Ragtime Oriole, Smiler Rag* and *Maple Leaf Rag*. *Five String Banjo*, LP album, Fred Van Eps, banjo, Robert Van Eps, piano, Van Eps Lab (Plainfield, N.J.), released 1956; ragtime selections include *St. Louis Rag* and *Ramshackle Rag*.

Ragtime Songs

Edward A. Berlin

Ragtime songs have often been overlooked in recent years. Edward A. Berlin sets the record straight in this newly written chapter, demonstrating that ragtime songs were an early and continuing part of ragtime throughout its history. He reviews the lyrics and racial imagery of the songs and shows that Alexander's Ragtime Band *was a major digression from the ragtime idea.*

Has the ragtime revival been a fraud? Have we, in disinterring the piano works of Joplin, Lamb, Scott, Matthews, Aufderheide, Lodge, *et al.*, and presenting these as the cream of ragtime, been perpetuating a false image of the phenomenon that set America to dancing and snapping to a new kind of syncopation? That pre–World War I America was turned on by ragtime is undoubtedly true, and is amply attested to by the contemporaneous raves for and ravings against the music. But as much as we would like to believe that the music that electrified the nation three-quarters of a century ago was the same that so charmed and intrigued us in the 1970s, the evidence suggests otherwise.

It seems that the great ragtime successes were not piano pieces at all (with the single exception of Scott Joplin's *Maple Leaf Rag*, which received an acclaim uncommon for a popular instrumental work), but songs—such as *Alexander's Ragtime Band, Waiting for the Robert E. Lee, Hitchy-Koo,* and *Hello! Ma Baby.* When Rupert Hughes, Hiram K. Moderwell, and countless others wrote about ragtime, their concern was with *songs;* when pianist Mike Bernard performed in the Tammany Hall ragtime contest, he won it playing *songs;* when composer Charles Ives directed his keen and unbiased ears toward the popular musical temper (captured and transformed in such works as his *Study No. 18* for piano), he heard *songs.* Pianist Ben Harney, long reputed to be the "originator" or "first popularizer" of ragtime, acquired his reputation by playing and *singing* ragtime, and his published compositions consist entirely of songs. Even Scott Joplin, the reigning prince of piano ragtime composition, discussed ragtime as a vocal music; the *New York Age,* one of America's leading Negro newspapers, quoted Joplin as saying, "Most people who say they do not like ragtime have reference to the *words* and not the music."[1] To consider only the piano masterpieces of ragtime and say, "This is ragtime," is clearly a distortion of history. Songs were an essential ingredient in the ragtime world, exceeding instrumental works in both numbers and renown, and must be included for a true picture of the musical style and the age.

It is often stated that ragtime emerged in publication with the piano rags of William Krell, Tom Turpin, Theodore H. Northrup, and then others, in 1897. But the previous year, 1896, witnessed the publication of several songs specifically labeled as ragtime. The first was Ernest Hogan's *All Coons Look Alike to Me* (copyright registered August 3, 1896), which presents its chorus in two versions, the second having a syncopated accompaniment and the caption: "Choice Chorus, with Negro 'Rag' Accompaniment Arr. by Max Hoffmann" (Example 16). W. T. Jefferson's *My Coal Black Lady* was similarly issued (copyright registered November 23, 1896) with a rag chorus arranged by Hoffmann, and Ben Harney's *You've Been a Good Old Wagon But You've Done Broke Down,* originally published in 1895 by Bruner Greenup of Louisville, was reissued by Witmark in October 1896 with a new cover and banner announcing "Original Introducer to the Stage of the New Popular 'Rag Time' in Ethiopian Song." Before any piano pieces were published as rags, ragtime songs had already established themselves.

Example 16. Ernest Hogan, *All Coons Look Alike to Me,* optional rag chorus, arr. Max Hoffmann, measures 1–4.

The racial character of early ragtime songs is immediately apparent. The covers often depict blacks in caricature, the lyrics are in what was considered Negro dialect, and the terms "coon song" and "Ethiopian song"—the latter for use by persons of genteel inclination—had long been common as nineteenth-century representations of Negro music. In the 1890s "coon song" was the more frequent expression, and it has been retained by present-day historians for reference to the Negro dialect songs of the minstrel, vaudeville, and other musical stages that usually depicted blacks in a flagrantly disparaging (and supposedly humorous) manner. In the lyrics the

One of the first published ragtime songs was Ben Harney's *You've Been A Good Old Wagon But You've Done Broke Down*, originally published in 1895. This edition was issued the following year. (*Library of Congress*)

words "coon" and "nigger" (or "niggah") are common; black men are portrayed as ignorant, gluttonous, thieving (stealing chickens, watermelons, and pork pies), gambling, cowardly, shiftless, and violent (most often wielding a razor); the women are sexually promiscuous and mercenary, often leaving one "honey" (which rhymes with "money") for another of greater generosity, thus precipitating an altercation between the men. Typical lyrics are as follows:

> A big black coon was lookin' fer chickens
> When a great big bulldog got to raisin' de dickens,
> De coon got higher, de chicken got nigher,
> Just den Johnson opened up fire.
> . . . .
> And now he's playing' seben eleben,
> Way up yonder in de nigger heabn,
> Oh! Mister Johnson, made him good.[2]
>
> I'se particular to mention,
> That it is my great intention

For to carve that yaller coon,
That tries to win this girl of mine
This little coal black valentine
My razor'll seal his doom.[3]

I don't like no cheap man
Dat spends his money on de 'stalment plan.[4]

All coons look alike to me,
I've got another beau, you see,
And he's just as good to me
As you, nig! ever tried to be,
He spends his money free.[5]

In the late 1890s virtually any Negro dialect song with a medium to lively tempo, or a syncopated rhythm, was called a ragtime song. In a few very early samples the music is modal, suggestive of folk or imitation-folk origins, but these songs are exceptions, as most pieces adhere to the more usual scale patterns of popular music. Syncopation is a common feature, identical to the types of syncopation characterizing piano ragtime, but even this element is not always required; many songs with square, on-the-beat articulations were labeled rags. The published form of a song, though, may not always reflect its manner of performance, and in at least one instance we can compare the sheet music with a transcription made from performance. The song is *I'm Livin' Easy* ("eatin' pork chops greazy"), published in 1899 and credited to Irving Jones, but apparently common property on the minstrel circuit for many years prior; the transcription, from a syncopated performance, was made by composer Charles Ives, who recalled having heard the song being "ragged" by minstrels in New Haven, Connecticut, around 1893–94 (Example 17).[6]

(a)

I'm liv - in' ea - - sy____

(b)

"I'm a-liv - in' ea - sy__

Example 17. Irving Jones, *I'm Livin' Easy,* opening chorus: (a) published version; (b) Ives transcription.

The performance of lyrics, too, might depart from the published version. Hughes notes the "curious feature" of interpolating extra syllables into the text,[7] and publisher Frank Witmark transcribed these "ragtime words" ("the words themselves, independent of the musical setting, were in the new zigzag rhythms")[8] as performed by Ben Harney, in the printing of Harney's *The Cake-Walk in the Sky;* consequently, the original lyric

> Put a smile on each face ev'ry coon now take your place
> becomes
> Pugut agey smigule ogon egeache fagace evvery cagoon
> tagake yougora plagace.[9]

As printed, these altered words look like a slightly complicated "pig Latin," or a "secret language" as still practiced by school children today, but one wonders if they are not actually a simplification of a form of verbal improvisation, of an incipient scat singing.

The "coon song" rage carried over well into the twentieth century, and the genre became as ubiquitous as the Sunday newspaper—literally. Major newspapers—the *New York World,* the *New York Tribune,* the *New York Journal & Advertiser,* the *Chicago American,* and others—included "coon songs" in their Sunday supplements. Such pieces as *Evah Dahkey is a King, The Lady with the Ragtime Walk, The Darkies' Rag Time Ball,* and *There Ain't No Use to Keep Hanging Around* were admitted regularly into millions of homes throughout America, a circulation exceeding by far the sales of all but the most popular musical hits of the day.

The trend after the turn of the century, though, moved away from the abusively racist lyrics in favor of words expressing more tasteful sentiments. Foremost among these was the Cole & Johnson Bros.'[10] *Under the Bamboo Tree,* a gentle tale of the courtship of a jungle maid of "dusky shade" by "a Zulu from Matabooloo." The chorus features both syncopations and the added syllables of ragtime lyrics (Example 18). So entranced was the public by this song that numerous imitations ensued. Songwriters created subcategories of "jungle" songs (*Down in Jungle Town, By the Light of the Jungle Moon, Moving Day in Jungle Town*) "under . . . jungle" songs (*Under the Jungle Moon, Under the Silv'ry Congo Moon*), and "under . . . tree" songs (*Under the Yum Yum Tree, Under the Matzos Tree, Under the Anheuser Bush*). *Under the Bamboo Tree* also made a lasting impression on Anglo-American poetry, being parodied by T. S. Eliot in his "Fragment of an Agon."

SONG BY WAUCHOPE AND HORSFALL

SWARTS AS TAMBO. SNOW AS BONES

> Under the bamboo
> Bamboo bamboo
> Under the bamboo tree
> Two live as one
> One live as two
> Two live as three
> Under the bam
> Under the boo
> Under the bamboo tree.[11]

Example 18. Cole & Johnson Bros., *Under the Bamboo Tree*, chorus, measures 1–8.

Gradually, in the course of the century's first decade, the ragtime idea came to be accepted as American rather than as the exclusive property of Negro, or Negro-imitated, music. Consequently, the "coon song" and its more respectable derivatives, which continued to flourish—especially in Negro shows and on the minstrel stage—came to share the ragtime label with songs that were racially neutral. Almost any American song with rhythmic life, particularly if it were danceable and in a duple or quadruple meter, was called a rag whether published with the designation or not. Some, such as Ted Snyder's *Wild Cherries Rag* (1908) and George Botsford's *Grizzly Bear Rag* (1910) were originally published as instrumentals, and later republished as songs (Irving Berlin providing the words in both of these instances), acquiring considerably more popularity in the transformation. The greater commercial reward of songs would help to explain why Scott Joplin, too, participated in this practice, reissuing such piano ragtime masterpieces as *Maple Leaf Rag* (1899) and *Pine Apple Rag* (1908) as songs, in 1904 and 1910, respectively; the latter follows the trends of the time in carrying no ethnic association.

With the beginning of the second decade of the century, there seems to have been an upsurge in the number of songs specifically published as rags, many emphasizing ragtime's new universality—including all nations, groups, and occupations—with such titles as *Parisian Rag* (1910), *That Italian Rag* (1910), *That Ragtime Suffragette* (1913), *That Paradise Rag* (1911, referring to the Pearly Gates), *The Hold Up Rag* (1912, a cowboy song), *The Ragtime Soldier Man* (1912), *Eskimo Rag* (1912), and topped off by Irving Berlin's all-inclusive *That International Rag* (1913).

By far the foremost ragtime song of the period was Berlin's *Alexander's Ragtime Band* (1911), another instance of a song that was originally published as an instrumental piece. So great was the success and renown of this work that many considered it the fulfillment of all ragtime that preceded it and the archetype for all that followed; for many writers in the 1920s and 1930s it typified the best (or the worst) in ragtime, and even a book devoted to black

Irving Berlin's phenomenally successful *Alexander's Ragtime Band* (1911) is, ironically, virtually nonsyncopated. (*John Edward Hasse Collection*)

music referred to *Alexander's Ragtime Band* as the culmination of the style and "that instrumental classic of matured ragtime."[12] Berlin himself helped to foster this myth and, ignoring the decade and a half of ragtime that preceded his celebrated work, stated, "I believe that such songs of mine as *Alexander's Ragtime Band, That Mysterious Rag, Ragtime Violin, I Want to Be in Dixie,* and *Take a Little Tip from Father* virtually started the ragtime mania in America."[13]

Rather than culminating all that preceded it, *Alexander's Ragtime Band* typified a major digression from the ragtime idea. Despite important exceptions, most prior rags were syncopated; Irving Berlin's hit tune seems to have shown that syncopation was not necessary, and from 1911 on there was an increase in both vocal and instrumental rags that feature dotted instead of syncopated rhythms. Thus, when Hiram Moderwell and others in the mid-1910s referred to *Waiting for the Robert E. Lee* (1912) and *Memphis Blues* (1912) as ragtime, they were doing so by the greatly altered standards of their day, accepting virtually all swinging popular music as ragtime. And this was not a misconception held only by the general public; *Memphis Blues,* the first important published blues, was actually subtitled "A Southern Rag," and W. C. Handy's later *Yellow Dog Blues* was originally titled *Yellow Dog Rag* (1914). It was not at all uncommon for blues compositions to present classic twelve-bar blues strains in alternation with sixteen-bar rag sections; before the blues was recognized as *sui generis,* it was often considered simply as a variant of the rag.

Many specialists today deny the legitimacy of the ragtime song and make a point of ignoring it in their studies. Clearly, the ragtime song is not what *they* mean by ragtime. But their definition is derived from the emphasis chosen by jazz buffs who were tuned into the traditional jazz revival of the 1940s, a movement that rediscovered the *Maple Leaf Rag,* the *12th Street Rag,* and other piano rags that lent themselves particularly to that neo-Dixieland style. Few ragtime songs had the qualities desired by the jazz revivalists, and consequently, most were excluded from the new, restricted definition of ragtime. But this narrow interpretation of the 1940s should not guide or restrict us as we attempt to understand ragtime in its fullest scope. The evidence is overwhelming that songs were integral to the Ragtime Era; despite substantial differences between instrumental and vocal rags, there were also significant junctures where the two genres overlapped and influenced each other. Early instrumental rags often concluded with a "coon song" chorus; piano pieces often acquired words; songs, especially those by major publishers, were frequently republished in piano arrangements in yearly collections—*Gem Dance Folio, Witmark Dance Folio, Star Dance Folio* (Jerome H. Remick & Co.), and the like. And even without such published arrangements, they were regularly played at the piano. Trends in one medium can be traced to the other as the cross-pollination between vocal and piano rags continued throughout the Ragtime Era.

The exclusive interpretation of ragtime as music only for the piano is both historically and musically false. Attempts to understand and explain one phase without the other must necessarily result in distortion. Ragtime must be studied not in its narrowest sense, but in its broadest. The original movement was so thoroughly integrated into American popular music and culture, so sweeping in its scope, that no other approach will suffice.

Notes

1. "Theatrical Comment," *New York Age*, 3 April 1913, p. 6. Emphasis added.
2. Ben Harney, *Mister Johnson* (New York: Harding's Music House, 1896; transferred to M. Witmark, 1896).
3. W. T. Jefferson, *My Coal Black Lady: Symphony de Ethiopia* (New York: M. Witmark, 1896).
4. [Bert] Williams and [George] Walker, *I Don't Like No Cheap Man* (New York: Jos. W. Stern, 1897).
5. Ernest Hogan, *All Coons Look Alike to Me* (New York: M. Witmark, 1896).
6. The Ives transcription is printed in Charles E. Ives, *Memos*, ed. John Kirkpatrick (New York: Norton, 1972), p. 56.
7. Rupert Hughes, "A Eulogy of Rag-Time," *Musical Record*, no. 447 (1 April 1899): 157–59.
8. Isidore Witmark and Isaac Goldberg, *The Story of the House of Witmark: From Ragtime to Swingtime* (New York: Lee Furman, 1939; reprint ed., New York: Da Capo Press, 1976), p. 154.
9. Ben Harney, *The Cake-Walk in the Sky* (New York: M. Witmark, 1899).
10. Bob Cole, James Weldon Johnson, and J. Rosamond Johnson.
11. T. S. Eliot, "Fragment of an Agon," *Criterion* 4 (January 1927); reprinted in T. S. Eliot, *The Complete Poems and Plays: 1909–1950* (New York: Harcourt, Brace & Co., 1952), p. 81.
12. Alain L. Locke, *The Negro and His Music* (Washington: Associates in Negro Folk Education, 1936), p. 62.
13. Irving Berlin, "Words and Music," *Green Book Magazine*, July 1915, p. 105.

Rags, the Classics, and Jazz

Gunther Schuller

This is a revision and expansion of the jacket notes Gunther Schuller wrote for the 1975 recording **The Road from Rags to Jazz** *by the New England Conservatory Ragtime Ensemble. Schuller illustrates the adoption of ragtime by "classical" composers; discusses "classical" influences on piano rags; and reasons that the distinctions between ragtime and early jazz had their origins more in practical, social, and technical factors than in any single creative/stylistic impulse.*

Though the entire history of mankind could be described as a process of relentless culture change, a significant part of human energies seems to be spent in resisting change, or at least one type of change—cross-fertilization or fusion. The history of Western art, with its twin concepts of the individual creator and the requirement of originality, offers evidence of our fundamental tendency to resist the process of cultural blending. Consciously, we seem always to have preferred the compartmentalization and segregation of our cultural expressions. But unconsciously, if only to assuage a basic need to communicate with our fellow beings, we seem to require—and thus in the end to accept—the subtle inroads of fusion. Starting with the melding of secular (and rather risqué) popular troubadour tunes with sacred motets seven centuries ago right up to the present-day efforts to achieve a jazz-rock fusion, Western musical history can be seen as a constant ebb-and-flow process of initial resistance to fusion, followed eventually by acceptance.

Of course, some strains resist cultural grafting and union more stubbornly than others. And if the social pedigree of one or the other is not acceptable to the prevailing tastes, then resistance is apt to be stronger. We seem to fear the hybrid, the eclectic, the mongrel, and to take refuge in the sanctity of the pure strain, even though there is not a shred of evidence that such "purity"—racial, genetic, social, or cultural—can actually be maintained or is, in fact, desirable.

The see-saw battle over the relationship between classical music and its neighbors from the wrong side of the track, ragtime and jazz, has raged for decades, and is still a matter of some controversy. It certainly was a point of contention at the beginning of the twentieth century when ragtime reigned supreme as America's popular music. The establishment taste makers of that day, well ensconced in their cultural citadels representing the fine arts, made every effort to avoid "contamination" by ragtimers and their ilk. The articles written *contra* ragtime, with its alleged malevolent influences, were legion. Much the same phenomenon occurred a generation later, when jazz was viewed as the new and dangerous intruder.

Add to this prejudice our disinclination, as Americans, to appreciate and cherish our indigenous cultural heritage, especially in its more popular manifestations, and we can understand how ragtime and jazz had to struggle merely to survive. We love the cultural import, almost always underrating our own homegrown product. Also, we Americans are the ultimate consumers, and what is no longer deemed of direct practical value we like to discard, be it our old buildings or last year's car, or a music we suddenly deem obsolete. That jazz and ragtime have survived (the latter by being recently *re*vived) is, under the circumstances, astonishing; it attests both to our best residual and unconscious instincts and to the quality and tenacity of these musics.

The quality of ragtime is, of course, what attracted not only musicians like Debussy, Stravinsky, Satie, Ives, and Sousa, but also millions of people here and abroad. Even so, many of these may have regarded ragtime as merely an ephemeral entertainment music, not realizing that even entertainment musics must have quality to achieve anything like durable success. And as to ragtime's relative durability, there can surely be little question. It was the most pervasive popular music for nearly two decades, yielding to its "successor" jazz only gradually and reluctantly. All the early jazz players thought of themselves as converted ragtime players; Rudi Blesh summed it up well in the title of his classic book, *They All Played Ragtime*.[1] Although most of them changed with the times as jazz found favor with the public in its various successive guises and expressions (New Orleans, Chicago, swing, Broadway show music, etc.), men as diverse as Jelly Roll Morton, Duke Ellington, Eubie Blake, George Gershwin, the great Kansas City band leader Bennie Moten, Bunk Johnson, James Europe, W. C. Handy, Fats Waller, James P. Johnson, Paul Whiteman, Ferde Grofé, and innumerable others all started out in ragtime. Obviously such a diversity of talents brought many new facets to the final stages of ragtime, a tradition never really as narrow as its detractors would have us believe. The range from Joplin and Turpin to Scott and Lamb and Matthews and Blake represents in itself a formidably wide spectrum of personal styles.

It is no wonder then that *some* musicians did take seriously this new music, born in the tenderloin districts of the Midwest and big cities of the East Coast. If we are surprised that Europeans took our humbly born popular music so to heart, we may recall that it was the Bohemian Dvořák who had to urge his American students in New York to listen to and *use* their own folk musics[2]; or that the first serious acceptance of jazz occurred in Europe, not America, and that the first course on jazz was given not in the United States but in Frankfurt, Germany, in 1931 by the Hungarian composer Matyas Seiber.

Were it not for Charles Ives (1874–1954), that remarkable innovator, iconoclast, and pluralist musician, we would have to cede the early recognition of ragtime to his European colleagues Debussy, Stravinsky, Satie, Milhaud, Walton, and others. One must give credit also to others like Arthur Farwell[3] and John Alden Carpenter (both composers) and Rupert

Charles Ives (right) and his friend Mandeville Mullally in their room at Yale University, ca. 1895. Ives was already aware of ragtime, and in a few years would begin composing works based on it. (*Courtesy Music Library, Yale University*)

Hughes (historian and encyclopedist) for promoting and defending ragtime at a time when that was risky business. But it was Ives who really loved the music. He consistently incorporated its quirky syncopated elements into his own works, not only in the several series of *Ragtime Dances* of 1902 to 1904 (lost), the first piano sonata, at least two of the violin sonatas, and *In the Inn* (1911), but later in such takeoffs as *Over the Pavements* (1913), *The See'r* (1913), and *Ann Street* (1922).

The latter two pieces, brief as they are, are instructive examples of how effectively Ives dealt with indigenous American musical idioms—not only ragtime, but the whole panoply of genres. *The See'r* is an epigrammatic takeoff on a small ragtime band (clarinet, cornet, euphonium, drums, and piano), raucously dissonant and brash, like some overly enthusiastic amateur group. A typically Ivesian touch is the cornet player's four-times-reiterated wind-up preparation for what promises to be a big solo. But alas, the poor cornetist can't think of anything to play, and gets stuck on one note, C, which he frantically punches out in odd rhythms that underscore his great distress, while the clarinet and baritone try to "get him back in" with ragtime licks; only they can't get together either, and the pianist and drummer finally crash in with a big cluster chord. The piece ends as abruptly as it began, leaving one a bit dazed and not quite sure that one actually heard right.

Ann Street gives us another cross-section of early twentieth-century musical Americana. An introduction, marked "fast and noisily," with two brash "harmonic series" trombone glissandi, gives way to a brief snatch of some quasipopular ditty. This in turn is interrupted by a "tailgate" trombone initiating a few bars of $\frac{7}{8}$ outlined by the piano. This leads to one solitary measure of jaunty jazz syncopation in the brass and piano, followed abruptly by a dreamily impressionistic phrase in which the flute in tranquil slow motion imitates the just-played jazz lick of the brass. The trumpet cuts in with an imperious three-note call (to what?) accompanied by a piano chord that seems Beethovenian yet is in A minor *and* A major. Five heavy chords in cornet and piano lead to a strange little vamp in $\frac{7}{16}$ meter. This gives way to a variant (in flute and piano) of the popular tune of the beginning, and the muted trumpet and piano conclude with a nostalgic phrase that is left suspended, unresolved in a typically Ivesian poignant gesture. All of this happens in twenty-two measures: a veritable kaleidoscope of dramatically contrasting musical strains, all compressed into a one-and-a-quarter-minute vignette.

By the time Claude Debussy (1862–1918) wrote his charming "Golliwog's Cake Walk" for his daughter in 1908, such genre and "characteristic" pieces constituted a well-established tradition (which was, incidentally, to be reborn with the American "novelty pieces" of the 1920s and 1930s ranging from Zez Confrey's *Kitten on the Keys* to Alec Templeton's *Bach Goes to Town*). Although it is unlikely that Debussy would have incorporated ragtime elements in his major orchestral scores, he did treat the subject respectfully and lovingly enough, not only in "Golliwog" but in two of his piano preludes ("Minstrels" and "General Lavine—eccentric"). After all, ragtime (although introduced to

Europe by Sousa during his European tour of 1900) was and is primarily a piano music, and it is logical that Debussy would have more readily thought of ragtime in connection with writing for the piano. It should also be noted that almost as if wishing to bring Wagner "down" to the level of ragtime, Debussy took his famous sideswipe at the German master by parodying the main motive from *Tristan und Isolde* and responding with his own derisive laughter, composed right into "Golliwog."

By the time Erik Satie (1866–1925) and Igor Stravinsky (1882–1971) came to the same crossroads more than ten years later, both the battles over Wagner and the absolute novelty of ragtime were things of the past. However, for Parisians like Satie, still in the midst of discovering African art and therefore loving this exotic new black music from America, ragtime as late as 1917 still had a certain shock value with which to *épater les bourgeois*. Satie's iconoclastic ballet *Parade* of that year became instantly notorious not only for its shocking Parisian music hall borrowings and slightly "seedy" ragtime sensationalism, but also for its futurist use of such noisemakers as sirens and typewriters. Actually, *Parade* wasn't all that shocking, but rather a suave and typically elegant Parisian view of *le ragtime americain*. Notable, incidentally, is the prominent use of the tuba, not as a bass but as a solo melodic instrument.

Igor Stravinsky's *Ragtime* (1918) was one of several ragtime-associated pieces from that period, including his *Rag Music* and the ragtime excerpt from *L'histoire du soldat*. I must confess that, despite many previous attempts to conduct this work, I feel I never really understood the piece until I had performed Joplin, Scott, and other classic ragtimers. Stravinsky based his ragtime pieces upon published rags that were sent to him from America and, to some extent, upon local European imitations of American ragtime bands. That Stravinsky was not interested in strict emulation of classic ragtime, but rather in a stylization of a new dance form, is shown in many ways, not the least of which is the inclusion of a French horn and, of all things, a cimbalom (the Hungarian national instrument) in his eleven-piece ensemble.

The opening flourish is strikingly similar to "Golliwog." Stravinsky's main opening section, recapitulated later, is full of jaunty, purposely awkward rhythmic syncopations. A quieter middle section follows, over a relentless ostinato bass of two alternating notes (G and E), interrupted several times by slashing, syncopated incursions. But these, too, lead to a sequence of brief episodes based partly upon earlier material. A mysterious-sounding low-register flute solo over quiet march rhythms in bass and drums leads to a strict recapitulation of the opening section. A coda, based on variants of the Debussy-like introductory measures, closes the work. In all of this, Stravinsky, with the masterful creations of *Petrushka* and *The Rite of Spring* behind him, exploits his instrumental resources, particularly the strings and drums, with ingenious and sophisticated virtuosity.

Cultural borrowing is, of course, not a one-way street. It would be quite erroneous to assume that the interaction between ragtime and classical music took only one form—that of classical musicians being captivated by this new American musical phenomenon. If anything, the traffic was heavier in the other direction. This was almost inevitable, since it was the rag composers, mostly black, who aspired to assimilate into the white musical culture. Classical influence took myriad forms, everything from the interpolation of little incidental classical touches or elements of compositional-technical sophistication all the way to complete changes of musical direction, as in the case of Joplin's nonragtime opera *Treemonisha* (1911) or Artie Matthews's complete abandonment of ragtime for the more "proper" climes of a classical music conservatory.

Classical influence could take even more unexpected and subtle forms, where the composer—perhaps unknowingly—juxtaposed musical materials and concepts never before integrated in just such a manner. An early case in point is the *Harlem Rag* (1897), the first published rag by a black composer, Tom Turpin (1873–1922). Indeed, its very earliness in ragtime's development may have allowed *Harlem Rag* to cast about for its style in such a kaleidoscopic way, before the preeminence of the *Maple Leaf Rag* (1899), when Joplin "fixed" the form and style of the piano rag for years to come.

In *Harlem Rag*, classical influences manifest themselves not so much in specific stylistic borrowings as in a general attitude that reveals well-learned lessons in harmony and form. Ironically, within the brevity of a three-minute piece, such elements almost collide with other materials that are neither classical nor even ragtime. These include Turpin's opening prelude and postlude, vestiges of an even earlier country music (mostly fiddle) that we recognize in pieces like *Turkey in the Straw* (a good indicator of how much jigs, clogs, polkas, and the like intermingled and coexisted with African or Afro-American musical traditions). From this innocent opening, Turpin moves abruptly into a surprisingly modern sequence of three themes. The first is hard-driving and jazzy, with more of a feeling of the early 1920s than pre-turn of the century. The second theme has an alternating call-and-response pattern between bass and treble. The third, a magnificent, imperious march theme, is embellished on its repeat by syncopated obbligato figures borrowed from the second theme.

What is perhaps most remarkable is the way the piece builds, development not being a prime characteristic of the "classic rag" form. Each successive "chorus" in *Harlem Rag* builds upon its predecessor, not of course in any sonata-form sense of development, but in some internal organic way that almost defies analysis. I think a good part of the success of this cohesion stems from the interesting way that Turpin—in the basic key of G—keeps returning to the bright tonality of E major (in the last four measures of the **A** theme, the first two measures of the **B** theme, and in the second measure of the marchlike **C** theme); and from the ingenious way in which the rapid-fire staccato rhythms of the **B** theme give way in rhythmic augmentation to the broader, statelier contours of the **C** theme. This section is almost grandiose, a true finale; the *Turkey in the Straw* postlude comes as a somewhat anticlimactic ending.

In the context of that turn-of-the-century era, composers like Louis Chauvin (1881–1908) and Robert 'Hampton (1890–1945) would probably have been surprised to find their creative offspring included in a musical grouping implying classical influence. (Or, not inconceivably, might they not have been proud at the recognition of such strivings?) However, the idea is not so farfetched as it might appear at first. Certainly Joplin, the co-author with Chauvin of *Heliotrope Bouquet* (1907), strove all his life to be accepted by the prevailing cultural/musical establishment, which to all intents and purposes meant the classical music establishment. As for Louis Chauvin, that tragic figure—"solitary wastrel Creole genius," Rudi Blesh has called him,[4] classical music was not all that remote. A pianist of extraordinary virtuosity, Chauvin had in his repertory everything from piano arrangements of Sousa marches to classical overtures, concert waltzes, and opera medleys. The vocal quartet that Chauvin helped to form was called the Mozart Comedy Four.[5] Quite apart from these career evidences, Chauvin's compositions, with their legato cantilena, as exemplified in the first theme of *Heliotrope Bouquet,* are abundant proof that musical lyricism and romanticism were not foreign to Chauvin's experience.

Rob Hampton, too, must have known his classical repertory, if only by ear (for it was his friend and colleague Artie Matthews who wrote out Hampton's *Cataract Rag* for publication). The third and fourth strains of *Cataract,* with their cascading thirty-second-note figurations, as well as the introduction and coda, show a strong classical influence, and sound for all the world like excerpts from a Beethoven piano concerto or Czerny etude.

Artie Matthews (1888–1958), the composer of the five *Pastime* rags, is another major star in the ragtime firmament—now unfortunately known only to a small audience. He certainly belongs with the "moderns," but he could just as easily have qualified in the category of "classical influence," since parts of his rags sound like early Kurt Weill. (Indeed, Matthews left ragtime around 1915, becoming first a church organist. A few years later he founded the Cosmopolitan Conservatory of Music in Cincinnati, and until he died in 1958, devoted himself exclusively to the classics.) And what of his modernistic "cluster" chords in the **A** strain of *Pastime Rag No. 4,* sonorities which in those days musicians referred to as "crazy chords"?

Matthews, born in Braidwood, Illinois, was certainly one of the best-trained and musically educated of the ragtimers. In his early days in Saint Louis, he was active as a composer and arranger for a number of Charlie Turpin's musical and theatrical enterprises, turning out entire shows, including orchestrations, once a week. He also worked for John Stark as an arranger, notating and preparing for publication rags of such colleagues as Rob Hampton and Charley Thompson. Matthews was among the first to publish a number bearing the title "blues"—even before W. C. Handy's *Memphis Blues*—a piece he called *Baby Seals Blues,* issued in August 1912. Later Matthews became famous in jazz circles for his *Weary Blues* (1915), really more ragtime than blues, which became a staple of the jazz repertory of the 1920s.[6]

It is ironic and tragic that the rejection of ragtime by proper musical circles as sinful and immoral music—indeed the segregation for decades (even into our own 1980s) of black musics from the established white culture—could have caused a gifted man like Matthews to turn his back on ragtime. In later years he taught classical theory at his own conservatory, made symphonic arrangements for the Cincinnati Symphony, and would hardly allow talk about ragtime in his presence, preferring to be associated only with the music of the classical masters such as Beethoven and Bach.

Matthews' *Pastime* rags, numbered 1 through 5, were all probably written around 1913. Some of these, including no. 4, were considered too advanced, even by a man as devoted to ragtime as publisher John Stark, who delayed the publication of *Pastime Rag No. 4* until 1920 when, in the context of newer styles coming in, Matthews' modernistic ideas would not seem quite so radical. The piece is startling enough as a piano work, but takes on even more striking dimensions when heard in an orchestral setting—an idea, one assumes, Matthews himself would have endorsed.[7]

Classical yearnings in ragtime may take another form of expression: in the overall mood or stance of a piece, as in the many romantic rags of Joseph Lamb (1887-1960). Take his moving, poignant *Ragtime Nightingale* (1915), an extensive mood "tone poem," albeit within the standard duration and multithematic form of the piano rag. Unhurried, contemplative, at once simple and grand, haunting, and at times vigorously swinging, *Ragtime Nightingale* embodies the full spectrum of ragtime's expressions. From the almost Tchaikovskian moodiness of the opening C-minor section with its graceful descending sixths in the middle measures, through the more energetic E-flat second theme to the scintillating Trio in A flat, the piece is a pure joy to hear. Lamb told Rudi Blesh that it was the name of *Ragtime Nightingale* that struck him first, inspired by Ethelbert Nevin's "Nightingale Song," which Lamb saw in his sister's copy of an issue of *Etude* magazine. From this germ evolved the whole piece.[8] And what an overpowering and joyous sense of completion one feels when the Trio strain reaches its climax and when the **B** theme returns to round out the piece.

To trace the transition from pure ragtime—notated, fixed, and played (more or less) the same way each time—to jazz—unnotated, improvised, and played differently each time—would go beyond the scope of this essay. It is too vast and complex a development to be dealt with so briefly. But something should be said, not to clarify or simplify, but rather to underscore the tangled and complex process that was nearly two decades in the making. Simplifying, one could say that "jazz is a successor to ragtime," that jazz grew out of the amalgamation of many musical elements, among which black ragtime, black blues, and the march tradition were undoubtedly the most significant and formative ingredients. It would be more accurate, however, to say that jazz in its several early forms was contained *within* ragtime from the very beginnings, with the boundaries often overlapping and at times probably even interchangeable. The distinctions were more on a practical, social, and technical level than on a stylistic level.

First, the distinctions were *practical.* The musicians played those instruments—a piano *or* a small instrumental group, a brass band *or* a string group—which their host had available or wanted to hear. In a hotel dining room or a theater pit, an instrumental ensemble was considered more appropriate than the average upright piano played by a "perfesser" in a New Orleans or Denver or Chicago "parlor house."

Second, the distinctions were *social.* The musician played what those who hired him wanted to hear and in the manner in which they wanted to hear it. It was the *milieu,* ranging from rough honky-tonks to the sedate salons of the rich gentry, that determined how and what he played. He might indeed play the *Maple Leaf Rag* in any and all of these establishments, but he'd play it one way here and another there. He'd clean it up there and dirty it up here. He'd play it straight here to impress his host, and he'd "fool around with it" there to arouse his clients to greater heights of spending.

Third, the distinctions were *technical.* The musician played according to his technical-musical talents or limitations, reading written music if that was his training, or improvising or playing by ear remembered tunes if such happened to be his background. Very few in those days combined both abilities. Jelly Roll Morton and James Europe were among those few, and one must note in passing that these musicians' knowledge of classical music was considerable.

Those early musicians were proud of their versatility. Indeed, it was necessary for their survival, since opportunities might knock at any door. Racial barriers generally kept things well segregated, yet black instrumentalists such as George Morrison (who was admired and given free lessons by Fritz Kreisler),[9] Ellington trombonist Lawrence Brown (who really wanted to play the cello in the symphony and solved that problem by learning to play the trombone as if it were a cello),[10] James P. Johnson (who as a young man strenuously practiced his classics and never missed a Hofmann or Rachmaninoff recital at Carnegie Hall), Jelly Roll Morton, James Reese Europe, W. C. Handy, and countless others all learned to handle a variety of musics. For them, going from ragtime to jazz was not so much a historical process as an everyday occurrence and necessity, depending primarily upon where the next dollar might come from.

Of course, there were some who were more determined and more creative than others. Morton, Ellington, Europe, Bennie Moten, and King Oliver really moved things along, while men like Earl Fuller, Wilbur Sweatman, Dave Peyton, and Doc Cook merely followed the prevailing musical winds. Other musicians like Eubie Blake, George Gershwin, William Grant Still (a versatile black instrumentalist and arranger who aspired to "assimilate"—not unlike Joplin—by becoming a classical composer, succeeding to the point where he is considered today the "dean of black composers"), and W. C. Handy went on to other fields—Broadway, publishing, the record business, arranging—or, in some less fortunate cases, oblivion.

Of the many examples one could cite of pieces illustrating the transition from ragtime to jazz, we have to limit ourselves to one—Eubie Blake's

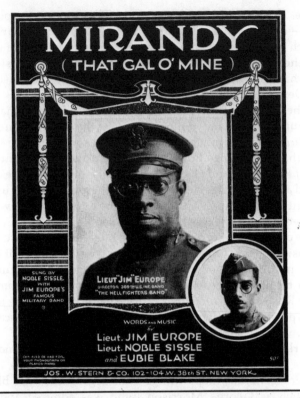

James Reese Europe, one of the most versatile and influential black musicians of the 1910s, was equally at home in ragtime, jazz, and symphonic music. Best known as a bandleader, he also composed instrumental works and songs, such as *Mirandy* (1918). (*John Edward Hasse collection*)

Charleston Rag, a gem of the ragtime repertory. Known as a "finger buster" and, as such, a fine example of the speedier, flashier Eastern ragtime school (out of Baltimore, New Jersey, and New York), *Charleston Rag* is a virtuoso instrumental piece. With its tricky walking bass in the **A** strain and its "hot jazz" feeling, it is a perfect example (like some of Jelly Roll Morton's pieces) of the transition of ragtime to early jazz. Eubie Blake (1883–1983) claims to have played *Charleston Rag* as early as 1899 in Baltimore, although it was not copyrighted until 1917. Eubie's own performances of this piece have never been precisely the same, as would have been expected in the older Midwest classic ragtime, although the overall format and key relationships are always retained; the "licks" and "breaks" are often interchanged and new variations are added *ad hoc*. In this sense, *Charleston Rag* grew, always drawing on its 1899 format, though it was more or less set for publication in a probably simplified and not necessarily *Urtext* edition in 1917 and then recorded in 1921 for the old Emerson label under its original title, *Sounds of Africa*.[11] In any case, *Charleston Rag* is a spectacular example not only of the aforementioned transition, but also of the complexity and rhythmic drive of Eastern ragtime, as contrasted with the more sedate, "not-to-be-played-fast" ragtime of the Saint Louis ragtime fraternity.

Viewed with the perspective of sixty to seventy years, it seems to be an altogether remarkable fact that jazz survived at all, or, to put it another way, that ragtime survived in the form of jazz. And what is remarkable is that, at a time when improvisatory techniques, dormant in Western music since the baroque era, were still an unappreciated medium of expression, it was the very spontaneity and uncontainability of jazz (i.e., ragtime in its freer, more unfettered form) that saved the music. I am convinced that straight, pure notated classical ragtime would have died (indeed, it did!), not only of its own ultimate limitations and inability to progress but, even before that, of the commercial strangulation visited upon it. It would have died of its own—or Joplin's—perfect vision. It was the "loosening up" represented by jazz that saved ragtime. Just as "ragging" the music had let in a fresh musical breath around 1900, so "jazzing it up" a generation or two later further opened the window—this time wide enough to allow a view all the way to the future.

Notes

1. Rudi Blesh and Harriet Janis, *They All Played Ragtime* (New York: Knopf, 1950).
2. See Antonin Dvořák, "Music in America," *Harper's New Monthly Magazine* 90 (February 1895): 428–34. This very influential article is reprinted in *The Negro and His Folklore in Nineteenth-Century Periodicals,* ed. Bruce Jackson (Austin: University of Texas Press, 1967), pp. 263–73.
3. Arthur Farwell's moving essays on American "native" music are, fortunately, available once again as a result of the recent republication of his entire Wa-Wan Press production—an eight-year labor of love on behalf of non-European-influenced American musics. See Vera B. Lawrence, ed., *Wa-Wan Press* (New York: Arno Press, 1970), vol. 4, p. 184 for Farwell's vigorous espousal of ragtime.
4. Rudi Blesh, Introduction, *Classic Piano Rags: Complete Original Music for 81 Rags* (New York: Dover, 1973), p. vii.
5. Blesh and Janis, *They All Played Ragtime,* pp. 57–58.
6. Ibid., pp. 262–63.
7. *Pastime Rag No. 4* has been arranged for sixteen-piece ragtime ensemble by Gunther Schuller and can be heard on *The Road from Rags to Jazz,* a two-record set recorded by the New England Conservatory Ragtime Ensemble, Golden Crest Records CRS-31042, 1975.
8. Blesh and Janis, *They All Played Ragtime,* p. 239.
9. Gunther Schuller, *Early Jazz: Its Roots and Musical Development* (New York: Oxford University Press, 1968), p. 368.
10. Stanley Dance, *The World of Duke Ellington* (New York: Charles Scribner's Sons, 1970), p. 119.
11. Eubie Blake's 1921 recording of *Sounds of Africa* was issued as Emerson 10434. It has been reissued as part of a two-disc album, *A Jazz Piano Anthology,* Columbia Records KG 32355, 1973.

Ragtime on Piano Rolls

Michael Montgomery, Trebor Jay Tichenor, and John Edward Hasse

Piano rolls were an important medium for disseminating ragtime. This chapter presents, for the first time, the story of ragtime on player piano rolls. The authors explain how player pianos work and examine the quantity of rags on rolls, the musical arrangements, the major roll recording artists, and the best-selling hits of piano roll ragtime.

Most ragtime appeared in printed sheet music form so it could be bought by those who could read music.[1] Many ragtime compositions also appeared on player piano rolls and this way *anybody* could buy and enjoy the sound of ragtime. This is why piano rolls were vital to carrying ragtime *sounds* to the general public. Before examining ragtime on piano rolls, however, let's look briefly at the player piano and the piano roll.

Player Pianos

Basically, here is what happens when a player piano "plays." The notes of the printed music become perforations in a long roll of paper which unwinds at a controlled speed over a "tracker bar." This is a machined metal "reader" with eighty-eight holes in it. The paper roll perforations are designed to register exactly with their corresponding tracker bar holes. When an operator pumps the player piano's foot pedals, an exhaust bellows pushes air out of the player mechanism to create a strong central vacuum. As a note hole in the moving paper roll reaches its corresponding hole in the tracker bar, air is let into the correct tracker-bar hole, and this triggers a pneumatic lifter bellows that makes the corresponding hammer strike the appropriate string or strings. (This also makes the piano key go down.) As the hole in the paper moves past the tracker bar, the hammer is deactivated (and the piano key goes back up).

The player piano, like many inventions, developed gradually. A Scottish-born American, John McTammany (1845-1915), was an early player pioneer and claimed to be the inventor of the player piano. About 1868 he constructed a mechanism for automatically playing small, hand-cranked table-top organs.[2] These organs used paper rolls to produce simple melodies with a limited range of notes. But McTammany was pushed aside by others.

By the late 1890s, the Aeolian Company brought out its "Pianola," for which inventor Edwin S. Votey (1856-1931) filed a patent application in 1897.[3] The Pianola was an early player mechanism housed in a varnished wooden cabinet, on casters, that the operator rolled up to the keyboard of a conventional piano. When operated, the Pianola's sixty-five wooden "fingers" depressed the middle sixty-five keys on the piano. The device was literally a "piano player." Soon afterward, the player mechanism was miniaturized and mounted out of sight inside the cabinet of the piano, so that when activated, the piano seemed to play by itself. This device was known as the "inner player" or more literally, the "player piano."

Another pioneer in the player piano industry was Melville Clark (1850-1918). Formerly with the firm of Story & Clark (established in 1875), Clark founded the Melville Clark Piano Company in 1900 to pursue his idea of building player pianos that would play the entire range of notes on the keyboard. Prior to 1900, the player would activate only fifty-eight or sixty-five notes of the eighty-eight note keyboard. This limitation resulted in rearranging and sometimes mutilating compositions written for more than a sixty-five-note range.[4] In 1901, Clark introduced his "Apollo" player with an eighty-eight note tracker bar and the first eighty-eight note music roll to utilize the full compass of the piano. In 1908, the rest of the player piano industry also adopted the eighty-eight note standard. This move gave great impetus to the growing player industry and "resulted in the formation of over fifty new companies operating solely in the roll business in the United States."[5]

A large number of patents were filed as more firms began manufacturing and improving the player piano. By 1904, according to Ehrlich, "there were more than forty different kinds of automatic pianos on the American market."[6] Table 14 lists some representative American manufacturers of player pianos. As players became more sophisticated, many established piano manufacturers responded by building their own player pianos or building their pianos so that player mechanisms built by other firms could be installed. Aeolian became the largest producer of player mechanisms. Their players were installed in Steinways, Webers, Stuyvesants, and other brands.

There were several different types of player pianos. Besides the standard home player, a variety of coin-operated piano (first marketed in 1898)

Table 14

Representative U.S. Player Piano Manufacturers, 1900–1930

MANUFACTURER	CITY*	BRAND NAMES
The Aeolian Co.	New York City	Pianola, Geo. Steck, Stroud, Stuyvesant, Weber
American Piano Co.	New York City	Electrelle, Knabe, Mason & Hamlin, Armstrong, Foster, Primatone
The Autopiano Co.	New York City	Autopiano, Pianista
The Baldwin Co.	Cincinnati	Manualo (installed in Baldwin, Ellington, Hamilton, and Howard), Monarch, Modello
The Cable Co.	Chicago	Carola, Conover, and Euphona Inner-Players
Melville Clark Piano Co.	Chicago (plant in DeKalb, Ill.)	Apollo, Solo Apollo
Gulbransen Co.	Chicago	Gulbransen Registering Piano
Hardman, Peck & Co.	New York City	Autotone, Playotone, Standard
W. W. Kimball Piano Co.	Chicago	Kimball
Krell-French Piano Co.	Connersville, Ind.	Auto-Grand, Auto-Player, Piano-Auto, Solo-Grand
The Packard Piano Co.	Fort Wayne, Ind.	Bond, Packard
Starr Piano Co.	Richmond, Ind.	Remington, Richmond, Starr, Trayser
Story & Clark Piano Co.	Chicago and Grand Haven, Mich.	Story & Clark, Repro-Phraso
Waltham Piano Co.	Milwaukee	Electratone, Waltham, Warfield, Wilson
The Wilcox & White Co.	Meriden, Conn.	Angelus
Rudolph Wurlitzer Mfg. Co.	Cincinnati and North Tonawanda, N.Y.	Pianino,† Wurlitzer

* The city of corporate headquarters is listed. Some pianos were built in locations other than the corporate headquarters. For example, Aeolian Company manufactured George Steck pianos in Neponset, Massachusetts, and American Piano Company manufactured Mason & Hamlin pianos in Baltimore.

†The Pianino was a coin-operated piano.

Sources: Alfred Dolge, Pianos and Their Makers (Covina, Calif.: Covina Publishing Co., 1911); Harvey N. Roehl, Player Piano Treasury, 2nd ed. (Vestal, N.Y.: The Vestal Press, 1973); and Presto Buyers' Guide to Pianos, Player-Pianos, and Reproducing Pianos (Chicago: Presto, 1926).

appeared and was used in commercial establishments. There were also "reproducing" pianos (first exhibited in Freiburg, Germany, in 1904), which, unlike others, reproduced subtle dynamics and phrasing. The reproducing piano was used primarily for classical and "serious" music, and few rag rolls were issued on the reproducing roll labels (Ampico, Duo-Art, Welte, Artrio-Angelus).

Novel and highly mechanical, the player piano spread from the United States to Britain and continental Europe. The Aeolian Company, the most successful manufacturer in the United States, opened a London showroom in 1899. Its Pianola did brisk business under the slogan, "So simple a child can play it."[7]

In the United States, player sales peaked between 1919 and 1923. The players were expensive (the Pianola retailed for two hundred and fifty dollars in 1898—a major investment in those days), and often represented a family's second or third largest single purchase, after a house and perhaps an automobile. The decline of the player piano resulted from the rising

THE
AMERICAN PLAYER PIANO

IN THE HOME

is the Delight of the AMERICAN GIRL

The absolute control of tempo and expression in the AMERICAN PLAYER PIANO particularly adapts it to the accompanying of the human voice, and this is one of the many reasons why it is so great a favorite in American homes and accounts in some degree for its tremendous and ever growing popularity.

THE AMERICAN PLAYER PIANO CO.
15-17-19 Canal Place, New York, N. Y.

As this advertisement (ca. 1905) implies, the player piano was a prized possession. Just as most amateur pianists were women, many operators of player pianos were young ladies. (*Courtesy Harvey N. Roehl*)

popularity of competing entertainment media—talking pictures (movies), radio, and the phonograph. By the middle 1930s, in the heart of the Depression, piano dealers were reportedly selling six-hundred-dollar player pianos for twenty-five dollars.[8]

Piano Rolls

The earliest piano rolls were not true recordings of someone's actual playing. A skilled music arranger had the job of planning and cutting the holes in a master roll, using a blank sheet of paper some thirty feet long and eleven and a quarter inches wide. The task of positioning the many perforations was solved in different ways. Basically, a roll company arranger knew how many inches of paper had to pass over the tracker bar for every measure of music. So within a given number of "measures" on the master paper, he or she could divide the notes on the sheet music into perforations of varying lengths, cut these "perfs" into the master so they would correspond with the notes to be activated, and produce a master roll of any composition the company wanted to reproduce.

The arranger's musical score told where to put the "perfs." No arranger, however, was bound by the musical notes on the page; the notes were merely a starting point. Where the sheet music showed a single note, for example, the arranger might cut in an octave. Some rolls are so heavily arranged, or rearranged, that they are called "orchestral" arrangements— every note on the keyboard seems to play during the performance!

During the 1910s, the public was eager to hear more lifelike "solo" performances. Several companies worked diligently to perfect machinery to properly record the playing of performing artists. In 1912, Melville Clark issued the first QRS hand-played roll made from a "live" performance, Lee Roberts's rendition of his own composition, *Valse Parisienne*. Later in 1912, QRS issued hand-played rolls by the black pianist from Missouri, John W. "Blind" Boone. Aeolian introduced its first hand-played rolls to the public early in 1913.

Clark devised a drum of paper that moved as the artist sat at the recording piano. The artist could hear the performance as it was being recorded. During the recording performance, pencil marks were made by eighty-eight tiny carbon markers as the piano keys were depressed. When the "recording" was finished, the result was a marked-up preliminary master roll. The next operation consisted of manually cutting out the marked spots with special die punches. After this step, the master roll was complete. Copying machinery could mass produce many copies at a time from the master.

In May 1923 a new employee named J. Lawrence Cook (1899–1977) began to arrange piano roll masters for QRS. Cook's arrangements were so skillful that the finished results sound hand-played even today. Cook stayed with QRS until the early 1960s, and produced most of the QRS "hand-played" rolls during the 1930s and 1940s.[9]

The other means of producing hand-played rolls was the direct-punch method. For this process, the artist recorded on a special piano. During the performance, high-speed die punches cut holes into the blank master paper as it moved along. Some master rolls were "playable," meaning the artist could hear, without delay, what had just been recorded by playing the new master on a regular player piano. Corrections could easily be made by taping over the wrong notes and cutting in the correct ones. Close examination reveals that many "hand-played" rolls were a combination of true hand-playing with some embellishment notes added by the roll editor (or arranger)—usually to emphasize the melody. Eubie Blake's rolls on the Mel-O-Dee label are prime examples of such editing room enhancements.[10]

American piano roll manufacture was concentrated in Chicago and New York City, as Table 15 shows. QRS, which began in Chicago, opened manufacturing plants in New York City, San Francisco, and Toronto, as well as in Sidney, Australia, and Utrecht, Holland. At the retail level, piano rolls were sold by piano stores and music dealers, as well as dime and department stores. Sears Roebuck, Montgomery Ward, and other big-city department stores carried low-cost rolls in their mail-order catalogs.

Table 15
Major U.S. Piano Roll Manufacturers, 1900–1930

MANUFACTURER	CITY	BRAND NAMES
The Aeolian Co.	New York City	Aeolian, Mel-O-Dee, Metro-Art, Universal, Duo-Art
American Piano Co.	New York City	American Piano Control, Ampico
Bennett & White Co.	Newark, N.J.	Artempo
The Cable Co.	Chicago	Diamond, Imperial, Recordo
Chase & Baker Co.	Buffalo, N.Y.	Chase & Baker, Melographic
Melville Clark Piano Co.*	Chicago	Autograph, QRS, Solo-Apollo
Columbia Music Roll Co. (later Capitol Roll and Record Co.)	Chicago	American, Capitol, Cecile, Challenge, Columbia, Sterling, Supertone, Syncronized
Connorized Co.	New York City	Cecilian, Connorized
W. W. Kimball Piano Co.	Chicago	Kimball
Pianostyle Co.	Brooklyn, N.Y.	Pianostyle, Majestic
Republic Player Roll Corp.	New York City	Republic
Rose Valley Co.	Philadelphia	Ideal
Staffnote Player Roll Co.	Milwaukee	Staffnote, Hitz, Playrite
Standard Music Roll Co.	Orange, N.J.	Arto, Electra, Perfection, SingA
United States Music Roll Co.	Chicago	Lakeside, U.S. Music
Vocalstyle Music Co.	Cincinnati	Vocalstyle
The Wilcox & White Co.	Meriden, Conn.	Angelus, Artrio-Angelus

*When Melville Clark died in 1918, the M.C.P.C. was reorganized. The piano factory was sold to another firm, and the roll part of the business became the QRS Company. In the 1920s, QRS purchased a number of smaller companies, including Connorized (ca. 1927), Imperial (1922), International (ca. 1930), Pianostyle (ca. 1930), Recordo (ca. 1925), United States Music (1926), and Vocalstyle (1927). This reduced competition by taking these roll brands off the market. The master rolls of the defunct firms were destroyed.

Ragtime on Piano Rolls

Piano rolls were essential in disseminating ragtime, especially to the non-piano-playing public. During the Ragtime Era, few cylinder or phonograph recordings of piano solos were made. Until the 1920s, the main ragtime piano soloist on discs was Mike Bernard (1881–1936). Although ragtime invariably could be heard in silent movie theaters as background music and in many saloons, these sources alone could not have made piano ragtime so popular. It was the player pianos and rag piano rolls that carried this happy sound into countless homes and parlors.

At least one thousand different rag compositions appeared on piano rolls, and many appeared on several different labels. Rags, however, comprised a small percentage of the total number of titles issued on piano rolls. From 1900 to 1910, the proportion of rags was probably between 1 and 3 percent of the total output of all available titles. The ratio rose slightly in the next decade. A 1916 United States Music Company catalog included about 265 piano rags (10 percent) in a total listing of 2,640 titles, and a 1918 QRS catalog lists 340 rag rolls (5.9 percent) in a total list of 5,320 titles.[11]

The low percentage of rag titles presents only part of the picture, because certain rags sold in huge quantities. The best clue to sales that we have is the number of months or years that a selection stayed in a company's catalog. In most catalogs, Scott Joplin's *Maple Leaf Rag* appeared early and remained for many years. Classic rags sold well on rolls and were issued by all major labels. The most popular rag rolls were those copyrighted by the major publishers.[12] Established publishers such as John Stark & Son and most of the Tin Pan Alley firms mailed out complimentary sheet music copies of their rags to the piano roll manufacturers. Because small-town publishers had limited promotion and distribution, the rags they published as sheet music rarely appeared on piano rolls.

Roll companies issued every type of music that was popular—marches, "coon songs," rags, two-steps, classics, syncopated songs, and a few syncopated waltzes, such as *Echoes from the Snowball Club* (Harry P. Guy).[13] Of piano rags, the runaway best-seller was Charles L. Johnson's hit *Dill Pickles Rag*, which was issued by at least ten different piano roll companies. One label, Supertone, offered *Dill Pickles* in two different arrangements (Supertone 95120 and 10013). Based on the number of copies surviving today, *Dill Pickles* was followed in sales by the cakewalk hit *At a Georgia Campmeeting* (Kerry Mills), and by *Maple Leaf Rag* (Scott Joplin) and *Black and White Rag* (George Botsford). In alphabetical order, other successful ragtime rolls were:

> *Everybody Two-Step* (Wallie Herzer)
> *Junk Man Rag* (Luckey Roberts)
> *Ragging the Scale* (Edward B. Claypoole)
> *Smokey Mokes* (Abe Holzmann)
> *St. Louis Tickle* (Barney & Seymore)
> *Temptation Rag* (Henry Lodge)
> *That Gosh-Darned Two-Step Rag* (M. K. Miller)
> *Très Moutarde (Too Much Mustard)* (Cecil Macklin)
> *Turkey in the Straw: A Rag Time Fantasy* (Otto Bonnell)
> *12th Street Rag* (Euday L. Bowman)
> *Wild Cherries Rag* (Ted Snyder)[14]

A minority of the major piano rag composers recorded piano rolls. Nevertheless, rolls have been found with credits naming the following ragtime composers as recording artists:

Felix Arndt (1889–1918)	James P. Johnson (1891–1955)
Roy Bargy (1894–1974)	Nat Johnson (1878–1921)
Eubie Blake (1883–1983)	Scott Joplin (1868–1917)
Blind Boone (1869–1927)	Jelly Roll Morton (1890–1941)
George Botsford (1874–1949)	Paul Parnell [pseudonym of Paul
Axel W. Christensen (1881–1955)	Pratt (1890–1948)]
Malvin Franklin (1889–1981)	Luckey Roberts (1887–1968)
George Gershwin (1898–1937)	J. Russel Robinson (1892–1963)
Albert Gumble (1883–1946)	Charley Straight (1891–1940)
Fred Heltman (1887–1960)	Fats Waller (1904–1943)

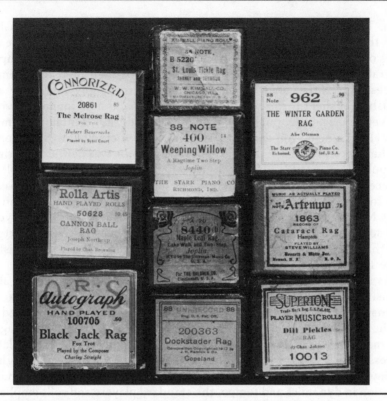

A selection of ragtime player piano rolls. (*John Edward Hasse collection*)

One cannot always believe the label credits, but they are accurate more often than not.

Rarely was a rag roll a note-for-note reproduction of the printed sheet music. Embellishments were often made in both arranged and hand-played rolls. An early technique was simply to double both bass and treble to achieve a fuller sound. Other embellishments were short fill-in runs and extensive use of the tremolo. The most popular device was the mid-range melody in tremolo with flashy embellishments carried on in the upper ranges. The most brilliant arranger was Mary E. "Mae" Brown, an organist, pianist, teacher, and songwriter who joined the staff of the United States Music Company in 1909.[15]

Each manufacturer developed its own style of arranging rolls. In many rag rolls issued by the Connorized Company, the bass note octave (the "oom" of the left-hand "oom-pah") is cut so that one octave note plays a fraction of a second earlier than the other. The "pah" is often cut so that the middle or upper note of the left-hand triad is delayed slightly. The effect is subtle, but it evokes the sound of a strummed stringed instrument such as banjo or guitar. This characteristic of Connorized rag rolls can be detected clearly by playing the rolls very slowly.

A tune issued on a piano roll almost always appeared first in sheet music form. The sheet music market was larger, sheets were less expensive to print than rolls were to manufacture, and a publisher could advertise other tunes on the inside and outside covers. In addition, the piano roll companies generally needed the sheet music as the basis for their own arrangements. Interestingly, few tunes appeared on piano rolls only and were never published in sheet form. Both QRS and National issued Joplin's *Silver Swan Rag*, yet it was neither published nor copyrighted.[16] QRS catalogs from 1905 to 1911 list a piano roll entitled *The Princeton Tiger*, credited to Scott Joplin—another piece, which if actually composed by Joplin, was neither copyrighted nor published. At this writing, however, no copies of the latter roll have surfaced. In the 1910s when there was a demand for one-step and fox-trot rolls for dancing, a number of tunes were written primarily for piano roll issue. Most of these pieces were also published in sheet music form, yet the rolls sold much better than the music sheets in these instances. Forty-odd rags that were never published as scores but were issued as rolls are listed in Table 16.

As noted above, the repertory on reproducing rolls was drawn almost exclusively from classical and "serious" music. Reproducing pianos, more expensive than standard players, were considered touches of class and taste for the wealthy. Since classical music required more dynamics than ragtime, the manufacturers may have regarded the monochromatic, relatively expressionless sound of the standard player pianos as "good enough" for ragtime. Indeed, it can be argued that with no variety in phrasing and little variation in dynamics and tempo, the standard players and rolls emphasized only the rhythmic and syncopated nature of ragtime rolls. The following rags are almost all that were recorded on reproducing rolls:

> *Charleston Rag* (Eubie Blake), played by Eubie Blake, Ampico 54174E
> *Desecration Rag* (Felix Arndt), played by Felix Arndt, Duo-Art 5716
> *Junk Man Rag* (C. Luckey Roberts), played by Felix Arndt, Duo-Art 5544
> *The Smiler Rag* (Percy Wenrich), played by Felix Arndt, Duo-Art 5551
> *Zu Zu Rag* (Max Fischler), played by Victor Arden, Ampico 52603

As jazz tunes began to replace rag titles in the late 1910s, fewer and fewer rags were issued on piano rolls. Several of James Scott's late rags—*Troubadour Rag* and *Rag Sentimental*—appeared on the Musicnote label in about 1919. James P. Johnson's stride pieces, such as *Carolina Shout* and *Harlem Strut*, appeared in the early 1920s, as the vogue of the pneumatic player piano reached its height.

Table 16
Unpublished Rags Issued on Piano Rolls

COMPOSER	TITLE	COMPANY AND NUMBER	RELEASE DATE
Baker, Edythe	Blooie-Blooie	Universal 203545 *	
Bargy, Roy	A Blue Streak	Imperial 513600 *	
	Omeomy	Imperial 513980 *	
Botsford, George	Universal Rag	Universal 100019, Metrostyle Themodist 300282	
Copeland, Les	Bees and Honey Rag	Universal 202759 *	
	Race Track Blues	Universal 202753 *	
	Rocky Mountain Fox	Universal 202725 *	
	Twist and Twirl	Universal 202755 *	1917
Delcamp, J. Milton	Rackety-Rag	Republic 47708 *	1920
Johnson, Arnold	Tek-Nik-Ality Rag	Imperial 51220 *	
Johnson, James P.	Caprice Rag	Perfection 87023 *	July 1917
	Daintiness Rag	Universal 203107 *	July 1917
	Harlem Strut	QRS 101014 *	
	Innovation	Universal 203255 *	
	Steeplechase Rag	Universal 203179 *	May 1917
	Twilight Rag	Metro-Art 203274 *	Nov. 1917
Joplin, Scott	Silver Swan Rag	QRS 31533, Master Record (National) 1239	
Kortlander, Max	Funeral Rag	QRS 100306 *	
	Hunting the Ball Rag	QRS 100470 *	
	Let's Try It	QRS 100660 *	
	Lil' Joe	QRS 100706 *	
Muth, Armand	Keen Kut-Ups	Staffnote 2039 *	
Ohman, Phil	Dixie Kisses	QRS 100884 *	
Pratt, Paul	Little Bit of Rag	U.S. Music 8005	
	Prattles	U.S. Music 7916	
	Wailana Rag	U.S. Music 7917	
Stover, Harry	Mel-O-Dee Rag	Mel-O-Dee 203557 *	
Straight, Charley	Black Jack Rag	QRS 100705 *	Nov. 1917
	A Dippy Ditty	Imperial 511770 *	Aug. 1918
	Fastep	Imperial 511560 *	Feb. 1918
	Itsit	QRS 100600 *	
	Lazy Bones	QRS 100500 *	
	Mitinice	QRS 100475 *	
	Nifty Nonsense	Imperial 511510 *	June 1918
	Out Steppin'	QRS 100571 *	
		Imperial 510000 *	May 1917
	Playmor	QRS 100571 *	
	Rag-A-Bit	Imperial 511760 *	Mar. 1918
	S'more	QRS 100409 *	
	Try Me	QRS 100406 *	
	Universal Rag	QRS 100801 *	
Straight, Charley & Rube Bennett	Mow 'em Down	Imperial 511940†	June 1918
Willet, Herb	Gulbransen Rag	U.S. Music 66036	
Woods, Clarence	Black Satin Fox Trot	U.S. Music 9235	

* Roll is played by the composer.
† This roll is played by Charley Straight.
Source: David A. Jasen and Trebor Jay Tichenor, *Rags and Ragtime: A Musical History* (New York: Seabury Press, 1978).

From 1930 to the 1950s there was little market for player pianos and rolls. From peak sales of nearly eleven million in 1926, QRS sales dropped to a low of two hundred thousand rolls per year in the early 1950s. Some resurgence of popularity occurred in the United States in the late fifties and sixties, and QRS began reissuing a few rags. In the 1970s, as a yearning for nostalgia swept the United States, QRS piano roll production approached one million rolls per year, and four manufacturers were producing over ten thousand new player pianos yearly.[17] The Joplin revival and the movie *The Sting* (1974) in particular helped create renewed demand for ragtime piano rolls by a new generation of player-piano owners. The Aeolian Company began manufacturing a spinet player piano named "The Sting," and the QRS catalog included piano rags played by Scott Joplin, Eubie Blake, Max Morath (b. 1926), and William Bolcom (b. 1938), among others.

In 1978, Superscope, Inc., introduced the "Pianocorder" reproducing system, which operates from computer-encoded cassettes rather than from piano rolls. The "Pianocorder" can be installed in standard pianos or is available already installed in the "Marantz Reproducing Piano." By arrangement with QRS, Superscope released over one hundred fifty rags on its special cassettes. Through a digital process, the company recreated these performances by adding expression dynamics not present in the original rolls. Old rag rolls can now be transformed, with the aid of a computer!

And so, in the 1980s, sixty years after the apparent demise of ragtime and fifty years after the decline of the player piano, ragtime and piano rolls once again join hands to carry jaunty syncopations across the land.

Notes

1. The authors wish to thank Harvey N. Roehl, president of the Vestal Press, for his suggestions concerning the manuscript.
2. Alfred Dolge, *Pianos and Their Makers* (Covina, Calif.: Covina Publishing Co., 1911), pp. 134–36, and John McTammany, *The Technical History of the Player* (New York: Musical Courier Co., 1915).
3. Dolge, p. 150.
4. Ibid., p. 154.
5. Dolge, p. 154; Nicholas Slonimsky, ed., *Baker's Biographical Dictionary of Musicians*, 6th ed. (New York: Schirmer Books, 1978), p. 326; and Harvey N. Roehl, "Re-enacting the Artist," in *The Pianocorder Story*, ed. James Turner, rev. ed. (Chatsworth, Calif.: Superscope, Inc., 1978), p. 20.
6. Cyril Ehrlich, *The Piano: A History* (London: J. M. Dent, 1976), p. 134.
7. David Wainwright, *The Piano Makers* (London: Hutchinson, 1975), p. 127.
8. Ehrlich, p. 136.
9. The expression "hand-played" appears in quotes because the rolls Cook made were not true recordings. The rolls were, however, issued with artist credits on them (*e.g.,* "Played by J. Lawrence Cook") and the public never knew the difference. The rolls *sounded* like someone was playing, and that was enough.
10. A thorough listing, compiled by Michael Montgomery, of Eubie Blake's piano rolls is included in Al Rose, *Eubie Blake* (New York: Schirmer Books, 1979), pp. 189–95.

11. *General Catalog, Perforated Music Rolls, Volume IV* (Chicago: United States Music Co., 1916), and *QRS Player Rolls* (Chicago: The QRS Co., 1918).

12. An exception seems to be some coin-operated rolls that contain more obscure rags, probably ones on which the publishers did not reserve mechanical reproduction rights.

13. For more complete citations of the following rolls, consult "A List of Player Piano Rolls" in Rudi Blesh and Harriet Janis, *They All Played Ragtime*, 4th ed., rev. (New York: Oak Publications, 1971), pp. 326–37; and David A. Jasen and Trebor Jay Tichenor, *Rags and Ragtime: A Musical History* (New York: Seabury Press, 1978), pp. 41, 87, 140, and *passim*.

14. John Hasse, telephone interview with Mike Schwimmer of Glencoe, Illinois, 14 November 1979. Schwimmer's selection of the best-selling ragtime rolls is based on his ten years' experience as a dealer in tens of thousands of antique piano rolls.

15. "United States Music Company Celebrates Twentieth Anniversary," *Music Trade Indicator*, 25 February 1925, p. 16.

16. A piano roll of *Silver Swan Rag* was discovered in 1970 and transcribed by Dick Zimmerman and Donna McCluer. It was published in *The Collected Works of Scott Joplin*, Vol. 1, ed. Vera Brodsky Lawrence (New York: New York Public Library, 1971), pp. 291–95.

17. *QRS Player Roll Catalog 1979–1980* (Buffalo, N.Y.: QRS, 1979).

The Reactions to Ragtime

Neil Leonard

During its heyday, ragtime was the subject of great controversy. Neil Leonard, in this new chapter, summarizes favorable and unfavorable reactions to ragtime, presents historical background for the controversy, and probes the racial, sexual, and religious implications of the debate.

In the dozen or so years since its latest rediscovery ragtime has achieved a surprising level of respectability. Ragtime has come out of the limbos of forgotten or ignored popular music to take its place in the concert hall, and its creators—men like Scott Joplin and Joseph Lamb—have been post-humously elevated from the status of mere piano players or popular-song writers to the standing of classical composers. It has found a wide appeal among discriminating segments of the music audience and has been recorded on numerous labels, including prestigious ones such as Angel and Nonesuch, ordinarily reserved for Western art music. Indeed, by 1974 ragtime had become so popular and its leading composer so esteemed that *Record World*, the trade magazine, called Scott Joplin "THE classical phenomenon of the decade" and pointed out that for several weeks of that year the "Best Seller" list in the classical category consisted wholly of recordings of Joplin compositions.[1]

In the midst of this growing respectability and esteem it is sometimes difficult to imagine how a music now so acceptable, at times even tame, could have generated such an angry controversy in the first two decades of this century. Who were the opponents of ragtime and what were they upset about?

For the most part they were of two types: first, people with a financial or emotional investment in cultivated music—musicians, music teachers, critics, and their followers; the second, guardians of public morality—clergymen, politicians, educators and their followers. Members of both groups were concerned that ragtime, which to them could mean any kind of syncopated popular music, threatened the appreciation and development of art music or, worse, contaminated social and moral behavior. Consequently they attacked the new music on several fronts.[2] They ridiculed its words and music as cheap, tawdry, dull, repetitious, and appealing to man's lower nature. They pandered to ethnic biases with slurs, however implicit, denigrating the music and its creators. They pointed to its supposed intellectual, moral, and physical perils, which evoked memories of degenerate times past. Not content merely to argue against it, they did what they could to suppress it, prohibiting it in certain locations, recommending that union musicians refuse to perform it, and sometimes taking dancers caught doing the Turkey Trot off to jail or dismissing them from their jobs.

During World War I the controversy engaged more thoughtful Americans. The most articulate spokesman for the pro-ragtime forces, Hiram K. Moderwell (1888–1945), noted that although well-known foreign musicians praised ragtime, our own musical authorities tended to isolate themselves from it, and indeed from all that was exciting in our native folk and popular music. Moderwell praised ragtime's technical resourcefulness in melody and, above all, rhythm, and undertook to explain its innovations and their intricacies which he held to be "the perfect expression of the American city with its restless, bustling motion."[3] He believed that the new music expressed our national character and provided the raw material for a native art music that our composers could not afford to ignore.

The most redoubtable spokesman for the anti-ragtime camp, composer Daniel Gregory Mason, (1873–1953) dismissed the idea of a national school of composition as fallacious. No school of composers, he maintained, could speak for our culture. Moreover, he found the "jerk and rattle" of ragtime to be ugly, representative not of our national virtues but our vices, characteristic of our restlessness, hustle, and "thoughtless superficial 'optimism.'"[4] Ragtime was simply a local idiom, a caricature with the vitality of the comic strip. The intensified national consciousness aroused by the war, concluded Mason, had blunted the discriminatory powers of men like Moderwell, for ragtime was but a vulgar cliché or musical trick of speech, full of gimmicky appeal but without possibilities for classical composition.

These were the main outlines of the ragtime controversy, which lasted until the 1920s when it became part of the larger battle over jazz. But to see the broad outlines of the argument is not to understand why the participants were so troubled, sometimes so vehement. To understand their agitation we need to look briefly at the background of Euro-American music, particularly art music, in this country and the strong feelings it generated.

There was little classical music played in the United States before the Civil War. A people concerned with making a living on land or sea, or in the busy mill and market towns, had little time for an abstract, cultivated art. The census of 1850 lists only twenty-six hundred men occupied as musicians, classical or otherwise.[5] With the exception of a few members of groups such as the Handel and Haydn Society, founded in Boston in 1815, and the New York Philharmonic Society, organized in 1842, classical musicians tended to be amateurs.

But after slow beginnings, interest in art music grew rapidly. In the years after Appomattox, changing social and economic circumstances encouraged development in many of the arts and provided a growing upper middle class with the wealth and leisure to support the arts. Art music was imported from abroad and superimposed uncomfortably on our culture. As the well-known conductor and taste maker Walter Damrosch (1862–1950) explained, "Instead of growing upward from the masses it was carefully introduced and nurtured by an aristocratic and cultural community."[6] Thus, it developed somewhat artificially instead of emerging naturally out of individual needs and resources.

Along with art music had come a relatively fixed set of musical values about composition and training, as well as some of the best musicians in Europe. These men not only defined good music for diffident American audiences but dictated how it should be played. Autocratic conductors like Theodore Thomas and members of the Damrosch family were trained in the idealism of German romanticism, which regarded music, in its highest forms, as the most spiritual of all the arts. These zealots set about to bring uplifting symphonic music in uncompromising programs to frequently indifferent and sometimes hostile audiences whose tastes ran to lighter fare.

But if ardent German-born conductors could tolerate light classical music, they had little sympathy for popular music, which seemed to flourish weedlike in American soil, the music of marching bands, minstrelsy, vaudeville, dance halls, cabarets, saloons and other unsavory places. Whereas art music was noble and uplifting, popular music was vulgar and, in its lowest forms, evil, something to be contained or stamped out.

These values predominated in intellectual and concert circles in the upper and middle classes, which were looking for fixed standards in the arts. They predominated, too, in the public schools from the early grades onward, and in college music departments and conservatories. And finally they prevailed in the growing world of musical journalism, which invariably featured the foreign-born musicians as the most gifted composers and performers and the final authorities on musical subjects.

But all of this is not to say that classical music flourished on this side of the Atlantic. I have already noted a lack of audience enthusiasm, and to this can be added other woes. Symphony orchestras, chamber groups, and opera companies generally operated in the red and had high mortality rates. A feeling persisted that music was woman's work, and a disproportionately large number of concertgoers were women. By the same token, men were discouraged·from a musical career by the belief that music was a suitable avocation but not a fit career for a gentleman, at least a red-blooded one. Those men who did become composers produced few works of distinction and had trouble getting a hearing when they did. Finally, the long shadow of the European tradition, whatever its benefits, had paralyzing disadvantages. Professional performers found they could not be accepted without European training and press notices. At the same time, many of our composers felt that they had to escape the German hegemony that seemed to deaden the creative impulse.

In an attempt to tap native roots, some of our composers—following Dvořák's use of "plantation melodies" in the "New World" Symphony—turned to American folk music. Despite the disdain of conservatives who found no inspiration in such sources—particularly black music—adventurous composers advocated the use of Indian music, cowboy songs, even popular music such as ragtime, as raw material for more refined works. This advocacy resulted in little music of lasting value and, as we have seen, contributed to an argument which was part of the broader ragtime controversy.

As the foregoing paragraphs imply, the ragtime controversy and its background were highly complex and admit to no simple interpretations. I think, however, that we can shed light on it by looking at it in religious terms. Religious implications in the background of the ragtime dispute are not hard to find. The German romantics who shaped our concert life were acutely aware of the closeness of religion and art, both of which provided access to the realm of the ideal. Of all the arts, music—and especially symphonic music, the purest kind—was the most spiritual, the most removed from the impurities of the material world. In a sense, the conductors who presided over our musical establishment resembled evangelical priests zealously bringing the Word to the wilderness, or at least to the cultural frontier, in order to uplift spiritually the semibarbarous audiences. When missionaries Theodore Thomas (1835–1905) and Karl Bergmann (1821–1876) heard that Americans disliked Wagner, they are reported to have said at different times, "Then they must hear him until they do."[7] The prevailing feeling about the ennobling nature of art music is aptly illustrated by Theodore Thomas's statement, "The man who does not understand Beethoven and has not been under his spell has not half lived his life. The masterworks of instrumental music are the language of the soul and express more than those of any other art. Light music, popular music, so called, is the sensual side of the art and has more or less devil in it."[8]

The sharp and often vehement distinction between holy, noble classical music and demonic, sensual popular music ran through much of the discussion of music in the years before and during the ragtime controversy and underlies much of its rhetoric. As one opponent of ragtime put it, "In

Christian homes, where purity and morals are stressed, ragtime should find no resting place. Avaunt the ragtime rot! Let us purge America and the Divine Art of Music from this polluting nuisance."[9] Another opponent of the new music said that "little by little the people at large have forgotten the noble melodies which used to interest them and have sold themselves body and soul to the musical(?) Satan."[10] Arguing against such assertions a proponent of the new music wondered "why the c-sharp minor chord . . . should be pure and holy and beautiful when used in the 'moonlight sonata' [sic] and poisonous and immoral when used in a ragtime piece."[11]

Émile Durkheim (1858–1917) in *The Elementary Forms of Religious Life*[12] points out that all religions make a sharp distinction between not only the religious and the profane but also between two kinds of religious forces. It is the two kinds of religious powers that concern us here, for traditionalists seem to have regarded both classical music and ragtime as having religious implications, albeit of opposite kinds. In speaking of the two kinds of religious forces, Durkheim distinguishes between the beneficent ones that promote physical and moral order and encourage life and health, and the evil, impure ones contributing to disorder, illness, fear, and death. On the one hand is the divine, on the other the diabolical, and while the two are radically antagonistic in one sense, their relationship is highly ambiguous because they come from the same sources and are even made from one another. Moreover, they are highly contagious, flowing into and infecting one another with disastrous results.

The fear of contagion explains much of the horror and vehemence which traditionalists felt toward popular music, which seemed not to be simply vulgar and impure but demonic and infectious. As early as 1853 the powerful Germanophile critic John Dwight (1813–1893) asserted in his *Journal of Music* that a popular tune such as *Old Folks at Home* "*breaks out* now and then, like a morbid irritation of the skin."[13] Popular music, then, was to some not simply cheap and tawdry but diabolical, with a magical, infecting quality that could contaminate pure and exalted things.

Any form of popular music was poisonous, but that of the Negro was especially frightening, particularly when it had the runaway infectiousness of ragtime. One alarmed observer exclaimed, "The counters of the music stores are loaded with this virulent poison which in the form of a malarious epidemic, is finding its way into the homes and brains of youth."[14] Another traditionalist declared, "It is an evil music that . . . must be wiped out as other bad and dangerous epidemics have been exterminated."[15] And classical pianist Edward B. Perry (1855–1924) felt that the new music could only be treated "like a dog with rabies, with a dose of lead. Whether it is simply a passing phase of our decadent art culture or an infectious disease which has come to stay, like la grippe and leprosy, time alone can show."[16]

But whether it was a passing illness or had come for good, many felt that ragtime's contagion was contaminating the sources and growth of much that was divine and good in American life. For one thing, it was ruining the taste of the young people who were the future supporters of classical music.

"I do not believe there is such a thing as *good* popular music," asserted Karl Muck (1859–1940), sometime conductor of the Boston Symphony Orchestra, in 1915. "I think that what you call . . . ragtime is poison. It poisons the very source of your musical growth, for it poisons the taste of the young."[17] Others complained that it would not only ruin the taste of young musicians but hurt their technique, too. In 1912, piano teacher Philip Gordon (b. 1894) wrote in the *Musical Observer* that "Ragtime will ruin your touch, disable your technic, misuse your knowledge of pedaling, and pervert whatever sense of poetry and feeling you have into superficial, improper channels. Shun it as you would the 'Black Death.'"[18]

Still more disturbing, the contagion of the demonic new sound was spreading uncontrollably beyond the music to the very bases of purity in society and in the individual. Some critics equated ragtime with the evils of alcohol. "A person innoculated with the ragtime-fever is like one addicted to strong drink!"[19] Others felt that syncopation caused permanent brain damage, and like Francis Toye (1883–1964), cited "scientific" data to this effect.[20] A German authority concurred, charging that ragtime would "eventually stagnate the brain cells and wreck the nervous system."[21] Yet others feared that it brought about moral disintegration, poisoning both personal and national standards. *"Its greatest destructive power lies in its power to lower the moral standards,"* claimed one writer, who went on to describe the social downfall of the younger generation.[22] At its most frightening, ragtime was a national poison that threatened to spread to the rest of the Western world and doom the civilization of the white man.

For the most part of the racism of the anti-ragtime camp was softened or veiled with euphemism or understatement. But occasionally the horror felt for the diabolical "coon" songs and other sounds fuzzily associated with ragtime, and black music generally, bared ethnic fears. Noting that some characteristics of ragtime resembled those of the hymns that Negroes sang in the "excesses" of camp meetings, Francis Toye explained that ragtime "show[s] precisely the kind of 'vitality' associated with Revivalism peculiar to the negro! What need have we of further witnesses? For of all hysteria that particular semi-religious hysteria is nearer to madness than any other."[23] For members of the establishment, used to staid and rational kinds of religion, the wild enthusiasms of less formal, ethnic religions were easy targets for bigotry, particularly when they were tied to a musical contagion that threatened the national welfare.

One troubled observer asked:

Can it be said that America is falling prey to the collective soul of the negro through the influence of what is popularly known as "rag time" music? . . . If there is any tendency toward such a national disaster, it should be definitely pointed out and extreme measures taken to inhibit the influence and avert the increasing danger—if it has not already gone too far. . . . [T]he American "rag time" or "rag time" evolved music is symbolic of the primitive morality and perceptible moral limitations of the negro type. With the latter sexual restraint is almost unknown, and the widest latitude of moral uncertainty is conceded.

This statement appeared in a letter to the editor of the Paris edition of the *New York Herald* in 1913 and was later reprinted in the *Musical Courier*, arousing a good deal of comment and indignation. It further claimed that "some sociological writers of prominence" and "all psychologists" agreed that America was succumbing to the evils of the Negro soul.[24] In some quarters, then, there seemed to be clear and overwhelming evidence of the spreading ragtime contagion, which was all the worse for its racial character.

Generally, traditionalists felt that the racial threat was related to sinful sexuality among blacks. To understand this point it is helpful to bear in mind how race and sex were tied together in the minds of "respectable" whites in the years after 1900.[25] Clergymen and others who considered themselves guardians of public morality took the findings of Darwin, Weismann, and other scientists to confirm their own belief that restraint was the self-evident rule of sexual morality (except for procreative purposes), to be supported by the dictates of private conscience and the laws of church and state. Continence was necessary not simply to limit the birth rate but to ensure a breed fit for the struggle for existence. But miscegenation was a constant threat, people fearing that "inferior" races, especially the black race, would endanger the purity of the blood. Stereotyped as childlike and sensual by nature, the Negro offered a strong sexual temptation to whites, and his brute passions could break out into frightful acts. Traditionalists feared that contagious black impurity would eventually outweigh the abstinence of the virtuous.

As early as the 1860s doctors and others had reported that the birth rate of white Protestants was declining while that of "inferiors" rose in numbers which threatened to overwhelm the European stock; the few strong would not be able to support the great mass of "inferiors" and degenerates, and the result would be the decline of white civilization in America. Therefore, the well-intentioned drew a sharp line between pure and impure, spiritual and sensual, in sexual mores, and sought tight restraints to guard against any threat to virtue.

Ragtime seemed to fly in the face of these restraints. Opponents of the music found the words, the melodies, and especially the rhythms offensive to conventional decency. Above all, ragtime's use of syncopation generated in some listeners an ecstatic response that far exceeded traditional bounds.

Looking back from our present vantage point, we regard the ecstatic response to ragtime as extremely mild. Certainly its contemporary *proponents* regarded it the same way, insofar as they considered it in these terms. One early enthusiast noted that the music "has a powerful stimulating effect, setting the nerves and muscles tingling with excitement."[26] Another, popular bandleader Martin Ballmann, exclaimed in 1912, "It certainly has a swing to it that sends one's blood tingling."[27] Speaking of the infectious appeal of ragtime, Hiram K. Moderwell wrote, "You simply can't resist it," and went on to describe his reactions to one performance:

> *I felt my blood thumping in tune, my muscles twitching to the rhythm. I wanted to paraphrase Shakespeare—"The man who hath no ragtime in his soul/ Who is not moved by syncopated sounds . . ." and so on. . . . This ragtime appeals to the primitive love of the dance—a special sort of dance in which the rhythm of the arms and shoulders conflicts with the rhythm of the feet, in which dozens of little needles of energy are deftly controlled in the weaving of the whole.*[28]

But the *opponents* of ragtime viewed its physical and psychological effects in less moderate terms. One German listener who eventually saw its artistic potential was at first alarmed at his reaction.

> *Suddenly I discovered that my legs were in a condition of great excitement. They twitched as though charged with electricity and betrayed a considerable and rather dangerous desire to jerk me from my seat. The rhythm of the music, which had seemed so unnatural at first, was beginning to work its influence over me. It wasn't that feeling of ease in the joints of the feet and toes which might be caused by a Strauss waltz, no, much more energetic, material, independent as though one encountered a balking horse, which it is absolutely impossible to master.*[29]

Gustav Kühl, the author of this statement, represents those initially ill disposed to the new musical but still susceptible to its effects. However, ragtime's most adamant opponents seemed to have no ecstatic response to the music and were appalled by the apparently uncontrollable contagion affecting those who did. For uncompromising traditionalists such as Francis Toye, the seemingly involuntary gyrations of ragtime dancers were such that "Any unsophisticated visitors from Mars, who did not know their excuse, would judge from their looks, their movements and their strident but pathetic yells that they were raving lunatics only fit for the Martian equivalent of a strait-jacket."[30] Not surprisingly, Toye linked ragtime to tarantism and the horrors of other historical lunacies which continued to haunt the memory of civilized man.

From the fifteenth century onward and in the wake of the Black Death there were outbreaks of tarantism, a form of acute, ecstatic trance or possession resembling Saint Vitus's dance. Emerging in areas where there had been great privation or death, it seized different kinds of people, peasants, housewives, children, artisans, and others who danced in bacchanalian revelry for hours, chanting, rhythmically clapping, screaming, foaming at the mouth, and having visions and convulsions. Ordinarily, such cathartic dances were of an erotic nature with the participants resembling Dionysian maenads. According to contemporary legend, this contagious frenzy resulted from tarantula bites, which the Catholic church took to be the working of the Devil or other evil spirits. Tarantism persists today in the south of Italy in cults of oppressed women.[31]

Tarantism was but one of the historical precedents of acute ecstasy that foes of ragtime could cite to justify their fears of the syncopated music. Today these people sound like rabid reactionaries, but it would be a mistake to dismiss them as such, because among the ranks of ragtime opponents were many moderate (and less vocal) citizens, community leaders, and clergymen.

In 1913 the *New York Times* reported that Canon Newboldt of Saint Paul's in London had assailed the ragtime wickedness in a sermon asking, "Would indecent dances, suggestive of evil and destructive of modesty, disgrace our civilization for a moment if professed Christians were to say: I will not allow my daughter to turn into Salome?" Responding to this sermon a day later, the *Times,* speaking for middle-class respectability, declared that Canon Newboldt was no sensational preacher but a staid and

The *Devilish Rag* (1908) pokes fun at critics' condemnation of ragtime as evil. Note the devil who, through his musical pipe, appears to be playing ragtime. (*John Edward Hasse collection*)

respected theologian not given to inflammatory statements. The editorial went on to say that "decent people in and out of the church are beginning to be alarmed" at the "rude" and "vulgar" music and "loose conduct" accompanying it with "dances defying all propriety." The *Times* concluded that the Canon's "example should be followed in all of the churches of England and the United States. We are drifting toward peril and the drift must be checked."[32] It was not simply the archconservatives or reactionaries who were troubled by ragtime, but more reasonable men, more guarded in sensitive questions, who looked to religion for guidance when confronted by the fearful specter of degeneracy.

We can get a broader perspective of the traditionalist response to ragtime by looking at it against the background of Max Weber's writings on sex, art and religion that appear in his *Religionsoziologie*, translated into English by Ephraim Fischoff as *The Sociology of Religion*.[33] Weber (1864–1920) showed that the privileged classes—which, as we have seen, provided the chief opponents of ragtime—required from religion the psychological assurance of legitimacy. Thus the orthodox morality offers a rationale for the accepted ethic (the Protestant ethic for many of ragtime's opponents) and for established ideas of social order. Whereas new sects and cults abound with ecstatic enthusiasm, the old, settled religions are staid and fixed in their ways, and slow to accept new ideas, particularly when they smack of irrational or highly emotive behavior. Accordingly upholders of long-standing Western religions, whatever their institutional affiliations, emphasize sober, purposeful action based on rational self-control and methodical planning. In sexual matters they usually demand not celibacy but avoidance of the erotic, since the unbridled sex drive returns man to the irrational level of animal behavior and poses a threat to the legitimacy of marriage.[34]

Because of the "undignified" response of some of its listeners and dancers, ragtime ran afoul of these strictures. It seemed to be the entering wedge of licentiousness or, worse, a sign that eroticism had found its way to the heart of the younger generation. And nothing could be better proof of this than the wild movements of the Bunny Hug, Devil's Ball, Grizzly Bear, or Baboon Baby Dance, whose very names reminded alarmists of Satanic or animal implications and whose gyrations seemed more appropriate to the brothel than the dance hall. As one observer exclaimed, "It has been discovered that many ragtime songs as well as dances receive their inspiration in the brothel [and are] tossed upon the market to corrupt the minds of the young. . . . Our police authorities have informed us that in the dens of vice and the vilest of cabarets, ragtime music, sporting papers and salacious novels are always found." No less shocking to the same writer was the sheet music to ragtime songs which had "title pages picturing contortioned, partly clothed dancers in attitudes suggesting inebriated Hottentots."[35] Whatever the degree of exaggeration in such remarks, it is clear that for sober-minded supporters of orthodox religion the ecstatic eroticism that went along with ragtime seemed sinfully irrational, and its associations with the black man and the brothel only served to dramatize its diabolical bestiality.

As Weber points out, art, like sex, has a strong irrational element and can involve powerful feelings inviting surrender to sensual impulses. Therefore, he argues, orthodox religion opposes unregulated artistic development as it does unbridled sex. Religion has not, of course, always confined and restrained the arts; at their outsets religions often have close ties with art, especially music, as did early Christianity. But, according to Weber, such connections may well disintegrate in time, particularly as art evolves in its own ways, autonomously creating unique esthetic values that strain or break religious links.

Then, too, as religion becomes more formal and rational it deemphasizes art along with magic, ecstasy, ritual, and orgy in favor of things ascetic, spiritual, and mystical. When rational values become entrenched in religion, art is suspect as an easy route back to the irrational, whether in the form of orgiastic and ritualistic behavior or in the shape of a religion of love culminating in the transcendence of the individual. Therefore, conservative Protestantism and like-minded faiths sought controlled development of art, which would direct its energies along acceptable emotional and intellectual lines and limit its growth to boundaries consistent with rational behavior.[36]

Obviously, European art music transplanted into American soil at the behest of cultivated people in the privileged class—the very ones who defined what was "officially" acceptable—fitted comfortably within the rational limits. But ragtime, which had emerged in the wild undergrowth of a racial subculture in response to the unconscious needs of the people, was beyond the pale. It aroused in some an ecstasy of seemingly atavistic sensualism that defied the sober, purposeful asceticism of the Protestant ethic, whose proponents provided the core of the anti-ragtime forces.

In looking at the traditionalist opposition to ragtime from a religious point of view, I do not mean to suggest that this angle of vision provides the only valid way to look at the controversy or that it explains it entirely. Obviously it is but one way to view some of the reactions to ragtime. But I think that it illuminates the highly spiritual and emotional tone of the argument and its core concerns of art, sex, race, class, and nationality, which lay not only at the center of the ragtime dispute but of other social and intellectual controversies of the day. These questions defined the contours of the skirmish lines between the pro- and anti-ragtime camps and the positions of persons in between who exchanged fire with both sides.

Notes

1. See Edward A. Berlin, "Piano Ragtime: A Musical and Cultural Study" (Ph.D. diss., City University of New York, 1976), p. 62 fn. I have relied heavily on Berlin's work, chapter 3 of which offers an excellent summary of the ragtime controversy.

2. Berlin, pp. 75-76, 116-17; see also Neil Leonard, *Jazz and the White Americans* (Chicago: University of Chicago Press, 1962), pp. 25-28.

3. Hiram K. Moderwell, "Two Views of Ragtime, I, 'A Modest Proposal,'" *Seven Arts* 2 (July 1917): 368, 370, 375; Moderwell, "Ragtime," *New Republic,* 16 October 1915, p. 286.

4. D. G. Mason, "Concerning Ragtime," *The New Music Review* 17 (March 1918): 116; Mason, "Folk-Song and American Music (A Plea for the Unpopular Point of View)," *Musical Quarterly* 4 (July 1918), pp. 324, 337.

5. U.S. Department of the Interior, Census Office, *The Seventh Census of the United States: 1850* (Washington, D.C.: Robert Armstrong, Public Printer, 1853), p. lxxiii.

6. Walter Damrosch, *My Musical Life* (New York: Charles Scribner's Sons, 1923), p. 334.

7. Theodore Thomas, *Theodore Thomas: A Musical Autobiography,* ed. George P. Upton, 2 vols. (Chicago: A. C. McClurg & Co., 1905), vol. 1, pp. 234–35; and John H. Mueller, *The American Symphony Orchestra: A Social History of Musical Taste* (Bloomington: Indiana University Press, 1951), p. 292.

8. Thomas, *Autobiography,* Vol. 1, epigraph.

9. Leo Oehmler, "Ragtime: A Pernicious Evil and Enemy of True Art," *Musical Observer* 11 (September 1914): 15.

10. Arthur Weld, "The Invasion of Vulgarity in Music," *Etude* 17 (February 1899): 52.

11. W. T. Gleeson, "Answering the Critics," *Ragtime Review* 3 (March 1917): 22–23.

12. Trans. Joseph Ward Swain (New York: The Macmillan Co., 1915).

13. John Tasker Howard, *Our American Music* (New York, Thomas Y. Crowell Co., 1931), p. 188.

14. "Musical Impurity," *Etude* 18 (January 1900): 16.

15. "Our Musical Condition," *Negro Music Journal* 1 (March 1903): 137–38.

16. Edward Baxter Perry, "Ragging Good Music," *Etude* 36 (January 1918): 372.

17. Karl Muck, "The Music of Democracy," *Craftsman,* December 1915, p. 227.

18. Philip Gordon, "Ragtime, Folksong and the Music Teacher," *Musical Observer* 6 (November 1912): 724–25.

19. Oehmler, p. 15.

20. Francis Toye, "Ragtime: The New Tarantism," *English Review,* March 1913, pp. 654–56.

21. "Music in America," *New York Times,* 9 October 1911, p. 10.

22. Oehmler, p. 15. Emphasis added.

23. Toye, p. 657.

24. Walter Winston Kenilworth, "Demoralizing Ragtime Music," *Musical Courier* 66 (21 May 1913): 22–23.

25. See Oscar Handlin, *Race and Nationality in American Life* (New York: Doubleday, Anchor Books, 1957), pp. 119–22.

26. "Questions and Answers," *Etude* 16 (October 1898): 285.

27. Rupert Hughes, "A Eulogy of Rag-Time," *Musical Record,* no. 447 (1 April 1899), p. 158.

28. Moderwell, "Ragtime," p. 285.

29. Gustav Kühl, "The Musical Possibilities of Rag-Time," trans. Gustav Saenger, *Metronome* 19 (March 1903): 11.

30. Toye, p. 657.

31. I. M. Lewis, *Ecstatic Religion: An Anthropological Study of Spirit Possession and Shamanism* (Baltimore: Penguin, 1971), pp. 37–66.

32. "Canon Assails Our New Dances," *New York Times,* 25 August 1913, p. 3; "Canon Newboldt's Warning," Editorial, *New York Times,* 26 August 1913, p. 8.

33. English translation (Boston: Beacon Press, 1964). First published in Germany in 1922.

34. Weber, *The Sociology of Religion,* pp. 236–39 and *passim.*

35. Oehmler, pp. 14–15.

36. Weber, *The Sociology of Religion,* pp. 242–45; see also Weber, *The Rational and Social Foundations of Music,* trans. and ed. Don Martindale, Johannes Riedel, and Gertrude Neuwirth (Carbondale: Southern Illinois University Press, 1958).

Major
Ragtime
Figures

Scott Joplin, Pioneer

Addison W. Reed

As "The King of Ragtime Writers," Scott Joplin warrants a major biographical chapter. Addison Reed traces Joplin's life from his humble boyhood in Texas and his early years as an itinerant musician, to the success of Maple Leaf Rag, *the strivings of his late rags, and the disappointments of his opera* Treemonisha. *This is a revision of an article published in 1975.*

Scott Joplin (1868–1917), once lost to obscurity, has finally found his place in the sun and been accorded his rightful position as one of the first truly American composers.[1] He was one of the nation's musical pioneers, for he was the first to develop fully that pianistic form which could be considered the initial American art form, the piano rag. On the one hand, it is amazing that it took such a long time for the genius of this black composer to be recognized; on the other, his recent rise from obscurity symbolizes the prevailing attitudes of our past and present society. Although Joplin was respected by his peers as "The King of Ragtime Writers," the musical establishment refused to acknowledge his work as a bona fide means of musical expression. Now, however, we have his collected works in print, as well as significant articles and books about him written by some of the foremost music authorities and critics in the nation. The continuing interest in Joplin is clearly based on the fact that the musical world has finally come to realize the uniqueness of his contributions to

From *The Black Perspective in Music* 3 (Spring 1975): 45–52; (Fall 1975): 269–77. ©1975 by *The Black Perspective in Music*. Reprinted by permission.

music. This essay offers a biographical sketch of this creative man whose music has made a comeback more than sixty years after his death.

Sometime during the 1850s, ex-slave Jiles Joplin (1842?–1922) left home in South Carolina and, migrating westward, settled in an area that borders northeast Texas and southwestern Arkansas.[2] There he met Florence Givens (1841?–1903?), a caretaker for one of the local churches. After a brief courtship they decided to get married. During the first decade of their marriage Scott Joplin was born.

According to the most frequent accounts, Scott was born on Tuesday, November 24, 1868, probably in Bowie County on the northeastern border of Texas. The first documented entry of the Joplin family occurs in a Cass County census of 1870 in which Scott and his father, mother, and older brother are listed.[3] In 1873, the area where the Joplins resided became a municipality and was named Texarkana because it straddled the Arkansas-Texas state line. The dividing line of the city is significant, for the Texas side was predominantly white and the Arkansas side predominantly black— as it is today. Scott was the second son of Jiles and Florence. The other children were Monroe, Robert, Willie, Ossie, and Myrtle, all of whom were musical except Monroe. Jiles Joplin had been a violinist for parties given at the "big house" during slavery. His mother sang and played the banjo. Robert and Willie were violin players like their father, and Robert even composed some. The daughters, Ossie and Myrtle, were excellent singers and are known to have sung in and around Texarkana during their adult life.[4]

If one would know about the milieu in which this family existed, it is important to understand the struggles of the black man in American society in the last half of the nineteenth century. During the 1860s the Civil War ended and slavery was abolished; the Ku Klux Klan, however, commenced its activities to disenfranchise Negroes. Reconstruction was in the air, and, for the first time in the history of the United States, Negroes were elected to state legislatures and to Congress. Southern Negroes were happy and confused at the same time; their freedom was restricted, and they had little means of support. These were people who had known only working in the fields, for the most part without wages. But as newly freed slaves they had to find some means of support for their families and for themselves. Without training or vocation, the ex-slaves went wandering in what was to them a foreign land—the United States. Meanwhile, the abolitionists and segregationists were working to achieve their own ends, which sometimes helped and sometimes hindered the Negro in his quest for sustenance.

The life of the Joplin family during Scott's early childhood was beset by the usual difficulties met by the typical black family in the late nineteenth century. The area where the Joplins decided to reside was small, poor, and segregated, and it provided few opportunities for a black man and his wife to sustain a sizable family. Procuring adequate housing or purchasing property was practically impossible for blacks, and this situation made the black man seek whatever kind of shelter he could find—usually a substandard and extremely crowded dwelling. Inadequate finance, lack of suitable work opportunities, and the general emasculation of the Negro placed seemingly impossible demands on the black man who wished to sustain and give comfort to his family.

To compound what already seemed to be insurmountable difficulties, early in Scott Joplin's life his father left the family.[5] Florence had to seek out some means to rear a family of seven. Her only salvation was domestic work, yet during this period domestic work did not provide financial stability. She also washed and ironed for people in the community. Stalwart and "a giant" she must have been, for she was able to rear her family and see them all reach adulthood. Soon after Jiles left the family he began railroad work and took another wife.

Despite the separation of Scott's mother and father in his early youth, he was influenced musically by both parents. Scott's father, as a violinist, acquainted Scott with many of the popular European musical forms that were current during the nineteenth century, such as waltzes, schottisches, polkas, and quadrilles. Through the singing and banjo playing of his mother, young Scott became familiar with the syncopated vocal line that was characteristic of many of the plantation melodies. Because Scott's mother was the caretaker of the local church prior to the separation, Scott learned firsthand the Negro method of superimposing syncopated patterns on the melodies and changing the words of the hymns sung in church.

When Scott and his brothers and sisters were very young their mother often took them to church, not only on Sundays but on weekdays as well. There, Scott heard the "patting Juba," spirituals, shouts and hollers, and there he probably participated in the ring plays. In these musical forms, developed and fostered by the Negro, Scott Joplin would have become aware of the folk melodies, the syncopated rhythms, and the repeated choruses, all of which were characteristic of Negro music in the nineteenth century. Joplin also became conscious of the never-relenting, strict background beat that may be considered a natural element of Negro music. This black heritage obviously influenced Joplin in his use of syncopated patterns, blue notes, and melodies reminiscent of fiddle and banjo tunes in his piano and vocal compositions.

Even before his adolescence, Joplin began to demonstrate his precocity, especially in playing the piano. Scott would accompany his mother to the various homes where she did domestic work and practice on the pianos. One of the families for whom Florence worked was the Cook family on Hazel Street; Mrs. Cook gave permission for Scott to play on the piano while his mother went about her chores.[6] It was here that he would imitate the music that he had heard in the church and add his own improvisations.

Because of the musical nature of the Joplin household, Florence was extremely pleased with her son's prowess at the piano; despite a scarcity of funds, she purchased a used piano so that Scott could practice at home. As Scott's ability matured, he began to play at churches and for socials in the Texarkana area. Through his popularity as a pianist, Scott becme known throughout southwest Arkansas and northeast Texas while he was still in his teens.

As Joplin's popularity increased he was noticed by various music teachers in the area, and at least one of them offered to teach him to read music and to play the standard piano literature. We still are not exactly certain with whom Joplin studied, but we do know the names of several Texarkana music teachers. One was Mag Washington, who taught music at the first of the black schools in the town. John C. Johnson, a light-skinned black, was known as "Professor" and is said to have performed classics as well as dance music.[7] Recent speculation has centered upon another Texarkana music teacher, Julius Weiss, as Joplin's primary piano instructor. Born in Germany, Weiss was employed by Colonel Robert W. Rodgers of Texarkana as a tutor for his children, and taught piano to these and other local youngsters. In a carefully documented article, Theodore Albrecht presents a substantially but not thoroughly convincing case that Weiss was Joplin's oft-mentioned "old German music teacher" to whom the composer felt indebted the rest of his life.[8]

Scott must have had also some training in fundamental theory in the Texarkana area, for later in his life he was able to enroll in advanced harmony and composition courses at the George R. Smith College for Negroes in Sedalia, Missouri.

It must be remembered that the world of secular music influenced Joplin's composition as much as or more than that of the church and the music studio. As do all youngsters, Scott liked to explore, and since music was his main concern, he began to listen to some of the music in the clubs, honky-tonks, and eating places of Texarkana and of the surrounding areas. Here Scott heard semblances of the blues and the "ragging" of marches and current piano literature of the day. Such performances have now been identified as the predecessors of ragtime.[9] In Joplin's time there was not a definite demarcation between the sacred and the secular (just as today soul music and gospel are musically similar). The music which came out of the homes, work areas, eating places and honky-tonks in the Negro sections of town was markedly similar to the music he heard in the church, except for the texts.

As Joplin developed, his popularity grew, and he began to play in various clubs and further develop his improvisational ability. In the clubs and honky-tonks, customers often would ask for selections of which he had never heard, but if the melody or a fragment of a melody was given to him, he could always satisfy the clientele with his performances.

This new venture of Joplin's was not approved by his father. As a matter of fact, it was the cause of a continuing argument that kept them at odds throughout their lives. Jiles Joplin did not see any future in piano playing as an occupation for his son and wanted him to take a job on the railroad. Scott's mother, on the other hand, was pleased to have her son add to the financial stability of the family by earning money playing the piano; she felt that through her teaching and her example Scott would remain a faithful and sincere person, always striving toward a commendable goal. Scott's mother was an inspiration to him throughout his life, and her influence was especially evident in the libretto of his final extended work, *Treemonisha*, the theme of which is education for the salvation of the Negro race.

Scott continued to play piano professionally during his early teens—despite his father's opposition—and at the same time attended school. Because of the paucity of written records and the conflicts in oral and documented accounts, the early location and name of Scott's school cannot as yet be completely stabilized. However, Scott's early schooling was achieved at either the Central "High" School or the Orr School.[10] We can judge by his later activities and accomplishments that, indeed, Scott Joplin did receive an adequate educational background at an early age. In addition to attending school and playing, he began to teach music. His gregarious nature brought him close to other young men in the community who had similar interests. One outcome of his new friendships was the organization of a vocal quintet, led by Joplin, which included Wesley Kirby, Tom Clark, Willie Joplin and Robert Joplin. The organization of this group inspired Scott to make his initial efforts at composition. Evidently the group performed first as a quartet, for Robert Joplin was not present at their first performance in Clarksville, Texas; Robert did join the group later, however, and the five young men traveled and sang in Texas, Arkansas, and Missouri.

The travels of the Texas Medley Quartette, as the group was called, helped Joplin at an early age to make great strides in his career. He already had become a well-known pianist in his home town, in the surrounding areas, and in some of the major cities of the West and Midwest. He also had shown himself and those around that he was adept as a composer and as the leader of a musical group which traveled and earned money. But the Texarkana area was small and provincial and did not provide the freedom and opportunity necessary for a composer-performer to grow, or excel, or to expand his horizons. Because of these limitations Joplin left his home in Texarkana when he was about sixteen or seventeen. Where he went and what he did must be left to conjecture, but it seems he made his way northeast as a vocalist with the Texas Medley Quartette and as an itinerant pianist.

Since very few records were kept by the Joplin family, it is difficult to ascertain exactly when Joplin left Texarkana or arrived in Saint Louis, Missouri. Probably sometime during 1885 he arrived in Saint Louis, known even then as the "Gateway to the West." That city in the late nineteenth century was the center for rail and riverboat travel in the Midwest—for those planning travel to the East or those daring to move to the far West. Because of a continuous influx of people from all levels of life, Saint Louis was a cosmopolitan city with recreational outlets for all. The section of Saint Louis that attracted Scott was considered one of the most prosperous sections of the city. Because of its proximity to the waterfront and its easy accessibility, the district, called Chestnut Valley, drew many tourists. Chestnut and Market Streets were regarded as the most notorious of the Valley, with their sporting houses and saloons where men could engage in nearly any kind of recreational activity they might desire. The area provided, however, a source of patronage for itinerant pianists, whose music was an indispensable element of sporting-house activity.

It was in Saint Louis's Chestnut Valley, then, that Scott Joplin finally settled as a café pianist, making his headquarters at the Silver Dollar Saloon. As a black pianist of the late nineteenth century, he had only two employment possibilities: to work either in the church or in the brothel. While the church could provide spiritual guidance, it could not provide a livelihood—only the red-light district could do that. "Honest" John Turpin, black owner of the saloon, was one of the important men of the district. Later, Joplin would become a very good friend of Turpin's sons Tom (1873–1922) and Charlie (ca. 1867–1935), but in 1885 they were off in Searchlight, Nevada, trying their luck at mining. They did not return until 1894.

Although Joplin made his home in Saint Louis for approximately eight years, he traveled away from the city a great deal during that time, playing piano and listening to pianists in other cities of Missouri and as far away as Louisville and Cincinnati. In 1893 he decided to go to Chicago, the site of the Columbian Exposition. The two years that he spent there would have far-reaching effects and influences on Joplin and the future of American music. The Chicago World's Fair was a grandiose affair that brought people—black and white—from far and near to sell their wares and their talents. But the Negro, especially the Negro of ragtime, not being an "acceptable" member of American society, was regarded as an oddity and, consequently, was forced to sell his talents on the outskirts of the fair. There sporting districts were set up, filled with pianists and other instrumentalists performing for the entertainment of those who became weary of the bustling fair.

Being outside of the mainstream of activity bothered Joplin, sensitive man that he was, but it did not deter him from trying to enhance his reputation as a good pianist and a bandleader. He met two of the "Windy City"'s most popular ragtime pianists, "Plunk" Henry and Johnny Seymour, and through them widened his knowledge of piano playing in general and ragtime in particular. During this period Joplin organized his first band, which seems to have been composed of a cornet, clarinet, tuba, and baritone horn.[11] Thus he became acquainted with a large amount of band literature—a significant acquisition, for the brass band music of this period is commonly regarded as one of the important precursors of rag. He also began to develop a skill in instrumentation that would find its culmination in the music he later wrote for the Queen City Concert Band of Sedalia, Missouri, and in the orchestration for his two operas.

Probably the most momentus and lasting friendship Joplin established in Chicago was with Otis Saunders, another rag pianist there during the fair. Joplin and Saunders were nearly the same age and became close friends. As Otis watched Joplin leading his band and playing piano in various establishments, he became more and more conscious of his friend's genius and began to persuade Joplin to write down and publish the compositions he had been improvising. Although Joplin's avowed goal in life was to make music his vocation, he was nevertheless reluctant to try to gain entry into a field where few blacks had succeeded. In 1894 Otis and Scott left Chicago, making their way south playing in various cities on the way until they arrived in Saint Louis. They went to the saloon of "Honest" John Turpin, Joplin's initial benefactor. There the Turpin brothers, who had recently returned from Nevada, heard Scott play, and they too began to encourage Joplin to think seriously about his compositions. The encouragement and prodding Scott received from Saunders and the Turpin brothers made him restless. His old yearning for travel returned, and he influenced Saunders to leave Saint Louis and travel with him west to Sedalia, Missouri.

In Sedalia, Joplin unknowingly moved a step closer to publishing his music and improving his compositional technique, for Sedalia had two music publishing firms, those of A. W. Perry and John Stark, and the George R. Smith College for Negroes, which contained a special department devoted to music. According to a recently found copy of the catalog for 1894–1895, the special department was headed by Reverend L. Weber, A. M., and included instruction in piano, organ, violin, guitar, mandolin, cornet, banjo, and voice.[12] The College was dedicated on March 26, 1894, and presumably the 1894–1895 catalog was the first issue. Although the exact year of Joplin's enrollment is not known, it can be reasonably assumed that he entered around 1897. It is quite possible that these few years allowed for an increase in musical offerings and the development of instructors capable of teaching Joplin the current vogue in piano literature and the fundamentals of theory and composition. Therefore, it is very possible that through the instruction gained at the George R. Smith College for Negroes, Scott developed more technical facility and learned how to notate the syncopations of rag, something which previously had eluded him.

Sedalia was one of the first cities above the Mason-Dixon line to establish a college for Negroes. The college was built by Sarah Smith as a memorial to her father, Colonel Smith, the founder of Sedalia.[13] Sedalia's fame did not come from the school, however, but rather from the fact that in the 1890s it had one of the largest red-light districts in Missouri. That was the prime reason that Saunders and Joplin had gone to Sedalia. In the district they could continue their usual way of making a living. So as soon as Joplin and Saunders arrived in Sedalia they began to look for work at the various taverns, saloons, and brothels in the city. Two clubs were especially significant during the last decade of the nineteenth century. One was called the Black 400 Club and was presumably owned by W. J. Williams and supervised by C. E. Williams. This club also was called, at times, the 400 Social Club and the 400 Special Club.[14] The other club, and perhaps the more significant of the two, was the now-famous Maple Leaf Club, which has heretofore eclipsed other important establishments considered so germane to the social and musical climate in which Joplin developed.[15] As Joplin moved in and out of the various saloons and cafés, his style of piano playing caught the fancy of the town, and he became the most sought-after pianist.

The tremendous popularity that Joplin was enjoying made him decide to make Sedalia his home for a few years. While he was attending the college, he continued his teaching and his performing. One of his first students in Sedalia was Arthur Marshall (1881–1968), who attended the college with Joplin. After the relationship between Joplin and Marshall had progressed from a teacher-student level to friendship, Joplin was invited to stay with Marshall's parents, who provided a home for him during most of his years in Sedalia. Another student of Joplin's during this period was Scott Hayden (1882–1915). Many were the nights that the Marshall and Hayden households would ring with the sounds of the trio playing rags. It was during these impromptu sessions that the idea of collaborating on the composing of rags came to Joplin and his two students. As the trio became closer they would often frequent the establishments where Joplin played, sometimes offering their own improvisations on the works of Scott Joplin.

Although it was probably the Black 400 Club that first enticed Joplin to its premises, it was the Maple Leaf Club that played a significant role in Scott Joplin's life. As is well known, Joplin's first successful and most popular rag was named after the club, and it was there that the publisher of the piece, John Stark, first heard Joplin play. The several physical descriptions of the club that are extant do not agree in all details, but it is impossible now to correct any inaccuracies since the building was torn down some time ago. Located on Main Street in Sedalia, the club in its heyday was an important center of political and social activity for both blacks and whites. It was not the noisy bar or sporting house described in some accounts, although parties were held at the club. A large room with a piano in one corner served as a rehearsal hall for the all-black Queen City Concert Band and for vocal groups. About 1959 the building was destroyed and a marker erected on the site:

```
┌─────────────────────────────────────┐
│                                      │
│              SITE OF THE             │
│           MAPLE LEAF CLUB            │
│          ─────────────────          │
│        ERECTED IN TRIBUTE TO         │
│            SCOTT JOPLIN              │
│              1868—1917               │
│              COMPOSER                │
│                                      │
│            JOHN STARK               │
│              1841—1927               │
│            PUBLISHER OF              │
│        THE MAPLE LEAF RAG           │
│                AND                   │
│       OTHER SEDALIA RAGTIMERS        │
│          ARTHUR MARSHALL            │
│           SCOTT HAYDEN              │
│          ─────────────────          │
│            THE CRADLE OF             │
│           THE CLASSIC RAGS           │
│          ─────────────────          │
│             ERECTED BY              │
│      THE SCOTT JOPLIN MEMORIAL       │
│        FOUNDATION COMMITTEE          │
│    SEDALIA CHAMBER OF COMMERCE       │
│                1961                  │
│                                      │
└─────────────────────────────────────┘
```

By 1896 Joplin had settled in Sedalia, and it was during his stay there that he first began to receive benefits from his original compositions. While touring with a vocal group earlier, he had published two songs at Syracuse, New York, in 1895 (*A Picture of Her Face* and *Please Say You Will*) and three piano pieces at Temple, Texas, in 1896 (*Combination March, Harmony Club Waltz,* and the *Great Crush Collision March*). These compositions are in the genteel tradition and contain little evidence of the personal style that was to emerge in his piano rags. The pieces have historical significance, however; the songs typify the kind of music performed by Joplin's vocal group, and the piano pieces represent the favorite pianistic forms of nineteenth-century America—the kinds of compositions that were being published during the latter part of the century and were selling well. Although Joplin began his ragtime career after publishing these five pieces, he never turned his back entirely on marches and waltzes. His published output includes a total of four marches and five waltzes. His vocal production includes nine songs, of which four belong to the genteel tradition, two are "coon" songs, and three are piano rags to which words were added.[16]

In 1898 Joplin submitted his first two rags, *Original Rags* and the *Maple Leaf Rag,* to Carl Hoffman of Kansas City for publication, but only *Original Rags* was accepted. Later, Joplin approached A. W. Perry of Sedalia with the *Maple Leaf Rag,* but he too rejected it. The piece became known to the black community of Sedalia, however, despite the fact that it was not available in published form, and it achieved a great deal of popularity. Negroes were proud that the rag bore the name of the most prominent Negro club of the city, especially one sanctioned by the city fathers.

It was in the summer of 1899 that John Stark (1841–1927) heard Joplin playing the *Maple Leaf Rag* at the club and was impressed by what he heard. Stark had moved to Sedalia from Chillicothe, Missouri, in 1883 as an agent for the Mason and Hamlin organ company; later he opened a music store.[17] After hearing Joplin perform, he invited the pianist to come to his store the next morning to play for his son, Will Stark. According to one version of the historic occasion—by now, a legend—Joplin brought a small boy with him, who danced while Joplin played the rag on the piano. Supposedly, the boy's dancing influenced the Starks to accept the piece for publication, despite their fears that the difficulty of the music might hinder sales.[18] Whatever the reason for the acceptance, Joplin and Stark signed a contract on August 10, 1899, agreeing to terms for the rag's publication. Joplin was to receive a royalty of one cent per copy sold. The *Maple Leaf Rag* marked the beginning of a five-year contractual agreement between Scott Joplin and John Stark and catapulted the composer to eventual worldwide fame.[19]

Rag compositions had been published prior to 1899. The first was *Mississippi Rag* by white songwriter-bandleader William H. Krell in January 1897, and the first published by a black man was *Harlem Rag*, by Tom Turpin (1873–1922) in December 1897. The earlier rags, however, lacked the drive and charm of Joplin's piece. The piece soon became a hit all over the nation and, later, in Europe. It found its way into the repertory of pianists, banjoists, marching bands, and theater orchestras, and was recorded dozens of times.

In addition to composing, teaching, and playing piano during these years, Joplin also found time to play second cornet in the Queen City Concert Band. During this period he became friendly with Ed Gravitt, the band's conductor, and George Ireland (1866?–1963), a ragtime clarinetist. Later, Ireland wrote in a letter to black poet Arna Bontemps that Joplin was not fond of (conventional) band music.[20] Joplin also formed his own small ensemble, using the same instruments he had had in his Chicago group—cornet, clarinet, tuba and baritone. This group performed Joplin's original compositions. Along with his instrumental activities, Joplin found time to lead and sing with a vocal quartet. There are extant newspaper references to the performances of the group, which was called the Sedalia Quartet. In 1899, for example, and again in 1904, the quartet performed for the August 4 celebrations of the Emancipation anniversary in Sedalia.[21]

Despite Joplin's deep involvement in Sedalia's musical life, the major concern of his life after the success of the *Maple Leaf Rag* was to publish his music. The relationship that existed between John Stark and Scott Joplin was novel and, at the same time, peculiar for the period. The wide gulf between black and white, dating from slavery and intensified by segregation and discrimination, was still largely uncrossable as the nation moved into the twentieth century. Yet in the small, racially split town of Sedalia a white man was becoming the benefactor of a black composer. Neither Joplin nor Stark allowed the relationship to become that of master and servant, as might have happened.²² The two men made the arrangement a lucrative business venture for each. Although the five-year contract was apparently not an exclusive one—Joplin published with several companies during his lifetime—Stark remained the composer's chief publisher until 1908.

In 1900 Stark moved to Saint Louis so that he could enlarge his publishing facilities, a move made necessary by the unprecedented success of the *Maple Leaf Rag*. Joplin moved to Saint Louis not too long afterward. About this time, he married Belle Hayden, a sister-in-law of Scott Hayden, his erstwhile student. It is not known whether they were married in Sedalia or in Saint Louis. Scott Hayden, who also had recently married, followed Joplin to Saint Louis, and the two families lived together in the same residence. In 1903 both couples moved to a thirteen-room house, which they used both as a residence and a boarding house.

The success of the *Maple Leaf Rag* did not by virtue of the contract itself provide financial security. Its success, however, ultimately brought Joplin fame, which allowed him financial security and a mobility heretofore unknown. It was during this time that he was dubbed "The King of Ragtime Writers." The title was given to him first in Sedalia, then later in all of the large cities where ragtime became popular. Joplin was invited to appear in various places as a pianist, as the leader of a vocal quartet, and as the renowned composer of the *Maple Leaf Rag*. He traveled a great deal during the early years of the century and revisited Sedalia several times. He had a special affection for the town where his rise to fame began.

Toward the end of 1899, Joplin made a notable accomplishment with his completion of an extended work in rag style, entitled *The "Rag Time Dance."* He wrote both the words and the music for this work (the only one of his songs for which he himself supplied lyrics) and indicated the kinds of dances to be performed. A notice published in the music states: "Complete directions for all the steps of the 'Ragtime Dance' are published by Scott Joplin—and can be obtained wherever this piece is for sale." Among the dances to be performed are the rag-time dance, the cake-walk prance, the clean-up dance, the Jenny Cooler dance, the slow drag, the back-step prance, and the Sedidus walk. Stark was not amenable to publishing such an extended work, so Joplin financed a performance of the work in an effort to convince Stark to publish it. Stark remained reluctant; he did not publish the work until 1902. As he had predicted, it was unsuccessful. The public wanted piano rags and ragtime songs, not extended "folk ballet."

Although shaken by Stark's negative attitude toward *The "Rag Time Dance,"* Joplin gained enough confidence in his compositional skills from the experiment to try another extended work, this time a ragtime opera to which he gave the title *A Guest of Honor*. A somewhat makeshift performance of the opera was staged in Saint Louis, according to some sources, and an application for copyright of the work was sent to the Copyright Office in Washington, D.C. on February 18, 1903. But copies of the music were never received by that office. It has been presumed that the music was lost in the mail. That every copy of the opera was lost is unlikely, for Joplin is sure to have made more than one copy. He would have kept at least one or more copies for his own use. It is highly probable that the work was performed by Joplin's Ragtime Opera Company, which toured during the fall of 1903 in Illinois, Kentucky, Missouri, Iowa and Nebraska.[23]

Despite his involvement with extended works, Joplin composed piano rags prolifically during this period. His music was published not only by Stark but also by A. W. Perry of Sedalia and in Saint Louis by S. Simon, Val. Reis, the Bahnsen Music Company, the Thiebes-Stierlin Music Company, the American Music Syndicate, and Joplin himself (*The Easy Winners*, 1901). Joplin's absorption in his music and his travel away from home for long periods of time inevitably became a source of friction in his family life. In 1905 a baby girl was born to the Joplins, but within several months, she died. This tragedy apparently was the breaking point in a marriage already characterized by the unsympathetic attitude of the wife toward her husband's career. In 1905 the couple separated, and Joplin sold the house to rag composer and pianist Arthur Marshall, who operated it as a boarding house until he and his wife moved to Chicago in 1906.

Joplin's whereabouts are difficult to ascertain after he sold his house. In 1905 he was listed in neither Sedalia nor Saint Louis. In 1906 he went to Chicago and stayed with the Arthur Marshalls for a short period, attempting to find work but to no avail. In 1906 and 1907 he was listed as living with the Tom Turpins in Saint Louis. But according to Joplin's nephew, Fred Joplin, Scott was in Europe during this time and returned to Texarkana in 1907 to visit his relatives.[24]

Another suggestion of a trip to Europe had appeared in a 1901 article in the *Saint Louis Post-Dispatch*. Titled "To Play Ragtime in Europe," the article quotes Alfred Ernst, director of the Saint Louis Choral Symphony Society, as intending to take copies of Joplin's works with him to Germany, "with a view to educating the dignified disciples of Wagner, Liszt, Mendelssohn and other European masters of music into an appreciation of the real American ragtime melodies. It is possible that the colored man may accompany the distinguished conductor."[25] We do not know whether Joplin ever actually traveled to Europe. Perhaps this mystery, and that of the lost *Guest of Honor*, will someday be solved.

Joplin composed prolifically up to this time in his life. The years 1899 to 1905 saw the publication of no fewer than five of his songs and twenty of his piano rags, including *The Entertainer* (1902). Significantly, 1906 was a barren year for Joplin publications. Only two pieces were issued, and one of these was not really new but rather a piano arrangement of the 1902 *Ragtime Dance*. Did Joplin's travels (including a possible trip abroad) during these years prevent him from composing and publishing? Or was it his despondency? Despite the fact that he had won recognition as "The King of

SCOTT JOPLIN.

It Was He Who Gave Us That Cleverest of Rags, "Maple Leaf"—Other Clever Numbers From His Pen.

The subject of this sketch, Scott Joplin, is a negro who is considered to be one of the greatest composers of rag-time music in this country. He gave us that clever and best of rags, "Maple Leaf," which has sold for years, and will sell for years to come.

One of his recent efforts is a march entitled "Antoinette," written in 6-8 time. It is an excellent composition and one that should become a favorite with bands and orchestras.

Scott Joplin has been working a considerable time on a grand opera which will contain music similar to that sung by the negroes during slavery days, the music of today, the negro ragtime, and the music that the negro will use in the future.

While in St. Louis the writer paid a visit to the John Stark Music Company, where he met and heard Mr. Joplin play the overture of his new opera, and to say that it was exceptionally good would be putting it mildly.

Scott Joplin considers it too hard work for him to sit at the piano and compose. He gets his inspirations while walking along the street or in his bed at night, and when a melody comes to him he immediately puts it down on music paper, which he always carries with him.

He is unassuming and never has much to say, and seldom speaks of his music. The Stark Music Company, of St. Louis, Mo., publishes his compositions.

A rare article about Scott Joplin from a New York music trade magazine of 1907. (*John Edward Hasse collection*)

Ragtime Writers," he had failed to find publication support for his extended works. He had failed in his personal relationship, having lost his wife and his child. He must have stopped to take stock of how much he had accomplished at this point in his career, and perhaps he dwelt too heavily on his failures.

By 1907 Joplin's anxiety had apparently run its course, and he began to look forward to new goals and accomplishments. During the years 1907 to 1909 he completed and had published fifteen rags, two of them in collaboration with others, and three songs. In addition, he crowned his career as a teacher by self-publishing a rag manual, the *School of Ragtime*, in 1908. The manual contains six exercises, and its introductory note indicates the serious attitude Joplin took toward ragtime.

> *What is scurrilously called ragtime is an invention that is here to stay. That is now conceded by all classes of musicians. That all publications masquerading under the name of ragtime are not the genuine article will be better known when these exercises are studied. That real ragtime of the higher class is rather difficult to play is a painful truth which most pianists have discovered. Syncopations are no indication of light and trashy music, and to shy bricks at "hateful" ragtime no longer passes for musical culture. To assist amateur players in giving the "Joplin Rags" that weird and intoxicating effect intended by the composer is the object of this work.* [26]

While acknowledging the popularity of ragtime, Joplin nevertheless was aware that its charm would be destroyed if the music were performed incorrectly. He cautioned against neglecting rhythmic matters:

> *It is evident that, by giving each note its proper time and by scrupulously observing the ties, you will get the effect. So many are careless in these respects that we will specify each feature. In this number* [i.e., Exercise no. 1], *strike the first note and hold it through the time belonging to the second note. . . . Play slowly until you catch the swing, and never play ragtime fast at any time.*

Above all, Joplin believed, the correct tempo should always be observed.

> *The instructions given* [i.e., for Exercise no. 6], *together with the dotted lines, will enable you to interpret this variety which has very pleasing effects. We wish to say here, that the "Joplin ragtime" is destroyed by careless or imperfect rendering, and very often good players lose the effect entirely, by playing too fast. They are harmonized with the supposition that each will be played as it is written, as it takes this and also the proper time divisions to complete the sense intended.*

Joplin's concern about the fast tempos used by many ragtime players is indicated also in the warning he began to have printed at the beginning of his publications:

NOTE: *Do not play this piece fast. It is never right to play Ragtime fast.*
Composer.

In 1905 Stark had moved his editorial offices to New York City, although he retained a printing plant in Saint Louis. From 1905 to 1910 his firm published six of Joplin's original or collaborative pieces; Joseph W. Stern published three; Joseph M. Daly, one; W. W. Stuart, one; and Seminary Music Company published the other eight. Joplin arrived in New York sometime during 1907 and remained there until his death in 1917. So Scott Joplin and John Stark were again together in the same city, but neither their friendship nor business relationship were to last very long. In 1909 the two men had a serious disagreement, which severed their hitherto rather amiable relationship. Joplin was eager to have his new opera published, but Stark was unwilling to take such a risk, as he had done with the unsuccessful *"Rag Time Dance"* (1902). In addition, Stark began to demand that Joplin sell his compositions outright without royalty arrangements. The disagreement dissolved a business-friendship association of ten years.[27] After his wife, Sarah, died in 1910, Stark returned to Saint Louis. After the break with Joplin, Stark published only three more Joplin works: the collaborative rag, *Felicity Rag* (1911), written by Joplin and Scott Hayden; *Kismet Rag* (1913) by Joplin and Hayden; and Joplin's *Reflection Rag*, published in 1917 after the composer's death.

During his New York years Joplin continued his warm relationships with his former students Scott Hayden and Arthur Marshall and made new contacts, meeting some of the well-known black musicians of his time. He is also known to have advertised to collaborate with other composers on ragtime arrangements.[28] He wrote a rag in collaboration with Louis Chauvin (1881–1908), a colorful rag pianist-composer who was noted for his skills in Saint Louis "cutting" contests. In these competitions, pianists were judged by how fast they could play, and Chauvin was one of the best. Another friendship that dated back to the Saint Louis days was that with James Scott (1886–1938), whom Joplin found to be as serious about ragtime as he was. Scott, born in Neosho, Missouri, received his early training from John Coleman, a local black pianist. About 1905, James Scott traveled to Saint Louis in order to meet, and possibly study with, Joplin. In 1908 Joplin met another musician who was serious about ragtime, at Stark's new publishing office in New York. Joseph Lamb (1887–1960), a white man, had studied Joplin's music before he met the composer, and was a great Joplin enthusiast. The two men became friends and played their compositions for each other. Joplin helped Lamb to publish his first rag, *Sensation—A Rag*, in 1908.

New York was an exciting place for black musicians and entertainers during the first decades of the century, and Joplin could not help but become involved to some degree in the intense musical activity of the blacks. It was the world of Will Marion Cook (1869–1944), Joe Jordan (1882–1971), James Reese Europe (1881–1919), Bob Cole (1863–1911), and the Johnson brothers—musician J. Rosamond (1873–1954) and poet James Weldon (1871–1938). It was the time of the Memphis Students and their talked-about concerts of syncopated music at Hammerstein's Victoria Theater on Broadway, of the celebrated musicals of Bert Williams (1874–1922) and George Walker (1871–1911), of the beginning of the Clef Club, one of the first Negro musicians' unions in the nation. In 1907 Joplin met Eubie Blake (1883–1983), one of the several rag-piano wizards who were becoming legendary in the East.[29] In 1912 Joplin talked with Harry Lawrence Freeman, who had been composing operas since 1892 and had staged several of his own works.[30] The two men must have had a serious discussion about opera, particularly from the standpoint of the black opera composer.

Soon after Joplin arrived in New York, he met Lottie Stokes (1873–1953), and they were married in 1909. She proved to be the exact opposite of Belle Hayden Joplin in regard to the interest she took in Joplin's music. Lottie was very enthusiastic about his work and encouraged him to try all avenues for publishing his music. His determination to succeed moved him to set up his own publishing house on West Forty-seventh Street.[31] He also maintained a studio.

The constant and driving preoccupation of Joplin during these years was his second opera, *Treemonisha*. No doubt he had been working on it for some time before moving to New York; perhaps he began to compose it soon after completing *A Guest of Honor*. Eubie Blake states that when he talked with Joplin in Washington, D. C. in 1907, Joplin was then discussing his desire to obtain a copyright for his opera. In 1908 Joplin played parts of the opera for Joseph Lamb, and by 1910 must have been giving all of his attention to it. Only two of his pieces were published that year, and one of those was an earlier piano rag, *Pine Apple Rag* (1908), to which lyrics were given. Joplin was more determined than ever to publish and produce the opera, despite Stark's refusal to publish it. Finally Joplin published the 230-page score himself in May 1911. Then followed an agonizing search for a producer for *Treemonisha*. The Joplins placed notices in the local papers and contacted potential producers, but no one came to the rescue. Benjamin Nibur, manager of the Lafayette Theater in Harlem, was reputed to be interested in staging the opera, but nothing came of it.[32]

As might have been anticipated from a man of Joplin's drive and determination, he decided to produce the opera himself. Sam Patterson, an old friend from the Saint Louis days, helped him to copy the orchestrations for the work and, more important, helped Joplin to keep up his spirits during this depressing period. Lottie Joplin also did everything she could to encourage Scott. He assumed the responsibility himself for rehearsing the singers and dancers, but his funds were low and the rehearsals were necessarily inadequate. Finally, Joplin was ready for the performance, which took place in 1915 in a Harlem hall with Joplin at the piano, substituting for an orchestra. The performance was doomed to failure from the beginning; it had none of the elements associated with an opera—scenery, costumes, orchestra. No producers were ever found for the opera during Joplin's lifetime.

The failure of *Treemonisha* in 1915 brought about Joplin's complete breakdown. He had shown disturbing signs of mental disintegration earlier, and it seems that the failure of his opera was the final blow. In 1916 Joplin was committed to Manhattan State Hospital. He died on April 1, 1917, the cause attributed to "dementia paralytica-cerebral" and a contributing cause, "syphilis."

Treemonisha was the culminating achievement of Joplin's life, a work that had been his obsession for almost a decade. The opera is composed in the "grand" manner, including an overture and preludes to the second and third acts. There are no spoken parts; the music comprises twenty-seven numbers—recitatives, arias, and ensembles—with accompanying dances for some of the numbers. The basic theme of the opera is that through education the ex-slaves can free themselves from superstition and servitude. Its message to the public was that education can be the salvation of the black people in the United States. I cannot help but reflect on Joplin's early life and the importance his mother gave to education as a way of life for her family. Although Joplin asserts in his preface to the score that the story of *Treemonisha* is fictitious, his descriptions of the characters and their occupations and actions mirror his own early life experiences and thus give the opera an autobiographical tone.

It is worthy of note that the opera is not a "ragtime" opera; only three numbers employ rag style. It was Joplin's aim to write a genuine opera, and he did not feel that he had to rely on any one stylistic idiom in order to express himself. In essence the opera is a dramatic statement of black music at the beginning of the twentieth century and includes references to all of the idioms associated with the music—even the blues.[33] To be sure, *Treemonisha* received at least one rave review in its time. A critic writing for the *American Musician* (24 June 1911) observed that Joplin "has created an entirely new phase of musical art and has produced a thoroughly American opera."[34]

Black New York paid little attention to Joplin's opera. The music that was being played and recognized by Negroes of New York in the early twentieth century was not rag opera nor ragtime. Though there were places where rag could be heard, it was not for consumption by sophisticated black listeners, for ragtime was associated with lowly origins. It is significant that Joplin is given little or no attention in the three major documents of black music history of this period: W. C. Handy's *Father of the Blues* and Tom Fletcher's *The Tom Fletcher Story: 100 Years of the Negro in Show Business!* devote only a few lines to Joplin; James Weldon Johnson's *Black*

Manhattan does not mention Joplin at all.[35] Generally, the music performed by the accepted black groups was that in the white European tradition, not the black folk music style. For a Negro to survive in the musical world, he had to adopt "white" standards; otherwise his music was relegated to the brothels and red-light districts. Joplin could not, and would not, accept this. But the time was not ripe for his stand; black militancy was not in vogue during his day.

Now, sixty-odd years after his death, the world is reevaluating this musical genius born of ex-slaves. Joplin's works have finally been hailed and the composer has been honored in many cities. In Astoria, Queens, New York, in October 1974, the American Society of Composers, Authors, and Publishers (ASCAP) held a service to install a bronze marker at Joplin's grave in Saint Michael's Cemetery. Texarkana, Arkansas-Texas, commissioned a bust of Joplin and named a park after him, and Orr School has been nominated for the National Register of Historical Places. In 1975 Chicago rededicated an elementary school and named it the Scott Joplin Elementary School, where ASCAP unveiled a bronze plaque honoring Joplin. In 1978, through the efforts of the Scott Joplin Landmark Preservation Society, Saint Louis began renovation of one of Joplin's old homes.[36] The highlights of posthumous honors came in 1976, with the awarding of a special Pulitzer Prize to Joplin for *Treemonisha*, and in 1983, with the issuance of a U.S. postage stamp for Joplin. What kind of man was he to have achieved so much under such unfavorable conditions?

Notes

1. This essay is based upon my Ph.D. dissertation, "The Life and Works of Scott Joplin" (University of North Carolina at Chapel Hill, 1973), and includes information which has recently come to light. The starting point for my research on the life of Joplin was the well-known book by Rudi Blesh and Harriet Janis, *They All Played Ragtime* (New York: Alfred A. Knopf, 1950).

2. James Haskins with Kathleen Benson, *Scott Joplin* (New York: Doubleday, 1978), p. 22.

3. Ibid., p. 32.

4. Jerry Atkins, "Scott Joplin and Texarkana," mimeographed [n.p.], 1 March 1972, pp. 3–4; Ann and John Vanderlee, "Scott Joplin's Childhood Days in Texas," *Rag Times* 7, no. 4 (November 1973): 5–7; Ann and John Vanderlee, "The Early Life of Scott Joplin," *Rag Times* 7, no. 5 (January 1975): 2–3; and interview with Donita Fowler and Mattie Harris, nieces of Scott Joplin, Texarkana, Arkansas, 25 July 1971.

5. Haskins, *Scott Joplin*, p. 54; Atkins, "Scott Joplin," p. 2; Vanderlee, "Scott Joplin's Childhood Days," p. 5.

6. Haskins, *Scott Joplin*, p. 56.

7. Ibid., p. 53.

8. Theodore Albrecht, "Julius Weiss: Scott Joplin's First Piano Teacher," *College Music Symposium* 19, no. 2 (Fall 1979): 89–105.

9. W. D. Hill, "Saga of Scott Joplin, Ragtime King," *The Sedalia Democrat*, 11 February 1962, p. 1.

10. Haskins, *Scott Joplin*, pp. 57–58.

11. Ernst Krohn, "Music Publishing in St. Louis," Papers of Ernst Krohn, Gaylord Music Library, Washington University, Saint Louis, p. 2; Haskins, *Scott Joplin*, p. 81.

12. *George R. Smith College, 1894–1895* (Sedalia, Mo.: George R. Smith College, 1894), p. 34.

13. S. Brunson Campbell, "Ragtime Begins," *Record Changer* 7 (March 1948): i.

14. Haskins, *Scott Joplin*, p. 91.

15. Documentation is not known to exist for the Black 400 Club, but in 1976 the articles of federation for the Maple Leaf Club were found, dated December 1898. See "Joplin Rag Respectable," *Saint Louis Post-Dispatch*, 1 March 1976, p. 3B. It can be conjected with a fair amount of certainty that the Maple Leaf Club existed prior to formal incorporation.

16. For an extensive discussion of the music of Joplin see Addison Walker Reed, Ph.D. diss., "The Life and Works of Scott Joplin." Joplin's known published works are reprinted in *The Complete Works of Scott Joplin*, ed. Vera Brodsky Lawrence, Volume I, *Works for Piano* and Volume II, *Works for Voice* (New York: The New York Public Library, 1982).

17. *Simmons and Kernodle's Pettis County and Sedalia City Directory, 1883–84*, identifies John Stark as follows: "genl agent Mason Hamlin Organ Company, also dealer in musical instruments and sheet music, 222 Ohio res. ss 4th, 2 W. Ohio."

18. Dorothy Brockhoff, "Missouri was the Birthplace of Ragtime," *Saint Louis Post-Dispatch*, 18 January 1961, p. 3.

19. "The Maple Leaf Rag Contract," *Rag Times* 9, no. 2 (September 1975). The contract is also reprinted in James Haskins, *Scott Joplin*, following p. 80 and in David A. Jasen and Trebor Jay Tichenor, *Rags and Ragtime: A Musical History* (New York: Seabury Press, 1978), preceding p. 77. See also "R. A. Higdon," *Rag Times* 9, no. 4 (November 1975): 11. The five-year contract is discussed by W. D. Hill, "Saga of Scott Joplin," p. 1.

20. Ireland to Bontemps, 19 July 1947, Arna Bontemps Papers, Special Collections, Fisk University Library, Nashville.

21. *Sedalia Daily Capital-Gazette*, 4 August 1899, p. 8; *Sedalia Evening Sentinel*, 4 August 1904, p. 5.

22. Such was the case of pianist Blind Tom, for example, who was an older contemporary of Joplin's. See Geneva Southall, "Blind Tom: A Misrepresented and Neglected Composer-Pianist," *The Black Perspective in Music* 3, no. 2 (May 1975): 141–59.

23. *New York Dramatic Mirror*, 12 September 1903, 17 October 1903, 24 October 1903.

24. Interview with Fred D. Joplin, Marshall, Texas, 31 July 1971. For speculation on a possible Joplin trip to England, see Edward S. Walker, "Scott Joplin in England," *Storyville* no. 68 (December 1976–January 1977), pp. 66–68.

25. "To Play Ragtime in Europe," *Saint Louis Post-Dispatch*, 28 February 1901.

26. Scott Joplin, *School of Ragtime: 6 Exercises for Piano* (New York: Scott Joplin, 1908). Reprinted in Scott Joplin, *The Complete Works of Scott Joplin*, Vol. 1.

27. Russell E. Cassidy, "Joseph F. Lamb: A Biography," *The Ragtimer* 5, no. 4 (Summer 1966): 32.

28. Advertisement, "Scott-Joplin," *American Musician and Art Journal* 23, no. 21 (8 November 1907): 12.

29. Interviews with Eubie Blake, Brooklyn, New York, 29 June 1971 and 24 December 1971.

30. Letter received from Valdo Freeman, son of H. Lawrence Freeman, dated 19 October 1971.

31. Haskins, *Scott Joplin*, p. 183; S. Brun Campbell, "From Rags to Ragtime: A Eulogy," *Jazz Report* 5, no. 5 [ca. 1967]: [5]–[6].

32. Samuel B. Charters and Leonard Kunstadt, *Jazz: A History of the New York Scene* (New York: Doubleday, 1962), p. 48.

33. Rudi Blesh, "Scott Joplin: Black American Classicist," in *The Complete Works of Scott Joplin*, Vol. I; Carman Moore, "Notes on Treemonisha," in *The Complete Works of Scott Joplin*, Vol. II.

34. "A Musical Novelty," *American Musician and Art Journal* 27 (24 June 1911): 7.

35. W. C. Handy, *Father of the Blues,* ed. Arna Bontemps (New York: Macmillan, 1941); Tom Fletcher, *The Tom Fletcher Story: 100 Years of the Negro in Show Business!* (New York: Burdge & Co., 1954); and James Weldon Johnson, *Black Manhattan* (New York: Alfred A. Knopf, 1930).

36. Daphne Walker, "Shepard Says Conway Veto Won't Stop Joplin Home Restoration," *Saint Louis Argus,* 14 September 1978, sect. 2, p. 1; Haskins, *Scott Joplin,* pp. 12–17.

James Scott

Marvin L. VanGilder

James Scott is frequently ranked second only to Joplin as a composer of enduring piano rags. Though there is relatively little published material on James Scott, Marvin L. VanGilder manages to reconstruct Scott's interesting life. VanGilder traces Scott's career from the small town of Carthage, Missouri, where he swept the floors of a music store, to Kansas City, where he composed his final "classic rags," taught piano, and played in a theater orchestra.

It seems inevitable that James Scott would rise to musical eminence. John Coleman, fine Missouri pianist, recognized the spark of genius in a barefoot boy who came to him for musical guidance. Charles "Charlie" R. Dumars, enterprising music publisher and local bandmaster in the mold of John Philip Sousa, detected the sound of artistic expertise in the practicing of a teen-age ex-bootblack. And Scott Joplin recognized a musician worthy of acceptance into his inner circle of keyboard masters. Some observers may conclude that this trio shaped the artistic success of James Scott, ranked by most scholars as second only to Joplin himself. Without those mentors, however, the pulse of artistic greatness in the "little professor"[1] would probably have sought and found other routes to the summit of musical expression.

James Scott's parents, James Sylvester Scott, Sr., and Mollie Thomas Scott, had both been born slaves in North Carolina. James was the second child of his parents; born in 1886, he joined a sister, Lena. Other children who followed were, consecutively, Douglas, Howard, Bessie, and Oliver, all born in Neosho, Missouri. Neosho in the 1880s was just beginning to emerge from frontier status. It was a rustic village with clusters of boxlike frame cottages and broad, tree-lined streets which, lacking hard surface paving, often turned to mud or dust. The business district was comprised largely of false-front frame buildings. Numerous fields and forested areas remained, in which a boy could pursue the delights of nature and escape from the rigid disciplines of a demanding household. Not all attractions were out of doors, however. Neosho also boasted several saloons and hotel bars, where black entertainers performed for tossed pennies, for beer or for an occasional cold-cut sandwich.[2] Among those entertainers was John Coleman, whose skill at the keyboard drew the attention of show business personalities from a wide area and who added to his meager income by serving as a teacher. One of his students was Jimmy Scott, who began study of the keyboard at least as early as he began learning the written word in Neosho's "colored" elementary school.[3]

Mollie Thomas Scott played plantation tunes, folk airs popular among the miners and farmers of southwest Missouri, blues melodies, and gospel laments by ear without benefit of formal training; her son, when little more than a toddler, began copying her technique.[4] The Scott family at Neosho owned no piano or organ; Jimmy practiced on public instruments and in the homes of more affluent neighbors.[5] Refinement of natural talent began when Coleman took the youngster under his wing, giving him some thirty formal lessons in classical piano technique with application to the developing idiom to be known as ragtime.[6] The learning process was accelerated by Scott's intense passion for knowledge[7] and by his rare gift of absolute pitch, which was so comprehensive that even as a child he could hear full chords and repeat them at will.[8] A few years later, at Carthage, Missouri, the practice became a serious competitive game in which he consistently bested every other music student, black and white, male and female.[9] Study of his scores suggests he also may have been blessed with ambidexterity.

About 1899, the family moved to Ottawa in southwest Kansas to join relatives. The period of residence at Ottawa was brief but significant. It was there that Jimmy produced his first composition, using a reed pump organ owned by an uncle and aunt, and shared with his first cousin Ruth (later Mrs. Callahan).[10] When both families moved to Carthage in about 1901, they transported the cabinet organ with them, and Scott was able to continue his keyboard practice and composition. A bit later, after Ruth Callahan's family moved from Carthage, taking the organ, James Scott, Sr., managed to purchase a used upright piano. Thereafter, music rolled forth almost constantly from the Scotts' frame cottage at Fifth and Valley streets. All the Scott children learned to play piano, although only Jimmy received formal training and developed music-reading skill. In addition, other Carthage musicians often visited the home to share in Jimmy's enthusiasm.[11]

Like Neosho and Ottawa, Carthage was on the fringe of the raucous, booming tri-state lead mining district of Missouri, Kansas, and Oklahoma. Unlike neighboring boom towns such as Joplin, Webb City, and Granby, the Carthage economy had a diverse base in agriculture, industry, and marble quarries, which were being developed into one of the largest building stone sources in the world. Carthage had acquired a metropolitan air along with widely shared visions of future metropolitan status, tempered somewhat by a Victorian conservatism that touched virtually every aspect of community life. Although the population was less than ten thousand, crowds on the streets and in the stores suggested a greater size. The elegant Harrington House Hotel attracted noted travelers from throughout the world. To the south, the new Delphus Theater drew both vaudeville headliners and the new silent celluloid marvels. Scattered throughout the downtown area were a number of saloons where men sought escape into alcohol or into the stirring music supplied by itinerant entertainers such as pianist John William "Blind" Boone (1869–1927). To the south and east were the Calhoun School of Music, the professional piano studio of Emma Johns (DeArmond) (1862–1936), and several churches with strong musical traditions. Electric-powered trolleys offered direct service to every boom town and camp in the Tri-State mining complex. It was possible for an enterprising youngster who could scrape up a single coin to board a car there and travel quickly to Lakeside Amusement Park at Webb City, Missouri, or to Joplin, Missouri, where pioneer ragtimers gathered in the lurid atmosphere of the House of Lords saloon. At Lakeside's pavilion, he was likely to hear the sparkling music of such keyboard wizards as Percy Wenrich, who already was gaining national notice as "The Joplin Kid." If the coin was not readily available, he could stroll the few blocks to City Park and listen to the Carthage Light Guard Band, directed by Dumars. Enrolled at overcrowded, segregated Lincoln School and nearing the end of his formal education, young James absorbed many stimuli of his lively environment and with quiet competence became a part of it.[12]

At age fifteen, already a skilled pianist who could read the most intricate Bach, Brahms, and Chopin scores as well as interpret the popular idioms of his time, Scott began to "sit in" between dance sets at the Lakeside Park pavilion and was cheered by older entertainers. This activity, however, brought him no income, so he went to work as a shoeshine boy for a Carthage barber. He supplemented the proceeds from that labor by playing piano at several Carthage saloons for any coins patrons chose to toss into the kitty. Scott was described as sitting at the keyboard with his left leg wrapped around a leg of the stool or bench and bouncing up and down with the beat as he played, his short, square-tipped fingers literally flying over the keys as he attempted to squeeze the greatest possible number of tones into the space of each beat. When thus occupied, he was lost to the world and the sordid atmosphere around him, totally absorbed with the wonder of his music. A quiet, studious, spiritual teenager, he was emotionally withdrawn except when seated at the piano, where he was transformed into a smiling, bouncing extrovert who sought and gained attention.[13]

Because music was the center of his being, he was drawn to the Dumars Music Company store at 109 South Main Street. There bandmaster Charles Dumars displayed the latest sheet music along with racks of violins, flutes, banjos, cornets, clarinets, accordions, harmonicas, and player piano rolls. Decorative picture frames were a nonmusical specialty. The rear room was filled with pianos and parlor organs. Professional musicians often paused there to visit with Dumars during their travels through the Midwest.[14]

In 1902, Dumars hired the sixteen-year-old Scott as a kind of general flunky. Jimmy washed windows and swept out the store daily, helped arrange promotional displays, dusted shelves, and was assigned as a trainee at the craft of picture framing.[15] At every opportunity, the youth slipped into the back room and applied his skill to the keyboard instruments in stock. When Dumars heard the brilliant sounds, he recognized Scott's great talents and reassigned him as sales clerk and instrument and song demonstrator.[16] There was a measurable increase in business volume, and many people came to the store merely to hear Scott play. His own compositions were among the most popular of the works he played and requests for printed copies stirred Dumars to consider expanding his business interests into the music publishing field.[17] While working for Dumars, Jimmy obtained supplementary employment at the Delphus Theater and at Lakeside Park. In addition, he was the pianist for a trio that also included mandolinist Walt Lewis and a now-forgotten banjoist.[18] His fame grew as his piano virtuosity attracted larger audiences and mature pianists began to visit Carthage to hear him play and to share musical ideas. Drawing upon Scott's growing reputation, Dumars launched his publishing career in March 1903 with issuance of Scott's rag *A Summer Breeze: March and Two-Step*. Dumars also published the work in band and orchestral arrangements, and advertised that the piece was "sold everywhere and pronounced by critics the cream of two-steps."[19] Sales were sufficient to inspire Dumars to further ventures; six months later, he published Scott's *The Fascinator: March and Two Step*, which the young composer dedicated "to my friend, Miss Daisy N. Pierce." In 1904, he issued a third Scott rag, *On the Pike*, in observance of the Saint Louis World's Fair, and *The Meteor March* by another young Carthaginian, white pianist Clarence Woods. Scott's *On the Pike* was "especially dedicated to visitors of the 'Pike'," the fair's amusement area, where a number of ragtime pianists performed.

In 1906 Scott went to Saint Louis and met Scott Joplin, and about this time, we are told, the two composers also had an encounter in Carthage.[20] Scott's scores thereafter became more complex and reveal some Joplin influence, although always retaining Scott's own thematic unity and brilliance. Interestingly, Joplin's scores about that time began to exhibit more intricate character. One can only speculate that, while Joplin was the mature and experienced teacher and Scott the young seeker for knowledge, the exchange of musical wisdom may have been mutual. Partly as a result of the contact with Joplin, Stark Music Company of Saint Louis and New York, Joplin's primary publisher, became Scott's main publisher as well. The Stark firm published Scott's *Frog Legs Rag* in 1906, and the sprightly piece became a success. In subsequent years, Stark would advertise *Frog Legs* as "one of the pioneer rag-classics."

Not yet twenty-one years of age, small in stature and emotionally introverted, Scott became somewhat of a celebrity, particularly among fellow musicians.[21] He accepted performing gigs in Kansas City, Sedalia, Saint Louis, and other cities, but continued to call Carthage home and to maintain his ties with the Dumars firm, working regular shifts with the sales and delivery crews when not otherwise occupied.[22] As a result of his performances, he found many eager friends and benefactors, including Mr. and Mrs. Mett Penn of Kansas City, Missouri, to whom he dedicated his *Kansas City Rag*, published in 1907 by the Stark firm.

For Scott's career as a composer, 1909 was a big year. Allen Music Company of Columbia, Missouri, issued his *Great Scott Rag*, with the composer retaining copyright. Stark published *Ragtime Betty, Sunburst Rag*, and *Grace and Beauty*, which several leading authorities consider his greatest rag. Apparently Stark thought highly of it too, for in his advertising he described *Grace and Beauty* as difficult, "heavy," "high-class," and "A rag as it ought to be," and admonished his customers, "Play every note of Grace & Beauty in slow March time and there is no person with soul so dead as not to like it." The 1909 rags contained the brightest, most optimistic sounds of an optimistic idiom; the work of Scott challenged all other ragtimers to strive for greater polish, complexity, and brilliance in both composition and performance.[23] Also in 1909, the Dumars-Gammon Music Company of Carthage, successor to Dumars Music Company at a new site on the town square, published two Scott songs with words by Dumars, *She's My Girl From Anaconda* and *Sweetheart Time*.

A youthful photo of James Scott, ca. 1904, about the time of Scott's third rag, *On the Pike*. (*Courtesy Rudi Blesh*)

Little affected by public attention, Scott continued to perform at the Delphus Theater and at Lakeside Park. In 1910, he composed *Calliope Rag* especially for Lakeside's steam-powered calliope. The unpublished and damaged manuscript was discovered years later and restored by Robert "Ragtime Bob" Darch. It was disseminated through publication in the third edition of *They All Played Ragtime.*[24]

In 1910 Stark published Scott's *Hilarity Rag, Ophelia Rag,* and *Hearts Longing Waltzes,* and in 1911 issued *Princess Rag, Quality,* and *Ragtime Oriole.* In 1912 the E. W. Berry Music Company released an orchestration of *The Fascinator,* and by about this time Stark issued, separately and as part of the "Red Back Book," orchestrations of four Scott rags: *Ophelia, Hilarity, Frog Legs,* and *Grace and Beauty.* About this time also Scott began his teaching career, tutoring pianists as part of his work with Dumars-Gammon.[25] The year 1914 saw the publication of his *Climax Rag,* later to become a favorite of traditional jazz musicians, *Suffragette Waltz,* and *Take Me Out to Lakeside,* the latter a song with lyrics by Ida Miller of Lawrence County, Missouri, and issued by Ball Music Company of Carthage. It was a period of excitement. "I remember when he was writing *Lakeside,*" said his sister Bessie in 1973. "It was a happy time!"[26]

During this period, Stark continued to publish most of Scott's compositions: *Evergreen Rag* in 1915, *Prosperity Rag* and *Honey Moon Rag* in 1916, *Efficiency Rag* and *Paramount Rag* in 1917, and *Rag Sentimental* in 1918. Another firm, Will L. Livernash Music Company of Kansas City, issued two Scott works in 1918: *Dixie Dimples Rag* and *Springtime of Love Waltz.* By the time Scott and his wife Nora Johnson, a slender, quiet woman[27] of whom little is known, elected about 1920 to transfer their principal residence to Kansas City, he already was known fondly as the "little professor." Scott set up a private teaching studio with adjoining living quarters at 402 Nebraska Street, Kansas City, Kansas,[28] where he installed a new grand piano, probably the most cherished material possession of his entire life.[29] His composing continued unabated. He "just wrote, wrote, wrote," said his cousin, Patsy Thomas.[30] As he settled into maturity, his piano scores grew more complex, featuring rhythmic and harmonic patterns so intricate as to tax the abilities of the most skillful pianists of any idiom. Scott's scores of this period reveal the nature of changing times, both in musical expressiveness and in the titles, most of which were chosen by John Stark:[31] *Troubadour Rag, New Era Rag* and *Peace and Plenty Rag,* 1919; *Pegasus, Modesty Rag,* and *Shimmie Shake,* a song with words by Cleota Wilson, 1920; *Victory Rag* and *Don't Jazz Me: Rag (I'm Music),* 1921 and *Broadway Rag,* 1922. As the title *Don't Jazz Me: Rag* suggests, Stark then was engaged in a futile battle against the trend towards more improvisation and less faithfulness to scores in the then-spreading jazz idiom, which, after all, partly grew out of ragtime. Indeed, many of Scott's scores, carefully unified and artistically precise, virtually defy attempts at improvisation, and in fact allow the performer relatively few choices in interpretation.

In the early 1920s, Scott resumed the work of theater musician launched at the Delphus in Carthage by signing on as pianist for the Panama Theater, a small silent-movie house on East Twelfth Street in Kansas City, Missouri. About 1924 Scott joined the "colored" Local 627 of the American Federation of Musicians and moved to the Lincoln Theater, Eighteenth and Lydia streets.[32] There he joined a seven-piece pit orchestra that provided music for silent films and accompanied vaudeville artists such as Bessie Smith and Gertrude "Ma" Rainey touring on the circuit of the TOBA (Theater Owners Booking Association). His contemporary, Lawrence Denton, who played with Scott at the Lincoln, remembers that Scott "had execution," enjoyed a reputation as a "number one" pianist, and played lots of classics— "all those big numbers . . . like Hungarian Rhapsody" of Franz Liszt.[33] Playing in the pit orchestra required Scott to be an expert sight reader from scores and an improviser from lead sheets. Nora, a modest but attractive woman, sometimes came to meet him after his night's work ended at the Lincoln, and at other times he left immediately to go home to her, avoiding the partying and boozing habitual to some performers.[34] "He wasn't a hang-around dude," notes one of his contemporaries.[35] James and Nora had no children; they gave their full attention to each other.

After some two or three years at the Lincoln, Scott transferred to the Eblon Theater, 1822 Vine, where he joined a six-piece theater orchestra. By November of 1928, the Eblon had discharged its orchestra and installed a new fifteen-thousand-dollar Wicks pipe organ to accompany silent movies.[36] By about 1930, sound movies edged out the silent films, and there was no further need for movie theater musicians. That development and the death of his beloved Nora marked the beginning of the end for James Scott. With an eight-piece band he had formed, he continued to play for dances and beer parks into the 1930s,[37] but the old verve was gone. The market for ragtime had disappeared and if he kept on composing, his works, shelved and unpublished, were lost. Scott may have been restless or financially troubled during his last eight years, for he lived in at least four different places in Kansas City, Kansas: in 1930 at 1930 North Hallock, in 1934 at 844 Freeman, and in 1936 at 634 Troup Avenue.[38] By 1938 he had moved with his pet dog and his grand piano into the home of his cousin Ruth Callahan at 1926 Springfield Street. Thus, he shared with Ruth the end of his career as he had shared with her its beginnings.[39] Old age quickly overtook Scott with premature infirmities: His fingers were stiffened by arthritis and his body weakened by dropsy.[40]

He is said to have continued nevertheless to create complex sounds at the keyboard until he was admitted to Douglas Hospital, Kansas City, Kansas, where he died on August 30, 1938, at age fifty-two.[41] Undoubtedly, much great music died with him. He was buried in Westlawn Cemetery beside Nora's grave. The graves, tragically, lay unmarked and abandoned for more than forty years until 1980, when a local group raised funds to mark James's grave; a handsome headstone was formally dedicated on May 3, 1981.[42] Even those few members of his generation still living have some difficulty remembering James Scott. He was so quiet and unobtrusive that he made a slight personal impression, leaving only the image of one who, at the keyboard, "had execution," but was otherwise shy, preoccupied, and devoted to his wife and to a world of melody unknown to others around him.

But Scott's music is not forgotten. The sensitivity, craftsmanship, and virtuosity of his piano rags is now recognized. *Frog Legs Rag, Grace and Beauty, Climax Rag, Hilarity Rag, Ragtime Oriole,* and others have now been reprinted and are recorded and performed again. The ex-bootblack from Missouri is hailed, albeit belatedly, as "the crown prince of ragtime." James Scott quietly enriched the realm of music, and his enchanting works are likely to endure for centuries.

Notes

1. Rudi Blesh and Harriet Janis, *They All Played Ragtime*, 4th ed., rev. (New York: Oak Publications, 1971), p. 115.
2. Interview with Thomas Hart Benton, native of Neosho, Missouri, May 1963.
3. Interview with Bessie Anna Geneva Scott Farris (1895–1978), sister of James Scott, Neosho, Missouri, 17 December 1973 (hereafter Bessie Farris).
4. Ibid.
5. Ibid.
6. Blesh and Janis, p. 112.
7. Interview with Bessie Farris.
8. Blesh and Janis, pp. 112–13.
9. Interviews with Bessie Walker Hickman (piano student of Emma Johns DeArmond at Carthage, Missouri, and acquaintance of James Scott from 1902 to 1915), 2 May 1969 and 8 April 1977. Odessa Wyman McBean (born 1890), in a letter to the author dated 15 April 1976 written for her by her daughter M. Pauline York, stated that she was one of a group of students, among whom also were James Scott and Clarence Woods, who played for each other and shared group criticism. Mrs. McBean later became a theater pianist-organist.
10. Blesh and Janis, pp. 112–13.
11. Interview with Bessie Farris.
12. Interview with Ray Rose, professional ragtime pianist, Carthage, Missouri, 18 May 1976. Marvin L. Van Gilder, *The Carthage Press Bicentennial Ragtime Festival Commemorative Edition*, 27 May 1976, pp. 28–30. *Carthage Souvenir Booklet* (*Carthage Democrat*, 1901). Interviews from 1958 to 1974 with Carl Fry, circus band cornetist, and Homer Clark, jazz clarinetist, both of whom worked with James Scott at Lakeside Park; with George McFadden (1876–1977), lifelong resident of Carthage and vicinity; with John H. Flanigan, Sr., Floyd Meador, and E. S. Glenn, members of pioneer Carthage families that knew James Scott; and with J. Byron Fly, judge of the Jasper County Court and veteran Joplin, Missouri, professional trombonist and official of Local 620, American Federation of Musicians.
13. Blesh and Janis, p. 115; interview with Bessie Farris.
14. Interview with Mary Kellogg (Carthage piano instructor and contemporary of James Scott as student in 1902 at Calhoun School of Music), July 1964.
15. Blesh and Janis, p. 113; interview with Vola Lindley Huggins (customer of Dumars Music Company from 1910 to 1917), 4 April 1976; telephone interview with Ed Stebbins (member of Carthage, Missouri, Fire Department, 1910–15), 5 March 1976.
16. Blesh and Janis, p. 113.
17. Ibid.
18. Interview with Vola Huggins; interview with Ed Stebbins.

19. The advertisement appeared on the front cover of Clarence Woods' *The Meteor: March and Two-Step* (Carthage, Mo.: Dumars Music Co., 1904).

20. Blesh and Janis, p. 114; interview with Bessie Farris.

21. Interviews with Robert R. Darch, professional ragtime pianist, Newtonia, Missouri, 1968, and Carthage, Missouri, 1974 and 1975.

22. Interview with Vola Huggins; interview with Mary Kellogg. Carthage city directories list James Scott as residing from 1910 to 1911 at 707 East Sixth Street and as employed by Dumars-Gammon Music Company, 123 East Third Street. From 1915 to 1916, James and Nora Scott had a residence at 501 Budlong Street in Carthage. In 1917 the Scotts were listed as residents of 729 East Sixth Street in Carthage and James was identified as a musician for the Delphus Theater, 114 East Fourth Street. The directories indicate that James and Nora Scott continued to maintain a Carthage residence until at least 1920.

23. Interview with Robert Darch.

24. Rudi Blesh and Harriet Janis, *They All Played Ragtime*, 3rd ed., rev. (New York: Oak Publications, 1966).

25. Interview with Bessie Hickman.

26. Interview with Bessie Farris.

27. Ibid.

28. Blesh and Janis (p. 115) indicate that Scott moved to Kansas City about 1914, but subsequent research suggests that it was not until about 1920 that Scott became a resident of Kansas City. He is listed in Carthage city directories through 1920. His first listing in city directories of Kansas City is in 1922, identified as a music teacher, 402 Nebraska Avenue, Kansas City, Kansas.

29. Blesh and Janis, p. 115.

30. Ibid. Another cousin was the noted blues singer Ada Brown (1890–1950).

31. Ibid., p. 117.

32. John Edward Hasse, telephone interview with Lawrence Denton (born 1893), Kansas City, Missouri, 28 December 1977.

33. Ibid.

34. Ibid.

35. John Edward Hasse, telephone interview with Herman Walder (black musician from Kansas City), 29 December 1977.

36. "New Music for Eblon Theatre," *Kansas City American*, 1 November 1928, p. 3.

37. Blesh and Janis, p. 118.

38. Kansas City, Kansas, city directories in the collection of the Kansas City, Kansas, Public Library.

39. Blesh and Janis, p. 118. In an interview, Bessie Farris said that Lena Scott King, Jimmy's older sister, also lived with Ruth and James.

40. Interview with Mrs. Farris; Blesh and Janis, p. 118.

41. State of Kansas, State Board of Health, Division of Vital Statistics, Standard Certificate of Death for James Scott.

42. "A Memorial for James Scott," *Rag Times* 13 (January 1980): 6; "James Scott Memorial Dedication Ceremony," *Rag Times* 15 (July 1981): 6.

The Ragtime Kid (An Autobiography)

S. Brunson Campbell

Brun Campbell reportedly was Scott Joplin's only white pupil. In this colorful article from 1952, Campbell provides firsthand information on Scott Joplin, the ragtime scene in Missouri, and the life of itinerant pianists. During the 1940s, he began a second career in ragtime, writing about the music and making recordings that document his style of early or "folk ragtime" playing.

I was born in Washington, Kansas, March 26, 1884, and as far back as I can remember I was raised in an atmosphere of excitement, my parents rushing me to the cyclone cellar everytime there was a bad wind or hail storm, or my grandfather telling me exciting stories of the "Old West": stories about the Gold Rush of '49, of Indians and outlaws and of the great herds of buffalo that roamed the plains. And I met many of the old pioneers as I was growing to manhood. My grandfather had purchased thousands of acres of Kansas land from the government for 50¢ an acre, and when he moved to Oberlin, a small town in northwestern Kansas, Decatur County, he brought father, mother and myself with him.

The railroad was pushing westward at the time, crossing his land, and he established two towns along the proposed right-of-way. One of the towns was named Allison. It was to be a railroad division town and was to have a roundhouse and machine shop. It quickly grew to about 500 inhabitants in anticipation of the railroad's coming. But heavy rain storms washed out the graded right-of-way and when a new survey was made grandfather's two towns were by-passed and left inland. Then a severe drought ruined all

From *Jazz Report* 6 [ca. 1967–68]: 7–12. Reprinted by permission.

western Kansas crops, caused great hardships and left my grandfather bankrupt. He returned to Rochester, N.Y., broken in health, and died there a few years later.

My parents decided to stay in Kansas and grow up with the country. Father turned to the barber trade and opened a one-chair shop in Oberlin. He became very popular with the yound blades of the town and in a short time had three other barbers working for him. He prospered and invested his money in town affairs and held various city positions. He played the guitar and sang and formed a real "barbershop quartet," which sang at parties and civic affairs. We were all very happy.

Dreaming of better things, father decided to move to St. Joseph, Mo., so we left the little town in Kansas. He hoped to find a position as a traveling salesman but was unable to do so and again turned to barbering. I was about nine years old then, and it was not long before I became one of St. Joseph's "Dead End Kids," selling newspapers and shining shoes on the streets. My father soon caught up with me and put me out of business.

The newspapers were running articles about the coming opening of the Cherokee Strip in Indian Territory and one day father came home all excited. He said to commence packing as we were moving to Arkansas City, Kansas, for the opening. In the spring of 1893 we arrived at Arkansas City, just four miles from the "Strip." It was one of the towns along the Kansas and Indian Territory line, where crowds of people were pouring in from all over to register for their right to take part. Father obtained a job barbering and was very busy, working all day and most of the night. . . .

On September 16, 1893, the signal shots rang out from the trooper's guns and these thousands of people started out as pioneers of the Cherokee Strip. My father made the run, but he must have gotten in his own road for he was not successful in staking out a claim. After the run many of those not fortunate enough to make a stake returned to their old states. Others stayed in the new country and worked and grew up with it. . . .

My parents decided to stay in Arkansas City, so we settled there and I entered school. I also began piano lessons and in a short time was playing the popular songs of the day. Father secured a position as traveling salesman for a wholesale grocery firm, doing well and receiving several salary raises, but eventually became involved in some sort of disagreement with the management of the firm and was discharged. Shortly thereafter he was engaged as salesman by the largest wholesale grocery firm in Indian Territory at Guthrie, Oklahoma, and in time transferred to the firm headquarters at Oklahoma City, then was assigned the territory west of El Reno, so we moved to El Reno, Oklahoma. As soon as we were settled in our new home I took more piano lessons. By this time I was playing pretty "hot" ragtime piano.

The following year the government opened up more land for settlement, but this time it was to be a drawing for claims instead of a "land rush" or "race." El Reno was the main town for the drawing. I was then 16 and clerking at the Kerfoot Hotel, the main El Reno hotel, where the sample room was used as the place for registering. Imagine the crowd of people that came to that Oklahoma town of 7500 for the drawing! It was estimated at one time that there were over one hundred thousand there. . . .

I saw one of the funniest jokes ever played in a saloon in El Reno. It was played on the customers by the bartender. He suspended a string from the ceiling and let it hang down to just within reach and on the end he tied a lead from a 44-calibre shell with a sign attached which read: "Don't touch! This is the bullet that killed Jesse James." You would see some customer slowly edge his way to where the bullet was suspended, and when he thought no one was watching he would jerk it from the string and sneak out the back door with the "bullet that killed Jesse James." The bartender told me that in one day he had replaced the bullet over one hundred times. You don't happen to have one of these "bullets that killed Jesse James," do you?

I saw Billie Morgan, a notorious gambler, operate a "drop-case" and take a "sucker" for several hundred dollars right on a street corner in the main part of town. I saw the original "Arkansas Kid" break the Attic Gambling House. I saw Frenchie La Britten, a high powered gambler, win ten thousand dollars on the cut of the cards. El Reno was sure a wild town during those days, with lots of gun fights, and on top of that the soldiers from Fort El Reno, when they had gotten around too much liquor would shoot up the town and the "red-light" district once in a while. Everyone seemed to be making money hand over fist, so I decided to make myself some easy money too. At every saloon that had a piano in it I would step in and play a few ragtime pieces and pick up a few dollars from the customers. One day I was playing some hot rags and some barbershop chord numbers for some fellows who had been drinking and felt like harmonizing, when in walked my father, hotter than some of the rags I had been playing. He and I really had a good time in the "old wood shed." He said it hurt him more than it did me to whip me, but I had heard that one before, so in a few days I would make the rounds of the saloons again and pick up some more easy money playing piano. In those days the laws were not as strict about a kid coming into a saloon or gambling house as they are today.

I met a young pianist by the name of Egbert Van Alstyne, who was the piano player for a musical show from New York that got stranded in El Reno. He stayed at my parents' home until he received funds to return to New York. Mr. Van Alstyne later became one of America's popular song writers. He wrote such hits as *In the Shade of the Old Apple Tree* and those early Indian song hits *Navajo* and *Cheyenne*. He told me in later years that his inspiration to write an Indian song came while he was watching the Cheyenne Indians as they passed through El Reno on their yearly visit to another tribe. He was a pioneer composer of Indian song hits.

One of my biggest thrills came when I played Scott Joplin's *Maple Leaf Rag* for Gordon Lillie (Pawnee Bill) in the Kerfoot Hotel. I played it just as Joplin had taught me a year or so before. He liked the way I played and twenty years later when I met him again in Tulsa he asked me to play *Maple Leaf* for him again. I think there will never be a musical number written that will last in popularity as Joplin's *Maple Leaf*. It is a great monument to a great Negro ragtime pioneer.

In course of time those who had come to El Reno for the drawing began to leave and it was not long before the city was back to normal. My father took to drink and gambling and lost his position with the grocery firm. He could not stand prosperity. Mother and he separated. She sold all our belongings, including my piano, and with my younger brother moved back to Arkansas City. I started out on my own. I played piano wherever I could find a job, and in about five years I was one of the best ragtime players in the middle west. I had been taught how to play by Scott Joplin, who taught me his *Maple Leaf Rag* and his other early numbers in 1898 when I was about fifteen years old. I pioneered the playing of ragtime along with those early Negro pianists and composers of Sedalia and Saint Louis.

Playing ragtime was an exciting life. I met and played for many notable people: Teddy Roosevelt, Bill Cody (Buffalo Bill), Gordon Lillie (Pawnee Bill), Governor Ferguson of Indian Territory, George Evans (Honey Boy Evans), Lew Dockstader, the great minstrel man. These last were mostly auditions. Salary differences kept me from signing contracts with them as a featured ragtime piano act. I realized later that I had made the greatest mistake of my life in not doing so. I also played ragtime for famous outlaws and other men, such as Frank Jones, Cole Younger, Emmet Dalton, Henry Starr, Old Bat Masterson, Bud Ledbetter, Heck Thomas, and many others including the famous Hobo A#1, who was in reality a railroad detective.

There is an old proverb, Arabian, I believe, to the effect that a man's fate is hung around his neck like a collar that cannot be removed, which amounts to saying we all have a destiny we cannot lose. It was my destiny to become one of the pioneer ragtime pianists of the 1890s.

It was in 1898 that fate introduced me to Negro ragtime. A friend and I ran away to Oklahoma City to a celebration being held there. We became separated and I wandered into the Armstrong-Byrd music store and began to play some of the popular tunes of the day. A crowd gathered to listen, encouraged me with applause and called for more. After a time a young mulatto, light complexioned, dressed to perfection and smiling pleasantly, came forward. He placed a pen-and-ink manuscript of music in front of me entitled *Maple Leaf Rag*, by Scott Joplin. I played it and he seemed impressed. (He afterwards told me I had made two mistakes.) He turned out to be Otis Saunders, a fine pianist and ragtime composer, a pal of Scott Joplin and one of ragtime's first pioneers. I learned from him that Joplin was then living in Sedalia and that he, Saunders, was joining him there in a few days.

I returned home, but a roaming propensity and a newly awakened interest in ragtime prompted me to run away again. This time I headed for Sedalia and after riding in box cars, cattle cars, and "blind baggage," I finally reached there and lost no time seeking out Otis Saunders and Scott Joplin, who was playing piano in a tavern there. At Saunders' request, I played for Joplin. They both thought I played fine piano and Joplin agreed to teach me

Brun Campbell, "The Ragtime Kid." (*Courtesy Rudi Blesh*)

his style of ragtime. He taught me how to play his first four rags, the *Original Rags*, *Maple Leaf Rag*, *Sun Flower Slow Drag*, and *Swipesy Cake Walk*. I was the first white pianist to play and master his famous *Maple Leaf*.

I became a kid ragtime pianist, the "Original Ragtime Kid" of the nineties, and met almost all of the early Negro pianists and composers of ragtime. Such greats as Tom Turpin, Scott Joplin, Otis Saunders, Scott Hayden, Arthur Marshall, Louis Chauvin, Tony Williams, Tony Jackson, Melford Alexander, Jelly Roll Morton, Jim and Ida Hastings and "Ink" Howard. Saint Louis, Sedalia, and Kansas City were the three most important cities of ragtime's beginning. Sedalia was the "hub" of the ragtime wheel, and the most important. The George R. Smith College, a higher educational college for Negroes, was located there and many Negroes came to Smith College to take courses in music. . . .

There were many fine Negro musicians in Sedalia in those days and Scott Joplin was the greatest. He was very studious, wanted to go places in music, and he did. He also played cornet and was something of a singer. Other Sedalia pianists who helped make a ragtime history were the previously mentioned Otis Saunders, Scott Hayden, Arthur Marshall, Tony Williams and Melford Alexander and Jim and Ida Hastings. Sedalia was a wide-open town in those days, with saloons, gambling houses, dance halls, a

red-light district and it was in these places the pianists could be found
selling their musical wares. Two very popular clubs were the Maple Leaf
and the 400 Special Club, run by the Williams brothers, friends of Joplin.

Sedalia prided itself as being first with ragtime band and orchestra as
well as ragtime piano. The Negro band organized at Sedalia in 1891, who
called themselves the "Queen City Negro Brass Band," [Ed. Note: Campbell
undoubtedly means "Queen City Concert Band"] was the first "Street and
Parade Band" in America to play Joplin's *Maple Leaf Rag, Sunflower Slow Drag,*
and Tom Turpin's *Bowery Buck,* three of the first rags written. Out of this
band Joplin took five pieces and formed the first ragtime orchestra in
America.

Not much happened along the ragtime route until 1897, when several
feeble attempts at ragtime composition took place. In that year Tom Turpin,
a Negro pianist of Saint Louis, wrote and had published [by Robert De Yong
of Saint Louis] a tune called *The Harlem Rag.* This was claimed to be the first
rag ever written. It *was* the first of a more advanced style and it wasn't long
before the district around Chestnut and Market and West 18th Streets was
rocking to Tom Turpin's *Harlem Rag.* While a good number, it was not in
true ragtime form, and it was rearranged three different times. Another
Negro musician, William Tyers, finally put it in the true ragtime mold and it
was published by Joseph Stern of New York.

It was Scott Joplin over at Sedalia who set the true ragtime pattern in
1897 with *Original Rags.* This was published in 1899 by Carl Hoffman of
Kansas City. If that rag did not convince the critics that Joplin was the
"ragtime master," then his next did, for it was his famous *Maple Leaf Rag* of
1899. It became the "classic" of all rags and today it is the most beloved of
the Ragtime Era. Ragtime was the Negro's music, but it was the white man
who made it popular. They first heard it in the Negro districts of Sedalia,
Kansas City and Saint Louis. They invited the Negro pianist into their
homes to play for their parties and dances, and with the publication of
Joplin's *Maple Leaf* ragtime spread like wild fire to all corners of the globe.

None of the original pianists played ragtime the way it was written.
They played their own style. Some played march time, fast time, slow time
and some played ragtime blues style. But none of them lost the melody and
if you knew the player and heard him a block away you could name him by
his ragtime style.

Ragtime piano contests originated in Sedalia and were later held in Saint
Louis and Kansas City and drew large crowds. Louis Chauvin, a great Negro
improvisor of natural ability, was top pianist around Saint Louis. He is
given credit for teaching Joplin to play ragtime, but that is not so. They did
exchange ideas about trick arrangements and difficult passages and other
points but to say he was Joplin's teacher is pure "bunk." Ragtime was a pool
of many men's ideas, and the one who could put it down on paper was
considered the rightful composer even if he did not originate the tune. . . .

Scott Joplin named me the "Ragtime Kid" after he had taught me to play
his first four rags, and as I was leaving him and Sedalia to return to my

home in Kansas he gave me a bright, new, shiny half dollar and called my attention to the date on it. "Kid," he said, "This half dollar is dated 1897, the year I wrote my first rag. Carry it for good luck and as you go through life it will always be a reminder of your early ragtime days here at Sedalia." There was a strange look in his eyes which I shall never forget.

Well, I carried that half dollar as a good luck pocket piece as Joplin suggested. Then in 1903 I met another pianist in a midwestern city and we became chums. One day we decided to go frog hunting down at the river near by. We got into a friendly argument as to who was the best shot, so I took my silver half dollar and placed it in a crack on top of a fence post as a target. We measured off and my friend fired and missed. I shot and hit it dead center. The impact of the bullet really put it out of shape, so on our return to the city I went to a blacksmith shop and with a hammer reshaped it as best I could and then carried it as a pocket piece as before. But one day I somehow spent it.

Years later I married and moved to California. On May 1, 1930, a customer came into my place of business and paid for a purchase with the same silver half dollar I had used for a target 27 years before. My lucky piece had returned to me. I could hardly believe my eyes, but there it was—right in my hand. As I kept looking at it and turning it over the panorama of my life as a ragtime pianist unfolded before me and I could see the strange look in Scott Joplin's eyes as he gave it to me, and that half dollar seemed to say: "Why don't you write about Scott Joplin and early ragtime. Write his biography and other articles and sell them to magazines and newspapers."

And then it seemed to say: "Don't you think it would be nice to make a piano recording of his *Maple Leaf Rag* just as he taught you back there in Sedalia, and use the money from these sources to erect a memorial monument over his unmarked grave for what he did in the field of early American music?" I did all that with the exception that I never erected the monument. Instead I sent the money to his widow to help her in an illness of long standing.

As early as the turn of the century Joplin had the idea that his fine ragtime music could stand up with the best of the so-called better music. In an attempt to prove it he wrote an opera entitled *A Guest of Honor*, in 1903. But it had weak lyrics and the publisher, John Stark & Sons of Saint Louis, withdrew it.* But he never gave up the idea, for in 1911 he published his second effort, a three-act ragtime opera called *Treemonisha*. It was performed once in New York at the Lincoln Theater but casting was poor and it did not come up to his expectations. He grieved himself to death. He thought his

---

* *Editor's Note: A Guest of Honor* was never published. The Copyright Office received an application dated February 18, 1903, but the music manuscript never arrived; it may have been lost in the mail. Campbell may here be confusing *A Guest of Honor* with Joplin's *The "Rag Time Dance,"* which Stark did publish and which proved commercially unsuccessful. See Addison W. Reed's chapter, "Scott Joplin, Pioneer."—*JEH*

music unappreciated and once said, "Maybe fifty years after I am dead it will be." He died in 1917.

Each carriage in his funeral procession carried the name of one of his compositions. *Maple Leaf Rag* was on the first. *Maple Leaf* was the true beginning of his career and was published by John Stark. Stark also published the composition that closed his career, *Reflection*, in 1917, the year of his death.

His widow once wrote me, "Of all Scott's old friends, you are the only one who has ever offered to do anything for him." It was the least the "Ragtime Kid" could do for an old friend.

May Aufderheide and the Ragtime Women

Max Morath

Though the best-known ragtime composers were men, many women wrote rags. In this new study, Max Morath chronicles the life of May Aufderheide, the most successful of the ragtime women, and describes some of the other women writers of rag. He explores sexual roles in American music of this era, and sets forth several seeming paradoxes in ragtime and musical culture of the Ragtime Era. As a supplement to this chapter, there is, at the back of the book, a first-ever listing of ragtime compositions by women.

It should come as no surprise that there were dozens of quality rags composed by amateur and professional female pianists in the early years of the twentieth century.[1] The wonder is that there were not *more*.

Belated discovery of the importance of the women of ragtime speaks not only of the indifference accorded these women and, indeed, female composers generally. It speaks also of the difficulty of drawing a clear line of development back to ragtime and other early forms of American popular music. It calls into question our oversimplified assumptions of neat and orderly cultural patterns and our quick-setting clichés on the roles of class, race, and gender in a musical history whose hearty disorder we try vainly to organize.

Curious paradoxes abound: Ragtime was "black," the ragtime women were white; ragtime, born tough and considered an underworld threat, matured quickly into middle-class gentility; women of the time were still "in the home," but thousands broke away and prospered in the tumultuous show business of the time. They equaled and often outnumbered men in many performing categories, but not, strangely, as pianists and composers, even though there were probably ten female pianists for every male pianist in the population generally.

Consider: A syncopated musical style that emerged from complex sources in nineteenth-century America matured around 1900 into a distinct genre for the piano. Developed by gifted young black musicians, and taking the curious name "ragtime," it then spread through middle-class America like a prairie fire. Its rampant success was due not only to undeniable musical appeal. Ragtime surfaced just as our mercantile nation was ready for the boosting of a national music. The tools for the job were then on hand: the phonograph, the five-and-ten-cent store, traveling salesmen and vaudeville troupers riding trains into village and town, and most important for ragtime, a prodigious production of pianos.

And who were the pianists of turn-of-the-century America? Women. The great majority of pianists were unquestionably middle-class white women, keyboard trained in the European manner, participating in America's booming quest for culture. It was mainly our grandmothers who purchased those colorful rags in hundred-thousand-copy lots, succumbing to ragtime's lure, often as not in the face of stormy parental objection. And it is the sweetest of ironies that they successfully conveyed this genial music of the sporting house and the wine shop to the parlor and the tea dance without knowing (or, what is more intriguing, not *caring*) about its racy genealogy.

Of course, there were men at the piano, too. The ragtime years coincide with a great era of piano virtuosity in classical music dominated by males. But this was the European tradition; we Americans were busy with our schizoid rejection of all that, slavishly adoring European tradition on one hand, scorning it on the other. In this brawling, free-wheeling young country a man ought to be playing cards, not piano!

The young black male pianist was less torn by this conflict, and it was perhaps the vigor of the black musicians, bringing ragtime and jazz, that restored a gender-balanced image to the piano. But at the turn of the century, piano lessons were for little girls; little boys played ball and went fishing. And if a stern parent insisted on musical training, violin lessons were usually prescribed for the male child.

Look at the old advertisements. Seated at the early-twentieth-century piano is a woman. And the piano, of course, is almost always an upright.

The upright piano was collectively invented in Europe and the United States in the nineteenth century, and by the late 1880s the complicated upright action had been thoroughly perfected.[2] And what a happy invention it was! Like its contemporary, the phonograph, and like the radio to come, it brought music to The People. The upright did not cost a fortune, nor did it demand a drawing room in which to reside, as did the imposing grand pianos that were the pride of the musical elite. The upright was designed to stand against a wall, as if its inventors had plotted its shape to fit a typical middle-class parlor in city or village. Sales figures are astonishing, reaching a peak of over 364,000 pianos sold in 1909, and averaging around 300,000 per year during the first two decades.[3] Of those five million or so pianos, most were hardy uprights.

So here was a lovely confluence of technical and economic and artistic forces: a new kind of piano, entering a consumer society now tied together by rails and sales; a new popular music, called ragtime, with a hustling trade to market it; and millions of piano-playing Americans, most of them female, with increasing hours of leisure time on their hands. Many of these female pianists played ragtime, and of course they wrote it, too!

Musically the women's rags reveal a wide range of style and quality, as would a similar sampling of rags by male composers, or for that matter of any brand of popular music in any period. For every good and inventive piece there are always dozens and dozens of stale and imitative ones, and the ladies of ragtime were just as capable as their gentlemen competitors of turning out syncopated potboilers.

With the exception of *Pickles and Peppers* (Adaline Shepherd) and a handful of others, the compositions of the ragtime women were not wildly popular across America, especially with the non-piano-playing citizen. But then it is worth recalling that the same was true of almost all piano rags in those first two decades. Only Scott Joplin's *Maple Leaf Rag* and a few others enjoyed great popularity. Until their subsequent revivals, piano rags generally found favor only with pianists. The public knew America's music was ragtime, all right, but to most people "ragtime" meant songs and, after 1910 or so, dances. Ragtime was *Waiting for the Robert E. Lee* or the *Grizzly Bear Rag*, not Joplin's *Gladiolus Rag* or Julia Niebergall's *Red Rambler Rag*. Even after his smash *Maple Leaf*, Joplin's rags probably enjoyed no greater sales than the rags of the more successful of the ragtime women—May Aufderheide, Adaline Shepherd, Charlotte Blake. Female composers of piano rags entered a well-defined marketplace that promised the same unpredictable success that music publishing has always offered. They took their chances, and they left their mark.

This essay on the ragtime women does not attempt anything beyond a partial listing of their works, and a cursory examination of some of their individual lives. All of those studied lived and worked at some point during the prime ragtime years of 1897 to 1917. Some of their compositions were quite successful in their time, measured by sales and popular impact.

Biographical research on these women began with my decision to record a complete long-playing album of rags by turn-of-the-century women composers, eventually released in October of 1977.[4] Inquiry into the lives of the women, to provide programing and promotional information, proved quite difficult and in some cases—Charlotte Blake, Mabel Tilton, Louise V. Gustin—yielded no details at all. For others—Adaline Shepherd, May Aufderheide, Muriel Pollock—information was forthcoming after considerable digging. As the deadline (July 15, 1977) for the album's liner notes was reached, sufficient information was available to provide thumbnail biographies of several composers. Some of these biographies have been fleshed out and updated here, and a few recently found nuggets of information on other ragtime women are presented.

I have elected to treat in detail the life of May Aufderheide of Indianapolis, Indiana, one of the prime figures—male or female—in piano ragtime. Her known published works number nineteen pieces, including seven rags, an output considerably more extensive than those of such acknowledged male figures as Louis Chauvin, Scott Hayden, or Clarence Woods. Happily, May Aufderheide has also proven to be the most accessible for biographical study, achieved mainly through interviews with surviving family members. Also, the past prominence of her family in Indianapolis society assured considerable coverage by newspapers and historical associations.

May Frances Aufderheide was born in Indianapolis, Indiana, on May 21, 1890, the daughter of John Henry and Lucy Deel Aufderheide. She had one brother, Rudolph (1891–1955). Her father (1865–1941) became a wealthy man in the small loan business, presiding over a company that grew eventually to eighty-one offices in eleven states. The Aufderheides could not be more typical of those middle-class American families from which the ragtime women emerged. John H., true to form, studied the violin as a child, and continued to play as an adult; as a member of the Art Association and the Orchestra Association of Indianapolis, he supported the musical and cultural life of the city.[5]

His sister May Kolmer (1877–1956) was a superb musician, typical of those middle-class white women of the late nineteenth century whose education inevitably incorporated a thorough musical training.[6] She achieved a high degree of professional musicianship: She performed with the Indianapolis Symphony at the old Tomlinson Hall, taught piano for many years at the Metropolitan School of Music, and then taught privately during much of her later life.[7] And it was she who taught piano to her niece, imparting to May a degree of that same solid grounding in classics and technique that she herself had encountered as a child. Young May, remembers her cousin, Mrs. Russell Veit, "played very well," though she "played only the popular things." This again fits the pattern, as women of May's generation were caught up in the craze for popular music, probably against the wishes of their elders.

In fields other than music May certainly received a much better than average education for a female of her time. She was sent east to Pelham Manor, a finishing school, and upon graduation was taken by her parents on a European tour. Her niece, Mrs. Joan Aufderheide Thompson, quotes from May's diaries many remarks reflecting her youthful excitement during this trip, her enthusiasm at being taken to the theater and to the opera in New York and abroad.[8]

In the brief period between her return from Europe to Indianapolis and her marriage in 1908, May Aufderheide must have been very busy with music and composition and enjoying life immensely. Her scrapbooks and diaries reveal an almost idyllic flurry of courtship and socializing. This was from 1906 to 1907; ragtime was a burgeoning force in popular music by then, if not the nationwide craze it would become a few years later when the publication of *Alexander's Ragtime Band* (Irving Berlin, 1911) made it a household word.

May Aufderheide's first application for copyright appears on February 6, 1908, for *Dusty Rag*, the two published copies being received at the Copyright Office on April 10 of that year. *Dusty* is a straightforward, solid rag, and, unlike most rags, it apparently lent itself well to the infant New Orleans jazz idiom, as did her later rag *The Thriller Rag* (1909): both pieces were played from memory thirty-odd years later by the great New Orleans trumpeter Bunk Johnson.[9] *Dusty* was originally issued by the Duane Crabb Publishing Company of Indianapolis, with Mr. Crabb designing the red and black sheet music cover. Sales figures are not available, but judging from the presence of *Dusty* copies in modern sheet music collections, it enjoyed steady sales. Steady enough, at least, to encourage John H. Aufderheide himself to enter the publishing business.

John H., already a rising executive and financier, opened his publishing company later in 1908, *Dusty Rag* being duly transferred to it late in that year. *Dusty* began a long list of compositions by May Aufderheide to be published by this, for a time, highly successful Indianapolis firm.

Upon discovering that May Aufderheide was published almost exclusively by a firm owned by her father, one is tempted to downgrade her work by dismissing her father's efforts as those of a doting parent, the publishing operation nothing more than a vanity press. John H. Aufderheide and Company, Music Publishers, however, quickly became the proprietor of a catalog listing many Indiana composers. If this were a vanity press, operated by a wealthy man for a dubiously talented daughter, its owner would certainly not have sought out and published so many other composers.

By the summer of 1909, news of May Aufderheide's rags and of the Aufderheide publishing enterprise had made the New York trade journals. The *American Musician and Art Journal* reported:[10]

"CLASSIC RAGS" COMPOSED
BY MAY AUFDERHEIDE

Talented Indianapolis Girl Is Achieving Enviable Reputation

That the syncopation in rag music does not necessarily mean that this class of music is unworthy and below the notice of lovers of good music is proven by the work May Aufderheide, the young Indianapolis composer, is doing.

Formerly very popular only as a pianist, she has of late doubled that asset by the success she is achieving as a "classic rag" writer. Her first important "rag," "Dusty," created such attention that her father, J. H. Aufderheide, decided to do a little publishing as a side line.

Miss Aufderheide truly saw that the sales of "Dusty" would be large and, encouraged, composed "Richmond Rag," which blossomed forth and attracted much popularity. Both "Dusty" and "Richmond Rag" are now in considerable demand.

Miss Aufderheide's compositions are invariably written in a popular vein, but, thorough and true artist that she is, there is much in her work that makes a strong appeal to lovers of true music. Her compositions take spontaneously with the public, so delightfully and persistently infectious are they.

About the time that "Richmond Rag" was produced, Mr. Aufderheide employed P. C. Pratt, a capable and enterprising manager, to look after his publishing interests and Mr. Pratt is gradually and surely working the business up to a broader standpoint, and a short time will see this house prominent among other leading publishers.

Miss Aufderheide has two new rags on the press that, judging from the past, will be sure winners: "Buzzer Rag" and "The Thriller" are the titles and our readers will surely not regret communicating with J. H. Aufderheide who has his offices in the Lemcke Building, Indianapolis, Ind.

Besides the lucrative business of publishing his daughter's compositions, Mr. Aufderheide is a small jobber in a way, handling other publishers' music. He also publishes the charming waltz song, "I'll Pledge My Heart To You," and the celebrated "Vanity Rag."

Keep your eye (and ears) on Miss Aufderheide's works.

(John Edward Hasse collection)

If May Aufderheide's upbringing and education were typical of the ragtime women, her adult life continued to reveal much in common with her sister composers. She entered into an early marriage, which was at first to affect her life positively and creatively, and then to draw her away from music and into tragedy and loneliness.

In 1908 she married a young architect, Thomas Kaufman, from Richmond, Indiana, home of the Starr Piano Company. Mrs. Russell Veit recalls her cousin May remarking that the days in Richmond "were the happiest of her life." This joyful state could well account for the relatively large number of compositions she produced during the four years following her marriage. In the year after her marriage came a rag named for her husband's hometown, *The Richmond Rag*. Two rags followed in 1909—*Buzzer Rag* and *The Thriller Rag*. *A Totally Different Rag* and *Blue Ribbon Rag* appeared in 1910; and *Novelty Rag* was published in 1911. Certainly these publication dates, indeed the dates of all her published works, coincide with those "happiest days of her life" in Richmond, Indiana.

This tranquil and creative period was to be short lived, however. The young Mr. and Mrs. Kaufman soon returned to Indianapolis, where Kaufman tried his hand, apparently without success, at a career in architecture in that city. For whatever reason—the hinted failure at his chosen profession or the lure of a position in his father-in-law's fast-growing loan company—Thomas Kaufman became associated with the Commonwealth Loan Company in 1916.[11] And in spite of the fact that May Aufderheide Kaufman now settled into a life of considerable affluence and social standing, her creative days waned, and she was to confront mounting frustration and eventual tragedy.

Of course, these teen years of the new century, during which the Aufderheide publishing company also closed its books, coincide with the twilight of ragtime popularity in the United States. May Aufderheide's creative decay may also have been influenced by this declining market. But then, popular music generally continued its booming growth, and May seemed unable, or unwilling, to attempt the transition into the newer forms of popular music, as did many other young composers, both male and female—Muriel Pollock, for instance.

The subsequent years—the 1920s, thirties and forties—reveal no musical activity from May Aufderheide Kaufman. Her cousin recalls that during the 1930s she cannot remember May's playing the piano at all; she seemed to have "given up on her music" totally. The Kaufmans were unable to have children of their own, and May's attentions were focused on their adopted daughter, Lucy. In early 1947 Thomas Kaufman resigned as board chairman of the Commonwealth firm, and he and May moved to California. But if the Kaufmans retired to California with substantial wealth, they also brought with them from Indiana mounting health problems and deteriorating family life. Family members acknowledge that Thomas Kaufman had long since become an incurable alcoholic; the Kaufman's daughter Lucy had developed deep personal problems, drinking among the least of them. During the 1950s May became increasingly withdrawn, suffered constantly from arthritis, and was overwhelmed by the problems of her husband and her daughter. Lucy Kaufman died in 1958, and Thomas Kaufman died a year or so later. May now "came out" somewhat, and regained a measure of the joviality and high spirits she had as a youth. She continued, however, to be plagued by arthritis and suffered a number of strokes, which confined her to a wheelchair during the last years of her life. She died in Pasadena on September 1, 1972.

May Frances Aufderheide had a strong creative urge that, nurtured by training at the piano, took musical form early in her life. She was fortunate enough to see publication of much of her work, and a relative degree of success for a few pieces. Had she been a man, would she have enjoyed a lifelong career in music or publishing? Might she, on the other hand, have gone into her father's booming loan business as did her brother Rudolph, who also displayed some musical talent? Success in popular music is tenuous, for men as well as women, and the prospect of financial security in other endeavors has led many composers and performers away from early promise and success in music.

The fact that ragtime was first a product of mid-America is substantiated over and over again as the women of ragtime emerge to join the already well-delineated male personalities. Detroit, Chicago, Kansas City, Nashville, Cincinnati, Saint Louis, Indianapolis—these were the early ragtime citadels.

Julia Niebergall and Gladys Yelvington, like May Aufderheide, were from Indiana. Julia Lee Niebergall (1886–1968) is reported by relatives "to have made her living by playing the piano all her life." She came from a musical home in which her father played the bass viol, her brother the drums, and a sister the piano. But she was the only professional musician to emerge from the family.[12]

There is a strong tone of independence in many of the ragtime women, typified in Julia Niebergall. Married once as a young woman, she sought a divorce shortly thereafter, and restored her maiden name. Maintaining her own home until she died at age eighty-two, she was reportedly one of the first women in Indianapolis to own an automobile. She was involved throughout her life in Indianapolis musical circles, was pianist at the Colonial Theatre in Indianapolis, and later earned a living as a professional accompanist for dance classes.

Gladys Yelvington (1891–1957) is another of the ragtime women whose musical career ended with marriage. She worked as a silent movie pianist in Elwood, Indiana, but never played professionally again after her marriage to Leo Parson in 1912. Although *Piffle Rag* was Yelvington's only published work, her family remembers that "she could make a piano or organ talk, laugh or cry—either rags or classics."[13]

Adaline Shepherd's *Pickles and Peppers* (1906) was evidently the biggest seller produced by any of the ragtime women; copies of this "ragtime oddity" still turn up with dependable regularity in stacks of old music. Published also for orchestra and for military band—as many of the rags were—it was in steady use by William Jennings Bryan in his 1908 drive for the presidency, and publisher Joseph Flanner of Milwaukee claimed sales of two hundred thousand piano copies early in that year.[14]

Adaline Shepherd composed and had published *Live Wires Rag, Wireless Rag*, and *Victory March*, but she disappeared from professional life after a brief flurry of success. She was born in Algona, Iowa, on August 19, 1883, and died in Milwaukee on March 12, 1950. In 1910 she married Fred S. Olson (1879–1956), who prospered in the insurance business. Adaline Shepherd Olson apparently lived out her life amid considerable wealth and comfort. She seems, however, to have drawn back from her musical ambitions, possibly due to the wishes of her husband. In this, and other respects, her life seems to parallel remarkably that of May Aufderheide. Relatives remember her, too, as "fun loving" and "spirited"— qualities that are captured in *Pickles and Peppers*. Many pianists consider it definitive ragtime. Its elaborate syncopations are carefully scored, and reveal themselves in straight reading without improvisation.[15]

While the rags of Adaline Shepherd and May Aufderheide were probably the best known by female composers during the ragtime years, the most famous professional musician who qualifies as a woman of ragtime was Muriel Pollock (1895–1971).

Born in Kingsbridge, New York, of parents who had emigrated from Kiev in the 1880s, she received extensive classical training in New York, and while still quite young established a professional reputation as a pianist, organist, and composer. *Rooster Rag* (1917) may well be her first published work. She followed it in the 1920s with songs and theatrical scores, including material in John Murray Anderson's *Jack and Jill*, and the score for the Broadway musical *Pleasure Bound*.

In 1933 she joined the NBC radio network as staff organist, and continued her composing with such efforts as the excellent *Piano Notions* suite (1935).[16] In 1938 she married songwriter Will Donaldson and the couple moved to the West Coast shortly thereafter, both continuing their careers in Hollywood.

Show business people who worked with "Molly" Pollock still express awe at her talent. She had all the pianist's skills, was a superb sight reader and fine accompanist as well as soloist, and was totally at ease with both jazz and the classics. In fact, she seemed to disagree with such imposed musical barriers. Her stepson Ted Donaldson says, "She had no patience with what she considered a snobbish attitude toward popular music. It was all music to her—good of its kind, or poor of its kind."[17]

Three of the ragtime women—Louise V. Gustin, Charlotte Blake, and Nellie M. Stokes—lived and worked in Detroit. Louise V. Gustin was a prolific composer, probably one of the oldest of the ragtime women, her

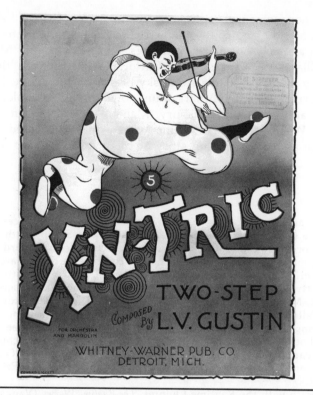

Louise V. Gustin was one of the early women composers of ragtime. Perhaps to conceal her gender, however, her publisher sometimes used only her initials, as above. *X-N-Tric* dates from 1900. (*Courtesy Max Morath*)

Topsy Turvy dating to 1899. She is listed in the 1895 Detroit City Directory as a music teacher, and four years later as a clerk. Her work triggers speculation about the practice of sex prejudice in the music business of the time, and perhaps equally about social attitudes regarding popular music. Gustin's name often appears as "L. V." rather than "Louise V." Did the publisher worry that a woman's name as composer discouraged sales? Or was the use of initials the woman's preference? Did she perhaps deem her efforts in popular two-steps and rags too frivolous for direct attribution? One becomes suspicious of all other initial-bearing composers of ragtime and early popular song (and there were many). How many were women? Were they hiding? Or being hidden?

According to Detroit city directories, both Charlotte Blake and Nellie M. Stokes worked as clerks, at least for a time, for the large publishing house of Jerome H. Remick & Company. In 1908 Blake is listed as a pianist for the Remick firm; Stokes is listed in 1901 as a music teacher and in 1904 as a musician. Except for their published compositions, nothing further is known about these women.

Many other women of ragtime appear in stacks of the old sheet music and in piles of old piano rolls—some briefly, for just one ragtime venture, others with a steady output of good rags. Libby Erickson of Minneapolis, Mamie Williams of Kansas City, Carlotta Williamson of Boston, Ella Hudson Day of Dallas, Sadie Koninsky of Troy, New York, Marcella A. Henry of Peru, Illinois, and others of unknown origins—Geraldine Dobyns, Mabel R. Kaufman, Cora Salisbury, Mabel Tilton, Kathryn L. Widmer, Florence M. Wood—these are ragtime women still awaiting rediscovery and performance as the fascinating story of this winsome music continues to unfold.

Notes

1. Research assistance for this essay has come from many sources. I especially appreciate the enthusiastic volunteer detective work of Susan Wirth, Milwaukee, into the life of Adaline Shepherd; and the research of John Edward Hasse, who accumulated much of the data on the Indiana composers. Thanks are also due to Edward A. Berlin, Rudi Blesh, Katherine Jay-Carroll, the late Dorothy Coats, Roy Guenther, David A. Jasen, Jay Joslyn, Dan Langan, Suzanne Lieberson, Frankie MacCormick, Michael Montgomery, Corbin Patrick, Chuck Thurston, Trebor Jay Tichenor, Walter Wager, Bob Wright, and especially Norma Morath.
2. Edgar Brinsmead, *The History of the Pianoforte* (Detroit: Singing Tree Press, 1969); and Arthur Loesser, *Men, Women, and Pianos* (New York: Simon & Schuster, 1954).
3. U.S. Bureau of the Census, *Historical Statistics of the United States, Colonial Times to 1970*, Bicentennial Edition, Part II (Washington, D. C.: Government Printing Office, 1975), p. 697.
4. Max Morath with the Ragtime Quintet, *The Ragtime Women* (Vanguard Records VSD 79402, 1977).
5. "J. H. Aufderheide Dies in His Home: Rites Tuesday for Head of Commonwealth Loan Company Board," *Indianapolis News*, 1 September 1941, part 2, p. 9; and Paul Donald Brown, ed., *Indianapolis Men of Affairs 1923* (Indianapolis: The American Biographical Society, 1923), pp. 26–27.
6. Telephone interview with Mrs. Russell Veit, Indianapolis, 11 April 1978. This and all succeeding references to Mrs. Veit are drawn from this interview.
7. "Mrs. Kolmer, Teacher Of Music, Dies," *The Indianapolis Star*, 27 February 1957.
8. Personal interview with Mrs. Joan Aufderheide Thompson, Little Rock, Arkansas, 5 November 1977. This and all subsequent references to Mrs. Thompson are based on this interview.
9. Rudi Blesh and Harriet Janis, *They All Played Ragtime* (New York: Knopf, 1950), p. 221.
10. *American Musician and Art Journal*, 13 August 1909, p. 20.
11. "R. C. Aufderheide Succeeds Kaufman At Commonwealth," *The Indianapolis Star*, 23 March 1947, section II, p. 45.
12. The information on Julia Niebergall is drawn mostly from letters and interviews by the author and John Hasse with Marilyn Niebergall, a niece, Indianapolis; and from the obituary, "Miss Julia Niebergall," *Indianapolis Star*, 20 October 1968, section 1, p. 26.
13. Telephone interview with Mrs. Joanne Cantwell, daughter of Gladys Yelvington, of Lake Station, Indiana, by John Edward Hasse, July 1977.
14. "Milwaukee Girl Author of Campaign Lyric," *American Musician and Art Journal*, 23 October 1908, p. 5; "Two Flanner Numbers," *American Musician and Art Journal*, 13 March 1908, p. 10.

15. Information on Adaline Shepherd is drawn from interviews and correspondence carried out in 1977 by Susan Wirth of Milwaukee with Shepherd relatives Betty Crotty Olson Hughes of Indianapolis, Ginny Bolte Bartel of Phoenix, and others. (Adaline Shepherd definitely spelled her name with two "a's," although it becomes "Adeline" on some of her later pieces. She was probably christened "Ada," and was known as "Addie" by her family. Perhaps the popularity of *Sweet Adeline* [1903] prevailed upon her, or her publishers, to change the spelling.)

16. The Lynn Farnol Group, Inc., comp. and ed., *The ASCAP Biographical Dictionary of Composers, Authors and Publishers*, 3rd ed. (New York: The American Society of Composers, Authors and Publishers, 1966), p. 576.

17. Personal interview with Ted Donaldson, stepson of Muriel Pollock Donaldson, Hollywood, California, 26 April 1977.

Conversations
with
James P. Johnson

Tom Davin

Sometimes called the "Father of Stride Piano," James P. Johnson (1891–1955) was a virtuosic exponent of this early style of jazz piano. "Stride" piano was a close cousin of ragtime and flourished in Harlem and other eastern locales. In this interview, published originally in 1959, Johnson provides rich details of the social setting of professional ragtime performers: the life, repertory, working conditions, nicknames, and dress of East Coast ragtime pianists or "'ticklers." He also tells of recording piano rolls.

In the December, 1958, *Jazz Review*, Dick Wellstood quoted Thelonious Monk's 1957 remark, made while listening to a playback of one of his solos: "That sounds like James P. Johnson."

Wellstood continued: "Strangely enough, Monk does sound like James P. from time to time, and so do Fats, Basie, Tatum and Duke (as well as Willie Gant and Q. Roscoe Snowden). Since James P. has had such a strong influence on so many well-known pianists, it is amazing that most people have never heard of him."

If this is so, perhaps an outline of his contributions may be helpful in showing his place in jazz history. Scott Joplin, Jelly Roll Morton, James P. Johnson—these are the three legs which support the grand piano of

From *The Jazz Review* 2 (June 1959): 14–17; (July 1959): 10–13; (August 1959): 13–15; (September 1959): 26–27; (March-April 1960): 10–13. Reprinted by permission of Martin T. Williams and Nat Hentoff, editors of *The Jazz Review*.

American jazz. Their influence will never disappear from the jazz scene for long.

From 1916 to 1930, James P. Johnson was the outstanding ragtime pianist and composer for piano in New York. During that time, he developed the New York style of "stride" piano from the rags of Scott Joplin and the southern Negro cotillion and set dances, embellished with the styles of a generation of café pianists from the South and West who came to New York in that era. Additional polish was contributed by the European concert and salon pianists who were heard everywhere in the city at that time, from De Pachmann and Hofmann on down.

Applying these techniques, James P. brought the full piano, or orchestral style of playing to its peak in the 1920's. It has not been surpassed since. True, the current trend in piano style has been toward the "thin" rather than the "fat" piano technique.

His greatest influence on pianists who were in their formative stage in 1916 or the following years was through his piano rolls for Aeolian and QRS, since he was the first Negro pianist to cut his own rags. Many other pianists learned to play by following them on the player piano. Later, his records had the same effect, even as records are still the schoolrooms of jazz, here and overseas. This pioneering, plus his rich and powerful style, caused the pianists who followed him to come up "sounding like James P." all or some of the time.

He taught this style to his apprentice, Fats Waller, who lightened it, simplified it and made it popular with the public through his exuberant, entertaining personality.

Playing behind Bessie Smith and Ethel Waters, James P. set standards for blues and novelty accompaniment that have never been equaled.

He was a composer of songs, show music, movie scores and symphonic works based on the themes of his piano music. . . .

In *The Story of Jazz,* Marshall Stearns writes:

"In the early 'fifties, James P. Johnson, old and sick, often wondered what could have happened to his beloved ragtime. For a brief moment, it seemed that the large compositions on which he had been working were about to be accepted and played, along with the time-honored classics of Mozart and Beethoven. Johnson's concertos were quite as complex and, in a sense, twice as difficult to play as Mozart's. Perhaps his Afro-American folk origins betrayed him, for the average classical musician is utterly incapable of the rhythmic sensitivity that is necessary to play Johnson's pieces. Only an orchestra composed of Smiths [Willie the Lion], Wallers, and Johnsons could have done it."

Two years before he died, I was fortunate to be able to interview him extensively about the early New York jazz scene, the people and music which influenced his style. From the notes on his career, these conversations emerge.

DAVIN: Did you learn your first piano at home?

James P. Johnson in 1921. He is considered the greatest player of the Harlem "stride" style of jazz piano, which was derived from ragtime. (*Courtesy Duncan P. Schiedt*)

JOHNSON: No, except for a few little tunes like *Little Brown Jug*. In 1902, when I was eight, we moved to Jersey City and there I first heard early ragtime. We sold our piano, then, to help pay the moving expenses and so we never had a piano in the house, until we moved to New York a few years later.

DAVIN: When did you first start to play ragtime?

JOHNSON: When we moved to Jersey City, my older brother met some ragtime piano players, or ticklers as they were called, and since they were popular fellows, always in demand socially, I looked up to them.

I became friendly with one tickler, Claude Grew, who could play anything in all keys. That was the mark of a cabaret player, who had to accompany different singers in their favorite keys. He taught me everything he knew. So did an older boy, George Perry, who was another real tickler. I remember another player, Floyd Keppard, a Creole with French background, sharp features and thick, good hair.

What they played wasn't ragtime as we know it now. It was mostly popular songs with a strong rhythm and with syncopated vamps, not a whole composition or arrangement. Scott Joplin's pieces were popular. They got around the country, but the ticklers I knew just played sections of them that they heard someplace. I never knew that they were Joplin's until later.

DAVIN: Were there many ticklers in Jersey City then?

JOHNSON: Yes, it was a temporary settlement for them. I guess at times there were more good ragtime players in Jersey City in those days than any other place in the United States.

DAVIN: How was that?

JOHNSON: Well, most of the ragtime players were working in sporting houses and cabarets in the South—Baltimore, Norfolk, Charleston, Atlanta—and in the Middle West—Pittsburgh, St. Louis, Memphis and other places.

Now, most of these fellows were big-time pimps or at least did a little hustling on their own. The ladies liked their music, so these boys would play slow drags, rags or songs that would touch the ladies' hearts—so they would get a woman or two or three to hustle for them. These ticklers didn't make much money, playing sometimes 12 hours a day in the houses or cafés—maybe $10 a week, and as much more in tips. Some had to work on tips alone. So they managed a few girls on the side.

Now, a good girl was measured by how much money she could draw, and the best kind of sporting woman was a thieving woman who knew how to get into a man's pocket and get his bankroll.

Sometimes, a girl would roll a live one and get $500 or $1,000. This usually brought a complaint to the police, so the girl and her tickler friend would have to leave town. They'd head north and east to New York and the last stop on the railroad was Jersey City. It still is for a lot of railroads.

DAVIN: When did you come to New York?

JOHNSON: We moved from Jersey City to New York in 1908 when I was 14. We had a piano in the house again. In Jersey City I heard good piano from all parts of the South and West, but I never heard real ragtime until we came to New York. Most East Coast playing was based on cotillion dance tunes, stomps, drags, and set dances like my *Mule Walk Stomp, Gut Stomp,* and the *Carolina Shout* and *Balmoral* [*Carolina Balmoral*—Ed.]. They were all country tunes.

In New York, a friend taught me real ragtime. His name was Charley Cherry. He played Joplin. First he played, then I copied him, and then he corrected me.

When I went to Public School 69, I was allowed to play for the Assembly and for the minstrel shows we put on there. I had a high soprano voice yet, so I was put into the school chorus. Once, Frank Damrosch (Walter Damrosch's brother) auditioned us for his production of Haydn's *Creation.* He used 100 boys in sections. I remember that he personally complimented me because I was singing so strong. We all got a bronze medal for taking part.

In New York I got a chance to hear a lot of good music for the first time. Victor Herbert and Rudolph Friml were popular and were played all the time. It seems they still are.

I used to go to the old New York Symphony concerts; a friend of my brother's who was a waiter used to get tickets from its conductor, Josef

Stransky, who came to the restaurant where he worked. I didn't get much out of them, but the full symphonic sounds made a great impression on me. That was when I first heard Mozart, Wagner, Von Weber, Meyerbeer, Beethoven and Puccini.

DAVIN: Was there much jazz or ragtime played in New York in the years before 1914?

JOHNSON: There weren't any jazz bands like they had in New Orleans or on the Mississippi river boats, but the ragtime piano was played all over in bars, cabarets and sporting houses. From what I have heard from older men who played in New York in 1890 and 1900, there was a kind of ragtime played then. W. C. Handy told me the same. A lot of early New Orleans tunes were played by bands and piano players around New York.

The other sections of the country never developed the piano as far as the New York boys did. Only lately have they caught up. The reason the New York boys became such high-class musicians was because the New York piano was developed by the European method, system and style. The people in New York were used to hearing good piano played in concerts and cafés. The ragtime player had to live up to that standard. They had to get orchestral effects, sound harmonies, chords and all the techniques of European concert pianists who were playing their music all over the city.

New York developed the orchestral piano—full, round, big, widespread chords and tenths—a heavy bass moving against the right hand. The other boys from the South and West at that time played in smaller dimensions— like thirds played in unison. We wouldn't dare do that because the public was used to better playing.

We didn't have any instruments then except maybe a drummer, so we had to use a solid bass and a solid swing to get the most colorful effects. In the rags, that full piano was played as early as 1910. Even Scott Joplin had octaves and chords, but he didn't attempt the big hand stretches. Abba Labba, Luckey Roberts and later ticklers did that.

When you heard the biggest ragtime specialists play, you would hear fine harmony, exciting touch and tone and all the themes developed.

DAVIN: Who were some of the ragtime pianists you heard in your early teens?

JOHNSON: In 1911, when I was still going to school in short pants, we lived on 99th Street, Manhattan, and I used to go to a cellar on 100th Street and 3rd Avenue, called The 100th Street Hall, run by a fellow nicknamed "Souser." I never knew his name; he was a juice hound. They had a four- or five-piece band there (piano, drums, violin, flute or clarinet). It was called the New Amsterdam Orchestra or Hallie Anderson's Orchestra. They played verses and choruses, in simple arrangements until 2 A.M. every night.

But after two, they pulled the piano out into the middle of the floor and "Souser" would play terrific rags. Then he'd let me play and I'd hit the piano until 4 A.M. I kept my schoolbooks in the coal bin there and went on to school after a little sleep.

In the same year, I was taken uptown to Barron Wilkins' place in Harlem. Another boy and I let our short pants down to look grown up and sneaked in. Who was playing there but Jelly Roll Morton! He had just arrived from the West and he was red hot. The place was on fire! We heard him play his *Jelly Roll Blues.*

I remember that he was dressed in full-back clothes and wore a light brown melton overcoat, with a three-hole hat to match. He had two girls with him.

Then I was just a short-pants kid in the back of the crowd and I never saw him again until 10 years later in Chicago. I was able to appreciate him then, but I couldn't steal his stuff. I wasn't good enough yet. In 1943, though, they picked me to impersonate his style at the New Orleans Jazz Carnival.

That same year, 1911, I heard Thad "Snowball" Wilkerson who played only by ear and in one key—B natural. He had taught Alberta Simmons to play rags. She was a fine instrumental pianist who played with Clef Club Bands. She lived at 8th Avenue, and 41st Street. Below her lived Willie Gant, then about 12 years old a very talented youngster, like Fats Waller was when I first met him. Incidentally, Russell Brooks, another fine pianist lived there, and it was in his flat on 133rd Street that I first met Fats in later years as a boy of 13. Raymond Boyette, called "Lippy," also lived there. He was a tickler, too. Years later, in the 1930's, he used to get me rent-party jobs in Harlem when the depression was on. Other players I heard in that house were Conky Williams, the great Dick Turpin and Nat Stokes, who came from Richmond, Virginia.

Alberta Simmons was kind enough to teach me the full Joplin rags that she played so well: *Frogs Legs . . . Maple Leaf Rag . . .* and the *Sunflower Slow Drag.*

DAVIN: James P., how did you get launched as a professional pianist?

JOHNSON: I told you before how I was impressed by my older brothers' friends. They were real ticklers—cabaret and sporting-house players. They were my heroes and led what I felt was a glamorous life—welcome everywhere because of their talent.

In the years before World War I, there was a piano in almost every home, colored or white. The piano makers had a slogan: "What Is Home Without A Piano?" It was like having a radio or a TV today. Phonographs were feeble and scratchy.

Most people who had pianos couldn't play them, so a piano player was important socially. There were so many of them visiting and socializing that some people would have their pianos going day and night all week long.

If you could play piano good, you went from one party to another and everybody made a fuss about you and fed you ice cream, cake, food and drinks. In fact, some of the biggest men in the profession were known as the biggest eaters we had. At an all-night party, you started at 1:00 A.M., had another meal at 4:00 A.M. and sat down again at 6:00 A.M. Many of us suffered later because of eating and drinking habits started in our younger socializing days.

But that was the life for me when I was seventeen.

In the summer of 1912, during high-school vacation, I went out to Far

Rockaway, a beach resort near Coney Island, and got a chance to play at a place run by a fellow named Charlie Ett. It was just a couple of rooms knocked together to make a cabaret. They had beer and liquor, and out in the back yard there was a crib house for fast turnover.

It was a rough place, but I got nine dollars and tips, or about eighteen dollars a week over all. That was so much money that I didn't want to go back to high school. . . .

DAVIN: Excuse my interruption. Tell me more about Far Rockaway.

JOHNSON: There was another place there called "The Cool Off," located down near the station. Some Clef Club members played there, and they used to come over after hours to hear me play dirty. Kid Sneeze was among them, and Dude Finley, a pianist who played a rag in D minor that had the same trio that was later used in *Shake It, Break It, Throw It Out The Window; Catch It Before It Falls.*

That fall, instead of going back to school, I went to Jersey City and got a job in a cabaret run by Freddie Doyle. He gave me a two-dollar raise.

In a couple of months, Doyle's folded up, and I came back to Manhattan and played in a sporting house on 27th Street between 8th and 9th Avenues, which was the Tenderloin then. It was run by a fellow named Dan Williams, and he had two girl entertainers that I used to accompany.

DAVIN: What type of music were you playing in 1912?

JOHNSON: Oh, generally popular stuff. I played [*Play*] *That Barbershop Chord* . . . *Lazy Moon* . . . Berlin's *Alexander's Ragtime Band.* Some rags, too, my own and others . . . Joplin's *Maple Leaf Rag* (everybody knew that by then) . . . his *Sunflower Slow Drag* . . . *Maori*, by Will Tyers . . . *The Peculiar Rag* and *The Dream*, by Jack the Bear.

Then there were "instrumentals"; piano arrangements of medleys of Herbert and Friml, popular novelties and music-hall hits—many by Negro composers.

Indian songs were popular then, and the girls at Dan Williams' used to sing *Hiawatha* . . . *Red Wing* . . . *Big Chief Battleaxe* . . . *Come With Me To My Big Teepee* . . . [*My*] *Pony Boy*—all popular in the music halls then.

Blues had not come into popularity at that time—they weren't known or sung by New York entertainers.

DAVIN: Had you done any composing by that time?

JOHNSON: No, but I was working out a number of rags of my own that they wanted to publish at Gotham & Attucks, a Negro music publishing firm whose offices were at 37th Street, off Broadway. I couldn't write them down and I didn't know anybody who would do them for me.

Cecil Mack was president of Gotham & Attucks. All the great colored musicians had gathered around the firm—Bert Williams, George Walker, Scott Joplin, Will Marion Cook, Joe Jordan, Tim Brymn.

They had a lot of hit songs . . . *Just* [*One*] *Word Of Consolation* . . . *Red, Red Rose* . . . *Down Among the Sugar Cane* . . . *Good Morning, Carrie.* Gussie L. Davis, who wrote white-style ballads for them, was the composer of [*In*] *The Baggage Coach Ahead*, the greatest tear-jerker of the time.

DAVIN: Were you long at Dan Williams' place?

JOHNSON: No, only a couple of months. I had a number of jobs in the winter of 1912–13. One was playing movie piano at the Nickelette at 8th Avenue and 37th Street. They had movies and short acts for short money. Many vaudeville acts broke in there. Florence Mills first sang there I recall.

In the spring of 1913, I really got started up in The Jungles. This was the Negro section of Hell's Kitchen and ran from 60th to 63rd Street, west of 9th Avenue. It was the toughest part of New York. There were two to three killings a night. Fights broke out over love affairs, gambling, or arguments in general. There were race fights with the white gangs on 66th and 67th Street. It was just as tough in the white section of Hell's Kitchen.

DAVIN: Where did you play there?

JOHNSON: In 1910 and 1911, I used to drop in at Jim Allan's place at 61st Street and 10th Avenue, where I'd wear my knickers long so they wouldn't notice that I was a shortpants punk. After they heard me play, they would let me come when I wanted.

So, in the spring of 1913, I went uptown and got a job playing at Jim Allan's. It was a remodeled cellar, and since it operated after hours, it had an iron-plated door—like the speak-easies had later. There was a bar upstairs, but downstairs there was a rathskeller, and in the back of the cellar there was a gambling joint.

When the cops raided us now and then, they always had to go back to the station house for axes and sledge hammers, so we usually made a clean getaway.

My "New York Jazz" album [on Asch] tried to show some types of music played in The Jungles at that time . . . Joplin's *Euphonic Sounds* . . . *The Dream* . . . Handy's [*Hesitating*] *Blues.*

One night a week, I played piano for Drake's Dancing Class on 62nd Street, which we called "The Jungles Casino." It was officially a dancing school, since it was very hard for Negroes to get a dance-hall license. But you could get a license to open a dancing school very cheap.

The Jungles Casino was just a cellar, too, without fixings. The furnace, coal, and ashes were still there behind a partition. The coal bin was handy for guests to stash their liquor in case the cops dropped in.

There were dancing classes all right, but there were no teachers. The "pupils" danced sets, two-steps, waltzes, schottisches, and "The Metropolitan Glide," a new step.

I played for these regulation dances, but instead of playing straight, I'd break into a rag in certain places. The older ones didn't care too much for this, but the younger ones would scream when I got good to them with a bit of rag in the dance music now and then . . .

DAVIN: Who were some of the other ticklers in The Jungles at that time?

JOHNSON: Well, there was Bob Gordon, the March King, who played at Allan's before me. He wrote *Oh, You Drummer!* which was popular because it had a lot of breaks for drums.

Then there was Freddie Singleton, who used to relieve me at The Jungles Casino now and then. When I would lay off at Allan's, I would play at Georgie Lee's near by, which was laid out the same as Allan's, except that it had a cabaret in the back room, instead of gambling.

About this time, I played my first "Pigfoot Hop" at Phil Watkin's place on 61st Street. He was a very clever entertainer and he paid me $1.50 for a night's playing with all the gin and chitterlings that I could get down.

This was my first "Chitterlin' Strut" or parlor social, but later in the depression I became famous at "Gumbo Suppers," "Fish Fries," "Egg Nog Parties," and "Rent Parties." I loved them all. You met people.

When I was at Allan's, I met Luckey Roberts at a party.

DAVIN: What was Luckey like in those days of his prime?

JOHNSON: Luckey Roberts was the outstanding pianist in New York in 1913—and for years before and after. He had composed *The Elks March . . . Spanish Venus . . . Palm Beach Rag . . . The Junk Man Rag.*

Luckey had massive hands that could stretch a fourteenth on the keyboard, and he played tenths as easy as others played octaves. His tremolo was terrific, and he could drum on one note with two or three fingers in either hand. His style in making breaks was like a drummer's: He'd flail his hands in and out, lifting them high. A very spectacular pianist.

He was playing at Barron Wilkins' place in Harlem then, and when I could get away I went uptown and studied him (I was working at Allan's from 9:00 P.M. to 7:00 A.M.). Later we became good friends, and he invited me to his home. Afterwards, I played at Barron Wilkins', too, as did my friend Ernest Green, who first introduced me to Luckey. Ernest was a good classic pianist. Luckey used to ask him to play the *William Tell* overture and the [*Light*] *Cavalry Overture*. These were considered tops in "classical" music amongst us.

Ernest Green's mother was studying then with a piano and singing teacher named Bruto Gianinni. She did house cleaning in return for lessons—several Negro singers got their training that way. Mrs. Green told me: "James, you have too much talent to remain ignorant of musical principles." She inspired me to study seriously. So I began to take lessons from Gianinni, but I got tired of the dull exercises. However, he taught me a lot of concert effects.

I was starting to develop a good technique. I was born with absolute pitch and could catch a key that a player was using and copy it, even Luckey's. I played rags very accurately and brilliantly—running chromatic octaves and glissandos up and down with both hands. It made a terrific effect.

I did double glissandos straight and backhand, glissandos in sixths and double tremolos. These would run other ticklers out of the place at cutting sessions. They wouldn't play after me. I would put these tricks in on the breaks and I could think of a trick a minute. I was playing a lot of piano then, traveling around and listening to every good player I could. I'd steal their breaks and style and practice them until I had them perfect.

From listening to classical piano records and concerts, from friends of

Ernest Green such as Mme. Garret, who was a fine classical pianist, I would learn concert effects and build them into blues and rags.

Sometimes I would play basses a little lighter than the melody and change harmonies. When playing a heavy stomp, I'd soften it right down—then, I'd make an abrupt change like I heard Beethoven do in a sonata.

Some people thought it was cheap, but it was effective and dramatic. With a solid bass like a metronome, I'd use chords with half and quarter changes. Once I used Liszt's *Rigoletto Concert Paraphrase* as an introduction to a stomp. Another time, I'd use pianissimo effects in the groove and let the dancers' feet be heard scraping on the floor. It was used by dance bands later.

In practicing technique, I would play in the dark to get completely familiar with the keyboard. To develop clear touch and the feel of the piano, I'd put a bed sheet over the keyboard and play difficult pieces through it.

I had gotten power and was building a serious orchestral piano. I did rag variations on *William Tell* overture, Grieg's *Peer Gynt Suite* and even a *Russian Rag* based on Rachmaninoff's Prelude in C-Sharp Minor, which was just getting popular then.

In my *Imitators' Rag* the last strain had *Dixie* in the right hand and *The Star Spangled Banner* in the left. (It wasn't the national anthem then.) Another version had *Home! Sweet Home!* in the left hand and *Dixie* in the right.

When President Wilson's "Preparedness" campaign came on, I wrote a march fantasia called *Liberty*.

From 1914 to 1916, I played at Allan's, Lee's, The Jungles Casino, occasionally uptown at Barron Wilkins', Leroy's and Wood's (run then by Edmund Johnson). I went around copping piano prize contests and I was considered one of the best in New York—if not the best. I was slim and dapper, and they called me "Jimmie" then.

DAVIN: Had you done any composing yet?

JOHNSON: I had started to compose my first rag about this time (1914), but nothing was done with it, and I threw it away. I also wrote and threw away a number of songs, although some people seemed to like them.

Entertainers used to sing blues to me, homemade blues, and I'd arrange them for piano, either to accompany them or play as solos. One of these homemade blues, *All Night Long*, was made into a song by Shelton Brooks, who also wrote *The Darktown Strutters' Ball*.

Then I met Will Farrell, a Negro song writer, and he showed me how to set my pieces down in writing. He also wrote lyrics for them. With him, I set down my first composition to be published, *Mamma's and Pappa's Blues*.

There had been a piece around at the time called *Left Her On The Railroad Track* or *Baby, Get That Towel Wet*. All pianists knew it and could play variations on it. It was a sporting-house favorite. I took one opening strain and did a paraphrase from this and used it in *Mamma's and Pappa's Blues*. It was also developed later into *Crazy Blues*, by Perry Bradford.

I had composed *Carolina Shout* before that. It wasn't written down, but was picked up by other pianists. My *Steeplechase Rag* and *Daintiness Rag* had spread all over the country, too, although they hadn't been published.

With Farrell, I also wrote *Stop It, Joe!* at this time. I sold it, along with *Mamma's and Pappa's Blues* for twenty-five dollars apiece to get enough money for a deposit on a grand piano.

In the summer of 1914, I went for a visit to Atlantic City and heard Eubie Blake (who composed *Shuffle Along* later), one of the foremost pianists of all time. He was playing at The Belmont, and Charles Johnson was playing at The Boat House, both all-night joints.

Eubie was a marvelous song player. He also had a couple of rags. One, *Troublesome Ivories,* was very good. I caught it.

I saw how Eubie, like Willie Smith and Luckey Roberts, could play songs in all keys, so as to be ready for any singer—or if one of them started on a wrong note. So I practiced that, too. I also prepared symphonic vamps—gutty, but not very full.

While in New Jersey that summer, I won a piano contest in Egg Harbor, playing my *Twilight Rag* (which had a chimes effect in syncopation), *Steeplechase Rag,* and [*When It's*] *Nighttime in Dixieland.*

There was a pianist there who played quadrilles, sets, rags, etc. From him, I first heard the walking Texas or boogiewoogie bass. The boogie-woogie was a cotillion step for which a lot of music was composed. I never got his name, but he played the *Kitchen Tom Rag* which was the signal for a "Jazz" dance.

When I came back to New York, I met the famous Abba Labba in the Chelsea district. To this day, I can't remember his right name, either. He was a friend and pupil of Luckey Roberts'.

Abba Labba was the working girls' Jelly Roll. His specialty was to play a lot of piano for girls who were laundresses and cooks. They would supply him with stylish clothes from their customers' laundry and make him elaborate rosettes for his sleeve guards. The cooks furnished him with wonderful meals, since they had fine cold kina (keena) then. Cold kina was leftover food from a white family's dinner that the cook was entitled to. This was an old southern cooks' custom: they fed their own family with these leftovers and they were sure to see that there was plenty of good food left. That's why old southern home cooking was so famous—the cook shared it.

Most of the full-time hustlers used to cultivate a working girl like that, so they could have good meals and fancy laundry.

Abba Labba had a beautiful left hand and did wonderful bass work. He played with half-tone and quarter-tone changes that were new ideas then. He would run octaves in chords, and one of his tricks was to play *Good Night, Beloved, Good Night* in schottische, waltz and ragtime.

I fell on his style and copied a lot of it.

DAVIN: What was Willie Smith like in his young days?

JOHNSON: Willie Smith was one of the sharpest ticklers I ever met—and I met most of them. When we first met in Newark, he wasn't called Willie

"The Lion"—he got that nickname after his terrific fighting record overseas during World War I. He was a fine dresser, very careful about the cut of his clothes and a fine dancer, too, in addition to his great playing. All of us used to be proud of our dancing—Louis Armstrong, for instance, was considered the finest dancer among the musicians. It made for attitude and stance when you walked into a place, and made you strong with the gals. When Willie Smith walked into a place, his every move was a picture.

DAVIN: You mean he would make a studied entrance, like a theatrical star?

JOHNSON: Yes, every move we made was studied, practiced, and developed just like it was a complicated piano piece. . . .

DAVIN: Let's see . . . What were you doing in 1914 and 1915?

JOHNSON: . . . . I also worked in a song and dance act with Ben Harney, who was one of the greatest piano players and who was supposed to be "the inventor of ragtime." He used to play two pianos together—one with each hand. Ben was also a great entertainer on the TOBA time, a southern vaudeville circuit. His big songs were: *I'm a Natural Born Cannon Ball Catcher,* and *Mister Johnson, Turn Me Loose.* . . .

I was getting around and known in the theatrical music field. One day I got a message to go see Mr. Fay at the Aeolian Company. He wanted someone to cut ragtime piano rolls.

Now, I had never cut a roll before. In fact, no Negro had ever cut his own compositions before. Mr. Fay at Aeolian set me down at a piano and I played a rag. Until he played it back at me, I didn't know I had cut a roll. Later, Russel Robinson, a white pianist, taught me how to run the piano roll cutter. From 1916 on, I cut one or two rolls a month of my own pieces at Aeolian. I wrote rags in every key in the scale. Every one of them had to be written out perfectly because the manuscript of each piece was used for correcting the rolls, if any note wasn't punched right.

Being the first Negro composer to cut his own rags, I saw them become famous and studied all over the country by young ticklers who couldn't read much music. Later I did the same type of rolls for QRS, which had a bigger circulation and really spread my rags around. These were all terrific rags. They have been recut and recorded on lp by Riverside Records. It was at Aeolian later, in 1920, that I met George Gershwin who was cutting "oriental" numbers there when I was making blues rolls which were popular then. He had written *Swanee* and was interested in rhythm and blues. Like myself, he wanted to write them on a higher level. We had lots of talks about our ambitions to do great music on American themes. In 1922, we had a show together in London. In 1917, I made my first record. It was for a company that had started up in the office building where Will Farrell and I had our office; it later became OKeh Records.

I cut a record for them, my *Caprice Rag,* which had a nocturne-like quality and sounded great. But the company never issued it. They had little faith in Negro compositions until 1920–21 when Mamie Smith and Perry Bradford made some records for them.

Rudi Blesh
and the Ragtime
Revivalists

John Edward Hasse

Ragtime music has undergone a series of revivals that have brought it renewed popularity and new audiences. This chapter comprises interviews, conducted for this book, with three leading figures in the revival of ragtime: "The Dean of Ragtime Historians," Rudi Blesh, the scintillating ragtime entertainer Max Morath, and the conductor-arranger-scholar Gunther Schuller. In addition, there are profiles of thirteen others who have played leading roles in reviving ragtime music.

Of the hundreds of musicians, researchers, and writers who have been involved in ragtime music since its rediscovery in the early 1940s, no one has done more to rescue, dignify, and champion this genre than Rudi Blesh. With his close friend Harriet Janis (1898–1963), he wrote its first history, *They All Played Ragtime,*[1] which became a classic and has remained in print for thirty years. In the intervening period, he has modestly expanded the book three times, and has engaged in a number of activities to further ragtime. For this chapter, I have interviewed Blesh and two other articulate, internationally known leaders of the ragtime revival—Max Morath and Gunther Schuller.[2]

The son of a surgeon, Rudolph Pickett Blesh was born in Guthrie, Oklahoma Territory, on January 21, 1899—the same year the *Maple Leaf Rag* was published. In 1910 his family visited Vienna, Austria, and this exposure greatly furthered young Rudi's budding interest in music and art. As a youth he studied piano, violin, and cello. He heard ragtime in his native Guthrie but was not allowed to play it at home. In 1917 he went East to study at Dartmouth College, and on a weekend trip to New York City, heard the Original Dixieland Jazz Band, bought one of their records and immediately became hooked on jazz. Dissatisfied with the curriculum of his English major, he dropped out of Dartmouth in 1920. Several years later, with his mother (now divorced) and younger brother, he moved to Berkeley, California. Blesh entered the University of California to study architecture, and in 1924 earned his B.S. with honors. He worked as an interior designer, and later as an industrial, furniture and architectural designer, until 1943.

His jazz record collection was wiped out in the Berkeley fire of 1924, and his interest waned until about 1935, when he started avidly collecting and listening to jazz discs. In 1943 he was invited to deliver a lecture series called "This is Jazz" at the San Francisco Museum of Art.[3] Because of the success of the lectures, Alfred Frankenstein, music critic of the *San Francisco Chronicle*, asked Blesh to become jazz critic for the newspaper. On a trip to the New York home of composer Virgil Thompson in 1944, Blesh was asked by Herbert Weinstock of Alfred A. Knopf to write a history of jazz, and Blesh

Rudi Blesh, "The Dean of Ragtime Historians," ca. 1960. (*Photograph by Hans Namuth, courtesy Rudi Blesh*)

began work on it shortly thereafter. Meanwhile, in 1945, Blesh met Harriet Janis, and soon moved to New York. She introduced him to the finer points of modern art, and he introduced her to jazz. Together they traveled to New Orleans, Chicago, and Washington for field interviews and library research for his jazz book, published in 1946 as *Shining Trumpets: A History of Jazz*.[4] Blesh and Janis founded Circle Records, a small but significant jazz label, which became the first to issue the Library of Congress recordings of Jelly Roll Morton. In 1953 they sold the Circle catalog—exclusive of the Morton sides—to Jazzology Records.

Blesh wrote and narrated radio programs on jazz and American folk music in the late 1940s and in the early 1960s, and beginning in the mid-1950s, taught at Queens College and New York University. He wrote seven more books on jazz, modern art, and cinema.[5] During this time he always maintained a special love for ragtime music. He contributed a major essay, "Scott Joplin: Black American Classicist," to *The Collected Works of Scott Joplin*[6] and in the 1970s annotated a number of recordings and worked in other ways to promote the rediscovery of ragtime. Like a benign patriarch, Blesh encouraged young ragtime performers and composers to pursue the music he loved—and still loves—so much.

The following interview took place at the Blesh summer home in Gilmanton, New Hampshire, on a warm summer day, July 16, 1978.

HASSE: What attracted you to ragtime music?

BLESH: The entire period, as a part of the art nouveau period, in which I'd become very interested, and the theatrical period that had people that I admired in it very much, like Anna Held and Lillian Russell. And all of the glamour and the romance of the period. It seemed to me that not only was ragtime our first really American music, but that it was beautiful music with charm and innocence, and that it would do the country good to have it again. [Laughs] Ragtime is the music of the art nouveau period, and the whole subject of art nouveau was the glorification of women. And jazz to me is the opposite. It's the glorification of the male. It's—of the more aggressive side. And put in the tritest of terms, it's like the difference between the nineteenth century and the twentieth. Actually, even though ragtime went on to 1917, it was still a part of a Victorian expression that I think is great in itself. In other words, ragtime wasn't seeking to startle anybody, to frighten them, to harm them, or anything. It was aimed to cajole and to seduce and to flirt with you. [Laughter]

HASSE: But if you listen to ragtime as opposed to, say, Sousa or a folk song or a spiritual or jazz, what particularly appeals to you in ragtime music?

BLESH: Well, that's very hard to say. It would be like asking if you have a garden full of flowers and you like all of them, why do you like this one better than the others? Because it's bigger, redder, or what, you know. There are very subtle, personal things involved there. I do think that it goes back into very early memories that I can't recall, because, after all, 1899 and

1900 [when Blesh was an infant] were very fecund ragtime years. And in a sense, unlike jazz ragtime seems like going home again.

HASSE: How did you come to write *They All Played Ragtime?*

BLESH: It was a form of a dare or a challenge, you might say, and it happened in this way. I had written *Shining Trumpets* in 1946 and then a couple of years had gone by and I wasn't doing any writing, except like magazine articles and things of that sort, but no full length book. And one day out in Long Island, in the summer of 1949, [my good friend Harriet "Hansi" Janis] turned to me and said, "Don't you think it's about time that you're doing another book? You've been letting a lot of time go by." She was a great one for books, because she would say, "Long after you're gone, your book will still be there, and don't forget that." I thought she was referring to jazz, and I said, "Well, Hansi, I really wrote everything I have to say about jazz, at least at this time in *Shining Trumpets.*" "Well," she said, "that's not the only music there is. What about ragtime?" I absolutely had not even thought of ragtime. And my first reaction was, "Well, there must have been dozens of books written on it." She said, "Don't you kid yourself. I'd like to bet you that there're none, because I've been looking around and there aren't any." Anyway, well that was sort of a challenge, but I knew it was going to be a heck of a research job. And I said, "I don't think that many of the people will be still alive." She said, "Well, that you would have to find out." I said, "Hansi, I won't do it unless you'll do it with me and we'll make it a collaborative effort." She said, "All right." So then we decided what to do, and it being at the end of summer, we decided before looking up survivors of the period and so forth that we had better read everything that had been written in the ephemera—magazines and newspapers and so forth—about ragtime, and we went first to Washington, D. C., to go to the Library of Congress. And we found a gal there by the name of Genevieve Norvell, whom I bless to the end of my days, because she became fired up about our project. She would hunt up material for us to read in every imaginable magazine—not merely the *American Musician* or *Etude,* but also obscure sources such as the *Chicago Interocean.* That has some of the early things. That's where the name ragtime is first, I think, supposed to have been used. She got us permission, or she wrangled it, or didn't bother to get permission to get out all the sheet music we wanted to look at and handle—take into rooms alone and look at. She allowed us to have anything photostatted that we wanted. And we spent every day there of the week for well over a month really combing the thing. Then we came back and went to the New York Public Library, did the same thing, also looking for pictures wherever we could find them. Then the next step was to see the live people. So we went to a friend of ours, the late Kenneth Lloyd Bright, a marvelous black friend of ours in Harlem whose father had owned (and then Kenneth subsequently owned) and ran the Lafayette Theater and Lafayette Rehearsal Hall, which is famous in jazz and blues annals. Bright said, "The man who could tell you where most of these people are is Shepard Edmonds—Shep Edmonds—out in Columbus, Ohio." And we immediately got in touch with Shep Edmonds, and went right out to see him, and he proved amenable to helping us. Shepard Edmonds had been a piano player and was in Chicago at the time of the 1893 World's Fair. He heard ragtime there and gave us the names of guys playing it there in the year of the exposition, 1893, which is four years before the first published rag. Plunk Henry and people of that sort were names that we were able to preserve, though we'll never hear their music. Shep Edmonds got out of piano playing when he became the first black private detective. That was his big pride. But when you got him on the subject of the players, it was another thing. And he would say that the last he had heard Arthur Marshall was in Kansas City, this guy was this, and that guy was that, and so forth. And he was the one that gave us the practical advice: How do you find the guys when you get there? He was a realist, and he didn't have any false racial pride—he talked about things the way they were. He said, "You know, some of these people may not be so well along in means now. You get to town and you won't find them in the phone book. They probably don't even have a phone. When that happens, go to the"—he still used the word "colored"—"go to the colored undertaker and say, 'Where will I find Arthur Marshall?' Well, Authur Marshall is getting along in years and the undertaker knows right where he is and the state of health he's in because he's watching him. He's his business." And it worked out unfailingly. We did get to Kansas City and saw the undertaker. He says, "Yes, Marshall lives on such and such a street. You can just go up there and call on him." Kenneth Lloyd Bright was of the very first importance, and he also made this remark: "It's a good thing that you two are working together, because getting in to see some of these people in black houses, if a white man comes alone they're immediately leery. He's a bill collector for someone, or he wants something, or he's got a warrant for arrest, or something. But," he says, "if there's a lady along with him, she'll always get in." And she always would. [Laughs] And, of course, that was before tape, and Mrs. Janis took all these things down in notebooks while we talked. And I have the notebooks here—some twelve or fourteen of them, which nobody's been able to translate. She not only used the two main systems of shorthand, but apparently had some shorthand symbols of her own. And we've had the best cryptologists look at it—they can't decipher it. There the material lies, and I still hope it can be translated. So after talking to Shep Edmonds, we doubled back and we made out our itinerary. And then we traveled for several months getting all this material. That brings us about into the holidays, and the actual writing began right around in December of 1949 or January of 1950. We turned the manuscript in the spring of 1950 and they published the same year.

HASSE: When you started, how long did it take you to write the manuscript?

BLESH: My memory is that we did all of the thing in under four weeks. I would write it out in longhand, then I would copy it myself on the typewriter with my hunt and peck system, which consists of editing because when you go from a handwritten thing to type you automatically edit. Then

Harriet Janis, ca. 1960, coauthor with Rudi Blesh of the pioneer history *They All Played Ragtime.*
(*Photograph by Hans Namuth, courtesy Rudi Blesh*)

Hansi looked it over and she did editing, and that night, then, the whole thing would get typed in its final version. I know we turned the whole manuscript in before or by the very early part of February, and Knopf was so enthusiastic about the book that they said they were going to get it out the same year, which they did.

HASSE: In the fall?

BLESH: In the fall, yes, October.

HASSE: And so the whole book from inception to publication took a year and a quarter.

BLESH: That's right.

HASSE: That's amazing!

BLESH: Yeah. And they got it out and they published all the pictures that we had—everything. . . . Mrs. Janis had a strong feeling about the effect that this book might have over a long period of time. She said, "I don't think it's going to do anything very much the first few years. There will be a revival of ragtime, but," she says, "it's going to take at least twenty-five years." Well, from 1949 to twenty-five years later is so close to the date that the way the thing worked out that it's amazing, you know. She said, "After all, it's been on the shelf now for over that length of time." And so she was right about that.

HASSE: Now, going back to your schedule, you weren't trying to push things along. It just fell into place so quickly.

BLESH: Well, it fell into place because the story seemed to tell itself in many ways. And, incidentally, we had these sessions nearly every day for a couple of weeks, taking rags—the music that we had gotten, the photostats from the Library of Congress, and everything—out to Ralph Sutton, who would play them for us. And, you know, he would sight read it and interpret it at the same time. He's an instant reader. It was uncanny how he would play it. Later on for the revised edition after Hansi was gone, Max Morath played the new things for me. But anyway, the story just seemed to want to tell itself, and we didn't seem to want to take a day off, and just found that going seven days a week, it just rolled. It was one of those fortunate things: the time was just right for us—the time was right all the way around.

HASSE: And you were able to devote full time.

BLESH: Full time, yeah.

HASSE: When you first began your work on ragtime, what assumptions did you have?

BLESH: Well, that it had been one of the great musical crazes of history. That it had got not only America but France and England and so forth completely involved in the thing. That it rode in with this dance craze of the cakewalk, and hit every level of society, and was even being played in China. And the thing that struck us most about it was that this sort of music, even just judged by its effects, is important. And the fact that no book had been written about it, we just couldn't believe. And the farther we got into it, the more exciting it was. Here was some real pioneering work that still could be done. There had been books on jazz; *Shining Trumpets* was not a pioneering effort, just what I brought to it was different.

HASSE: Did you go into your research with any definable theories, hypotheses?

BLESH: No, we didn't expect to find it as a music to be taken as seriously as music, as it turned out to be. We didn't expect, for example, that we were going to find out that the works of a Joplin or a Lamb were truly classical. That was a revelation to us, you know. You begin to analyze the compositions and they're marvelous. And they represent a whole school of creativity that was new. And, honestly, they began to make most jazz, except that in the hands of the masters, sound just happenstance and chancy, you know, and almost sloppy. I'm not certainly including a Dizzy Gillespie or a Louis Armstrong or a Sidney Bechet, but rather the usual jam thing. You could get some little pianist sitting down and just playing Scott Joplin as he saw it from the score, and it came out better than those jam sessions. [Laughter]

HASSE: So that was one of the surprises that you had in the course of your research?

BLESH It was a revelation.

HASSE: A revelation?

BLESH: Yes, it was a revelation. That's right, it was a revelation. To find out, you see, that within the core of all this commercial claptrap that was being issued by Tin Pan Alley and so forth, was a core of fine, serious, enduring work. That was the real revelation. And to see that the usual picture was there: The genuine, worthwhile thing is in the middle, just a small amount of it at any time, and a tremendous amount of junk goes along with it. And the fact that, as far as the public is concerned, they couldn't care less whether it was by Joplin or Joe Doakes, just as long as it went "dooh de la da da"—that honky-tonk, ragtime feeling.

HASSE: What other major surprises did you have in the course of your research and writing that might have changed your assumptions or the ideas that you began with?

BLESH: Well, I don't know of any particular thing that happened, but there were a lot of very interesting things that developed. One was finding how many important people were still alive. When you figure that we were able to personally interview around one hundred people that were all very intimately connected one way or another with ragtime. There were ones who wouldn't see us, who wouldn't be interviewed, but they were very, very, very few. For the most part, they were—well, like Joe Lamb. When we went to see Joe Lamb, he was genuinely surprised that anybody could ever be interested in ragtime anymore. When he found out that we weren't kidding him or pulling his leg, he just wanted to open up. [Laughs] And there was among a whole lot of people a feeling of happiness that something was being done about ragtime, because it's a music that attracted people's love. . . . Incidentally, years after Joplin died, Lottie Joplin still had unpublished pieces by Joplin. She let us borrow things like *Pretty Pansy Rag, Recitative Rag,* and others, and we took them to James P. Johnson, who played them for us. Now you know, James P. was the most generous of men, and he was by no means not some big shakes as a player and a composer himself. But he said, "There's only one Scott Joplin, and how great he was."

HASSE: And he thought those manuscripts were good.

BLESH: Yes, he thought they were good, and the way he played them they were good. But why weren't we a little less ethical and had them photostatted and kept them until such a time as we could see what would happen to the originals? What happened to the originals was when Lottie [Joplin] died they were turned over to Wilbur Sweatman as executor and they disappeared. And with his death they're gone.

HASSE: While we're on the subject, what do you consider some of the unsolved mysteries of ragtime?

BLESH: One, of course, is the famous *Guest of Honor*—Scott Joplin's lost opera. Where is it? That's one of the mysteries. And it was probably full of beautiful music. Then there's the business of Scott Joplin's trunk with unpublished manuscripts and family photographs and all sorts of things that Lottie said they had left for an unpaid board bill in a rooming house in Pittsburgh. No amount of search could find it, because the interval of time was too great.

HASSE: If a young researcher came to you and said, "Mr. Blesh, are there any areas in ragtime that you think still should be explored?", what would you say?

BLESH: Well, there're quite a few leads to follow up, and I think that a good, thorough search for the *Guest of Honor* might just turn it up. I just have a feeling it's still in existence. . . . What should be started is a thorough history of the ragtime revival itself. Keep it like an open-ended file until there's enough to do. I think it's extremely interesting that a thing can be dormant all those years and then can take hold again, and people find it just as fresh and beautiful as it ever was. It makes you wonder about fashion. And I think that that's a project that I'm sure that if Mrs. Janis were here— well, we'd probably be already collating something on the revival. But I think that having men like Donald Ashwander composing ragtime means a great deal at this point. There's a lot of material being put down on paper that's going to be of value. . . . I know now that there's been a tendency on the part of a few people to criticize *They All Played Ragtime* in that it's not a musical history but a social history. Well, we had our reasons for that. If ragtime as a music had fallen into neglect and nobody was interested in it, a musical history was not going to revive it. But if the time itself, the social background, and the characters were interesting enough, then it would lead to a desire to hear their music, which is a way that I think it did work out. Also, we had a feeling that you can't really describe music. You can say it's beautiful, or it stinks. What else can you say? That "in the third movement Beethoven unexpectedly inverts the augmented seventh, creating an effect?" Something like that doesn't mean a damn thing. In other words— and I know that we did the same thing in our art books and I did in my own *Modern Art U.S.A.*, the artist comes before the art or there wouldn't be the art. The musician or composer comes before the music, or there wouldn't be the music. The human element is very important, I think. And, if more of that had been done in the past on some of the great figures in history, we would be much richer.

Like Rudi Blesh, Max Morath "soaked up" ragtime as a child, and as an adult pursued it partly because of his interest in its era. Like Blesh, he is keenly interested in the human element and social history of the music.

Max Morath is as engaging and multi-talented a person and ragtime entertainer as can be found anywhere. Max Edward Morath was born October 1, 1926, in Colorado Springs, Colorado, the son of a real estate broker and a woman who had once played piano for the silent movies. His mother had performed ragtime and while she never formally taught it to her son, Morath feels it "soaked" into him as a child. He also received some formal piano training in those years, and as a teenager, studied music theory and composition privately.

He worked his way through Colorado College as a radio announcer, and received his B.A. in English in 1948. He worked for several years as a television director, announcer, and entertainer, and performed in summer stock melodramas, where he began specializing in performing American popular music from the early twentieth century. From 1959 to 1960 he wrote and performed a lively twelve-program series for National Educational Television called *The Ragtime Era*, and from 1961 to 1962, a second series of fifteen programs, *Turn of the Century*. He kept busy performing at colleges and industrial conventions with his unique one-man shows blending ragtime piano and singing, vintage song-slides, theatrical sets and costumes, social commentary, and humor.

Morath has tirelessly sought to make ragtime music come alive by reconstructing its era and by presenting the music and its social times in vibrant shows readily accessible to the general public. He toured the nation with his show *Ragtime Revisited* from 1964 to 1967, and after a successful four-month off-Broadway run of *Max Morath at the Turn of the Century*, he toured with that show for three years. In recent years he has taken his shows *The Ragtime Years* and *Living a Ragtime Life* on the road, and has made numerous television appearances, including a public broadcasting special, *Max Morath and the Boston Pops*. He has recorded over a dozen record albums, for Epic, RCA, Vanguard, and New World Records, and has collated and edited six ragtime music folios, described elsewhere in this book.

Morath is a man of great energy and enthusiasm, and it was with

Max Morath at Columbia Records' Thirtieth Street Studio, New York City, 1963. (*Courtesy CBS Records*)

pleasure that I welcomed him into my home in Bloomington, Indiana, on September 26, 1977, for the following interview.

MORATH: I don't think that there's any way to make a hard and fast rule about performing ragtime, because each performer approaches a given rag at a given concert with a different background of discipline and years at the piano. So, a Josh Rifkin would approach a concert in which he played Scott Joplin's *Euphonic Sounds* differently than I would, or Butch Thompson would, or pianists that have come to ragtime through all the disciplines that you can come. I would like to have that real deep, way-down subconscious training that gives me the command of the notes that a concert pianist has, so that when he comes to his audience he's not thinking about the notes, he's thinking about his interpretation, his dynamics, his pedaling, the tiny nuances of performance. I don't have that kind of discipline—never have had. My piano education is sketchy, and my piano playing for money—or to audiences—until I was thirty years old was still improvisational.

HASSE: Well, how did you get into ragtime piano then in such a big way?

MORATH: I got into it because I got interested in the period, and my historical interests and my interests in a whole lot of things that have nothing to do with ragtime centered on that period. And, meanwhile, remember the most practical reason for it all was, after all, I was making my living at this. I began to find that by specializing in a certain type of music and a certain type of approach to comedy—still exemplified in the shows I do which kind of unite history as entertainment, or entertainment as history, and amalgamate, so that an audience doesn't quite understand what the hell's happening except they pick up some laughs, and they hear a few familiar things, and they hear a few things that seem kind of arty, and you lay it on them and if you're successful, you give them a two-hour bath that involves what show business is all about. Music, laughs, a few dropouts of serious moments, a little satire and a little information. But I really, truly *am* interested on a personal level in those many things that historically make up the period that produced ragtime. I've always considered it a beautiful piece of dumb luck that the music of that period happened also to be solo piano style predominantly, or at least one great area of it was a solo piano style. And that the vocal styles fit my kind of voice. If a guy's going to go out and do a show about those years, which, as we've said, may be roughly the 1880s to the 1920s, then one can do it as a *soloist*. I've had a lot of people say, "Why don't you go into the twenties? Do the same thing, treat the twenties like you do?" And it's a great idea, except you've got to have a *band*. You cannot do the music of the twenties with any kind of—I won't even use the word "authenticity"—I don't even care about authenticity—but with any kind of *fun*, and any kind of real treatment of that music. You cannot do it as a soloist. Vocally, I could do it. I've got the "pipes" for that part, but you've got to take a band on, and I don't *want* to take a band on. . . . We use the word "entertainment" for what I do, and I've always tried to feel that way—

I do not want to aim any portion of the show that I do at a specialized audience. I don't want anybody in that theatre to have had to come in and sit down in that seat, for which he paid five or ten dollars, and have to have done any *homework*. I don't want them to necessarily be "into" Scott Joplin or Bert Williams. That's unfair, and it's also very self-destructive, because if you've got to work to a specialized audience, you're working to a few thousand people. I don't want to do that. I want to work to a *general* audience. Now, sure, it's specialized in this sense—the theatre-going public, the people who are willing to get up from a dinner table and get in the car and drive to the theater and lay down a few dollars and walk in and say, "Okay, on with the show." *That* is a somewhat specialized audience, and obviously those people are people who do follow certain theatrical or musical events and have certain predispositions. But, I find, many times an audience that has no specialized interest whatsoever is the *best* audience. Many times I've played to people that are ragtime aficionados, and they come up to me after the show and say, "Well, gee, we like the show; but, you only played six or seven rags. How come? We thought you'd play all the Joplin rags." And I say, "Well, I'm sorry to disappoint you, but I never have done that." And I never have. The major problem that I have in public and press relations is to get the idea across that my show is an entertainment, not a concert of piano or vocals, or some kind of musicological trip to the past, or an illustrative lecture. All those deadly things that would keep people away in droves.

HASSE: Earlier, before we put on the tape recorder, we were talking about the way one learns to play piano rags.

MORATH: Well, I used the expression that I always find it necessary to "blood" a rag, and by that I mean to get it as much under one's fingers as you think one can. You're sitting at home in your studio and you think you have it *cold,* and then you go out and put it up in front of even ten people, and you fall completely apart. Right? And you have to keep going and you maybe make horrible mistakes, but you do indeed finish it and come up to a conclusion, and the audience perhaps isn't any the wiser. And, after you've done that two or three times, you have "blooded" the rag. Again, I go back to the fact that I have not had an intensive ten-year or fifteen-year period of disciplined digital training, and yet I work pretty hard at the piano and I think I have a pretty good command of it. But I still find with the rags, as opposed again to improvisational things, that I get them down until I can play them perfectly in rehearsal, but I still am terribly nervous about presenting them to an audience under close scrutiny in a concert. Not a nightclub audience, because there people are talking and waiters coming back and forth—hey, that's no problem at all. But if you're up there on a stage and people are sitting out in their "big black cave" and you're up there under the lights and you say, "I will now play—" then you're under a microscope. I find that after having done that and gone through the torture of putting those things up front three or four times, I pass through a kind of vale of tears and come out the other side in command of that particular rag.

HASSE: Does it take you a long time to work up a rag to the point where you can play for the public?

MORATH: Well, it varies. It depends on the difficulty of the piece. Sometimes it's a couple of months. Now, rags that I get up for a recording, the day I record them, that's it—forget them. I don't play them again. Because I don't *have* to. Come up to them for the recordings, do the best you can in the studio, and make as little use of the razor blade as you can—but still you know it's there—and the retake, and then goodbye. But I always find that there are certain rags that penetrate a recording rehearsal schedule, and you think, "Hey, that's a good rag. I'm going to put that in such-and-such a position in the show. I think it would function there." I work with a metronome a lot, by the way.

HASSE: In rehearsing?

MORATH: Yes.

HASSE: Rehearsing for public performance or recording?

MORATH: Both. I find that rags tend to rush. Most performers that I've ever talked to find that rags rush, particularly under performing exigencies; and, therefore, I find that rehearsing with a metronome, while it certainly isn't the thing you want to do too close to a performance, is a good way to get tight with it. So I do that. Then, at a certain point, if I'm going to go out in front of an audience, I'll pick myself a kind of out-of-the-way date somewhere, and I'll slip one of these new rags in. And, I'll probably make a mess of it. And I'll do it again somewhere, and eventually I'll get it so securely under my fingers that it no longer is a threat, and I enjoy playing it then.

HASSE: You practice two hours a day?

MORATH: I try to. When I'm working on some specific project, I practice more than that. There are times when I practice not anywhere near that much. Being on the road is one of the most difficult times to get practice time.

HASSE: How do you do it?

MORATH: Well, what I try to do if I'm in a run some place, like a theatrical run for a couple of weeks, I have the great luxury of going over to the theater when there's nobody else there at eleven o'clock in the morning and practicing for three or four hours. I mean, that's fun.

HASSE: Do you think that performing piano rags requires precision?

MORATH: Well, I like to quote Josh Rifkin, who put it so succinctly: "In playing ragtime, you're so exposed." Of course, he meant classic rags, and he was specifically speaking of Joplin, but I think that's true, you know. Piano rags, especially what are called classic rags, are very transparent, and allow very little room for covering up one's mistakes.

HASSE: You can't pedal your way through them.

MORATH: You can't pedal or "chromatic" your way through things. [Laughs] So, if you get lost, you better be improvising in the genre, you know.

HASSE: That's tough.

MORATH: It is hard to get those things—it is hard for me. . . . Before we rolled the tape, we were talking about a jazz set. You're playing a set and you're playing some standard, and it's your turn to take a solo and you start to execute something that your mind tells you would be nice, and you *miss* it. Well, that's not really a mistake, because you're going to play *something*, and you may all of a sudden simplify four bars and come back around to the beginning of the ninth bar and you decide you're going to do something else. But you went out and tried something, and decided not to and came back—an improvisational technique. You can't do that with rags.

HASSE: No. You were saying that playing a rag in a nightclub where the waiters are clinking around taking orders, people are talking, is different than playing it in a concert situation. Would you say you would play it differently, or would you say it's just a different demand?

MORATH: Well, no, I don't think you'd necessarily play it differently. I mean, if you'd decided you were going to play a James Scott rag, and you were working in a saloon, and some of the people were listening and some weren't, I suppose you'd still try to play it well. But the pressure's off.

HASSE: Yeah, although—now this is something I've found: I play some of the rags quite a bit differently at a supper club for a crowd of people who are drinking and eating and talking than I do in concert.

MORATH: In what way is it different?

HASSE: Well, I would play them fairly classically on the concert stage, not really like Rifkin, but with a lot of dynamics, almost too much expression, if you can say that—phrasing, long lines—and then when I play at a nightclub I'd find that to get the people's attention—because I'm competing against the din, the food, the liquor—I'd have to play them more loudly, more percussively and sometimes a little faster. But I wouldn't have to do that on a concert stage because I had their attention.

MORATH: Of course, I'll tell you this. You'd also make this difference: There are certain rags that you would *not play* in one of those situations.

HASSE: That's right.

MORATH: In the dinner-booze situation, you probably wouldn't play Joplin's *Magnetic Rag*, let's say. Whereas in a concert audience, if you had that audience right where you want them, and you want to say something about Joplin's musicality or his abilities or his progress as a composer, and you lay *Magnetic* back to back to with *The Entertainer* or *Easy Winners*, you can accomplish something in a concert sense that you could never begin to accomplish in a nightclub sense. So I think you'd pick your material differently, too.

HASSE: You practice with a metronome. What else do you go through in learning a new rag?

MORATH: I wouldn't really dignify it by putting any kind of study technique on it, John. I'm a fairly fast memorization study. As you know rags are fifty percent repetition, so you get the main theme in the first four bars, and it repeats. Well, let's face it, there's nothing alarmingly difficult about ragtime harmonies—you go about where you think you're going. So I find, especially if I'm in a hurry, I can memorize a rag in a big hurry.

HASSE: In one week?

MORATH: Oh, less than that. I can learn it in a day, but I wouldn't want to play it in a recording session. I don't like to be dependent on printed music. There are times when I have done so, but I'd rather play it by memory, so I try to get the thing by memory first, and then practice and get it under my fingers. Well, you know, there's not that much happening in a rag. You're doing what—sixty-four measures of music, half of which repeats itself almost totally.

HASSE: But I find, at least in some of the rags, that exact memorization isn't always easy. There are little surprises, for example, in the left hand.

MORATH: Well, I'll tell you, I don't necessarily abide religiously by bass lines. I don't go out of my way to invent new bass lines, but in a tonic chord if the composer happened to use two fifths in the bass in a particular measure, and I use a fifth and a root, I don't think that the ghost of Scott Joplin is going to descend on me. [Laughs] I don't mean that to be flippant, but I think there's so much evidence that ragtime composers and publishers, with a few exceptions, were so negligent about such things, and bass lines in ragtime were not that important most of the time. After all, they functioned more for rhythm than for tone.

HASSE: Why do you think the composers and publishers were negligent?

MORATH: Well, because it was a popular field and nobody gave a damn. There were certain exceptions. I think one of the great things about Joplin is that he and John Stark, and other publishers that Joplin worked for, insisted on a greater degree of scoring accuracy than did most others. Eubie Blake has told me about having to simplify his rags *Fizz Water* and *Chevy Chase* for their publication in 1914. Eubie put it beautifully. He said, "We were advised we had to write for the girl in the five-and-ten-cent store."

HASSE: Sales clerks in the sheet music departments?

MORATH: Exactly—sight readers. So Eubie simplified. He had to.

HASSE: As a pianist, how do you view piano rags?

MORATH: I think of piano rags as essentially entertainments *for oneself*. I think that's their joy, and I think that's why people enjoyed them greatly in those days. And ragtime is so deliciously pianistic that there's a great element in playing rags that is very close to those skills that come close to working out puzzles, and finishing drawings, or writing limericks, or little exact things like cabinet making. I know this sounds terribly unmusical, but I really think of ragtime that way. It's so beautifully precise and so symmetrical, yet there's a great, great satisfaction in simply mastering that symmetry just for yourself and feeling the completeness that mastering a rag gives you. There's something extremely mathematical about ragtime. There's a chess game element. And I think that that's the fun of it, and I think that most people are probably not going to perform rags in public; and if they do, they've got to work out their own emotional approach to that, and the best thing to think about in playing rags is simply to enjoy them and just delight in that pianistic "rush" that you get from rags.

HASSE: Yeah. That's interesting. I think that there's a whole body of people out there (that we don't have any way to count) who are performing ragtime in their own homes. It's an amateur music movement that has not really been chronicled, but it's there.

MORATH: Well, see, the thing that I have often thought of—so important here—is that for a long time—forty years, maybe—the piano has been an orphan in popular music. The piano has been overshadowed. First it was the big band sound in which the piano was a merely rhythm instrument. There were, of course, some jazz pianists that were important—but most people who play piano cannot master that kind of improvisation. They can listen to Teddy Wilson or Bill Evans and get listening pleasure, but they cannot go to the piano and move in that direction. Therefore, after years and years in which the piano dominated, or certainly stood high in popular music all the way through the ragtime years, through all that beautiful stuff that was written in the twenties—not only the novelties and the raggy things, but a lot of gorgeous impressionistic things by people like Rube Bloom and Peter DeRose—piano music, in other words, that you could go down to the store and buy, take home, put up on the piano, play, it was written for *that* instrument—it disappeared, and it's still gone. Tell me about the *new* things and the new styles and the new piano music that is being written, published, and is available today for the *average* pianist to take home, set up on his music rack, and play. There isn't anything in that light. So the rediscovery of ragtime has been a boon to your frustrated keyboardist.

If Rudi Blesh almost singlehandedly rescued ragtime from likely historical oblivion, and Max Morath was the first to carry it anew to a mass public through numerous tours and especially on television, it was Gunther Schuller who, along with Joshua Rifkin, in the 1970s brought ragtime new respectability and audiences in the United States and Europe.

Schuller, my third interview subject, is a major American composer, a well-known conductor and educator, and a jazz scholar. The son of a violinist who played in the New York Philharmonic, he was born in New York City on November 22, 1925. During the 1940s and 1950s, he performed as horn soloist with the Cincinnati Symphony and the Metropolitan Opera. Schuller taught horn at the Manhattan School of Music and composition at Yale University, and from 1967 to 1977 was President of the prestigious New England Conservatory of Music.

Since about 1950 he has been actively involved in various fusions of jazz and classical music, and in 1957 coined the term "third stream" to denote such blends. Schuller has composed more than eighty-five works, including several operas and numerous chamber and symphonic works, a number of which include jazz elements. He is also a scholar of jazz, and his important book *Early Jazz* (1968) includes numerous references to ragtime.[7]

In 1972, Schuller founded the New England Conservatory Ragtime Ensemble, and, through its zestful performances and recordings (on Angel and Golden Crest records), brought orchestrated ragtime a new popularity and status. He and his ensemble played concerts across the country, appeared several times on public television, made a four-week tour of the Soviet Union in May and June of 1978, and were heard worldwide via shortwave radio on the Voice of America. Schuller has a hectic schedule that includes frequent trips to Europe; since I was unable to arrange a face-to-face meeting, we conducted our interview by telephone between Boston, Massachusetts, and Bloomington, Indiana, on October 1, 1978.[8]

HASSE: When and how did you first become interested in ragtime?

SCHULLER: My interest in ragtime coincides and starts with my interest in jazz, which, of course, goes way back into my own teen years, although I must admit that in those earlier years—I'm speaking about the 1940s—I was much more intensely involved with the jazz of the then-new music, called bebop, and the music of Duke Ellington and people like that. And my interests in ragtime, at that time, were somewhat peripheral, and I can't claim that I was very knowledgeable. But later, as I began to study the subject more and read more, I also came under the influence of Martin Williams. I think that he was the first one to really make me aware of the unusual qualities, especially the structural qualities of ragtime. This was in the middle or late fifties. He had been writing occasionally on ragtime and doing interesting structural and formal analyses of some of the rags of Joplin. We were working together on the *Jazz Review*, a very good magazine of that period. We saw a lot of each other and, of course, exchanged ideas a lot. So from him I got a deeper and better understanding of ragtime. And this coincided with my reading Rudi Blesh's book *They All Played Ragtime*, a book that has been a revelatory experience for thousands of people, I imagine, in regard to ragtime. So, those two things together—Martin's somewhat more analytical approach to the actual music and Rudi Blesh opening up that whole world to me—made me very keenly interested in the music.

But I am a French horn player, and with a French horn there isn't a lot you can do with ragtime. If you're a pianist, you can play it. But I'm not a pianist at all, and so there was always this gap between what I *knew* about the music on the one hand, and on the other hand my ability to do something about that. So, to make a long story very short, my first chance to actually do something with ragtime occurred when through Vera [Brodsky] Lawrence I got some copies of the "Red Back Book," which I had heard about through all those years. But whenever anyone mentioned it, it was always understood that all copies of the "Red Back Book" had disappeared from the face of the earth, and that it was pointless to look for

it. But when these arrangements came into my hands through Vera
Lawrence, I seized the opportunity to get personally involved with ragtime
as a performer. And I guess the rest is history: the formation of the New
England Conservatory Ragtime Ensemble in 1972, the concert that we gave
at the Smithsonian (again, Martin Williams was the instigator of that), then
the record companies picking up on it—and Angel [Records] being one of
those—and recording us, and then the Grammy Award, and that led to *The
Sting*, and so on. (You know the rest of the history.) So to answer your
question, one summary way is to say that I always had been interested in
ragtime. I wish to emphasize that it wasn't something that suddenly
happened to me in 1972, when I started the Ragtime Ensemble. It had been
an abiding interest, about which, however, I couldn't do anything
specifically as a performer until the vehicle in the form of the "Red Back
Book" arrangements came along. The circumstances I've recounted made it
finally possible to express my interest in ragtime in specific tangible terms.

HASSE: Would you say that the first thing that attracted you to it was
the musical sound of it? Or was it the study of it?

SCHULLER: It was a combination of both. I don't think I can ever separate
those aspects in my own studies of anything. I'm a composer, a creative

Gunther Schuller conducts the New England Conservatory Ragtime Ensemble in its recording
of original orchestrations from Scott Joplin's "Red Back Book," Jordan Hall, Boston, February,
1973. (*Courtesy Angel Records*)

person, and I tend also to be quite analytical. But at the same time, I'm also a performer; and I'm always making the translation from the one realm, the creative, to the other, the recreative. But what attracted me when I was merely studying and enjoying the music as a listener (of the old piano rolls, for example) was the perfection of the materials, even though the means used were very simple. The forms were very simple, closely related to the march forms, also very simple melodic and harmonic ideas, and essentially a very simple structural approach—but perfect! So I always appreciated this music as a kind of perfection in miniature—the small form carried to a very high level of skill and of beauty, as high as one finds in classical composers, many of whom, like Chopin or Delius or composers like that, also worked very well in small forms and were often not particularly successful in the large extended forms. So this kind of miniaturized perfection is something that I appreciated, particularly since I'd already been for many, many years a very keen student and performer of Anton Webern, who is probably the greatest small-form miniaturist composer of the twentieth century. So that was one element of my appreciation. But when I performed the music, I learned to love and appreciate another level of the music which really had to do more with the inner essence of it, and that is that whole fantastic combination of an endlessly *joyous* music, *perfectly* put together; in other words, a music which one can appreciate on the most analytical intellectual level, if one wants to, but which one can also enjoy purely as a perfectly made *entertainment* music. And this is, I think, the reason that ragtime enjoys now, in this revival, such an enormous success. It really speaks to both types of listeners—those of a more intellectual or culturally experienced background, but also to those who just simply go to music, whatever it might be—whether it's jazz or rock or a Strauss waltz or a Beethoven symphony— who go to music as consumers and as enjoyers and as listeners. They can enjoy it on a sort of surface level, without even being particularly conscious of the wonderful compositional niceties of the music. And that is a very rare, almost unique, combination. I think most musics that I know of in the world—I mean if you look at the entire spectrum of musics from all kinds of popular musics to ethnic musics and to the art musics and so on—there are very few that combine those two levels of perfection in such a brilliant way. That was really a revelation to me when I began to perform the music. And, of course, when I saw the audiences' reactions and the reactions of my musicians and myself, I knew that this was a unique kind of music. I think the most startling thing that I learned about ragtime since I began performing it is that it is the *only* music—and I really want to emphasize this—it is the *only* music that I know of (and I know almost every kind of music; I have enormous catholicity of taste and I have studied everything from the *ars nova* to the most advanced combinatorial serialism and all kinds of Third-World musics, African, Japanese, you name it—I've tried to study and get to know everything), I know of no music other than ragtime that I could perform *so consistently* over *so many years* and *so many times* the same pieces—I mean the *Maple Leaf Rag*, *The Entertainer*, or *Pine Apple Rag*, or whatever—and *never once* fail to enjoy it. Never once! I just cannot understand it. It is to me totally incomprehensible. I have played almost every kind of music. After all, I played for fifteen years in the Metropolitan Opera, and I must have played *La Traviata* three hundred times; I played with the New York Philharmonic, and the Cincinnati Symphony where I played Tchaikovsky symphonies, Mendelssohn, or Beethoven many times; and I must say, even in those very high realms of music—the great classical masterpieces—there is a limit as to how many times you can play those works and still fully enjoy them. I remember specifically a tour with the Cincinnati Symphony when I was seventeen years old and playing first horn there. We did the Tchaikovsky Fifth Symphony more than a dozen times, and by about the eighth performance, although I loved the piece— and the Fifth Symphony is, after all, for a horn player a delight because it features that great horn solo in the second movement—after about the eighth performance, I almost couldn't stand the piece any more. And I can cite literally hundreds of examples of music that I've performed where after a certain amount of time it just begins to bore or pale or lose its original captivation.

Now I can say truthfully that in these countless ragtime performances that I've done with my ensemble, this has *never* happened, even for one fleeting moment. In fact, the contrary. I can come to a ragtime concert totally exhausted from an impossible day—everything's gone wrong, and I'm tired, and I haven't had any sleep—and after ten seconds of the *Maple Leaf Rag* I feel refreshed and alive. It's like a tonic. I'm suddenly elated and in physically and mentally superior spirits. It's the most amazing thing! I don't fully understand it, but I think it's attributable to this rare combination of a kind of technical perfection of works like those of Joplin and to this other mysterious quality: the inner and genuine and irresistible joy in this music.

HASSE: That is remarkable. Have you noticed this same effect on any other people?

SCHULLER: The kids in my ensemble virtually all feel the same way, and most of them feel it to the very same extent that I do. A few perhaps not quite to that extent. And, of course, everything I'm saying is also borne out by the audiences to which we play, for example, at Wolf Trap [Farm] where we've played for seven years in a row—and where a good part of that audience comes back *every year*. To me they confirm the same thing. They also are somewhat amazed that no matter how often they hear this music, it doesn't pale on them. I have heard some people say, "Well, I'm getting pretty tired of ragtime," but if I were to look into that more closely, I probably would find that they have either heard some shoddy performance, or some other extenuating factor has come into it.

HASSE: It is very interesting to hear you say this, because this has been my experience, too. I play piano in a supper club on weekends, and the same people show up week after week asking for the *Maple Leaf Rag, The Entertainer*. They just don't get tired of it. It's just such a fine music.

SCHULLER: Yes. Perfectly crafted but with a human quality in it which is beyond examination. The two combine together into something that's really unique.

HASSE: Besides classical music, third stream, and modern jazz, you have been involved as a performer and a conductor in a number of other, sometimes older, American musics—ragtime, the opera *Treemonisha*, Sousa and march music, country fiddle band music, the music of Paul Whiteman, Duke Ellington, and Jelly Roll Morton. That's quite a variety of musics. In the course of your work with these musics, how have you come to perceive their similarities?

SCHULLER: Well, it's like anything else—there are similarities and there are dissimilarities. One could argue it either way. One could find certain common threads through many of those musics that you just enumerated; and then, on the other hand, I think what is probably more important is not so much the similarities, but the things that make them *distinctive,* because it is *those* qualities which made those musics survive in their time and beyond into our own time. So it is the distinctive qualities of an Ellington or Whiteman or Jelly Roll Morton or Joplin or Ives, or whoever, that makes us talk about them still in 1978. The similarities are the very same things that to a large extent also exist in all kinds of second rate and mediocre music. So those are not as interesting. But, of course, what all these musics do have in common, except that they present it in different and personal ways, is an enormous rhythmic vitality, which we now regard as a particularly or peculiarly American contribution. And, indeed, that is a contribution which, again, comes to a large extent from the black people, and which is not common to the European classical tradition, at least not to that extent. And to this very day most Europeans have great trouble performing American music, whatever kind—classical or popular—with that true rhythmic vitality, not because they're not musically skilled or because they're incompetent, but because that kind of rhythmic vitality is just not in their bones and in their blood. So that is one particularly American element which one could say is common to all these composers, to all these musicians. But then there's a vast difference between the harmonies and melodies of a Duke Ellington, let's say, as opposed to those arrangers who worked for Paul Whiteman, Grofé, and Challis. And yet, in my view, they are of almost equal quality as styles, just different.

HASSE: Yes. Do you see yourself in part as a champion of neglected American musics?

SCHULLER: Yes, I do. I don't wish to make a whole career of it or do *only* that, but amongst the many things that I do, I definitely do see myself as a champion of that music (a) because I find much of the music has great merit and value and beauty and, therefore, it deserves to be performed and heard; and (b) because I know from studying the whole history of the development of the arts in the United States that we have suffered for a long time (and still do to some extent) from a tremendous inferiority complex about our own music. That's partially understandable when one realizes that we are a very young country and we had, in fact, to import our musical traditions primarily from Europe in order to have any; and that whole development has got to take a long time—several centuries perhaps. Before one can establish one's own tradition, there's a lot of importing and acquiring and imitating and borrowing and stealing that has to take place. During that period one tends to be aware of that, and so one tends to develop a sense of inferiority about that. But I think those days are long gone now, and I think it's high time that America be quite proud of its musical traditions—past and present, classical and popular—in their best forms, of course. I mean, there's a lot of crap which is produced all the time in *all* periods and in *all* generations and in *all* styles and perhaps, more today than ever before. So one can't be proud of *everything*. But one can be proud of the best things, and I think one should be. And in recognition of that, I certainly would champion all good music without going to the extreme of saying our older music is better than someone else's.

In the last three decades since *They All Played Ragtime*, many others besides Blesh, Morath, and Schuller have helped to breathe new life into ragtime, have explored, presented, and disseminated the music. Among these others are performers, conductors, composers, arrangers, researchers, writers, concert promoters, magazine editors, music publishers, record company executives, and broadcasters. You will find most of these people elsewhere in this book—mentioned in various chapters, listed in the bibliography or discography, included as authors of essays. Among the hundreds of individuals, I have selected thirteen for special mention. These are thirteen genuine ragtime partisans who have had probably the most impact in preserving, regenerating, and presenting ragtime before a wide public. Each of them has been involved in more than one facet of the ragtime revival—in performing, composing, collecting, researching, writing, lecturing, and/or promoting. They are discussed below in alphabetical order.[9]

EUBIE BLAKE became in the 1970s and 1980s the ragtime performer most familiar to the public at large—through numerous appearances on television and a successful Broadway tribute, *Eubie!*. Many people, even if pressed, could name no other living ragtime musician. He was born James Hubert Blake in Baltimore on February 7, 1883. While early in his career Eubie left ragtime to go on to musical comedy and popular songwriting, it is his ragtime contributions that brought him fame late in his life. The longest-living ragtimer from the original era, he kept up an ambitious schedule late into his nineties, with appearances on the "Today" and "Tonight" television programs, at the White House Jazz Festival, and on many other stages and screens, in the United States and Europe. On his 100th birthday, on February 7, 1983, he was honored with several gala concert tributes in New York. Five days later, on February 12, he died.

WILLIAM ELDEN BOLCOM is a composer and pianist who has made a substantial impact in ragtime. He was born in Seattle, Washington, on May 26, 1938.

Trained in composition at the University of Washington (B.A.), Mills College (M.A.), and Stanford University (D.M.A.), he has taught composition at the University of Michigan since 1973. In 1967 he became interested in ragtime and stimulated the interest of such figures as Joshua Rifkin and Vera Brodsky Lawrence (both discussed below). Bolcom ranks as one of the leading composers of ragtime since its rediscovery; he has recorded his works on Nonesuch and Jazzology and many of his rags have been published by Edward B. Marks. Beginning with his 1971 recording *Heliotrope Bouquet* (Nonesuch H-71257), Bolcom was, along with Joshua Rifkin, influential in gaining acceptance of ragtime by the academic and classical music communities. He co-authored (with Robert Kimball) *Reminiscing with Sissle and Blake* (1973),[9] which did much to promote new interest in Eubie Blake, and in the late 1970s Bolcom contributed the essay on ragtime to *The New Grove Encyclopedia of Music and Musicians*.[10] A pianist of grace and élan, Bolcom and his wife, singer Joan Morris, perform recitals of American popular songs written since the 1890s.

LOUIS FERDINAND BUSCH, born in Louisville, Kentucky on July 18, 1910, was better known by his inimitable pseudonym, Joe "Fingers" Carr. A self-taught arranger and accompanist, Busch worked in artists and repertory for Capitol Records beginning in 1949. In April 1950, he created his colorful pseudonym and began recording ragtime piano, eventually releasing fourteen albums and thirty-six singles. He composed and recorded about twenty of his own rags and recorded more published rags than anyone else, giving a number of these works their first recordings. As Jasen and Tichenor have written, "he was a major rediscoverer of ragtime at a time" when few people had been interested.[11] In the 1950s his many recordings helped expose a new public to ragtime, and though they emphasized the happy aspects of the music, they also—for better or worse—helped promulgate for ragtime a "rinky-tink" image. Busch died in an auto accident on September 18, 1979.

ROBERT DARCH has probably traveled more miles to perform ragtime than any other revivalist. Born in 1920 in Detroit, "Ragtime Bob" Darch has been spreading the effervescence of ragtime since the mid-1950s to audiences throughout the United States and Canada. One of the first professional ragtime entertainers since the music's heyday, Darch has specialized in the saloon circuit, where he feels ragtime songs and instrumentals are most at home. Darch helped revive the careers of Eubie Blake and Joe Jordan, discovered "lost" rag manuscripts of James Scott and Scott Hayden, and helped organize ragtime festivals in the late 1950s and early 1960s in several communities in Missouri. He also influenced a number of younger musicians, including Trebor Tichenor and Steve Spracklen, to become involved with the music. Darch has recorded albums for United Artists, Jan Productions, and Mekanisk Music Museum.

RICHARD ROVEN HYMAN, better known as Dick Hyman, was born in New York City on March 8, 1927. He studied piano with Teddy Wilson and since 1948 has extensively recorded and performed jazz and popular music. An unusually versatile musician, he performs most if not all the styles in the history of jazz piano. In the 1950s, using the pseudonyms Knuckles O'Toole, Willie "The Rock" Knox, and Slugger Ryan he recorded piano rags in a honky-tonk style on a tinny-sounding piano. In the 1970s, under his own name, he took a dramatically different, more sensitive approach to performing ragtime on the critically successful *Scott Joplin: The Complete Works for Piano*, a handsomely packaged five-record set from RCA Red Seal (CRL 5-1106). Hyman has also become a leading champion of the music of Jelly Roll Morton and other ragtime-influenced jazz pianists such as James P. Johnson, and has been active in the jazz repertory movement. Hyman arranged and, off camera, performed the music for the 1977 motion picture *Scott Joplin*, which starred Billy Dee Williams and Art Carney.

DAVID ALAN JASEN pursues ragtime on many fronts—including performing, producing record reissues, writing, researching, and collecting. Born in New York City on December 16, 1937, he early came under the influence of recordings of Joe "Fingers" Carr. Meanwhile he earned a B.A. in Communication Arts from American University and an M.L.S. from Long Island University, and he now teaches at C. W. Post Center. As a performer, he has two albums on Blue Goose, and one each on Folkways and Euphonic Records. Jasen has built one of the world's largest collections of ragtime records, sheet music, and documentary materials, and has compiled a pioneer discography, *Recorded Ragtime, 1897-1958* (1973). With Trebor Jay Tichenor, he co-authored the important book *Rags and Ragtime: A Musical History* (1978), and he has compiled and edited the folio *Ragtime: 100 Authentic Rags* (1979).[12] Jasen has been most prolific as the producer-annotator of dozens of historical reissues of vintage recordings of ragtime, novelty piano, and early jazz for Folkways, RBF, and Herwin records.

VERA BRODSKY LAWRENCE is a historian and editor of American music. She was born on July 1, 1909, in Norfolk, Virginia, and received musical training at the Juilliard Foundation. She was a concert pianist from 1930 to 1965, and then changed careers to edit contemporary classical music publications and the piano works of American composer Louis Moreau Gottschalk. Her primary and lasting contribution to ragtime and the ragtime revival was her compiling and painstaking editing of *The Collected Works of Scott Joplin.* (two volumes, 1971). This major work, for the first time, made nearly all of Joplin's piano works, in definitive editions, easily available to a wide public. It did much to make Joplin acceptable to the classical music world, and sent other music publishers scrambling to issue their own ragtime folios; within a few years ragtime musicians had literally hundreds of new publications from which to choose.[13] Lawrence was also instrumental in reviving Joplin's long-dormant opera *Treemonisha* and shepherding it to a brilliant recording by Gunther Schuller and the Houston Grand Opera (Deutsche Grammophon 2707 083, 1976).

R. MICHAEL MONTGOMERY was born in Chicago on March 9, 1934, and as a teen-ager became hooked on the sound of player pianos. He began collecting, and imitating at the keyboard, old player piano rolls. After earning a B.A. in English from the University of Michigan in 1955, he began working for Michigan Bell. Montgomery's contributions to ragtime are multifaceted. In the late 1950s, he became one of the first to write about Joseph Lamb following that composer's rediscovery. Beginning in 1959 he contributed a number of pioneering piano rollographies—on Scott Joplin, Eubie Blake, and others—to specialist magazines and to various books. Conscientiously striving to preserve, understand, and disseminate ragtime and early jazz and blues on piano rolls has been his main interest. He has produced or coproduced sixteen albums of vintage piano roll recordings for Biograph Records, including five LPs of Scott Joplin rolls and one of James Scott. Montgomery has amassed an outstanding collection of five thousand piano rolls and ten thousand pieces of sheet music from the Ragtime Era and the 1920s. Another major contribution has been his energetic and generous behind-the-scenes help with the research of many authors, including Rudi Blesh, Trebor Tichenor and David A. Jasen, and the present author. To those who know him, he is a source of contagious enthusiasm for researching and appreciating ragtime and related musics.

MELVIN E. "TURK" MURPHY, trombonist and band leader, was born in Palermo, California, on December 16, 1915, and grew up just as the Ragtime Era gave way to the novelty piano and jazz of the 1920s. Murphy was one of the earliest to research and resurrect vintage ragtime for presentation to the public. In about 1940 he helped organize the Lu Watters jazz band, and in 1941 participated in its influential recordings of such ragtime tunes as *Maple Leaf Rag, At a Georgia Campmeeting, Black and White Rag,* and *Smoky Mokes.* This band, more than any other single force, was responsible for the reawakening of worldwide interest in traditional jazz. Since 1947 he has led his own traditional jazz band, and has recorded LPs for Columbia, RCA, Verve, Atlantic, and Good Time Jazz, among others. Since 1960 his band has performed regularly at Earthquake McGoon's, a San Francisco night club owned jointly by Murphy and his pianist, Pete Clute. Through his recordings, tours, and appearances at such festivals as the National Ragtime Festival, Murphy has built a large following in the United States, Europe, and Australia. For more than forty years, he has been researching and collecting vintage ragtime music, and his band performances feature healthy portions of classic rags. In 1972 Atlantic Records issued his *The Many Faces of Ragtime* (SD 1613), a delightful album of jazz band ragtime (Joplin, Scott, Aufderheide, and others), which won many new friends for the band and for ragtime as jazz.

JOSHUA RIFKIN was born in New York City in 1944 and earned degrees in composition from the Juilliard School and in musicology from Princeton University. His 1970 record *Scott Joplin: Piano Rags* (Nonesuch H-71248) helped launch a major Joplin revival in the 1970s, and was honored with a Record of the Year Award by *Stereo Review*. The disc, the best-selling record in the history of Nonesuch Records, reached a wide audience, and was followed by two subsequent volumes in 1972 and 1974. Rifkin's careful, note-for-note renditions served to legitimize Joplin and ragtime as respectable material for classical musicians and for the concert hall, and helped establish a school of ragtime performance which emphasized literal, slow readings with careful attention to dynamics and phrasing. Rifkin began concertizing in 1972, and in the fall of 1973 and the spring of 1975 toured the United States. He made a substantial impact in England, where he toured in December 1973 and in the spring of 1974, and where he made numerous radio and television appearances, including two of his own specials for the BBC. Rifkin has lectured on Joplin at several German universities, including Frankfurt, Saarbrücken, Cologne, and Marburg. In 1980 Angel Records, another respected classical label, released a special digital recording of Rifkin's interpretations of Joplin rags.

TREBOR JAY TICHENOR has worn many ragtime hats—as editor, writer, historian, collector, pianist, recording artist, and producer. He was born in Saint Louis on January 28, 1940, and at the age of thirteen, discovered ragtime through the recordings of Joe "Fingers" Carr. In 1963 he earned a B.A. degree from Washington University. Tichenor began composing his own "folk"-style rags in 1961, and has completed more than two dozen of them. In 1961, he co-founded and co-edited the *Ragtime Review*, the first regular periodical on ragtime since the 1910s, and that same year helped organize the Saint Louis Ragtimers, for whom he has played piano ever since. He has recorded three albums as solo pianist, and five with the Ragtimers. Tichenor owns the largest collection of ragtime piano rolls, and has collaborated with Michael Montgomery on six important record reissues of the rolls of Scott Joplin and James Scott. He is the co-author of *Rags and Ragtime: A Musical History* (1978) and has compiled and edited two folios of rare piano rags, *Ragtime Rarities* (1975) and *Ragtime Rediscoveries* (1979).[14] He co-authored the essay on ragtime piano rolls that appears in this book, and hosts a weekly ragtime radio program in Saint Louis. Tichenor is such a ragtime partisan, even addict, that he has said, "I'm like Will Rogers: I never heard a rag I didn't like."

TERRY WALDO, whose real name is Ralph Emerson Waldo III, was born in 1944 in Ironton, Ohio. He earned a B.A. and M.A. in communications from Ohio State University. As a pianist, Waldo "paid his dues" playing Shakey's pizza parlors and Red Garter banjo bars. He has performed as a jazz pianist with his own Gutbucket Syncopators and other groups, and has recorded a number of albums as soloist and band member. His greatest contribution to the ragtime revival was his 1974 series for National Public Radio, "This is Ragtime," for which he traveled the nation to interview performers, critics, and researchers. This series helped legitimize ragtime and bring its music and history to a sophisticated new radio audience. Waldo wrote a witty, lively book, also called *This is Ragtime* (1976),[15] based on his radio series. A prótegé of Eubie Blake, Waldo has worked to promote and recognize Blake's unique music and transcribed and edited a folio of Blake's rags (1975), making available for the first time accurate transcriptions of Blake's complex playing style. Waldo is a regular performer at festivals such as the National Ragtime Festival, held each summer in Saint Louis.

RICHARD ZIMMERMAN, ragtime pianist, advocate, writer and editor, was born on August 11, 1937, in Charleston, West Virginia. He began piano lessons at the age of eight and at the age of sixteen began playing ragtime. He earned a B.S. in civil engineering and an M.S. in structural engineering, both from Stanford University. He worked for twelve years at Mattel as a game designer, and since then has freelanced as a professional magician and designer of magical illusions. In 1967 he helped found the Maple Leaf Club, a Los Angeles-based organization of ragtime players and aficionados. This club, along with the Canadian-based Ragtime Society, has fostered the growth of an international ragtime fraternity. Under Zimmerman's editorship, the club's periodical, the *Rag Times,* has developed into the leading vehicle for the dissemination of news of the ragtime revival, and has stimulated much valuable research into the history of ragtime. Zimmerman has also made his mark as a pianist, becoming the first to record Joplin's entire known ragtime output in a five-record boxed set (Murray Hill 931079). He also recorded *The Collector's History of Ragtime,* another five-record set (Murray Hill M-60556/5). Zimmerman has built a fine collection of ragtime sheet music and documentary materials, and has aided other researchers with their work.

There they are: Rudi Blesh, dean of ragtime historians and patriarch of the ragtime revival; Max Morath, ragtime spokesman and entertainer extraordinaire; Gunther Schuller, conductor-scholar and eloquent champion of ragtime. And thirteen other dedicated apostles of this syncopated sound who have expended great time and poured enormous energy into rekindling and recounting the music. Despite differences in age, musical training, and profession, these sixteen Americans share devotion to this joyful, scintillating style. I like to believe that the Western world is slightly happier, more optimistic and reminiscent, because of their efforts on behalf of the jaunty music called ragtime.

Notes

1. Rudi Blesh and Harriet Janis, *They All Played Ragtime* (New York: Alfred A. Knopf, 1950; 2nd ed., rev., New York: Grove Press, 1959; 3rd ed., rev., New York: Oak Publications, 1966; 4th ed., rev., New York: Oak Publications, 1971).

2. The conversations printed in this chapter represent edited excerpts from the original interviews. The tape recordings and complete transcripts of these interviews are on deposit at the Indiana University Archives of Traditional Music, Bloomington. See also *Who's Who in America 1980-81* (Chicago: Marquis Who's Who, 1980) and Nicholas Slonimsky, *Baker's Biographical Dictionary of Musicians* (New York: Schirmer Books, 1978; London: Collier Macmillan, 1978).

3. Blesh subsequently collected and published the lectures as *This is Jazz: A Series of Lectures Given at the San Francisco Museum of Art* (San Francisco: The author, 1943; London: Jazz Music Books, 1945).

4. (New York: Knopf, 1946; London: Cassell, 1949).

5. *Modern Art, U.S.A.* (New York: Knopf, 1956); *Stuart Davis* (New York: Grove Press, 1960); *Keaton* (New York: Macmillan, 1966); *Combo U.S.A.* (Philadelphia: Chilton, 1971); and with Harriet Janis, *De Kooning* (New York: Grove Press, 1960) and *Collage: Personalities, Concepts, Techniques* (Philadelphia: Chilton, 1962).

6. In *The Collected Works of Scott Joplin*, ed. Vera Brodsky Lawrence, Volume I: Works for Piano; Volume II: Works for Voice (New York: New York Public Library, 1971). The introduction is also included in *The Complete Works of Scott Joplin*, ed. Vera Brodsky Lawrence, Volume I: Works for Piano; Volume II: Works for Voice (New York: New York Public Library, 1982).

7. *Early Jazz: Its Roots and Musical Development* (New York: Oxford University Press, 1968).

8. Portions of the interview were published in John Edward Hasse, "An Interview with Gunther Schuller," *Annual Review of Jazz Studies* 1 (1982): 39–58.

9. For the capsule biographies of these twelve, I have drawn upon the following sources: John Chilton, *Who's Who of Jazz: Storyville to Swing Street* (Philadelphia: Chilton, 1972); Leonard Feather, *The New Edition of the Encyclopedia of Jazz* (New York: Bonanza Books, 1960); Leonard Feather, *The Encyclopedia of Jazz in the Sixties* (New York: Bonanza Books, 1966); David A. Jasen and Trebor Jay Tichenor, *Rags and Ragtime: A Musical History* (New York: Seabury Press, 1978); Nicholas Slonimsky, *Baker's Biographical Dictionary*; Terry Waldo, *This is Ragtime* (New York: Hawthorn Books, 1976); *Who's Who in America 1980-81*; and upon my own correspondence and/or interviews between 1978 and 1980 with David A. Jasen, Vera Brodsky Lawrence, Michael Montgomery, Turk Murphy, Joshua Rifkin, Trebor Jay Tichenor, Terry Waldo, and Dick Zimmerman.

10. Robert Kimball and William Bolcom, *Reminiscing with Sissle and Blake* (New York: Viking, 1973); William Bolcom, "Ragtime," in *The New Grove Encyclopedia of Music and Musicians*, ed. Stanley Sadie, 20 vols. (London: Macmillan, 1980; Washington, D.C.: Grove's Dictionaries of Music, 1980; Hong Kong; Peninsula Publishers, 1980), 15: 537–40.

11. Jasen and Tichenor, *Rags and Ragtime*, p. 268. For additional biographical information on Busch, see David A. Jasen, "Our Friend, Lou," *Rag Times* 13, no. 4 (November 1979): 1.

12. Jasen, *Recorded Ragtime, 1897-1958* (Hamden, Conn.: Archon Books, 1973); Jasen and Tichenor, *Rags and Ragtime*; and Jasen, comp., *Ragtime: 100 Authentic Rags* (New York: The Big 3, 1979).

13. Eventually Lawrence added three rags which had not been available for the *Collected Works*. The result was the publication of *The Complete Works of Scott Joplin*, ed. Vera Brodsky Lawrence, Volume I: Works for Piano; Volume II: Works for Voice (New York: New York Public Library, 1982).

14. *Ragtime Rarities: Complete Original Music for 63 Piano Rags* (New York: Dover, 1975) and *Ragtime Rediscoveries: 64 Works from the Golden Age of Rag* (New York: Dover, 1979).

15. Terry Waldo, *This is Ragtime* (New York: Hawthorn Books, 1976).

The
Music
of
Ragtime

The Grace and Beauty of Classic Rags: Structural Elements in a Distinct Musical Genre

Roland Nadeau

Roland Nadeau surveys the musical elements of piano rags, examining their rhythms, melody, texture, harmony, and form. Nadeau also offers advice on how a piano rag should be performed. This article originally appeared in 1973, just as the Scott Joplin revival was beginning.

From *Music Educators Journal* 59 (April 1973): 57–64. Copyright © 1973 by Music Educators National Conference. Used with permission.

Ragtime has come home, perhaps to stay. Authentic performances—both live and on discs—have brought it back the way it was, and recent publications have given a good deal of information on the literature of ragtime and how the style developed. Most of the writing on rag, however, has been historical, and only a few exceptions have included technical or analytic information. With the renewed interest in ragtime, there is a practical need for a discussion of the structural elements of the style that will aid the performer and enhance the enjoyment of the listener. An understanding of such elements as tempo, meter, syncopation, melody, and form as they are used in ragtime will advance the appreciation and performance of one of the first distinctly American musical genres.

Rhythmic Elements

Because ragtime generates great rhythmic motion, the unknowing player tends to play a rag as fast as his fingers will allow. Ragtime should never be played in a very fast tempo, and the evidence on this point is convincing. Scott Joplin, in his *School of Ragtime*, stated categorically, "Play slowly until you catch the swing, and never play ragtime fast at any time." One of his favorite indications was "Slow March Tempo" (see *Sugar Cane* and *Pine Apple Rag*). Joplin's admonition makes sense because the rag came in part from the march, and marches are obviously not played in running tempo. It also makes sense for more cogent reasons. The textural web of ragtime is intricate, with much for the ear to assimilate—both strong rhythmic counterpoint of accents and sophisticated melodic figuration. The harmonic rhythm sometimes is quick, and incipient countermelodies periodically crop up in both treble and bass.

On the other hand, ragtime must not be played too slowly. Its tempo should range from a moderato to an easy allegro. Whether a rag is graceful or raucous, the player discovers its tempo by a combination of musical intuition and an analysis of its structure. In general, the more subtle and sophisticated the interaction of rhythmic, melodic, textural, and harmonic factors is, the more conservative the tempo must be. No matter what the tempo, the beat is almost always rigorously steady.

The classic rag is in duple meter, as were its ancestors, the march, cakewalk, quadrille, polka, and jig. The quarter note is the usual beat unit, and the meter signature, $\frac{2}{4}$. When notated in four quarter notes, a rag is played in cut time, $\frac{2}{2}$, and the effect is the same. In the right-hand part, the quarter note is subdivided into eighths, dotted eighths, and sixteenths in different syncopated combinations. Sometimes the dotted sixteenth with a thirty-second appears, but the eighth-note triplet is seldom present. (The triplet division of the basic beat was to become important later, in jazz.)

All rags contain syncopation, but, whereas the duple meter is used motorically throughout, the use of syncopation is partial. Syncopated measures are dispersed throughout each rag, and in nonsyncopated

Grace and Beauty (1910) is a ragtime masterpiece by James Scott. *(John Edward Hasse collection)*

measures, accents in the right-hand part coincide with strong metric accents in the left. The proportion of syncopated to nonsyncopated measures is roughly four to one. For example, Joplin's *Maple Leaf Rag* shows sixty-seven syncopated measures out of a total of eighty (not counting repeated parts). The percentage of syncopated measures in James Scott's *Grace and Beauty* is seventy-nine and that of Joseph Lamb's *Top Liner Rag* is eighty-two.

Of course, syncopation is not unique to ragtime; it also occurs in keyboard music of the European tradition. Such pieces as J. S. Bach's two-part invention no. 6, in E major, and Chopin's etude in A Minor, Op. 25, No. 4, are heavily syncopated. The *Etude* contains syncopation in every measure but the last three (sixty-two out of sixty-five measures). Although much syncopation is present in both the Bach and Chopin pieces, neither of these compositions resembles ragtime. It follows then that ragtime syncopation must be different from that found in earlier styles of music.

Ragtime syncopation is distinguished by the consistent use of a variety of accents on the weak part of the divided quarter-note unit. In practice, accents appear either on the second eighth, or on the second, third, or fourth sixteenth. The basic generative rhythmic pattern that underlies ragtime syncopation (Example 19) may have evolved from the iambic pattern. Both patterns were well known in preragtime American dances and in European music. The pattern in Example 20, called the "Scotch snap," was as common in Baroque music as it was in the early American jig. The fact that both patterns (Examples 19 and 20) are also basic to certain West African dances supports the belief that ragtime is a product of sociomusical syncretism.

Example 19.

Example 20.

Other patterns also appear regularly. Several make use of tied notes or a rest on the beat (Example 21). All of these patterns, and a few others, are then used by the composer to energize his melodic line. (The passage in Example 22 shows a mixture of several of the patterns shown in Examples 19 through 22). This mixture of selected syncopated patterns, more than any other factor, distinguishes ragtime rhythm from that found in traditional music.

Example 21.

The example in Example 23 is different from the previous figures, yet related to them. The right hand plays several groups of four even notes arranged so that melodic accents do not coincide with metric accents in the bass. Thus, instead of the normal pattern of accents (Example 24), the melodic grouping in three's produces accents opposed to those in the bass (Example 25).

A sophisticated variant of the bimeter in Example 25 occurs when the values in the right-hand part are not even, but nevertheless establish a feeling of meter opposed to that in the bass (Example 26).

Melody and Texture

Rag melody is strictly instrumental and pianistic, and its contour is characteristically disjunct. By contrast, European piano literature of the

Example 22. Joseph F. Lamb, *Excelsior Rag*, **B** strain, measures 7–16.

Example 23. George Botsford, *Black and White Rag*, **A** strain, measures 1–4.

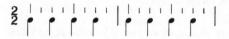

Example 24.

Example 25.

Example 26. James Scott, *Hilarity Rag*, **D** strain, measures 1–6.

nineteenth century often contains conjunct melodic lines. A familiar example is Chopin's waltz in C-sharp minor, Op. 64. The first and second strains are disjunct, but the third (D-flat major) is essentially conjunct and song-like.

Consistent with the disjunct contour of rag melody is its wide range. The melodic line can cover more than three octaves, which allows considerable figural contrast. Its basic soprano register is sometimes divided into lower and upper soprano. Typically, a kind of "call and response" dialogue occurs where short melodic fragments are tossed from lower to upper soprano (Example 27).

Example 27. James Scott, *Prosperity Rag*, **C** strain, measures 1–4.

The pianistic figuration in ragtime is rich and varied. Melodic runs that traverse diatonic and chromatic scale patterns or outline chords are common. Single notes alternating with octaves are used to add brilliance to the sound. When this happens, as in the second strain of *Maple Leaf Rag*, the octave often sounds on the weak part of the beat, reinforcing the feeling of syncopation. Harmonic thirds and fourths, as well as full chords, serve to thicken the melodic line and enrich the textural sound.

One interesting device in ragtime is the use of a short, temporary

Example 28. Joseph F. Lamb, *Cleopatra Rag*, B strain, measures 1–4.

counterline set against the main melody (Example 28). These are seen below or above the main line, always within the compass of five fingers.

The primary role of the left-hand part is to establish and maintain the duple meter. Much of the time it articulates either a down-up, down-up accompaniment pattern in even eighth notes or a variation (see Examples 22, 23, 26, 27, and 28). By no means is the left hand limited simply to marking the beat. At certain points it plays short melodic scale passages against the line in the soprano (Example 29). This incipient counterpoint supplies considerable interest to a bass part whose function essentially is one of support. At times, the left-hand part is made melodically equal to the soprano line and a true contrapuntal dialogue is established (Example 30). It is rare, however, to see the main melody in the bass with the accompaniment in the soprano, as in the third strain of Lamb's *Ethiopia Rag*. Rag melody normally requires the brightness of the soprano register to give it the typical ragtime sound.

Example 29. Joseph F. Lamb, *American Beauty Rag*, C strain, measures 1–4.

Example 30. James Scott, *Prosperity Rag*, B strain, measures 1–4.

Harmonic Elements

Ragtime is rigidly tonal, its key scheme, chord structures, and chord progressions derived essentially from traditional European models. Consistent with its usual happy moods, the key/mode is predominantly major. There is some pentatonic feeling but little or no suggestion of blue-note melody or harmony.

The use of different keys within one rag is limited. Each major rag is divided roughly into two key areas—tonic and subdominant. Within these key areas, short temporary modulations to related keys occur frequently.

Chords are conventional in interval structure and are no more dissonant than those in early Romantic keyboard music. Considerable dissonance is provided, however, by nonchord tones. These dissonant nonchord tones become especially dynamic when they receive syncopated accents. In Example 31 the tones with arrows are both syncopated and nonchordal.

Example 31. Scott Joplin and Scott Hayden, *Sunflower Slow Drag*, **B** strain, measures 5–8.

The chord vocabulary of ragtime consists of triads; dominant sevenths, diminished sevenths, and secondary sevenths; ninth chords; and triads with the added sixth. Chord syntax is highly derivative from models in earlier styles. The way the chords are connected is no more adventuresome than in the more conventional works of Mozart and Haydn. Chord roots consistently follow the three standard diatonic progressions—up a fifth or down a fourth, down a third, and up a second. Cadences at the joints of the form are usually authentic (dominant to tonic) or half (ending on the dominant).

Interspersed within strong diatonic chord relationships is much chromatic harmony. Secondary-dominant-seventh and diminished-seventh chords are abundant and resolve dutifully to a chord with root a perfect fourth or a minor second above. Augmented sixth chords and borrowed chords from the parallel minor are also common. Chromatic progressions, such as those in Example 32, often are found in the most original rags and resemble the close barbershop harmony of the period.

Form

The piano rag is cast in a part-form similar to those found in the march, waltz, and traditional dances. Normally there are four parts (strains), and they often follow this letter scheme: **AA BB A / CC DD.** (A

Example 32. James Scott, *Grace and Beauty*, **D** strain, measures 13–16.

sampling of fifty-two classic rags showed twenty-six in this pattern and five others in similar form.) Each part has its own rhythmic, harmonic, and melodic character. Thus, a rag in this part-form—**AA BB A / CC DD**—consists of four clearly separated and contrasted strains, most of them repeated before the next begins.

Each strain is square and symmetrical, almost always sixteen measures in length and divided evenly into groups of four or eight measures. Many rags also include an introduction before the first strain and one or two transitions between later strains. Normally, these are four measures long. On a higher structural level, the rag is organized into two sections:

Section 1—**AABBA**
Section 2 (trio)—**CCDD**

No matter what the pattern of parts may be, the second section (trio) begins with part **C**. The accompanying charts show relationships of sections, parts, measure groups, and key schemes.

At this point an interesting question arises. Within the most characteristic rag pattern (**AABBA/CCDD**), why doesn't the **A** strain return as it does in traditional forms containing a trio? If we consider that the rag's trio, which is normally the concluding section, begins and ends in the *subdominant key*, the question becomes more intriguing. Here is a form that not only ends with a trio, but ends in a key other than the tonic.

We can dismiss immediately the possibility that ragtime composers were not aware of ternary structure in preragtime forms. In several of the rags sampled, either the **A** or **B** strain does return at the end (see Figure 11), sometimes in the tonic key. The rag composers certainly knew the effect of circular ternary structure, but they preferred something else. Intuitively, they grasped that the exciting, sometimes euphoric rag expression they desired could be enhanced by a key shift up to the subdominant that stays to the end.

It is possible that the subdominant key of the trio section functions as the true tonic and that the key area of the first section really is dominant. Looked at this way, a standard major rag in two flats and then three flats such as *Sun Flower Slow Drag*, might function tonally this way:

Section 1—**AABBA**, B-flat major (dominant function)
Section 2 (trio)—**CCDD**, E-flat major (tonic function)

Sunflower Slow Drag, by Joplin and Hayden

Sections	Section 1				Section 2 (Trio)		
Parts*	Intro.	A	B	A	Trans.	C	D
Measures	4	16	16	16	4	16	16
Key scheme	B♭	B♭	B♭	B♭	E♭	E♭	E♭

*Repeats not shown

Ragtime Nightingale, by Joseph Lamb

Sections	Section 1				Section 2 (Trio)		
Parts*	Intro.	A	B	A	C	Trans.	B
Measures	4	16	16	16	16	4	16
Key scheme	Cm	Cm	E♭	Cm	A♭	E♭	E♭

*Repeats not shown

Another analytic approach is to hear the rag in two tonic keys a perfect fourth apart. Of the two tonic sections, the second is especially exciting because of its higher key level. If we look at a rag this way, we need not worry that it does not return to the tonic, for there are two tonic sections, each ending in the key in which it began:

Section 1—**AABBA**, B-flat major (tonic function)
Section 2—**CCDD**, E-flat major (tonic function)

Thus, while the inner strains of rag form are extremely symmetrical and square, its sectional structure—when tonal function is considered—is original and perhaps even prophetic.

Scores and Performance

As yet, little research is available on printed rag scores and manuscripts as they relate to ragtime performance of the time, but there is little doubt that some printed rags, including original editions of sheet rags of the period, only approximate what was actually played or was meant to be played by their creators. Many were simplified for practical reasons. (Max Morath reports Eubie Blake's work on the simplified rags, "We were advised in those days to write for the girl in the five-and-ten-cent store."

Presumably, what could be negotiated by the pianist-saleslady could be managed at home by the amateur.)

However, many printed rags—especially those by Joplin, Lamb, and Scott—represent carefully worked out, finished compositions. Although it is probable that these compositions were subject to some modifications when played by their composers, the printed versions represent an authentic ragtime style if they are faithfully realized.

Performance indications for tempo, dynamics, and phrasing on rag scores show that "loud and fast" interpretations are not adequate. Phrasing and balance of tone should be as carefully handled by the player as in other "classic" keyboard genres. When this is done, the rag emerges as the expressive and exciting music imagined by its composers.

Ragtime has been removed from the shelf, and we are beginning to understand it in terms of its structure, origins, social background, and performance. Certain elements of the rag are innovative and forward-looking, but others are highly derivative. The rag's unique syncopated melodic patterns operating over steady beats in duple meter contributed to Dixieland and later jazz genres. Other elements restricted ragtime and finally ended its role as a continuing force in American music.

Ragtime had a relatively short life span of approximately twenty years. When the rag perished early in the twentieth century, it bequeathed musical forces to the newly emerging jazz that are perhaps indispensable to its essence. To the degree that it influenced jazz, rag continued to affect music even after its death. It perhaps was the first truly American music— beautiful, finished, and complete in itself, pointing to new directions still not fully explored.

Hot Rhythm in Piano Ragtime

Frank J. Gillis

Rhythm is what gives ragtime its distinctive character. This article, first published in 1967 and revised in 1980, clarifies how piano rags worked their rhythmic magic. Using numerous musical examples, Frank J. Gillis establishes the basic motif of rag rhythms, and shows how it was varied and extended. He uses as his starting point the concept of "hot rhythms"— especially offbeat rhythmic and melodic phrasing.

It was Richard A. Waterman who first applied the concept of "hot" to African rhythms found in the New World in a paper read at the ninth annual meeting of the American Musicological Society in New York City on December 28, 1943.[1] The concept has been discussed in subsequent writings by Waterman (1914–1971) and Alan P. Merriam (1923–1980)[2] and is treated, in reference to nineteenth-century music in the United States, in Hans Nathan's *Dan Emmett and the Rise of Early Negro Minstrelsy.*[3]

This paper intends to extend our knowledge of "hot" rhythms through an examination of piano ragtime. Attention will be focused primarily on the rhythmic aspects of the music, particularly syncopated phrases and patterns, rather than on ragtime's melodic, harmonic, or formal aspects. In general, the discussion will be limited to the works of three significant composers: Scott Joplin (1868–1917) and James Scott (1886–1938), black composers from Missouri, and Joseph Lamb (1887–1960), a white musician

From *Music in the Americas*, ed. George List and Juan Orrego-Salas. (Bloomington: Indiana University Research Center in Anthropology, Folklore, and Linguistics, 1967), pp. 91–104. Reprinted by permission of Indiana University Research and Graduate Development.

from New Jersey. These men created the majority of the "classic" rags, compositions considered by music historians and critics to have more esthetic value than the superficial product of most Tin Pan Alley popular composers.

Ragtime appears to have arisen concurrently in a number of cities in the United States during the 1890s. Elements of the music can be found in early prototypes of New Orleans jazz, in the rural music of the southern highlands, in the pre-1900 music of the Mississippi–Missouri River area, and in the minstrel-based songs of New York City and the Atlantic Coast region. There are cross-influences existing between these musics that have not yet been studied in detail.

Ragtime is basically a composed piano music, written in $\frac{2}{4}$, in which the left hand maintains a regular and steady fundamental beat against which the right hand plays a wide variety of syncopated phrases. It deviates from the strict accent on the first and second pulse common to marches and other European-oriented music of the nineteenth century. In its day, ragtime was an exciting and provocative music, with its shifting accents and other rhythmic innovations, and was a vital part of the revolutionary movements taking place in the arts at the turn of the century.

Since ragtime represents an artistic attempt to apply Western esthetic and technical principles of composition, it lies more within the realm of art music than of folk music. The leading ragtime composers searched for immortality as "great ragtime composers,"[4] and sought to make permanent contributions to the musical literature in the European tradition.[5] Although the ragtime writers used a number of techniques and materials drawn from Western art music, the stylistic elements with which they worked came from folk and popular music. Hans Nathan (b. 1910), in his work on Dan Emmett, discusses how rhythmic devices—irregular stresses and offbeat accentuations taken from Scotch and Irish dance tunes—were tempered with syncopations of early rural Negro banjoists (Examples 33 and 34).[6] Subsequently, this banjo music proceeded, as Nathan tells us, "to an idiom infinitely more complex in rhythm than could have originated within a predominantly white cultural milieu."[7] The offbeat phrasing of melodic accents falling between the down beats and the up beats, a major aspect of what Waterman terms "hot" rhythms, is found in a number of the Negro

Example 33. Excerpt from *Clem Titus' Jig.*

(a)   (b)

Example 34. Excerpts from *Hell on the Wabash Jig.*

banjo tunes contained in Nathan's work. These rhythmic patterns were more fully developed in ragtime, and the extensive and varied use of such syncopated motifs and phrases is the essence of ragtime's individuality and the basis of its artistic value.

A constantly recurring rhythmic pattern, one that might be called the rhythmic leitmotiv of ragtime, is a figure composed of three notes, the second having twice the value of the first or third, thus: ♫ . This syncopated figure first appeared, minus the third note, in an 1834 minstrel tune entitled *Zip Coon*. In a later variant, known today as *Turkey in the Straw*, this figure appears in full form at the beginning of the refrain. From its first use, such a short-long-short motif can be found in a wide variety of Negro and Negro-influenced music expressions in the United States: dance music, minstrel tunes, spirituals, and popular songs.[8] This figure thus appears as part of the musical tradition in an area bounded roughly by lines drawn from the Georgia Sea Islands, through New Orleans, Saint Louis, Chicago, New York, and to the point of beginning.

It should be noted now that this seminal rhythmic device has been known in other parts of the New World for a number of years. It underwent perhaps an earlier development in the Caribbean, and in several South American countries under Negro influence, which was closely parallel to its expansion and elaboration in the United States. Gilbert Chase, in his *America's Music*, discusses the application of this figure in the *habanera* bass and its use in New Orleans.[9]

In ragtime, both the ♫ motif and its counterpart, ♪♩♪ , appeared as "hot" elements in the earliest compositions. They were used extensively in the first published work in the new idiom, W. H. Krell's *Mississippi Rag* (1897). In the ragtime compositions which followed, the motif was developed by a multitude of techniques: through accumulation, variation, and modification, in both short and long rhythmic patterns (Examples 35, 36, and 37).

Example 35. Scott Joplin, *The Easy Winners*, **A** strain, measures 1-3.

In Scott Joplin's first published ragtime composition, his *Original Rags* of 1899, and in Tom Turpin's *Bowery Buck* of the same year, the early motif is extended: ♫♩ . This adds to the offbeat character by taking the listener one step further from the fundamental pulse, not returning to it until the final beat of the measure. Again, we have variations of this motif. In

Example 36. Arthur Marshall, *Kinklets,* **A** strain, measures 3–4.

Example 37. James Scott, *Hilarity Rag,* **A** strain, measures 1–3.

combination with rests, and beginning on strong and weak beats, it is used in all parts of the measure, and eventually it carries across the bar line. In a Scott Hayden and Joplin collaboration, *Sunflower Slow Drag* (1901), this motif, stated in two different patterns, is used extensively in all themes (Example 38). It is intensified through accumulation in Joe Jordan's *Pekin Rag* (Example 39), where the pattern is repeated continuously in every measure of the sixteen-bar Trio section, and in James Scott's *Grace and Beauty* (Example 40)

Example 38. Scott Joplin and Scott Hayden, *Sunflower Slow Drag,* (a) **A** strain, measure 1; (b) **B** strain, measure 2.

Example 39. Joe Jordan, *Pekin Rag,* **C** strain, measures 1–3.

Example 40. James Scott, *Grace and Beauty*, **B** strain, measures 1-4.

Example 41. James Scott, *Hilarity Rag*, **B** strain, measures 1-4.

and *Hilarity Rag* (Example 41). Such accumulated rhythmic patterns are an important stylistic element of Scott's music.

A major variation of the early motif appears in 1903 when Joplin, in *Weeping Willow*, carries the upbeat still further so that it does not resolve until the first beat in the following measure (Example 42). Here, the composer-pianist is toying with the listener's perception of the fundamental beat before returning to the basic pulse. In the opening bars of Lamb's *American Beauty Rag* (Example 43), the same syncopated pattern is carried over the bar line; and in the total complex phrase of which it is a part, the balance is not satisfactorily restored until we come to the third measure, where there is a return to the regular accent. A variant of this stress on the upbeat appears in Joplin's *Elite Syncopations* (Example 44) and Lamb's *Sensation* (Example 45). Here, the technique of offbeating is not so pronounced, nor is the balance disturbed so much as it is when the offbeats are used with the "swing" or "'oom-pah" bass, that is, with the bass note struck on the strongly accented first and second beats and intervening chords on the weaker upbeats.

Example 42. Scott Joplin, *Weeping Willow*, **A** strain, measure 3.

Example 43. Joseph F. Lamb, *American Beauty,* **A** strain, measures 1–3.

Example 44. Scott Joplin, *Elite Syncopations,* **A** strain, measures 1–3.

Example 45. Joseph F. Lamb, arr. Scott Joplin, *Sensation,* **A** strain, measures 7–8.

In another syncopated figure, the upbeat is struck only before the strong first and second pulses, thus appearing but twice in each measure: ♫♩♫⌐♩♪. A number of composers—Joseph Northrup in his *Cannon Ball* (Example 46), Joplin in his *Eugenia* (Example 47) and *Fig Leaf Rag,* Lamb in his *Ethiopia Rag* (Example 48)—utilize variations of this type of syncopation repeatedly. Similar repetitions of a melodic or, as in the case of *Cannon Ball,* of a more

Example 46. Joseph Northrup, *The Cannon Ball,* **C** strain, measures 1–2.

Example 47. Scott Joplin, *Eugenia*, **A** strain, measures 1–2.

Example 48. Joseph F. Lamb, *Ethiopia Rag*, **D** strain, measures 1–2.

purely percussive rather than melodic character were later called "riffs" and served to provide a compelling rhythmic background for the jazz soloist.

The extensive use of patterns containing offbeat stresses, in conjunction with numerous other rhythmic devices, resulted, chiefly in the hands of Lamb, in complicated rhythmic phrases. I have already mentioned the rhythmic complexity of one phrase in Lamb's *American Beauty* (Example 43). His *Excelsior Rag* (Example 49) and *Patricia Rag* (Example 50) also contain a variety of shifting accents.

Offbeat phrasing, arrived at through the use of syncopated motifs— varied, extended, and accumulated—appears throughout piano ragtime. It is one of the identifying characteristics of the music and the chief rhythmic device that produces the quality referred to as "hot."

Another Africanism that can be found in ragtime is the "metronomic sense." As Waterman defines this concept, it is the ability of the listener to supply a basic beat when the musician, in performance, is concentrating on rhythmic patterns and phrases without explicitly stating a regular and

Example 49. Joseph F. Lamb, *Excelsior Rag*, **A** strain, measures 5–8.

Example 50. Joseph F. Lamb, *Patricia Rag,* **A** strain, measures 13–15.

steady pulse. As Nathan informs us, in early minstrel music the banjo and fiddle tunes were accompanied by the tapping of the instrumentalist's foot. Throughout ragtime's history the fundamental beat is explicitly stated in the left hand. However, deviations from this basic rhythmic principle are found in a few ragtime compositions.

As early as 1906, Tom Turpin departs from the standard use of the left hand in the third theme of his *Bowery Buck* (Example 51), which is composed of a passage repeated three times with slight variations. Though it is not difficult to feel a fundamental beat in this section, at certain points the stronger accents on beats 1 and 2 and the weaker stresses on the intervening upbeats are missing. Thus, there are no explicitly stated beats on beat 2 in the first, third, and fifth measures, and secondary accents are lacking in the first, second, or both halves of measures 2, 4, 6, 7, and 8. With the strong accent mark on the initial upbeat of the first, third, and fifth measures and a commonly felt metrical accent at the beginning of the second and fourth measures, a sense of imbalance is created by the loss of the regular pulse customarily expressed in ragtime. Along with this, measures 6, 7, and 8 have a mixture of marked as well as irregular accents, not commonly found in ragtime, which adds to the offbeat character of the entire eight-bar section.

Example 51. Tom Turpin, *Bowery Buck,* arr. D. S. DeLisle, **C** strain, measures 1–8.

The opening phrases of *Heliotrope Bouquet* (Example 52), a Scott Joplin–Louis Chauvin collaboration of 1907, also lacks the precise, regular pulse found in the left hand of piano ragtime.[10] The bass part employed at the beginning of the composition (♪♫♪♫) is closely associated with Latin American music. Although such deviations from the normal ragtime bass pattern were occasionally used, it is not a characteristic of the style. In his *Pastime Rag No. 3* (1916), Artie Matthews pays so little regard to the explicit statement of the pulse that his composition can hardly be classified as a rag in the "classic" tradition of Joplin, Scott, and Lamb. His *Pastime* rags, of which there are five, are filled with rhythmic patterns and techniques uncommon to ragtime, but very much a part of later jazz piano styles.

Example 52. Scott Joplin and Louis Chauvin, *Heliotrope Bouquet,* **A** strain, measures 1–3.

Since ragtime is based to a large degree on Western dance music characterized by a strong duple meter, it does not employ mixed meters, which would tend to confuse not only the dancers but listeners as well. There are occasions, however, when it would appear that the ragtime composers are "playing" with ternary time. The bass pattern opening Joplin's *Maple Leaf Rag* (Example 53) exemplifies a technique in which a strong accent on the first beat and minor accents on the second half of the first beat and second basic beat give a feeling of $\frac{3}{4}$ meter. Such a bass line is used extensively in Arthur Marshall's *The Pippin* (1908). In the Trio section of *Nappy Lee: A Slow Drag* (Example 54) by Joe Jordan, the $\frac{3}{4}$ statement is made in both the upper and lower voices. There has perhaps been no conscious effort on the part of the composer here to work in more than one meter. However, with the written accent on the upbeat of measure 1 and the downbeat of measure 2, both of these getting equal stress, it would appear that there was a possible intent on the part of the composer to mix meters.

Example 53. Scott Joplin, *Maple Leaf Rag,* **A** strain, measures 1–4.

Example 54. Joe Jordan, *Nappy Lee: A Slow Drag*, **C** strain, measures 1–4.

Such experiments with rhythmic patterns were the stock in trade of the ragtime composer.

Another type of binary-ternary mixture found in this music is the use of a three-note melodic cycle against the duple-metered ragtime bass, the so-called secondary rag rhythmic pattern.[11] In 1905, we find Percy Wenrich employing this pattern for one measure of a two-bar phrase that is repeated throughout the final theme of his *Peaches and Cream* (Example 55) and Joseph Northrup taking up two measures with this motif in his *Cannon Ball* (Example 56). It is true that there is no accent placed on the first note of each cycle to give it a strong polyrhythmic character, but the use of the octave, here playing a different accentual role each time it appears, functions in the same manner. Perhaps the best-known example and most extensive employment of this rhythmic device is in the *12th Street Rag* of Euday Bowman (Example 57). Frequently found in ragtime and in jazz, the three-note cycle used in conjunction with a binary bass pattern is rhythmically exciting and, though mild in comparison to melodic-rhythmic figures found in present-day jazz, it still has meaning for a wide listening audience today. The "secondary rag" motif was but one of a number of

Example 55. Percy Wenrich, *Peaches and Cream*, **D** strain, measures 1–3.

Example 56. Joseph Northrup, *The Cannon Ball*, **A** strain, measures 5–6.

12th Street Rag, originally published in 1914, is the most familiar work featuring the three-note rhythmic figure called "secondary rag." This edition was published in 1919. (*John Edward Hasse collection*)

Example 57. Euday L. Bowman, *12th Street Rag*, **A** strain, measures 1–4.

rhythmic devices characteristic of ragtime which brought about a revolution in Western music.

In summary, Richard A. Waterman isolated certain aspects of rhythmic behavior found in West African music—offbeat rhythmic and melodic phrasing, a deviation from the explicit statement of the fundamental pulse, and an attempt at the use of more than a single meter—which give the music a "hot" or "compelling" quality. These characteristics spread, through the "dynamics of musical diffusion," into various portions of the New

World, among which was an area in the central United States. Here a new music called ragtime, which utilizes to some degree the "hot" elements of African rhythmic style, was developed among black pianists and composers. An analysis of rhythmic ornamentation found in "classic" ragtime compositions shows clearly that this music stands firmly in the "hot" tradition of Afro-American music.

Notes

1. This paper was published as "Hot Rhythm in Negro Music," *Journal of the American Musicological Society* 1 (Spring 1948): 24–37.
2. Richard A. Waterman, "African Influence on the Music of the Americas," in *Acculturation in the Americas,* ed. Sol Tax (Chicago: University of Chicago Press, 1952), pp. 207–18; Alan P. Merriam, "African Music," in *Continuity and Change in African Cultures,* ed. William R. Bascom and Melville J. Herskovits (Chicago: University of Chicago Press, 1959), pp. 49–86; Merriam, "The African Idiom in Music," *Journal of American Folklore* 75 (April–June 1962): 120–30.
3. Hans Nathan, *Dan Emmett and the Rise of Early Negro Minstrelsy* (Norman: University of Oklahoma Press, 1962). See Chapter 13 and *passim*.
4. Joseph Lamb once told Rudi Blesh, "I didn't want to make any money on my things. I only wanted to see them published because my dream was to become a great ragtime composer." See Rudi Blesh and Harriet Janis, *They All Played Ragtime,* 4th ed., rev. (New York: Oak Publications, 1971), p. 239.
5. Scott Joplin wrote several extended ragtime compositions and two operas, *A Guest of Honor* (1903) and *Treemonisha* (1911).
6. Nathan, *Dan Emmett,* pp. 196–97.
7. Ibid., pp. 205–6.
8. See, for example, spirituals as printed in William Francis Allen, Charles P. Ware, and Lucy McKim Garrison, eds., *Slave Songs of the United States* (New York: Simpson, 1867. Repr. New York: Smith 1929; New York: Books for Libraries, 1971); Theodore F. Seward, comp., *Jubilee Songs as Sung by the Jubilee Singers of Fisk University* (New York: Biglow & Main, 1872); Gustavus D. Pike, *The Jubilee Singers and Their Campaign for Twenty Thousand Dollars* (Boston: Lee and Shepard, 1873; London: Hodder and Stoughton, 1874. Repr. New York: AMS Press, 1974); and J. B. T. Marsh, *The Story of the Jubilee Singers, With Their Songs* (London: Hodder and Stoughton, 1875; rev. ed. Boston: Houghton Mifflin, 1880). This same motif can be found in dance and minstrel tunes appearing in Nathan, *Dan Emmett,* and in ragtime and popular music compiled in numerous collections. See the appendix of this book for a listing of ragtime music anthologies.
9. Gilbert Chase, *America's Music: From the Pilgrims to the Present* (New York: McGraw-Hill, 1955), pp. 309–11.
10. The opening theme is undoubtedly Chauvin's contribution to the joint effort since it is known his father was a native of Mexico. Joplin, however, employs this same figure in the left hand of the first section of his *Euphonic Sounds* (1909), and throughout his *Solace: A Mexican Serenade* (1909).
11. The concept of "secondary rag" is discussed by Lowell H. Schreyer in footnote 29 to his chapter, "The Banjo in Ragtime," in this book.

Joplin's Late Rags: An Analysis

Guy Waterman

Originally published in 1956, this article was the first serious attempt to analyze the music of the greatest ragtime composer. Guy Waterman argues that Joplin's late rags—Euphonic Sounds, Wall Street Rag, Magnetic Rag, and so on—attempt to synthesize "classical" music with ragtime. Waterman finds that in his late rags, Joplin allowed greater freedom for the left hand, strove for implicit rather than explicit rhythmic momentum, and grew more concerned with structure.

John Stark, the ragtime publisher, wrote in his famous obituary on Scott Joplin, "he left his mark on American music." Joplin (1868–1917) was unquestionably the foremost figure in the story of ragtime. Historians have usually counted Joplin and Tom Turpin as the most important influences on the composers of the 1900–10 period. If their work is taken as a whole, he and James Scott were probably the greatest writers in the idiom. And, since ragtime contributed much to jazz of its time and later, Stark's generosity is well founded.

But there is another part of Joplin's legacy which is equally important—his effort late in life to synthesize the ragtime he helped to create with certain methods and devices of concert composition. This part of Joplin's

From *Record Changer* 14, no. 8 [ca. 1956]: 5–8. Used by permission of the author.

work left no mark on American music—it has been almost completely ignored. Indeed, its only publicity has been a handful of recordings, none of which has received much notice.

Before we begin to examine his efforts, we should have a clear picture of his previous career and, to see things in perspective, of the contemporary developments in his musical environment.

Back at the turn of the century, Joplin had been one of the founding fathers of written ragtime. The early rags established the basic principles of the style—multi-theme structure, harmonic orthodoxy, simple syncopation, and the other elements usually associated with the term "ragtime." It is difficult to single out particular tunes as typical, but these include most of the more familiar rags, like Turpin's *St. Louis Rag*, Joplin's *Maple Leaf Rag*, and the Joplin–Scott Hayden collaboration, *Sunflower Slow Drag*.

In the years just preceding 1909 (when Joplin was to embark on his great experimentation), ragtime was raised to a somewhat higher plane than that of melodious Turpin two-beat. James Scott published his first rag in 1903. In 1906 his electric *Frog Legs Rag* appeared, and was followed immediately by such classics as *The Ragtime Betty*, *Grace and Beauty*, and *Hilarity Rag*. Joseph Lamb started in 1908 with *Sensation*. Joplin himself had a banner year in 1907 with six of his best rags (including the Chauvin collaboration, *Heliotrope Bouquet*), each of which reveals greater powers of expression than those of his earlier years. Three more followed in 1908, including the monumental *Fig Leaf Rag*. This was the golden age of ragtime proper.

Another trend was developing simultaneously. This was the so-called Saint Louis school of sensationalistic, showy display. This trend proved stronger than the work of Scott and Joplin's 1907–08 period, since its appeal was infectious and immediate.

Scott and Lamb had established themselves as writers of "classic ragtime." Joplin had written some of the greatest rags—*Rose Leaf Rag*, *Gladiolus Rag*, *Fig Leaf Rag*. Scott and Lamb continued to write in much the same way. They wrote uniformly fine rags, but no first-rate composer will stay long in one groove. Joplin's position was that great things had been said in the ragtime style of the time, and that truly fresh creation required new resources.

No art may remain static. Internal development is necessary if it is to continue vital. Joplin had already participated in one great transformation of rag style, that which occurs between his works of 1904 and 1907, between Turpin and Scott. He now embarked on a new course, that which begins with the five 1909 rags and continues until his death in 1917.

What one first notices about late Joplin rags is the "serious" cast. Syncopation, while remaining an essential part of his musical equipment, is almost deliberately toned down, phrasing is longer, harmonies more complex. Modulation is more extensive and foreign keys are occasionally established within the sixteen-bar framework. Specifically, three main features of the style stand out: increased freedom in the left hand; the attempt to keep rhythmic momentum implicit rather than explicit; and a new, or at least increased, concern with structure.

One of the chief weaknesses of strict ragtime (though probably one of its strong points as well) was its reliance on the "oom-pah" left-hand pattern. From this straight jacket Joplin now sought emancipation. The left hand assumed a more independent character, carrying melodic passages and delineating harmonies more specifically. A good contrast between the earlier role of the left hand and its new importance is provided in the opening bars of *Rose Leaf Rag* (1907) and *Euphonic Sounds* (1909). The former is one of the most contrapuntal of the pre-1909 rags, yet, after four bars of sixteenth-note runs, the left hand lapses into the safe and sane "oom-pah." *Euphonic Sounds* opens with an equally moving left hand, but at the fifth bar, and again at the thirteenth, the "oom-pah" is not required. It should be stressed that in the majority of late rags, Joplin retained the crutch, and in the Hayden collaborations, *Kismet* and *Felicity,* used it almost exclusively. It should also be pointed out that in some cases, other devices were used as rather lame substitutes—the straight chords of the trios in *Paragon* and *Euphonic Sounds* and the arpeggios that too often passed for Joplin counterpoint. Nevertheless, the problem is squarely faced in enough passages to make the point.

The attempt to maintain rhythmic momentum without explicit delineation is not peculiarly Joplin's. The same problems confront the ultramoderns of today—Gerry Mulligan, the Modern Jazz Quartet, Hall Overton's group. The beat was central to ragtime as it has been to jazz. In both, of course, it has been used as a positive force. Nevertheless, it is significant that in both cases musicians have appeared who felt its obvious statement to be a restriction. Aside from isolated passages in *Solace, Wall Street Rag,* and *Reflection Rag,* Joplin's most basic efforts in this line occur in the first two strains of *Euphonic Sounds* and the last of *Magnetic Rag.* The usual procedure is to curve the moving voice so that it syncopates the third beat. Typical examples are from the trio of *Solace* and the opening of *Wall Street Rag* (Example 58). I shall discuss the second theme of *Euphonic Sounds* at greater length below. (It should be mentioned that Hines and almost all modern jazz since Thelonious Monk is also concerned with making the beat implicit— but with a view to heightening the rhythmic sense, not subduing it, as in Joplin.)

Example 58. Scott Joplin, *Wall Street Rag,* **A** strain, measures 1–4.

The structure of a rag had been one of the most firmly entrenched traditions. There were two accepted formulas: **ABACD** and **ABCD.** In his last period, Joplin became aware of structure as an end in itself and used it with more care than it has ever received in jazz. (By structure I simply mean the large-scale organization of a tune—as opposed, perhaps, to "phrasing," on a smaller scale.) *Euphonic Sounds* is the first rag, so far as I know, to be cast in truly cyclical form. Earlier rags had used phrases that repeated through several themes—in *Sunflower Slow Drag,* for example. In *The Entertainer,* he inserted a section of the second theme just before the last. But *Euphonic Sounds* is a full-blown model rondo: **ABACA.** Three other rags used the cyclical technique—*Kismet, Scott Joplin's New Rag,* and *Magnetic Rag.* Since *Kismet* and *Magnetic Rag* state the theme only at the beginning and the end they are not authentic rondos. The *New Rag* is a special case. The form would seem to be **ABACDA.** But the **D** theme has the quality of an interlude, since it is entered by a three-bar fragment in the dominant of the new key and since it ends with an irreversible lead into the recapitulation of **A.** It is the only theme in Joplin's work which is not repeated. One might therefore characterize the *New Rag* either as a standard rag with recapitulation added or as a rondo with extended second interlude. Another structural innovation of late Joplin is the coda. It cannot be said that Joplin ever learned to use this device effectively. The only purpose it seems to serve—in *Euphonic Sounds, New Rag,* and *Magnetic Rag*—is the avoidance of too abrupt an ending. A corollary of this attention to structure was an interest in key relationships: in tonal music the two usually go together.

Notice that Joplin's change of rag form is directly opposed to the transformation wrought by jazz pianists. Jazz, seeking one theme as a center for improvisation, tended to weaken the sense of form that it inherited from ragtime. Jelly Roll Morton was the last pianist to make a serious thing of it. Joplin's efforts obviously strengthen this sense of form. One has only to hear the blazing return of the first theme of *Magnetic Rag*—the restoration of major tonality, the momentum of the renewed beat—to recognize the power of recapitulation in ragtime.

Joplin's struggles were not all successful. There are several aspects of his late writing which betray something less than finished artisanship. I have mentioned that he never really found what to do with the beat. A similar question he raised concerned the sixteen-bar limit, and this also remained unanswered. Only once did Joplin break through that barrier—in the third theme of *Magnetic Rag* (Example 59)—although portions of *Magnetic Rag, Euphonic Sounds,* and the *New Rag* do not sound tied down. In general, one might say that the various ideas with which Joplin was working were not sufficiently synthesized into a unified style. Perhaps the enormity of the task required more time than he was permitted (only seven active years followed 1909 before he was committed to an asylum). One might also notice a loss of drive, a running down of energy in the late rags as compared with *Maple Leaf, Sunflower Slow Drag,* and *Gladiolus Rag.*

Perhaps the most unfortunate aspect of the late period is the uneven

Example 59. Scott Joplin, *Magnetic Rag*, **C** strain.

quality of the rags. This is in striking contrast with the Joplin of earlier days who turned out quality rags as effortlessly as Bach his 371 chorales or Haydn his symphonies. Any specific comment along these lines, of course, is partly subjective. I would say that only *Euphonic Sounds* and *Scott Joplin's New Rag* are real *tours de force*. *Magnetic Rag*, his most ambitious in conception, falls a little short in execution. *Solace* is frankly experimental. Some of the less pretentious rags, like *Paragon* and *Kismet*, are thoroughly enjoyable, but they are colorless next to *Euphonic Sounds* and *Magnetic Rag* on the one side and *Rose Leaf Rag* and *Fig Leaf Rag*, or even the earlier rags, on the other.

The reader will notice that I am omitting the opera *Treemonisha* from my discussion. This gigantic thing is almost completely unexplored territory. Doubtless there is much of both grain and chaff therein—it is an inviting task for the adventurous—but until it is more familiar to both the reader and this writer it is best left alone.

Example 59. (*continued*)

An intensive study of *Euphonic Sounds* shows what heights Joplin achieved in his last period. Perhaps it would be more accurate to say it shows what potentialities his new ideas suggested, since it cannot be said that he fully realized these thoughts in his lifetime. Since *Euphonic Sounds* has received some notice in recent years, it has been attacked in some quarters, just as Louis Armstrong and, more recently, Jelly Roll Morton have been subjected to excessive counterattack after years of unqualified critical praise. It is damned with the faint praise of such terms as "interesting," with the implication that it is not really very profound. Nevertheless, as with Louis and Jelly, realistic examination of the music itself reaffirms the more generous appraisal.

As I pointed out above, *Euphonic Sounds* is cast in rondo form. The principal theme is stated three times with two subordinate sections sandwiched between. It is interesting to notice the ways the composer

Euphonic Sounds (1909), a *tour de force* of Joplin's late period, and one of his most ambitious compositions. (*John Edward Hasse collection*)

contrasts this theme with the other two. The home tonic is B major, and no real modulation takes place within the first theme. Throughout the other two this key is never established—they pass through several others, mostly minor. The interludes are themes of conflict, of disturbance. The main theme is one of resolution, of redemption. The returns from the middle themes to the main one use this contrast to great artistic effect.

A further contrast lies in the internal structure of the themes. The first is the only one of the three that can be subdivided into the two traditional eight-bar sentences. The second works through an uninterrupted climax to the twelfth bar, then settles down, builds up through the repeat and returns once again to the opening theme. The third works to a climax earlier, in bar 7, then works its way into position for the return. These asymmetrical frames heighten the feeling of restlessness, the regular composition of the home theme strengthening its calm.

Internally, the first theme is a masterpiece. Each of the two sentences opens with a flowing contrapuntal phrase. The first time this is followed by a quiet four-bar phrase (Example 60), suggesting a modulation to the relative minor, a suggestion quickly rejected by the reappearance of the opening bars. After the second statement, a two-bar outburst vindicates the

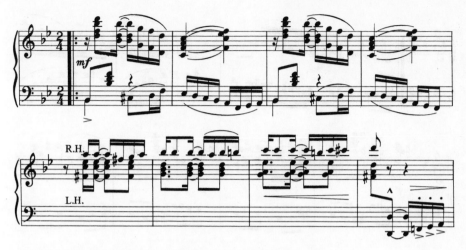

Example 60. Scott Joplin, *Euphonic Sounds*, **A** strain, measures 1–8.

tonality beyond question, ending on the cadential six-four chord, which is easily resolved to the end.

The second theme has no such supreme confidence. It is important to follow the tonality through this section (Example 61), for it is extremely well worked out to give great emotional effect.

The theme is introduced by a descending passage which leads to a low B♭ on the first note. From here until the climactic twelfth bar is a constant ascent in the treble and, most of the way, an equally towering descent in the bass. Almost immediately a minor key (B minor) is established. In bar five, C minor appears, in a magnificent modulation designed to suit the nature of the climax. Technically the six-four chord of B minor becomes, by a chromatic alteration as simple as it is effective, the dominant ninth of the new key, flatted and with root omitted. (Joplin always approaches a key through its dominant, after the fashion of the great tonal composers and Beethoven in particular.) The change into G minor in bar nine is accomplished by the dramatic augmented six-four-three chord leading to the dominant—notice that each new modulation is increasingly imperative, driving the motion to its apex in bar twelve.

Up to bar eleven, each new key had been minor. Bar thirteen asserts D♭ major, next to G♭the richest and deepest of all keys, although the theme is not yet home. Bar twelve is a brilliant stroke. Besides the tonal changes, it is the focal point in two other ways—up to that point the melody rises, thereafter it descends, and up to that point is a constant crescendo, thereafter diminuendo. It is therefore a crucial measure, and the composer is equal to the task. Such a touch as this is not susceptible to cold analysis. The reader should notice two things, however, with reference to the passages on either side—the dynamics indicated for that measure, and the position of the two notes in the chords that immediately precede and follow. It is not too much to say that this one measure, in context, is sufficient evidence of Joplin's claim to greatness.

Example 61. Scott Joplin, *Euphonic Sounds*, **B** strain.

The third theme is not so successful. Again the modulations are interesting, rotating around F major, which ultimately serves as the dominant of the home key for the final return. But the construction is not so dramatic, and in places, bars seven and eight in particular, the conception seems to presuppose a fuller treatment (more notes) than Joplin was prepared to introduce.

Incidentally, examination of rags like this explodes two theories which unfortunately still claim adherents: (a) that early ragtime and jazz were very simple affairs devoid of subtlety; and (b) that Joplin was a tune thief, not responsible for all the compositions that bear his name. The first contention appears for example, in Barry Ulanov's [*A History of Jazz in America*]: "Nothing especially important musically happened to jazz on the piano until the music got to Chicago and Earl Hines. . . ." Such a judgment seems rather blind when we realize that by itself even such a masterpiece as *Euphonic Sounds* does not measure up to the great rags of Joplin's earlier years or those of Scott at his best, and, further, that no ragtime composer crammed such towering musical logic into his work as did the purportedly uncomplicated Jelly Roll Morton. In saying this, one takes nothing away from the standing of the great revolutionist Hines or his successors.

The second contention, based mostly on some undocumented claims of one Otis Saunders, has been backed by the English historian Rex Harris, among others. The only answer is that if Saunders is to take Joplin's place, he, Saunders, must prove he wrote practically all Joplin's work. Not only are they all fine rags, but the development from *Original Rags* in 1899 to *Reflection Rag* in 1917 is clearly that of one man working out his musical ideas. If this man's name was not Joplin, that is a matter of semantics.

It is obvious from such analysis as I have suggested that Joplin's late work was a tremendous undertaking. *Euphonic Sounds* is his biggest achievement after 1908, but *Magnetic Rag* is even more ambitious, and *Scott Joplin's New Rag, Solace,* and the posthumous *Reflection Rag* reward study.

When we remember that Joplin was established as "King of Ragtime Writers" when he *began* this experimentation, we realize that it was more than a whim which led to the development. Scott continued to the end in the same pattern. This dynamic quality of Joplin's musical personality is the true measure of his stature. Every outstanding composer of the Western world maintained a fresh outlook throughout his career—from Bach and Haydn to the twentieth-century leaders, Schoenberg, Stravinsky, Hindemith. It is this quality more than the merits of *Maple Leaf Rag* or any other rag that sets Joplin above his contemporaries.

Unfortunately, jazz musicians seem to die at the wrong time. Bix Beiderbecke, Fats Waller, and Tony Jackson, as well as half a dozen modernists, all died much too soon. On the other hand, from musical considerations alone, many would say that Louis Armstrong, Sidney Bechet, and some others are long overdue. Joplin belongs in the former category. He was almost fifty when he died—not young perhaps, but he had barely started on a line of development which required much time and experimentation to complete. More important, Joplin alone was equipped to work it out. The musical trends of his time and later were such that no one could follow in his path. The course which he blazed resulted from his own mind, and it diverged from the main road—jazz—which caught up the younger musicians in its headlong course. The discipline of ragtime was too sophisticated for the new jazz; it was not sophisticated enough for Joplin. He was a true prophet in the wilderness, but where in 1899 and 1907 others

The Musical Legacy of Joe Lamb

Joseph R. Scotti

Joseph F. Lamb was one of the most accomplished, prolific, and long-lived of rag composers. In a study written for this book, Joseph R. Scotti explores Lamb's musical motivations, style periods, and individual stylistic traits. Scotti also compares the works of Lamb with those of Scott Joplin and James Scott. This chapter is both a summary of Lamb's ragtime contributions and a model that could be adopted for other ragtime studies.

Joseph F. Lamb (1887–1960) led a unique musical life, became recognized as one of the greatest ragtime composers, and left a rich legacy. His earliest and most enduring musical motivation was his exciting discovery that the notes he scrawled on paper could adequately represent his musical concepts. From the moment his sisters played the round little black dots of his childhood attempts at composition through his final years and last piano rags, Lamb remained captivated by the printed score. Lamb did not conceive of a dichotomy between musical concepts and their notation; improvisation seemed baffling, awkward, redundant. In this respect Lamb realized Scott Joplin's vision of ragtime as a notated art form more thoroughly than did Joplin himself. Joplin (1868–1917) assimilated ragtime as an itinerant musician, finally committing the music to paper with his *Original Rags* and *Maple Leaf Rag* of 1899. In contrast, Lamb's fundamental exposure to music, including ragtime, came from playing and studying sheet music, a piano primer, and musical excerpts from such magazines as *The Etude*.

By 1904 the young composer had returned from a Catholic prep school in Canada to which his mother had sent him when his father died several years before. Commuting from New Jersey to New York City to a job in the wholesale dry goods business, the sixteen-year-old began buying sheet music at Gimbel's and Macy's, particularly on Saturdays, the seven- and eight-cent sale days.

Like Joplin, Lamb began composing by writing songs and miscellaneous piano pieces and, in the process, mastered the essential skills of notation. In 1905, H. H. Sparks of Canada published his *Celestine Waltzes* and *Lilliputian's Bazaar,* both multipartite compositions. The latter, subtitled "a musical novelty," has mild syncopations resembling those of turn-of-the century cakewalks. Lamb's *Florentine Waltzes,* published by Sparks in 1906, shows him in full command of melody, harmony, modulation, texture, accompaniment patterns, and overall form and tonal plan. It is likely that Lamb wrote these pieces at an earlier date, perhaps between 1901 and 1903 while still in Canada, and that Sparks delayed their publication, for it has been common for publishers to defer publication for reasons of budget or market.

It was his encounter in 1904 with *Maple Leaf Rag* and other published Negro rags that became the second powerful motivation in the musical life of Joe Lamb. As he later confided to jazz critic Whitney Balliett, "I found I was partial to rags, particularly the harder kind, and then Scott Joplin's *Maple Leaf Rag* hit me good and proper. Ninety-five percent of the best rags were written by Negroes, you know, and I seemed to fall right in with their things."[1] After Joplin's *Maple Leaf Rag* hit him "good and proper," Lamb began a long-term love affair with, and commitment to, classic ragtime as conceived by Joplin and proselytized by publisher John Stark (1841–1927).

Lamb composed a number of rags, as yet unpublished, which were experimental in both overall structure and tonal plan. *Joe Lamb's Old Rag,* for example, has the unusual form **A B CC A DD E**, with the subdominant key not appearing until **D** instead of at **C**, as was usual in his published rags. *Chasin' the Chippies* has the uncommon scheme **Intro AA BB CC A DD EE B**, with all strains in the original tonic except **D**, which begins in relative minor and ends in the home key. *Jersey Rag* has a startling tonal plan: The first section, **AA BB A**, is in six flats (G-flat major) while the second section, **CC DD**, is in one sharp (G major). Lamb may have been merely avoiding the cumbersome keys of C-flat major, the true subdominant, or B major, the enharmonic subdominant, at the trio. He could have easily transposed the entire piece, but we have explicit testimony from Lamb that he purposefully selected rags' keys for their individual sonorities.[2]

According to Lamb, about eleven unpublished rags sort of accumulated from 1907 to 1914 and, after looking them over fifty years later, he was rather sorry that he had not submitted them for publication.[3] *The Old Home Rag* was finally published in the posthumous *Ragtime Treasures* of 1964.[4] This composition and *Sensation,* Lamb's first published rag (discussed below) provide us with a glimpse of Lamb's style before he met Joplin. Another ten polished and robust rags remain, unfortunately, in manuscript. When the thorny questions of copyright ownership for these unpublished rags are finally resolved, the ragtime community will behold a previously unknown dimension of Lamb's creativity. We shall never know, however, what other arcane forms and tonal plans Lamb might have evolved had he not met Scott Joplin.

Lamb's coincidental meeting with Joplin in 1907 in the New York office of publisher John Stark became Lamb's third strong musical motivation. It is little understood that though Joplin's intercession on Lamb's behalf resulted in Stark's publication of *Sensation: A Rag* and subsequent rags by Lamb, it also inhibited Lamb's innovative experimentations with the large form, or macroform, the tonal plan, and the phrase structure of piano rags. From then on, Lamb's published rags are bisectional and in five parts, in keeping with the form crystallized by Joplin. Lamb's treble lines assume a melodic lyricism also attributable to Joplin's imposing influence, and Lamb's strains, like those of Joplin, James Scott (1886–1938), and other ragtime composers, become parallel double periods. Absent in Lamb's rags published after he met Joplin are the contrasting double periods, through-composed strains, expansive macroforms, unusual modulations, run-in codas, parodistic treatments of preexisting materials, and shifted accents of "secondary rag" that characterize such unpublished rags as *The Old Home Rag, Joe Lamb's Old Rag, Greased Lightning Rag, The Jersey Rag, Rapid Transit Rag, The Bee-Hive, The Ragtime Special*, and *Chasin' the Chippies*. Lamb tells us that *Old Home* and *Joe Lamb's Old Rag* were also endorsed for publication by Joplin; Lamb did not submit them to Stark because, shortly after the publication of *Sensation*, he completed *Ethiopia Rag* and *Excelsior Rag* and liked them better.

Lamb's twelve rags published by John Stark from 1908 to 1919 fall into two groups: (1) the "heavy" rags in which Lamb synthesized the styles of Joplin and Scott (*American Beauty Rag, Ethiopia Rag, Excelsior Rag, Ragtime Nightingale*, and *Top Liner Rag*), and (2) the "light" rags in which he culminated the cakewalk tradition[5] (*Bohemia Rag, Champagne Rag, Cleopatra Rag*, and *Reindeer: Ragtime Two Step*).[6] *Contentment Rag* and *Patricia Rag* fall in between the two groups.

Lamb fuses the melody-dominated style of Joplin with Scott's expansive use of the keyboard registers in such instances as the first strains of *Excelsior, American Beauty, Patricia*, and *Top Liner*. Lamb replaces Joplin's typical *a a' a b* double-period construction for a strain with *a b a c*, making the first period contrasting rather than parallel. He imitated and developed in many of his own strains the compression of small bar form (*a a b*) used by Scott in the first period of *Frog Legs Rag*, which was one of Lamb's favorite rags.[7] The narrow-range melodies of Joplin probably inspired the first strains and trios of Lamb's "light" rags, *Champagne, Reindeer, Cleopatra*, and *Bohemia*. Scott's propensity for rhythmic exuberance and call-and-response patterns appears, among other places, in the trio and last strain of Lamb's *American Beauty*, and in the last strains of *Sensation, Ethiopia*, and *Patricia*. Since one of the distinguishing characteristics of classic rags is the conscious striving for cohesion in the macroform—as Lamb put it, the strains have to be

Joseph Lamb (seated), with friends, 1908. Note the upright piano piled high with sheet music. (*Courtesy Rudi Blesh*)

"compatible"[8]—Lamb's sophisticated synthesis of the widely divergent styles of Joplin and Scott is impressive.

Among Lamb's individual stylistic traits are his use of the sequence for development purposes (*e.g.*, *Sensation* and *Ethiopia*, last strains; *Bohemia*, interlude; *American Beauty*, second phrase, second strain; and *Patricia*, second phrase, first strain) and his emphasis on the harmonic sonority of the diminished seventh with upper-neighbor appoggiatura (*e.g.*, *American Beauty*, second phrase, second strain; *Patricia*, second phrase, first strain; *Top Liner*, fourth measure, first strain). Whereas Scott's phrase structure is based on two-measure motives and Joplin's on four-measure phrases, Lamb's phrase structure, particularly in the "heavy" rags, has a constant thrust toward the eight-measure period, characterized by shifted cadences and prolonged cadence chords.

Lamb made two unique contributions to the ragtime literature. First, he employed a tremendous diversity of texture from rag to rag (*e.g.*, his "light" rags as opposed to his "heavy" rags), from strain to strain (Examples 62–65), and even from phrase to phrase (Examples 66–67). Second, in several instances Lamb was able to transcend ragtime's usual four-measure phrase structure, for example, in the first strains of *American Beauty*, *Top Liner*, *Cottontail*, and *Arctic Sunset* (Examples 68–71).

After a stint of approximately ten months as a Tin Pan Alley song plugger and arranger about 1910, Lamb decided to keep music as an

Example 62. Joseph F. Lamb, *Bohemia Rag*, **A** strain, measures 1–4.

Example 63. Joseph F. Lamb, *Bohemia Rag*, **B** strain, measures 1–4.

Example 64. Joseph F. Lamb, *Ragtime Nightingale*, **B** strain, measures 1–4.

Example 65. Joseph F. Lamb, *Ragtime Nightingale*, **C** strain, measures 1–4.

avocation and to make his living in the dry goods business. Though Lamb eschewed musical night life to stay at home with his family and, as far as we know, met only one classic ragtimer—Scott Joplin—Lamb was not completely dependent for inspiration on the notated rags of Joplin and other composers. The usual portrayal of Lamb as musically insular oversimplifies the evidence. His esoteric commitment to classic ragtime isolated him from Tin Pan Alley exploitation, and his residing in New York City precluded his

Example 66. Joseph F. Lamb, *Excelsior Rag,* **A** strain, measures 1–8.

Example 67. Joseph F. Lamb, *Ethiopia Rag,* **C** strain, measures 1–8.

participation in the Midwestern ragtime community; yet, he became familiar with much published ragtime and with other musics as well. As a lad he had listened to German folk singers in Berlin, Ontario, and later he learned the music of Sissle and Blake, amassed an impressive library of

Example 68. Joseph F. Lamb, *American Beauty Rag*, **A** strain, measures 1–8.

Example 69. Joseph F. Lamb, *Top Liner Rag*, **A** strain, measures 1–8.

popular songs and all types of rags, listened to black religious singing at a camp meeting ground, and participated in family sings and parish minstrel shows.[9] His experience with music was multifaceted.

In the 1920s Lamb approached the Mills Music company, hoping to find an outlet for his rags when John Stark went out of business. Mills was not interested in rags but in the then-current piano novelty, or "novelette." Again demonstrating his adaptability, Lamb obliged with fifteen novelties, all of which perished when Mills moved its offices in 1935. Samples of Lamb's novelty style survive in *Arctic Sunset* and *Hot Cinders* (Examples 71 and

Example 70. Joseph F. Lamb, *Cottontail Rag*, **A** strain, measures 1–8.

72), posthumously published by Mills in *Ragtime Treasures*. In both compositions, Lamb combines the novelty texture with traditional ragtime texture, demonstrating again his ability to manipulate widely disparate musical materials into an organic, esthetically convincing whole.

Lamb's fourth and most rewarding musical motivation occurred when Rudi Blesh (b. 1899) and Harriet Janis (1898–1963) rediscovered him in 1949 living in a modest frame house in Brooklyn. They informed him that he was considered one of the three most important ragtime composers, and asked if they could interview him for the first comprehensive study of ragtime music and musicians. Not until then did Lamb receive any critical acclaim besides that of Joplin and Stark over fifty years earlier. With the publication of *They All Played Ragtime* in 1950[10] the name and music of Joe Lamb were accorded the attention they had long deserved. Lamb's modest home on East Twenty-first Street became a point of pilgrimage for ragtime scholars and enthusiasts. Most importantly, Lamb was encouraged to complete the fragmentary rags he had carried in his memory for decades and to compose new ones, extending and consummating the genre of piano ragtime generations after its cultural demise.

The fruit of this rediscovery was the collection *Ragtime Treasures* (posthumously published in 1964), and *Alaskan Rag*, published posthumously in the third edition of *They All Played Ragtime*.[11] *Ragtime Treasures* contains

Example 71. Joseph F. Lamb, *Arctic Sunset*, **A** strain, measures 1–8.

thirteen pieces that Lamb wrote in his prime (some of which he revised), or completed or composed following his rediscovery. These compositions are richly varied. *Firefly Rag, Good and Plenty Rag,* the *Old Home Rag, Thoroughbred Rag,* and *Toad Stool Rag* constitute Lamb's revival of the robust style he abandoned in favor of Joplin's melodic lyricism. *Hot Cinders* and the first strain of *Arctic Sunset* exemplify his piano novelty style. *Cottontail Rag, Blue Grass Rag,* and *Ragtime Bobolink* reveal his important final legacy—his metamorphosis of the piano rag. Generally thinning out its texture, Lamb distilled and refined the legato-style rag into a *camerata* art for the ragtime connoisseur.

In several of the *Ragtime Treasures* pieces, left-hand tenths moving in quarter-note rhythms replace the typical oom-pah bass patterns, filling out the harmony and often leaving the general pulse implied through interaction with the treble line, as in the second strain of *Cottontail* and the trio of *Arctic Sunset*. Three-voiced chords without bass accompaniment constitute the entire texture in the first phrases of *Alabama Rag* and *Ragtime Bobolink*, the highest notes of each chord yielding a melodic line.

Flashes of the rhythmic bombast of Lamb's style before he met Joplin occur most brilliantly in *Old Home Rag* and in the second strain and trio of *Good and Plenty*. Other examples of Lamb's return to techniques of his earliest rag style are found in *Chimes of Dixie*, which has a parodistic treatment of the Dixie theme in all strains, recalling the "ragged" parody of

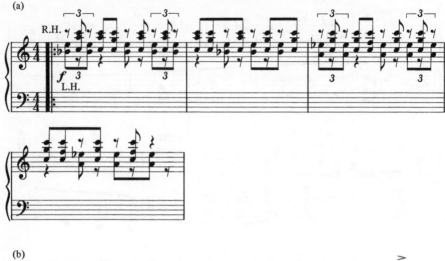

Example 72. Joseph F. Lamb, *Hot Cinders*, **B** strain, measures (a) 1-4 and (b) 9-12.

Home! Sweet Home! in the last strain of *Old Home Rag*; in the second strain of *Ragtime Bobolink*, which begins in relative minor and ends on the dominant of the relative major; and in the trio of *Ragtime Bobolink*, which is through-composed—an atypical procedure for piano rags that Lamb first used in the fourth strain of *Joe Lamb's Old Rag*.

Like *Hot Cinders*, *Arctic Sunset*—Lamb's ultimate achievement with diverse texture—combines the novelty style with traditional oom-pah ragtime, as mentioned above. Whereas *Hot Cinders* juxtaposes the two styles within each strain, the four strains of *Arctic Sunset* are texturally autonomous. The first strain (see Example 71), in novelty style, abandons the explicit pulse completely, relying on a chromatically descending harmonic passage followed by a simple, diatonically ascending arpeggio in octaves. Sharply contrasting with the first strain is the second, with its strong emphasis of the duple pulse and simple I–V chords in slow harmonic rhythm. The imaginative bass line and differentiated treble rhythms of the second and fourth phrases ingeniously salvage this toe-tapping strain from the category of ricky-tick "junk rag."

The trio, explicitly designated "Serenade—Slow," brings back melodic and harmonic chromaticism, has an implied pulse, is only half as long (eight measures) as the usual strain, and sings with a languid, long-lined theme in quasiperpetual motion; the strain ends in a shifted cadence, another prominent feature of Lamb's late rags. The last strain is boisterous—a throwback to the rollicking verve of Lamb's pre-Joplin rags. Although innocuously marked "Allegretto," it has a driving self-propulsion created by the rhythmic interplay of bass and treble. Whether viewed as a suite or a tone poem, *Arctic Sunset* is aesthetically cohesive despite its texturally disparate components—a tribute to the imagination and craftsmanship of its composer.

Lamb was proudest of his *Alaskan Rag,* newly composed after his rediscovery and published after his death. The piece abounds in long-lined melodic arches, left-hand tenths, judiciously nuanced textures, exploitation of the lower registers of the treble, and melodic/harmonic sequences. A haunting rag, it is unanimously respected as the quintessence of the lyric, legato-melodic rag style pioneered by Joplin and culminated by Lamb.

Far more than other composers of piano rags, Lamb treated introductions as integral, sometimes crucial, elements of the form. On the downbeat of the first strain of *Alaskan Rag,* each hand unexpectedly has a rest. The introduction, melodically and harmonically related to the first strain, makes possible this ingenious surprise by supplying the expected downbeat in the accompaniment. Thus, in this most *cantabile* of rags, Lamb injected one of the most startling rhythmic phenomena in the ragtime literature, a syncopation highlighted by the structural interdependence of the introduction and strain, displaying a finesse verging on the magical.

Although in some ways *Alaskan Rag* summarizes Lamb's contributions to the ragtime repertoire, it does not contain his most significant structural contribution—transcending the convention of four-measure phrases in piano rags. Concentrating on texture, voicing, rhythm, and melody, Lamb sidestepped the structural implications of transcending the four-measure phrase. These implications, which included endlessly elided cadences, erosion of the phrase structure, and eventual dissolution of tonally oriented form, were seized upon by such European art music composers as Wagner, Strauss, and Schoenberg. It is almost as though Lamb were saying to the modernists and atonalists, "Wait a minute, boys. Maybe it doesn't have to go that way."

Pursuing such structural possibilities was more in keeping with the inclinations of Joplin, who sought to dignify ragtime not only through the expanded forms of his late rags but also through association with the sophisticated European genres of opera (*Guest of Honor*, 1903, and *Treemonisha*, 1911), ballet or, more properly, "folk ballet"[12] (*Ragtime Dance*, 1902), and even symphony.[13] James Scott and Joe Lamb climaxed their composing careers within the context of the ternary form with trio, the prototypical mold of the piano rag. Scott consistently produced brilliant and inspired rags from

Frog Legs Rag (1906) to *Broadway Rag* (1922) with little stylistic change. Lamb's rag production, more sporadic though eventually more profuse than either Joplin's or Scott's, encompassed radical mutations: the pre-Joplin rags (1904–1907), the Stark rags (1908–1919), the Mills novelties (early 1920s), and the syntheses and metamorphoses represented in the posthumous *Ragtime Treasures*.

A close comparison of the rags of Lamb, Joplin, and Scott demonstrates that each of the three brought something to the classic rag indicative of his own musical environment and activities. Joplin's well-honed melodies bespeak his years of roaming Middle America, collecting folklike strains with blue notes and pentatonic contours—strains which were eventually blended in the five-part classic rag. Scott's rhythmic drive, deployment of "jazz breaks," and virtuosic use of the keyboard attest to his reputed dexterity at the piano and foreshadow his long career as theater organist, arranger, and orchestral pianist in the silent movie houses of Kansas City. Lamb's "light" rags (*Bohemia, Champagne, Cleopatra,* and *Reindeer*), his use of harmonic, melodic, and rhythmic clichés from the popular songs and vaudeville music of the time,[14] and the preponderance of diatonic and chromatic melodic contours in his rags as opposed to the considerably greater use of pentatonicism and blue notes in Joplin's and Scott's works, point toward Tin Pan Alley.

The crucial historical significance of Joe Lamb is that, after Joplin's *Maple Leaf Rag* hit him "good and proper," this white Easterner eagerly embraced classic ragtime as conceived by Joplin and Midwest publisher John Stark. Lamb took up ragtime not as a tantalizing fancy, not for commercial expediency, not from a lust for esthetic battle, and not because of social sympathy for blacks or ideological convictions about American popular music. Lamb adopted ragtime out of a love of the music and an artistic commitment to it. Joplin and Stark promoted ragtime as a notated piano genre worthy of comparison to the high artistic achievements of European art music. Because Lamb never separated musical concepts from their notation, he—more than any of the other well-known classic ragtime composers—absorbed the music the way that Joplin and Stark dreamed it should be transmitted: through meticulous realization of the printed score.

When Joe Lamb died in 1960 at the age of 72, he left a rich legacy. A composer almost solely by avocation, he in fact produced thirty-six piano rags, seventeen piano novelties—including the rag/novelties *Hot Cinders* and *Arctic Sunset,* twenty-odd miscellaneous pieces, and forty-three songs. Lamb was a composer of imagination, craftsmanship, experimentation, and longevity. He synthesized the widely divergent styles of Joplin and Scott with the idioms of commercial ragtime, manipulated disparate musical materials into organic wholes, and utilized a tremendous diversity of textures. By thinning out its texture, Lamb distilled and culminated the legato piano rag style. He was able to break through the rag's convention of four-measure phrase lengths, and brought tonal and structural sophistication to the piano rag. A white emulator of a black musical tradition, Joe Lamb took for granted the very respectability of ragtime, which his black hero, Scott Joplin, died proving.

Notes

1. Whitney Balliet, "The Ragtime Game," *The New Yorker*, 2 July 1960, pp. 20–21.
2. Russ Cassidy, "Joseph Lamb—Last of the Ragtime Composers," *Jazz Monthly*, November 1961, p. 10. Cassidy's serialized biography first appeared in *Jazz Report* 1 (January, February, March, April, and August 1961) and was reprinted in *Jazz Monthly* 7 (August 1961): 4–7; (October 1961): 12–15; (November 1961): 9–10; and (December 1961): 15–16. It was also reprinted in *Ragtime Society* 5 (Summer 1966): 29–42. Quotations will be from the *Jazz Monthly* reprint, which is more widely available in public and college libraries than are *Jazz Report* and *The Ragtimer*.
3. Ibid.
4. Joseph F. Lamb, *Ragtime Treasures: Piano Solos by Joseph F. Lamb*, Foreword by Rudi Blesh (New York: Mills Music, 1964).
5. Although "rag" and "cakewalk" were semantically confused during the late 1890s and early 1900s, there seems to be a notable textural differentiation in syncopated piano music of this period. Rag's instrumental texture is characterized by shorter note values, full chord sonorities, changes of register, adoption of broken-chord banjo figurations in the treble, and imaginative bass lines in octaves which are often quasicontrapuntal and/or abandon their monotonous oom-pah function for more intricate interplay with the treble. The transference of the banjo figurations to the treble part of the piano is nowhere better exemplified than in the first three strains of Joplin's *Maple Leaf Rag*; the textures are more specifically pianistic in later works of Joplin and in the rags of Tom Turpin, Charles L. Johnson, and James Scott. Cakewalk, on the other hand, is characterized by a lilting, singable treble line of one or two notes, narrow in range, in relatively longer note values accompanied by simple chords of three notes or less, and usually one-note basses in an interminable oom-pah pattern. This texture seems to have strong associations with ragtime's vocal genres. "Cakewalk tradition" here refers to the latter texture, found in many mildly syncopated turn-of-the-century cakewalks and in the delightfully transparent rags of Charles Hunter. It should be understood, however, that cakewalk titles died out around 1903, and that most rags combine the two textures in various ways (e.g., the treble part of the fourth strain of *Maple Leaf* has a lilting tune in relatively longer note values than the treble parts of the other strains, accompanied by a very ambitious "rag"-like left hand).
6. Letter from Joe Lamb to Thornton Hagert, 21 October 1959. Lamb tells Hagert that his "heavy" rags lack the easily discernible melodic line of his "light" rags. Further stylistic distinctions and the subclassifications of *Patricia* and *Contentment* are mine.
7. Lamb's use of imitation can be found, for example, in the first period, first strain of *Excelsior Rag*, and his use of expansion or "development" in the first period, trio of *Patricia Rag*.
8. Cassidy.
9. Further information on Lamb's song plugging and arranging is provided in Cassidy, "Joseph F. Lamb." Lamb's Tin Pan Alley activities are discussed in Joseph R. Scotti, "Joe Lamb: A Study of Ragtime's Paradox" (Ph.D. diss., University of Cincinnati, 1977), pp. 61, 77, 81–84. Lamb's familiarity with the music of Sissle and Blake and his amassment of a voluminous library of sheet music, particularly rags, are documented in a letter from the composer to ragtime enthusiast Allen Meyer,

quoted in Scotti, pp. 77 and 102. The minstrel shows are chronicled in Cassidy, "Joseph Lamb," and more thoroughly in Marjorie Freilich Den, "Joseph F. Lamb, A Ragtime Composer Recalled" (M.A. thesis, Brooklyn College, 1975), pp. 22–23.

10. Rudi Blesh and Harriet Janis, *They All Played Ragtime* (New York: Alfred A. Knopf, 1950).

11. Blesh and Janis, *They All Played Ragtime,* 3rd ed., rev. (New York: Oak Publications, 1966), following p. 209.

12. Ibid., p. 68.

13. An unidentified article of 7 September 1916 announces: "Scott Joplin, the composer, has just completed his music comedy drama 'If,' and is now writing his Symphony No. 1. He has studied symphonic writing." This statement is quoted by Samuel B. Charters and Leonard Kunstadt in *Jazz: A History of the New York Scene* (Garden City, N.Y.: Doubleday, 1962), p. 49.

14. Examples include the introduction and last phrase of the first strain of *Reindeer.*

Jelly Roll Morton and Ragtime

James Dapogny

Though primarily a jazz musician, Jelly Roll Morton is also significant to ragtime. His musicianship and style were deeply indebted to ragtime; his repertory included a number of piano rags; and he clearly articulated the differences between ragtime and jazz. After reviewing Morton's career in this new chapter, James Dapogny explores Morton's conception of, debt to, and departures from, ragtime. In the process, Dapogny illuminates some differences and similarities between ragtime and jazz piano.

Ferdinand "Jelly Roll" Morton's career as a composer and pianist spanned much of the Ragtime Era and the early years of jazz. The time and place of Morton's birth and the circumstances of his youth made it possible for him to become familiar with the elements of ragtime, of jazz, and of the blues. He came to know at first hand the range of styles of the vital, increasingly visible black music tradition. Morton considered himself to be first and foremost a jazz pianist, though he is significant to the history of both ragtime and jazz. His ideas on ragtime and jazz are important, for he knew and understood both, loved both, could illustrate the differences between them, and had evolved a jazz style much indebted to ragtime's usages.

Morton was born Ferdinand Joseph Lamothe on October 20, 1890, probably in New Orleans, Louisiana.[1] He was raised in New Orleans with two sisters, mainly by a great-grandmother and an aunt and uncle. In his youth, he enjoyed the advantages of music lessons and opportunities to attend the French Opera. When he was seventeen years old, however, his great-grandmother learned that he worked as a sporting-house pianist and expelled him from her home.[2]

He then began traveling, acquiring a repertoire of alternate vocations. For perhaps ten years he traveled as a pool hustler, gambler, pimp, singer, vaudeville performer, pianist, and bandleader. He visited, apparently not for more than a few months at a time, Mobile, Memphis, New York, Chicago, Saint Louis, Detroit, Tulsa, and Denver. During this traveling period, his repertoire included the music of Scott Joplin, James Scott, and Artie Matthews, and he met and absorbed the styles of many other musicians. During this period, too, he composed *New Orleans Blues, Jelly Roll Blues, King Porter Stomp, Frog-I-More Rag,* and perhaps *Wolverine Blues, Bert Williams,* and *The Crave.* It is of course possible that he composed other pieces, some lost and others now well known, at this time. *Jelly Roll Blues* was published in 1915 by Will Rossiter of Chicago.

In 1917 Morton went to California for what was to be about a five-year stay. He lived with his business partner, Anita Johnson Gonzales—whom he sometimes referred to as his wife—and used Los Angeles as a home base for further travel to Canada, Alaska, and Mexico. Between 1917 and 1923, Morton composed *Kansas City Stomp, The Pearls,* and probably *Mamanita,* and, in 1918, copyrighted *Frog-I-More Rag*—whose copyright manuscript is the first notation we have in his hand.

In 1923, at the age of about thirty-seven, Morton returned to Chicago, and began twin careers as a recording soloist and bandleader, and as composer for publication. During the next six years, the Melrose Brothers Music Company published more than thirty Morton compositions for various media. By 1929, Morton had recorded and/or had published many of his older pieces and several works for which there is no earlier record: *Big Foot Ham, Grandpa's Spells, London Blues, Shreveport Stomp, Perfect Rag, Stratford Hunch, Dead Man Blues, Black Bottom Stomp, Soap Suds, Hyena Stomp, Billy Goat Stomp, Jungle Blues,* and *Wild Man Blues.* Of these, the last seven might well date from the Chicago period, although *Grandpa's Spells* and, in particular, *Perfect Rag* seem to be older compositions.

Early in 1923, at the peak of his success with his Victor records, Morton moved to New York with his new wife, Mabel Bertrand. There he had much less artistic and financial success for a variety of reasons: the more formidable competition in New York; jazz's new stylistic frame of reference, to which Morton was unwilling to adapt; his inability to keep a band working; and his personality, which New Yorkers considered abrasive. According to Mabel, he continued to earn a good living in music until the early 1930s[3], but by 1935 he encountered very hard times and decided to leave New York City.[4] From this New York period date his compositions *Buffalo Blues, Boogaboo, Georgia Swing, Pep, Seattle Hunch, Frances, Freakish,* and about thirty other pieces of varied type and quality (including a few of disputed authorship).

Morton spent at least two years, part of 1935 to the end of 1938, in Washington, D.C., eventually playing in—and managing—a mediocre

Jelly Roll Morton. (*John Edward Hasse collection*)

nightclub. While in Washington, however, he made his historic Library of Congress recordings for Alan Lomax.[5] In them, Morton talked about his life and travels and played a great deal, recording the previously unknown *Bert Williams, The Crave, Creepy Feeling*, and *Spanish Swat*. Among the many fine performances is a pair of recordings of *Maple Leaf Rag*, one in "Missouri" style and the other in his own. In 1938, he also made four commercial solo recordings, including the only one of *Fingerbuster*, probably an earlier piece.

In late December, 1938, Morton returned to New York City to try to capitalize on the renewed interest in his work. His health was very bad, and his days seem to have been filled with an unrelenting series of disappointments. But he made some fine recordings—piano solo, piano-vocal, and band—and did attract some attention. He and his band also made some poor recordings, which, despite the indifferent playing of the ensemble, show that Morton still had, and knew how to use, musical ideas.

In November, 1940, he returned to Los Angeles without Mabel. The return was motivated in part by his continuing failing health. On July 10, 1941, after more disappointments and hardship, Morton died in Los Angeles County General Hospital in Anita Gonzales's arms.

Jelly Roll Morton is widely regarded as a transitional figure between ragtime and jazz. But Morton himself had no doubts about his musical identity: He was a jazz pianist and composer. However he admired such men as Joplin, Scott, Matthews, Turpin, and Chauvin; however familiar he was with their music (evidently to a great extent);[6] however much his playing and composing might seem conditioned by ragtime—especially to younger musicians who found his playing dated—Morton appears consciously to have taken a musical path different in many respects from that of ragtime. His music is more fundamentally different from ragtime than is immediately obvious. Morton recognized this deep difference—the basis of his claims about his place in jazz history—but the essential difference was and is lost to many for whom the ragtime surface of some aspects of his playing and composing mask a natively jazz-styled conception.

Much of what Morton believed about ragtime can be learned from the Library of Congress recordings.[7] His comments reveal a view of ragtime somewhat different from that held by most modern scholars of the subject; at the least, his is a different use of the term "ragtime."

On the Library of Congress recordings, Morton tells us of having known, before his arrival in Missouri, the music of Turpin, Joplin, Chauvin, Matthews and Scott.[8] He identifies these men as good composers—it is obvious that he is not merely being reserved in his use of only "good"—even while casting doubt on the musical literacy of some of them. (Morton also talked of knowing such "Tin Pan Alley" rags as *Black and White Rag* by George Botsford and *The Russian Rag* by George L. Cobb.[9])

Undoubtedly, Morton was familiar with the tradition of "ragging" preexisting nonragtime melodies, just as he, in his words, "swung" the "Miserere" and the "Anvil Chorus" from *Il Trovatore*.[10] But for him, "ragtime" seems to have meant not a way of playing, but rather the great notated ragtime classics, the music of the men he identified as good composers. Although a contemporary understanding of the term "ragtime" might be broad enough to include varieties of improvised music, Morton's conception was, perhaps not surprisingly, one of the music as a body of literature; compositions with fixed structure and detail that nevertheless permitted some freedom of interpretation. When Morton gives us his evocations of great New Orleans pianists he remembers—Morton spoke of the good *composers* of Missouri and the great *pianists* of New Orleans—he plays what we might well think of as ragtime in recalling Tony Jackson,[11] Alfred Wilson,[12] Buddy Carter,[13] Albert Carroll,[14] and Sammy Davis.[15] Yet he refers to the Buddy Carter example as a "hot honky-tonk number" and as a "stomp," and calls Tony Jackson's *Naked Dance* simply a "fast-speed tune." He refers to none of his imitations, except that of Sammy Davis, as ragtime, and then with some apparent reservations: After Lomax asks Morton if the music he had just performed was ragtime, Morton says, "Yeah, that's considered ragtime." Even his choice of the word "considered" suggests that Morton deemed crucial elements of ragtime to be missing: In my opinion, what Morton misses is composition. So it seems that for

Morton the presence of surface elements of ragtime style, particularly figuration in the right hand, does not make the music "ragtime."

Morton's relationship to ragtime is most tellingly illustrated in his two Library of Congress performances of *Maple Leaf Rag*.[16] They show us much about the creation of his piano style and give us some clues about his compositional thinking. The two versions have been variously labeled and discussed, but Morton's own brief comments at the end of each version make clear what he was attempting to show. After playing the first version, Morton says, "That was the way they played it in Missouri. Of course I played the same tune: I had played it in a different tempo; that is, on the version of my creation of jazz music. In fact, I changed *every* style . . . to mine." After playing the second version, Morton declares, "That was the style that I played in New Orleans. In my estimation, it's a vast difference." Thus Morton does not claim his second version to be in New Orleans style: it is *his* style.

Morton executes the Missouri version seriously and well, without a hint of the parody he uses to illustrate the shortcomings of Benny Frenchy[17] or pianists with inaccurate left hands[18] or those who sped up tempos.[19] This version may or may not represent common practice in Missouri in 1904, and certainly anyone familiar with Morton's playing will recognize him as the performer here. What is most important about these two performances is the differences they reveal between, on the one hand, Morton's conception and memory of what is presumably "orthodox" ragtime style and, on the other hand, his own jazz style.

An easily noticeable difference is the tempo: The Missouri version is faster. Whether or not this quicker tempo is really an accurate reflection of the Missouri style Morton was attempting to demonstrate, it does show us, by contrast, Morton's preference for a slower tempo, something that he refers to elsewhere in the Library of Congress recordings. This difference might not seem significant except that it is clearly the result of a deliberate, judicious choice Morton made in the service of developing a new style. Although the faster tempo is more impressive technically, the slower tempo gives Morton the opportunity to swing eighth notes in a more pronounced and modern way. Morton's interest was not at all in technical display.

The two recordings of *Maple Leaf Rag* demonstrate differences in Morton's control of musical texture; in his own style he worked toward more textural contrast—a crucial element in Morton's playing *and* composing. He shaped performances and compositions with juxtapositions of quite different textures. This is not to say that such contrasts do not exist in notated ragtime—indeed, Morton probably learned some basic lessons there—but merely to observe that Morton placed them into greater relief. In these two performances, the greater emphasis on textural contrast is perhaps most obvious in Morton's left hand.

Since Morton claimed that jazz piano, properly played, imitates a band,[20] it might be useful to describe his left-hand styles by analogy to band playing. In Morton's first *Maple Leaf Rag* rendition, his left hand functions much as would a band's rhythm section; by stating the bass line and the complete harmonies as well as by maintaining the pulse, it combines the functions of bass, drums, and guitar or banjo. In the second version, his left hand becomes less predictable, more active, and more melodic—a low-register complement to the melody—playing the kinds of figures that have been likened to those of New Orleans–style trombone lines. This technique causes syncopation, already characteristic of ragtime's upper register, to appear—with the addition of swung eighth notes—in a lower stratum of the texture. There are whole measures, and in other pieces longer segments, in which Morton abandons explicit articulation of the pulse. In the Missouri version, for instance, Morton's left hand states the pulse explicitly for the first four measures of the first strain (Example 73). There is a vast difference in Morton's second version (Example 74). He maintains the quarter-note pulse, of course, but no longer states it explicitly throughout. He does not use attacks to emphasize the pulse, not even at the strong-beat points in the measure, which are indicated by asterisks in Example 74. The syncopation and feeling of swing have penetrated to the very bottom of the texture, and the left hand no longer supplies a rhythmic basis against which all syncopation is heard.

Example 73. Jelly Roll Morton performance of *Maple Leaf Rag*, "Missouri" version, **A** strain, measures 1–4.

Example 74. Jelly Roll Morton performance of *Maple Leaf Rag*, "Jelly Roll Morton" version, **A** strain, measures 1–4.

A further difference between the two performances, dependent upon this new left-hand style, is that the new low-register syncopations call for a new use of dynamics. Single loud notes, such as the anticipations, and quiet notes, such as the repeated notes on the second halves of beats, provide a wide range of dynamics and articulation within a very short span of time. For instance, in measure 3 of Example 74, the A-flat octave on the second half of beat 3 is the quietest note in the measure, and the A natural and B flat following are the loudest notes, showing great contrast within a short time.

The two renditions also show some significant differences in pitch use. Melodically, the Morton-style performance admits the characteristic jazz-scale flatted notes—something Morton's own compositions also do. They are especially prominent in the last statement of the last strain, though

Morton also uses them in the third strain statement of the Saint Louis version.

Another pitch usage, more typical of the style of Jelly Roll Morton and later jazz pianists than of earlier ragtime (though here again Morton uses it in the Saint Louis version as well), is the harmonization and lengthening of passing notes in the bass. To make the relationship of Morton's versions to Joplin's original clearer, Joplin's measure 1 is renotated (Example 75) in $\frac{4}{4}$ meter instead of the original $\frac{2}{4}$. Morton harmonizes Joplin's last-beat A natural with a diminished seventh chord and puts this passing A natural onto the strong beat, making the bass line more evenly paced—with a half-note harmonic rhythm—and giving the bass line a more modern sound (Example 76).

Example 75. Scott Joplin, *Maple Leaf Rag,* **A** strain, measures 1–2 renotated in $\overset{4}{4}$ meter.

Example 76. Jelly Roll Morton performance of *Maple Leaf Rag,* "Missouri" version, **A** strain, measure 1.

This kind of harmonization and transfer of position can be heard in several other places in both *Maple Leaf* performances. Morton did not always use this procedure, however. He often preferred to use ragtime's quarter-note passing tones, a usage that probably made him seem old-fashioned in later years.

In these two renditions there are important, though subtler, differences in right-hand style, too. Morton's right-hand melodic style departs from that of ragtime perhaps even more than does his left-hand lower-register syncopation. A feature of his right-hand style is the strong playing of the melody in octaves. Figuration, based on arpeggiation of the harmony, is reduced to what are now commonly called "ghost notes," or it is transformed into a very melodic—that is, truly linear, not arpeggiated—light, eighth-note filigree.

Clearly, Morton the melodist wanted an unequivocal presentation of the melody. For his own pieces, this often meant a kind of melody not characteristic of ragtime. But, perhaps from ragtime itself, he had also developed a taste for the motor-rhythm effect of much ragtime, the infectious, propulsive sound of lengthy, unbroken spans of eighth notes. One accommodation to the two conflicting values—not unique to Morton though he must have been an early exponent—was the development of a style in which the melody, strongly played in octaves with ghost notes between, replaces, in an understated way, the piano rag's figuration. Later pianists, such as Earl Hines, would reduce the use of ghost notes, further stripping jazz piano style of ragtime elements. Morton's other accommodation to conflicting values of melody and rhythm occurred in the development of a flow of eighth notes that was genuinely melodic, often providing the "clarinet part" of Morton's jazz-piano-as-band-imitation style. However different in conception Morton's use of these eighth notes was, it still gave to his piano playing much of ragtime's rhythmic veneer, which later musicians found dated.[21]

This view of Morton's melodic style may help to explain some interesting opinions he expressed. In 1938, Morton told Lomax that all the current jazz pianists he heard were merely "ragtime pianists in a very fine form."[22] How could, for instance, Fats Waller or Art Tatum, of whom Morton must have been aware, have been thought of as ragtime—as opposed to jazz—pianists? Morton was alluding, I think, to stride piano styles such as Waller's and James P. Johnson's, which really *were* closely allied to ragtime's melodic tradition, and to what *he* heard as the figuration-dominated playing of pianists influenced by Teddy Wilson and Art Tatum. (Here *Morton* had failed to recognize the emergence of new melodic ideas.) To Morton, his principle, "Always have the melody going some kind of a way,"[23] was not being observed. Melody was lost in right-hand figuration. And the left hand? These pianists had clean, light, functional left-hand styles, which were fine embodiments of an ideal of the pianist's left hand as rhythm section. Morton, however, had discarded this "too-simple" style thirty to thirty-five years earlier.

Perhaps Morton's convictions concerning melodic style help to explain why he spoke well of pianist Bob Zurke (1912–1944), who had a strongly melodic, octave-dominated right hand and an active, involved left hand.[24] In concept, if not in detail, Zurke's approach to piano playing was similar to that of Morton.

Finally, the comparison of the two Morton performances of *Maple Leaf Rag* reveals important differences in the overall textural and dynamic shaping of the performances. In my opinion, the Saint Louis version is more even in every detail from beginning to end. It flows steadily, uninterrupted by the emphasis of one strain over another. Morton's own version, in contrast, contains many small interior climaxes and, most importantly, treats the arrival of the third strain, in the subdominant key, as a major dividing point. This multistrain format, a piano rag element, is a feature of the Jelly Roll style and is found in many Morton compositions.

Morton continued to publish and record multistrain pieces all his life, even in the face of a very clear general trend away from this format. However, his adherence to this multistrain format in his own pieces tends to obscure his very important compositional innovations within that format, which might be summarized as follows:

1. his introduction of unique ways of composing strains and of relating them to one another

2. his use of functionally different types of strains: some for literal statement, some for paraphrase or thematic variation, and some for free harmonic improvisation
3. his emphasis upon the last strain as a climactic segment of improvisation

With some of these differences put into relief, we can see more clearly what Morton's composing and playing has in common with ragtime:

1. considerable reliance on sixteen-measure strains (though Morton's climactic last strains are often thirty-two measures long)
2. multistrain compositions, with contrasts of melody and texture an important premise (though Morton also wrote very fine pieces that are constructed differently)
3. a sensitivity to chord inversion—expressed through the bass line—that disappears (or at least changes) in much jazz from the later 1920s onward, except in that of some fellow ragtime-grounded pianists[25]
4. a motor-rhythm effect
5. some use of quarter-note passing tones in the bass
6. a concentration on the middle range of the piano keyboard

Are Morton's compositions, therefore, truly rags? Some, even such early works as *Jelly Roll Blues* and *New Orleans Blues*, obviously are not, nor are such later pieces as *London Blues*, *Hyena Stomp*, and *Wild Man Blues*. But others—*King Porter Stomp* and *Wolverine Blues*, and even *Pep* and *Freakish*, written later when Morton was absorbing some modern influences—certainly have at least some ragtime characteristics of surface and structure.

Morton does seem to have eliminated in his playing the more obvious elements of ragtime melody. The most overtly midwestern rag-styled melodies are the ones he cast aside. He abandoned *Perfect Rag* after its first recording in 1924 and revived it, as *Sporting House Rag*, only for a nostalgic series of recordings in 1939.[25] Morton's later recordings of *King Porter Stomp* do not present the melody of the second strain as literally as do the earlier 1920s recordings. Significantly, other musicians omitted this strain altogether when playing this popular piece. The raggy portions of the melody of the first strain of *Grandpa's Spells* (it is raggy as Morton played it but not as it was published) were replaced on the 1926 Red Hot Peppers recording of the piece by solo and duo breaks. Still, such a work as *Frances*, in its second strain, reflects the stride tradition, a descendant of another branch of ragtime. It would be hard to conclude that any Morton composition, even perhaps *Perfect Rag*, is truly a rag in the sense of the notated midwestern ragtime tradition with which Morton seems to have associated the term. As much as Morton may have retained, he added, removed, or changed many elements.

Commentators have often referred to the difficulty of separating fact from fiction in Morton's life and to the consequent difficulty of attributing to Morton specifically, or to jazz practice in general, the nonragtime features of his style. An examination, however, of what he accomplished and of the times in which he did it—the evidence is a good deal more solid than many have realized—shows him to have been both a pioneer in technique and an accomplished artist.

Long before his recording career began, Jelly Roll Morton had departed from notated ragtime conventions: he had integrated the jazz-blues scale into his music (*New Orleans Blues, Jelly Roll Blues*); had developed composed, rather than improvised, variations on melodies and devised new ways of relating ideas from different strains (*Jelly Roll Blues, Frog-I-More-Rag*); had developed a rifflike compositional phrase structure (*King Porter Stomp*); had created new approaches to melody and new ways for the pianist's left hand to operate; and had made a place *in composed music* for varied kinds and amounts of improvisation.

But all of Morton's music and his Library of Congress commentary suggest that ragtime contributed importantly to his overall development as a musician. To his technical musicianship, ragtime provided musical literacy, a sense of harmony, and the development of pianistic technique and self-discipline. Toward his compositional artistry, ragtime gave basic lessons in musical form and in improvising disciplined thematic variation. While ragtime was still a powerful, living tradition, Morton used the lessons learned from ragtime to develop a distinctly new piano style, making syncopation a pervasive part of the music's fabric. He had done this before 1907, when he left New Orleans for the last time.

Notes

1. Lawrence Gushee, "Would You Believe Ferman Mouton?" *Storyville* 95 (June–July 1981): 164–68; 98 (December 1981–January 1982): 56–59.

2. Biographical information on Morton is drawn from Alan Lomax, *Mister Jelly Roll: The Fortunes of Jelly Roll Morton, New Orleans Creole and "Inventor of Jazz"*, 2nd ed. (Berkeley: University of California Press, 1973); Jelly Roll Morton, "A Fragment of an Autobiography," *Record Changer*, March 1944, pp. 14–16, April 1944, pp. 27–28; Jelly Roll Morton, "I Created Jazz in 1902," letter to Robert Ripley reprinted in its entirety in *The Jazz Record*, April 1945, pp. 4, 5, 15, May 1945, pp. 10, 11; Kenneth Hulsizer, "Jelly Roll Morton in Washington," *Jazz Music* 2 (February–March 1944): 109–116; George W. Kay, "Final Years of Frustration (1939–1941), as told by Jelly Roll Morton in his letters to Roy J. Carew," *Jazz Journal* 21, no. 11 (November 1968): 2–5 and 21, no. 12 (December 1968): 8–9; Karl Kramer, "Jelly Roll Morton in Chicago; The Missing Chapter," *The Ragtimer* 6, no. 1 (April 1967): 15–22.

3. Lomax, *Mister Jelly Roll*, p. 216.

4. Ibid., p. 228.

5. During May and June of 1938, Alan Lomax recorded 104 acetate sides of Morton talking, singing, and playing (Library of Congress, Archive of Folk Song master discs 1638–88, 2787–89). Most, but not all, of the recordings were subsequently released commercially, first on 78 rpm by Rudi Blesh's Circle Records, and later on long-play discs by Riverside Records (9001–9012) and several foreign labels.

6. Lomax, *Mister Jelly Roll*, pp. 148–49.

7. Jelly Roll Morton, recorded by Alan Lomax at Coolidge Auditorium, Library of Congress, Washington, D.C., 1938, master discs 1653 and 1654. These *Maple Leaf Rag* performances are included on Riverside 9003 and on Herwin 401.

8. Morton, Library of Congress master discs 1653 and 1654.
9. Lomax, *Mister Jelly Roll*, p. 162.
10. Morton, Library of Congress master disc 1668.
11. Ibid., discs 1642, 1643.
12. Ibid., disc 1642.
13. Ibid., disc 1647.
14. Ibid., disc 1688.
15. Ibid., disc 1642.
16. Ibid., discs 1653, 1654.
17. Ibid., disc 1666.
18. Ibid., disc 1650.
19. Ibid., disc 1649.
20. Ibid.
21. Lomax, *Mister Jelly Roll*, p. 218; Elmer Snowden quoted in Chris Albertson's brochure notes to *Jelly Roll Morton* (Giants of Jazz), Time-Life Records STL-J07, 1979, p. 45; James Dapogny, interview with Franz Jackson, Hinsdale, Illinois, Fall 1958.
22. Morton, Library of Congress master disc 1649.
23. Ibid.
24. Ibid.
25. The piano rag's use of the "tonic" six-four chord at cadences is already absent in Morton's compositions.
26. Morton's recording of *Sporting House Rag*, "lost" for forty years, was issued in 1979 on Jelly Roll Morton, *New Orleans Memories Plus Two*, Commodore XFL 14942.

Band and Orchestral Ragtime

Thornton Hagert

Though instrumental ragtime was primarily a piano style, thousands of bands and small orchestras played it, too. In this trailblazing essay, Thornton Hagert examines these ensembles' makeup, performance practices, and performance settings. He also describes the roles of the various instruments, the shortcomings of the notation, the influences of popular dances, and the publication of the "Red Back Book" and other collections.

During the period when ragtime was first popular—from the late 1890s until World War I—it was performed for popular audiences throughout the nation, not only by pianists and singers, but also by literally thousands of instrumental groups. The main categories of such instrumental groups were: mandolin clubs and other aggregations of fretted instruments; bands of wind instruments (usually with drums); and orchestras of mixed instrumentation that featured the violin and cello. Publishers of popular music customarily issued—in addition to sheet music versions for piano and song—"instrumentations" designed for all such groups. In this form, ragtime was widely performed at concerts, dances, and as incidental music at public gatherings. This exposure of ragtime music to the mass of

Portions of this chapter appeared as notes to the recording *Classic Rags and Ragtime Songs*, The Smithsonian Collection N 001, 1975. Used by permission of the Smithsonian Institution Press.

performing musicians and their audiences facilitated the general acceptance of the persistent syncopation and rhythmic thrust that in time became a major distinguishing characteristic of American music. The music for fretted instruments is treated in the chapter "The Banjo in Ragtime" by Lowell H. Schreyer. This chapter discusses the instrumentations of ragtime pieces published for popular bands and orchestras.

By 1900, many different types of bands performed at all sorts of public functions, particularly those held out of doors. To simplify matters, there were: (1) old-style brass bands, probably most common in towns and small cities; (2) brass-and-reed bands; and (3) grand concert bands such as those of John Philip Sousa (1854–1932), Frederick Innes (1858–1927), and Alessandro Liberati (1847–1927)—to name only a few of those which became nationally known.[1]

By this time, the old-style brass bands (made up of a family of similar brass wind instruments in B flat and E flat) had been largely superseded by the "military" brass-and-reed bands, which mingled various valved brass instruments from different families, including a variety of bass instruments, some in C and some in F. They also included D-flat piccolos and

Arthur Pryor (1870–1942) was assistant conductor for John Philip Sousa, and beginning in 1903, led his own band which recorded many cakewalks and rags. Pryor was also a composer of instrumental rags. (*John Edward Hasse collection*)

B-flat and E-flat clarinets. The brass-and-reed band had a repertoire that included selections from opera, funeral dirges, quick-step marches, mildly syncopated "Ethiopic" numbers, and popular waltzes, schottisches, and Bohemian polkas. The instrumentations published for these groups were written in such a way that they could still be used by the old-style brass band comprised of E-flat and B-flat cornets, E-flat alto, B-flat tenor, and E-flat baritone horns.[2]

The famous concert bands—with strong orchestral components of slide trombones (instead of the valved trombones or tenor horns still favored by the other bands), double-bass instruments, and many woodwinds (including flutes, oboes, bassoon, a dozen or more clarinets and some saxophones) were still quite exceptional. They normally performed as touring groups at special concerts or in extended engagements at expositions, summer resorts, or amusement parks. These bands almost never played for marching or dancing. Their repertoires ran the gamut from transcriptions of symphonic pieces, opera overtures, and artistic solos, with brilliant variations, to popular novelties such as modern march two-steps, cake-walks, and Bowery waltzes. In the major cities, there were similar, though generally smaller, resident groups, many of whose men worked in orchestras in the winter season and in concert bands in the summer.[3]

In addition, every hotel, theatre, restaurant, and dance hall of any pretension had a small orchestra made up of most of the instruments used in a symphonic or operatic orchestra—strings, brass, woodwinds, percussion, and perhaps piano. While in practice the size of these orchestras varied considerably, the ideal included fifteen or more musicians playing: first and second violins, viola, cello, string bass, flute, first and second clarinets, oboe, bassoon, first and second cornets (or trumpets), slide trombone, F horns, drums (bass, cymbal and snare), and also piano.[4]

According to theatrical directories of the period, an orchestra of this size was the norm only in the best theatres of New York and Boston. In the theatres of Brooklyn, Chicago, San Francisco, and Washington, for example, an orchestra more commonly consisted of nine or ten men, and in a small city, it often had fewer than that.[5] A concert program by such an orchestra typically included "selections" from (or an overture to) a popular musical show or opera, a concert version of a Strauss or Waldteufel waltz set, and a "characteristic" intermezzo or descriptive fantasy.

A dance orchestra was also variable in size and makeup. It often included a fretted instrument such as mandolin, guitar, or one of a variety of banjo-type instruments, and it often did not use a piano. A dance program by such an orchestra would probably include a military two-step in $\frac{6}{8}$ time or a "ragtime" two-step in syncopated $\frac{2}{4}$ time, a schottische or barn dance in $\frac{4}{4}$, and a waltz in $\frac{3}{4}$ time, most likely a medley of popular songs.[6]

We are accustomed to hearing ragtime played on the piano, but what did ragtime sound like when played by bands and orchestras such as these? To be truthful, we cannot be very sure about that. In his discography, *Recorded Ragtime, 1897–1958*, David A. Jasen lists hundreds of ragtime and cakewalk recordings made in the United States before World War I, the bulk of them by soloists on the banjo or accordian, or by oddly constituted military bands.[7] Before the early 1910s, there are only a handful of recordings of groups with violins playing ragtime.[8] In the earliest days, it was nearly impossible to record bands and orchestras as they normally performed. Except when performing solos with unobtrusive accompaniment, or in duets or trios, most band and orchestra instruments were almost impossible to record with any clarity. These "almost impossible" instruments included violin, viola, cello, and string bass; flute, clarinet, saxophone, oboe, and bassoon; alto, baritone, and French horn; guitar and mandolin; and piano and drums. Ruling out all these instruments left only piccolo, cornet, trombone, and brass bass—instruments that dominate the earliest recordings of large groups playing ragtime. Clarinets, baritones, and raspy Stroh violins could be employed in exposed situations where the other instruments were very subdued. Occasionally, one can hear a "boom" on a small bass drum or a passage with snare drumming prominent. In addition to having uncharacteristic instrumentation, the early recordings were further compromised by a general lack of dynamic contrast, and by infrequent use of tempos intended for dancing.[9]

Fortunately for us, the orchestral and band ragtime of those days has been preserved in the form of the "stock" instrumentations which were published to meet the requirements of the music trade. From these, we can reconstruct the sound of the popular band and orchestra to a remarkable degree—as long as we do not allow ourselves to forget that nothing in music today is quite what it was in 1900. The instruments themselves are different, and instrumental styles of performance have changed greatly over the intervening years. Our notions of tempo, pitch, tone production, vibrato, articulation, phrasing, and rhythmic emphasis are different, and our views of what function each instrument is supposed to serve have altered radically. All these things varied widely even at the time. It seems fairly obvious that a black orchestra playing in a dance hall in San Francisco might sound very different from a white orchestra performing in a theater in Philadelphia, even though each was using identical orchestrations on the same day in 1913. To reconstruct either one of these performances would require more than merely reading the notes on the page.

Indeed, some of the notation itself will leave a modern performer wondering what was meant. Tempo indications, when given at all, were apt to be "moderato" or "slow march tempo," terms which are no longer clear. The tempos actually used varied between the East and the Midwest; varied among social classes according to the manner of dancing favored; and varied, of course, depending on the complexity of the rhythms in the written parts. The parts for the strings were generally devoid of any bowing indications. Markings for dynamics were of the crudest sort, generally limited to "mf/p" for the entire group, all at once. There was no conductor's score, and no general indication that any one part contained the melody or some other important line that ought to stand out. The parts for the snare drum were seldom in "universal notation," but generally in various sorts of shorthand that reflect the great changes taking place within drumming.

All in all, reconstruction of the sound of the old instrumental groups is difficult for even the most skilled musicians, and any claims of authenticity may well be viewed with some skepticism. Perhaps the most we can hope for today is a sincerely performed and satisfyingly musical interpretation of a composition that was written sufficiently well that it survives the translation into present-day conventions.

All of these shortcomings in the notation of the parts are further confounded by the fact that the composition itself was apt to have been compromised or modified in order to make it accessible to the general public. Virtually all ragtime, including "classic" ragtime, seems to have been strongly influenced by the prevailing fashion in dance music. Beginning in the 1890s, there was a tremendous vogue for a peppy dance called the two-step. It consisted of a simple step-close-step movement in each bar and was at first danced to the music of the military quick step march in $\frac{6}{8}$ meter at about sixty bars per minute, although after a while almost anything in $\frac{2}{4}$, ₵, or $\frac{4}{4}$ would serve. There were thousands of two-step numbers of the $\frac{6}{8}$ variety, and thousands more of others in varying time signatures and of diverse types, including cakewalks, *habaneras*, slow drags, and ragtime pieces. Many of these appear to have developed within entirely different traditions from the military quick step, and required slower tempos and an internal rhythmic sense at great odds with the simple alternating beat of the two-step. Nevertheless, the two-step was *the* prevailing dance for over twenty years, and publishers of popular music aggressively marketed all sorts of novelties as two-steps, not only in sheet music form, but also as instrumentations for bands and orchestras, and for fretted instruments.[10]

It is hard to know for certain to what degree ragtime was compromised by this situation, but certainly part of the price that it paid for riding the crest of the two-step wave was that it was often played too fast (despite the advice frequently printed at the beginning of the music). Further, because the more complex or eccentric ragtime pieces became quite ungainly at such tempos, they were neglected in favor of the simpler, more formulaic pieces. The tendency in polite dance music to reduce vigorous and "tricky" rhythms to a smoother, quicker, alternating beat has been very persistent and may be observed since about 1825 in the popularization of the galopade, waltz, polka, and schottische. In more recent times, as in the early 1910s, even those popular songs which were published in $\frac{4}{4}$ time (and clearly required it) were routinely converted to a simpler $\frac{2}{4}$ when published in dance form: Examples include Irving Berlin's *Alexander's Ragtime Band* (1911) and Newton and Seibert's *Casey Jones* (1909).

By the end of the first decade of the 1900s, other dances began to find increasing favor, including the turkey trot, the grizzly bear, the glide, and the revived barn dance. By the midteens this culminated in the widely popular one-step and then the fox trot. The broadly syncopated one-step (at about sixty or more bars per minute) was especially interesting because the familiar rhythmic figurations of cakewalk and ragtime were now stretched out over twice as many bars, and thus ended up being played about half as fast and with more powerful accents than in the old two-step variety. Such a practice had occurred for years in black dance music, the most common example being the strutting finale of a cakewalk, which was done in "half-time." The new way of writing ragtime seems to represent a growing comprehension that the two-step conception was inadequate for that ragtime which was slow and powerfully accented. The beauty of the new system was that it overcame this inadequacy while preserving both the accepted $\frac{2}{4}$ notation and the convention of having one dance step on each principal beat. This method did not attract the interest of the "classic" rag writers such as Scott Joplin (1868–1917), James Scott (1886–1938), and Joseph Lamb (1887–1960), who continued to compose within the gentler two-step and slow march traditions, but it did suit some of the Eastern writers, such as Eubie Blake (1883–1983), whose *Fizz Water* (1915) is a nice example of the genre.

In a similar manner, the fox trot was played slower than a two-step and included more accented beats in a phrase. It came to be written in $\frac{4}{4}$ or in ¢ and was initially played at about forty bars per minute, the familiar point of reference for the general public being the barn dance out of the old military schottische. Public acceptance of all this was nevertheless very slow, despite the apparent vogue for fox trots in the 1910s. The result was that fox trot numbers were often performed as one-steps or even two-steps, the number of accented beats being cut in half, and the tempo speeded up, some examples being Wilbur Sweatman's *Down Home Rag* (1911) and Euday Bowman's *12th Street Rag* (1914).

Quite apart from these tendencies, we know from comparing variant editions that publishers generally "simplified" ragtime syncopations so that the novice pianist would have less difficulty with them. They routinely eliminated large intervals such as octaves or tenths in the bass, reduced the bass part to the standard two-step rhythm, and avoided extreme registers and "difficult" key signatures. From the 1890s until well after World War I, the publishers' instrumentations for band and orchestra were, of course, prone to the same kinds of modification and simplification that befell the piano scores from which they normally were developed. Instrumentations—prepared, after all, largely for professional musicians—*could* have restored some of the elements edited out of the popular solo piano versions, but, in fact, almost never did. Sometimes an arranger did provide some additional interest in the form of countermelodies or *obbligatos* that were not in the original piano version. They were most apt to do this in the "trio" strain, or in some other loosely organized strain where such liberties seemed appropriate. Harry L. Alford's orchestration of Percy Wenrich's *The Smiler* (1907) is a good example of this practice, resulting in an orchestral rag that is much more interesting than the published piano version. And while we might expect that published instrumentations would occasionally include some rhythmic development (such as intensifying the syncopations) or rhythmic expansion (such as going into half-time) or at least "ragging" a simple melody, they almost never did unless those things were an essential part of the original composition. A rare example of "ragging" a melody may be found in the violin, flute, and drum parts of a dance orchestration by Harry L. Alford of Shelton Brooks' *Some of These Days* (1910).

In what follows, I have tried to describe typical instrumentations of the period for band and orchestra, showing what instruments were provided for and the nature of the parts distributed among them. I have included three musical examples: one from a band number of 1900 (Example 77), the second from an orchestration of 1899 (Example 78), and the third from an orchestration of 1910 (Example 79). I have segregated the individual parts according to their function and have written them all in concert key at their correct pitch (except for the string bass, which should be read an octave lower). These excerpts display general characteristics of band and orchestra music that held true from the mid-1890s through the mid-1910s. My comments here are necessarily very general; they describe tendencies, and many exceptions can be found. For us, the most important difference between a band and an orchestra of 1900 is that some instruments they had in common are given different roles. The most striking difference is that the "solo" B-flat cornet in the band is the primary melody instrument and, although not apparent here, had the liberty of embellishing the melody. The "solo" B-flat clarinet in the band is given not the melody proper, but a rather independent elaborated part mixing upper harmony with references to the melody. In an orchestra, all the drumming was apt to be done by a single musician playing snare drum and bass drum, the latter with a foot pedal.

By about 1900, a published band instrumentation of the popular two-step variety commonly included over twenty different parts with enough duplication that it could be used by an old-style brass band, or by a brass-and-reed band, or by a large concert band. To state the matter in the simplest terms, the parts were divided up in this fashion: the melody (generally duplicated at three levels); an assortment of harmony parts (either supporting the melody or as a generalized background); perhaps a counter part or solo in the lower register; and the downbeat and upbeat rhythms. The principal melody part usually lay in the range of the treble clef and was played by B-flat cornets and clarinets, and also by the E-flat cornet and the oboe. The melody was duplicated an octave or two higher by the D-flat piccolo and E-flat clarinet, and an octave lower by the E-flat baritone (unless it was assigned a solo or counter part), by the B-flat tenors, and sometimes by the first and second trombones. The first and second trombones generally played upbeats, as did the E-flat altos and B-flat tenor horns. The downbeats were played in the upper bass by the third and fourth trombones, bassoon, sometimes the E-flat baritone, and a variety of tubas and euphoniums. The bass was sometimes duplicated an octave below by the helicon or another double-bass instrument.

But I have left out something very important: Below the principal melody, other cornets and clarinets played supporting harmony and generalized background harmony. Above the principal melody, the solo B-flat clarinet played an upper harmony part. Such upper harmony parts were unique to band arrangements at that time but, as we shall see, became common in orchestra music within ten years. D-flat piccolos were sometimes given an elaborate *obbligato* part to play when the melody was not very busy—as in a "trio" section of a march two-step.

In the following excerpt (Example 77) from the band version of *Remus On Broadway* (1900), the cakewalk melody is played by the solo B-flat cornet, first B-flat cornet, and first B-flat clarinet, oboe, and E-flat cornet, all in unison. The E-flat clarinet is playing the melody an octave higher, and the

Example 77. M. Clark, *Remus on Broadway*, arr. for band, **A** strain, measures 3–4.

D-flat piccolo an octave higher still. Above the principal melody parts is an elaborated part for the solo B-flat clarinet. The second and third B-flat cornets are playing (in unison) a supporting lower harmony to the melody. The second and third B-flat clarinets are playing a generalized harmony background. The E-flat baritone horn in this instance is playing the melody an octave below the B-flat cornet, but often played counter parts. The four E-flat alto horns (and the first and second B-flat trombones) are playing upbeats. The third and fourth B-flat trombones and the bassoon are playing an upper bass part, and the unpredictable "tuba" has a part written at essentially the same pitch. (In later years, the tuba would probably be played an octave lower.) The snare drummer plays upbeats and a roll, and the bass drummer plays downbeats. There are no indications for the cymbal, but it generally followed the bass drum part.

Orchestrations of about 1900 also took into account the fact that a performance would usually involve less than the full complement of fifteen instruments and piano. One could buy a "small" version of the orchestration that simply omitted the parts for oboe, bassoon, horns, and second clarinet. What remained was written in a fashion that would allow it to be played by fewer instruments. Consequently, these orchestrations were not prescriptive in the sense of requiring a specific instrumentation, nor were they "arrangements" that set out to exploit coloristic differences between the different families of instruments.[11]

To state the matter in the simplest terms, the orchestrator assigned the melody and its harmonies to one group of instruments, and the underlying rhythmic part and its harmonies to another group of instruments, and to each in such a way that there was a great amount of duplication of parts. This allowed different combinations of instruments to perform the piece successfully in a more or less complete manner. For example, the treble clef of the original piano score (the pianist's right-hand part)—which generally contained the melody, full of syncopations and close harmonies (or octaves)—was usually assigned to seven of the instruments in this way: the melody (usually the "top line") was assigned to the violin and flute, either in unison or an octave apart. Depending on its register, the melody was also divided between the first clarinet and first cornet, each of these alternating from phrase to phrase or even from bar to bar between melodic and harmonic passages. The second clarinet and second cornet were given the job of supporting the firsts, generally with a simplified part in unison or an octave apart, or in harmony with the first part. Thus it was possible to play the melody with only a violin or a flute, or with only a clarinet *and* a cornet. (The oboe also had melody parts.)

Similarly, the bass clef of the original piano score (the pianist's left-hand part) was generally limited to downbeats and upbeats in the customary two-step pattern, with an occasional melodic passage at octaves. In the orchestrations, this part was assigned to no less than nine instruments. Specifically, the downbeats were assigned to the cello, trombone, string bass, bassoon, bass drum, and the pianist's left hand; the upbeats were given to the second violin, viola, horns, snare drum, and the pianist's right hand. The snare drum part often included rhythms in imitation of the melody. Thus, it was possible for the bass clef to be played by only the piano, or by a combination of trombone (or cello) or string bass and drums—and, in fact, it often was.

If doubling of parts allowed performance by a smaller group, it also gave the fuller orchestra the option of a considerable variety of combinations. Even during a performance, the leader could assign the prominent parts to one of several instruments, thereby producing a more varied effect. For example, a strain might first be stated by only the strings, and then repeated by the wind instruments and drums, or perhaps by the solo piano. There was no conductor's score to indicate to the leader when this might be done. Since the leader in the early days was almost invariably the first violinist and since he generally had the entire melodic line in his own part, he could— knowing the conventions of the day—usually anticipate when the clarinet or cornet would be doubling the line. In later days, the pianist often became the musical director of the orchestra. Instead of being a mere accompaniment, his part often became a complete part, with sufficient cues for the other instruments that the pianist could call the shots or play solos.

The expression "to play second fiddle" had a dire meaning in these orchestrations. Instead of playing a continuous line in harmony with the first violin (as they would normally do in a Mozartian sonata) both the second violin and viola were restricted to an unrelenting accompaniment role that placed them squarely in the rhythm section.[12]

In the following excerpt (Example 78) from the orchestration of *A Warm Reception* (1899), the melody is played by the violin and clarinet with the flute an octave above; there is nothing in between them. The first and second cornets are playing partly harmony, and partly melody with its lower harmony. Later in the orchestration, the cornet will have melody that is not in the clarinet part. The oboe and second clarinet are playing a sustained harmony, which is quite unusual at this time. The cello and bassoon have an important counter part. The second violin and viola and two F horns are playing upbeats. The trombone has an upper bass part, an octave higher than the string bass. Not shown here are the trombone's "cues" for the important counter part, which would be played if there were no cello. The piano is performing a rhythmic accompaniment with downbeats in the bass and upbeats in the treble. The snare drum is imitating the rhythms of the melody, in this case without the customary downbeats on the bass drum and fixed cymbal. It is unusual for an orchestra of this period to be playing in B flat. Most orchestrations were published in the keys of C, G, D, or A for a better sound from the strings. In such cases, the clarinetist and cornetist would play instruments pitched in A instead of in B flat.

By the end of the first decade of the 1900s, nearly every instrument in the orchestra was changing markedly in its function and in its manner of performance. Many of these changes seem to have been introduced by musicians who had crossed over from band music. Thus, by 1910, the

Example 78. Bert R. Anthony, *A Warm Reception,* arr. for orchestra by M. I. Brazil, **A** strain, measures 1–2.

cornet was increasingly the primary wind instrument playing melody, and the clarinet was more and more relegated to a role of playing upper harmony parts and piccololike elaborations. The cello, and to some extent, the bassoon were often assigned the more melodic role of playing extended lines in harmony with, or counter to, the melody lines in the treble clef. These extended lines constituted another voice rather than mere accompaniment, and trombonists took pride in being able to read cello parts as well as their own. The trombone, indeed, was asserting itself in other ways.

Instead of rendering only routine upper bass parts, it was often featured prominently, playing humorous sliding solo passages, or harmonies and connective phrases.[13]

Even the manner of playing the violin began to change during this period. No longer was the first violin master of the dance orchestra. He was now compelled to compete for the melody with the powerful cornet and for the upper harmony part with the clarinet; in addition, he was now being challenged—sometimes by the tenor banjo being strummed tremolo with a plectrum, and sometimes by the aggressive piano, no longer content to play mere accompaniment rhythms. Drummers were revelling in new equipment—wire rather than gut snares, minstrel-band woodblocks, gongs, tom-toms, orchestra bells, and rapid-fire bass drum pedals. Violinists were forced to give up the older style or playing which had used so much *portamento*, and to develop new bowing tactics that rendered the strongly accented and eccentrically syncopated figures in a more convincing (and audible) fashion. Some violinists even resorted to metal strings.

In the following excerpt (Example 79) from the orchestration of *Knock-Out Drops*, 1910, we have a clear demonstration of some of the changes which occurred in orchestra music: the piano is now important, and elements of band music are being adopted by the dance orchestra.[14] Though it is not apparent in this two-bar excerpt, the orchestration features the trombone playing comic slides. The cornet plays the ragtime melody while the clarinet performs a simple upper harmony part with imitative rhythms. The second clarinet and second cornet are playing lower harmonies in support of the melody. There is a horn part for a sustained harmony, which in 1910 was still unusual for an orchestra. At this point, there is also a strong counter part being played by the cello, horn, trombone, and piano. The piano has cues for the melody that are not shown here. The drums have an imitative part on the snare (with stroke rolls) and downbeats on the bass. A few years later, drum parts often included explosive upbeat accents on the bass and traps.

In further response to the varying requirements of orchestras all over the nation, publishers began to issue orchestra folios in which the individual instruments' parts for a dozen or so compositions were gathered into one folio. Thus, an orchestra leader could buy one book of violin parts, one of piano, and any others that he needed, and have usable orchestrations for a dozen compositions. In 1907, *Jacobs' Dance Folio No. 1* was available for all "fifteen instruments and piano," and included twelve selections in each book of parts. By 1912 the *Remick Orchestra Folio* was available for only "eleven instruments and piano," the oboe, bassoon, horns, and second clarinet parts now no longer furnished.

By no later than very early 1915, John Stark (1841–1927) the pioneer publisher of ragtime, issued his own orchestra folio, called *Standard High-Class Rags*, which he described as "an orchestra book for all time" with the claim that "Hits may come and hits may go, but these classics go on forever." Often referred to as the "Red Back Book of Rags" because of the

Example 79. F. Henri Klickmann, *Knock-Out Drops: Rag,* arr. for orchestra by Harry L. Alford, **A** strain, measures 1–2.

color of its cover, this collection included some of the choicest items in the Stark catalog, ranging in original publication date from 1899 (*Maple Leaf Rag*) to 1911 (*The Minstrel Man*).[15] They had all been published before as individual orchestrations and the practical Stark simply reused the printing plates for this publication. Only eleven books of parts (including piano) were available; the parts for oboe, bassoon, horns, second cornet, and second clarinet were omitted, even though the original orchestrations had generally included them. It is a testimony to John Stark's lack of business acumen that none of the fifteen selections included in the folio were ever recorded at the time—with the lone exception of *Maple Leaf Rag*, which by 1915 had been recorded a total of seven times, mostly by banjoists and military bands. Despite the almost legendary status given the "Red Back Book" by jazz historians, it was, in fact, never in wide use—although several influential orchestra leaders did use it, including John Robichaux (1866-1939) in New Orleans and Charles Elgar (1885-1973) in Chicago. From reading the testimonials Stark printed, one gets the impression that his orchestrations sold better in Europe and in the Antipodes than they did in the U.S.[16]

In 1947, several attempts were made to record groups playing classic rags from the "Red Back Book," using veteran musicians who had played the complex orchestrations when they were first published. The instrumentation in each case was: trumpet, clarinet, trombone, guitar, string bass, piano, and drums. The intent was not to re-create the original sound of the old-style orchestras, but rather to demonstrate ragtime elements of the

The John Robichaux Orchestra, 1896, which performed in fine restaurants and hotels in New Orleans from about 1895 to 1927. Known for its up-to-date repertory, the orchestra performed a wide variety of popular music, including ragtime. Seated (from left): Dee Dee Chandler, Charles McCurdy, John Robichaux, Wendell MacNeil. Standing (from left): Baptiste DeLisle, James Wilson, James MacNeil, Oak Gaspard. (*John Edward Hasse collection*)

early jazz band repertoire.[17] Bunk Johnson's band recorded *The Entertainer* (1902), *The Minstrel Man* (1911), *Kinklets* (1906), and *Hilarity Rag* (1910), and Mutt Carey's New Yorkers recorded *Sensation* (1908), *The Entertainer* (1902), and *The Chrysanthemum* (1904).

In the early 1970s, in conjunction with the concert performances and recordings by the New England Conservatory Ragtime Ensemble, the indefatigable Gunther Schuller (b. 1925) also edited for publication all of the orchestrations of Joplin compositions found in Stark's *Standard High-Class Rags*, and also Joplin's *Sugar Cane*, which was originally published not by Stark but rather by Seminary Music.[18] Since the original orchestrations are quite scarce, Schuller's publication for the first time makes readily available to the general public a handful of the choicest pieces from the era of orchestrated ragtime. For the most part, Schuller's editing is limited to correcting errors in notation and providing expression marks. He occasionally tinkers with form, such as not repeating a strain, or ending on a return to an earlier strain not indicated in the original score; but these alterations are consistent with the performance practice of the period. The most drastic deviation from the original scores occurs when Schuller at times reassigns the melody (on a repeat) to a new instrument—a procedure seldom found in published orchestrations prior to World War I. What would generally have been done at the time would be for one of the duplicate melody instruments to drop out, leaving the other a clear field. In such a case, one of the first violins might fake a harmony part, counter part, or *obbligato*. The performances on Schuller's recordings are sympathetic attempts to show that classic ragtime has qualities that are "artistic" and within the salon orchestra tradition. On its *Red Back Book* LP, Schuller's ensemble performs with some expression, with varied dynamics, and with reasonable alternations of tempo.[19]

Other modern recordings of original orchestrations have been made that provide a fairly good sense of how orchestras of the period dealt with various types of ragtime—from the cakewalks, "classic" rags, and slow drags to the one-steps and fox trots. These are honest attempts at reconstruction, directed by T. J. Anderson, Jr., Gerard Schwarz, Dick Hyman, and Albert White.[20] Unhappily, I am not able to cite any published recordings of comparable attempts to reconstruct authentic band performances of ragtime.

By 1917, the time of America's entry into World War I, the old idea of the through-composed multistrain rag or dance composition had nearly died, although vestiges would persist through the mid-1920s. In its place increasingly came the notion of the more simply constructed basic tune on which variations were to be worked. Paraphrasing of melodies, developing new counter melodies and *obbligatos*, and altering tonality were the new vogue. By the early 1920s, "arrangements" that exploited the varied tone colors of the brass and reed instruments (including saxophones) became common. In the popular mind, it was the Jazz Age, and ragtime was a relic of a bygone era.

Notes

1. See H. W. Schwartz, *Bands of America* (Garden City, N.Y.: Doubleday, 1975) and Kenneth Berger, *Bandmen* (Evansville, Ind.: Berger Band, 1955). For an overview of certain band activities in one particular city, see William J. Schafer with assistance from Richard B. Allen, *Brass Bands and New Orleans Jazz* (Baton Rouge and London: Louisiana State University Press, 1977).

2. See *Quick Step Journal for Brass and Reed Bands* (Philadelphia: J. W. Pepper, 1887), a publisher's catalog; T. H. Rollinson, *Treatise on Harmony, Counterpoint, Instrumentation, and Orchestration* (Philadelphia: J. W. Pepper, 1886); and L. P. Laurendeau, *The Practical Band Arranger* (New York: Carl Fischer, 1911).

3. See *Band Leader's Guide,* 8 vols. (New York: Carl Fischer, 1879–1907), a publisher's catalog.

4. See the widely used instruction book by Henri Kling, *Professor H. Kling's Modern Orchestration and Instrumentation,* trans. Gustav Saenger, 2nd ed. (New York: Carl Fischer, 1905).

5. Julius Cahn, *The Julius Cahn Theatrical Guide and Motion Picture Directory,* published annually (New York: Julius Cahn, 1896–1919).

6. See *Advance Agent: The MarkStern* [sic] *Popular and Operatic Successes* (New York: Jos. W. Stern & Co., 1903), a publisher's catalog.

7. David A. Jasen, *Recorded Ragtime, 1897–1958* (Hamden, Conn.: Archon Books, 1973). Note that Jasen carefully excludes ragtime songs, blues, one-steps, and many cakewalks. Note also that record companies often identified a performing group as an "orchestra" even when it had no strings and sounded indistinguishable from a band.

8. By the early 1910s, however, particularly in England, there were numerous ragtime recordings of orchestras with violins prominent. Some British examples are included on the recording *Those Ragtime Years,* World Records SHB 41. An occasional item may be found in the LPs cited below in Note 9.

9. Recordings may be heard on the LPs: *The Sousa and Pryor Bands,* New World Records NW 282; *Too Much Mustard,* Saydisc SDL 22; *When Grandma was a Teenager,* Vintage Jazz Music VLP-2; David A. Jasen, comp., *Ragtime Entertainment,* Folkways RBF 22; and *Ragtime: A Recorded Documentary,* Piedmont 13158.

10. See the discussion of "The Two-Step" and "The Ragtime Dances" in Thornton Hagert, jacket notes to *Come and Trip It,* New World Records NW 292.

11. Frank Powers, "Ragtime Stock Orchestrations," *Ragtime Society* 5 (November 1966): 44–48.

12. I should remind the reader than an orchestra may have *several* first violins, playing melody in unison or with one or more ad-libbing harmony parts or counter parts, but a "second violin" is limited to a mind-numbing accompaniment part.

13. Such changes as these were once commonly cited as the innovations of New Orleans jazz musicians. In fact, these changes appear to have been developing steadily throughout the country and were widely reflected in orchestrations.

14. See also an excerpt from an incomplete band instrumentation of *Knock-Out Drops* that appears in Frank Tirro, *Jazz: A History* (New York: Norton, 1977), pp. 152–53.

15. See also Samuel B. Charters, "Red Backed Book of Rags," *Jazz Report* 2 (July 1962): 7–8.

16. I have found nothing to corroborate modern rumors that Stark published several differing editions of the "Red Back Book of Rags," even one in the 1920s as one story has it. The back of the original folio carries an advertisement that at first seems to suggest that two other folios were available: "Ten Best Rags by Scott Joplin" and "Ten Best Rags by James Scott," the most recent rag from which was published in 1911. The advertisement appears to be from an old printing plate that Stark resurrected in his haphazard fashion, so I think these are simply lists of piano items that were still available.

17. Recordings may be heard on Bunk Johnson, *Last Testament,* Columbia Special Products JCL 829 (some pressings defectively mastered) and Mutt Carey's New Yorkers, *Jazz: New Orleans Vol. 1,* Savoy MG 12038.

18. Scott Joplin, *The Red Back Book,* ed. Gunther Schuller, is actually a series of eight separately published orchestrations (Melville, NY: Belwin-Mills, 1974).

19. New England Conservatory Ragtime Ensemble, conducted by Gunther Schuller, *Scott Joplin: The Red Back Book,* Angel S-36060, 1973.

20. T.J. Anderson and ensembles, *Classic Rags and Ragtime Songs,* The Smithsonian Collection N 001, 1975; [The Federal Music Society,] Dick Hyman and his dance orchestra, and Gerard Schwarz and his dance orchestra, *Come and Trip It: Instrumental Dance Music 1780s–1920,* New World NW 293, 1978; Albert White and the Gaslight Orchestra, *Your Father's Moustache,* Vols. 1, 2, and "2" [actually 3], Barbary Coast 33002, Barbary Coast 33008, and Fantasy 8040.

Novelty Piano Music

Ronald Riddle

Piano ragtime, by the early 1920s, had been eclipsed by Kitten on the Keys *and other piano novelties. In this first serious study of the style, Ronald Riddle explains that novelty piano music developed from piano rags but added sophisticated harmonic devices. Riddle reveals piano novelty influences in George Gershwin's work and shows that piano novelties reflected the ethos of the 1920s.*

By the early 1920s the sound of piano ragtime already evoked nostalgia. The associations were set that endure to the present day—barrooms, player pianos, cinematic chase scenes, and slapstick. In 1923 composer Zez Confrey published a piece entitled *Nickle in the Slot*, which uses the tricky new style of "piano novelty" to poke gentle fun at both piano ragtime and the player piano—two institutions without which the piano novelty could not have come to pass.

Shortly after *Nickle in the Slot* was published, Confrey (1895-1971) was featured as a pianist in a historic concert heralded by the announcement: "Paul Whiteman and His Palais Royal Orchestra Will Offer An Experiment in Modern Music, Assisted by Zez Confrey and George Gershwin," with the event scheduled for February 12, 1924 at Aeolian Hall in New York.[1]

Confrey's contribution to the concert was similar in character to *Nickle in the Slot*—a virtuoso parody of the sound of ragtime and the player piano. The composer's piano-playing enlivened the first part of the program, which was devoted largely to the past, as a sort of clownish prologue to the symphonic extravaganzas to come. In the second half, Whiteman brought in a battery of violins and cellos and proceeded—with the help of Victor

Herbert, George Gershwin, and Sir Edward Elgar—to make a lady out of jazz, or at least to dress her as such.

The program's climax was, of course, the premiere of Gershwin's *Rhapsody in Blue*, an inspired mélange of blue tonality, harmonies derived from Ravel and the barbershop, and keyboard techniques that emanated in large part from the new vogue of novelty piano music. Zez Confrey, who was now presumably listening from the wings, had sprung the piano novelty on the world three years earlier with the publication of *Kitten on the Keys*. Subsequently he had published a fifty-page instruction manual of novelty-piano technique and licks,[2] many of which were now being immortalized in the piano part to *Rhapsody in Blue*. We know Confrey to have been a quiet and reflective man. His ruminations during the *Rhapsody's* premiere have not been recorded.

Confrey's role in both *Nickle in the Slot* and the Aeolian Hall appearance seems to have been that of providing a sort of whimsical requiem for old-hat ragtime-style piano. In reality his efforts presaged also the soon-to-come decline and near-extinction not only of the player piano but of the piano itself, as an important product of American industry and as a prime component and symbol of cultivated middle-class life. And together with this decline and fall would go the important and presumably final genre of American notated popular solo-piano music, the piano novelty, which Confrey had brought to brief incandescent prominence.

Kitten on the Keys sold over a million sheet-music copies in its first year of publication,[3] eclipsing even the enormous initial sales of Scott Joplin's *Maple Leaf Rag* (1899) a generation earlier. In the words of Henry Osgood: "Probably no other piano solo ever leaped into such widespread popularity in so short a time."[4] And for a brief few years, piano novelties—hundreds upon hundreds of them—were the hottest thing on the market. The style would leave its mark, more or less permanently, on jazz piano style, in popular song, and in concert music both here and abroad.

The very word "novelty" sold sheet music, as had "rag" and "blues" in earlier years. Since publishers are ever-alert for magic words, one finds that the term "novelty" covers a generous field. I note for instance in a 1923 listing of the "Jack Mills Edition of Modern American Piano Novelties" a piece called *Magnetic Rag*, by Scott Joplin, in company with a number of interspersed items that look suspiciously like recycled schottishes and parlor-piano bagatelles from an earlier time.

By and large, however, the term "novelty" refers to a distinct and flashy new approach in which are found—to quote a publisher's advertisement—"new ideas in rhythm and execution, as well as novel and tricky effects for pianists who strive to be versatile." The same ad promises: "Tricky themes, exceedingly appropriate for dancing, sparkling and scintillating novelettes and reveries that are reminiscent of the works of the old masters. . . ."[5]

Among these old masters ought to be included the ragtime composers of the preceding two decades, since the novelty piano tradition is really a sort of refined, white suburban extension of ragtime. From ragtime, novelty

Zez Confrey's *Kitten on the Keys* was a best seller, even eclipsing the initial sales of *Maple Leaf Rag*. (*John Edward Hasse collection*)

piano derives such features as sectional form, stride bass, duple meter (usually), and very pervasive syncopation—especially of the variety that results from the use of phrase groupings of three within a four-beat context, a device often referred to as "secondary rag."[6] Like ragtime, novelty piano is largely pentatonic in its melodic and ornamental makeup; and it very rarely uses blue tonality.

Unlike most of the older ragtime, however, novelty piano style incorporates a number of purely *harmonic* attention-getting devices, such as higher-interval chords (the ninth particularly), the prominent use of minor modality, augmented triads and whole-tone-scale effects, and sudden unprepared shifts of key. It is an eminently "tricky" sort of music, as the publisher's ad suggests, and its ambiguities and surprises are intended to throw the listener off balance and to induce a happy state of vertigo, as suggested by titles like *Giddy Ditty, Dizzy Fingers, Skidding, Stumbling, Meandering,* and *Rambling in Rhythm.*

The dizzying effects were intensified through sheer speed of execution, reflected in names like *Racing Down the Black and Whites, Shootin' the Chutes, Cyclone,* and *Blue Tornado.* The reader will look in vain for any Joplinesque warnings against playing too fast.

In fact, the novelty was a very self-consciously show-off sort of genre, even smugly so, as in the Phil Ohman title, *Try and Play It*. Actually novelties are never as hard to play as they sound, but the effect is always striven for. Not only were there *Dizzy Fingers*, but *Fancy Fingers*, *Feather Fingers*, and *Hot Fingers*, not to speak of *Loose Elbows*, *Nervous Knuckles*, and *The Arm Breaker*. Both *Breakin'* and *Jugglin'* the piano were in vogue, as ivories were *Teased*, *Coaxed*, *Whipped*, *Sailed* over, and *Bounced* upon. Performers who were able to indulge in this *Piano Phun* were afflicted with *Piano Mania* and performed in *Pianoflage*.

The puns and other verbal high jinks of the titles are in accord with the flashy legerdemain of the style. The move from ragtime to the novelty was a move from humor to wit—or some fraction of it—and from the relaxed and good-natured sallies of pre-war innocence to the wordly and jaded ambience of the Prohibition speakeasy. Novelty piano was directed to an increasingly urbanized society, which valued the Jazz Age sophistication of F. Scott Fitzgerald and the sardonic intellectual horseplay of H. L. Mencken.

Of course, mere titles are often the creation of trend-conscious publishers; but they caught the fancy of consumers for whom the piano was an ubiquitous part of home entertainment. And the briefly rocketing sales of player pianos suggests a need for a type of music whose sheer rapidity and breathtaking effects were beyond the means of most domestic practitioners.

But the often programmatic titles of piano novelties perhaps reflect as well certain contrasting aspects of American thought and values in the 1920s. On the one hand we find the sort of wise-guy, slangy expressions that exemplified the postwar boom-times, a mood of audacity and defiance, and a pervasive loss of innocence; on the other hand, a longing for that very innocence. The brassy cockiness of the new age is expressed in titles like *Smart Alec*, *High Hattin'*, *Jay Walk*, *You Tell 'Em, Ivories*, and—inevitably—*The Cat's Pajamas*. But the ingenuous images of the nursery and playroom are projected in *The Doll Dance* and in *Rag Doll, Rag Doll Dimples, Rag Doll Carnival, Marionette, Puppets' Suite*; these are joined by *Jumping Jacks, Jumping Beans, Jack in the Box*; while *Kitten on the Keys* shares billing with *Dog on the Piano, Putting on the Dog, My Pet, Mouse's Hooves*, and even a *Chocolate Bunny*.

This curious contrast of brazen wisecracking on one side and ineffable cuteness on the other seems to mirror the divided nature of a society in transition that at once embraced the voluptuous Clara Bow—the "It" girl of the twenties—while at the same time cherishing the image of the maidenly Mary Pickford, "America's Sweetheart" of an era that was vanishing. In similar fashion, the lively new dances like the fox trot and the Charleston coexisted with the older waltz and other stately dances. And even the music of jazz, which definitively set the pace for the age, was itself regarded in categories of "sweet" on the one hand and "hot" on the other.

The piano novelty, both hot and sweet, was widely considered to be part of the jazz idiom in the 1920s. The critic Henry O. Osgood, one of the first to publish a book-length study of jazz, observed in 1926 that: "For a long time there was no piano idiom in jazz. Finally some one came along and invented one. The some one appears to be Zez Confrey."[7] Osgood refers specifically to *Kitten on the Keys,* which he describes as the first jazz piece that was distinctly pianistic. Osgood thus fatuously waves aside a whole generation of ragtime artists; but his criterion bears reflection. Previous idioms, he felt, sounded as good and usually better when orchestrated, whereas Confrey's art was not readily translatable to any other instrument or combination.

Whatever the validity of Osgood's period-piece judgments, it is clear that the novelty-piano style capitalized on the idiomatic possibilities of the keyboard. The whole genre rests, however, on the earlier innovations of classic ragtime, which in turn derive from a variety of syncopated and pentatonic songs and dance-types of the late nineteenth century. The conjunction of African polyrhythms with European harmonies and sectional form underlies what might be viewed as the earliest or prototypical examples of what would become known as the piano novelty. In such pieces as Henry Cohen's *Canadian Capers* of 1915 and Felix Arndt's *Nola* of the following year, a smoothness of phrasing and a classical-piano decorum were imposed on the ragtime structural framework, while syncopated phrasings prevailed. Another early piece with strong novelty overtones was the *Rialto Ripples* of George Gershwin and Will Donaldson, published in 1917, in which minor modality—very rare in classic ragtime—is featured with syncopated figures in a basic rag format.

At the time that Gershwin was writing *Rialto Ripples,* he was already a featured artist on piano rolls, having thus joined a profession that would be common for novelty-piano composers. Out in Chicago, a young conservatory-trained pianist named Edward E. Confrey was signed up to cut piano rolls for the QRS company in 1918. Within a year he had made rolls of a number of his own compositions. *Kitten on the Keys* was one of these, but it was not until two years later that the work was put into sheet-music form. It was a historic occasion—the birth, in effect, of a minor industry. Confrey followed with other successes in short order. His song *Stumbling,* also issued as a piano solo, was the first hit vocal work that made use of rhythmic patterns of three over a four-beat pulse, antedating Gershwin's *Fascinatin' Rhythm* by two years. Confrey's *Dizzy Fingers* of 1923 became almost as well known as *Kitten on the Keys,* and like the earlier work, has never been out of print to this day. In all, he published some thirty-five piano solos and songs during that decade, in addition to his course in *Novelty Piano Playing,* which came out in 1923 and remained in print for over forty years.

Confrey's early works were the inspiration for a multitude of other novelty composers in the twenties. Confrey's counterpart at a rival piano-roll firm in Chicago was Roy Bargy (1894–1974), who scored successes with such pieces as *Rufenreddy, Jim-Jams,* and *Sunshine Capers.* Other prominent early names in the field were the New York–based composers Rube Bloom (1902–1976), Phil Ohman (1896–1954), and Arthur Schutt (1902–1965). In England the genre was promoted by Billy Mayerl (1902–1959), who published a dozen of what he called "Syncopated Impressions."

Among the more successful novelty pieces was Jesse Greer's (1896–1970) *Flapperette* of 1926. In the same year Nacio Herb Brown (1896–1964) published *The Doll Dance*, which, like *Flapperette*, has never been out of print. Another notable work incorporating novelty-piano style was Bix Beiderbecke's harmonically adventurous *In a Mist*, published in 1928.

The piano novelty shared the stage with a number of other variously successful keyboard genres to which it was related. Classic ragtime was, naturally, a close cousin; and contemporaneous pieces by such Harlem stride pianists as James P. Johnson and Fats Waller were being published in the twenties as well. All of these types share more features than not, but there are a handful of keyboard idioms that serve to identify and enliven novelty style as such. Some of these appear right off the bat in *Kitten on the Keys*. The first thing that strikes the ear is the parallel fourths in the right-hand part (Example 80). This device becomes almost a trademark of novelty-piano style, to the point where its absence would be conspicuous (see also, for instance, the introductory bars to *The Doll Dance* or the first strain of Harold Potter's *Rippling Waters*, Example 81). I can find no precedent for this device in earlier ragtime piano.

Example 80. Zez Confrey, *Kitten on the Keys*, Introduction, measures 1–2.

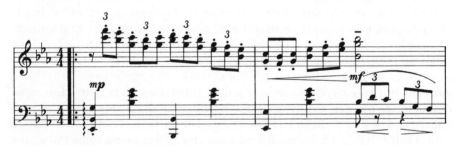

Example 81. Harold Potter, *Rippling Waters*, **A** strain, measures 1–2.

Another frequent device is the tritone closing up on a minor third—the little flourish that flavors the whole first strain of *Kitten on the Keys*. This is particularly pianistic, like the parallel fourths: done in rapid alternation, up or down the keyboard, the figure sounds hard to play but fits the fingers beautifully. This is a very old device indeed (compare the passages immediately following the slow introduction of Beethoven's "Pathétique" Sonata, first movement) and is found in ragtime as early in 1901, in Joplin's *The Easy Winners* (Example 82).

Example 82. Scott Joplin, *The Easy Winners,* **A** strain, measures 1–2.

Rapid alternation of chords or single notes between two hands is also frequently used, as in the opening passage of Confrey's *My Pet* (Example 83) and in similar fashion, the second strain of the same composer's *Coaxing the Piano* (Example 84).

Example 83. Zez Confrey, *My Pet*, Introduction, measures 1–2.

Example 84. Zez Confrey, *Coaxing the Piano,* **B** strain, measures 1–2.

Flashy chromatic passages are often used for introductory, interspersed, and climactic episodes. The introduction to *Coaxing the Piano,* for instance, features an ascending figure (Example 85); and the same piece later contains a descending example, this time on augmented triads (Example 86).

No feature is more pervasive, however, than "secondary rag"—the use of groups of three within a metrical framework of four. A simple illustration may be drawn from the second-strain melody of Vee Lawnhurst's *Keyboard Konversation* (Example 87). More-complex examples abound in virtually every piece by Zez Confrey. The figure is the veritable *raison d'être* of *Stumbling,* for instance, and is used to flamboyant effect in the second strain of *Dizzy Fingers* (Example 88).

None of these devices originates with the piano novelty, but it is in this genre that they are used to full effect in conjunction with glittering arpeggio-work, frequent excursions into minor modality, and harmonic

Example 85. Zez Confrey, *Coaxing the Piano*, Introduction, measures 1–2.

Example 86. Zez Confrey, *Coaxing the Piano*, Interlude: Introduction to **C** strain, measures 1–2.

Example 87. Vee Lawnhurst, *Keyboard Konversation*, **B** strain, measures 1–4.

Example 88. Zez Confrey, *Dizzy Fingers*, **B** strain, measures 1–4.

departures from the more strictly diatonic harmony and pentatonic melody of classic ragtime.

The direct and indirect influence of novelty-piano techniques may be seen in a variety of works by European and American composers of concert music. The piano works of George Gershwin, who acknowledged his debt to Zez Confrey, are teeming with novelty devices, many of them clearly laid out in Confrey's instruction course of 1923. Gershwin's works may well have served as the principal conduit through which these devices were brought to other parts of the world. To cite only two examples, we definitely hear piano novelty figures in Ravel's G-major concerto of 1931 and in Bohuslav Martinů's *Eight Preludes* of 1929.

The destiny of the piano novelty was of course tied inextricably to that of the piano itself. When the style first arose, sales of pianos were already on the decline, having reached their peak in 1909.[8] The widening availability of home phonographs presumably helped cause the slow decline of sales through the ensuing decade, but the slope became even steeper after 1921, when radio broadcasting and the ownership of sets became widespread.

The player piano enjoyed a vogue which helped boost piano sales in general from 1919 through 1925, a period during part of which player pianos actually outsold conventional instruments. But the bottom dropped out of the piano market in the second half of the decade. Well in advance of the Great Depression of the thirties—and in the midst of an economic boom—pianos simply stopped selling. By 1929 piano-makers were able to retail scarcely more than a third of the instruments sold in 1925; and of those sold, only 28 percent were player pianos. With the onset of the Depression, the piano business was reduced to near-oblivion, and the player piano itself became commercially extinct after 1932. Accordingly, the market for the piano novelty simply disappeared.

And the genre itself became a period piece almost overnight, as anachronistic as the coonskin coat or the Stutz Bearcat. Though a handful of novelty-piano compositions would remain in print to our own day, and its influence lives on in more durable forms, the novelty simply disappeared into the void, like so many artifacts of the Jazz Age. During its mayfly existence it dominated the market for popular piano music and has clearly left its influence, to one degree or another, on a variety of musical styles. It deserves far more than a footnote to the ongoing history of American music. But in the end, the piano novelty suffered a sad but predictable fate: it lost its novelty. While it lasted it was great fun, no matter how you spell it, but it was too hot *not* to cool down.

Notes

1. The Aeolian Hall concert has been re-created from vintage recordings in *An Experiment in Modern Music: Paul Whiteman at Aeolian Hall,* issued by the Smithsonian Collection of recordings, 2028.

2. Zez Confrey, *Zez Confrey's Modern Course in Novelty Piano Playing* (New York: Mills Music, 1923).

3. David A. Jasen and Trebor Jay Tichenor, *Rags and Ragtime: A Musical History* (New York: Seabury Press, 1978), p. 215.

4. Henry O. Osgood, *So This is Jazz* (Boston: Little, Brown, and Co., 1926), p. 79.

5. "Modern American Piano Novelties," advertisement for the Jack Mills Edition, 1923.

6. "Secondary rag" is discussed in footnote 29 of Lowell H. Schreyer's chapter "The Banjo in Ragtime," in this book.

7. Osgood, p. 78.

8. The sales of the piano and the player piano are presented in the graph on page 15, in John Edward Hasse's introductory chapter, "Ragtime: From the Top."

Ragtime in Early Country Music

Norm Cohen and David Cohen

Ragtime music affected many aspects of American culture, including white country music. Norm and David Cohen present a first-time exploration of ragtime's influence on early country recordings, finding that country musicians adopted a number of ragtime songs and instrumental hits, borrowed and modified the word "rag," and created their own pieces, called "rags."

In the early 1920s, there emerged a new category of phonographically recorded music in the United States. Variously labeled "hillbilly" or "old-time" music, or "old familiar tunes," it represented not new music, but rather the first attempt to record such music for local consumption in the rural South, featuring singers and instrumentalists right out of that milieu.[1]

The musicians involved in this development, accustomed to playing in front of courthouses and on street corners as much as in barns and schoolhouses, heard black street musicians, and vaudeville and medicine show performers, as well as classical musicians in opera houses, on records, and at chautauquas. Old-time fiddler Clayton McMichen numbered violin virtuoso Fritz Kreisler among his influences; country banjoist Charlie Poole idolized early banjo star Fred Van Eps; and singer Jimmie Rodgers learned his first songs from cylinder recordings by artists such as dialect and "coon song" performer Arthur Collins.

Given this state of affairs, it is not surprising that ragtime, the major musical novelty of the turn of the century, should have left its imprint on American country music. And if the imprint is only slightly visible today, it is because for the past three decades country music has been dominated by vocalists. Aside from occasional instrumental renditions of songs and excepting nonmainstream branches such as bluegrass and Western swing, country music has virtually no instrumental tradition. Thus, scholarship tends to focus on the idiom's textual rather than musical characteristics. Further, if the imprint has not been commented upon often, it is because scholarship has concentrated on the Anglo-American folk ancestry of country music.[2]

An investigation into the influence of ragtime on country music naturally begins in about 1922, with the first recordings of hillbilly music by traditional Southern rural musicians. Although providing fifty-seven years of data as of this writing, this span is still shorter than those of other recorded genres. Blues were first recorded two years earlier; jazz, five years earlier; ragtime, about twenty-five years earlier; and the first commercial recordings were made about thirty-two years earlier.

In principle, there might be other, pre-1920s sources to which to turn: newspaper and magazine accounts of public dances, fiddle contests, and other musical events; private diaries and letters; later interviews with musicians and audiences who participated in country music events prior to 1920. For data from the 1920s and after, the phonograph recordings might be supplemented by radio broadcasts, either preserved on transcription discs or home cylinder (and later acetate disc) dubs, or described in print; and by field recordings by folklorists or other music researchers. Unfortunately, our first examinations of these potential sources have not found them helpful—the subject of ragtime does not turn up. Hence, with very few exceptions, our conclusions are based entirely on commercial phonographic recordings, most of which were produced between 1922 and 1942.

Although this is not the place to offer a definition of "ragtime music," some general remarks are necessary to establish a working definition for the reader's benefit. To the listener of the 1970s, ragtime was generally taken to mean the instrumental rags of Scott Joplin and his peers of the period from just before the turn of the century through the late 1910s. However, it is now generally accepted that to the public at that time, the term "ragtime" had a much broader reference—to almost any tune syncopated in a characteristic way. In particular, many "coon songs" of the late 1890s and early 1900s were considered ragtime. Furthermore, in many people's minds, any piece could be "ragged," or rendered in ragtime rhythms—from "coon songs" to the overture from *Tannhäuser* to the *Merry Widow* waltz. In this light, hillbilly music of the 1920s was full of raggy elements. Such syncopated popular songs as *Razors in the Air* (1880), *Hand Me Down My Walking Cane* (1880), *Bill Bailey, Won't You Please Come Home?* (1902), *The Preacher and the Bear* (1904), *Moving Day* (1906), *Casey Jones* (1909), *Alexander's Ragtime Band* (1911), *Alabama Jubilee* (1915), and *Are You From Dixie?*

(1915) all became hillbilly standards in the 1920s. From this perspective early hillbilly music was indeed saturated with ragtime.

However, this essay makes use of a narrower focus: instrumental tunes that were either themselves titled, or considered to be, rags. During the twenty-year period from 1922 to 1942, there were some ten to twenty thousand recordings made that are generally classed as "hillbilly" or "country" music. Of these, about two hundred can be identified as either (1) well-known published piano rags; (2) tunes identified in Jasen's discography, *Recorded Ragtime 1897–1958*[3]; (3) pieces with the words "rag," "stomp," "strut," "shuffle," or "wobble" in the title; or (4) works that have other titles yet which are known to have ragtime characteristics. More than one hundred of these records were available for auditioning for this study. The recordings were examined with an ear to determining just how raglike each one is, based upon the presence or absence of several characteristics of piano rags: certain syncopated rhythms[4] and certain characteristic harmonic progressions.[5]

Interestingly, those pieces in our sample which we determined to be the most raglike were mostly original country tunes not taken from sheet music: *Beaumont Rag* (Smith's Garage Fiddle Band, originally issued on Vocalion 5268, and others), *Cotton Patch Rag* (John Dilleshaw and String Marvel, OKeh 45328), *Japanese Breakdown* (Scottdale Stringband, OKeh 45509), *Ozark Rag* (East Texas Serenaders, Brunswick 538), *Oompah Rag* (Farr Brothers, JEMF LP 107).

Speaking more generally, the salient observations emerging from our study can be summarized as follows:

1. A good half of the country tunes titled "rags" had none of the characteristics of the piano rags, though many had syncopations and "bluesy" elements characteristic of ragtime or "coon" songs. The reason for the popularity of such titles is itself worthy of examination: perhaps it can be taken as an indicator of the popularity of real rags at that period. In many cases, these were original compositions, but in others they were simply retitled older tunes. For example, *Choctaw County Rag* by the Ray Brothers (Victor V-40313) is actually *At a Georgia Campmeeting; Wednesday Rag* by Bob Dunn's Vagabonds (Decca 5772) is *Wednesday Night Waltz* jazzed up; *Searcy County Rag* by Ashley's Melody Men (Victor V-40158) is *Chicken Reel;* and Hank Garland's *Sugarfoot Rag* is in fact *Pretty Little Widow*. Possibly either the recording artists or the record company executives (the "A & R" men) *titled* them "rags" in the hope of encouraging sales.

Another explanation, offered by several veteran western swing musicians to Fred Hoeptner when he interviewed them some two decades ago, is that there was a dance called the "rag" that was popular in the 1920s and 1930s, for which that type of music was appropriate.[6] In any case, in the past few decades, by "rag" most country musicians mean a fast instrumental piece that affords an opportunity for demonstrating musical virtuosity. As Merle Travis, an articulate and knowledgeable country performer and composer, declared, ". . . a rag is a snappy little ditty that an instrumentalist plays to show off his ability to play."[7]

2. Complex characteristic piano rag forms such as **AA BB A CC DD** were nonexistent in the country ragtime pieces, both the original compositions and also the few renditions of piano rags. In general, the structure of pieces titled "rags" tended to be no more complex than the older Anglo-American fiddle tunes (*i.e.,* **AB, ABC,** or rarely, **ABCD**). It should be noted, however, that the musicians—from various idioms—who have recorded piano rags over the years have frequently omitted repeats and sometimes dropped, or changed the order of, strains.

3. In contrast to the large number of ragtime and "coon" songs, very few piano rags found their way into the recorded country music repertoire: *Dill Pickles* (by far the favorite with nearly a dozen recordings), *Black and White Rag, St. Louis Tickle,* and *12th Street Rag* practically exhaust the list. Some of the most oft-recorded piano rags—*Maple Leaf Rag, Canadian Capers, King Porter Stomp, Kitten on the Keys, Temptation Rag*—do not turn up at all in recorded country tradition. In some cases the absence is not surprising, in view of the paucity of country recordings with piano lead before the mid-1940s. Piano novelties (sometimes called "novelty rags") such as *Kitten on the Keys* do not readily lend themselves to performance with country music instrumentation. Several pre-rag cakewalks—which, in their original form, had the classic rag format and most of the other ragtime characteristics—entered the hillbilly tradition also: *At a Georgia Campmeeting* and *Whistling Rufus* were the most popular; *Eli Green's Cake Walk* was also recorded. The **B** section melody of the cakewalk hit *Creole Belles* (1900) turns up in a variety of guises: as *Rubber Dolly Rag, Back Up and Push, Goodbye Booze, Choc'late Ice Cream Cone,* and even—if we stretch it a bit—*Midnight Special.* Except for some versions of *Rubber Dolly* all of these disguised *Creole Belles* are quite unraggy.

4. Perhaps the most distinctive characteristic of the country ragtime pieces was the use of the circle of fifths chord progression. The origins of this pattern have eluded us; it is not at all common in either classic rags or in Tin Pan Alley "coon songs." On the other hand, it did occur in a large body of songs in the Afro-American preblues folk tradition (*e.g., Ella Speed, Cocaine Blues, Pick Poor Robin Clean, Salty Dog Blues*) that seems to have emerged toward the end of the nineteenth century. The progression was widely borrowed by jazz and white country musicians.

The last three observations together strongly imply that the piano rags of the 1897–1920 period had little impact on country music. There was, however, a pronounced body of country ragtime pieces that utilized the syncopations and other devices characteristic of both piano rags and the Afro-American folk tradition that preceded the Ragtime Era (and, in fact, outlived it). The conclusion that country music ragtime derived from this pre-1890s folk tradition seems both ineluctable and unsurprising. In this connection, it is interesting to note that *Maybelle Rag,* the first country recording of a piece titled "rag," is strongly syncopated, has the circle of

Table 17
A Chronology of Early Country Ragtime and Related Recordings, 1922–26

YEAR	TITLE	RECORDING ARTIST	ARTIST'S HOME	VOCAL	RECORD CO. AND NUMBER	COMMENTS
1922	Ragtime Annie	A. C. Robertson	Texas	No	Victor 19149	Syncopated instrumental tune of unknown origin, probably composed by Texas folk musicians, ca. 1900–1910.
1924	Snow Deer	Ernest Thompson	N. Carolina	Yes	Columbia 190-D	Popular ragtime compositions rendered as vocals with rather (metrically) square guitar/harmonica accompaniments.
1924	At a Georgia Campmeeting	Ernest Thompson and Connie Sides	N. Carolina	Yes	Columbia 206-D	
1924	Alexanders' Ragtime Band	Ernest Thompson	N. Carolina	Yes	Columbia 15002-D	
1924	Chicken Reel	E. R. "Poss" Acree	(unknown)	No	OKeh 40197	A popular two-step from 1910 with some ragtime syncopations; possibly a country performer.
1924	Casey Jones	Riley Puckett	Georgia	Yes	Columbia 113-D	A pop hit from 1909 with some ragtime syncopations.
1925	Maybelle Rag	Young Brothers and Homer Davenport	Tennessee	No	Gennett 3077	First hillbilly recording of a tune titled "rag." It has circle of fifths progression and some ragtime syncopations.

298

Year	Title	Artist	Location		Record	Notes
1925	Don't Let Your Deal Go Down	Charlie Poole and the North Caroline Ramblers	N. Carolina	Yes	Columbia 15038-D	Immensely popular country tune built on circle of fifths chord progression; the first influential such hillbilly piece recorded.
1925	Medley—Dill Pickles, Turkey in the Straw, Swanee; b/w St. Louis Tickle	Jim Couch	(unknown)	No	OKeh 40456	Medley includes one rag hit, Dill Pickles; both sides of disc performed as harmonica instrumentals.
1925	Whistling Rufus	J. D. McFarlane	N. Carolina?	No	OKeh 40027	A cakewalk hit from 1899.
1925	Chicken Reel	Dr. Claude Watson	Texas?	No	OKeh 45020	A 1913 pop hit, considered by some a ragtime song, but not very syncopated.
1925	Snow Deer	Jimmie Wilson's Catfish Band	Oklahoma	(un-known)	OKeh 45019	
1925	Atlanta Special	Dixie String Band	Georgia	No	Paramount 33164	A variant of the popular, rather unraglike Chinese Breakdown—also known as Chinese Rag, Georgia Bustdown, Shanghai Rag, and That Old Tiger Rag.
1926	Goodbye Booze	Gid Tanner and Fate Norris	Georgia	No	Columbia 15105-D	Based on Creole Belles.
1926	Hickman Rag	Charlie Bowman	Tennessee	No	Vocalion 15377	Second original (i.e. not sheet-music derived) hillbilly recording of a tune titled "rag." Has circle of fifths progression, but is not very raglike.

fifths progression, and was learned by Jess Young, fiddler on the recording, from a black fiddler in about 1910.[8] While one should not make too much of a single instance, it is nevertheless a striking one, and certainly is consistent with our previous comments.

The first hillbilly recordings (*i.e.*, the first commercial records by white rural Southern folk musicians) were made in the summer of 1922 by two fiddlers: A. C. "Eck" Robertson and Henry Gilliland. Between that date and the end of 1924, some two hundred eighty hillbilly recordings were made and issued. Of these, only six have ragtime elements in the narrower sense that we use the term. There were a few more in 1925 and 1926, including some genuine rags and some very raglike pieces. All of these are listed in Table 17.

In general, as Table 17 illustrates, there was a paucity of ragtime music in the recorded hillbilly repertoire prior to 1927. From this observation, we conclude that either (1) ragtime music was not firmly entrenched in the idiom before the advent of the hillbilly record industry; or (2) ragtime was not considered appropriate for hillbilly musicians to record in those years. The latter explanation seems unlikely, inasmuch as everything we know about the operation of the early "A & R" men indicates that during those formative years they knew little about the music they were recording and exercised little control over it.

Ragtime country music seems to have flourished in Texas, home of the East Texas Serenaders (above). This string band began recording rags in the late 1920s. (*Courtesy County Records*)

Starting in about 1927 or 1928, ragtime began to emerge with more conviction in recorded hillbilly music. There were three recordings of *Dill Pickles* in 1927 and 1928 and four more in 1929 and 1930 (see Table 18). *Black and White Rag* and *St. Louis Tickle* were both recorded in 1930; *At a Georgia Campmeeting*, once each in 1927, 1928, and 1929; and *Whistling Rufus* twice in 1928 and once in 1929. More important, what were evidently original raglike compositions began to appear as well—at least they are not identifiable as having appeared in sheet music versions.

Bands with a significant number of ragtime tunes in their recorded repertoires appeared all over the map—the Scottdale Stringband in Mississippi; Seven Foot Dilly in Atlanta; Jack Cawley's Oklahoma Ridge Runners; the Grinnell Giggers from Missouri. But best represented was Texas, where perhaps more than anywhere else, ragtime country music flourished. By 1930, the East Texas Serenaders, Smith's Garage Fiddle Band, and the Harper Brothers had all recorded country rags. In 1928, there appeared for the first time on disc what has since become the best-known country rag, *Beaumont Rag* (see Table 19). Its origin is unknown; it may have been the creation of Smith's Garage Fiddle Band, which first recorded it in Dallas. Another country tune with strong ragtime elements that was frequently recorded was *Stone's Rag*, written by Oscar Stone and first recorded in 1928 (later recorded under the alternate titles of *Stone Mountain Rag*, *Whiskers*, and *Lone Star Rag* as well).

Table 18
Pre–World War II Country Recordings of *Dill Pickles*

DATE OF RECORDING	RECORDING ARTIST	RECORD COMPANY AND NUMBER	COMMENTS
1925 Aug.*	Jim Couch	OKeh 40456	Included in medley. Couch is probably a country musician.
1928 Jan.	Billy Milton and his One Man Band	Gennett 6318	
1928 Feb.	McLaughlin's Old Time Melody Makers	Victor 21286	
1928 Mar.	Dr. Humphrey Bate and his Possum Hunters	Brunswick 243	
1929 Feb.	Kessinger Brothers	Brunswick 315	LP reissue: RBF Records RF 18.
1929 Jun.	Texas Night Hawks	OKeh 45363	Titled *Crazy Rag*.
1929 Nov.	East Texas Serenaders	Brunswick 379	Part of *Three-In-One Two-Step* medley. LP reissue: County 410.
1929 Mar.*	Smith's Garage Fiddle Band	Vocalion 5306	
1932 Apr.	Corn Cob Crushers	Champion 16373, Superior 2794	
1936	Sanford Rich	Lib. of Congress AFS 3306 A2	Unissued field recording made by Charles Seeger in Arthurdale, West Virginia.
1939 July	Swift Jewel Cowboys	Vocalion 05309	
1939 Aug.	Four Pickled Peppers	Bluebird B08518	

*Approximate date.

Table 19
Pre–World War II Country Recordings of *Beaumont Rag*

DATE OF RECORDING	RECORDING ARTIST	RECORD COMPANY AND NUMBER	COMMENTS
1928 Oct.	Smith's Garage Fiddle Band	Vocalion 5268	LP reissue: County 517
1929 June	Texas Nighthawks	OKeh 45363	Titled *Possum Rag*
1929 Nov.	Oscar & Doc Harper	OKeh 46397	
1931 Mar.	Jack Cawley's Oklahoma Ridge Runners	Victor 23521	Titled *White River Stomp*
1934	East Texas Serenaders	Decca 5408	LP reissue: County 410
1935 Aug.*	Leon's Lone Star Cowboys	Decca 5433	Titled *White River Stomp*
1937 Mar.	Bill Boyd's Cowboy Ramblers	Bluebird B-6959	Titled *Beaumont.* LP reissue: Bluebird AXM2-5503
1937 June	Light Crust Doughboys	Vocalion 03645	
1937 Dec.	Cliff Bruner's Texas Wanderers	Decca 5474	LP reissue: MCA (Japan) VIM 4016
1938 Nov.	Bob Wills and his Texas Playboys	Vocalion & OKeh 04999, Conquerer 9718, Columbia 37642 & 20241	LP reissue: Old Timey 117
1940	Woodrow (Woody) Wilson Guthrie	Library of Congress AFS 3408 B3	Recording was first publicly issued on Elektra LP 271/272

*Approximate date.

Since pianos were rare in recorded early country music (Texas and southwestern Virginia may have been exceptional areas), on all of the early country rags the lead melodies were taken, as in older tunes, primarily by fiddles. In the late 1920s and the 1930s, mandolins, banjo-mandolins, ukuleles, and similar instruments rose to great popularity, and these seemed better suited to rags than to older Anglo-American string band tunes. Nevertheless, there was no sudden increase in frequency of recorded rags, partly because of a growing number of recordings featuring vocalists with only incidental background accompaniment, and the concomitant decline in recordings featuring old-time string bands.

The main source for commercially recorded rags during the 1930s gradually became the newly emerging style of music known as western swing, featuring large dance bands that blended elements of Southwestern country music with big band swing. Such groups recorded many tunes titled "rags," but, as noted above, for the most part the term was used very broadly. Such recordings as Bill Boyd's *Barn Dance Rag* (Bluebird B-6177), Bob Wills' *Steel Guitar Rag* (OKeh 03394), Adolph Hofner's *Alamo Rag* (Columbia 20255), and Cliff Bruner's *Tequila Rag* (Decca 5953) are syncopated and/or bluesy, but are unlike the more restricted form of the classic piano rags. A few important rags did find favor in the Southwest: *Beaumont Rag*, *Dill Pickles*, and *Black and White Rag* were among the most popular.

In the 1950s, in association with bluegrass music, there began to emerge a style of virtuoso flat picking on guitar. Lead guitarists transcribed fiddle tunes for the guitar, and many of the fast, flashy instrumental pieces that were so adapted were titled "rags." But again, the term was used in a very broad sense. Hence, one finds many post–World War II recordings of "rags"—Hank Garland's *Sugarfoot Rag,* Merle Travis' *Cannon Ball Rag,* Earl Scruggs' *Randy Lynn Rag,* Woody Guthrie's *Woody's Rag,* Leslie Keith's *Black Mountain Rag,* and the Lonesome Pine Fiddlers' *Five String Rag*—but none of these is very raglike. Our analysis for the postwar period is cursory, but we suspect that a more thorough search would not reveal piano rag elements to be any more prominent than they were in the 1920s and 1930s.

In conclusion, ragtime influenced white country music in divers ways. Such rhythmic or syncopated "ragtime songs" as *Bill Bailey, Alexander's Ragtime Band,* and *Alabama Jubilee* all became country standards. Instrumental ragtime—the focus of our essay—suffused country music in several respects, though not very deeply. The musical term "rag" was adopted by country music, but its meaning changed. The word came frequently to mean a fast and flashy instrumental showpiece in duple meter, sometimes multisectional, sometimes not; in country usage, syncopation was no longer the *sine qua non* of "rag." The intricate, pianistic works of Scott Joplin and his fellow "classic ragtime" composers are, not surprisingly, virtually absent from country music repertory. A number of the most famous cakewalk and rag hits—*At a Georgia Campmeeting, Black and White Rag, Creole Belles, Dill Pickles, 12th Street Rag,* and *Whistling Rufus*—became perennial country favorites. And country music produced some of its own genuine instrumental rags— syncopated and multisectional—including *Cotton Patch Rag, Ozark Rag,* and the enormously popular *Beaumont Rag.* And so ragtime, which affected so many aspects of American culture, also penetrated into early white country music.

Recommended Listening

The East Texas Serenaders: 1927–1936 (County Records 410, 1977). Fourteen selections by one of the first recorded Texas stringbands that show, by our standards, strong ragtime influences. The album includes several excellent examples: *Ozark Rag, Arizona Stomp, Beaumont Rag,* and *Acorn Stomp,* all of which ranked as very raglike in our analysis. Jacket notes by Nancy Fly Bredenberg give biographical background and discuss the music in its original social context.

Maple Leaf Rag: Ragtime in Rural America (New World Records NW 235, 1976). Sixteen selections recorded from the 1920s to the 1960s, side 1 by black artists, side 2 by white. Compiled and annotated by Lawrence Cohn, whose conception of ragtime is again broader than our own. Includes several unraglike postwar selections: *Steel Guitar Rag, Cannon Ball Rag, Bugle Call Rag,* and *Randy Lynn Rag.*

Old-Time Mountain Guitar (County Records 523, 1972). Thirteen selections of guitar solos and duets recorded in the late 1920s. Four pieces were titled "Rag." Excellent jacket notes by Robert Fleder on early country guitar styles and origins.

Old-Time Southern Dance Music: The String Bands (Old Timey X 100, ca. 1962). Reissue of sixteen selections from the 1920s and 1930s, mostly by white artists. Of particular interest is the Scottdale String Band's *Japanese Breakdown,* an excellent example of country ragtime. Other "rag" selections—*Allen Brothers Rag, Chinese Rag,* and *Hawkins' Rag*—are not very raggy by our criteria. Brief brochure notes by Chris A. Strachwitz.

Ragtime 2: The Country—Mandolins, Fiddles, & Guitars (RBF 18, 1971). Fourteen selections originally recorded in the 1920s, about half by white artists, the remainder by black. Compiled and annotated by Samuel Charters, whose conception of ragtime here is far broader than that of this chapter. Nevertheless, the disc does include one good example of what changes take place when a classic rag is performed by a traditional country fiddler—the Kessinger Brothers' *Dill Pickles Rag*.

Texas Farewell: Texas Fiddlers Recorded 1922–1930 (County Records 517, 1969). This collection of fourteen string band recordings is of interest for including the first recording of *Beaumont Rag*, by Smith's Garage Fiddle Band. Also contains two selections by the East Texas Serenaders (both also available on County 410, see above).

Notes

1. This bifurcation is discussed in more detail in Anne and Norm Cohen, "Folk and Hillbilly Music: Further Thoughts on Their Relation," *JEMF Quarterly* 13 (Summer 1977): 50–57.
2. To date the only scholarly book-length history of country music is Bill C. Malone, *Country Music, U.S.A.* (Austin: University of Texas Press, 1968). Another important source is Archie Green, *Only a Miner* (Urbana: University of Illinois Press, 1972), chapter 2.
3. David A. Jasen, *Recorded Ragtime, 1897–1958* (Hamden, Conn.: Archon Books, 1973).
4. These include what we call the "cakewalk rhythm," ♫♩; a "delayed cakewalk rhythm," · ♫♫ ; a "Charleston rhythm," which appears in several forms: ♫♩ or ♫♫♩ or ♫♩; a grouping of sixteeth notes into threes: ♫♫♫♩; and the device of the strongly accented second eighth note of the measure:| ♪♪ .
5. These are the circle of fifths chord progression (I–VI⁷–II⁷–V⁷–I) and a V–I progression.
6. Telephone interview with Fred Hoeptner, August 1979, based on interviews he conducted in the late 1950s.
7. Letter from Merle Travis to Norm Cohen, 11 September 1979.
8. Charles Wolfe, jacket notes to *Tennessee Strings*, Rounder Records 1033, 1979. *Maybelle Rag* by the Young Brothers and Homer Davenport is reissued on this LP.

Checklist of Compositions

The following is a list of compositions mentioned in the text of this book. This list excludes "classical" works but includes all other compositions for which facts of publication could be determined. Unless otherwise indicated in the title or annotation, all works are published for piano solo. Generally, only first publication is listed; no effort has been made to trace subsequent reissues. For works that were not published, copyright data is generally given. In the few cases of a work neither published nor copyrighted, recording information is provided. Pieces which are traditional are identified as such.

African Pas'. Maurice Kirwin. Saint Louis: John Stark & Son, 1902.

African Pas'. Maurice Kirwin. Arranged for orchestra. Saint Louis: John Stark & Son, 190-.

After the Cake Walk. Nathaniel Dett. Arranged by Lee Orean Smith. New York and Williamsport, Penn.: Vandersloot Music Co., 1900.

Alabama Echoes (for banjo). Paul Eno. Philadelphia: Paul Eno, 1894.

Alabama Jubilee (song). Words: Jack Yellin; music: George L. Cobb. New York and Detroit: Jerome H. Remick & Co., 1915.

Alabama Rag. Joseph F. Lamb. Published in *Ragtime Treasures: Piano Solos by Joseph F. Lamb* (New York: Mills Music, 1964), pp. 6–9.

Alabama Rag Time: Cake Walk (for banjo). J. E. Henning. Chicago: Henning Music Co., 1897. Published in *The Chicago Trio* 1, no. 2 (December 1897–January 1898), p. 17.

Alamo Rag (song). Words: Ben Deely; music: Percy Wenrich. New York and Detroit: Jerome H. Remick & Co., 1910.

Alaskan Rag. Joseph F. Lamb. Published in Rudi Blesh and Harriet Janis, *They All Played Ragtime*, 3rd ed., rev. New York: Oak Publications, 1966.

Alexander (song). Words: Andrew B. Sterling; music: Harry Von Tilzer. New York: Harry Von Tilzer Music Publishing Co., 1904.

Alexander's Ragtime Band (song). Irving Berlin. New York: Ted Snyder Co., 1911.

Alexander's Ragtime Band: March and Two-Step. Irving Berlin. Arranged for orchestra by William Schulz. New York: Ted Snyder Co., 1911.

All Coons Look Alike to Me (song). Ernest Hogan. "Choice Chorus, with Negro 'rag' accompaniment arranged by Max Hoffman." New York: M. Witmark & Sons, 1896.

All in Down and Out (Sorry I Ain't Got It, You Could Get It, If I Had It) (song). Words: R. C. McPherson; music: Smith, Johnson, and Elmer Bowman. New York: The Gotham-Attucks Music Co., 1906.

All Night Long (song). Shelton Brooks. Chicago: Will Rossiter, 1912.

American Beauty Rag: A Rag of Class. Joseph F. Lamb. Saint Louis: Stark Music Co., 1913.

Arctic Sunset. Joseph F. Lamb. Published in *Ragtime Treasures: Piano Solos by Joseph F. Lamb* (New York: Mills Music, 1964), pp. 46–49.

Arm Breaker, The. Fred Rose. New York: Jack Mills, Inc., 1923.

At a Georgia Campmeeting: A Characteristic March. Kerry Mills. New York: F. A. Mills, 1897.

At a Rag Time Ball (for banjo). J. H. Jennings. Providence, R. I.: J. H. Jennings, 1900.

Atlanta Special. Traditional.

Auld Lang Syne (song). Words: Robert Burns; music: traditional. London: Preston & Smith, [1799].

Auntie Skinner's Chicken Dinners (song). Words: Arthur Fields and Earl Carroll; music: Theodore Morse. New York: M. Witmark & Sons, 1915.

Babes in Toyland: Selection: Victor Herbert. Arranged for orchestra by Otto Langey. New York: M. Witmark & Sons, 1903.

Baby, Get That Towel Wet (song). Traditional.

Baby Seal Blues: Sing 'Em—They Sound Good to Me. Baby F. Seals, arranged by Artie Matthews. Saint Louis: Seals and Fisher, 1912.

Bach Goes to Town: Prelude & Fugue in Swing. Alec Templeton. New York: Sprague-Coleman, 1938.

Ballin' the Jack (song). Words: Jim Burris; music: Chris Smith. New York: Jos. W. Stern & Co., 1913.

The Banjo: Grotesque Fantasie. Louis Moreau Gottschalk. New York: William Hall & Son, [ca. 1855].

Banjo Twang: Danse Negre. Charles Drumheller. Saint Louis: Drumheller Music Co., 1893.

Banjoisticus. Paul Eno. Philadelphia: Maximum Publishing Co., 1909.

The Barn-Yard Rag (song). Billy Johnson and Chris Smith. Chicago: Harold Rossiter Music Co., 1911.

Beaumont Rag. Traditional.

The Bee-Hive. Joseph F. Lamb. Composed ca. 1908–14; not published.

Bees and Honey Rag. Les C. Copeland. Not published. Issued on piano roll: Universal 202759.

Belle of the Cakewalk (song). Words: F. C. Lowder and W. M. Lind; music: L. B. O'Connor. Boston: Wood, 1898.

Ben Harney's Rag Time Instructor. Ben Harney, arranged by Theo. H. Northrup. Chicago: Sol Bloom, 1897.

Bert Williams. Ferdinand "Jelly Roll" Morton. © 1948 by the Estate of F. J. Morton, Los Angeles. Originally titled *Pacific Rag*.

Bethena: A Concert Waltz. Scott Joplin. Saint Louis: T. Bahnsen Piano Mfg. Co., 1905.

Big Chief Battleaxe (song). Thomas S. Allen. Boston: Walter Jacobs, 1909.

Big Foot Ham. Ferdinand "Jelly Roll" Morton. © 1923 by Lloyd Smith, Chicago.

Bill Bailey, Won't You Please Come Home? (song). Hughie Cannon. New York: Howley, Haviland & Dresser, 1902.

Billy Goat Stomp. Ferdinand "Jelly Roll" Morton. Chicago: Melrose Bros. Music Co., 1927.

Bird-Brain Rag. Joseph F. Lamb. Published in *Ragtime Treasures: Piano Solos by Joseph F. Lamb* (New York: Mills Music, 1964), pp. 10–14.

Black and White Rag. George Botsford. New York and Detroit: Jerome H. Remick & Co., 1908.

Black Bottom Stomp. Ferdinand "Jelly Roll" Morton. Chicago: Melrose Bros. Music Co., 1926.

Black Diamond Rag. Henry Lodge. New York: M. Witmark & Sons, 1912.

Blue Grass Rag. Joseph F. Lamb. Published in *Ragtime Treasures: Piano Solos by Joseph F. Lamb* (New York: Mills Music, 1964), pp. 30–34.

Blue Ribbon Rag. May Aufderheide. Indianapolis: J. H. Aufderheide & Co., 1910.

Blue Tornado. Zez Confrey. New York: American Academy of Music, 1935.

Bohemia Rag. Joseph F. Lamb. Saint Louis: Stark Music Co., 1919.

Boogaboo. Ferdinand "Jelly Roll" Morton. Chicago: Melrose Bros. Music Co., 1928.

Bouncing on the Keys. Ed Claypoole. New York: Jack Mills, Inc., 1924.

Bowery Buck. Tom Turpin. Saint Louis: Robert De Yong & Co., 1899.

Brainard's Ragtime Collection, Being a Collection of Characteristic Two-Steps, Cake Walks, Plantation Dances, Etc. New York: S. Brainard's Sons, 1899.

Breakin' the Piano. Billy James. New York: Jack Mills, Inc., 1922.

A Breeze from Alabama: A Ragtime Two Step. Scott Joplin. Saint Louis: John Stark & Son, 1902.

Briggs' Banjo Instructor (for banjo). Thomas F. Briggs. Boston: Ditson, 1855.

Briggs' Jig (for banjo). [Thomas F. Briggs?] Published in Thomas F. Briggs, *Briggs' Banjo Instructor*. Boston: Ditson, 1855, p. 24.

Broadway Rag: A Classic. James Scott. Saint Louis: Stark Music Co., 1922.

Buffalo Blues. Ferdinand "Jelly Roll" Morton. © 1928 by Triangle Music Publishing Co., New York. Later retitled *Mister Joe*, © 1939 by Tempo-Music Publishing Co., New York.

The Buffalo Rag. Tom Turpin. Chicago: Will Rossiter, 1904.

A Bunch of Rags: Rag Medley. Arranged by Ben M. Jerome. New York: Howley, Haviland, & Co., 1898.

A Bundle of Rags. Robert S. Roberts. Cincinnati: Philip Kussel, 1897.

Buzzer Rag. May Aufderheide. Indianapolis: J. H. Aufderheide & Co., 1910.

By Heck. S. R. Henry. New York: Jos. W. Stern & Co., 1914.

By the Light of the Jungle Moon (song). Words: Powell I. Ford; music: J. C. Atkinson. New York and Detroit: Jerome H. Remick & Co., 1911.

The Cake-Walk in the Sky (song). Ben Harney. New York: M. Witmark & Sons, 1899.

Canadian Capers. Gus Chandler, Bert White, and Henry Cohen. Chicago: Roger Graham, 1915.

Cannon Ball: Characteristic Two Step. Joseph C. Northup. Arranged by Thomas R. Confare. Chicago: Victor Kremer Company, 1905.

Caprice Rag. James P. Johnson. Published in *Ragtime Piano: A Collection of Standard Rags for Piano Solo* (Melville, New York: Belwin Mills Publishing Corp., 1963), pp. 62–65.

De Captain of de Coontown Guards. Dave Reed, Jr. New York: M. Witmark & Sons, 1897.

Carolina Balmoral. James P. Johnson. Not copyrighted or published. Recorded in November 1943 on Blue Note 25.

Carolina Shout. James P. Johnson. New York: Clarence Williams Music Publishing Co., 1925.

The Cascades: A Rag. Scott Joplin. Saint Louis: John Stark & Son, 1904.

The Cascades. Scott Joplin. Arranged for orchestra by E. J. Stark. Saint Louis: John Stark & Son, 190-.

Casey Jones (song). Words: T. Lawrence Seibert; music: Eddie Newton. Los Angeles: Southern California Music Co., 1909.

Casey Jones. Eddie Newton. Arranged for orchestra by M. L. Lake. New York: Carl Fisher, 1911.

Cataract Rag. Robert Hampton. Saint Louis:

Stark Music Co., 1914.

Cat's Pajamas, The. Harry Jentes. New York: Jack Mills, Inc., 1923.

Celestine Waltzes. Joseph F. Lamb. Toronto: H. H. Sparks, 1905.

Champagne Rag: March and Two-Step. Joseph F. Lamb. Saint Louis: Stark Music Co., 1910.

Champion Wing Dance (for banjo). Thomas J. Armstrong. Philadelphia: S. S. Stewart, 1888. Also published in *S. S. Stewart's Banjo and Guitar Journal* 4, no. 8 (February–March 1888), p. 11.

Charleston Rag (also known as *Sounds of Africa*). Eubie Blake. © 1917 by M. Witmark & Sons, New York. First published in *Sincerely, Eubie Blake,* transcribed by Terry Waldo. Brooklyn, New York: Eubie Blake Music, 1975, pp. 4–9.

Chasin' the Chippies: Two Step. Joseph F. Lamb. Composed 1914; not published.

Chatterbox Rag. George Botsford. Detroit and New York: Jerome H. Remick & Co., 1910.

Checker: Rag Two Step. Bulah Arens. Arranged by Julia Rosenbush. Indianapolis: Carlin & Lennox, 1908.

Chevy Chase. Eubie Blake. New York: Jos. W. Stern & Co., 1914.

Cheyenne (song). Words: Harry H. Williams; music: Egbert Van Alstyne. Detroit and New York: Jerome H. Remick & Co., 1906.

Chicken Reel: Two Step and Buck Dance. Joseph M. Daly. Boston: Daly Music Publisher, 1910.

Chicken Reel: Song. Words: Joseph Mittenthal; music: Joseph M. Daly. Boston: Daly Music Publisher, 1911.

Chimes of Dixie. Joseph F. Lamb. Published in *Ragtime Treasures: Piano Solos by Joseph F. Lamb* (New York: Mills Music, 1964), pp. 40–45.

Chinese Breakdown. Traditional.

Chinese Rag. Traditional.

Chocolate Bunny's Love Song. Zez Confrey. New York: Mills Music, Inc., 1949.

Christensen's Rag-Time Instruction Book for Piano. Axel W. Christensen. Chicago: Axel W. Christensen, 1904.

The Chrysanthemum. Scott Joplin. Arranged for orchestra. Saint Louis: John Stark & Son, 1905.

The Chrysanthemum: An Afro-Intermezzo. Scott Joplin. Saint Louis: John Stark & Son, 1904.

Climax Rag. James Scott. Saint Louis: Stark Music Co., 1914.

Cleopatra Rag. Joseph Lamb. Saint Louis: Stark Music Co., 1915.

Coaxing the Piano. Zez Confrey. New York: Jack Mills, Inc., 1922.

The Colored Major: Characteristic March and Two-Step. S. R. Henry. New York: Lyceum Publishing Co., 1900.

Combination March. Scott Joplin. Temple, Texas: Robert Smith, 1896.

A Coon Band Contest: Cake Walk Two Step. Arthur Pryor. New York: The Bell Music Co., 1899.

The Coons' Frolic (for band). George Southwell. Kansas City, Missouri: George Southwell, 1897.

De Coontown Jubilee Cakewalk (for banjo). C. L. Partee. Kansas City, Missouri: C. L. Partee Music Co., 1897.

Cotton Blossoms: March Comique. Milton H. Hall. Cincinnati: John Church & Co., 1898.

Cottontail Rag. Joseph F. Lamb. Published in *Ragtime Treasures: Piano Solos by Joseph F. Lamb* (New York: Mills Music, 1964), pp. 15–19.

Covent Garden: Ragtime Waltz. Marcella A. Henry. Chicago: Christensen School of Popular Music, 1917.

The Crave. Ferdinand "Jelly Roll" Morton. © 1939 by Tempo-Music Co., New York.

Crazy Blues (song). Perry Bradford. New York: Williams Music Co., 1920.

Crazy Bone Rag. Charles L. Johnson. Chicago: Forster Music Publisher, 1913.

Creepy Feeling. Ferdinand "Jelly Roll" Morton. © 1944 by Roy J. Carew, Washington, D.C.

Creole Belles: March–Two-Step. J. Bodewalt Lampe. Buffalo, New York: The Lampe Music Co., 1900.

Cyclone. Ferde Grofé. New York: Jack Mills, Inc., 1923.

Dakota Jig (for banjo). Ed. H. Hulse. Published in S. S. Stewart, *The Minstrel Banjoist* (Philadelphia: S. S. Stewart, 1881) p. 24.

Darkies Cake Walk (for banjo). William A. Huntley. [n.p.]: [n.p.], 1896.

The Darkie's Dream. George L. Lansing. Chicago: National Music Co., 1889.

The Darkie's Dream (for banjo). George L. Lansing. Boston: L. B. Gatcomb & Co., 1887.

The Darkies' Patrol. E. A. Phelps. New York: S. Brainard's Sons, 1892.

The Darkie's Rag Time Ball (song). Words: Jack Drislane; music: George W. Meyer. New York: F. B. Haviland Publishing Co., 1912.

Darktown Capers: An Original Southern Rag. Walter Starck. Saint Louis: Shattinger Music Co., 1897.

Darktown Jubilee Patrol (for banjo). Paul Eno. Philadelphia: F. H. Griffith and Co., [1894?].

Darktown Strutters' Ball (song). Shelton Brooks. Chicago: Will Rossiter, 1917.

Dat's Ma Honey Sho's Yo' Born (song). Joe Jordan. Chicago: Will Rossiter, 1912.

Daughters of Dahomey: Rag-Time Waltz. Harry P. Guy. Detroit: Harry P. Guy, 1902.

Day Dreams: Syncopated Waltz. Maxwell Gordon. Saint Louis: Buck & Lowney, 1912.

Dead Man Blues. Ferdinand "Jelly Roll" Morton. Chicago: Melrose Bros. Music Co., 1926.

Dill Pickles. Charles L. Johnson. Kansas City, Missouri: Carl Hoffman Music Co., 1906.

Dinah's Jubilee: Characteristic March and Two Step. Jacob H. Ellis. New York: Howley, Haviland, 1897.

Dixie. See *I Wish I Was in Dixie's Land.*

Dixie Dimples: Novelty Rag Fox Trot. James Scott. Kansas City, Missouri: Will L. Livernash Music Co., 1918.

Dizzy Fingers. Zez Confrey. New York: Jack Mills, Inc., 1923.

Doc Brown's Cake Walk. Charles L. Johnson. Arranged for banjo by Clarence L. Partee. Kansas City, Missouri: J. W. Jenkins' Sons Music Co., 1899.

Dog on the Piano. Ted Shapiro. New York: Jack Mills, Inc., 1924.

The Doll Dance. Herb Nacio Brown. San Francisco: Sherman, Clay & Co., 1927.

Don't Jazz Me: Rag (I'm Music). James Scott. Saint Louis: Stark Music Co., 1921.

Don't Let Your Deal Go Down (song). Traditional.

Down Among the Sugar Cane (song). Words: Avery and Hart; music: Cecil Mack and Chris Smith. New York: The Gotham-Attucks Music Co., 1908.

Down Home Rag. Wilbur Sweatman. Chicago: Will Rossiter, 1911.

Down in Jungle Town (song). Words: Edward Madden; music: Theodore Morse. New York: F. B. Haviland Publishing Co., 1908.

Dusty Rag. May Aufderheide. Indianapolis: Duane Crabb Publishing Co., 1908.

Dynamite Rag (Joe Lamb's Old Rag). Joseph F. Lamb. Composed 1907; not published.

The Easy Winners: A Ragtime Two Step. Scott Joplin. Saint Louis: Scott Joplin, 1901.

The Easy Winners. Scott Joplin. Arranged for orchestra. Saint Louis: Shattinger Piano & Music Co., 1903.

Echoes from the Snowball Club: Ragtime Waltz. Harry P. Guy. Detroit: Willard Bryant, 1898.

Echoes of the Congo. Lylian M. Chapman. Arranged by Carl Frolich. Detroit: Whitney-Warner Publishing Co., 1903.

Efficiency Rag. James Scott. Saint Louis: Stark Music Co., 1917.

Elaine: Syncopated Waltz. E. J. Stark. New York: Jos. W. Stern & Co., 1913.

Eli Green's Cake Walk. Sadie Koninsky. Arranged for banjo by Ruby Brooks and Harry Denton. New York: Jos. W. Stern & Co., 1899.

Eli Green's Cake Walk: March & Two Step. Sadie Koninsky. Arranged by Charles E. Pratt. New York: Jos. W. Stern & Co., 1898.

Elite Syncopations. Scott Joplin. Saint Louis: John Stark & Co., 1902.

Ella Speed (song). Traditional.

The Entertainer: A Rag Time Two Step. Scott Joplin. Saint Louis: John Stark & Son, 1902.

The Entertainer. Scott Joplin. Arranged for orchestra by D. S. DeLisle. [Saint Louis: John Stark & Son, 190-].

The Entertainer's Rag. Jay Roberts. Oakland: Pacific Coast Music Co., 1910.

Eskimo Rag (song). Words: Jean C. Havez; music: George Botsford. New York and Detroit: Jerome H. Remick & Co., 1912.

Ethiopia Rag. Joseph F. Lamb. New York and Saint Louis: Stark Music Co., 1909.

Eugenia. Scott Joplin. Chicago: Will Rossiter, 1905.

Euphonic Sounds: A Syncopated Novelty. Scott Joplin. New York: Seminary Music Co., 1909.

Evah Dahkey Is a Lady (song). Words: E. P. Moran and Paul Laurence Dunbar; music: John H. Cook. Chicago: Harry Von Tilzer Music Publishing Co., 1902.

Evergreen Rag. James Scott. Saint Louis: Stark Music Co., 1915.

Everybody Twostep: Rag. Wallie Herzer. © 1910 by Wallie Herzer. New York and Detroit: Jerome H. Remick & Co., 1911.

Excelsior Rag. Joseph F. Lamb. New York and Saint Louis: Stark Music Co., 1909.

Fancy Fingers. Burn Knowles. New York: ABC Standard, 1936.

Fascinating Rhythm (song). Words: Ira Gershwin; music: George Gershwin. New York: Harms, 1924.

The Fascinator: March and Two-Step. James Scott. Carthage, Missouri: Dumars Music Co., 1903.

The Fascinator: March and Two-Step. James Scott. Arranged for orchestra by E. W. Berry. Kansas City, Missouri: E. W. Berry Music Co., 1912.

Fat Frances. See *Frances.*

Feather Fingers. Claude Lapham. New York: Alfred & Co., 1928.

Felicity Rag. Scott Joplin and Scott Hayden. Saint Louis and New York: Stark Music Printing and Publishing Co., 1911.

Fickle Fay Creep. See *Soap Suds.*

Fig Leaf Rag: A High Class Rag. Scott Joplin. Saint Louis and New York: Stark Music Co., 1908.

Fingerbreaker. See *Fingerbuster.*

Fingerbuster. Ferdinand "Jelly Roll" Morton. © 1942 by Roy J. Carew, Washington, D.C. Also known as *Fingerbreaker.*

Firefly Rag. Joseph F. Lamb. Published in *Ragtime Treasures: Piano Solos by Joseph F. Lamb* (New York: Mills Music, 1964) pp. 60-64.

Fizz Water. J. Hubert Blake. New York: Jos. W Stern & Co., 1914.

Flapperette. Jesse Greer. New York: Jack Mills, Inc., 1926.

Flaxy Cunninghams Cake Walk (for banjo). E. H. Frey. © 1897 by S. S. Stewart. Published in

S. S. Stewart's Banjo and Guitar Journal 14, no. 1 (April–May 1897), pp. 9–11.

Floreine: Syncopated Waltz. E. J. Schuster. Indianapolis: Warner C. Williams & Co., 1908.

Florentine Waltzes. Joseph F. Lamb. Toronto, Canada: H. H. Sparks, 1906.

Florida Rag. George L. Lowry. New York: Jos. W. Stern & Co., 1905.

Forest & Stream: Polka or Two-Step. William H. Tyers. New York: F. A. Mills, 1897.

Frances. Ferdinand "Jelly Roll" Morton. © 1931 by Southern Music Co., New York. Also known as *Fat Frances.*

Frankfort Rag. Maude M. Thurston. Arranged by Harry L. Alford. Chicago: Maude M. Thurston, 1909.

Freakish. Ferdinand "Jelly Roll" Morton. © 1929 by Southern Music Co., New York.

Frog Legs Rag. James Scott. Saint Louis and New York: Stark Music Co., 1906.

Frog Legs Rag. James Scott. Arranged for orchestra by Scott Joplin. Saint Louis: Stark Music Printing & Publishing Co., 1906.

Frog-I-More Rag. Ferdinand "Jelly Roll" Morton. © 1918 by Ferd Morton, Los Angeles. Washington, D. C.: R. J. Carew, 1948.

The Gaby Glide (song). Words: Harry Pilcer; music: Louis Hirsch. New York: Shapiro, Bernstein, 1911.

Georgia Bustdown. Traditional.

Georgia Swing. Ferdinand "Jelly Roll" Morton. Chicago: Melrose Bros. Music Co., 1928.

Giddy Ditty. Zez Confrey. New York: American Academy of Music, 1935.

Gladiolus Rag. Scott Joplin. New York: Jos. W. Stern & Co., 1907.

Golden Rod Reel (for banjo). Edith E. Secor. Philadelphia: S. S. Stewart, 1889.

Good and Plenty Rag. Joseph F. Lamb. Published in *Ragtime Treasures: Piano Solos by Joseph F. Lamb* (New York: Mills Music, 1964), pp. 56–59.

Goodby Booze (song). Traditional.

Good Morning, Carrie (song). Words: R. C. McPherson; music: Smith and Bowman. Chicago: Windsor Music Co., 1901.

Good Night, Beloved, Good Night (song). Words: Jack Everett Fay; music: James Oliver. New York: M. Witmark & Sons, 1904.

Grace and Beauty. James Scott. Arranged for orchestra by E. J. Stark. Saint Louis: Stark Music Printing and Publishing Co., [n.d.].

Grace and Beauty: A Classic Rag. James Scott. Saint Louis and New York: Stark Music Co., 1909.

Grandpa's Spells. Ferdinand "Jelly Roll" Morton. Chicago: Melrose Bros. Music Co., 1923.

Greased Lightning Rag. Joseph F. Lamb. Composed ca. 1908–1914; not published.

Great Crush Collision March. Scott Joplin. Temple, Texas: John R. Fuller, 1896.

Great Scott Rag. James Scott. Columbia, Missouri: Allen Music Co., 1909.

Grizzly Bear Rag. George Botsford. New York: Ted Snyder Co., 1910.

Grizzly Bear Rag (song). Words: Irving Berlin; music: George Botsford. New York: Ted Snyder Co., 1910.

A Guest of Honor: A Ragtime Opera. Scott Joplin. © 1903 by Scott Joplin; not published.

Gut Stomp. James P. Johnson and Willie "the Lion" Smith. Not copyrighted or published. Recorded by James P. Johnson in November 1943 on Blue Note 24.

Happy Little Nigs: Ragtime Two Step. George Elliott. Saint Paul: George Elliott, 1897.

Harlem Rag. Tom Turpin. Arranged by D. S. DeLisle. Saint Louis: Robert De Yong & Co., 1897. Rev. ed., arranged by Will Tyers. New York: Jos. W. Stern & Co., 1899.

Harlem Strut. James P. Johnson. Not copyrighted or published. Recorded September 1921 on Black Swan 2026.

Harmony Club Waltz. Scott Joplin. Temple, Texas: Robert Smith, 1896.

The Hat He Never Ate (song). Words: Howard S. Taylor; music: Ben Harney. Chicago: Home Music Co., 1899.

He Done Me Wrong (Death of Bill Bailey) (song). Hughie Cannon. New York: Howley, Haviland, Dresser Co., 1904.

Hearts [sic] *Longing Waltzes.* James Scott. Saint Louis and New York: Stark Music Co., 1910.

Heliotrope Bouquet: A Slow Drag Two-Step. Scott Joplin and Louis Chauvin. Saint Louis and New York: Stark Music Co., 1907.

Hello! Ma Baby (song). [Joseph E.] Howard and [Ida] Emerson. New York: T. B. Harms & Co., 1899.

The Hesitating Blues (song). W. C. Handy. Memphis: Pace & Handy Music Co., 1915.

Hiawatha: A Summer Idyl. Neil Moret. Saint Louis: Daniels & Russell, 1901.

Hiawatha (His Song to Minnehaha) (song). Words: James O'Dea; music: Neil Moret. Detroit: Whitney-Warner Publishing Co., 1903.

High Hattin'. Zez Confrey. From *African Suite.* New York: Jack Mills, Inc., 1924.

Hilarity Rag. James Scott. Saint Louis: Stark Music Co., 1910.

Hilarity Rag. James Scott. Arranged for orchestra by Rocco Venuto. Saint Louis: Stark Music Printing & Publishing Co., 191.

Hitchy-Koo (song). Words: L. Wolfe Gilbert; music: Lewis F. Muir and Maurice Abrahams. New York: F. A. Mills, 1912.

The Hold-Up Rag (song). Words: Edward Madden; music: Egbert Van Alstyne. New York: Jerome H. Remick & Co., 1912.

Home! Sweet Home! (song). Words: John Howard Payne; music: Henry R. Bishop. London:

Goulding, D'Almaine, Potter & Co., 1823.

Honey Moon Rag. James Scott. Saint Louis: Stark Music Co., 1916.

Honeysuckle Rag. George Botsford. New York and Detroit: Jerome H. Remick & Co., 1911.

Honolulu Rag (song). Words: Harry Williams; music: Egbert Van Alstyne. New York and Detroit: Jerome H. Remick & Co., 1910.

Hot Cinders. Joseph F. Lamb. Published in *Ragtime Treasures: Piano Solos by Joseph F. Lamb* (New York: Mills Music, 1964), pp. 20–25.

Hot Corn (for banjo). Paul Eno. Philadelphia: Stewart & Bauer, 1899.

Hot Fingers. Joe Gold. New York: Jack Mills, Inc., 1925.

Hot Fingers. Robert Marine. New York: Robert Marine, 1928.

Hot Foot Ike Cake Walk (for banjo). J. E. Agnew. Des Moines: J. E. Agnew, 1901.

Hotfoot Sue. [composer, publisher, copyright date unknown.] Recorded by banjoist Vess Ossman in 1897 on Berliner 475.

Hot House Rag. Paul Pratt. Saint Louis: Stark Music Co., 1914.

Hunky Dory Darky. [composer, publisher, and copyright date unknown.] Recorded by banjoist Will Lyle in 1889 on a North American Phonograph Company cylinder.

Hungarian Rag. Julius Lenzberg. New York: Jerome H. Remick & Co., 1913.

Hyacinth: A Rag. Joseph F. Lamb. Composed ca. 1908–14; not published.

Hyena Stomp. Ferdinand "Jelly Roll" Morton. Chicago: Melrose Bros. Music Co., 1927.

I Don't Like No Cheap Man (song). [Bert] Williams and [George] Walker. New York: Jos. W. Stern & Co., 1896.

I Don't Understand Ragtime (song). Irving Jones. New York: Jos. W. Stern, 1899.

I Hates to Get Up Early in de Morn (song). Words: John Queen; music: Hughie Cannon. New York: Howley, Haviland and Dresser, 1901.

Il Trovatore: Syncopated Waltz. Warner C. Williams. Indianapolis: Warner C. Williams & Co., 1912.

Imitation of the Banjo. W. K. Batchelder. Boston: Nathan Richardson, 1854.

I'm Livin' Easy (song). Irving Jones. New York: F. A. Mills, 1899.

In a Mist. Bix Beiderbecke. New York: Robbins Music Corp., 1928.

The Incandescent Rag. George Botsford. New York and Detroit: Jerome H. Remick & Co., 1913.

In the Baggage Coach Ahead (song). Gussie L. Davis. New York: Howley, Haviland & Co., 1896.

In the Shade of the Old Apple Tree (song). Words: Harry H. Williams; music: Egbert Van Alstyne. New York: Shapiro, Remick &

Co., 1905.

Irresistible Fox Trot Rag. Lora M. Hudson. Not published. Issued on piano roll: U.S. Music 7589.

Irresistible Rag. W. C. Powell. New York: Church, Paxson and Co., 1910.

It's Moving Day. See *Moving Day.*

I Want to Be in Dixie (song). Irving Berlin and Ted Snyder. New York: Ted Snyder Co., 1911.

I Wish I Was in Dixie's Land (song). D. D. Emmett. Arranged by W. L. Hobbs. New York: Firth, Pond & Co., 1860. Also published as *I Wish I Was in Dixie.* Words: W. H. Peters; music: J. C. Viereck. New Orleans: P. P. Werlein, 1860. Also published with the latter title, publisher, and year but with words credited to J. Newcomb.

Jack in the Box. Zez Confrey. New York: Jack Mills, Inc., 1927.

Jacobs' Dance Folio No. 1. Arranged for orchestra. Boston: Walter Jacobs, 1907.

Japanese Breakdown. Traditional.

Jay Walk. Zez Confrey. New York: Jack Mills, Inc., 1927.

Jelly Roll Blues. See *Original Jelly Roll Blues.*

The Jersey Rag. Joseph F. Lamb. Composed ca. 1908–1914; not published.

Jim-Jams. Roy Bargy. Cleveland: Sam Fox Publishing Co., 1922.

Jinx Rag. Lucian P. Gibson. Arranged by Artie Matthews. Saint Louis: Lucian P. Gibson, 1911.

Juggling the Piano. Sam P. Perry. New York: Jack Mills, Inc., 1924.

Jumping Jack. Rube Bloom, Bernie Seaman, and Marvin Smolev. New York: ABC Standard, 1928.

Jungle Blues. Ferdinand "Jelly Roll" Morton. Chicago: Melrose Bros. Music Co., 1927.

The Jungle Rag (for banjo). Parke Hunter. Published in *Dallas' Artistic Banjoist, No. 370* (London: J. E. Dallas, [n.d.]).

The Junk Man Rag. C. Luckeyth Roberts. New York: Jos. W. Stern & Co., 1913.

Just One Word of Consolation (song). Words: Tom Lemonier; music: Frank B. Williams. New York: Chas. K. Harris, 1906.

Kalamity Kid. Ferd Guttenberger. Arranged by J. Russel Robinson. Macon, Georgia: Ferd Guttenberger, 1909.

Kansas City Rag. James Scott. Saint Louis and New York: Stark Music Co., 1907.

Kansas City Stomp. Ferdinand "Jelly Roll" Morton. Chicago: Melrose Bros. Music Co., 1923. Also known as *Kansas City Stomps.*

Keyboard Konversation. Vee Lawnhurst. New York: Jack Mills, 1923.

King Porter Stomp. Ferdinand "Jelly Roll" Morton. Chicago: Melrose Bros. Music Co., 1924.

Kinklets. Arthur Marshall. Arranged for orchestra by E. J. Stark. Saint Louis: Stark Music Printing & Publishing Co., 1906.

Kismet Rag. Scott Joplin and Scott Hayden. Saint Louis: Stark Music Co., 1913.

Kitten on the Keys. Zez Confrey. New York: Jack Mills, 1921.

Knock Out Drops: Rag. F. Henri Klickmann. Arranged for orchestra by Harry L. Alford. Chicago: Victor Kremer, 1910.

Kullud Koons' Kake Walk (for banjo). Dan Emerson. New York: Wm. A. Pond & Co., 1892.

The Lady with the Ragtime Walk (song). Armstrong Brothers. New York: W. B. Gray & Co., 1898. Reprinted in a supplement of the *New York Journal & Advertiser,* 18 June 1899.

Lazy Moon (song). Words: Bob Cole; music: Rosamond Johnson. New York: Jos. W. Stern & Co., 1903.

Left Her on the Railroad Track (song). Traditional.

Levee Rag: Dance Characteristic. Charles E. Mullen. Chicago: Will Rossiter, 1902.

The Lilliputian's Bazaar. Joseph F. Lamb. Toronto: H. H. Sparks, 1905.

Lily Queen: A Ragtime Two-Step. Arthur Marshall and Scott Joplin. New York: W. W. Stuart, 1907.

The Lily Rag. Charles Thompson. Arranged by Artie Matthews. Saint Louis: Syndicate Music Co., 1914.

Lion Tamer Rag. Mark Janza. Louisville: A. F. Marzian, 1913.

The Little Brown Jug (song). R. A. Eastburn. New York: J. E. Winner, 1869.

Live Wires Rag. Adaline Shepherd. Chicago: Adelphi Publishing Co., 1909.

Log Cabin Rag. Ferd Guttenberger. Arranged by J. Russel Robinson. Macon, Georgia: Ferd Guttenberger, 1908.

Lolly Pops (for banjo). Harry Reser. New York: Harry Reser, 1924.

London Blues. Ferdinand "Jelly Roll" Morton. Chicago: Melrose Bros. Music Co., 1923. Also known as *London Cafe Blues.* Also published as *Shoe Shiner's Drag.* Chicago: Melrose Bros. Music Co., 1928.

London Cafe Blues. See *London Blues.*

Loose Elbows. Billy Mayerl. London: Keith-Prowse & Co., 1926.

Loose Fingers. Stanley C. Holt. London: Lawrence Wright Music Co., 1923.

Louisiana Rag. Theodore H. Northrup. Chicago: Thompson Music Co., 1897.

Love Dreams: Syncopated Waltz. Joseph F. Cohen. Indianapolis: Warner C. Williams & Co., 1915.

Love in Absence (song). Words: M. A. O'Reilly; music: Joseph F. Lamb. Montclair, New Jersey: Gordon Hurst, 1909.

Lovie Joe (song). Words: Will Marion Cook; music: Joe Jordan. New York: Harry Von Tilzer Music Publishing Co., 1910.

Magnetic Rag. Scott Joplin. New York: Scott Joplin Music Publishing Co., 1914.

Mamanita. Ferdinand "Jelly Roll" Morton. © 1949 by the Estate of Ferdinand J. Morton, Los Angeles.

Mamma's and Pappa's Blues. James P. Johnson. New York: F. B. Haviland, 1916.

Mandy's Ragtime Waltz. J. S. Zamecnik. Cleveland: Sam Fox Publishing Co., 1912.

Maori: A Samoan Dance. Will H. Tyers. New York: Attucks Music Co., 1908.

Maple Leaf Rag. Scott Joplin. Sedalia, Missouri: John Stark & Son, 1899.

Maple Leaf Rag (song). Words: Sydney Brown; music: Scott Joplin. Saint Louis: John Stark & Son, 1903.

Maple Leaf Rag. Scott Joplin. Arranged for orchestra. [Saint Louis: John Stark & Son, ca. 1901].

Marionette: Fox Trot. Felix Arndt. Cleveland: Sam Fox Publishing Co., 1914.

Meandering. Zez Confrey. New York: Jack Mills, Inc., 1921.

Melody in F: (Syncopated) Waltzes. Will B. Morrison. Indianapolis: Warner C. Williams & Co., 1913.

The Memphis Blues: A Southern Rag. W. C. Handy. Memphis: Handy Music Co., 1912.

The Meteor March. Clarence Woods. Carthage, Missouri: Dumars Music Co., 1904.

Midnight Special. Traditional.

The Minstrel Man. J. Russel Robinson. Arranged for orchestra by E. J. Stark. Saint Louis: Stark Music Printing and Publishing Co., [191-].

Mississippi Rag. William H. Krell. Chicago and New York: S. Brainard's Sons, 1897.

Mister Joe. See *Buffalo Blues.*

Mister Johnson Turn Me Loose (song). Ben Harney. New York: Harding's Music House, 1896. Transferred to M. Witmark, 1896.

The Mobile Buck: The Famous Mississippi Steamboat Dance (for banjo). [Composer not identified]. Arranged by G. L. Lansing. Published in *Gatcomb's Musical Gazette* 5, no. 4 (December 1891), p. 9.

Mobile Persuasion (for banjo and piano). W. H. Sleider. Philadelphia: S. S. Stewart, 1890. Also published in *S. S. Stewart's Banjo and Guitar Journal* 14, no. 2 (June–July 1897), p. 5.

Modesty Rag: A Classic. James Scott. Saint Louis: Stark Music Co., 1920.

Mouse's Hooves. Zez Confrey. New York: American Academy of Music, 1935.

Moving Day (song). Words: Andrew B. Sterling; music: Harry Von Tilzer. New York: Harry Von Tilzer Music Publishing Co., 1906.

Moving Day in Jungle Town (song). Words: A. Seymour Brown; music: Nat D. Ayer. New York and Detroit: Jerome H. Remick & Co.,

1909.

Mr. Music Master Play That Rag Some Faster (song). Words: Lew Brown; music: Albert Von Tilzer. New York: The York Music Co., 1911.

Mule Walk Stomp. James P. Johnson. Not copyrighted or published. Recorded by James P. Johnson on 14 June 1939 for Columbia Records.

My Coal Black Lady: Symphony de Ethiopia (song). W. T. Jefferson. "Rag accompaniment to Chorus 'Coal Black Lady' arr. by Max Hoffman." New York: M. Witmark & Sons, 1896.

My Gal Is a High Born Lady (song). Barney Fagan, arranged by Gustav Luders. New York: M. Witmark & Sons, 1896.

My Gal Sal (song). Paul Dresser. New York: The Paul Dresser Publishing Co., 1905.

My Pet. Zez Confrey. New York: Jack Mills, Inc., 1921.

My Pony Boy (song). Words: Bobby Heath; music: Charley O'Donnell. New York: Up To Date Music Publishing Co., 1909.

The Naked Dance. Tony Jackson. Not published or copyrighted by Jackson. Jelly Roll Morton's arrangement was copyrighted in 1939 by Tempo-Music Publishing Co., Washington, D. C., and was subsequently published in 1950.

Nappy Lee: A Slow Drag. Joe Jordan. Des Moines: James E. Agnew, 1903.

Navajo (song). Words: Harry H. Williams; music: Egbert Van Alstyne. New York: Shapiro, Bernstein & Co., 1903.

Nervous Knuckles. Norman J. Elholm. New York: Jack Mills, 1923.

New Coon in Town. J. S. Putnam. Chicago: Sol Bloom, 1883.

New Coon in Town. Otto Gunnar. New York: S. Brainard's Sons, 1884.

New Era Rag. James Scott. Saint Louis: Stark Music Co., 1919.

New Orleans Blues. Ferdinand "Jelly Roll" Morton. Chicago: Melrose Bros. Music Co., 1925.

Nice and Easy: Rag Fox Trot. Cliff McKay. Arranged by Paul Pratt. New York and Detroit: Jerome H. Remick & Co., 1916.

Nickle in the Slot. Zez Confrey. New York: Leo Feist, 1923.

Nifty Notes (for banjo). Bill Bowen. New York: J. Pitman Grant, 1925.

Night on the Levee. Theodore H. Northrup. Chicago: Sol Bloom, 1897.

Nightingale Rag. See *Ragtime Nightingale.*

Nobody's Looking But de Owl and de Moon (song). Words: J. W. Johnson and Bob Cole; music: Rosamond Johnson. New York: Jos. W. Stern & Co., 1901.

Nola. Felix Arndt. Cleveland: Sam Fox Publishing Co., 1916.

No Place Like Home. See *Home! Sweet Home!.*

Nonpareil (None to Equal). Scott Joplin. Saint Louis and New York: Stark Music Co., 1907.

Novelty Rag. May Aufderheide. Indianapolis: J. H. Aufderheide & Co., 1911.

Oh! Swing Me Honey (for banjo). George L. Lansing. Boston: E. F. Delano, 1885.

Oh That Navajo Rag (song). Words: Harry Williams; music: Egbert Van Alstyne. New York and Detroit: Jerome H. Remick & Co., 1911.

Old Black Joe (song). Stephen C. Foster. New York: Firth, Pond & Co., 1860.

Old Folks Jig (for banjo). Arranged by S. S. Stewart. Published in *S. S. Stewart's Banjo and Guitar Journal* 2, no. 11 (August–September 1884), p. 13.

The Old Home Rag. Joseph F. Lamb. Published in *Ragtime Treasures: Piano Solos by Joseph F. Lamb* (New York: Mills Music, 1964), pp. 2–5.

One More Rag. Minnie Berger. Arranged by Arthur Campbell. Saint Louis: Stark Music Co., 1919.

On the Pike. James Scott. Carthage, Missouri: Dumars Music Co., 1904.

Ophelia Rag. James Scott. Saint Louis and New York: Stark Music Co., 1910.

Ophelia Rag. James Scott. Arranged for orchestra by Rocco Venuto. Saint Louis: Stark Music Co., 191-.

Original Jelly Roll Blues. Ferdinand "Jelly Roll" Morton. Chicago: Will Rossiter, 1915. Also known as *Jelly Roll Blues.*

Original Rags. Scott Joplin. Arranged by Charles N. Daniels. Kansas City, Missouri: Carl Hoffman, 1899.

Over There (song). George M. Cohan. New York: Leo Feist, 1917.

Pacific Rag. See *Bert Williams.*

Palm Beach Rag. Luckey Roberts. New York: Jos. W. Stern, 1914.

Palm Leaf Rag: A Slow Drag. Scott Joplin. Chicago and New York: Victor Kremer Co., 1903.

Parade of the Jumping Beans. Zez Confrey. New York: Mills Music, Inc., 1944.

Paragon Rag. Scott Joplin. New York: Seminary Music Co., 1909.

Paramount Rag. James Scott. Saint Louis: Stark Music Co., 1917.

Parisian Rag (song). Branen and Lange. New York: Jeff T. Branen Music Publishing Co., 1910.

Pastime Rag No. 1: A Slow Drag. Artie Matthews. Saint Louis: Stark Music Co., 1913.

Pastime Rag No. 1: A Slow Drag. Artie Matthews. Arranged for orchestra. Saint Louis: Stark Music Co., 1913.

Pastime Rag No. 2: A Slow Drag. Artie Matthews. Saint Louis: Stark Music Co., 1913.

Pastime Rag No. 3: A Slow Drag. Artie Matthews. Saint Louis: Stark Music Co., 1916.

Pastime Rag No. 4: A Slow Drag. Artie Matthews. Saint Louis: Stark Music Co., 1920.

Pastime Rag No. 5: A Slow Drag. Artie Matthews. Saint Louis: Stark Music Co., 1918.

Patricia Rag. Joseph F. Lamb. Saint Louis: Stark Music Co., 1916.

Peace and Plenty Rag. James Scott. Saint Louis: Stark Music Printing and Publishing Co., 1919.

Peaches and Cream. Percy Wenrich. Detroit and New York: Jerome H. Remick & Co., 1905.

The Pearls. Ferdinand "Jelly Roll" Morton. Chicago: Melrose Bros. Music Co., 1923.

Pegasus: A Classic Rag. James Scott. Saint Louis: Stark Music Co., 1920.

Pekin Rag. Joe Jordan. Chicago: Jordan & Motts Pekin Publishing Co., 1904.

Pep. Ferdinand "Jelly Roll" Morton. © 1931 by Southern Music Co., New York, but not published.

Perfect Rag. Ferdinand "Jelly Roll" Morton. © 1949 by the Estate of Ferdinand "Jelly Roll" Morton, Los Angeles. Also known as *Sporting House Rag.*

Pianoflage. Roy Bargy. Cleveland: Sam Fox Publishing Co., 1922.

Piano Mania. William Fazioli. New York: Jack Mills, Inc., 1922.

Piano Phun. Louis Alter. New York: Robbins-Engel, Inc., 1925.

Pick Poor Robin Clean (song). Traditional.

Pickles and Peppers: A Rag Oddity; March and Two Step. Adaline Shepherd. Milwaukee: Joseph Flanner, 1906.

A Picture of Her Face (song). Scott Joplin. Syracuse, New York: Leiter Bros., 1895.

Piffle Rag. Gladys Yelvington. Indianapolis: J. H. Aufderheide & Co., 1911.

Pine Apple Rag. Scott Joplin. New York: Seminary Music Co., 1908.

Pine Apple Rag: Song. Words: Joe Snyder; music: Scott Joplin. New York: Seminary Music Co., 1910.

The Pippin: A Sentimental Rag. Arthur Marshall. New York and Saint Louis: Stark Music Co., 1908.

Plantation Echoes: Rag Two-Step. Theodore H. Northrup. Chicago: Sol Bloom, 1897.

Play That Barber Shop Chord (song). Words: William Tracey; music: Lewis F. Muir. New York: J. Fred Helf & Co., 1910.

Play That Barber Shop Chord: Introducing Oh You Bear Cat Rag; Rag Two Step. Lewis F. Muir. New York: J. Fred Helf & Co., 1910.

Pleasant Moments: Rag-Time Waltz. Scott Joplin. New York: Seminary Music Co., 1909.

Please Say You Will: Song and Chorus. Scott Joplin. Syracuse, New York: M. L. Mantell, 1895.

Pleasure Bound (musical comedy). Words: Max and Nathaniel Lief; music: Muriel Pollock, Phil Baker, and Maury Rubens. New York: Shubert Music Publishing Co., 1929.

Pork and Beans. Theron C. Bennett. Chicago: Victor Kremer Co., 1909.

The Preacher and the Bear (song). Joe Arzonia. Philadelphia: Arthur Longbrake, 1904.

Pretty Little Widow. Traditional.

Pretty Pansy Rag (song). Scott Joplin. Unpublished manuscript, incomplete.

Pride of Bucktown. Robert S. Roberts. Cincinnati: Philip Kussel, 1897.

The Princess Rag. James Scott. Saint Louis: Stark Music Co., 1911.

Prosperity Rag. James Scott. Saint Louis: Stark Music Co., 1916.

Puppets Suite. Billy Mayerl. London: Keith-Prowse & Co., 1927.

Putting on the Dog. Ted Shapiro. New York: Jack Mills, Inc., 1923.

Quality: A High Class Rag. James Scott. Saint Louis: Stark Music Co., 1911.

Racing Down the Black and Whites. Adam Carroll. New York: Harms, Inc., 1926.

Rag Doll. Herb Nacio Brown. San Francisco: Sherman, Clay & Co., 1928.

Rag Doll Carnival. Zez Confrey. New York: Mills Music, Inc., 1945.

Rag Doll Dimples. Zez Confrey. New York: American Academy of Music, 1935.

Ragging the Scale. Edward B. Claypoole. New York: Broadway Music Corp., 1915.

Raggy Rastus (for banjo duet). Gatty Jones. Published in *S. S. Stewart's Banjo, Guitar, and Mandolin Journal* 18, no. 1 (December 1900).

Rag Medley. Max Hoffman. New York: M. Witmark & Sons, 1897.

Rag Pickings (for banjo). George L. Lansing. New York: M. Witmark & Sons, 1898.

Rag Sentimental. James Scott. Saint Louis: Stark Music Co., 1918.

Ragtime Annie. Traditional.

The Ragtime Betty. James Scott. Saint Louis and New York: Stark Music Co., 1909.

Ragtime Bobolink. Joseph F. Lamb. Published in *Ragtime Treasures: Piano Solos by Joseph F. Lamb* (New York: Mills Music, 1964), pp. 26–29.

Ragtime Cowboy Joe (song). Words: Grant Clarke; music: Lewis F. Muir and Maurice Abrahams. New York: F. A. Mills, 1912.

The Ragtime Dance. Scott Joplin. Saint Louis and New York: Stark Music Co., 1906. See also *The Rag Time Dance.*

The Rag Time Dance (song). Scott Joplin. Saint Louis: John Stark & Son, 1902.

The "Rag Time Dance". Scott Joplin. Arranged for orchestra by D. S. DeLisle. Saint Louis: John Stark & Son, 191-.

A Rag Time Episode (for banjo). Paul Eno. New York: Jos. W. Stern & Co., 1899.

Rag Time March. Warren Beebe. Chicago: Will

Rossiter, 1897.

Ragtime Medley (for banjo). Arranged by Vess Ossman. London: Clifford Essex, [n.d.].

Ragtime Nightingale. Joseph F. Lamb. Saint Louis: Stark Music Co., 1915.

A Rag-Time Nightmare: March and Two-Step. Tom Turpin. Saint Louis: Robt. DeYong & Co., 1900.

Ragtime Oriole. James Scott. Saint Louis: Starl Music Co., 1911.

The Rag Time Patrol. R. J. Hamilton. Chicago National Music Co., 1897.

The Rag-Time Queen (song). Irving Jones. Nev York: Feist & Frankenthaler, 1901.

A Ragtime Skedaddle (for banjo). George Rosey New York: Jos. W. Stern & Co., 1899.

Rag Time Skedaddle (for banjo). George Rosey. Arranged by Ruby Brooks and Harry Denton. New York: Brooks & Denton, [1902?]. See also *A Ragtime Skedaddle.*

A Ragtime Sneeze (for banjo). Bill Bowen. New York: Wm. J. Smith Music Co., 1926.

The Ragtime Soldier Man (song). Irving Berlin. New York: Waterson, Berlin & Snyder, 1912.

The Ragtime Special. Joseph F. Lamb. Composed ca. 1908-1914; not published.

Ragtime Turkey Trot (song). Words: Julian Eltinge and Jack Mahoney; music: Percy Wenrich. Chicago: Windsor Music Co., 1913.

Rambling in Rhythm. Arthur Schutt. New York: Jack Mills, Inc., 1927.

Randy Lynn Rag. Earl Scruggs. © 1956 by Peer International Corp., [New York?].

Rapid Transit Rag. Joseph F. Lamb. Composed ca. 1908-1914; not published.

The Ragtime Violin (song). Irving Berlin. New York: Ted Snyder Co., 1911.

Rastus on Parade. Kerry Mills. New York: F. A. Mills, 1895.

Rattle the Banjo (for banjo). [Composer, publisher, and copyright date unknown.] Recorded by banjoist Will Lyle in 1889 on a North American Phonograph Co. cylinder.

Razors in the Air. J. E. Murphy. Brooklyn, New York: Wm. H. Kennedy, 1880.

A Real Slow Drag (song). Scott Joplin. New York: Scott Joplin Publishing Co., 1913.

Recitative Rag (for orchestra). Scott Joplin. Unpublished manuscript; incomplete.

The Red Mill (operetta). Victor Herbert. New York: M. Witmark & Sons, 1906.

Red Pepper: A Spicy Rag. Henry Lodge. New York: M. Witmark & Sons, 1910.

Red Red Rose (song). Words: Alex Rogers; music: Will Marion Cook. New York: Gotham-Attucks Music Co., 1908.

Red Rose Rag (song). Words: Edward Madden; music: Percy Wenrich. New York and Detroit: Jerome H. Remick & Co., 1911.

Red Wing (song). Words: Thurland Chattaway; music: Kerry Mills. New York: F. A. Mills,

1907.

Red Wing: An Indian Intermezzo. Kerry Mills. New York: F. A. Mills, 1907.

Reflection Rag: Syncopated Musings. Scott Joplin. Saint Louis: Stark Music Co., 1917.

Reindeer: Rag Time Two-Step. Joseph F. Lamb. Saint Louis: Stark Music Co., 1915.

Remick Orchestra Folio. Arranged for orchestra. Detroit and New York: Jerome H. Remick & Co., 1912.

Remus on Broadway. M. Clark. Arranged for band. New York: F. A. Mills, 1900.

Rhapsody in Blue. George Gershwin. New York: Harms, Inc., 1925.

Rialto Ripples. George Gershwin and Will Donaldson. New York: Jerome H. Remick & Co., 1917.

Richmond Rag. May Aufderheide. Indianapolis: J. H. Aufderheide & Co., 1908.

Rippling Waters. Harold Potter. New York: Jack Mills, 1923.

Robardina Rag. E. Warren Furry. Arranged by Arthur B. Mooney. Saint Louis: Balmer & Weber Music House, 1902.

Roll Them Cotton Bales (song). Words: James W. Johnson; music: J. Rosamond Johnson. New York: Jos. W. Stern & Co., 1914.

Rooster Rag. Muriel Pollock. New York: Jos. W. Stern & Co., 1917.

Rose Leaf Rag. Scott Joplin. Boston: Jos. M. Daly Music Publishing Co., 1907.

Roustabout Rag. Paul Sarebresole. New Orleans: Gruenewald, 1897.

Rufenreddy. Roy Bargy and Charley Straight. Cleveland: Sam Fox Publishing Co., 1921.

Russian Rag. George L. Cobb. Chicago: Will Rossiter, 1918.

Sailing Over the Keys. Silvio De Rienzo. New York: Bibo, Bloedon & Lang, 1928.

Salty Dog Blues (song). Traditional.

Scott Joplin's New Rag. Scott Joplin. New York: Jos. W. Stern & Co., 1912.

School of Ragtime: 6 Exercises for Piano. Scott Joplin. New York: Scott Joplin, 1908.

Searchlight Rag: A Syncopated March and Two Step. Scott Joplin. New York: Jos. W. Stern & Co., 1907.

Seattle Hunch. Ferdinand "Jelly Roll" Morton. © 1929 by Southern Music Co., New York.

Sensation: A Rag. Joseph F. Lamb. Arranged by Scott Joplin. New York and Saint Louis: Stark Music Co., 1908.

Sensation. Joseph F. Lamb. Arranged for orchestra by E. J. Stark. [Saint Louis and New York: Stark Music Printing & Publishing Co., 19—].

Shamrock Rag. Euday L. Bowman. Fort Worth: Euday L. Bowman, 1916.

Shanghai Rag. Traditional.

Shave 'em Dry: Rag Fox Trot. Sam Wishnuff. Saint Louis: Stark Music Co., 1917.

She's My Girl from Anaconda (song). Words:

Charles Dumars; music: James Scott. Carthage, Missouri: Dumars-Gammon Music Co., 1909.

Shifty Shuffles: Buck Dance. Eva Note Flennard. Philadelphia: Welch & Wilsky, 1897.

The Shimmie Shake (song). Words: Cleota Wilson; music: James Scott. Saint Louis: Stark Music Co., 1920.

Shoe Shiner's Drag. See *London Blues.*

Shootin' the Chutes. Larry Briers. New York: Jack Mills, Inc., 1924.

Shreveport Stomp. Ferdinand "Jelly Roll" Morton. Chicago: Melrose Bros. Music Co., 1925.

The Sick Indian (for banjo). Horace Weston. Published in *S. S. Stewart's Banjo and Guitar Journal* 3, no. 12 (October-November 1886), p. 21.

Silver King Polka-March. Mamie A. Gunn. Saint Louis: Thiebes-Stierlin Music Co., 1897.

Silver Swan Rag. Attributed to Scott Joplin. © 1971 by the Trust of Lottie Joplin Thomas.

The Skeleton Rag (song). Words: Edward Madden; music: Percy Wenrich. New York and Detroit: Jerome H. Remick & Co., 1911.

Skidding. Ed Claypoole. New York: Jack Mills, Inc., 1923.

Slippery Elm Rag. Clarence Woods. Dallas: Bush & Gerts Piano Co., 1912.

Smart Alec. Zez Confrey. New York: Jack Mills, Inc., 1933.

The Smiler: (Joplin-Rag). Percy Wenrich. Chicago: Arnett-Delonais Co., 1907.

The Smiler. Percy Wenrich. Arranged for orchestra by Harry L. Alford. Chicago: Arnett-Delonais Co., 1907.

Smoky Mokes. Abe Holzmann. New York: Feist and Frankenthaler, 1899.

Smoky Mokes (for banjo). Abe Holzmann. New York: Feist and Frankenthaler, 1901.

Snow Deer: Indian Song (song). Words: Jack Mahoney; music: Percy Wenrich. New York: Wenrich-Howard Co., 1913.

Soap Suds. Ferdinand "Jelly Roll" Morton. © 1949 by the Estate of Ferdinand J. Morton, Los Angeles. Also known as *Fickle Fay Creep.*

Solace: A Mexican Serenade. Scott Joplin. New York: Seminary Music Co., 1909.

Some of These Days. Shelton Brooks. Arranged for orchestra by Harry L. Alford. Chicago: Will Rossiter, 1910.

Sounds from the Cottonfields (for banjo). J. H. Jennings. Providence, Rhode Island: Jennings, 1893.

Sounds of Africa. See *Charleston Rag.*

Spaghetti Rag. George Lyons and Bob Yosco. New York: Maurice Shapiro, 1910.

Spanish Swat. Ferdinand "Jelly Roll" Morton. © 1948 by the Estate of Ferdinand J. Morton, Los Angeles.

Spanish Venus: Tango. Luckey Roberts. Not copyrighted or published.

Sporting House Rag. See *Perfect Rag.*

Springtime of Love: Valse. James Scott. Kansas City, Missouri: Will L. Livernash Music Co., 1918.

Star and Garter Ragtime Waltz. Axel W. Christensen. Chicago: Christensen School of Popular Music, 1910.

The Star Spangled Banner (song). Words: Francis Scott Key; music arranged by Thomas Carr. Baltimore: Carrs [sic] Music Store, 1814.

The Stars and Stripes Forever. John Philip Sousa. Cincinnati: The John Church Co., 1897.

Steel Guitar Rag. Leon McAuliffe. New York: Irving Berlin, 1944.

Stepping Out (for banjo). Bill Bowen. New York: Wm. J. Smith Music Co., 1926.

Steeplechase Rag. James P. Johnson. Not copyrighted or published. Recorded in May 1917 on piano roll: Universal 203179. Recorded on disc in August 1944 as *Over the Bars,* Decca 24884.

St. Louis Blues (song). W. C. Handy. Memphis: Pace & Handy Music Co., 1914.

St. Louis Rag. Tom Turpin. New York: Sol Bloom, 1903.

St. Louis Tickle. Barney & Seymore. Chicago: Victor Kremer Co., 1904.

Stone's Rag. Oscar Stone. Not copyrighted or published, but recorded in 1928.

Stop It, Joe! (song). Words: William Farrell; music: James P. Johnson. New York: F. B. Haviland, 1917.

Stratford Hunch. Ferdinand "Jelly Roll" Morton. Published, in slightly different version from original piano solo called *Stratford Hunch,* as *Chicago Breakdown* (Chicago: Melrose Bros. Music Co., 1926).

The Strenuous Life: A Ragtime Two Step. Scott Joplin. Saint Louis: John Stark & Son, 1902.

Stumbling. Zez Confrey. New York: Leo Feist, 1922.

St. Vitus Rag (song). Words: J. Leubrie Hill; music: J. Rosamond Johnson. New York: Jerome H. Remick & Co., 1912.

Suffragette Waltz. James Scott. Saint Louis: Stark Music Co., 1914.

Sugar Cane. Scott Joplin. New York: Seminary Music Co., 1908.

Sugar Cane. Scott Joplin. Arranged for orchestra. New York: Seminary Music Co., [19—].

Sugarfoot Rag (song). Words: George Vaughn; music: Hank Garland. Hollywood: Forrest Music Corp., 1950.

A Summer Breeze: March and Two Step. James Scott. Carthage, Missouri: Dumars Music Co., 1903.

Sunburst Rag. James Scott. Saint Louis and New York: Stark Music Co., 1909.

Sunflower Slow Drag: A Rag Time Two-Step. Scott Joplin and Scott Hayden. Saint Louis: John Stark & Son, 1901.

Sunflower Slow Drag. Scott Joplin and Scott Hayden. Arranged for orchestra by D. S. DeLisle. Saint Louis: John Stark & Son, 1902.

Sunshine Capers. Roy Bargy: Cleveland: Sam Fox Publishing Co., 1922.

Swanee (song). Words: Irving Caesar; music: George Gershwin. New York: T. B. Harms and Francis, Day & Hunter, 1919.

Sweetheart Time (song). Words: Charles Dumars; music: James Scott. Carthage, Missouri: Dumars Music Co., 1909.

Swipesy Cake Walk. Scott Joplin and Arthur Marshall. Saint Louis: John Stark & Son, 1900.

Take a Little Tip from Father (song). Irving Berlin and Ted Snyder. New York: Ted Snyder Co., 1912.

Take Me Out to Lakeside (song). Words: Ida Miller; music: James Scott. Carthage, Missouri: Dumars Music Co., 1914.

Take Your Clothes and Go (song). Irving Jones, arranged by W. H. Tyers. New York: Jos. W. Stern & Co., 1897.

Teasing the Cat. Charles L. Johnson. Chicago: Forster Music Publisher, 1916.

Teasing the Ivories. Arthur Schutt. London: Francis, Day & Hunter, 1924.

Temptation Rag. Henry Lodge. New York: M. Witmark & Sons, 1909.

That Beautiful Rag (song). Words: Ted Snyder; music: Irving Berlin. New York: Ted Snyder Co., 1910.

That Devil Rag (song). Words: Edward Madden; music: Egbert Van Alstyne. New York and Detroit: Jerome H. Remick & Co., 1913.

That Eccentric Rag. J. Russel Robinson. Indianapolis: I. Seidel Music Publishing Co., 1912.

That Fascinating Rag. Walter Rolfe. Kansas City, Missouri: J. W. Jenkins Sons Music Co., 1911.

That Good Old Irish Rag (song). Words: Jack Mahoney; music: Theodore Morse. New York: Theodore Morse Music Co., 1910.

That Gosh-Darned Two Step Rag. M. Kendree Miller. Dallas: Bush & Gerts, 1913.

That International Rag (song). Irving Berlin. New York: Waterson, Berlin & Snyder Co., 1913.

That Irresistible Rag (song). Words: E. R. Wright; music: Paul Eugene. New York: John T. Hall, 1913.

That Italian Rag (song). Words: Edgar Leslie; music: Al Piantadosi. New York: Leo Feist, 1910.

That Mysterious Rag (song). [Irving] Berlin and [Ted] Snyder. New York: Ted Snyder Co., 1911.

That Nifty Rag. S. E. Roberts. New York: George F. Briegel & Co., 1911.

That Old Tiger Rag. Traditional.

That Paradise Rag (song). Words: Joe Goodwin; music: George W. Meyer. New York: F. B. Haviland Publishing Co., 1911.

That Raggedy Rag: Ragtime Dance Song (song). Joe Jordan. New York: Harry Von Tilzer Music Publishing Co., 1912.

That Ragtime Suffragette (song). Words: Harry Williams; music: Nat D. Ayer. New York: Harry Williams Music Co., 1913.

That Teasin' Rag. Joe Jordan. New York: Jos. W. Stern & Co., 1909.

That Texas Rag. Nell Wright Watson. Arranged by Phil Epstein. Fort Worth: Philip Epstein, 1913.

There Ain't No Use To Keep On Hanging Around (song). Irving Jones. New York: Feist & Frankenthaler, 1899. Composed for and printed in a supplement to the *New York World*, 17 September 1899.

Thoroughbred Rag. Joseph F. Lamb. Published in *Ragtime Treasures: Piano Solos by Joseph F. Lamb* (New York: Mills Music, 1964), pp. 35–39.

The Thriller Rag. May Aufderheide. Indianapolis: J. H. Aufderheide & Co., 1909.

Tickled to Death. Charles H. Hunter. Nashville: Frank G. Fite, 1899.

Tiger Jig: Old Time Banjo Jig (for banjo). [Composer unknown.] Published in *S. S. Stewart's Banjo and Guitar Journal* 8, no. 5 (December 1891–January 1892), p. 22.

Toad Stool Rag. Joseph F. Lamb. Published in *Ragtime Treasures: Piano Solos by Joseph F. Lamb* (New York: Mills Music, 1964), pp. 51–55.

Tobasco: Rag-Time Waltz. Charles L. Johnson. New York: Jerome H. Remick & Co., 1909.

Too Much Mustard. See *Très Moutarde.*

Top Liner Rag. Joseph F. Lamb. Saint Louis: Stark Music Co., 1916.

Topsy-Turvy Two-Step. L. V. Gustin. Detroit: Whitney-Warner Publishing Co., 1899.

Topsy Two Step. Libbie Erickson. Arranged by William B. Fassbinder. Chicago: W. C. Polla Co., 1904.

A Totally Different Rag. May Aufderheide. Indianapolis: J. H. Aufderheide & Co., 1910.

Treemonisha: Opera in Three Acts. Scott Joplin. New York: Scott Joplin Music Publishing Co., 1911.

Très Moutarde (Too Much Mustard). Cecil Macklin. New York: Edward Schuberth & Co., 1911.

Trixy Two Step. Libbie Erickson. Arranged by William B. Fassbinder. Chicago: W. C. Polla Co., 1904.

Troubadour Rag. James Scott. Saint Louis: Stark Music Co., 1919.

Troublesome Ivories. Eubie Blake. Published in *Giants of Ragtime* (New York: Edward B. Marks Music Corp., 1971), pp. 28–33.

True Love: Syncopated Waltz. F. Henri Klickmann. Chicago: Frank K. Root, 1913.

Try and Play It. Phil Ohman. New York: Richmond-Robbins, 1922.

Turkey in the Straw (song). See *Zip Coon.*

Turkey in the Straw: A Rag Time Fantasy. Otto Bonnell. New York: Leo Feist, 1899.

Tutor for the Banjo (for banjo). Otto Langey. Philadelphia: Harry Coleman, 1894.

12th Street Rag. Euday L. Bowman. Fort Worth, Texas: Euday L. Bowman, 1914.

Twilight Rag. James P. Johnson. Not copyrighted or published. Issued on piano roll: Metro–Art 203274, November 1917.

Uncle Joe's Cake Dance (for banjo). C. S. Patty. Published in *S. S. Stewart's Banjo and Guitar Journal* 7, no. 4 (October–November 1890), p. 8.

Under the Anheuser Bush (song). Words: Andrew B. Sterling; music: Harry Von Tilzer. New York: Harry Von Tilzer Music Publishing Co., 1903.

Under the Bamboo Tree (song). Words: James Weldon Johnson; music: Bob Cole and J. Rosamond Johnson. New York: Jos. W. Stern & Co., 1902.

Under the Jungle Moon (song). Words: Edward Madden; music: Max Hoffman. New York: Rogers Bros. Music Publishing Co., 1907.

Under the Matzos Tree (song). Fred Fischer. New York: Fred Fischer Music Publishing Co., 1907.

Under the Silv'ry Congo Moon (song). Lawrence B. O'Connor. Boston: Walter Jacobs, 1907.

Under the Yum Yum Tree (song). Words: Andrew B. Sterling; music: Harry Von Tilzer. New York: Harry Von Tilzer Music Publishing Co., 1910.

Valse Parisienne. Lee Roberts. Fort Wayne, Indiana: Will A. Young, 1912.

Victory March. Adaline Shepherd. Chicago: National Music Co., 1908.

Victory Rag. James Scott. Saint Louis: Stark Music Co., 1921.

Waiting for the Robert E. Lee (song). Words: L. Wolfe Gilbert; music: Lewis F. Muir. New York: F. A. Mills, 1912.

Walk Baby Walk or The Pickaninny Cake Walker. Theo. C. Metz. New York: Primrose & Rose, 1897.

Wall Street Rag. Scott Joplin. New York: Seminary Music Co., 1909.

A Warm Reception. Bert R. Anthony. Arranged for orchestra by M. I. Brazil. Fall River, Massachusetts: G. H. Munroe & Co., 1899.

A Warm Reception (for banjo). Vess Ossman. London: Clifford Essex Co., [n.d.]. Recorded by Vess Ossman in 1900 on Edison cylinder 7452. Also published in *BMG* 3, no. 30 (March 1906), p. 89.

The Washington Post: March. John Philip Sousa. Philadelphia: Harry Coleman, 1889.

Weary Blues. Artie Matthews. Saint Louis: Stark Music Co., 1915.

Weeping Willow: Ragtime Two Step. Scott Joplin. Saint Louis: Val A. Reis Music Co., 1903.

What You Goin' To Do When the Rent Comes 'Round? (Rufus Rastus Johnson Brown) (song). Words: Andrew B. Sterling; music: Harry Von Tilzer. New York: Harry Von Tilzer Music Publishing Co., 1905.

When It's Night Time in Dixieland (song). Irving Berlin. New York: Waterson, Berlin & Snyder Co., 1914.

When Ragtime Rosie Ragged the Rosary (song). Words: Edgar Leslie; music: Lewis F. Muir. New York: F. A. Mills, 1911.

Whipping the Keys. Sam Goold. New York: Stark & Cowan, 1923.

Whistling Rufus. Kerry Mills. New York: F. A. Mills, 1899.

The Whitewash Man. Jean Schwartz. New York: Cohan and Harris Publishing Co., 1908.

Who'll Win de Cake Tonight? Ethiopian Schottische. Walter Hawley. New York: George L. Spaulding, 1897.

"Wiggy Waggy" Rag. Mattie Harl Burgess. Arranged by William H. Tyers. New York: Leo Feist, 1910.

Wild Cherries Rag. Ted Snyder. New York: Ted Snyder Co., 1908.

Wild Cherries: That Cooney, Spooney Rag (song). Words: Irving Berlin; music: Ted Snyder. New York: Ted Snyder Co., 1909.

Wild Man Blues. Ferdinand "Jelly Roll" Morton and Louis Armstrong. Chicago: Melrose Bros. Music Co., 1927.

Wippin' the Ivories. Henry Lange. New York: Waterson, Berlin & Snyder Co., 1923.

Wireless Rag. Adaline Shepherd. Chicago: Standard Music Publishing Co., 1909.

Wolverine Blues. Ferdinand "Jelly Roll" Morton. Chicago: Melrose Bros. Music Co., 1923.

Woody's Rag. Woody Guthre. © 1957 by Sanga Music, [n.p.].

The Yellow Dog Rag (song). W. C. Handy. Memphis: Pace & Handy Music Co., 1914.

You Tell 'Em Ivories. Zez Confrey. New York: Jack Mills, Inc., 1921.

You're in the Right Church, But the Wrong Pew (song). Words: Cecil Mack; music: Chris Smith. New York: The Gotham-Attucks Music Co., 1908.

You've Been a Good Old Wagon But You've Done Broke Down (song). Ben Harney. Louisville: Bruner Greenup, 1895. Rev. version, New York: M. Witmark & Sons, 1896.

Zez Confrey's Modern Course in Novelty Piano Playing. Zez Confrey. New York: Jack Mills, Inc., 1923.

Zip Coon (song). Authorship claimed by George Washington Dixon, and also by Bob Farrell and George Nichols. First published in 1834 by five different publishers.

Zu Zu Rag. Max E. Fischler. New York: The John Franklin Music Co., 1916.

Select Bibliography

This is a select bibliography of ragtime literature primarily published as books or periodical articles. Some book chapters on ragtime are included, but generally only when the entire chapters concern ragtime. Therefore, the reader will want also to consult histories of jazz, popular song, and American music, for many of these include ragtime. He or she should also check music reference works, especially those in jazz and popular music. The reader may also wish to refer to general reference works, including encyclopedias, periodical indexes, and biographical dictionaries.

Entries are organized into the following categories:

General Reference
Ragtime in General
Sources and Origins of Ragtime
Early Comment
Musical Description/Analysis
Ragtime and Region
Ragtime Repertory
Ragtime Piano Performance
Orchestrated Ragtime
Ragtime Guitar
Ragtime Recordings
Ragtime Piano Rolls
Ragtime and Classical Music
Ragtime Festivals and Concerts
Ragtime Revivals
Ragtime Figures

General Reference

ASCAP Biographical Dictionary. 4th ed. New York: Bowker, 1980. 589 pp.

de Lerma, Dominique-René. *Bibliography of Afro-American Music; Volume 2: Afro-American Idioms*. The Greenwood Encyclopedia of Black Music. Westport, Conn.: Greenwood Press, 1982. 220 pp.

Hefele, Bernhard. *Jazz Bibliography: International Literature on Jazz, Blues, Spirituals, Gospel and Ragtime Music*. Archon, Conn.: Shoe String Press, 1981. 368 pp.

Jablonski, Edward. *The Encyclopedia of American Music*. Garden City, N.Y.: Doubleday, 1981. 629 pp.

Sadie, Stanley, ed. *The New Grove Dictionary of Music and Musicians*. 20 vols. London: Macmillan, 1980. Passim.

Skowronski, JoAnn. *Black Music in America: A Bibliography*. Metuchen, N.J.: Scarecrow Press, 1981. 733 pp.

Southern, Eileen. *Biographical Dictionary of Afro-American and African Musicians*. The Greenwood Encyclopedia of Black Music. Westport, Conn.: Greenwood Press, 1982. 479 pp.

Ragtime in General

Ashforth, Bob. "On Classic Ragtime." *Ragtimer*, March–April 1970, p. 7.

Berlin, Edward A. "Piano Ragtime: A Musical and Cultural Study." Ph.D. diss., City University of New York, 1976. 432 pp.

———. *Ragtime: A Musical and Cultural History*. Berkeley and Los Angeles: University of California Press, 1980. 248 pp.

———. "Ragtime and Improvised Piano: Another View." *Journal of Jazz Studies* 4, no. 2 (1977): 4–10.

Bessom, Malcolm E. "From Piano Thumping to the Concert Stage: The Story of Ragtime." *Music Educators Journal* 59 (April 1973):

53-56.

Blesh, Rudi. "Ragtime Revaluated." *Playback* 2 (May 1949): 5-6.

———, and Harriet Janis. *They All Played Ragtime*. New York: Alfred A. Knopf, 1950; 4th ed., rev. New York: Oak Publications, 1971. 347 pp.

Borneman, Ernest. "From Minstrelsy to Jazz." *Record Changer*, January 1945, p. 3.

Brown, Sterling. "Negro Producers of Ragtime." In *The Negro in Music and Art*, edited by Lindsay Patterson, pp. 49-50. International Library of Negro Life and History, vol. 16. New York: Publishers Co., 1967.

Campbell, S. Brunson. "Early Great White Ragtime Composers and Pianists." *Jazz Journal* 2 (May 1949): 11-12.

———. "Looking Backwards: Round the 'Houses.'" *Jazz Journal* 2 (June 1949): 9-10.

———. "More on Ragtime." *Jazz Journal* 4 (May 1951): 4.

———. "Ragtime." *Jazz Journal* 2 (April 1949): 9-10. Reprinted in *Ragtime Society* 2 (October 1963): [5-6].

Carew, Roy J. "Assorted Rags." *Record Changer* 7 (February 1949): 6. Reprinted in *Ragtime Society* 3 (November 1964): 75.

———. "Euphonic Sounds." *Record Changer* 4 (December 1945): 40-41.

———. "Historic Corner." *Jazz Forum*, no. 4 (April 1947): 9.

———. "Hodge Podge." *Jazz Report* 2 (September 1961): 5-7.

———. "New Orleans Recollections." *Record Changer*, February 1943, pp. 28-29. Reprinted in *Record Changer* 6 (July 1947): 9; reprinted in *Ragtime Society* 3 (March 1964): 22.

———. "New Orleans Recollections." *Record Changer* 7 (December 1948): 12. Reprinted in *Ragtime Society* 3 (May 1964): 36.

———. "Random Recollections." *Jazz Forum*, no. 3 (January 1947): 1-2.

———. "Those Days are Not Gone Forever." *Playback* 2 (July 1949): 6ff.

Charters, Ann. *The Ragtime Songbook*. New York: Oak Publications, 1965. 112 pp.

Charters, Samuel. "Ragtime: Pristine and Pre-Sting." *New York Magazine*, 15 July 1974, p. 57.

Chase, Gilbert. "The Rise of Ragtime." Chapter 21 in *America's Music: From the Pilgrims to the Present*, pp. 429-47. 2nd ed., rev. New York, Toronto, London, and Sydney: McGraw-Hill, 1966.

Cole, Russ. Untitled letter. *Ragtime Society* 4 (March-April 1965): 19-20.

Collier, James Lincoln. "Scott Joplin and the Ragtime Craze." In *The Making of Jazz: A Comprehensive History*, pp. 43-53. Boston: Houghton Mifflin, 1978.

David, John R. "Tragedy in Ragtime: Black Folktales from St. Louis." Ph.D. diss., Saint Louis University, 1976. 323 pp.

Davis, Charles B., Jr. *Ragtime Piano Music in Print*. Midway Park, N.C.: Charles B. Davis, Jr., 1982. 32 pp.

Dennison, Sam. *Scandalize My Name: Black Imagery in American Popular Music*. New York: Garland Publishing, 1982. 608 pp.

Dickinson, Peter. "The Achievement of Ragtime: An Introductory Study with Some Implications for British Research in Popular Music." *Proceedings of the Royal Musical Association* 105 (1978-79): 63-76.

Dexter, D. "Ragtime Future is with Femmes, Morath Says." *Billboard* 89 (2 July 1977): 42f.

Dykstra, Brian. "Should Your Foot Tap at a Piano Recital?" *Clavier* 11 (December 1972): 18-20.

Ewen, David. "'Oh, that beautiful rag.'" In *The Life and Death of Tin Pan Alley: The Golden Age of American Popular Music*, pp. 168-78. New York: Funk and Wagnalls, 1964.

Featherstone, J. G. "Ragtime: A Comment." *Storyville*, no. 11 (June-July 1967): 29-30.

Flowitt, Dave. "Ragtime in Retrospect." *Storyville*, no. 36 (1 August 1971): 203-6.

Fox, Charles. "Ragtime Revisited." *Jazz & Blues* 2 (January 1973): 4-5.

Franks, Percy. Untitled letter. *Ragtime Review* 4 (January 1965): 4.

———. Untitled letter. *Ragtimer*, January-February 1971, p. 12.

Gammond, Peter. *Scott Joplin and the Ragtime Era*. New York: St. Martin's Press, 1975. 223 pp.

Goldberg, Isaac. "The Rise of Tin Pan Alley: Ragtime." Chapter 6 in *Tin Pan Alley: A Chronicle of American Popular Music*, pp. 139-77. With a supplement by Edward Jablonski. New York: Ungar, 1961.

Harding, Walter N. H. Untitled letter. *Ragtime Society* 3 (April 1964): 24-25.

Hasse, John Edward. "The Study of Ragtime: A Review and a Preview." In *Discourse in Ethnomusicology: Essays in Honor of George List*, edited by Caroline Card, John Hasse, Roberta Singer, and Ruth M. Stone, pp. 161-90. Bloomington: Indiana University Ethnomusicology Publications Group, 1978.

Hayes, C. "Joplin Boosts Piano Sales." *Melody Maker* 49 (20 April 1974): 47.

Jasen, David A. "Another Look at Ragtime." *Rag Times* 3 (August-September 1969): 6-7.

———. "Ragtime—A Re-Evaluation." *Ragtimer* 6, nos. 5-6 (1967): 26-28. Reprinted in *Jazz Journal* 21 (April 1968): 22-23.

———. "Ragtime Explained." *Storyville*, no. 37 (October-November 1971): 4-7.

_____, and Trebor Jay Tichenor. *Rags and Ragtime: A Musical History*. New York: Seabury Press, 1978. 310 pp.

Kay, George W. "Ragged but Right." *Record Changer* 9 (March 1950): 5. Reprinted in *Ragtime Society* 3 (January 1964): 7–8.

Kramer, Karl. "Influence of Ragtime on Stage Music." *Ragtime Society* 4 (January 1965): 4–5.

Marks, Edward B. *They All Sang: From Tony Pastor to Rudy Vallee*. As told to Abbott J. Liebling. New York: Viking Press, 1934. 321 pp.

McNeil, W. K. "Syncopated Slander: The 'Coon Song,' 1890–1900." *Keystone Folklore Quarterly* 17 (Summer 1972), 63–82.

Mitchell, Bill. "Those Ragtime Years." *Jazz Report* 1 (June 1961).

Møldrup, Erik. *Ragtime*. Århus, Denmark: Publimus, 1975. 141 pp. Text in Danish.

Morath, Max. "Any Rags Today?" *Music Journal Magazine* 18 (October 1960): 76–77. Reprinted as Introduction to *34 Ragtime Jazz Classics*. New York: Edwin H. Morris, Melrose Music, 1964.

_____. "First There Was Ragtime." *Jazz Report* 2 (January 1962): 8–9.

_____. "Ragtime—Folk Music of the City." *Music Journal* 22 (November 1964): 29–30, 64–65.

"'Morath: 'Ragtime Was for Women.'" *Kansas City* (Missouri) *Star*, 12 February 1978, p. 25H.

Norris, John. "They Still Play Ragtime." *Down Beat* 35 (17 October 1968): 7, 41.

Pearsall, Ronald. "The Coming of Ragtime." In *Edwardian Popular Music*, pp. 181–92. Rutherford, New Jersey: Fairleigh Dickinson University Press, 1975.

Raichelson, Richard. "Ragtime: Its Folk Roots and Influence on American Popular Music." Paper presented at the Annual Meeting of the American Folklore Society, Salt Lake City, Utah, 1978. 14 pp.

"Ragtime." *Jazz Forum*, no. 4 (April 1947): 5–7.

"Ragtime." *Record Changer* 10 (July–August 1951): 12–13.

"Ragtime." *Ragtime Review* 1 (January 1962): 2.

"The Ragtime Society." *Musicgram* 1 (October 1963): 51–53.

"Ragtime Wins Approval in USSR." *Ragtimer*, January–February 1976, p. 11.

Rogers, Charles Payne. "Ragtime." *Jazz* 1 (June 1942): 10–12. Reprinted in *Ragtimer* 2 (March 1963): 3–4.

_____. "Ragtime." *Jazz Forum*, no. 4 (April 1947): 5–8.

Rose, F. "Good Rag Times." *Ragtimer*, March–April 1977, pp. 9–11.

Rose, Frank. "These Rag Times Are Back Again." *Zoo World*, no. 56 (11 April 1974): 17–19.

Rusch, Robert D. "Rusch on Ragtime." *Jazz Journal* 26 (April 1973): 22–23.

Saal, Hubert. "Glad Rags." *Newsweek*, 5 August 1974.

Sampson, Henry T. *Blacks in Blackface: A Source Book on Early Black Musical Shows*. Metuchen, N.J.: Scarecrow Press, 1980.

Sandner, W. "Ragtime—Zur Geschichte einer nationalen amerikanischen Musik." *Musik und Bildung* 8 (June 1976): 314–20.

Schafer, William J. "'Fizz Water': Ragtime by Eubie Blake, Luckey Roberts, and James P. Johnson." *Mississippi Rag* 3 (December 1975): 1–2.

_____. "Ragtime: Changing White Views of Black Music." *Theology Today* 31 (January 1975): 346–49.

_____, and Johannes Reidel, with assistance from Michael Polad and Richard Thompson. *The Art of Ragtime: Form and Meaning of an Original Black American Art*. Baton Rouge: Louisiana State University Press, 1973. 249 pp.

Shapiro, Elliott. "'Ragtime' USA." *Notes* 8 (June 1951): 457–70.

Shapiro, Richard, and Esther Mayesh Shapiro. *Minstrel Man: A Novel from Their Teleplay by Richard Shapiro and Esther Mayesh Shapiro*. New York: Popular Library, 1976. 189 pp.

Shaw, Arnold. "The Scott Joplin Renaissance; Ragtime: The Missing Link in Pop and Jazz." *High Fidelity* 22 (October 1972): 81–83.

Simms, Bartlett D., and Ernest Borneman. "Ragtime: History and Analysis." *Record Changer* 4 (October 1945): 4–9.

Stearns, Marshall W. "Ragtime." In *The Story of Jazz*, pp. 104–10. New York: Oxford University Press, 1956.

Suthern, Orrin Clayton II. "Minstrelsy and Popular Culture." In *Remus, Rastus, Revolution*, edited by Marshall Fishwick, pp. 57–72. Bowling Green, Ohio: Bowling Green University Press, [1971?].

Thompson, Kay C. "More on Ragtime." *Record Changer* 8 (October 1949): 9–10.

_____. "Ragtime Vs. The Blues." *Jazz Journal* 3 (November 1950): 2–3.

Tirro, Frank. "Ragtime." Chapter 4 in *Jazz: A History*, pp. 88–113. New York: W. W. Norton, 1977.

Traill, Sinclair. "Jig-Piano or Ragtime—It Still Has a Beat." *Melody Maker* 26 (23 December 1950): 654–58.

Tudor, Dean. "Play That Ol' Ragtime Revival." *Library Journal/School Library Journal Previews* 4 (December 1972): 5–17.

Turner, Peter. "Introduction to Ragtime."

Footnote 1, no. 3 (1970): 6-8; no. 4 (1970): 4-5.

Waldo, Terry. *This is Ragtime.* New York: Hawthorn Books, 1976. 244 pp. Reprint. New York: Da Capo, 1984.

Walker, E. S. "Early Jazz/Ragtime." *Jazz Monthly*, no. 186 (August 1970): 28.

Waterman, Guy, "Ragtime." In *Jazz*, edited by Nat Hentoff and Albert J. McCarthy, pp. 34-58. New York: Rinehart, 1959. Reprint. New York: Da Capo Press, 1974.

———. "A Survey of Ragtime." *Record Changer* 14, no. 7 [ca. 1955-56]: 7-9. Reprinted in *The Art of Jazz*, edited by Martin Williams, pp. 11-18. New York: Oxford University Press, 1959.

Whitcomb, Ian. "America's Sin." *Rag Times* 7 (November 1963): 3.

———. "Ragtime." In *After the Ball: Pop Music from Rag to Rock*, pp. 16-40. New York: Simon & Schuster, 1973.

White, John Alfred. "A Dialogue on Ragtime." *Mississippi Rag* 1 (August 1974): 2-4.

Wilford, Charles. "Ragtime: An Excavation." *Piano Jazz*, no. 2 (1945): 9-12. Reprinted in *Ragtime Society* 1 (December 1962): [3]; (January 1963): [4]; 2 (February 1963): [2]; (March 1963): [5].

———. "Ragtime Classics: Ten Piano Rags." *Jazz Journal* 30 (February 1977): 40.

Williams, Martin. "The Same Old Story." *Down Beat*, 7 September 1967, 14.

Willis, D. K. "Soviets Sample Ragtime Rhythm." *Christian Science Monitor* 70 (June 26, 1978): 2.

Willmorth, N. E. "Cakewalks." *Rag Times* 9 (July 1975): 6-7.

Witmark, Isidore, and Isaac Goldberg. *From Ragtime to Swingtime: The Story of the House of Witmark.* New York: Furman, 1939. Reprint. New York: Da Capo Press, 1976. 480 pp.

Zimmerman, Dick. "The Original Maple Leaf Club." *Rag Times* 8 (May 1974): 3.

Sources and Origins of Ragtime

"Again the Origin of Ragtime." *Melody* 2 (December 1918): 4.

Cable, George W. "The Dance in the Place Congo." *Century Magazine*, February 1886, 517-32.

"The Cake Walk." *New York Times*, 28 February 1892, 4.

"Cake Walk Broken Up." *New York Times*, 13 February 1898, 2.

"The Cake Walk A 'Fake' Walk." *New York Times*, 28 February 1892, 5.

"The Cake Walk in Vienna." *New York Times*, 1 February 1903, 5.

"Cakewalk Trust the Latest." *New York Times*, 26 November 1900, 3.

Campbell, S. Brunson. "Ragtime Begins." *Record Changer* 7 (March 1948): 8, 18; reprinted in *Ragtime Society* 2 (November 1963): 4-5.

Cook, Will Marion. "Clorindy, the Origin of the Cakewalk." *Theatre Arts* 31 (September 1947): 61-65; reprinted in *Readings in Black American Music*, edited by Eileen Southern, pp. 217-23. New York: W. W. Norton, 1971.

"Fun at the Cake Walk." *New York Times*, 4 May 1895, 6.

Hasse, John Edward. "The Genesis of a Musical Genre: Classic Ragtime." Paper presented at the annual meeting of the Society for Ethnomusicology, Philadelphia, 12 November 1976. 14 pp.

Kern, F. "The Roots of Classical Ragtime." *Ragtimer*, May-June 1976, 9-12.

Narodny, Ivan. "The Birth Processes of Ragtime." *Musical America* 17 (29 March 1913): 27.

Nathan, Hans. "Early Banjo Tunes and American Syncopation." *Musical Quarterly* 42 (October 1956): 455-72.

"An Old-Time Cake Walk." *New York Times*, 2 March 1895, 6.

"The Origin of Rag Time." *Metronome* 17 (August 1901): 7.

"Origin of Rag Time." *Musician* 6 (September 1901): 227.

"The Origin of Ragtime." *New York Times*, 23 March 1924, section 9, 2.

"Questions and Answers." *Etude* 16 (October 1898): 285.

"Questions and Answers." *Etude* 18 (February 1900): 52.

Rosenfeld, Monroe H. "'Ragtime'—A Musical Mystery: What It Is and Its Origin." *Tuneful Yankee* 1 (January 1917): 9-10. Reprinted in *Rag Times* 6 (March 1973): 6-7.

Thacker, Eric. "Gottschalk and a Prelude to Jazz." *Jazz & Blues* 2 (March 1973): 10-12, 17.

———. "Ragtime Roots: African and American Minstrels." *Jazz & Blues* 3 (December 1973): 4-6.

———. "Ragtime Roots: The Classical Succession." *Jazz & Blues* 3 (November 1973): 6-7.

Thompson, Kay C. "Early Cakewalks: The Roots of Ragtime." *Jazz Journal* 5 (March 1952): 14-15; reprinted in *Ragtime Society* 3, (February 1964): 7-8.

———. "The Pre-History of Ragtime." *Ragtimer* 6, no. 3 (1967): 16-19.

"Walking for a Cake." *New York Times*, 7 February 1897, 2.

Early Comment

For a more complete listing, see the bibliography in Edward A. Berlin, *Ragtime: A Musical and Cultural History* (Berkeley and Los Angeles: University of California Press, 1980), pp. 215–226.

"About 'Ragtime.'" *Ragtime Review* 2 (August 1916): 6.

"American Music and Ragtime." *Music Trade Review* 37 (3 October 1908): 8.

"Another Defender of Ragtime." *Ragtime Review* 1 (April 1915): 3.

Autolycus [pseud.]. "'Rag-time' on Parnassus." *Musical Opinion* 36 (February 1913): 328–29.

Bickford, Myron A. "Something about Ragtime." *Cadenza* 20 (September 1913): 13; (November 1913): 10–11.

Bickford, Zarh Myron. "Ragtime as an Introduction and Aid to Better Music." *Melody* 2 (January 1918): 7.

Buchanan, Charles L. "The National Music Fallacy: Is American Music to Rest on a Foundation of Ragtime and Jazz?" *Arts and Decoration* 20 (February 1924): 26, 62.

Cadman, Charles Wakefield. "Cadman on 'Ragtime.'" *Musical Courier* 69 (12 August 1914): 31.

"Canon Assails Our New Dances." *New York Times*, 25 August 1913, 3.

"Canon Newboldt's Warning." *New York Times*, 26 August 1913, 8.

"'Coon Songs' on the Wane." *American Musician and Art Journal* 22 (12 June 1906): 26a.

"Crime of Ragtime." *Ragtime Review* 2 (May 1916): 2.

"Der Cake Walk." *Illustrierte Zeitung* (Leipzig), 5 February 1903, 202–03.

Christensen, Axel. "Chicago Syncopations: An Open Letter to Orpheus on Ragtime." *Melody* 3 (January 1919): 21.

———. "Chicago Syncopations: Ragtime Demoralizing." *Melody* 2 (November 1918): 22.

———. "Popular Music an Absolute Necessity." *Melody* 2 (October 1918): 6.

———. "The Popularity of Ragtime." *Christensen's Ragtime Review* 1 (December 1914): 1–2. Reprinted in *Melody* 2 (January 1918): 8.

———. "Ragtime: A Few Remarks in Its Favor." *Christensen's Ragtime Review* 1 (December 1914): 20.

———. "Ragtime Pianists I Have Known." *Melody* 2 (December 1918): 5.

———. "A Talk on Ragtime." *Melody* 2 (September 1918): 2. Reprinted in *Rag Times* 9 (November 1975): 4–5.

"Concerning Ragtime." *Musical Monitor* 8 (September 1919): 619.

Converse, C. Crozat. "Rag-Time Music." *Etude* 17 (June 1899): 185; (August 1899): 256.

"'Coon Songs' on the Wane." *American Musician and Art Journal* 22 (12 June 1906): 26a.

Curtis, Natalie. "The Music America Buys." *Craftsman* 23 (January 1913): 390–400.

———. "The Negro's Contribution to the Music of America: The Larger Opportunity of the Colored Man of Today." *Craftsman* 23 (15 March 1913): 660–69.

"Ducasse Uses Ragtime in New Tone Poem." *Musical America* 17 (10 March 1923): 15.

[Editorial]. *American Musician and Art Journal* 26 (13 August 1910): 19.

"Editorials." *New Music Review and Church Music Review* 22 (December 1923): 542; 22 (October 1924): 464.

"The Ethics of Ragtime." *Jacobs' Orchestra Monthly* 3 (August 1912): 27–29.

"Ethics of Ragtime." *Literary Digest*, 10 August 1912, 225.

Farjeon, Harry. "Rag-Time." *Musical Times and Singing-Class Circular* 65 (1 September 1924): 795–97. Reprinted in *New Music Review* 23 (November 1924): 513–15.

Farwell, Arthur. "Apaches, Mollycoddles and Highbrows." *Musical America* 16 (17 August 1912): 2.

———. "The Popular Song Bugaboo." *Musical America* 16 (6 July 1912): 2.

———. "The Popular Song Bugaboo: No. 2." *Musical America* 16 (27 July 1912): 2.

———. "Where Professors and Socialists Fail to Understand Music." *Musical America* 16 (31 August 1912): 26–27.

Gardner, Carl E. "Ragging and Jazzing." *Metronome* 35 (October–November 1919): 34.

Gates, W. F. "Ethiopian Syncopations—The Decline of Ragtime." *Musician* 7 (October 1902): 341.

Gleeson, W. T. "Answering the Critics." *Ragtime Review* 3 (March 1917): 22–23. Reprinted in *Melody* 3 (February 1919): 22–23; reprinted in *Ragtimer*, November–December 1968, pp. 4–5.

Gluck, Alma. "America and Good Music." *Musical Courier* 66 (28 May 1913): 22–23.

Goodrich, A. J. "Syncopated Rhythm Vs. 'Rag-Time.'" *Musician* 6 (November 1901): 336.

Gordon, Philip. "Ragtime, The Folk Song and the Music Teacher." *Musical Observer*, November 1912. Reprinted in *Rag Times* 6 (September 1972): 12–13; reprinted in *Ragtimer*, May–June 1973, pp. 8–10.

Goodrich, A. J. "Syncopated Rhythm Vs. 'Rag-Time.'" *Musician* 6 (November 1901): 336.

Hanson, Bessie. "Ragtime, the American National Music." *Ragtime Review* 1 (March 1915): 8.

Henderson, W. J. "Ragtime, Jazz, and High Art." *Scribner's Magazine,* February 1925, 200–203.

Hubbard, W. L. "A Hopeful View of the Ragtime Roll." *Musician* 25 (August 1920): 6.

Hubbs, Harold. "What is Ragtime?" *Outlook* 27 (February 1918): 345.

Hughes, Rupert. "A Eulogy of Rag-Time." *Musical Record,* no. 447 (1 April 1899): 158.

―――――. "Will Ragtime Turn to Symphonic Poems?" *Etude* 38 (May 1920): 305.

Kaufman, Philip. "Why Ragtime Benefits the Classical Scholar." *Ragtime Review* 1 (April 1915): 2.

Kenilworth, Walter Winston. "Demoralizing Rag Time Music." *Musical Courier* 66 (28 May 1913): 22–23.

Kramer, W. Walter. "Extols Ragtime Article." *New Republic* 5 (4 December 1915): 122.

Kühl, Gustav. "Rag Time." *Die Musik* 1 (August 1902): 1972–76. Reprinted as "The Musical Possibilities of Ragtime," translated by Gustav Saenger. *Metronome* 19 (March 1903): 11; (April 1903): 8.

Kussel, Phil. "Phil Kussel's Retort." *Music Trades,* 1 February 1902.

Lanseer-MacKenzie, J. "Ragtime as National Music." *Musical Monitor* 8 (May 1919): 401–02.

Liebling, Leonard. "The Crime of Ragtime." *Musical Courier* 72 (20 January 1916): 21–22.

"Martin Ballmann's Rag-Time Philosophy." *American Musician and Art Journal* 28 (28 September 1912): 5.

Mason, Daniel Gregory. "Concerning Ragtime." *New Music Review and Church Music Review* 17 (March 1918): 112–16.

―――――. "Folk-Song and American Music (A Plea for the Unpopular Point of View)." *Musical Quarterly* 4 (July 1918): 324, 337.

―――――. "Prefers Demonstration to Cheers." *New Republic* 5 (4 December 1915): 122.

Miller, Kelly. "Artistic Gifts of the Negro." *Voice of the Negro* 3 (April 1906): 252–57.

"Mission of Popular Music." *American Musician and Art Journal* 26 (11 March 1910): 23.

Moderwell, Hiram K. "Ragtime." *New Republic,* 16 October 1915, p. 286.

―――――. "Two Views of Ragtime, I, 'A Modest Proposal.'" *Seven Arts* 2 (July 1917): 368, 370, 375.

Muck, Karl. "The Music of Democracy." *Craftsman,* December 1915, p. 227.

"Music in America." *New York Times,* 9 October 1911, p. 10.

"Music of Today." *American Musician and Art Journal* 26 (25 March 1910): 23.

"Musical Impurity." *Etude* 18 (January 1900): 16.

"Must Avoid Ragtime." *Musical Courier* 69 (12 August 1914): 10.

Narodny, Ivan. "The Birth Processes of Ragtime." *Musical America* 17 (29 March 1913): 27.

Oehmler, Leo. "Ragtime: A Pernicious Evil and Enemy of True Art." *Musical Observer* 11 (September 1914): 15.

"Our Musical Condition." *Negro Musical Journal* 1 (March 1903): 137–38.

Perry, Edward Baxter. "Ragging Good Music." *Etude* 36 (January 1918): 372.

"Philosophizing Rag-Time." *Literary Digest* 46 (15 March 1913): 574–75.

"Psychological and Socialistic Aspects of the Problems of Ragtime." *Musical America* 16 (13 August 1912): 26–27. Includes articles by Arthur Farwell, Rudolph von Liebich, and Alexander Thompson.

"Ragtime." *Ragtime Review* 2 (May 1916): 4.

"Rag-Time." *Times* (London), 8 February 1913, p. 11.

"Ragtime at the Indianapolis Fair." *Christensen's Ragtime Review* 1 (August 1915): 14.

"A Ragtime Communication." *Musical Courier* 40 (30 May 1900): 20.

"Rag-Time Hurts Classics." *American Musician and Art Journal* 28 (13 July 1912): 3.

"Rag-Time Loses Favor." *American Musician and Art Journal* 28 (27 July 1912): 11.

"Ragtime Music and Directoire Gowns Flayed." *Indianapolis Freeman,* 21 November 1908.

"'Ragtime—No! Never!'" *Ragtime Review,* March 1915, p. 6.

"The Ragtime Rage." *Musical Courier* 40 (23 May 1900): 20.

"Ragtime Symphony Played . . ." *Ragtime Review* 1 (April 1915): 3.

"A Rag-Time Victory." *Brainard's Musical* 2 (November 1900): 31.

"Ragtime Wrangling." *Literary Digest* 52 (8 January 1916): 68–70.

"Requiescat, Ragtime!" *American Musician and Art Journal* 26 (13 August 1910): 19.

Sachs-Hirsch, Herbert. "Dangers That Lie in Ragtime." *Musical America* 16 (21 September 1912): 8.

Scoggins, Charles H. "The Ragtime Menace." *Musical Progress* 2 (April 1914): 3–4.

"Scores of Popular Songs Coming Out." *American Musician and Art Journal* 23 (14 March 1907): 26.

"Sees National Music Created by Ragtime." *New York Times,* 9 February 1913, section 4, p. 5.

Sherlock, Charles Reginald. "From Breakdown to Ragtime." *Cosmopolitan,* October 1901, 631–39.

"Songs without History." *American Musician and Art Journal* 26 (22 April 1910): 23.

Stark, John. "Ragtime." *Intermezzo* 1 (April

1905): [2].

———. "Respectability of Ragtime." *Christensen's Ragtime Review* 2 (March 1916): 5–6.

"Syncopated Music Not Negro Music." *Music Trade Review* 48 (20 February 1909): 15.

"'To Jazz' or 'To Rag.'" *Literary Digest* 73 (6 May 1922): 37.

Toye, Francis. "Ragtime: The New Tarantism." *English Review* 13 (March 1913): 654–58.

Visscher, William Lightfoot. "Syncopation." *Christensen's Ragtime Review* 1 (August 1915): 5.

Walker, George W. "The Real 'Coon' on the American Stage." *Theatre* 6 (August 1906): 224 and i–ii of *Theatre Magazine Advertiser.*

"War on Ragtime." *American Musician* 5 (July 1901): 4.

Weld, Arthur. "The Invasion of Vulgarity in Music." *Etude* 17 (February 1899): 52.

"What Rags Will Live Forever?" *Christensen's Ragtime Review* 1 (October 1915): 6.

"Why Ragtime Is the True Music of 'Hustlers.'" *Christensen's Ragtime Review* 1 (December 1914): 3–4.

Wise, C. Stanley. "'American Music is True Art,' Says Stravinsky." *New York Tribune*, 16 January 1916, section 5, 3.

Musical Description/Analysis

Bolcom, William. "Review Essay: Ragtime Revival; *The Collected Works of Scott Joplin.*" *Yearbook for Inter-American Musical Research* 8 (1972): 147–61.

Charters, A. R. Danberg. "Negro Folk Elements in Classic Ragtime." *Ethnomusicology* 5 (September 1961): 174–83. Reprinted in *Ragtime Review* 4 (July 1965): 7–12.

Doerschuk, Bob. "Two Views of Eubie Blake's Piano Style: Terry Waldo & William Bolcom." *Contemporary Keyboard* 8 (December 1982): 59–60, 62, 70. Reprinted in *The Ragtimer*, January–February 1983.

Evans, David. "Folk Elements in American Dance Music, Ragtime, and Jazz." *Journal of American Folklore* 92 (July 1979): 365–69.

Floyd, Samuel A., Jr. and Marsha J. Reisser. "Social Dance Music of Black Composers in the Nineteenth Century and the Emergence of Classic Ragtime." *Black Perspective in Music* 8 (Fall 1980): 161–93.

Gillis, Frank. "Hot Rhythm in Piano Ragtime." In *Music in the Americas*, edited by George List and Juan Orrego-Salas, pp. 91–104. Bloomington: Indiana University Research Center in Anthropology, Folklore, and Linguistics, 1967.

Grossman, Stefan. "Stefan Grossman on Blind Blake's Music." *Guitar Player* 8 (July 1974): 48.

Gushee, Lawrence. "Ragtime Instrumental Style." Paper presented at the Annual Meeting of the Society for Ethnomusicology, Saint Louis, Missouri, 28 October 1978.

Hebert, Rubye Nell. "A Study of the Composition and Performance of Scott Joplin's Opera *Treemonisha.*" D.M.A. dissertation, Ohio State University, 1976.

Howard, Laura Pratt. "Ragtime." Master of Music thesis, Eastman School of Music, University of Rochester, 1942. 141 pp.

Nadeau, Roland. "The Grace and Beauty of Classic Rags: Structural Elements in a Distinct Musical Genre." *Music Educators Journal* 59 (April 1973): 57–64.

Newberger, Eli H. "The Development of New Orleans and Stride Piano Styles." *Journal of Jazz Studies* 4, no. 2 (Spring/Summer 1977): 43–71.

———. "The Transition from Ragtime to Improvised Piano Style." *Journal of Jazz Studies* 3, no. 2 (Spring 1976): 3–18.

Waterman, Guy. "Joplin's Late Rags: An Analysis." *Record Changer* 14, no. 8 [ca. 1956]: 5–8. Reprinted in *The Art of Jazz*, edited by Martin Williams, pp. 19–31. New York: Oxford University Press, 1959.

Wiggins, Gene. "Popular Music and the Fiddler." *JEMF Quarterly* 15, no. 55 (Fall 1979): 144–51.

Ragtime and Region

Baldwin, Rebecca. "Bittersweet Rag: The Story of Ragtime—Missouri's Contribution to the Music World." *Bittersweet* 5 (Winter 1977): 4–21.

Berlin, Edward A. "Ragtime in Old New York." *NYC Jazz* 3 (2 June 1980): 22.

Campbell, S. Brunson and Roy J. Carew. "Sedalia . . . Missouri, the Cradle of Ragtime." *Record Changer* 4 (May 1945): 3.

"Chicago Had its Ragtime Days." *Ragtimer*, January–February 1976, pp. 14–15. Reprinted from *Down Beat.*

Comiskey, Nancy L. "Historic Indianapolis: The Two-Step, Toe-Tapping Tempo of Ragtime." *Indianapolis Monthly*, March 1982, pp. 54–59.

Gregg, Dave. "Joplin is Labeled Birthplace of Jazz. . . ." *Joplin* [Missouri] *Globe*, 9 March 1958.

Hasse, John Edward. *Cincinnati Ragtime.* Cincinnati: John Edward Hasse, 1983. 39 pp.

———. "The Creation and Dissemination of Indianapolis Ragtime, 1897–1930." Ph.D. diss., Indiana University, 1981. 323 pp.

———. *Hoosier Ragtime: A Discography.* [Bloomington: Indiana University Archives of

Traditional Music], 1980. 6 pp.

―――. *Hoosier Ragtime: A Listing of Ragtime Compositions from Indiana.* [Bloomington: Indiana University Archives of Traditional Music], 1980. 6 pp.

―――. "Indianapolis and the Rise of Ragtime." Paper presented at conference, American Popular Music and Its Impact on World Culture. Inaugural meeting of the American chapter of the International Association for the Study of Popular Music, Dartmouth College, Hanover, New Hampshire, 14 May 1983. 23 pp.

―――. "New Info on Midwest Ragtime." *Rag Times* 14 (March 1981): 7.

LaBrew, Arthur. *Before and After the Advent of Ragtime in Detroit, Michigan: "The Ragtime Era in Detroit."* Detroit: Arthur LaBrew, 1973. Revised 1977. 29 pp.

Melton, Larry. "Sedalia Addresses." *Rag Times* 10 (November 1976): 9.

Neibarger, Clyde B. "Ragtime Pioneers in Sedalia." *Kansas City* (Missouri) *Star,* April 16, 1951. Reprinted in *Musicgram* 1 (February 1964): 103–05.

Powers, Frank. "Ragtime Antecedents in Cincinnati." *The Classic Rag,* Part 1, July–August 1977, p. 4; Part 2, April 1978, pp. 4–5. Reprinted in *Rag Times* 12 (May 1978): 4–5.

"Ragtime Lafayette." *Hoosier Rag* 3 (May 1981), pp. 3–4.

"Ragtime Music (Invented in St. Louis) Is Dead." *Saint Louis Post-Dispatch,* 4 April 1909, Sunday magazine section, p. 1.

"Ragtime Music Was Born in Sedalia." *Sedalia Democrat,* 16 October 1960.

"Sedalia, Missouri Stakes Claim as Birthplace of Ragtime: Pitches for Historical Status." *Variety* 240 (10 November 1965): 1ff.

"St. Louis Just a Ragtime City." *Saint Louis Post-Dispatch,* 22 October 1901, p. 1.

Tichenor, Trebor Jay. "Missouri's Role in the Ragtime Revolution." *Missouri Historical Bulletin* 17 (April 1961): 239–44.

Trexler, Connie. "Hoosier Ragtime Women." *Fort Wayne News-Sentinel,* 19 November 1977, p. 2W.

Young, Fletcher. "St. Louis and All That Jazz." *Saint Louis Magazine* 2 (September 1964): 18–19, 44, 46–48.

The Ragtime Repertory

Hankins, Roger. "The Nine Lives of *Maple Leaf Rag.*" *Ragtimer* January–February 1972, pp. 4–7; March–April 1972, pp. 4–10.

Laird, Landon. "*The 12th Street Rag* Story." *Kansas City* (Missouri) *Times,* 23 October 1942. Reprinted in *Rag Times,* May 1979, pp. 1, 2.

Mitchell, Bill. "The *Maple Leaf Rag* Story." *Rag Times,* March–April 1969, pp. 7–8.

Montgomery, Michael. "The Story of 'Ragging the Scale.'" *Ragtime Society* 5, May–June 1963: 6–7.

Tichenor, Trebor. "Weeping Willow: An Analysis." *Rag Times* 6 (March 1973): 4–5. Reprinted from *Ragtime Review,* April 1965.

―――. "Who *Really* Wrote the *St. Louis Tickle?*" *Ragtime Review* 3 (April 1964): 6. Reprinted in *Rag Times* 3 (January–March 1970): 4.

―――, and Bob Wright. "Joplin's *Eugenia:* Analysis." *Ragtimer* 6, nos. 5–6 (1967): 17–18.

Walsh, Jim. "'Alexander's' Musical History." *Hobbies* 87 (December 1982): 58, 59, 71; (January 1983): 62–67, 70, 75; (February 1983): 62–65, 67.

Ragtime Piano Performance

Christensen, Axel. "A Course in Vaudeville Piano Playing." Arrangements by John S. Meck. *Christensen's Ragtime Review* 1–2 (December 1914–March 1916): passim.

―――. "Tone and Touch for Ragtime." *Christensen's Ragtime Review* 1 (July 1915): 5–6.

Dykstra, Brian. "Playing a Rag." *Clavier* 11 (December 1972): 29.

Hasse, John Edward. *Playing Ragtime Piano.* Bloomington, Indiana: John Edward Hasse, 1981. Reprint ed. Indianapolis: Hoosier Ragtime Society, 1983. 14 pp.

Winn, Edward R. "'Ragging' the Popular Song Hits." *Melody* 2 (January–September 1918): passim.

―――. "Ragtime Piano Playing." *Cadenza* 21–23 (March 1915–October 1916): passim.

―――. "Ragtime Piano Playing: A Practical Course of Instruction for Pianists." *Tuneful Yankee/Melody* 1–2 (January 1917–June 1918): passim.

Orchestrated Ragtime

Charters, Samuel B. "Red Backed Book of Rags." *Jazz Report* 2 (July 1962): 7–8.

Lampe, J. Bodewalt. "The Art of Arranging Music." *Tuneful Yankee* 1 (1917); reprinted in *Rag Times* 7 (January 1974): 4–5.

Powers, Frank. "Come On and Hear Waldo's Ragtime Band." *Classic Rag,* October–November 1981, 3–4.

―――. "Ragtime Stock Orchestrations." *Ragtime Society* 5 (November 1966): 44–48.

Schafer, William J. "Ragtime Arranging for Fun and Profit: The Cases of Harry J. Alford and J. Bodewalt Lampe." *Journal of Jazz Studies* 3 (Fall 1975): 103–17.

Thompson, Butch. "Ragtime, Cakewalk & Stomps: Dusting off the Red Back Book." *Mississippi Rag* 1 (November 1973): 5–7.

Ragtime Guitar

Griffith, Ellen. "The Real Ragtime Guitar." *Rag Times* 11 (November 1977): 5–7.

Grossman, Stefan. "Stefan Grossman on Classic Ragtime Guitar" [title varies]. *Guitar Player* 9 (June–October 1975): passim.

———. "Stefan Grossman on Raggin' the Blues." *Guitar Player* 10 (April 1976): 71.

Rummel, Jack T. "The Ragtime Guitar: An Overview." *Rag Times* 15 (March 1982): 3–4.

Ragtime Recordings

Carey, Dave. "A Listing of Ragtime Recordings." *Jazz Journal* 3 (February 1950): 6–7.

Davis, C. B. "Ragtime on Record." *Audio* 58 (June 1974): 50–52.

"Discography of Ragtime Recordings." *Jazz Forum* 4 (April 1947): 7–8.

Englund, Bjorn. "Ragtime Comes to the Far North." *Talking Machine Review*, no. 54–55 (October–December 1978), pp. 1434–35.

Goodfriend, James. "Ragtime: The Last Roundup." *Stereo Review* 33 (September 1974): 130–31.

Hitchcock, H. Wiley. "'Ragtime of the Higher Class.'" *Stereo Review* 26 (April 1971): 84.

Jasen, David A. "Original Ragtime Released." *Rag Times* 11 (May 1977): 11.

———. *Recorded Ragtime 1897–1958.* Hamden, Conn.: Archon Books, 1973. 155 pp.

Koenigsberg, Allen. *Edison Cylinder Records, 1889–1912: With an Illustrated History of the Phonograph.* New York: Steller Productions, 1969.

Kresh, Paul. "First Annual Ragtime Roundup." *Stereo Review* 32 (April 1974): 116–17.

Lotz, Rainer E. *Grammophonplatten aus der Ragtime-Ära.* Dortmund, West Germany: Harenberg Kommunikation, 1979.

Moe, Phil. "Ragtime on Record: A Classic Rag Discography." *Mississippi Rag* 1 (March 1974): 8–9.

Offergeld, Robert. "Scott Joplin's Orchestrated Ragtime." *Stereo Review* 30 (June 1973): 116–17.

Paget, Daniel. "From the Saloon to the Salon: Rifkin's Genteel Joplin." *High Fidelity*, November 1980, pp. 66–67.

Rust, Brian. "Ragtime on Records," *Storyville*, no. 27 (February–March 1970): 110–13.

Salzman, Eric. "The Second Annual Ragtime Roundup." *Stereo Review* 32 (June 1974): 126–27.

Smart, James R. *The Sousa Band: A Discography.* Washington, D.C.: Library of Congress, 1970. 123 pp.

Spottswood, Richard, and David A. Jasen. "Discoveries Concerning Recorded Ragtime." *Jazz Journal* 21 (February 1968): 7.

Tudor, Dean and Nancy Tudor. "Ragtime," in *Jazz*, pp. 45–54. American Popular Music on Elpee. Littleton, Colo.: Libraries Unlimited, 1979.

Walker, Edward S., and Steven Walker. *English Ragtime: A Discography.* Woodthorpe, Mastin Moor, Derbyshire, England: Edward S. Walker, 1971. 104 pp.

Wyndham, Tex. "Ten Years of Ragtime LP's." *Rag Times* 11 (May 1977): 8–9.

Ragtime Piano Rolls

"The Jelly Roll Morton Piano-Rollography." *Record Research* 1 (December 1955): 11–12.

Montgomery, Michael. "Eubie Blake Piano Rollography (Revised)." *Record Research*, no. 159–160 (December 1978): 4–5.

———. "James P. Johnson Rollography." *Record Research*, no. 20 (November–December 1959): 16.

———. "More Rolls by Morton." *Record Research*, no. 49 (March 1963): 6–7.

———. "Rags to Riches: The Odyssey of Player Piano Rolls." *American Life: A Collector's Annual* 4 (1964): 144–47.

———. "Scott Joplin Rollography." *Record Research*, no. 2 (April–May 1959): 2.

"On 65 Note Piano Rolls." *Ragtime Review* 1 (July 1962): 8–9.

Piano Roll Albert [Albert Huerta]. "Ten Years of Piano Rolls." *Rag Times* 11 (May 1977): 20–22.

Sherman, Charles. "Old Piano Roll Buffs: Two St. Louis Fanciers of Ragtime Perforate Music for Player Instruments." *Saint Louis Post-Dispatch*, 15 September 1964.

Simone, R. "Jelly Roll Morton Rollography." *Matrix*, no. 51 (February 1964): 14–17.

Spear, Horace L. "Jelly Rolls." *Storyville*, no. 32 (1 December 1970): 47–50.

Sprankle, Edmund J. "Nickel Jazz." *Jazz Report* 9, no. 6 [1979].

Zimmerman, Dick. "Ms. M.E. Brown, Piano Roll Arranger." *Rag Times* 7 (January 1974): 8.

Ragtime and Classical Music

Baskerville, David. "The Influence of Jazz on Art Music to Mid-Century." Ph.D. diss., University of California at Los Angeles, 1965.

Burk, John N. "Ragtime and its Possibilities."

Harvard Musical Review 2 (January 1914): 11–13; reprinted in *Opera Magazine* 2 (June 1915): 24–26.

Cadman, Charles Wakefield. "Cadman on Rag-Time." *Musical Courier* 69 (12 August 1914): 31.

Copland, Aaron. "Jazz Structure and Influence on Modern Music." *Modern Music* 4 (January–February 1927): 9–14.

Damon, S. Foster. "American Influence on Modern French Music." *Dial*, 15 August 1918, 93–95.

Downes, Olin. "An American Composer [Henry F. Gilbert]." *Musical Quarterly* 4 (January 1918): 23–36.

Gilbert, Henry F. "Folk-Music in Art Music— A Discussion and a Theory." *Musical Quarterly* 3 (October 1917): 577–601.

"Great American Composer: Will He Speak in the Accent of Broadway?" *Current Opinion* 63 (November 1917): 316–17.

Heyman, B. B. "Stravinsky and Ragtime." *Musical Quarterly* 68 (1982): 543–62.

Hughes, Rupert. "Will Ragtime Turn to Symphonic Poems?" *Etude* 38 (May 1920): 305.

Judson, Arthur L. "Works of American Composers Reveal Relation of Ragtime to Art-Song." *Musical America* 15 (2 December 1911): 29.

Mason, Daniel Gregory. "Folk-Song and American Music (A Plea for the Unpopular Point of View)." *Musical Quarterly* 4 (July 1918): 323–32.

"Rag-Time." *Times* (London), 8 February 1913, 11; reprinted in *Boston Symphony Orchestra Programmes* 32 (19 February 1913): 1186–96.

"Ragtime as a Source of National Music." *Musical America* 17 (15 February 1913): 37.

"Rag-Time Hurts Classics." *American Musician and Art Journal* 28 (13 July 1912): 3.

Rogers, M. Robert. "Jazz Influence on French Music." *Musical Quarterly* 21 (January 1935): 53–68.

Tick, Judith. "Ragtime and the Music of Charles Ives." *Current Musicology* 18 (1974): 105–13.

"Will Ragtime Save the Soul of the Native American Composer?" *Current Opinion*, December 1915, 406–07.

Ragtime Festivals and Concerts

Bell-Smith, P. "The Scott Joplin Ragtime Festival, Sedalia, Mo., July 25–28, 1974." *Ragtimer*, September–October 1974, pp. 10–11.

Brown, Karen. "Sedalia Swings to Joplin's Ragtime." *Kansas City* (Missouri) *Times*, 27 July 1974.

———. "Tunes of Ragtime Hero Resurrected." *Kansas City* (Missouri) *Star*, 28 July 1974, p. 6A.

Kisselgoff, Anna. "Dance: 'Elite Syncopations' Premiere." *New York Times*, 6 May 1976.

"Prodigal Son [ragtime ballet]." *Melody Maker* 49 (22 June 1974): 66.

Willmorth, Gus. "Sedalia Ragtime Festival." *Rag Times* 17 (July 1983): 2–3.

Ragtime Revivals

Affeldt, Paul. "Editorial." *Jazz Report* 1 (January 1961): 20–21.

"Angel Records: Joplin's 'Classical' Status." *Record World*, 6 July 1974, p. 22.

"Belwin-Mills Starts Revival by the Book." *Record World*, 6 July 1974, p. 26.

Cassidy, Russ, and Trebor Tichenor. "Are We Ready for an International Ragtime Fraternity?" *Jazz Report* 1 (April 1961): [13–14].

Fox, Charles. "Raggedy but Right." In *Jazz Now: The Jazz Centre Society Guide*, edited by Roger Cotterrell, pp. 16–23. London: Quartet Books, 1976.

Freedland, Nat. "Joplin's Rags Rule Roost in May with Popular 'Sting.'" *Billboard* 86 (18 May 1974): 6.

Hasse, John Edward. "The Research and Revival of Ragtime." Paper presented at the annual meeting of the Society for Ethnomusicology meeting jointly with the College Music Society, Saint Louis, 28 October 1978.

"The International Ragtime Society on Launching Pad." *Jazz Report* 2 (November 1961): 22.

Kovner, B. "Music: The Ragtime Revival." *Commentary* 61 (March 1976): 57–60.

Lucas, John. "Ragtime Revival." *Record Changer* 7 (December 1948): 8. Reprinted in *Ragtime Society* 3 (Summer 1964): 50.

"Maple Leaf Club Goals." *Rag Times* 1 (September 1967): 7.

"MCA and 'The Sting.'" *Record World*, 6 July 1974, 20, 24.

Mitchell, Bill. "The Maple Leaf Club [Los Angeles-based ragtime fraternity]: A Capsule History." *Jazz Report* 9, no. 4 (1977): 13–14.

———. "Those Ragtime Years." *Jazz Report* 1 (June 1961): [9–10].

"Nonesuch and the Scott Joplin Craze." *Record World*, 6 July 1974, pp. 20, 22.

Norris, John. "They Still Play Ragtime." *Down Beat* 35 (17 October 1968): 14, 41.

Scott, Patrick. "The Temperanceville Rag." *Saint Louis Globe-Democrat*, 27 March 1965.

West, Hollie I. "Ragtime Enjoys a Revival." *Washington Post*, 9 April 1972.

Wilford, Charles. "Ragtime: The Astonishing Boom." *Jazz Journal*, May 1974, pp. 4–6. Reprinted in *Ragtimer*, September–October 1974, pp. 4–9.

Ragtime Figures

AUFDERHEIDE, MAY

"'Classic Rags' Composed by May Aufderheide: Talented Indianapolis Girl is Achieving Enviable Reputation." *American Musician and Art Journal*, 13 August 1909, 20.
"May Aufderheide Honored." *Rag Times* 15 (May 1981): 1.

BARGY, ROY

Arneson, Bruce, and Tom Arneson. "The Roy Bargy Story." *Rag Times* 6 (September 1972): 8–10.
Mitchell, Bill. "Elite Syncopations: An Open Letter from Roy Bargy." *Jazz Report* 4 (September–October 1965): [5].

BENNETT, THERON

Wilkes, Galen. "Theron Bennett Remembered." *Rag Times* 17 (May 1983): 5–7.

BERLIN, IRVING

"Berlin Calls Jazz American Folk Music." *New York Times*, 10 January 1925, p. 2.
Freedland, Michael. *Irving Berlin*. New York: Stein and Day, 1974. 224 pp.
Jay, Dave. *The Irving Berlin Songography, 1907–1966*. New Rochelle, N.Y.: Arlington House, 1969. 172 pp.
Smith, Frederick James. "Irving Berlin and Modern Ragtime." *New York Dramatic Mirror*, 14 January 1914, 38.

BERNARD, MIKE

"Bernard is King of Rag-Timers." *New York Dramatic Mirror*, 3 February 1900, pp. 18–19; reprinted in *Ragtime Review* 1 (October 1962): 10–11.
Heermans, Jerry. "Mike Bernard: The Ragtime King." *Rag Times* 6 (November 1972): 6–8.

BLAKE, EUBIE

Ackerman, P. "Eubie Blake Takes a Session at Studio in Stride." *Billboard* 81 (22 February 1969), 6ff.
Bailey, Peter. "A Love Song to Eubie." *Ebony* 28 (July 1973): 94–96, 98–99.
Ballad, Richard. "Penthouse Interview: Eubie Blake." *Penthouse* 5 (March 1974): 57–60, 95–96.
Bellantonio, D. D. "Eubie Blake." *Jazz and Pop* 8 (March 1969): 24–26.
"Birthday Party." *New Yorker* 52 (8 March 1976): 30–32.
Blesh, Rudi. "Little Hubie." In *Combo USA: Eight Lives in Jazz*, pp. 187–217. Philadelphia: Chilton, 1971.

Bolcom, Williams, and Robert Kimball. *Reminiscing with Sissle and Blake*. New York: Viking Press, 1973. 256 pp.
———. "The Words and Music of Noble Sissle and Eubie Blake." *Stereo Review*, November 1972, pp. 56–64.
Carter, Lawrence T. *Eubie Blake: Keys of Memory*. Detroit: Balamp Publishing, 1979. 116 pp.
Choice, Harriet. "Eubie: Ragtime to Broadway and Back Again." *Chicago Tribune*, 4 February 1973. Reprinted in *Ragtime*, January–February 1975, 4–7.
Davies, J. R. "Eubie Blake, His Life and Times." *Storyville*, no. 6 (August 1966): 19–20; no. 7 (October 1966): 12–13ff.
"The Dean of Ragtime (95th Birthday Celebration)." *Ragtimer*, January–February 1978, pp. 8–9.
"Good Looking." *New Yorker* 54 (25 December 1978): 25–26.
Hession, Jim and Martha. "Eubie Blake: An Inspiration." *Rag Times* 3 (September 1983): 1–2.
Hollie, Pamela. "The Comeback Kid." *Wall Street Journal*, 23 October 1973, pp. 1, 16.
Hyder, William. "The Roaring Ragtime Odyssey of Eubie Blake." *Ragtimer*, January–February 1973, 4–10.
Hyman, Dick. "Keyboard Journal: Onstage with Eubie." *Contemporary Keyboard* 8 (December 1982): 70.
Isacoff, Stuart. "Eubie Blake: Playing and Writing Great Ragtime for Eighty Years." *Contemporary Keyboard* 3 (August 1977): 8–9.
Kimball, Robert. "Eubie Blake at 95." *ASCAP Today* 9 (Spring 1978)::20–22.
———, and William Bolcom. *Reminiscing with Sissle and Blake*. New York: Viking Press, 1973. 256 pp.
King, Bobbi. "Conversation with Eubie Blake (Continued): A Legend in His Own Lifetime." *Black Perspective in Music* 1 (Fall 1973): 151–56.
Klee, Joe H. "A Very Special Celebration." *Mississippi Rag* 10 (March 1983): 2.
McPartland, Marian. "At the Piano with Eubie Blake: An Informal Interview by Marian McPartland." *Contemporary Keyboard* 8 (December 1982): 56–58. Reprinted in *The Ragtimer*, January–February 1983.
Morath, Max. "93 Years of Eubie Blake: Interview." *American Heritage* 27 (October 1976): 56–65.
"Profile: Eubie Blake—Ragtime Giant." *International Musician* 77 (September 1978): 8ff.
"Rebirth of Ragtime: A Gay Nineties Rhythm Sets Toes to Tapping," *Life* 73 (21 July 1972): 46–47, 49.
Robinson, L. "Eubie Blake Remembers Ragtimes." *Billboard* 86 (26 October 1974): 32ff.
Rose, Al. *Eubie Blake*. New York: Schirmer

Books, 1979. 214 pp.

Saal, Hubert. "Mr. Ragtime," *Newsweek,* 22 February 1971, 99.

Southern, Eileen. "Conversation with Eubie Blake: A Legend in His Own Lifetime," *Black Perspective in Music* 1 (Spring 1973): 50–59.

"Still Shuffling." *Time,* 18 December 1972, 97.

Vogel, Frederick G. "Eubie!!" *Jazz Magazine* 2 (September 1978): 32–35.

Waldo, Terry. "Eubie Blake, 1883–1983." *Mississippi Rag* 10 (March 1983): 2.

Wilson, John S. "Age Fails To Dim Sparkle of Eubie Blake at Piano." *New York Times,* 3 March 1972.

BOONE, BLIND

"Blind Missouri Musician Wins International Fame." *Sedalia Capital,* 4 December 1959.

Darch, Robert R. "'Blind' Boone: A Sensational Missourian Forgotten." *Ragtimer* 6, nos. 5–6 (1967): 9–13.

Harrah, Madge. "The Incomparable Blind Boone." *Ragtimer,* July–August 1969, pp. 9–12.

———. "Wayne B. Allen: 'Blind' Boone's Last Manager." *Ragtimer,* September–October 1969: 10–15.

Parrish, William. "'Blind' Boone's Ragtime." *Missouri Life* 7 (November–December 1979): 17–23.

Rice, Patricia. "Blind Boone: Link to Ragtime Origins." *Rag Times* 11 (March 1978): 1–2. Reprinted from the *Saint Louis Post-Dispatch.*

BOTSFORD, GEORGE

Zimmerman, Dick. "George Botsford, 1874–1949." *Rag Times* 7 (January 1974): 9.

BOWMAN, EUDAY L.

"Burial Set for Euday Bowman, 'Twelfth Street Rag' Composer." *Fort Worth Star Telegram,* 27 May 1949.

Campbell, S. Brunson. "Euday Bowman and the '12th Street Rag.'" *Jazz Journal* 4 (January 1951): 14.

Laird, Landon. "The 12th Street Rag Story." *Kansas City* (Missouri) *Times,* 23 October 1942; reprinted in *Rag Times* 13 (May 1979): 1–2.

Mitchell, Bill. "Virginia City Ragtime: A Visit with Harry Bruce, with Some New Light on Euday Bowman." *Jazz Report* 5, no. 3 (1966); reprinted in *Rag Times* 1 (January 1968): 5–6.

"More About Bowman." *Rag Times* 17 (November 1983): 1–2. Reprinted from *Fort Worth Star Telegram,* 1 July 1937.

P.V.M. "He Gave Twelfth Street New Fame in His Jazz Tune." *Kansas City (Missouri) Star,* 5 June 1949, p. 8D.

BROOKS, SHELTON

"Shelton Brooks, 1886–1975." *Rag Times,* November 1975, 8.

"Shelton Brooks is Alive & Strutting." *Jazz Report* 7, no. 2 [ca. 1970].

CAMPBELL, BRUN

Affeldt, Paul E. "Brun Campbell." *Rag Times* 16 (May 1982): 4–5. Reprinted from *Jazz Report.*

———. "Last of the Professors." *Jazz Report* 2 (October 1961): [9–10].

Campbell, S. Brunson. "The Ragtime Kid (An Autobiography)." *Jazz Report* 6 [ca. 1967–68]: 7–12.

———, and Roy J. Carew. "How I Became . . . A Pioneer Rag Man of the 1890's." *Record Changer* 6 (April 1947): 12.

Lasswell, Paul. "Some Thoughts about Brun Campbell & Ragtime." *Rag Times* 14 (May 1980): 3.

Levin, Floyd. "Brun Campbell: The Original Ragtime Kid of the 1890s." *Jazz Journal* 23 (December 1970): 26–27.

Thompson, Kay C. "Reminiscing in Ragtime: An Interview with Brun Campbell." *Jazz Journal* 3 (April 1950): 4–5.

CANNON, HUGHIE

"A Song Writer's Message to the Boys: The Composer of 'Bill Bailey' and Other Songs Enters a Poorhouse in Detroit." *American Musician and Art Journal,* 11 February 1910, p. 17.

Durst, Don. "Bill Bailey Really Did Come Home: The Story of Jackson and All-Time Hit Song." *Jackson* (Michigan) *Citizen Patriot,* 30 January 1966, section 3, p. 27. This is the first of nine articles, each with a different title, on Cannon that were published daily (except February 5) through 8 February 1966.

"Stencils and Booze His Undoing." *Presto,* 10 February 1910, p. 26.

"Yes, Bill Bailey Has Gone Home: Hughie Cannon, Who Wrote Famous Songs, Dies in Infirmary." *Toledo Blade,* 18 June 1912, p. 8

CAREW ROY J.

Carew, Roy J. "A Tribute to Roy Carew Not Forgetting Jelly Roll." Introduction by George W. Kay. *Jazz Journal* 21 (May 1968): 22–23.

Kay, George W. "Reminiscing in Ragtime: An Interview with Roy J. Carew." *Jazz Journal* 17 (November 1964): 8–9; reprinted in

Ragtime Society 5 (December 1966): 67–69.
"Roy J. Carew, 1884–1967." *Ragtimer* 6, no. 3 (1967): 19.

CARR, JOE "FINGERS"

"Joe 'Fingers' Carr Killed in Auto Accident." *Ragtimer*, January/February 1980, 9.
Joseph, Tony. "Busch Goes from Ragtime to Riches." *Ventura* (California) *Star Free Press*, 24 November 1978. Reprinted in *Jazz Report* 9, no. 6 (1979).

CHRISTENSEN, AXEL

Christensen, Axel. "Teasing the Ivories: How I Broke In." *Melody* 3 (March 1919): 4.
———. "Teasing the Ivories, No. 2." *Melody* 3 (May 1919): 5.

COLE, BOB AND J. ROSAMOND JOHNSON

"Robert (Bob) Cole, Actor, Dead." *Chicago Defender*, 12 August 1911, 1.
Simmons, R. C. "Europe's Reception to Negro Talent." *Colored American Magazine* 9 (November 1905): 635–42.

CONFREY, ZEZ

Jasen, David A. "Zez Confrey, Creator of the Novelty Rag." *Storyville*, no. 40 (1 April 1972): 140–144.
———. "Zez Confrey, Creator of the Novelty Rag: Preparatory Research." *Record Research*, July 1971, 5, 10.

COTA, EL

Zimmerman, Dick. "'El Cota': 60 Years Later." *Rag Times* 3 (March 1970): 4.

DANIELS, CHARLES N.

"Charles N. Daniels." *New York Times*, 24 January 1943, p. 42.

DARCH, BOB

"Bob Darch Unearths Treasures." *Ragtimer*, September–October 1970: 8.
Schubert, Arnold. "'Ragtime Bob' Breezes Through Our Town and Stirs the Dust from Our Memories of 'Blind' Boone." *Columbia* (Missouri) *Tribune*, 28 July 1961.

DENNEY, HOMER

"Homer Denny [sic]." *Rag Times* 16 (July 1982): 2–3.

EDMONDS, SHEPHARD

Carew, Roy J. "Shephard N. Edmonds." *Record Changer*, December 1947: 13–14.

EUROPE, JAMES REESE

"Lieut. James Reese Europe: Master of Syncopated Rhythms." *Melody* 3 (July 1919): 3.

FEIST, LEO

"Leo Feist, Ragtime Publisher." *Metronome*, September 1923; reprinted in *Rag Times* 6 (March 1973): 10–11.

FILLMORE, HENRY J.

Bierly, Paul E. *Hallelujah Trombone!* Columbus, Ohio: Integrity Press, 1982. 156 pp.
———. *The Music of Henry Fillmore and Will Huff.* Columbus, Ohio: Integrity Press, 1982. 156 pp.

GIBLIN, IRENE

Huling, Jean. "Let's Remember Irene Giblin!" *Ragtimer*, September/October 1983, pp. 4–7.

GILBERT, L. WOLFE

Bourne, Dave. "L. Wolfe Gilbert, 1886–1970." *Rag Times* 3 (September 1970): 3.

GREEN, GEORGE HAMILTON

Powers, Frank. "George Hamilton Green." *Rag Times* 14 (July 1980): 2–3.

HAHN, TEDDY

Zimmerman, Dick. "Teddy Hahn and the Amazon Rag." *Rag Times* 16 (May 1982): 1–2.

HAMLISCH, MARVIN

Adels, Robert. "Marvin Hamlisch: 'The Entertainer' Comes Back Smiling." *Record World*, 6 July 1974, 28.

HARNEY, BEN

"Ben Harney Pioneer Exemplar of Ragtime Music." *Variety* 129 (9 March 1938), 46.
Blesh, Rudi. "Benjamin Robertson Harney." In *Dictionary of American Biography, Supplement 2,* edited by Robert L. Schuyler and Edward T. James, p. 286. New York: Scribner, 1958.
Bourne, Dave. "The Ben Harney Years (A Continuing Interview with George Orendorff)." *Rag Times* 4 (November 1970): 11–12.
———. "Touring with Ben Harney." *Rag Times* 16 (March 1983): 2–3.
Shirley, Wayne D. "More on Ben Harney." *Sonneck Society Newsletter* 6 (Spring 1980): 14.
Tallmadge, William H. "Ben Harney: Passing for Black." *Sonneck Society Newsletter* 6 (Summer 1980): 7.

———. "Ben Harney: White? Black? Mulatto?" *Sonneck Society Newsletter* 5 (Fall 1979): 16–17. Reprinted in *Rag Times* 13 (March 1980): 4–5.

HOFFMAN, ROBERT

Rose, Al. "New Orleans Rags and Robert Hoffman." *Rag Times* 9 (September 1975): 4–5.

HOLZMANN, ABE

M. H. R. "German Composer Who Writes American Cakewalk Music." *New York Herald,* 13 January 1901 [section 6], p. 3.

IRWIN, MAY

Walsh, Jim. "May Irwin." *Hobbies,* June 1963; July 1963.

JACKSON, TONY

Carew, Roy J. "'He Knew a Thousand Songs': A Recollection of Tony Jackson." *Jazz Journal* 5 (March 1952): 1–3.
Kay, George W. "Basin Street Stroller: New Orleans and Tony Jackson." *Jazz Journal* 4 (June 1951): 1–3; (August 1951): 1–2; (September 1951): 1–2.
———. "Remembering Tony Jackson." *Second Line* 15, nos. 11–12 (1964): 5–8ff.

JASEN, DAVID

Wilson, John S. "Dave Jasen, a Lecturer-Broadcaster-Writer, Leads Ragtime Revival on Long Island." *New York Times,* 14 November 1971; reprinted in *Rag Times* 5 (January 1972): 5.

JENTES, HARRY

Collins, Treve, Jr. "Concerning Harry Jentes." *Melody* 2 (September 1918): 4–6.

JOHNSON, CHARLES L.

"Charles L. Johnson." *American Musician and Art Journal* 25 (11 June 1909): 19.
"Charles L. Johnson." *Variety,* 10 January 1951, p. 63.
"More about Chas. L. Johnson." *Rag Times* 14 (January 1981): 7.
Zimmerman, Dick. "Charles L. Johnson—The Happy Ragtimer: An Interview with His Nephew." *Rag Times* 2 (July 1968): 6–7.

JOHNSON, JAMES P.

"An Interview with James P. Johnson." *Jazz Notes* 4 (January 1959): 1–4, 8.
Davin, Tom. "Conversations with James P. Johnson." *Jazz Review* 2 (June 1959): 14–17; (July 1959): 10–13; (August 1959): 13–15;

(September 1959): 26–27; 3 (March–April 1960): 10–13. Reprinted in part in *Jazz Panorama,* edited by Martin Williams, pp. 44–61. New York: Collier Books, 1964.
Hadlock, Richard. "Fats Waller and James P. Johnson." In *Jazz Masters of the Twenties,* pp. 145–71. New York: Macmillan, 1965.
Hammond, John. "Talents of James P. Johnson Went Unappreciated." *Down Beat* 19 (November 1955): 12.
Harrison, Max. "James P. Johnson." *Jazz Monthly* 5 (September 1959): 4–9.
Kirkeby, Ed, in collaboration with Duncan P. Schiedt and Sinclair Traill. *Ain't Misbehavin': The Story of Fats Weller.* New York: Dodd, Mead, 1966. pp. 52–57 and passim. Reprint ed. New York: Da Capo, 1975.
Lyttleton, Humphrey. "James P. Johnson." In *The Best of Jazz: Basin Street to Harlem; Jazz Masters and Masterpieces, 1917–1930,* pp. 23–35. New York: Taplinger, 1982.
Russell, Ross. "Grandfather of Hot Piano—James P. Johnson." *Jazz Information* 2 (November 1941): 20–24. Reprinted in *Frontiers of Jazz,* ed. Ralph de Toledano. 2nd ed., rev. New York: Frederick Ungar, 1962, pp. 170–76. Reprinted as "James P. Johnson" in *The Art of Jazz: Essays on the Nature and Development of Jazz,* ed. Martin T. Williams, pp. 49–56. New York: Oxford University Press, 1959.
Trolle, Frank H. *James P. Johnson: Father of the Stride Piano,* with contributions by Bill Moss, Kenneth G. Noble, and Michael Montgomery. Edited and annotated by Dick M. Bakker. Two vols. Alphen aan de Rijn, Netherlands: Micrography, 1982.
Vance, Joel. *Fats Waller: His Life and Times.* Chicago: Contemporary Books, 1977. pp. 33–35 and passim.
Waller, Maurice, and Anthony Calabrese. *Fats Waller.* New York: Schirmer Books, 1977. London: Cassell. pp. 26–31 and passim.
Wellstood, Dick. "W. C. Handy Blues." *Jazz Review* 1 (December 1958): 34–35.

JONES, CLARENCE M.

Powers, Frank. "Clarence Jones of Wilmington, Ohio." *Classic Rag,* February 1979, p. 6.

JOPLIN, LOTTIE

Goodman, Solomon. "Lottie Joplin." *Rag Times,* September 1976: 3.
Thompson, Kay C. "Lottie Joplin: Scott's Widow Reminisces on the Ragtime King." *Record Changer* 9 (October 1950): 8, 18.

JOPLIN, SCOTT

Adels, Robert. "Joplin Dominates Classical Sales." *Record World,* 6 July 1974, 20, 26.

Adams, Stanley. "Scott Joplin and Today's Composer." *Record World,* 6 July 1974, 24, 28.

Affeldt, Paul E. "Scott Joplin: His Story." *Jazz Report* 5 (August 1957): 3–4, 7–9.

Albrecht, Theodore. "Julius Weiss: Scott Joplin's First Piano Teacher." *College Music Symposium* 19 (Fall 1979): 89–105.

Anderson, T. J. "Scott Joplin and the Opera *Treemonishha.*" Paper presented at a meeting of the Association for the Study of Afro-American Life and History, Chicago, 30 October 1976. 8 pp.

Ainscough, Mike. "Some Brief Notes on Ragtime: The Influence of Scott Joplin." *Clanfolk,* Easter 1971, 22–25.

Atkins, Jerry L. "Early Days in Texas: New Notes on Scott Joplin's Youth." *Rag Times* 6 (September 1972): 1–3.

Barnes, Harper. "Scott Joplin: From Ragtime to Riches." *Saint Louis Post-Dispatch,* 13 February 1977.

"A Belated Note of Tribute Paid To Ragtime's Scott Joplin Here." *New York Times,* 19 August 1974, p. 28.

Belt, Byron. "Ragtime Great's Opera Disappoints Reviewer." *New Orleans Times-Picayune,* 20 August 1972, section 2, p. 17.

Bender, William. "Scott Joplin: From Rags to Opera." *Time,* 15 September 1975, 85–86.

Blesh, Rudi. "Scott Joplin." *American Heritage* 26 (June 1975): 26–32ff.

Bolcom, William. "Orchestrating *Treemonisha.*" *Performer Magazine for Wolf Trap Farm* 11, book 3 (second season 1972): 8.

Brockhoff, Dorothy. "Missouri was the Birthplace of Ragtime: Widow of Music Publisher Recalls Legendary Scott Joplin and How His Music Took Country by Storm." *Saint Louis Post-Dispatch,* 18 January 1961, p. 137.

Campbell, Brun. "From Rags to Ragtime: A Eulogy." *Jazz Report* 5 [ca. 1967]: 5–6.

———. "From Rags to Ragtime and Riches." *Jazz Journal* 2 (July 1949): 13, 14, 16.

———. "Ragtime Begins: Early Days with Scott Joplin Recalled." *Record Changer* 7 (March 1948): 8, 18. Reprinted in *Ragtimer* 2 (November 1963): 4–5.

Carew, Roy J. "Scott Joplin." *Jazz Record,* no. 60 (November 1947): 6–7.

———. "Treemonisha." *Record Changer* 5 (October 1946): 17.

———, and Don E. Fowler. "Scott Joplin: Overlooked Genius." *Record Changer* (September 1944): 12–14; (October 1944): 10–12; (December 1944): 10–11.

Charters, Ann. "The First Negro Folk Opera! *Treemonisha.*" *Jazz Monthly* 8 (August 1962): 6–11.

Collier, James Lincoln. "The Scott Joplin Rag."

New York Times Magazine, 21 September 1975, 18–20, 22, 24, 26, 28, 30ff.

"Composer of Ragtime Now Writing Grand Opera." *New York Age,* 5 March 1908.

Current, G. B. "Scott Joplin." *Crisis* 82 (June 1975): 219–21.

Daily, Georgia. "Childhood Friend Remembers Joplin." *Texarkana Gazette,* 6 May 1976.

Davis, Peter G. "Treemonisha—An Innocent Dream Come True." *New York Times,* 1 June 1975.

de Lerma, Dominique-René. "A Musical and Sociological Review of Scott Joplin's 'Treemonisha.'" *Black Music Research Newsletter* 5 (Spring 1982): 1, 9–10.

de Veaux, Scott. "Scott Joplin and the Development of Ragtime." B.A. thesis, Princeton University, 1976.

"Did You Know Ragtime Music Was Born in Sedalia?" *Sedalia Democrat,* 29 June 1947, pp. 1, 6.

"'Euphonic Sounds,' A Syncopated Two-Step, by Scott Joplin." *American Musician and Art Journal,* 6 May 1910, p. 5.

Evans, Mark. *Scott Joplin and the Ragtime Years.* New York: Dodd, Mead, 1976. For adolescents.

Fleming, S. "Joplin's *Treemonisha:* A Patchwork of Styles, Touching and Trying." *Hi Fi/Musical America* 26 (July 1976): 72–73.

Freed, Richard. "More on the Joplin Renascence." *Stereo Review* 29 (October 1972): 108.

"From Rags to Rags." *Time,* 7 February 1972, pp. 89–90.

Fuld, James J. "The Few Known Autographs of Scott Joplin." *American Music* 1 (Spring 1983): 41–48.

Giddins, Gary. "'Treemonisha' From on High Breaks Loose." *Village Voice,* 24 May 1976, p. 90.

Goldman, Arnold. "Scott Joplin's Dream." *Atlas,* September–October 1974.

Hebert, Rubye Nell. "A Study of the Composition and Performance of Scott Joplin's Opera *Treemonisha.*" D.M.A. dissertation, Ohio State University, 1976. 57 pp.

Hertzberg, Dan. "One Last Hand for the Entertainer." *Newsday,* 1 August 1974.

Hill, W. D. "Saga of Scott Joplin." *Sedalia Democrat,* 11 February 1962, p. 1.

Hoefer, George. "Missouri Group Honors Memory of Scott Joplin." *Down Beat,* 25 January 1952, p. 9.

Jacobson, Bernard. "Was Joplin Our Great Composer?" *Washington Star,* 19 March 1972, p. B8.

Jones, R. "'Treemonisha': Scott Joplin's Ragtime Opera Struts its Stuff on Broadway." *Opera News* 40 (September 1975): 12–15.

"Joplin, 'Father of Ragtime,' Honored," *Indianapolis News,* 26 November 1975.

"Joplin's Black Gold." *Newsweek*, 22 September 1975, p. 62.

Kunstadt, Len. "Scott Joplin Has Arisen . . ." *Record Research*, February 1972, pp. 3–4.

Kupferberg, Herbert. "Joplin's Opera Finally Makes It Big." *National Observer*, 27 September 1975.

Lawrence, Vera Brodsky. "Program Notes for *Treemonisha*." *Atlanta Arts* 4 (January 1972).

———. "Scott Joplin." *BMI*, Spring 1976, pp. 38–39.

Lentz, Paul. "Cashing in on Joplin." *Dixie*, 24 November 1974.

"Man Who Knew Joplin is the Man of the Hour." *Washingtonian*, 11 August 1972, p. B1.

"Maple Leaf Rag by Scott Joplin." *Ragtimer*, March–April 1977, p. 8.

"Marker for Joplin." *Long Island Press*, 2 August 1974, p. 2.

Marranca, B. "The Compleat Scott Joplin, if Rag is Your Bag." *Crawdaddy* 37 (June 1974): 82–84.

Moore, Carman. "Scott Joplin: Rags & Riches." *Village Voice*, 28 October 1971.

"A Musical Novelty." *American Musician and Art Journal*, 24 June 1911, p. 7.

Obika, D. D. "Citizen Group Plans to Restore Joplin's Home." *Saint Louis Post-Dispatch*, 27 March 1977, p. 3A.

"Once Ragtime King of Market Street Immortalized in Fisk Library." *Saint Louis Argus*, 4 June 1948, 1, 8.

"Orr School is Nominated for National Historic Site." *Texarkana* (Arkansas) *Gazette*, 2 May 1976.

Oswald, Charles J. "Joplin's St. Louis Home Designated a Landmark." *Saint Louis Globe-Democrat*, 18 March 1977.

"Ragtime Opera." *BMI*, Fall 1975, 30–31.

Raney, Carolyn. "Ragtime Makes a Comeback: New York's New Passion—Scott Joplin (1868–1917)." *Baltimore Sunday Sun*, 14 November 1971, section D, p. 1.

Reed, Addison Walker. "The Life and Works of Scott Joplin." Ph.D. diss., University of North Carolina, 1973. 212 pp.

———. "Scott Joplin, Pioneer." *Black Perspective in Music* 3 (Spring 1975): 45–52; (Fall 1975): 269–77.

Rich, Alan. "Rags to Rip-Offs: Scott Joplin's Music." *New York*, 10 June 1974.

———. "Scott Joplin's 20/20 Vision." *New York*, 3 November 1975, p. 83.

Rosenfeld, Monroe H. "The King of Rag-Time Composers is Scott Joplin, a Coloured St. Louisan." *Saint Louis Globe-Democrat*, 7 June 1903, Sporting Section, p. 5.

Rowley-Rotunno, Virginia. "Scott Joplin: Renascence of a Black Composer of Ragtime and Grand Opera." *Negro History Bulletin* 37 (January 1974): 188–93.

Saal, Hubert. "Glad Rags." *Newsweek*, 5 August 1974, p. 60.

———. "King of Rag." *Newsweek*, 1 November 1971, 97–98.

Schafer, William J. "Scott Joplin: 'Shake de Earth's Foundation.'" *Mississippi Rag* 2 (July 1975): 10–11.

Schonberg, Harold C. "Music: *Treemonisha*." *New York Times*, 31 January 1972.

———. "Scholars, Get Busy on Scott Joplin." *New York Times*, 24 January 1971, p. D15.

———. "The Scott Joplin Renaissance Grows." *New York Times*, 13 February 1972, p. 15.

Schuller, Gunther. "Scott Joplin's Operatic Vision Comes to Life." *New York Times*, 18 May 1975.

Schulz, R. E. "Rites in Ragtime." *Music Ministry* 8 (May 1976): 2–4.

"School Named for Scott Joplin." *New York Amsterdam News*, 8 February 1975, p. D-11.

"Scott Joplin." *American Musician and Art Journal*, 8 November 1907, 12.

"Scott Joplin and the Ragtime Revival." *Record World*, 6 July 1974, 20.

"Scott Joplin as N.B.C. 2 Hour Spec." *Variety* 282 (31 March 1976).

"Scott Joplin Awarded a Special Pulitzer Prize." *Texarkana Gazette*, 5 May 1976.

"The Scott Joplin Collection." *Musicgram* 1 (October 1963): 51–53.

"Scott Joplin Dies of Mental Troubles." *New York Age*, 5 April 1917, p. 1.

"Scott Joplin: From Rags to Opera." *Time*, 15 September 1973, p. 85.

"Scott Joplin Is Dead." *Ragtime Review* 3 (July 1917): 13.

"Scott Joplin's Old Home on Delmar Designated as National Landmark." *Saint Louis Post-Dispatch*, 18 March 1977.

"St. Louis and Scott Joplin." *Saint Louis Post-Dispatch*, 2 February 1972.

"To Play Ragtime in Europe." *Saint Louis Post-Dispatch*, 28 February 1901, p. 3.

Vanderlee, Ann, and John Vanderlee. "The Early Life of Scott Joplin." *Rag Times* 7 (January 1974): 2–3.

———. "Scott Joplin's Childhood Days in Texas." *Rag Times* 7 (November 1973): 5–7.

Walker, Edward S. "Scott Joplin in England: An Investigation." *Storyville* no. 68 (December 1976–January 1977): 66–68.

Walters, Bob. "Joplin's Ragtime Jazz Is Revived." *Texarkana Gazette*, 2 January 1972, pp. 1, 2A.

Walton, Lester A. "Music and the Stage: Composer of Ragtime Now Writing Grand Opera." *New York Age*, 5 March 1908, p. 6.

Williams, Martin. "Scott Joplin: Genius Rediscovered." *Down Beat*, 25 November 1971, pp. 16, 38.

_____. "Scott Joplin, the Ragtime King, Rules Once More." *Smithsonian*, October 1974, pp. 108-20.

"A Wreath, and a Prayer for the Father of Ragtime," *New York News*, 18 August 1974, section 2, p. 2.

Wren, George R. "Scott Joplin's *Treemonisha* has Premiere Performance in Atlanta." *Storyville*, no. 40 (1 April 1972): 147-48.

Zimmerman, Dick. "Saga of the Silver Swan." *Rag Times* 4 (July 1970): 1.

_____. "*Treemonisha* Charms the Critics." *Rag Times* 5 (March 1972): 7.

_____. "*Treemonisha* Premieres." *Rag Times* 5 (March 1972): 1-6.

JORDAN, JOE

"Joe Jordan (1882-1971)." *Rag Times* 5 (November 1971): 1.

"Joe Jordan: Mr. Music Officer." *Ragtimer*, July-August 1970, 9-11.

Johnson, Leslie Carole. "The Remarkable Joe Jordan." *Mississippi Rag* 5 (June 1978): 1-4.

Zimmerman, Dick. "A Visit with Joe Jordan." *Rag Times* 2 (September 1968): 6.

_____. "Joe Jordan and Scott Joplin." *Rag Times* 2 (November 1968): 5.

KELLY, E. HARRY

Pash, Dennis. "E. Harry Kelly." *Rag Times* 10, Part 1 (March 1976): 2-4; Part 2 (May 1976): 2-3.

KLICKMANN, F. HENRI

Zimmerman, Dick. "F. Henri Klickmann." *Rag Times* 7 (November 1973): 9.

KRELL, WILLIAM H.

"Wm. H. Krell." *Brainard's Musical* 1 (Autumn 1899): 1.

LAMB, JOSEPH F.

Balliet, Whitney. "Ragtime Game." *New Yorker*, 2 July 1960, pp. 20-21.

Blesh, Rudi. "Notes on an American Genius." Foreword to Joseph F. Lamb, *Ragtime Treasures: Piano Solos by Joseph F. Lamb*. New York: Mills Music, 1964.

Cassidy, Russ. "Joseph Lamb: Last of the Ragtime Composers." *Jazz Report* 1 (January, February, March, April, and August 1961). Reprinted in *Jazz Monthly* 7 (August 1961): 4-7; (October 1961): 11-15; (November 1961): 9-10; (December 1961): 15-16. Reprinted as "Joseph F. Lamb: A Biography." *Ragtime Society* 5 (Summer 1966): 29-42.

"The Compositions of Joseph F. Lamb." *Ragtime Society* 2 (January 1963): 5-6.

Den, Marjorie Freilich. "Joseph F. Lamb: A Ragtime Composer Recalled." M.A. thesis, Brooklyn College, 1976.

Eccles, William. "Mr. Ragtime Comes Home: After 50 Years, Ragtime's Pioneer Makes a Canadian Comeback." *The* (Toronto) *Star Weekly*, 21 November 1959.

"Inside Stuff: Music." *Variety* 216 (7 October 1959): 65.

"Joseph Francis Lamb Dies." *Second Line*, nos. 3-4 (1961): 15.

Montgomery, Mike. "Joseph F. Lamb: A Ragtime Paradox, 1887-1960." *Second Line*, nos. 3-4 (1961): 17-18.

_____. "A Visit with Joe Lamb." *Jazz Report*, December 1957.

Schafer, William J. "Joseph Lamb: 'Sensation.'" *Mississippi Rag* 2 (September 1975): 6-7.

Tichenor, Trebor J. "The World of Joseph Lamb: An Exploration." *Jazz Monthly* 7 (August 1961): 7-9; (October 1961): 15-16; (November 1961): 10-11; (December 1961): 16-17.

LAMPE, J. BODEWALT

"J. B. Lampe, 1869-1929." *Rag Times* 7 (January 1974): 5.

"J. Bodewalt Lampe." *American Musician and Art Journal* 28 (27 April 1912): 3.

LAWRENCE, VERA BRODSKY

Jenkins, Speight. "A Talk with Vera Brodsky Lawrence." *Record World*, 6 July 1974, pp. 20, 24, 28.

Phillips, McCandlish. "Music Sleuth Traces America's Past." *New York Times*, 28 June 1972, p. 36.

LODGE, HENRY

Goodman, Solomon. "Henry Lodge." *Rag Times* 10 (March 1977): 9.

Zimmerman, Dick. "The Henry Lodge Story." *Rag Times* 9 (January 1976): 1-6.

MADDOX, JOHNNY

McLellen, Joseph. "'Crazy Otto' at the Keyboard," *Washington Post*, 26 November 1979; reprinted in *Ragtimer*, January-February 1980, pp. 9-12.

MARSHALL, ARTHUR

Bradford, Robert Allen. "Arthur Marshall: Last of the Sedalia Ragtimers." *Rag Times* 2 (May 1968): 5.

MATTHEWS, ARTIE

"Artie Matthews." *Rag Times* 15 (March 1982): 5.

"Artie Matthews' Rites To Be Friday." *Cincinnati Post & Times-Star*, 27 October 1958, p. 6.

Fox, Frank M. "Artie Matthews, A Cincinnati Legend." *Classic Rag*, February 1978, pp. 5-7.

MONTGOMERY, MIKE

Byler, Bob. "Piano Man and Scholar." *Mississippi Rag*, (March 1980): 1-5.

MORATH, MAX

"Concert Reviews." *Variety* 282 (18 February 1976): 108.

Curtis, Olga. "The Ragtime Music of Max Morath." *Ragtimer* 6, nos. 5-6 (1967): 4-8.

"Dynamic and Exciting Ragtime Beat Returns." *Christian Science Monitor*, 13 January 1975, p. 3A.

Grey, G. "Public Television Presents Max Morath in One Hour Special—*The Ragtime Years*." *Ragtimer*, March/April 1976: 7-9.

Haskins, John. "Max Morath Calls Show Ragtime, Not Nostalgia." *Kansas City* (Missouri) *Star*, 28 December 1971.

Horowitz, I. "Max Morath: Story of Rags to Riches." *Billboard* 86 (25 May 1974): 8.

Hutton, Jack. "Max Morath: The Finest Ragtime Entertainer of Them All." *The Ragtimer*, March–April–May–June 1984.

Johnson, Ron D. "Max Morath: Living a Ragtime Life." *Mississippi Rag* 1 (October 1974): 6-7.

"Learn Along with Max." *Newsweek*, 19 March 1962, p. 82.

"Max Morath and the Ragtime Years." *Jazz Report* 9, no. 1 (1975): 8.

Max Morath at the Turn of the Century. New York: Dunetz & Lovett, 1970. [16] pp.

Meness, Charles. "Max Morath Revives 'The Ragtime Era.'" *Saint Louis Post-Dispatch*, 17 January 1961.

"Morath Still Pushing Rag." *Variety* 289 (21 December 1977): 63.

"Rag Peddler." *Time*, 22 February 1963, p. 42.

"The Ragtime Years with Max Morath." *Variety* 280 (22 October 1975): 148.

Reffkin, David. "The Entertainer: An Update; Interview by David Reffkin." *Mississippi Rag* 11 (November 1983): 1-2.

Tallmer, Jerry. "Across the Footlights: Best Parlay in Town—Max and Max." *New York Post*, 15 June 1964.

Thompson, Butch. "The Entertainer." *Mississippi Rag* 1 (November 1973): 1.

Wilson, John S. "Max Morath in Rag and 'Unragtime.'" *New York Times*, 30 January 1982, p. 20.

———. "Quartet Revives Classic of Ragtime." *New York Times*, 24 June 1964.

———. "Turn-of-the-Century Music Sparkles." *New York Times*, 7 September 1963.

MORTON, JELLY ROLL

Albertson, Chris. Brochure notes to *Jelly Roll Morton*, Time-Life Records STL-J07, 1979. 52 pp.

Balliett, Whitney. "The Whiskey is Lovely." *New Yorker* 34 (22 March 1958): 137-38.

Barker, Danny. "Jelly Roll Morton in New York." In *Jazz Panorama*, edited by Martin Williams, pp. 13-20. New York: Collier Books. 1964.

Brown, Sterling A. "Portrait of a Jazz Genuis: 'Jelly Roll' Morton (1885?-1941)." *Black World* 23 (February 1974): 28-48.

"Bury Jelly Roll Morton on Coast." *Down Beat* 8 (1 August 1941): 13.

Carew, Roy J. "New Orleans Recollections: About Jelly-Roll." *Record Changer*, December 1948. Reprinted in *Ragtimer* 3, no. 5 (May 1964): 36.

———. "Of This and That and Jelly Roll." *Jazz Journal* 10, no. 12 (1957): 10-12.

Cusack, Thomas. *Jelly Roll Morton: An Essay in Discography.* London: Cassell, 1952.

Dance, Stanley. "Lightly and Politely: The Jelly Roll Stakes." *Jazz Journal* 27 (April 1974): 14.

Emge, Charles. "Seriously Ill, Jelly Roll Fights an Unfriendly World." *Down Beat* 8 (1 April 1941): 13.

Goodfriend, James. "The Triumphant, if Slightly Overdue, Return of Mr. Jelly Lord." *Stereo Review* 32 (June 1974): 110-11.

Hill, Michael and Eric Bryce. *Jelly Roll Morton: A Microgroove Discography and Musical Analysis.* Occasional Papers, no. 16. Salisbury East, South Australia: Salisbury College of Advanced Education, 1977.

Kay, George W. "An Interview with Roy Carew." *The Ragtimer* 5, no. 6 (December 1966): 67-69.

———. "Final Years of Frustration (1939-1941) as Told by Jelly Roll Morton in His Letters to Roy J. Carew." *Jazz Journal* 21 (November 1968): 2-5; (December 1968): 8-9.

Kramer, Karl. "Jelly Roll in Chicago: The Missing Chapter." *Ragtimer* 6 (April 1967): 15-22.

Kumm, Bob. "The Strange Case of Jelly's Will as Told to Bob Kumm by Harrison Smith." *Storyville*, no. 25 (October–November 1969): 8-9.

Lomax, Alan. *Mister Jelly Roll: The Fortunes of Jelly Roll Morton, New Orleans Creole and "Inventory of Jazz".* New York: Duell, Sloan and Pearce, 1950; 2nd ed. Berkeley: University of California Press, 1973. 318 pp.

Lyttleton, Humphrey. "Jelly Roll Morton." In *The Best of Jazz: Basin Street to Harlem; Jazz Masters and Masterpieces, 1917-1930*, pp. 86-98. New York: Taplinger, 1982.

Lucas, John S. "Lord and Lion: Let the Records Set the Record Straight." *Second Line* 16 (May/June 1965): 61–64ff.

Merriam, Alan P. "Jelly Roll Morton: A Review Article." *Midwest Folklore* 8 (Winter 1958): 217–21.

Morton, Jelly Roll. "Fragment of an Auto-biography." *Record Changer* (March 1944): 15–16; (April 1944): 27–28.

———. "I Discovered Jazz in 1902." *Down Beat*, August 1938. Reprinted in *Frontiers of Jazz*, edited by Ralph de Toledano, pp. 104–07. New York: Frederick Ungar, 1947.

Russell, W. "Albert Nicholas Talks about Jelly Roll." *Second Line* 30 (Spring 1978): 3–10.

———. "Jelly Roll Morton and the *Frog-I-More Rag*." In *The Art of Jazz*, edited by Martin Williams, pp. 33–41. New York: Oxford University Press, 1959.

Schulberg, Budd. "What Made Tiger Rag?" *Esquire* 34 (September 1950): 47.

Schuller, Gunther. "The First Great Composer." Chapter 4 in *Early Jazz: Its Roots and Musical Development*, pp. 134–74. New York: Oxford University Press, 1968.

Smith, Charles Edward. *Jelly Roll Morton's New Orleans Memories*. New York: Consolidated Records, [n.d.].

———. "Oh, Mr. Jelly!" *Jazz Record*, no. 17 (February 1944): 8–10. Reprinted in *Jazz Piano*, no. 2 (1945): 17–19.

Souchon, Edmond. "Doctor Bites Doctor Jazz (and Apologizes)." *Record Changer*, February 1953, p. 6.

Spear, Horace L. "Some Notes on Jelly Roll." *Storyville*, no. 33 (1 February 1971): 88–89.

Thompson, Kay C. "Rag-Time and Jelly Roll." *Record Changer* 8 (April 1959): 8, 23.

Townley, Eric. "Bob Greene and Mister Jelly Lord." *Storyville*, no. 62 (December 1975–January 1976): 67–71.

Waterman, Guy. "Jelly Roll Morton." In *Jazz Panorama*, edited by Martin Williams, pp. 31–38. New York: Collier Books, 1964.

Williams, Martin. *Jelly Roll Morton*. New York: A. S. Barnes, 1961.

———. "Jelly Roll Morton: Three-Minute Form." Chapter 3 in *The Jazz Tradition*, rev. ed., pp. 16–46. New York: Oxford University Press, 1983.

MURPHY, TURK

Goggin, Jim. *Turk Murphy: Just for the Record*. San Leandro, Calif.: San Francisco Traditional Jazz Foundation, 1982. 356 pp.

Millstein, Gilbert. "Turk Murphy," in *Jam Session: An Anthology of Jazz*, edited by Ralph J. Gleason, pp. 95–97. London: Peter Davies, 1961.

OSSMAN, VESS L.

Walsh, Jim. "George N. & Audley F. Dudley." *Hobbies*, February 1953.

———. "Sylvester Louis Ossman (Banjo King)." *Hobbies*, September, October, November 1948; January, February 1949.

PARKER, KNOCKY

Cundall, Tom. "'The Strenuous Life': Knocky Parker." *Jazz Journal* 5 (September 1952): 1–2.

Daugherty, Jane. "Ragtime Revival Makes Sense to Knocky." *Saint Petersburg Times*, 6 November 1974.

"Knocky Parker." *Playback* 2, no. 6 (June 1949): 13.

Robertson, C. A. "Knocky Parker: Old Rags." *Audio* 42 (February 1958): 44.

Skerret, Frank. "Some Present-Day Pianists." *Jazz Journal* 3 (July 1950): 2.

PRATT, PAUL

"Paul Charles Pratt." *Indianapolis Star*, 8 July 1948, p. 12.

Parrish, Terry. "The Paul Pratt Story." *Rag Times* 17 (January 1984): 2–5; (March 1984): 3–6.

PRYOR, ARTHUR

Ames, J. Scott. "Arthur Pryor, A Little biography." *Music World*, November 1907.

"Arthur Pryor." *Metronome*, June 1905, pp. 10–11.

"Arthur Pryor." *Metronome*, October 1907, pp. 9–10.

"Arthur Pryor and His Band." *Metronome*, February 1905, p. 13.

"Growth of Arthur Pryor and His Band." *Metronome*, May 1909, p. 10.

"No Ragtime for Pryor." *Rag Times* 13 (November 1979): 4–5.

RIFKIN, JOSHUA

Dallas, K. "Rifkin's Ragtime Finale." *Melody Maker* 50 (25 January 1975): 41.

Dexter, D. "Rifkin Checks Out as Ragtime Virtuoso." *Billboard* 87 (12 April 1975): 66.

Johnson, Leslie Carole. "Rifkin on Ragtime." *Mississippi Rag* 2 (March 1975): 1–3.

Pleasants, Henry. "Rifkin, Ragtime Ambassador." *Stereo Review* 32 (April 1974): 52.

Zimmerman, Dick. "Rifkin Talks Ragtime." *Rag Times* 12 (January 1979): 2–3.

ROBERTS, DAVID THOMAS

Rummel, Jack T. "An Interview with David Thomas Roberts." *Rag Times* 16 (November 1982): 4–6.

ROBERTS, LUCKEY

"Charles Luckeyeth (Luckey) Roberts (1893–1968)." *Ragtimer* 6, nos. 5–6 (1967): 13.

Hoefer, George. "Luckey Roberts." *Jazz Journal* 16 (March 1963): 7–9.

Vinding, Terkild. "Forgotten People." *Second Line* 23 (May–June 1970): 329–31, 340.

ROBERTS, ROBERT

Walsh, Jim. "'Ragtime' Robert Roberts." *Hobbies*, April 1944.

ROBINSON, J. RUSSEL

"In Memoriam: J. Russel Robinson." *Ragtime Review* 2 (October 1963): 6.

Parker, John W. (Knocky). "J. Russel Robinson . . . An Overdue Tribute." *Ragtime Review* 1 (October 1962): 4–5.

Robinson, J. Russel. "Dixieland Piano," as told to Ralph auf der Heide. *Record Changer*, August 1947, pp. 7–8.

"Russel Robinson, Song Writer, Dies." *New York Times*, 2 October 1963, p. 42.

ROYE, RUTH

"The Princess of Ragtime." *Christensen's Ragtime Review* 1 (June 1915): 16.

RUSSELL, WILLIAM

Maher, Marileen. "Ragtime—Keeping It Alive." *Courier* 11 (22 May 1975).

Turner, Frederic. *Remembering Song: Encounters with the New Orleans Jazz Tradition*. New York: Viking Press, 1982, pp. 61–70.

SCHULLER, GUNTHER

Battisti, F. "Gunther Schuller and his Many Worlds of Music." *Instrumentalist* 32 (June 1978): 44.

Hasse, John Edward. "An Interview with Gunther Schuller." *Annual Review of Jazz Studies* 1 (1982): 39–58.

Palmer, R. "Gunther Schuller on the American Musical Melting Pot." *Down Beat* 43 (2 February 1976): 12–15ff.

Reffkin, David. "The Ragtime Machine." *Mississippi Rag* 11 (November 1983): 9–11.

Ryan, Barbara Haddad. "Schuller Sets Pace in Ragtime Renaissance." *Rocky Mountain News* (Denver, Colorado), 17 April 1979, pp. 50–51.

Wilson, John S. "Gunther Schuller." *BMI*, Spring 1975, pp. 44–45.

SCOTT, JAMES

Affeldt, Paul. "James Scott, 'Crown Prince of Ragtime.'" *Jazz Report* 1 (October 1960): 7–9.

"James Scott Memorial Dedication Ceremony." *Rag Times* 15 (July 1981): 6.

Morgan, Ray. "James Scott Marker Completed." *Rag Times* 14 (November 1980): 1. Reprinted from the *Kansas City* (Missouri) *Times*, 2 October 1980.

"Ragtime Musicians To Play in a James S. Scott Tribute." *Kansas City Times*, 2 May 1981, p. B8.

Schafer, William J. "Grace and Beauty: The Case of James Scott." *Mississippi Rag* 2 (August 1975): 7–8.

VanGilder, Marvin. "He Remembers James Scott." *Rag Times* 12 (September 1978): 1.

———. "James Scott." *Rag Times* 11 (May 1977): 14–18. Reprinted from the *Carthage* (Missouri) *Press*.

Wright, Bob, and Trebor Tichenor. "James Scott and C. L. Johnson: An Unlikely Musical Kinship." *Ragtime Review* 5 (January 1966): 7–8; reprinted in *Rag Times* 6 (September 1972): 4.

SHEA, TOM

Willick, George C. "The Dean of Folk Ragtime." *Mississippi Rag* 9 (April 1982): 1–2.

SMITH, WILLIE "THE LION"

Clayton, Steve. "Homage to Willie "the Lion" Smith." *Rag Times* 7 (July 1973): 6–8.

Smith, Willie "the Lion." *Music on My Mind: The Memoirs of an American Pianist*. With George Hoefer. Garden City, N.Y.: Doubleday, 1964. 318 pp.

"Willie the Lion Smith, 1897–1973." *Ragtimer*, July–August 1973, pp. 15–16.

SNYDER, TED

"Ted Snyder Talks about the Old Days." *Metronome Orchestral Monthly* (1923). Reprinted in *Rag Times* 10 (September 1976): 4–5.

Zimmerman, Dick. "A Visit with Mrs. Ted Snyder." *Rag Times* 4 (May 1970): 2–4.

SOUSA, JOHN PHILIP

Bierly, Paul E. *John Philip Sousa: American Phenomenon*. New York: Appleton-Century-Crofts, 1973.

Newsom, Jon, ed. *Perspectives on John Philip Sousa*. Washington, D.C.: Library of Congress, Music Division, 1983. 144 pp.

"'Ragtime Has Had Its Funeral,' Declares John Philip Sousa." *American Musician*, 26 March 1909, p. 15.

"Sousa at the Hippodrome." *New York Times*, 15 January 1906, p. 9.

STARK, E. J.

Cassidy, Russ. "Obituary of Etilman J. Stark." *Ragtime Review* 1 (January 1962): 3–4.

STARK, JOHN

"Best Songs Never Make a Hit." *Christensen's Ragtime Review* 1 (June 1915): 12.

Christensen, Axel. "Chicago Syncopations: John Stark Pioneer Publisher." *Melody* 2 (October 1918): 8.

"The Interviewer Talks With . . ." *American Musician and Art Journal* 24 (11 December 1908): 13.

"A Ragtime Pioneer." *Ragtime Review* 1 (September 1915): 8.

"Stark Music Company." *American Musician and Art Journal,* 27 August 1909, p. 30.

"Stark Music Printing Company's New Home." *American Musician and Art Journal* 20 (26 June 1906): 6.

"The Starks' First Decade in St. Louis." *Rag Times* 10 (January 1977): 1–2.

THOMPSON, CHARLES

Grove, Thurman, and Mary Grove. "St. Louis Piano: The Story of Charles Thompson." *Playback* 3 (January 1950): 3–6.

"Ragtime Piano Era in St. Louis Recalled in Jazz Course Here: Charley Thompson Tells Class of Competing With Other Top Pianists of That Time." *Saint Louis Post-Dispatch,* 1 March 1956.

Rogers, Charles Payne. "Charles Thompson, Ragtime Pioneer." *Record Changer* 9 (May 1950): 13. Reprinted in *Ragtimer* 6 (April 1967): 8.

Tichenor, Trebor J. "'The Real Thing' as Recalled by Charles Thompson." *Ragtime Review* 2 (April 1963): 5–6. Reprinted in *Rag Times* 5 (November 1971): 3–4.

TICHENOR, TREBOR JAY

"Trebor Jay Tichenor Turns 'Living a Ragtime Life' Into an Active Reality." *Ragtimer,* July–August 1975, pp. 10–11.

Wierzbicki, J. "His 'Piano Roll Blues': Trebor Tichenor Lives, Breathes and Collects Ragtime Music." *Ragtimer,* July–August 1978, pp. 11–13.

TURPIN, TOM

"Mr. Tom Turpin: A Rosebud Novelty." *Saint Louis Palladium,* 24 December 1904, p. 1.

"The Rosebud Ball." *Saint Louis Palladium,* 27 February 1904, p. 1.

Young, Nathan B. "Charlie and Tom" and "The Father of the Jazz Age" in *Your St. Louis and Mine,* pp. 39 and 62. Saint Louis: N. B. Young, [ca. 1937].

VAN EPS, FRED

Walsh, Jim. "Fred Van Eps." *Hobbies,* January, February, March, and April 1956.

WALDO, TERRY

Byler, Bob. "A Multitude of Talents." *Mississippi Rag* 4 (September 1977), pp. 10–12.

WENRICH, PERCY

"Percy Wenrich & Dolly Connolly." *Rag Times* 7 (September 1973): 6.

Tichenor, Trebor Jay. "Percy Wenrich: 'Chestnuts, Crabapples, and Sweet Cider.'" *Jazz Report* 1 (December 1969): [4]–[6].

Walsh, Jim. "Dolly Connolly and Percy Wenrich." *Hobbies* 78 (June 1973): 37, 38, 98F, 98G, 98X, 98Y, 98FF; (July 1973): 37, 38, 98F, 98G, 98X, 98Y, 98EE, 98FF.

WHITE, ALBERT

Martin, Peter. "The Ragtime Years as Lived by Albert White." *Mississippi Rag* 9 (August 1982): 1–3.

WILLIAMS, BERT

Charter, Ann. *Nobody: The Story of Bert Williams.* New York: Macmillan, 1970.

Walsh, Jim. "Bert Williams, The Thwarted Genius." *Hobbies,* September, October, and November 1950.

WOODS, CLARENCE

"Ragtime Wonder of South," *Ragtime Review* 3 (January 1917): 19.

VanGilder, Marvin. "The Childhood of Clarence Woods." *Rag Times* 11 (March 1978): 3. Reprinted from *Carthage (Missouri) Press.*

———. "Clarence Woods: 'The Ragtime Wonder of the South.'" *Rag Time* 11 (January 1978): 1–2. Reprinted from the *Carthage (Missouri) Press.*

WOOLSEY, CALVIN L.

Zimmerman, Dick. "C. L. Woolsey." *Rag Times* 10 (May 1976): 4–5.

ZIMMERMAN, DICK

Feather, Leonard. "Ragtime Enters Another Childhood." *Los Angeles Times,* 7 October 1968.

Ragtime Music Folios and Method Books

This is intended to be as thorough as possible a list of ragtime music collections and method books for piano, piano and voice, and other instruments. Besides ragtime, the related styles of novelty piano and stride piano are also included. Ragtime arrangements for ensembles larger than five pieces—for example, full band or orchestra—are not included. Also excluded are "classical" compositions, such as those by Charles Ives and Claude Debussy, that incorporate ragtime. Folios that include both vocal and piano ragtime are classified in the section into which they predominantly fall.

New as well as old ragtime compositions are included. Thus, the revival of ragtime composition, beginning in the 1960s, by William Albright, William Bolcom, Brian Dykstra, Peter Howard, Max Morath, James Tenney, and others is represented in a number of folios.

Series titles, if any, appear in parentheses. Where the publisher is not the distributor, the distributor, if known, is listed. Note that all Edward B. Marks Music Corporation publications are distributed in the United States by Belwin-Mills Publishing Corporation, Melville, New York 11746.

Titles known to be out of print are marked **OP**. An * following the entry indicates that I have not personally seen the item, and am relying on secondary sources of information. Those in-print piano folios that form the basic ragtime piano music collection are marked with a dagger (†).

The Sting folio is available for many different instruments. Besides those listed below, John Cacavas has made the following arrangements (all published by MCA/Mills): "All C Instruments," "All Bb Instruments," "All Eb Instruments," "All Bass Clef Instruments," (all the preceding with or without piano accompaniment), and "Piano Accompaniment for Instrumental Books."

My sources of information include: music publishers' catalogs, the Library of Congress, U.S. Copyright records, the Archive of Popular American Music (UCLA), the New York Public Library, and the private collections of Edward A. Berlin, Michael R. Montgomery, Trebor Jay Tichenor, and the present author. Also, *Ragtime Piano Music in Print* by Charles B. Davis, Jr., (Midway Park, N.C.: Charles B. Davis, Jr., 1982) and other published ragtime books were consulted.

The listings are organized as follows:

Solo Piano Collections
Ragtime Piano Method Books
Piano Duet Arrangements
Simplified Piano Collections
Ragtime Song Collections
Collected Organ Arrangements
Collected Guitar Arrangements
Collected Banjo Arrangements
Collected Arrangements for Violin and Piano
Collected Arrangements for Two Flutes or Two Violins
Collected Arrangements for B-flat Clarinet and Piano
Collected Arrangements for Flute or Clarinet and Piano
Ragtime Saxophone Methods
Collected Arrangements for Trombone and Piano
Collected Arrangements for Brass Quintet
Collected Arrangements for String Quartet
Collected Arrangements for Woodwind Quintet
Collected Arrangements for "German Band"
Collected Arrangements for C Instruments
Collected Arrangements for C, B-flat, or E-flat Instruments
Collected Arrangements for Recorder Quartet
Collected Arrangements for Chromatic Harmonica

Solo Piano Collections

Albright, William. *The Dream Rags for Piano.* New York: Edward B. Marks Music Corp., 1980. 25 pp.

———. *Grand Sonata in Rag for Piano.* Paris: Société des Editions Jobert, 1974. 21 pp. Distributed in the United States by the Theodore Presser Co., Bryn Mawr, Pa.

———. *Three Novelty Rags for Piano.* Paris: Société des Editions Jobert, 1973. 17 pp. Distributed in the United States by the Theodore Presser Co., Bryn Mawr, Pa.

Album of Rags, Vols. 1 and 2. New York: RFT Music Publishing Corp., 1973.*

Alpert, Pauline. *Pauline Alpert Folio of Modern Piano Solos.* New York: Mills Music, [ca. 1935]. 32 pp. **OP.**

Atwell, Winifred. *Francis & Day's Souvenir Album of Winifred Atwell.* London: Francis, Day & Hunter, [n.d.].*

———, comp. *Francis & Day's Album of Rags, Nos. 1, 2, and 3.* London: Francis, Day & Hunter, [n.d.].

†*The Best of Ragtime Favorites and How to Play Them.* New York: Charles Hansen, [197-]. 161 pp. Spiral-bound.

†Blake, Eubie. *Sincerely Eubie Blake: 9 Original Compositions for Piano Solo.* Transcribed by Terry Waldo. New York: Eubie Blake Music, 1975. 72 pp.

†Blesh, Rudi, comp. *Classic Piano Rags: Complete Original Music for 81 Rags.* New York: Dover Publications, 1973. 364 pp.

———. *The Ragtime Current: Piano Solos by a Mainstream of Today's Ragtime Composers.* New York: Edward B. Marks Music Corp., 1976.

Bolcom, William. *The Garden of Eden: Four Rags for Piano.* New York: Edward B. Marks Music Corp., 1974. 20 pp.

Brainard's Ragtime Collection, Being a Collection of Characteristic Two-Steps, Cake Walks, Plantation Dances, Etc. New York: S. Brainard's Sons Co., 1899. 96 pp. **OP.**

Carr, Joe "Fingers." *Bar Room Piano Solos: Original Compositions by Joe "Fingers" Carr, as Recorded on Capitol Records.* New York: Chatsworth Music, 1952. 31 pp. **OP.**

Classic Rags, Waltzes and Characteristic Music Especially Arranged for Professional and Theatre Pianists. Saint Louis: Stark Music Co., [ca. 1910]. 40 pp. **OP.**

Confrey, Zez. *African Suite, for Piano.* New York: Jack Mills, 1924. 16 pp. **OP.**

———. *The Exciting Era of Zez Confrey.* New York: Mills Music, 1963. 65 pp.

———. *Lawrence Wright's First Album of Famous Novelty Piano Solos by Zez Confrey.* London: Lawrence Wright, [ca. 1924]. 28 pp.

———. *Modern Folio of Novelty Piano Solos.* New York: Mills Music, [1930s?]. **OP*.**

†———. *Ragtime, Novelty and Jazz Piano Solos.* Edited by Ronny S. Schiff. Introduction by David A. Jasen. Melville, N.Y.: Belwin-Mills, 1982. 329 pp.

———. *Three Little Oddities.* Boston: Boston Music Co., [n.d.].*

———. *Zez Confrey's Novelty Piano Solos.* New York: Mills Music Co., [ca. 1933]. 32 pp. **OP.**

Dance Folio of Modern Dances; Tango, Maxixe, Fox Trot, One Step, Two Step, Hesitation Waltz. Saint Louis: Syndicate Music Co., [191-]. **OP.**

Dickie, Neville, arr. *The Neville Dickie Album of Rags and Standards.* London: Campbell, Connelly & Co., 1971. 27 pp.*

Dykstra, Brian. *Eight Concert Rags.* Wooster, Ohio: Brian Dykstra, [ca. 1980]. [83] pp. Available from Brian Dykstra, 1529 Cleveland Road, Wooster, Ohio 44691.*

EMI Book of Rags. London: EMI, [n.d.].*

Forster's Vocal and Instrumental Folio of Copyright Hits, No. 1. Chicago: Forster, [1911]. Unpaginated. **OP.**

Forster's Theater-Pianist's Folio of Copyrighted Hits, Nos. 2, 3, and 4. Chicago: Forster, [1912–14]. Unpaginated. **OP.**

Golden Encyclopedia of Ragtime, 1900–1974. New York: Charles Hansen, [1974]. (Memory Lane Series.) 367 pp.*

Heltman, Fred. *Six Rags for the Piano.* Cleveland: Fred Heltman Co., [ca. 1918]. 24 pp. **OP.**

Hoefer, George, ed. *The Ragtime Folio.* New York: Melrose Music Corp., 1950. (The Morris-Mayfair-Melrose Series of Famous Blues, Stomps, and Ragtime.) 33 pp. **OP.**

Howard, Peter. *Three Rags for Piano.* New York and London: G. Schirmer, 1979. 11 pp.

———. *Three More Rags for Piano.* New York and London: G. Schirmer, 1981. 12 pp.*

Ingraham, Herbert. *Herbert Ingraham's Classic Rags: A Collection of New and Original Ragtime Compositions for Piano.* New York: Maurice Shapiro, 1909. **OP.***

Isacoff, Stuart, comp. *From Rags to Jazz.* New York: Consolidated Music Publishers, 1976. (Music for Millions Series, Vol. 66.) 96 pp.

Jack Mills Incomparable Folio [of] Rags and Blues for the Piano, Vol. 1. New York: Jack Mills, [ca. 1925]. **OP.**

Jack Mills Modern Folio of Novelty Piano Solos, Nos. 1, 2, 3, 4, 5, and 6. New York: Jack Mills, [192-]. **OP.***

Jacobs' Piano Folio of Rags for Comedy, Acrobatic and Other Lively Scenes, 1, 2, 3, and 4. Boston: Walter Jacobs, [ca. 1920–24]. **OP.**

†Jasen, David A., comp. *Ragtime: 100 Authentic Rags.* New York: The Big 3 Music Corp., 1979. 408 pp.

Jo Ann Castle, Ragtime Piano Gal: 12 More Hits in Ragtime, as Recorded and Featured on the Lawrence Welk TV Show. Arranged by George N.

Terry. Santa Monica, Calif.: Harry Von
Tilzer Music Publishing Co., 1965. 47 pp.
Johnson, James P. *James P. Johnson's Piano Jazzfest.*
New York: Bregman, Vocco, and Conn,
1946. **OP*.**
_____. *Piano Solos by James P. Johnson.* Tran-
scribed from his Decca Records by Dick
Meares and David LeWinter. New York:
Clarence Williams Music Publishing Co.,
1945. **OP.**
Joplin, Scott. *Best of Ragtime.* Hialeah, Fla.:
Columbia Pictures Publications, 1980. (Uni-
versal Favorites Series, Vol. 15.)
_____. *The Best of Scott Joplin: A Collection of
Original Ragtime Piano Compositions.* Edited by
Bill Ryerson. New York: Charles Hansen
Music and Books, 1973. 97 pp. Spiral-
bound.
_____. *The Best Ragtime Originals: Advanced Piano.*
Miami: Screen Gems-Columbia Publica-
tions, 1974. 72 pp.
_____. *The Collected Works of Scott Joplin.* Edited
by Vera Brodsky Lawrence; Introduction
by Rudi Blesh. Vol. I: *Works for Piano.* New
York: New York Public Library, 1971. 305
pp. Hard cover. Also published in a paper-
bound edition as *Collected Piano Works.* New
York: New York Public Library, 1972.
_____. *The Complete Works of Scott Joplin.* Edited
by Vera Brodsky Lawrence; Introduction
by Rudi Blesh. Vol. I: *Works for Piano.* New
York: New York Public Library, 1982. (The
American Collection Music Series, No. 1.)
327 pp.
_____. *Complete Ragtime Piano Solos, Including
Waltzes, Marches, and Song Editions—and a Vocal
and Original Piano Solo of The Entertainer—
Motion Picture Award Winner.* New York:
Charles Hansen, 1974. 177 pp. Spiral-
bound.
_____. *Easy Winners: Nine Piano Rags.* Seven-
oaks, Kent, England: Paxton, [1978]. 37 pp.
Distributed in the U.S. by the Theodore
Presser Co., Bryn Mawr, Pa.
_____. *The Entertainer: Scott Joplin with a Difference.*
Arranged by David Kay. New York:
Charles Hansen, [1974]. 25 pp.*
_____. *The Entertainer und andere Ragtimes von
Scott Joplin.* Arranged by Ernst August
Quelle. München: BZ-Musik, Birnbach and
Zimmerhansl, 1974. 28 pp.
_____. *The Entertainer und weitere 9 bekannte Rags
von Scott Joplin.* Berlin: Rolf Budde Musikver-
lage, 1974. 44 pp.
_____. *King of Ragtime.* [Compiled by Albert
Gamse.] Carlstadt, N.J.: Lewis Music Pub-
lishing Co., 1972. 159 pp.
_____. *King of Ragtime Writers.* New York:
Charles Hansen, [1972?]. London: Hansen
House, [1972]. (Hansen House No. 11.) 72
pp.

_____. *The Missouri Rags, for Piano.* Selected by
Max Morath. New York and London: G.
Schirmer, 1975. 66 pp.*.
_____. *Piano Rags.* New York: Chappell Music
Co., [1974]. 48 pp.
_____. *Piano Rags, Book 1.* London: Chappell &
Co., 1973.*
_____. *Piano Rags, Book 2.* London: Chappell &
Co., 1973.*
_____. *Piano Rags, Books One, Two, and Three.*
Sevenoaks, Kent, England: Paxton, 1974.
Distributed in the U.S. by the Theodore
Presser Co., Bryn Mawr, Pa.
_____. *Piano Rags, Book No. 2: A Collection of Piano
Rags, Waltzes, and Marches.* New York:
Charles Hansen, 1973. 103 pp. Spiral-
bound.
_____. *Ragtime King.* New York: Carl Fischer,
1982. 120 pp.
_____. *Ragtime für Klavier/for Piano, Vols. I and II.*
Edited by Eberhardt Klemm. Leipzig: Edi-
tion Peters, 1977. Vol. I: 1899-1906. 90 pp.
Vol. II: 1907-1917. 79 pp.
_____. *Scott Joplin Presents 42 Entertaining Songs,
Including Visual Chord Charts, and Special School
of Ragtime Exercises by Scott Joplin; a Play-by-
Chords Edition for Piano or Organ.* New York:
Charles Hansen, [1973]. 65 pp.
_____. *Scott Joplin's World Famous Jazz Classics for
Piano.* Saint Louis: Stark Music Co., 1928.
34 pp. **OP*.**
_____. *13 Rags & Waltzes.* Hollywood, Calif.:
Beechwood Music Corp., 1974. 49 pp.
_____, et al. *Collaboration Rags: Six Piano Rags.*
Sevenoaks, Kent, England: Paxton, [ca.
1974]. 26 pp. Distributed in the U.S. by
the Theodore Presser Co., Bryn Mawr, Pa.
†Lamb, Joseph F. *Ragtime Treasures: Piano Solos by
Joseph F. Lamb.* Foreword by Rudi Blesh.
New York: Mills Music, 1964. 64 pp.
*Lawrence Wright's Albums of Famous Novelty Piano
Solos.* Nos. 2-5. London: Lawrence Wright,
[192-].
Little, Tiny, Jr., arr. *Lawrence Welk Favorites for
Honky-Tonk Piano.* New York: Remick Music
Corp., [1962?].*
Lopez, Vincent, comp. *A Folio of Vincent Lopez
Novelty Piano Solos; by Mel Kaufman, Harry
Jentes and Others.* New York: Robbins-Engel,
Inc., 1925. **OP*.**
*The Mark Stern Instrumental "Ragtime" Folio, No. 4:
Eighteen Famous Instrumental Ragtime Successes.*
New York, London, Chicago: Jos. W. Stern
& Co., [ca. 1901]. 60 pp. **OP.**
Martin, Gerald, comp. *Dizzy Piano: Famous Nov-
elty Solos from the Golden Age of Jazz.* New
York: Sam Fox Publishing Co., 1960. 64 pp.
_____. *Jazz Gallery: Piano Portraits in Rhythm;
Ragtime, Blues, Swing, Modern Jazz.* New
York: Sam Fox Publishing Co., 1961. 64 pp.
Masterpieces in Ragtime by the World's Most Famous

Writers. Saint Louis: Stark Music Co., 1929. 38 pp. **OP.**

Mayerl, Billy. *The Jazz Master: A Collection of Famous Piano Solos by Billy Mayerl from the Golden Age of Jazz.* New York: Sam Fox Publishing Co.; London: EMI Music Publishing, 1972.

†Morath, Max, comp. *Max Morath's Giants of Ragtime: Scott Joplin, Eubie Blake, Luckey Roberts, Jim Europe, Tom Turpin.* New York: Edward B. Marks Music Corp., 1971. 64 pp.

———. *The Mississippi Valley Rags for Piano.* New York and London: G. Schirmer, 1975.*

———. *One Hundred Ragtime Classics.* Denver: Donn Printing, 1963. **OP.**

†———. *Ragtime Guide: A Collection of Ragtime Songs and Piano Solos.* 2nd ed. New York: Hollis, 1964. **OP.**

Morton, Jelly Roll. *Blues, Stomps and Ragtime.* New York: Edwin H. Morris & Co., [197-]; distributed by Charles Hansen, New York. (Jazz Giants.)

†———. *The Collected Piano Music.* Transcribed and edited by James Dapogny. Washington, D.C.: Smithsonian Institution Press; New York and London: G. Schirmer, 1982. 513 pp.

———. *"Jelly Roll" Morton's Famous Series of Blues & Stomps for Piano, Vols. 1, 2 and 3.* Chicago: Melrose Bros. Music Co., [1930s?]. London: Herman Darewski Music Publishing Co., [n.d.]. 20, 28, and 20 pp. respectively. **OP.**

———. *"Jelly Roll" Morton's Folio.* Edited by George Hoefer. New York: Melrose Music Corp., 1949. (The Morris-Mayfair-Melrose Series of Famous Blues, Stomps, and Ragtime.) 45 pp. **OP.**

———. *Just Jazz, Blues and Stomps.* New York: Edwin H. Morris & Co., [197-]; distributed by Charles Hansen, New York. 64 pp.

———. *The Original Mr. Jazz.* Mary Allen Hood and Helen M. Flint, eds. New York: Edwin H. Morris & Co., 1975; distributed by Charles Hansen, New York, 143 pp.

Nothing But Rags: A Collection of Syncopated Piano Pieces. Chicago, New York, London, Sydney: Victor Kremer Co., [ca.1910]. 32 pp. **OP.**

Olsen, David C., ed. *45 Ragtime Classics.* [New York]: Big 3, 1983. (Mammoth Series, No. 28.) Distributed by Columbia Pictures Publications. 160 pp.

Pioneer Ragtime Folio. New York: M. Witmark, 1897. **OP*.**

The "Pioneer" Rag-Time Folio: A Collection of Original Rag-Time Compositions and Novelties by the Best Rag-Time Players and Composers in the Country. New York: Shapiro, Bernstein & Co., 1902. 73 pp. **OP.**

Pioneer Rag-Time Folio No. 2. Detroit: Whitney-Warner Publishing Co., and New York: Shapiro-Remick & Co., [190-]. **OP.**

†*Play Them Rags: A Piano Album of Authentic Rag-Time Solos.* New York: Mills Music, 1961. 49 pp.

The Rag Bag: A Collection of Ragtime Numbers by Popular Composers. New York: Leo Feist, 1910. 32 pp. **OP.**

†*Rag Time: 37 Renowned Rags for Piano.* New York: Warner Bros. Publications, [197-?]. 96 pp.

Rag & Dixieland: Album Piano Solo. Paris: Publications Francis Day, [197-?]. 16 pp.

†*Ragtime Piano: A Collection of Standard Rags for Piano Solo.* New York: Mills Music, 1963. 65 pp.

Sam Fox Popular Standard Rag Folio for the Piano, Vols. 1 and 2. Cleveland and New York: Sam Fox Publishing Co., 1922 and 1924. **OP.**

Schiff, Ronny S., ed. *Jazz, Blues, Boogie & Swing for Piano: "The Jazz of an Era".* Melville, N.Y.: MCA/Mills, 1977. 159 pp.

Shealy, Alexander, comp. *Ragtime: World's Favorite Music and Songs.* Carlstadt, N.J.: Ashley Publications, 1973. (World's Favorite Series, no. 73.) 160 pp.

The Sting, Featuring the Music of Scott Joplin. Melville, N.Y.: MCA/Mills, 1974. 34 pp.

Stokes, Samuel J. *Stokes' New Orleans Ragtime Music Album.* Covington, La.: Samuel J. Stokes, Jr., [1982]. 32 pp. Available from Samuel J. Stokes, Jr., P.O. Box 392, Covington, La. 70433.

Tenney, James. *Three Rags for Pianoforte.* Toronto: E. C. Kerby, 1981. 13 pp.

Terry, George N., arr. *Honky-Tonk Rag Time Piano.* New York: Remick Music Corp., 1962. 33 pp.

———. *12 Great Hits in Rag-Time as Played by Jo Ann Castle on the Lawrence Welk TV Show.* Santa Monica, Calif.: Harry Von Tilzer Music Publishing Co., 1963. 40 pp.

†*34 Ragtime Jazz Classics for Piano.* New York: Melrose Music Corp., 1964. 137 pp.

†Tichenor, Trebor Jay, comp. *Ragtime Rarities: Complete Original Music for 63 Piano Rags.* New York: Dover Publications, 1975. 305 pp.

†———. *Ragtime Rediscoveries: 64 Works from the Golden Age of Rag.* New York: Dover Publications, 1979. 296 pp.

TV Favorites in Ragtime Featured on the Lawrence Welk TV Show by Jo Ann Castle. Santa Monica, Calif.: Harry Von Tilzer Music Publishing Co., [196-].*

Waller, Fats. *Jazz Giants.* New York: Charles Hansen, [197-].*

———. *The Music Maker.* London: EMI, 1978. 64 pp.

———. *Reminiscences of Fats Waller.* New York: Charles Hansen, [197-].*

Wilford, Charles, comp. *Ragtime Classics*. Sevenoaks, Kent, England: Paxton [ca. 1975]. 36 pp.*

†Zimmerman, Richard, comp. *A Tribute to Scott Joplin and the Giants of Ragtime*. New York: Charles Hansen, 1975. 160 pp.

Ragtime Piano Method Books

Christensen, Axel W. *Christensen's Rag-Time Instruction Book for Piano*. Chicago: Axel W. Christensen, 1904. Later editions were published in 1906, 1907, 1908, 1909, 1915, 1919, and 1920. By 1920 the title had changed to *Axel Christensen's New Instruction Book for Rag and Jazz Piano Playing*. **OP.**

———. *Christensen's Rag Time Instructor No. 2, For Advanced Pianists*. Chicago: Axel W. Christensen, 1909. Later editions were published in 1924 and 1925. 34 pp. **OP.**

Confrey, Zez. *Zez Confrey's Modern Course in Novelty Piano Playing*. New York: Jack Mills, 1923. 51 pp. **OP.**

Harney, Ben. *Ben Harney's Rag Time Instructor*. Arranged by Theodore H. Northrup. Chicago: Sol Bloom, 1897, 10 pp. **OP.**

Joplin, Scott. *School of Ragtime: 6 Exercises for Piano*. New York: Scott Joplin, 1908. 4 pp. Reprint ed. New York: Charles Hansen, 1973.

Kail, Bob. *How to Play Ragtime Piano: For the Advanced Pianist*. New York: Charles Hansen, 1974. 32 pp.

Kay, David. *How to Play Ragtime: Intermediate Piano*. New York: Charles Hansen, 1976. 49 pp.

Klaphake, Lillian Rose. *Improved, Rapid System of Ragtime Piano Playing*. Cincinnati, Cincinnati School of Popular Music, 1910. 20 pp. **OP.**

Learn to Play the Alfred Way: Ragtime Piano. Port Washington, N.Y.: Alfred Publishing Co., 1975. 40 pp.

Novy, Lew J. *Novy's Greatest Book of Ragtime: The World's Simplified System*. Chicago: Lew J. Novy, 1915. **OP*.**

Rag-Time Instruction Book for the Piano as Used Exclusively by the Franklin Schools of Popular Music. New York: The Ragtime Music Publishing Corp., 1914. **OP*.**

Thomas, S. A. *Artist's Style Instruction Book: For Popular Music, Rag-Time and Jazz Piano Playing*. Milwaukee: Sidney A. Thomas, 1921. 16 pp. **OP.**

Winn, Edward R. *Winn's How to Play Ragtime*. New York: Winn School of Popular Music, 1913. Later editions were published in 1915, 1917, and 1923. A reprint edition is available from Jerry Vogel Music Co., New York.

Piano Duet Arrangements

Agay, Denes, arr. *Ragtime Duets: One Piano—Four Hands*. New York: Edward B. Marks Music Corp., 1975. 63 pp.

———. *Scott Joplin Ragtime Classics for Piano Duet, Arranged for One Piano—Four Hands*. New York: Edward B. Marks Music Corp., 1974. 65 pp.

Simplified Piano Collections

Agay, Denes, ed. *The Joy of Ragtime: A Graded Collection of Classic Piano Rags by Scott Joplin, James Scott, Joseph F. Lamb, Charles Hunter, Percy Wenrich, and Many Others*. New York: Yorktown Music Press, 1974. 80 pp.

———, arr. *Scott Joplin's Classic Rags*. New York: Edward B. Marks Music Corp., [197-].*

Allen, Jerry, arr. *Hot Rags & Slow Drags*. Oskaloosa, Ia.: Writers' Equity, 1975. Sole Selling agent: Frank Music Affiliates, Boston. (Piano Styles by Jerry Allen.) 32 pp. Spiral-bound.

Booth, Frank, arr. *It's Easy to Play Ragtime*. New York: Amsco Music Publishing Co., 1979. London: Wise Publications, 1976. (Everybody's Favorite Series, No. 240.) 59 pp.

Bradley, Richard, arr. *Ragtime Joy*. Hialeah, Fla.: Columbia Pictures Publications, 1978. (Columbia Easy Piano Line.) 24 pp.

Brimhall, John, arr. *John Brimhall Presents Ragtime*. Miami Beach: Hansen House, [198-?].*

———. *John Brimhall Presents the Best of Ellington, Eubie & Scott Joplin*. Miami Beach, Fla.: Hansen House, [1983]. 33 pp.

———. *John Brimhall Presents the Best of "Jelly Roll," "Pine Top" & Scott Joplin*. New York: Charles Hansen, [197-].*

———. *John Brimhall's Best of Ragtime*. New York: Charles H. Hansen, 1974. 23 pp.

———. *The Rage is Rag*. New York: Charles Hansen, [197-].*

Caramia, Tony. *Rag Times Four*. San Diego, Calif.: Neil A. Kjos Music Co., 1983. 16 pp.

Chagy, John. *Ragtime Festival: Five Piano Rags*. Boulder, Colo.: Myklas Press, 1979. 11 pp.

Dennis, Matt. *Mel Bay's Ragtime Piano Styles*. Kirkwood, Mo.: Mel Bay Publications, 1973. 40 pp.

Draeger, Jürg. *Ragtime for Fans: Rags for Pianist in Progressive Orders, [Vols.] 1 and 2*. Zürich: Edition Melodie, 1981.

Dykstra, Brian. *Great Ragtime Tunes by Scott Joplin & Others Simplified and Arranged for Piano by Brian Dykstra*. Fullerton, Calif.: Centerstream Publications, 1983. Distributed by Columbia Pictures Corporation. 47 pp.

Grove, Roger. *The Riches of Rag: Seven Solos for the*

Intermediate Piano Student. Evanston, Ill.: Summy-Birchard Co., 1976. (Frances Clark Library Supplementary Collection.) 15 pp.

Hinson, Maurice and David Carr Glover, comps. *An Adventure in Ragtime.* Melville, N.Y.: Belwin-Mills Publishing Corp., 1975. (David Carr Glover Piano Library Entertainment Series.) 32 pp.

Joplin, Scott. *The Easy Winners, Elite Syncopations, The Ragtime Dance: Ragtime Piano Solos by Scott Joplin.* Arranged for easy piano by John Brimhall. New York: Charles Hansen, 1974. (Brimhall Piano Series.) 8 pp.

_____. *The Entertainer, Easy Winners, Maple Leaf Rag: Ragtime Piano Solos by Scott Joplin.* Arranged for easy piano by Lawrence Grant, Carlstadt, N.J.: Lewis Music Publishing Co., 1974. 8 pp.

_____. *The Entertainer, Maple Leaf Rag, Peacherine Rag: Ragtime Piano Solos by Scott Joplin.* Arranged for easy piano by John Brimhall. New York: Charles Hansen, 1974. (Brimhall Piano Series). 7 pp.

_____. *The King of Ragtime Writers; Easy Piano.* Arranged by Lawrence Grant. Carlstadt, N.J.: Lewis Music Publishing Co., 1974. 32 pp.

_____. *Learn to Play the Alfred Way: Ragtime Piano.* Arranged by Allan Small. Sherman Oaks, Calif.: Alfred Publishing Co., 1978. 64 pp.

_____. *Matt Dennis Plays Scott Joplin: Intermediate.* Kirkwood, Mo.: Mel Bay Publications, 1974. 48 pp.

_____. *Ragtime Hits.* Selected, arranged, and edited by Herwin Peychär. Zürich: Edition Melodie, 1976, 28 pp.

_____. *Ragtime Piano Solos.* Arranged for easy piano by John Brimhall. New York: Charles Hansen, [1974]. 88 pp.*

_____. *Ragtime Piano Solos: Easy Piano.* Arranged by Allan Small. Sherman Oaks, Calif.: Alfred Publishing Co., 1974. 49 pp.

_____. *Ragtime Piano Solos, No. 2.* Edited by John Brimhall. New York: Charles Hansen, [197-].*

_____. *Ragtime Rage: Seven Fun-to-Play Piano Transcriptions, Books 1 and 2.* Compiled and arranged by John W. Schaum. Milwaukee: Schaum Publications, 1974.

_____. *Scott Joplin Arranged for Easy Piano.* Arranged by John Brimhall. New York: Charles Hansen, 1974. 32 pp.

_____. *Scott Joplin Favorites.* Arranged by James Bastien. Park Ridge, Ill.: General Words & Music Co., [1975]. 17 pp.

King, Stanford. *I'm Playing Ragtime: 12 Easy-to-Play Piano Pieces.* New York: Carl Fischer, 1975. 15 pp.

Schaum, John W., arr. *The Ragtime Book.* Melville, N.Y.: Belwin Mills, 1956. (Solo Piano Albums for the Young Student.) 23 pp.

Small, Allan, arr. *Ragtime Piano Solos: Easy Piano.* Port Washington, N.Y.: Alfred Publications, 1974. 48 pp.

The Sting, Featuring the Music of Scott Joplin. Arranged for easy-to-play piano by David Carr Glover. Melville, N.Y.: MCA/Mills, 1974. 23 pp.

Waldman, Robert. *A Rag Bag: For Piano.* Illustrated by Isadore Seltzer. New York and London: G. Schirmer, 1977. 24 pp.

Ragtime Song Collections

Bert Williams Folio of Ne'er-to-be-Forgotten Songs. New York: Robbins-Engel, 1925. 36 pp. **OP.**

Charters, Ann, comp. *The Ragtime Songbook: Songs of the Ragtime Era by Scott Joplin, Hughie Cannon, Ben Harney, Will Marion Cook, Alex Rogers and Others.* New York: Oak Publications, 1965.

Cole & Johnson [Bob Cole, Rosamond Johnson, and James Weldon Johnson]. *The Evolution of Ragtime.* New York: Jos. W. Stern & Co., 1903. 23 pp. **OP.**

Cole & Johnson Vocal Folio: A Superior Collection of Quaint and Classic Negro Songs by the Famous Writers Bob Cole, Rosamond Johnson, Jas. W. Johnson. New York: Jos. W. Stern & Co., 1904. (The Mark Stern Edition.) ca. 81 pp. **OP.**

The "Mark Stern" Ragtime Folio No. 1: A Collection of the Best Negro Melodies of the Day by Such Composers as Williams & Walker, Irving Jones, Barney Fagan, Monroe H. Rosenfeld, Gussie L. Davis, Al. Johns, Ed. Rogers, Tom Logan and other Famous Writers of Ragtime Successes. New York: Jos. W. Stern & Co., [ca. 1899]. 78 pp. **OP.**

The Mark Stern "Rag-Time" Song Folio No 2: Fifteen Late Popular Ragtime Successes by Williams & Walker, Heelen & Helf, Ed. Rogers, Bowman & Johns, Irving Jones, Hogan & Northrup, Monroe H. Rosenfeld, Bob. Cole, Deas & Wilson. New York: Jos. W. Stern & Co., [ca. 1902]. 79 pp. **OP.**

The Mark Stern Vocal "Ragtime" Folio, No. 3: Twenty-Three Latest Popular "Ragtime Hits" by Williams and Walker, Ernest Hogan, Paul Lawrence Dunbar, Max S. Witt, Jean C. Havez, and Other Prominent Writers of Favorite Negro Melodies. New York, London, Chicago: Jos. W. Stern & Co., [ca. 1903]. **OP.**

Morath, Max, comp. *Max Morath's Guide to Ragtime: A Collection of Ragtime Songs and Piano Solos.* New York: Hollis Music, 1964. 128 pp. **OP.** Revised edition published as *Max Morath's Ragtime Guide: A Collection of Ragtime Songs and Piano Solos.* New York: Hollis Music, 1972. 127 pp.

_____. *Max Morath's Songs of the Early 20th Century Entertainer.* New York: Edward B.

Marks Music Corp., 1977. 64 pp.

Original Ragtime Songs, Nos. 1 and 2. London: Francis, Day & Hunter, [n.d.].*

Rag Classix: More Than 40 Renowned Rags for Singing and Playing. New York: Warner Brothers, 1973. 144 pp.

Strictly "Rags": Memory Lane in Rag-Time (A Vocal-Piano Collection). New York: Remick Music, 1960.*

The "Up-to-Date" Coon Song Folio. New York: Shapiro, Bernstein & Co., [ca. 1902]. **OP***.

Whitcomb, Ian, comp. *I Remember Ragtime.* New York: Charles Hansen, [ca. 1973]. 96 pp. Spiral-bound.

Collected Organ Arrangements

Biggs, E. Power, arr. *Scott Joplin for Organ.* New York and London: G. Schirmer, 1976. (Great Performers' Edition.) 34 pp.

Bob Ralston, Ragtime Organ Man. Arranged for all organs by Mark Laub. Santa Monica, Calif.: Harry Von Tilzer Music Publishing Co., [196-?].*

The Entertainer and other Great Ragtime Songs. Arranged for Magnus and all other chord organs. New York: Charles Hansen, [197-].*

Erwin, Lee, arr. *Rosebud: Marches & Rags of Scott Joplin & Kerry Mills, Eubie Blake, Harry Guy, Arranged for All Organs.* New York: Edward B. Marks Music Corp., 1974. 48 pp.

Joplin, Scott *E. Power Biggs Plays Scott Joplin.* Registrations and editorial by Mark Laub. New York: Charles Hansen, 1974. 80 pp.

————. *The Entertainer and Other Scott Joplin Rags.* Advanced all-organ solos arranged by Richard Bradley. Miami: Screen Gems-Columbia Pictures Publications, 1974. 48 pp.

————. *The Entertainer, Maple Leaf Rag, Peacherine Rag: Ragtime Organ Solos by Scott Joplin.* Arranged for all organs by Mark Laub. New York: Charles Hansen, 1974. (Mark Laub All Organ Solos.) 7 pp.

————. *Great Scott! Play by Chords.* New York: Charles Hansen, 1974. 48 pp.

————. *Great Scott! Ragtime for Organ. Book One.* Arranged by Robert Hilf. New York: Charles Hansen, 1973. 49 pp. Spiral-bound.

————. *Great Scott! The Best of Ragtime.* Arranged for Magnus chord organ. New York: Charles Hansen, 1973.

————. *King of Ragtime: Easy Organ.* Arranged by Lawrence Grant. Carlstadt, N.J.: Lewis Music Publishing Co., 1975. 32 pp.

————. *The King of Ragtime Writers: For All Organs.* Arranged by Lawrence Grant. Carlstadt, N.J.: Lewis Music Publishing Co., 1974. 128 pp. Spiral-bound.

————. *Ragtime Classics for All Organs.* Arranged by Dick Hyman. New York: Edward B. Marks Corp., 1973. 30 pp.

————. *Scott Joplin Highlights.* Arranged by Ethel Tench Rogers, with registrations for all organs. Westbury, N.Y.: Pro Art Publications, 1975. 32 pp.

The Sting, Featuring the Music of Scott Joplin. Arranged for all organs by David Carr Glover. Melville, N.Y.: MCA/Mills, 1974. 30 pp.

The Sting, Featuring the Music of Scott Joplin. Easy-to-play arrangements for all organs by David Carr Glover. Melville, N.Y.: MCA/Mills, 1974. 36 pp.

Collected Guitar Arrangements

The Art of Ragtime Guitar. By the staff of Green Note Music Publications. New York: Schirmer Books, 1974. Berkeley, Calif.: Green Note Music Publications, 1974. Includes soundsheet. 96 pp.

Barter's Finger-Picking Blues & Ragtime Manual. New York: Amsco Music Publishing Co., [197-]. 128 pp.*

Block, Claudia. *Ragtime for Guitar in Special Easy Arrangements.* New York: Edward B. Marks Music Corp., 1974. 16 pp.

Camp, Charles. *How to Play Ragtime Guitar: For Group or Individual Instruction.* New York: Acorn Music Press, 1976, 64 pp.

Criswick, Mary, arr. *Ragtime for Guitar Ensemble.* London: Chappell, 1975. 35 pp. Distributed in the U.S. by Theodore Presser Co., Bryn Mawr, Pa.

Grossman, Stefan. *Contemporary Ragtime Guitar.* New York: Oak Publications; London: Music Sales Ltd., 1972. 112 pp.

————. *Ragtime Blues Guitarists.* New York: Oak Publications, 1970. 132 pp.

Joplin, Scott, *Classical Guitar.* Arranged by Mario Abril. Miami Beach: Hansen House, 1974. 16 pp.

————. *The Entertainer, Maple Leaf Rag, The Easy Winners.* Transcribed for guitar by Jerry Snyder. New York: Charles Hansen, 1974. (Jerry Snyder Guitar Series.) 7 pp.

————. *Ragtime Guitar: Selected Works of Scott Joplin.* Arranged by Paul Lolax. New York: Charles Hansen, 1975. (Hansen House No. 55.) Includes 7" sound sheet. 72 pp. Spiral-bound.

————. *Ragtime: Two Pieces for Guitar.* Arranged by Ferenc Foder. Budapest: Editio Musica, 1981. [6] pp.

————. *Ragtimes: The Entertainer, Maple Leaf Rag, Weeping Willow.* Transcribed by Deiter Kreidler. Mainz, West Germany: B. Schott's Söhne, 1979. 8 pp.

Karp, Michael, arr. *Rags for Guitar by Scott Joplin and Tom Turpin.* New York and London: G. Schirmer, 1977. 28 pp.

Silverman, Jerry. *Jerry Silverman's Ragtime Guitar: Complete Instructions and Exercises; 37 Raggy Songs with Lyrics, Music, and Chords; 23 Scott Joplin Rags Transcribed for Guitar; The Scott Joplin School of Ragtime Transcribed for Guitar.* New York: Chappell Music Co., 1976. 191 pp.

_____, [arr.]. *Sing & Play Ragtime for Guitar.* Los Angeles: United Artists Music, [1979]. 47 pp.

The Sting, Featuring the Music of Scott Joplin. Arranged for two guitars by Ronnie Charles. New York: MCA/Mills, 1974. 35 pp.

Collected Banjo Arrangements

Bay, Mel and Roy Smeck, comps. *Mel Bay's Ragtime Banjo.* Kirkwood, Mo.: Mel Bay Publications, 1974. 32 pp.

Joplin, Scott. *Great Scott! Songs and Solos for Banjo.* New York: Charles Hansen, 1973. 32 pp.

Sokolow, Fred, arr. *12 Ragtime Tunes Arranged by Fred Sokolow for Bluegrass Banjo Pickers.* Berkeley, Calif.: Kicking Mule Records, [197-]. Companion cassette available.*

Collected Arrangements for Violin and Piano

Joplin, Scott. *Ragtime Classics for Violin and Piano.* Arranged by Paul Zukofsky. New York: Edward B. Marks Music Corp., 1974. 12, 22 pp.

_____. *Ragtime for Violin: 6 Scott Joplin Rags.* Arranged by Itzhak Perlman. New York and London: G. Schirmer, 1977. Violin part, 19 pp.; piano part, 40 pp.

Collected Arrangements for Two Flutes or Two Violins

Joplin, Scott. *Seven Scott Joplin Rags for Two Flutes or Two Violins.* Arranged by Jean Chandler. Delaware Water Gap, Pa.: Shawnee Press, 1975. 31 pp.

Collected Arrangements for B-flat Clarinet and Piano

Joplin, Scott. *Ragtime Classics for B-flat Clarinet and Piano.* Arranged by Michael G. Frank. New York: Edward B. Marks Music Corp., 1974. Clarinet part, 11 pp.; piano part, 20 pp.

Collected Arrangements for Flute or Clarinet and Piano

Joplin, Scott. *Sechs Ragtimes für Flöte oder Klarinette in B und Klavier.* Arranged and edited by Dieter H. Forster. 4 vols. Adliswil, Switzerland: Albert J. Kunzelman, 1980.

Ragtime Saxophone Methods

Thompson, K. E. *The Rag-time Saxophonist: Suggestions and Models for "Ragging" on the Saxophone.* Los Angeles: Kathryne E. Thompson, 1920. 16 pp. **OP.**

Winn, Edward R. *Winn's How to Rag and Jazz on the Saxophone.* New York: Winn School of Popular Music, 1925.*

Collected Arrangements for Trombone and Piano

Fillmore, Henry. *Henry Fillmore's Lassus Trombone Plus 14 Other Hot Trombone Rags.* New York: Fillmore Music House/Carl Fischer, 1978. Piano part, 48 pp.; trombone part, 16 pp.

Collected Arrangements for Brass Quintet

Glad Rags Suite for Brass Quintet. Arranged by Arthur Frackenpohl. New York: Edward B. Marks Music Corporation, 1974. 19 pp. plus parts.

Joplin, Scott. *Sunflower Slow Drag/The Chrysanthemum.* Arranged by Philip Stansfeld. Seattle: Stansfeld Music Co., 1975. 6 pp. plus parts.*

_____. *Three Rags for Five.* Arranged by John Iveson. London: Chester Music, 1978. (Just Brass, no. 25.) 12 pp. plus parts.*

_____. *Three Scott Joplin Rags for Brass Quintet.* Arranged by Arthur Frackenpohl. New York: Edward B. Marks Music Corp., 1973. 15 pp. plus parts.

Ragtime Suite for Brass Quintet. Arranged by Arthur Frackenpohl. New York: Edward B. Marks Music Corp., 1974. 20 pp. plus parts.

Collected Arrangements for String Quartet

Joplin, Scott. *String Along with Scott: 10 Ragtime Pieces.* Arranged by Jerry Silverman. New York and London: G. Schirmer, 1978. 88 pp. plus parts. For string quartet with double bass, guitar and piano ad-lib or string orchestra with guitar and piano ad-lib.*

Zinn, William, arr. *Ragtime Favorites for Strings, as Performed by Zinn's Ragtime String Quartet.* Melville, N.Y.: Belwin-Mills Publishing Corp., 1974. 39 pp. plus parts (with optional double bass).*

Collected Arrangements for Woodwind Quintet

Joplin, Scott. *Two Joplin Rags.* Transcribed by Arthur Frankenpohl. Delaware Water Gap, Pa.: Shawnee Press, 1974. 16 pp. plus parts.

Collected Arrangements for "German Band"

Hungry Five Plays Ragtime. New York: Charles Hansen, [196-?]. Fifteen ragtime pieces arranged for five-piece "German band."

Collected Arrangements for C Instruments

Silverman, Jerry, arr. *Ragtime Solos & Duets: 20 Scott Joplin Favorites; Arranged for Flute, Recorder,* *Oboe, Violin, Mandolin, Harmonica, with Guitar Chords.* New York and London: G. Schirmer, 1978. 62 pp.

Collected Arrangements for C, B-flat, and E-flat Instruments

Joplin, Scott. *Scott Joplin's Entertainer and other Ragtime Hits.* Arranged by Denny Johns. Carlstadt, N.J.: Publisher Sales, 1974. "Solos/duets for C, B-flat, and E-flat instruments. Compatible combos played by any combination of instruments." B-flat volume has 41 pp.

Collected Arrangements for Recorder Quartet

Joplin, Scott. *Ragtimes.* Arranged by Christa Sokoll. Wilhelmshaven, West Germany: Otto Heinrich Noetzel Verlag, 1980. 24 pp.

Collected Arrangements for Chromatic Harmonica

The Sting, Featuring the Music of Scott Joplin. Arranged by Bob Bauer. New York: MCA/ Mills, 1974. 24 pp.

Rags on Record: An LP Discography

Philip J. Moe

This discography concerns ragtime as a body of syncopated, multisectional compositions (rags), rather than as a popular performance style or as an influence on jazz piano style, or as a body of music, including pop songs of the day, that may at one time (say, 1900–1920) have been referred to as "ragtime." I have therefore omitted (1) most recordings by "honky-tonk" pianists who perform such pop tunes as *Down Yonder* and *Red Wing* in a bouncy style sometimes called "ragtime," and (2) most recordings by the early stride or jazz pianists such as Jelly Roll Morton, James P. Johnson, and Willie "the Lion" Smith (for by the time most of them began to record, the rags in their repertoires were in little demand and there are therefore few rags on their available recordings),[1] and (3) collections of pop or vaudeville songs of the Ragtime Era that do not also include rags (with or without lyrics).

I do include recordings of the body of ragtime-derived novelty pieces (sometimes called "novelty rags") identified with such virtuosi as pianists Zez Confrey and Billy Mayerl, xylophonist George Hamilton Green, or banjoist Harry Reser. Recordings of transcriptions, arrangements, and orchestrations of ragtime are included. Some of the more interesting curiosities inspired by the Joplin revival are included. I have not attempted to list every LP on which one or more rags appear. Generally I include only those LPs which contain mostly ragtime *unless* (1) the LP includes one or more performances of historic interest, (2) the LP features a performer who has been particularly influential on contemporary performance style or has particular authority, or (3) the LP includes at least one composition or example of a genre which has seldom been recorded elsewhere by an authoritative performer.

Several discographies may be found useful as supplements to this one. The most extensive discography of early ragtime recordings is David A. Jasen's *Recorded Ragtime* (Hamden, Conn.: Archon Books, 1973). LP discographies compiled on somewhat different principles than this one appear as appendices to *Scott Joplin and the Ragtime Era* by Peter Gammond (New York: St. Martin's Press, 1975), *This Is Ragtime* by Terry Waldo (New York: Hawthorn Books, 1976), and *They All Played Ragtime* by Rudi Blesh and Harriet Janis (New York: Oak Publications, 1971).[2]

Within the limits I have set, this is intended to be as complete a listing as possible, as of May 31, 1984, of ragtime LPs issued in the United States and, when I know about them, elsewhere.

Several small labels whose issues appear several times in this discographer sell their records primarily by mail. The address of Jazzology Records (also producers of GHB and Audiophile records and owners of the Circle catalog) is 3008 Wadsworth Mill Place, Atlanta, Georgia 30032. MMM Records are available from Mekanisk Musik Museum, Vesterbrogade 150, Copenhagen, Denmark; from The Vestal Press, P.O. Box 97, Vestal, New York 13850; or from Sheldor and Associates, 523 25th Street, Ames, Iowa 50010. For Ragtime Society Records, contact The Ragtime Society, Inc., P.O. Box 520, Station A, Weston, Ontario M9N 3N3, Canada. For Stomp Off records, write P.O. Box 342, York, Pennsylvania 17405. Addresses for other suppliers are included below only for private-issue or limited-distribution records.

The discography is organized as follows:

Historical Performances
   Reissues of Early Ragtime Recordings
      General Anthologies
      Early Piano Recordings
      Early Banjo and String Band Recordings
      Early Xylophone Recordings
   Recordings of Player Pianos, Orchestrions, and Music Boxes
      Player Piano Recordings
      Orchestrions
      Music Boxes

Late Recordings by Early Ragtime Performers and Composers
   Solo Piano, or Piano with Accompaniment
   Banjo
   Band
Modern Performances
   Solo Piano, Duo Piano, and Piano (with Accompaniment) Performances of Mostly Vintage
   Rags
   Other Keyboard Instruments
   Ragtime Transposed or Arranged for Diverse Instruments
   Solo Performers
      Violin with Piano
      Guitar
      Banjo
      Flute
   Ensemble performances
      Strings, or Piano with Strings
      Percussion
      Brass
      Woodwinds
      Synthesizers
      Orchestras and Jazz Bands
   Contemporary Ragtime Compositions
   Joplin Curiosities

The following abbreviations are used in this discography:

OP   Record is out of print.
OP?   Record may be out of print.
OP+ Record is long out of print and scarce.
*   I have not had an opportunity to examine this recording and am therefore relying on a secondary source such as a record review, release announcement, or discography listing. I thus cannot vouch for the completeness or absolute accuracy of the information given.

Bracketed dates which immediately follow the album title are those of the original recordings. In instances where more than one recording by the same performer is cited, the entries are listed in chronological order of release.

Notes

1. The happy exception is, of course, Eubie Blake, who lived long enough for his ragtime compositions to regain their popularity.
2. The following performers (pianists or band leaders) appear in one or more of the discographies I have listed (and others) but do not individually appear in this one: Marvin Ash, Winifred Atwell, Jan August, Burt Bales, Kenny Ball, Chris Barber, Jimmy Blythe, Jaki Byard, Ken Colyer, Al "Spider" Dugan, Hank Duncan, Don Ewell, Will Ezell, Ray Foxley, Harry Gold, Bob Greene, Pete Handy, Armand Hug, Cliff Jackson, Merle Koch, Stephen Kovacs, Donald Lambert, Yank Lawson/Bob Haggart, George Lewis, Jelly Roll Morton, Red Nichols, Brooke Pemberton, Ragtime Rheingold, Luckey Roberts, Slugger Ryan, San Francisco Harry, Frank Signorelli, Willie "the Lion" Smith, Sammy Spear, Joe Sullivan, The Temperence Seven, Butch Thompson, Fats Waller, and Ian Whitcomb. Joe "Fingers" Carr, James P. Johnson, Johnny Maddox, Knuckles O'Toole, The St. Louis Ragtimers, Ralph Sutton, and Lu Watters make only token appearances in this discography.

Historical Performances

REISSUES OF EARLY RAGTIME RECORDINGS

General Anthologies

1. Charters, Sam, comp. *Ragtime 1, The City: Banjos, Brass Bands, & Nickel Pianos.* [ca. 1904–31] Folkways RBF 17. 1971. Brochure notes by Sam Charters, 2 pp.
2. *Cylinder Jazz: Early Jazz and Ragtime Recordings from Phonograph Cylinders, 1897–1928.* Saydisc [U.K.] SDL 210. [ca. 1967] Jacket notes by Brian Rust.
3. *An Edison Memorabilia of Musical Performances, Volume Two: Ragtime to Dance Music of the Twenties.* Mark 56 Records 727. 1976. Side One: Ragtime from Edison Blue Amberol Cylinders

1912-13. Side Two: Dance music from Edison discs of the twenties (1925-28).

4. Ellis, Chris, comp. *Those Ragtime Years: 1899/1916.* Two discs. E.M.I. World Records [U.K.] SHB 41. [1977?] (Retrospect Series, Series Coordinated by Michael Kennedy.) Jacket notes by Brian Rust, photos. British recordings of ragtime played on the banjo, concertina, and piano accordion; played by bands and orchestras; and ragtime-flavored songs with various accompaniments.

5. Hasse, John Edward and Frank J. Gillis, compilers and annotators. *Indiana Ragtime: A Documentary Album.* [1910-1981] Two discs, boxed. Portions in mono. Indiana Historical Society IHS 1001. 1981. Includes twenty-eight-page booklet, illustrated with sixty color and black and white photographs, and with bibliography and discography. Documents ragtime of Indiana composers, including May Aufderheide, J. Russel Robinson, Abe Olman, Paul Pratt, Russell Smith, etc. Total of thirty-three selections, nineteen newly-recorded for the album, fourteen reissued. Performers include Hasse, Gillis, Max Morath, New Orleans Rhythm Kings, Jesse Crump, Wally Rose, Knocky Parker, the Indiana University Ragtime Orchestra, Turk Murphy Jazz Band, and others. Side A: Piano and banjo soloists. Side B: Player piano rolls. Side C: Orchestra. Side D: Military, dance, and jazz bands. Available from the Indiana Historical Society, 315 West Ohio Street, Indianapolis, Indiana 46202.

6. *I'll Dance Till De Sun Breaks Through, 1898-1917: Ragtime: Cakewalks and Stomps, Vol. 2.* Saydisc [U.K.] 210. [ca. 1967] Jacket notes by Brian Rust.

7. Jasen, David A., comp. *Ragtime Entertainment.* [1901-1922] Folkways RBF 22. 1973. Brochure notes by David A. Jasen, 2 pp. Mostly recordings by bands and orchestras.

8. _____, comp. *Toe-Tappin' Ragtime: Original Recordings of Orchestrated Ragtime, Played by Dance Bands and Jazz Bands, Mostly from the Twenties.* Folkways RBF 25. (Ragtime Series, vol. 4.) 1974. Brochure notes by David A. Jasen, 2 pp. Mostly "novelty rags."

9. _____, comp. *Early Syncopated Dance Music: Cakewalks, Two-Steps, and Glides.* [ca. 1910-1922] Folkways RBF 37. 1978. Brochure notes by David A. Jasen, 6 pp. Early recordings by Sousa's Band, Pryor's Band, Walter B. Rogers Band, *et al.*

10. _____, comp. *Early Band Ragtime.** [ca. 1906-1913] Folkways RBF 38. 1979. Brochure notes by David A. Jasen, 4 pp. Side One: "Ragtime's Biggest Hits, 1899-1909," Side Two: "Obscure Rags Rarely Recorded."

11. _____, comp. *Late Band Ragtime.** Folkways RBF 39. 1979. Brochure notes by David A. Jasen.

12. *Jazz in Deutschland, v. 1: Vom Ragtime zum Hot Jazz, 1912-1928.** Electrola [West Germany] 1C134-32447/48m. [1979?] Recordings made in Germany by German bands and visiting performers (*e.g.,* Jack Hylton, Al Bowlly, Sam Wooding). Includes a few rags.

13. *A Programme of Ragtime, Vol. 1.** (Vintage Jazz Music) VJM [U.K.] VLP-1. [OP+] [ca. 1955-60].

14. *Ragtime: A Recorded Documentary (1899-1929).* Piedmont PLP 13158. [OP+] [ca.. 1955?] Brochure notes by Louisa Spottswood, 4 pp.

15. *Ragtime and Novelty Music: Vol. 1 (1906-1934).* RCA [France] FXM 1 7185. (Black and White Series, vol. 152.) [1976] Jacket notes in French by Pierre-François Cangardel; translation to English by Don Waterhouse. Selections feature chiefly piano or banjo.

16. *Ragtime: "Cake-Walks, Military Bands, Ragtime Orchestras, Coon Contests, Blues and Jass," Vol. 2 (1900-1921).** RCA [France] PM 42402. (Black and White series, vol. 190.) [1979?] Jacket notes in French by Daniel Nevers, translation into English by Don Waterhouse.

17. *Ragtime: Pianos, Banjos, Xylophones et Saxophones, Cake-Walks, Ragtime Orchestras, Coon-Contest, Military & Brass Bands, Blues, Jass et Novelty Music (1900-1930).* Two discs. RCA [France] PM 45687. (Black and White series; Jazz Tribune, no. 42.) [1983] Jacket notes in French by Daniel Nevers, translation into English by Don Waterhouse. Some, but apparently not complete, duplication of items 15 and 16.

18. *Rusty Rags: Ragtime, Cakewalks & Stomps, Vol. 4—1900-1917.* Saydisc [U.K.] SDL 253. [ca. 1974] Jacket notes by Brian Rust. Mostly bands and orchestras.

19. *Steppin' on the Gas: Rags to Jazz—1913-1927.** New World Records NW 269, 1977. Notes, tipped in and on jacket, by Lawrence Gushee, 6 pp., bibliog., discog., photos. Mostly jazz and dance numbers by various bands and orchestras. A few rags. Available only to libraries and educational institutions; not sold to individuals.

20. *Too Much Mustard: The Bands of Jim Europe & Arthur Pryor, 1907-1919: Ragtime, Cakewalks & Stomps, Vol 3.* Saydisc [U.K.] SDL 221. [ca. 1972] Jacket notes by Brian Rust. Side One: bands led by black bandleader James Reese Europe; Side Two: bands led by Arthur Pryor.

21. *When Grandma Was a Teenager: A Programme of Ragtime Music, with Minstrel and Gospel Songs (Vol. Two).* [1902-1914] (Vintage Jazz Music Society Records) VJM [U.K.] VLP 2. [ca. 1960?] Jacket notes by Brian Rust.

Early Piano Recordings

22. Bargy, Roy. *Piano Syncopations.* [ca. 1919-1924] Folkways RBF 35. 1978. Compiled and annotated by David A. Jasen. Brochure notes, 6 pp. Six studio recordings, eleven recordings

of player piano rolls cut by Bargy.

23. **Bloom, Rube, and Arthur Schutt.** *Novelty Ragtime Piano Kings Rube Bloom and Arthur Schutt.* Folkways RBF 41. 1980. Compiled and annotated by David A. Jasen. Side One: eight solos by Bloom, including six originals. Side Two: six Schutt solos, two duets with Jack Cornell (with drum accompaniment).

24. **Confrey, Zez.** *Creator of the Novelty Rag.* [recordings from 1921–24; piano rolls from 1918 and 1927] Compiled by David A. Jasen. Folkways RF 28. 1976. Brochure notes by Jasen, 2 pp. Side One: piano solos; Side Two: orchestra with piano.

25. **Jasen, David A.,** comp. *Black & White Piano Ragtime.* [1921–1943] Biograph BLP-12047. 1972. Jacket notes by Jasen. Side One: ragtime/jazz piano; Side Two: piano novelties.

26. _____, comp. *Ragtime Piano Originals: 16 Composer-Pianists Playing Their Own Works.* [ca. 1915–1930] Folkways RF 23. 1974. Brochure notes by Jasen, 2 pp.

27. _____, comp. *Ragtime Piano Interpretations.* [ca. 1912–1929] Folkways RF 24. 1974. Brochure notes by Jasen 4 pp. Solo and duo-piano recordings, mostly of virtuoso piano-novelty performers.

28. _____, comp. *Red Onion Rag: Piano Ragtime of the Teens, Twenties & Thirties.* [ca. 1917–1939] Herwin 402. [ca. 1974] Jacket notes by Jasen.

29. _____, comp. *Piano Ragtime of the Forties.* [1941–49] Herwin 403. [ca. 1975] Jacket notes by Jasen. Side One: recordings by famous ragtime and stride pianist/composers—Luckey Roberts, James P. Johnson, *et al.* Side Two: recordings by ragtime/jazz revival pianists such as Ralph Sutton, as well as Freeman Clark and J. Lawrence Cook.

30. _____, comp. *Piano Ragtime of the Fifties.* [1950–56] Herwin 404. [1976?] Jacket notes by Jasen. Side One: classic and novelty rags performed by interpreters of the 1950s—Winifred Atwell, Ray Turner, *et al.* Side Two: original rags of the 1950s performed by their composers—Bill Krenz, Lou Busch, *et al.*

31. _____, comp. *Early Ragtime Piano: 1913–1930.* Folkways RF 33. 1977. Brochure notes by Jasen, 2 pp. Mostly piano novelties performed by vaudeville or orchestra pianists.

32. _____, comp. *Late Ragtime Piano.* [1930s–1950s] Folkways RF 34. 1977. Brochure notes by Jasen, 2 pp. Surveys adventures and misadventures of ragtime in and at the hands of late novelty ragtime performers, traditional jazz revival pianists, skilled studio musicians, etc.

33. _____, comp. *Piano Ragtime of the Teens, Twenties & Thirties, Volume 2.* Herwin 405. [1978] Jacket notes by Jasen. Various artists.

34. _____, comp. *Piano Ragtime of the Teens, Twenties, & Thirties, Volume 3.* Herwin 406.

[1978] Jacket notes by Jasen. Various artists. Nine of the sixteen selections on this album were also included on OJL 16 (see 39).

35. _____, comp. *Ragtime Piano Novelties of the 20's.** Folkways RBF 42. 1981. Brochure notes by Jasen. Sixteen novelty piano selections, mostly played by now-obscure performers (*e.g.,* Jay Wilbur, Pauline Alpert, Henry W. Lange, Frank Herbin, Cecil Norman, Sid Reinherz, Patricia Rossborough).

36. _____, comp. *Ragtime Piano Revival.** [1940s–1950s] Folkways RBF 49. 1983. Brochure notes by Jasen, 4 pp. Recordings made during the first "ragtime revival" of the 1940s and 1950s.

37. **Mayerl, Billy.** *The King of Syncopation.* Compiled by Chris Ellis. World Record Club [U.K.] SH 189. (WRC Historical Series; Michael Kennedy, Series Coordinator.) [ca. 1974] Jacket notes, dated 1973, by Irene Ashton.

38. _____. *The Syncopated Impressions of Billy Mayerl.* Folkways RF 30. 1976. Compiled and annotated by David A. Jasen. Brochure notes, 2 pp. Recording dates not given, probably 1930s.

39. *Ragged Piano Classics* [1923–1943]. Origin Jazz Library OJL 16. [ca. 1969] Jacket notes by Dick Raichelson. Folk ragtime's last gasps.

40. *They All Played the Maple Leaf Rag.* [1907–1969] Herwin 401. [ca. 1972] Jacket notes by David A. Jasen. Fifteen versions of the *Maple Leaf Rag,* ranging from banjo to piano to swing band.

Early Banjo and String Band Recordings

41. **Charters, Sam,** comp. *Ragtime 2, The Country: Mandolins, Fiddles, & Guitars.* [ca. 1925–1935] Folkways RBF 18. 1971. Brochure notes by Charters, 2 pp.

42. **Cohn, Lawrence,** producer. *Maple Leaf Rag: Ragtime in Rural America.** New World Records NW 235. 1976. Jacket notes by Cohn, bibliog., discog. Side One: "Black Tradition," 1927–1964. Side Two: "White Tradition," 1929–1962. Available only to libraries and educational institutions; not sold to individuals.

43. **Jasen, David A.,** comp. *Those Ragtime Banjos** [1903–1926, 1951]. Folkways RBF 40. 1980? Various artists. Brochure notes by Jasen. [Note that a broad survey of early banjo recordings including some rags, as well as marches, pop tunes, and showpiece arrangements (*e.g., Carnival of Venice*) entitled *Banjo Greats* (no number) is available from Merritt Sound Recordings, 223 Grimsby Road, Buffalo, New York 14223. Merritt specializes in providing tape dubs (cassette, cartridge, or reel-to-reel) of early recordings, especially the

otherwise neglected sentimental pop and novelty songs.]

44. _____, and Nick Perls, producers. *String
Ragtime: To Do This You Got To Know How.* [ca.
1915–1935] Yazoo L-1045. 1974. Jacket notes.
String bands, harp, mandolin, Hawaiian guitar,
etc.

45. Reser, Harry. *Banjo Crackerjax, 1922–
1930.* Yazoo L-1048. [1975] Jacket notes by
David Jasen. Mostly Reser compositions.

46. Smeck, Roy. *Roy Smeck Plays the Hawaiian
Guitar, Banjo, Ukelele and Guitar.** Yazoo 1052.
[ca. 1978] Jacket notes by Stephen Calt. Includes five popular rags recorded between
1928 and 1937.

47. Stevens, Norman and Ron Jewson,
comp. *They All Played Banjo.* [1904–1916] Re-
trieval [U.K.] FG-403. [1976?] Jacket notes by
J. McNaghten. Early British banjo recordings
by Charlie Rogers, Joe Morley, Olly Oakley,
Burt Earle, John Pidoux, and others.

48. Van Eps, Fred and Vess L. Ossman.
Kings of the Ragtime Banjo. [1900–1923]. Comp.
and annotated by David A. Jasen. Yazoo 1044.
[1974?] Side One: Ossman. Side Two: Van
Eps. Banjo with piano or orchestra. See also
78.

Early Xylophone Recordings

49. Green, George Hamilton. *The Xylophone
Genius of George Hamilton Green.* Conservatory
7101M. (Collectors' Series). [ca. 1970?] Unsigned jacket notes. Brochure notes, 4 pp.,
illus., comprising advice by Green on xylophone technique. Xylophone solos with piano
accompaniment. Probably originally recorded
in the 1920s or early 1930s. Side One: classical
transcriptions, two Green compositions. Side
Two: xylophone novelties composed by Green.
Obtainable from: Lew Green, Sr., P.O. Box
234, Arlington Heights, Illinois 60006. See
also 251 and 252.

RECORDINGS OF PLAYER PIANOS,
ORCHESTRIONS, AND MUSIC BOXES

Player Piano Recordings

50. Jasen, David A., comp. *Unknown Piano
Rags.** Herwin 407. 1983. Piano rolls of vintage
rags which were never issued in sheet music
form. Composers include Paul Pratt, James
Reese Europe, and George Botsford. Side One:
rolls hand-played by the composers; Side Two:
arranged rolls. All performances declared to be
new to disc.

51. Johnson, James P. *James P. Johnson
1917—Vol. 2: His Earliest Ragtime Piano Rolls.*
Rolls selected, tempos chosen, and piano
pumped by Michael Montgomery. Biograph
BLP-1009Q. 1973. Jacket notes by Michael
Montgomery. Rolls originally hand played by
Johnson.

52. Kortlander, Max. *Max Kortlander: Piano
Roll Artistry.** Comp. and annotated by David
A. Jasen. Folkways RBF 43. 1981. Recordings
of eighteen Kortlander piano rolls including
seven pop tunes, six Kortlander compositions,
and five rags.

53. *Piano Roll Ragtime.* Sounds 1201. [**OP?**]
[ca. 1965?].

54. *Pianola Jazz: Early Piano Jazz and Ragtime
Played on Pianola Rolls.* Research and playing by
Rodney King. Saydisc [U.K.] SDL-117. [ca.
1965?] Jacket notes by Gef Lucena.

55. *Pianola Ragtime: Early Piano Ragtime from
Pianola Rolls.* Playing by Rodney King. Saydisc
[U.K.] SDL 132. (The Golden Age of Mechan-
ical Music, vol. 1.) [ca. 1966] Jacket notes by
Gef Lucena.

56. *Ragtime Piano Rolls.* Jazz Piano [U.K.?] JP
5001. [**OP?**] [ca. 1960?].

57. Straight, Charley. *The Piano Roll Artistry
of Charley Straight.** Presumably compiled and
annotated by David A. Jasen. Folkways RBF
44. 1982. Features eighteen hand played performances by Straight, including ten pieces
composed by Straight.

58. Tichenor, Trebor, and Michael Mont-
gomery, comps. *Scott Joplin—1916: Classic Solos
Played by the King of Ragtime Writers and Others from
Rare Piano Rolls.* Rolls selected and tempos
selected by Trebor Tichenor and Michael
Montgomery; piano pumped by Montgomery.
Biograph BLP-1006Q. 1971. Jacket notes by
Montgomery in collaboration with Tichenor.
Side One: six rolls apparently cut by Joplin
himself in 1916. Side Two: rolls of other Joplin
compositions, hand played by W. Arlington or
Wm. Axtmann in 1916–17.

59. _____. *Scott Joplin Ragtime, Volume 2.*
Selected and edited and tempos chosen by
Michael Montgomery and Trebor Tichenor;
piano pumped by Montgomery. Biograph
BLP-1008Q. 1971. Jacket notes by Tichenor
and Montgomery. Arranged rolls originally
issued ca. 1900–1910.

60. _____. *Scott Joplin Ragtime, Volume 3.*
Selected and tempos chosen by Trebor Tichenor and Michael Montgomery; piano pumped
by Montgomery. Biograph BLP-1010Q. 1972.
Unsigned jacket notes presumably by Tichenor
and Montgomery. Arranged rolls originally
issued between about 1900 and 1920.

61. _____. *Scott Joplin, "The Entertainer":
Classic Ragtime from Rare Piano Rolls.* Selected and
tempos chosen by Trebor Tichenor and
Michael Montgomery; piano pumped by Mont-
gomery. Biograph BLP-1013Q. (Vol. 4.) 1974.
Jacket notes by Tichenor and Montgomery.
Piano rolls cuts by Hal Boulware for his
Classics of Ragtime series, probably in the late
1950s or early 1960s.

62. _____. *Scott Joplin, "Elite Syncopations":
Classic Ragtime from Rare Piano Rolls.* Selected and
tempos chosen by Trebor Tichenor and

Michael Montgomery; piano pumped by Montgomery. Biograph BLP-1014Q. (Vol. 5.) 1974. Jacket notes by Tichenor and Montgomery. All but one roll cut by Hal Boulware.

63. _____. *James Scott: Classic Ragtime from Rare Piano Rolls.* Selected and tempos chosen by Trebor Tichenor and Michael Montgomery; piano pumped by Montgomery. Biograph BLP-1016Q. 1975. Jacket notes by Tichenor and Montgomery. Note that prior to the Biograph series, the most extensive series of recordings of ragtime piano rolls was that issued by Riverside Records during the 1950s. Riverside's material subsequently reappeared in a variety of authorized and unauthorized reissues, both complete and incomplete, mostly in Europe. Some rags also appear in the Johnny Maddox "World's Greatest Piano Rolls" series (Dot Records), played at improbable speeds with, I am told, capricious retitlings.

Orchestrions

64. *Ragtime Cabaret.* (Mechanisk Musik Museum) MMM Records [Denmark, but apparently manufactured in U.S.] LP-203. [ca. 1975] Jacket notes by Q. David Bowers. Ragtime and other period music performed by the Phillipps Orchestrion. A less hackneyed program than is usual for such productions.

Music Boxes

65. *Ragtime and Cakewalks: Played by Antique Musical Boxes from the Musical Wonder House, Wiscasset, Maine.* Album No. 1103. [ca. 1976] Jacket notes. Available from: The Merry Music Box, 20 McKown Street, Boothbay Harbor, Maine 04538.

LATE RECORDINGS BY EARLY RAGTIME
PERFORMERS AND COMPOSERS

Solo Piano, or Piano with Accompaniment

66. Blake, Eubie. *The Wizard of the Ragtime Piano.* 20th Fox 3003. [OP] [1958] Jacket notes. Various combinations of piano with vocal, drums, bass, guitar, and clarinet. Blake also recorded a second album for 20th Fox, 3009, *The Marches I Played on the Old Ragtime Piano.* Both records are now available as French RCA reissues: T609 (*Wizard . . .*) and T610 (*Marches . . .*) with new jacket notes.

67. _____. *The Eighty-Six Years of Eubie Blake.* Two discs. Columbia C2S 847. 1969. Jacket notes by Robert E. Kimball, photos. Solo piano with occasional vocals by Noble Sissle.

68. _____. *Eubie Blake: Volume 1, Featuring Ivan Harold Browning.* Eubie Blake Music EBM 1. [1971] Jacket notes, art, engineering, and production by Carl Seltzer. Side One: piano solos; Side Two: vocals with piano accompaniment.

69. _____. *Rags to Classics.* Eubie Blake Music EBM-2. [1972] Jacket notes, art, engineering, and production by Carl Seltzer.

70. _____. *Eubie Blake: Live Concert.* Eubie Blake Music EBM-5. [1974] Jacket notes by Lee R. Munsick.

71. _____. "91 Years Young." RCA [France] FXM1 7157. [ca. 1975] Jacket notes in French by Jean-Pierre Daubresse and Daniel Nevers, translation into English by Don Waterhouse. Recorded live in July, 1974, at the Nice jazz festival. Seven Blake originals, a Gershwin medley, and a Sousa transcription.

72. _____, Joe Jordan, Charles Thompson, and "Ragtime" Bob Darch. *Golden Reunion in Ragtime: Eubie Blake, Joe Jordan, and Charles Thompson Playing and Reminiscing with "Ragtime" Bob Darch.* Stereoddities C 1900. [OP] [1962] Jacket notes. According to the notes, Darch recorded additional material that was to be subsequently released. A few selections from the additional material were included in a promotional package Stereoddities produced for distribution to radio stations. In recent years, several other Blake albums—older recordings, piano rolls, and new recordings—have been issued. Blake albums containing relatively little ragtime include: *Eubie Blake and his Friends Edith Wilson & Ivan Harold Browning* (EBM-3); *Early Rare Recordings with Noble Sissle* (EBM-4); *Eubie Blake Introducing Jim Hession* (EBM-6); *Early Rare Recordings, Vol. 2* (EBM-7); *Eubie Blake and his Proteges* (EBM-8); *Song Hits* (EBM-9); *Eubie Blake: Blues & Ragtime, Vol. 1* (Biograph 1011Q); *Blues and Spirituals, Vol. 2* (Biograph 1012Q); *Shuffle Along: An Archival Recreation . . .* (New World NW 260) [available only to libraries and educational institutions]. See also 255.

73. Campbell, Brun, and Dink Johnson. *The Professors.* [1940s] Euphonic ESR 1201. [ca. 1962] Jacket notes by Paul Affeldt. After their rerelease in the 1960s, Campbell's recordings, in particular, were very influential in forming modern opinions of Midwest folk ragtime style.

74. Campbell, Brun, Euday Bowman, and Dink Johnson. *The Professors, Volume 2.* [1940s] Euphonic ESR 1202. [ca. 1963] Jacket notes by Paul Affeldt.

75. Filmer, Vic. *The Saga of Vic Filmer.* Jazzology JCE-58. (Jazz Piano Heritage Series, vol. 8.) [1975?] Jacket notes by Alasdair Fenton and George H. Buck, Jr. Recordings by a venerable British pianist who was purportedly, in 1910, the first British pianist to play ragtime (from newly arrived sheet music).

76. Lamb, Joseph. *Joseph Lamb: A Study in Classic Ragtime.* Folkways FG 3562. 1959. Brochure notes by Samuel B. Charters, 4 pp., photos. Solo piano and spoken reminiscences.

77. Thompson, Charles. *The Neglected Professor.** Euphonic ESR 1221. 1981. Home recordings from the early 1960s. See also 72.

Banjo

78. Van Eps, Fred. *5 String Banjo.* Van Eps Lab 711/2. [**OP?**] [n.d.] No notes, indeed no jacket. Private issue, presumably recorded in the 1950s and at one time available from Robert Van Eps, the performer's son and accompanist. See also 48.

Band

79. Bocage, Peter. *Peter Bocage with His Creole Serenaders and the Love-Jiles Ragtime Orchestra.* Riverside 9379/379. [**OP**] (New Orleans/The Living Legends.) [Recorded in 1961] Jacket notes by Herb Friedwald. Notable for three recordings of Joplin rags from the "Red Back Book."

80. *Jazz New Orleans, Vol. 1: Featuring Punch Miller & Mutt Carey* [ca. 1947]. Savoy MG-12038. [**OP**] [ca. 1955?] Jacket notes by H. Altbush. Carey plays three Joplin rags with a seven-piece jazz band.

81. Johnson, Bunk. *The Last Testament of a Great Jazzman* [1947]. Columbia Special Products JCL 829. (Collector's Series.) 1974. Jacket notes by George Avakian. Includes four or five selections from the "Red Back Book" played by a seven-piece jazz band. Johnson had played rags with New Orleans orchestras in the very early twentieth century.

Modern Performances

SOLO PIANO, DUO PIANO, AND PIANO
(WITH ACCOMPANIMENT) PERFORMANCES
OF (MOSTLY) VINTAGE RAGS

82. Abadi, Marden. *The Classic Joplin.* Orion ORS 76215. 1976. Jacket notes by Marden Abadi. Subsequently reissued in 1978 as Sine Qua Non Superba SAS 2020.

83. Albright, William. *Sweet Sixteenths: A Ragtime Concert; Works by Joplin, Lamb, Scott, Blake, Albright, and others.* Musical Heritage Society MHS 4578. 1982. Also issued as Musicmasters 20033 (1981). See also 90, 301, and 316.

84. Arpin, John. *Concert in Ragtime by John Arpin.* Scroll [Canada] LSCR 101. [**OP**] 1965. Produced in cooperation with the Ragtime Society. Jacket notes by Bob Ashforth.

85. _____. *The Other Side of Ragtime.* Scroll [Canada] LSCR 103. [**OP**] 1966. Jacket notes by Bob Ashforth.

86. _____. *Solo Piano.* Eubie Blake Music EBM-10. 1976. Jacket notes by Rudi Blesh. Novelty piano, jazz, and ragtime-influenced compositions.

87. Bennett, Richard Rodney. *Richard Rodney Bennett Plays George Gershwin and Billy Mayerl.* Polydor Select [U.K.] 2460 245. [ca. 1976] Jacket notes by Charles Fox. Side One: Gersh-

win's song arrangements; Side Two: eight Mayerl compositions.

88. Bolcom, William. *Heliotrope Bouquet: Piano Rags.* Nonesuch H-71257. 1971. Jacket notes by William Bolcom.

89. _____. *Pastimes & Piano Rags: Artie Matthews, James Scott.* Nonesuch H-71299. 1974. Jacket notes by William Bolcom.

90. _____ and William Albright. *Ragtime: Back to Back.* University of Michigan School of Music SM 0004. 1976. Jacket notes by William Bolcom and William Albright. Side One: Bolcom playing rags written by Scott Joplin in collaboration with either Arthur Marshall or Scott Hayden. Side Two: Albright playing stride compositions by James P. Johnson. Also issued as Musical Heritage Society MHS 4022 and Musicmasters 20002. See also 305 and 312.

91. Bolcom, William, Mary Lou Williams, Joshua Rifkin, *et al. An Evening with Scott Joplin at the Library and Museum of the Performing Arts, Lincoln Center, New York, October 22, 1971.* New York Public Library NYPL-SJ. [**OP**] [ca. 1972] Jacket notes by Vera Brodsky Lawrence. Limited edition.

92. Bolling, Claude. *Original Ragtime.* Columbia PC 33277. [1976] Jacket notes. Originally recorded by French Philips in 1966 and released as Philips 840.583/70.341. May subsequently have been reissued in France with Philips number 849.454. Repackaged in France with *Original Boogie-Woogie* as Philips 6641.142 (two discs).

93. _____. *Ragtime.** CY Records [France] CYL 6408. (Distributed by French RCA.) 1977. Classic, novelty, and original rags. Apparently reissued as CY 733.607 (WE 341) (distributed by French WEA) under the title *Ragtime Bolling,* jacket notes by Jean-Christophe Averty.

94. Carr, Joe "Fingers" [pseud. of Louis Busch]. *Brassy Piano.* Warner Bros. WS 1456. [**OP+**] 1962. Jacket notes. Standard piano rags with unidentified brass accompaniment.

95. _____. *Hits of Joe "Fingers" Carr.* Capitol SM-2019. [ca. 1974] No jacket notes. Reissue of Capitol (S)T 2019. Recordings made, presumably, during the mid- to late 1950s.

96. _____. *The Black & White Rag & Other Classic American Rags (1899–1918).* Capitol ST-11303. [**OP**] 1974. Jacket notes. Reissued from Capitol recordings, probably from the late 1950s. Carr released many other albums, first on Capitol and later, primarily on Warner Bros., most of which are long out of print and many of which may contain at least some ragtime.

97. Castle, Jo Ann. *Ragtime Piano Gal.* Ranwood 8011. [ca. 1970] Reissue of Dot DLP 25249, originally issued ca. 1964. Some of the material on this LP is also repackaged on *22 of*

the Greatest Ragtime Hits, two discs, Ranwood R-7007.

98. Charters, Ann. *Essay in Ragtime: Ragtime Piano Classics Played by Ann Charters.* Folkways FG 3563. 1961. Brochure notes by Samuel B. Charters, 8 pp., music, photos.

99. _____ *et al. Scott Joplin, American Folk Composer: Selections from the Ragtime Opera "Treemonisha" (1911) . . . [and] Five Classic Rags (1899–1917). . . . Treemonisha* selections performed by Carolyn Lewis, soprano, and the Utah State University concert Chorale, Ted Puffer, director and piano. Rags performed by Ann Charters, piano. Portents 3. [**OP+**] [ca. 1966] Jacket notes by Samuel Charters.

100. _____. *A Joplin Bouquet: Rags for Flowers and Leaves with Some Pleasant Moments of Euphonic Sounds.* GNP Crescendo GNP 9021. 1973. Jacket notes by Sam Charters. Recorded in 1958 and originally released ca. 1963 as Portents 1. Also available in the U.K. as Sonet SNTF 631.

101. _____. *The Genius of Scott Joplin.* GNP Crescendo GNPS 9032. 1974. Jacket notes by Sam Charters.

102. _____. *Scott Joplin and His Friends.* Sierra Wave SW-101. [ca. 1976] Jacket notes by Sam Charters. Released in England in 1974 as Sonet SNTF 682.

103. Christensen, Steen. *A Danish Tribute to Classical Ragtime.** LB Specialty [Denmark] LBS-1. [**OP**] [1972] Accompanied by Mr. Joe's Ragtime Group: piano, banjo, bass and washboard.

104. _____. *The Many Faces of Ragtime.* (Mekanisk Musik Museum) MMM Records [Denmark] LP-201. 1974. Biographical jacket notes by Claes O. Friberg. Notes on the music by Steen Christensen. Solo piano, except three selections that are duets with a player piano.

105. _____. *Livin' a Ragtime Life.* Jazz Crooner Vol. 7, JC 155771. 1977. Jacket notes by Steen Christensen. Solo piano except Side One, track one, piano duet with Neville Dickie and rhythm accompaniment; two other selections on Side One are multitracked. Issued by Stichting Jazz Crooner, P.O. Box 1920, Breda, The Netherlands. May also be available from MMM (see introduction).

106. Coffman, Bill, and Kathy Craig. *Concert Time and the Old Town Music Hall.** OTMH 101. 1980. Organist Coffman and pianist Craig playing seven duets and five solos. According to a review in the March, 1981, *Mississippi Rag,* the record is supplied in a plain white jacket with no notes. Available from Old Town Music Hall, 140 Richmond Street, El Segundo, California 90245. See also 167–169 and 237.

107. Darch, Bob. *Ragtime Piano.* United Artists UAS 6120/UAL 3120. [**OP**] 1960. Jacket notes.

108. _____ and his Ragtime Band and featured guests Joe Jordan, Eubie Blake, Sally Heiss, Steve Spracklen, *et al. A Febrisacient, Splendiferous Evening in a Fine Saloon.** Jan Productions JLP 160. [ca. 1971] Inquire about availability from: Jan Productions, 412 North Elmwood Road, Omaha, Nebraska 68132. See also 72. Darch has also recorded, with Steve Radecke, *The Ragtime Saloon.* Mekanisk Music Museum MC-230 (cassette only). [1982?] Piano and vocals, recorded in live performance.

109. Davies, William, with the recorded voice of Eubie Blake. *Scott Joplin and the Ragtime Era.* Produced by Peter Gammond. Discourses All About Music ABK 19. 1975. Jacket notes. An illustrated booklet is apparently enclosed with some or most copies. The record is programmed to illustrate Peter Gammond's book of the same title.

110. Dean, Paul. *Ragtime Favorites, Featuring Paul Dean.* Scrapbook 4497. 1978. Mostly Joplin rags. An obscure budget label which I have only seen offered in publishers' overstock catalogs.

111. Delano, Lois. *The Music of Joe Jordan [Played] by Lois Delano.* Arpeggio ARP 1205. [**OP**] (Produced in cooperation with the Ragtime Society.) 1968. Jacket notes by Dan Grinstead.

112. Dickie, Neville. *Ragtime Dance.* (Mekanisk Musik Museum) MMM [Denmark] LP-210. [Recorded in 1975] Includes a higher proportion of ragtime than most of Dickie's recent LPs.

113. _____ and his Ragtime Piano. *Rags and Tatters.** Contour 287 190. [ca. 1970?].

114. _____, Quentin Williams, and Pete Davis. *Ragtime Piano: Neville Dickie, Quentin Williams and Pete Davis Play Ragtime.* Saydisc [U.K.] SDL-118. [ca. 1966] Jacket notes by Gef Lucena. Four original rags played by Williams, nine classic rags performed by Dickie and Davis. See also 128.

115. Dykstra, Brian. *American Beauty: 12 Ragtime Classics.* Unnumbered private recording. [**OP**] [ca. 1973] Jacket notes by Brian Dykstra. See also 307.

116. _____. *The Riches of Rags.** Orion ORS 83449. [1982?]

117. Ferrell, Betty. *Ragtime Reflections by Betty Ferrell, Ragtime Pianist.* Private issue, no label or number. [1981?] Available from: Betty Ferrell, Route 1, Box 672, Delray Beach, Florida 33345.

118. Folds, Chuck. *It's Rag Time.** Jazzways JW 106/4. [**OP?**] [ca. 1975?] Accompanied by Jackie Williams, drums.

119. Frost, David Andrew. *Scott Joplin Piano Music.* Musical Heritage Society MHS 3201. [1975] Jacket notes by Thomas Frost.

120. Gogerty, Patrick. *The Classical Rags of Joseph F. Lamb.* Sound Current Records [unnumbered]. 1976. Brief jacket notes by Patrick K. Gogerty. Available from: Sound Current

Records, 81984 N. Fairfax Ave., #5, Los Angeles, California 90046.

121. Hasse, John. *ExtraOrdinary Ragtime: Choice Piano Rags by Scott Joplin, James Scott, Irving Berlin, &c.* Sunflower 501. 1980. Jacket notes by John Edward Hasse. Includes three rags by Indiana composers, one Hasse original. Available from: Sunflower Records, 41 Fendall Avenue, Alexandria, Virginia 22304.

122. Hersh, Paul and David Montgomery. *The Great Ragtime Classics.* RCA ARL 1-0364. [OP] 1974. Jacket notes by David Montgomery. Piano four-hands. See also 147 and 151.

123. Hicks, George. *George Hicks, Ragtime: Tickled Pink.* Folkways FS 3165. 1983. Brochure notes by David A. Jasen, 2 pp. Mostly novelty piano works.

124. Hyman, Dick. *Scott Joplin: The Complete Works for Piano.* Five discs, boxed. RCA CRL 5-1106. 1975. Brochure notes by Rudi Blesh, 8 pp., photos. Includes the solo piano compositions grouped by genre: rags, marches, waltzes, the *School of Ragtime* exercises (with instructions read by Eubie Blake), and twelve jazz improvisations by Hyman on Joplin themes. Selections from this set appear on Hyman's *Scott Joplin: 16 Classic Rags* (RCA ARL 1-1257).

125. _____. *Kitten on the Keys: The Music of Zez Confrey.* RCA Red Seal XRL1-4746. 1983. Jacket notes by Richard D. Sudhalter. Hyman has made many other albums as a jazz and pop pianist or as an arranger/conductor. Two other albums containing some ragtime are *Dick Hyman Plays Ragtime, Stomps and Stride* (Project 3 PR 5080 SD) and *Dick Hyman Plays Keyboard Classics of the Nostalgia Years,** two discs (Cadence CR 2001). Hyman is also reputed to have made some or all of the recordings attributed to "Knuckles O'Toole" (see 160 and 331).

126. Jasen, Dave. *Rompin', Stompin' Ragtime by Dave Jasen.* Blue Goose 3002. 1974. Jacket notes by Stephen Calt.

127. _____. *Rip-Roarin' Ragtime.* Folkways FG 3561. 1977. Brochure notes by Alan Douglas, 3 pp. Piano accompanied by Ed McKee, tuba, and Mike Schwimmer, washboard. See also 313.

128. _____, and Neville Dickie. *Creative Ragtime: David Jasen, The Rebel Regent of Ragtime Versus Neville Dickie, Pride of the British Isles.* Euphonic ESR 1206. [ca. 1968] Jacket notes by Paul E. Affeldt and autobiographical sketches by the composers. See also 112–114.

129. Jenks, Glenn. *The Ragtime Project.* [Bonnie Banks Productions] ᗺB 103. 1983. Brief jacket notes by Glenn Jenks. Nine classic rags, plus one original waltz. Obtainable from Bonnie Banks Productions, P. O. Box 811, Camden, Maine 04843.

130. Jensen, John. *Piano Rags by James Scott.* Genesis GS 1044. 1974. Jacket notes by Rudi Blesh.

131. _____. *Piano Rags by Joseph Lamb.* Genesis GS 1045. 1974. Jacket notes by Earl Rosenbaum.

132. _____. *Zez Confrey: Novelty Piano Solos.* Genesis GS 1051. 1974. Jacket notes by David A. Jasen.

133. Jones, hank. *This is Ragtime Now.* ABC-Paramount ABCS-496. [OP] 1964. Jacket notes by George Hoefer.

134. Jones, Jazzou. *Riverboat Ragtime.* High Water Records HW 101. 1983. Rags by Lamb, Scott, Joplin, Blake, *et al.*, as well as one original by Jones. Available from High Water Records, P. O. Box 13126, Hamilton, Ohio 45013.

135. Kaye, Milton. *The Classic Rags of Joe Lamb.* Two discs. Golden Crest CRS-4127. [1974?] Jacket notes by Rudi Blesh, 3 pp. Sides One and Two: piano solos. Side Three: Blesh and Kaye discussing Joseph Lamb and the interpretation of piano rags. No fourth side.

136. _____. *The Classic Rags of Joseph Lamb, Volume II.* Produced by Rudi Blesh. Golden Crest CRS-31035. [1975] Jacket notes by Rudi Blesh.

137. _____. *Ragtime at the Rosebud.* Two discs. Golden Crest CRS-31032. [1975?] Jacket notes by Rudi Blesh.

138. _____. *You Tell 'Em Ivories: Milton Kaye Plays Zez Confrey.* Golden Crest CRS-31040. [1975?] Jacket notes by Rudi Blesh.

139. Kleiner, Arthur. *Music for Silent Comedies.* Golden Crest CR 2004. (Collector's Series.) [ca. 1968] Back jacket cover contains reprint of *New York Times* article on Kleiner by Howard Thompson; inside jacket panels contain silent movie stills. Mostly piano novelties by Confrey.

140. Krenz, Bill. *Oh Willie, Play that Thing.** MCM E-184. (10" LP) [OP+] David Jasen credits Krenz with having written several interesting rags; this LP may contain some of them.

141. Kroekel, Dick. *Echoes from Lulu White's Mahogany Hall.* Ragtime CRU 1930. [1977] Jacket notes credited to Baron von Heisterkampt. Ragtime and period pop tunes; piano accompanied by Steve Ashton, drums. Available from: Grassroots Projects Unlimited, P.O. Box 4689, San Francisco, California 94101.

142. Labeque, Katia and Marielle. *Gladrags.* EMI Angel S-37980. 1983. Two-piano duets arranged by François Jeanneau. Jacket notes by John McLaughlin. Mostly Joplin rags.

143. Larsen, Morton Gunnar. *Don't You Leave Me Here.** Sonet SLP 1450. [1980?] Approximately one-half rags and one-half early

jazz tunes. A review by David Thomas Roberts in the July, 1980, *Rag Times* refers to an earlier recording by Larsen titled *Classic Rags and Stomps*, which was released in Scandinavia (Norway?), but gives no other particulars.

144. _____. *Morton Gunnar Larsen Plays Roberto Clemente, Poor Jimmy Green, and other Jazz/Ragtime Compositions.** Stomp Off S.O.S. 1009. 1981.

145. Levine, James. *James Levine Plays Scott Joplin.* RCA ARL 1-2243. 1977. Jacket notes by Peter Dellheim.

146. Lingle, Paul and Bill Mitchell. *Vintage Piano.* Euphonic ESR-1203. (Piano Series, vol. 3.) [ca. 1964] Jacket notes by Paul E. Affeldt. Lingle and Mitchell have one side each; the Mitchell side is mostly ragtime. A mimeographed letter from Affeldt apologizing for poor mastering is enclosed with at least the first pressing. Two subsequent recordings by Lingle (Euphonic 1217 and 1220), reputedly with superior sound, have been issued, but include few rags. See also 150.

147. Lytle, Cecil and David Montgomery. *Rags, Blues, the Boogie Bougaloo* [sic] *and a Sweet Goodnight—Amen!* Klavier KS 533. 1974. Jacket notes by David Montgomery. Duo piano and piano four hands. About one-half the contents is ragtime. See also 122 and 151.

148. Maddox, Johnny. *Tres Moutarde.* Paragon SG-102. 1978. Maddox recorded numerous albums for Dot in the 1950s and 1960s. Commercial exigencies and performance customs of the period caused few rags to be included on any one album (even when the word "ragtime" appeared in the title) and emphasized display of digital dexterity, but this record and another release, *Amoureuse* (Paragon SG-101, originally Redstone RSS 101) have been praised for choice of material and performance. Available from: Pragaon Productions, 1240 Krameria Street, Denver, Colorado 80220. Most recently Maddox has recorded *Johnny Maddox Plays Ragtime Favorites.* Mekanisk Music Museum MC-240 (cassette only).

149. Mandel, Alan. *An Anthology of American Piano Music* (1780-1970). Three discs, boxed. Desto DC 6445/47. 1975. Brochure notes, 6 pp., by Alan Mandel. Disc Two includes four classic rags. Mandel was one of the first contemporary classical pianists to regularly include rags in recital programs. See also 316.

150. Mitchell, Bill. *Ragtime Recycled.* Ethelyn Records ER 1750. 1972. Jacket notes by David E. Bourne. Piano with banjo, tuba and percussion accompaniment. See also 146.

151. Montgomery, David, and Cecil Lytle. *Piano Rags: Ragtime Piano for Four Hands.* Sonic Arts laboratory series Number 6. Direct to Disc Records. 1976. Jacket notes unsigned and by Leo De Gar Kulka. See also 122 and 147.

152. Morath, Max. *Max Morath Plays The Best of Scott Joplin and Other Rag Classics.* Two discs. Vanguard VSD 39/40. 1972. Jacket notes by Rudi Blesh. Record One: solo piano. Record Two: Morath arrangements of classic rags for piano, banjo, guitar, and string bass. Record Two is a reissue of Arpeggio ARP 1204 S, originally released by the Ragtime Society in 1968.

153. _____. *The World of Scott Joplin.* Vanguard Everyman SRV 310 SD. 1973. Jacket notes by Max Morath.

154. _____. *The World of Scott Joplin, Vol. 2.* Vanguard Everyman SRV 351 SD. 1975. Jacket notes by Lois Gertsman. SRV 310 and 351 were also packaged together in 1976 under the title *Max Morath Plays Ragtime* (Vanguard VSD 83/84, two discs). Morath has also issued a number of other recordings that document his work as singer, personality, and cultural historian/entertainer. The Max Morath/Wally Rose LP, *Ragtime Favorites of Scott Joplin and Other Great Piano Rags* (Columbia Harmony KH 32421) reissues three of the four piano rags from Morath's *Oh Play That Thing! The Ragtime Era* (Epic 26106) plus one rag from Epic 26066. *Max Morath at the Turn of the Century* (RCA LSO-1159) is a recording of portions of one of Morath's one-man shows and includes four rags. The RCA, the Epics, and probably the Harmony are out of print. More recently, on *Living a Ragtime Life* (Vanguard VSD 79391, 1978), Morath again records portions of a one-man show, including a few songs contained on albums now discontinued and three rags. On *The Great American Piano Bench: A Turn-of-the-Century Keyboard Sampler* (Vanguard VSD 79429, 1979), Morath supplies part of the original context of ragtime—some of the "other" piano works ragtime composers wrote and the "other" popular piano pieces that amateur pianists and professional entertainers performed. See also 245 and 272.

155. Morgan, Russ & Eddie Wilser. *Kitten on the Keys.* Decca DL 8746. [OP] [ca. 1955?] Jacket notes. Piano duets with rhythm accompaniment. Mostly Zez Confrey compositions.

156. Nadeau, Roland L. *Grace and Beauty: Classic American Ragtime.* Sounds of Northeastern CSRV 2625. (Sounds of Northeastern University Series, first volume.) 1979. Jacket notes, "The Ragtime Milieu," by Gerald Herman. Brochure notes by Roland Nadeau and William Tesson, 2 pp. Side One: piano rags by Joplin, Scott, and Lamb. Side Two: "Inside Ragtime: [spoken] Analysis and Commentary." Available from: Sounds of Northeastern, P.O. Box 116, Boston, Massachusetts 02117.

157. Nichols, Keith. *Keith Nichols Plays Scott Joplin and the Classic Rag Masters.* One-Up [U.K.]

OOU 2035. 1974. Jacket notes by Charles Fox.

158. _____. *Cat at the Keyboard.* One-Up [U.K.] OU 2085. 1975. Jacket notes by Charles Fox. Solo piano and piano with rhythm accompaniment. Mostly piano novelties. See also 283.

159. O'Boyle, Tom. *Nine Ragtime Masterpieces of Scott Joplin.* Devlin Productions [unnumbered]. 1974. Jacket notes by Susan Daniels. Available from: Devlin Productions, P. O. Box 9424, Colorado Springs, Colorado 80909.

160. O'Toole, Knuckles. *Knuckles O'Toole Plays the Greatest All-Time Ragtime Hits.* (ABC) Westminster/Grand Award WGAS 68003. [OP] 1974. Jacket notes by Tucker Inge. Reissue of Grand Award GA 209 SD, issued ca. 1960. Several other albums by "O'Toole" in a honky-tonk vein were also issued. See also 125.

161. Ott, Daryl. *Daryl Ott Plays and Sings Riverfront Rags and Blues.* Dirty Shame DSRC 1238. 1978. Jacket notes on the music by Trebor Jay Tichenor, and unsigned biographical notes. Program contains about one-half rags and one-half period pop songs. Notable for consistent choice of obscure and seldom-recorded material.

162. _____. *Friday Night Live!.* Uplift R-0180/DA-32880. 1980. Jacket notes by Ott. A half-dozen rags plus period pop, blues, and jazz songs. Available from Daryl Ott, 6451 Gildar Street, Alexandria, Virginia 22310.

163. Parker, John W. (Knocky). *Old Rags.* Audiophile AP 49. [OP] [ca. 1957?] Unsigned jacket notes.

164. _____. *The Complete Piano Works of Scott Joplin.* Two discs. Audiophile AP 71-2. [OP] [ca. 1960] Unsigned jacket notes. Contains most of the same solo piano works included in the five-disc sets performed by Dick Hyman (see 125) and Richard Zimmerman (see 205), but Parker shortens the pieces by omitting repeated strains.

165. _____. *The Complete Piano Works of James Scott.* Two discs. Audiophile AP 76-7. [OP] [ca. 1962] Brief notes by E. D. Nunn.

166. _____. *Golden Treasury of Ragtime.* Four separate discs. Audiophile AP 89, 90, 91, and 92. [OP] [ca. 1968] Brief, unsigned notes reprinted on each jacket. Composers are not identified in notes or on the discs. No duplication with Parker's complete Joplin and Scott sets. Excludes rags by Joseph Lamb and Artie Matthews. Parker performs on piano, celeste, and harpsichord (sometimes within a single rag), with rhythm accompaniment.

167. _____, and Bill Coffman. *Classic Rags and Nostalgia at the Old Town Music Hall; Knocky Parker at the Bösendorfer Grand Piano, Bill Coffman at the Mighty Wurlitzer Theatre Pipe Organ.* Euphonic ESR-1216. 1978. Jacket notes by Bill Mitchell.

Piano/organ duets including five Joplin rags and five period pop tunes. Parker has also recorded another album of duets, *Eight on Eighty-Eight* (Euphonic 1215), comprising two duets each with eight different California pianists, which includes a few rags.

168. _____. *From Ragtime to Ballroom.* Jazzology JCE-82. (Jazz Piano Heritage Series, vol. 32.) [1979] Jacket notes by Parker on ragtime as dance music. Brief jacket notes by George H. Buck, Jr., about the album and its companion. Duets by Parker (piano) and Coffman (organ).

169. _____ and Robbie Rhodes. *From Cakewalk to Ragtime.* Jazzology JCE-81. (Jazz Piano Heritage Series, vol. 31.) [1979] Jacket notes by Parker about the music; brief notes by George H. Buck, Jr., on the album and its companion (see 168); and unsigned notes on the artists. Duets by Parker (piano) and Coffman (theater organ), except Rhodes (piano) replaces Coffman on *Smoky Mokes*. See also 106.

170. Pistorious, Steve. *Classic Piano Rags Played by New Orlean's [sic] Own Steve Pistorious, The Creole Kid.* Jazzology JCE-78. (Jazz Piano Heritage Series, vol. 28.) [1977] Jacket notes by Al Rose and, briefly, George H. Buck, Jr. The artist's name is spelled "Pistorius" in the notes and the release announcement, but "Pistorious" on the cover.

171. Polad, Mike. *The Cascades and Other Ragtime Extravaganzas.* Jazzology JCE 77. [ca. 1972] Jacket notes by William J. Schafer.

172. Price, Ronnie. *The Scott Joplin Ragtime Album.* (CBS) Embassy [U.K.] EMB 31043. 1974. Jacket notes by Rex Oldfield. Ronnie Price, piano, accompanied by Derek Price, drums, Joe Mudele, bass, and Terry Walsh, guitar/banjo.

173. Rasch, Charlie. *Ragtime Down the Line.* Ragtime Society Records RSR-4. [OP] 1966. Jacket notes by Tom Shea and Charlie Rasch. Other records by Rasch that may contain some ragtime have been issued by CK Records and Society Bear Records.

174. Rifkin, Joshua. *Piano Rags by Scott Joplin.* Nonesuch H-71248. 1970. Jacket notes by Joshua Rifkin.

175. _____. *Piano Rags by Scott Joplin, Volume II.* Nonesuch H-71264. 1972. Jacket notes by Rifkin. Volumes one and two are also available packaged together as Nonesuch HB 73026, with brief additional notes by Alan Rich.

176. _____. *Piano Rags by Scott Joplin, Volume III.* Nonesuch H-71305. 1974. Jacket notes by Rifkin.

177. _____. *Digital Ragtime: Music of Scott Joplin.* Angel DS-37331. 1980. Unsigned jacket notes. Nine digitally recorded Joplin works, most of which Rifkin previously recorded for Nonesuch.

178. Roberts, David Thomas. *An Album of Early Folk Rags.* Stomp Off S.O.S. 1021. 1981. Jacket notes by David Thomas Roberts.

179. Rogers, Alan. *From Rags to Riches.* Polydor Select [U.K.] 2460 227. [ca. 1974] Brief jacket notes. Piano with drums and clarinet or pennywhistle.

180. Rogers, Eric. *Great Scott . . . The Music of Scott Joplin Played by Eric Rogers.* London SPC 21105. [OP] 1974. Jacket notes by Eric Rogers.

181. Rose, Wally. *Ragtime Classics Played by Wally Rose.* Good Time Jazz S 10034. 1960. Jacket notes by Lester Koenig. Piano with rhythm accompaniment.

182. ———. *Wally Rose on Piano.* Blackbird C 12007. 1970. Jacket notes by Paul Tuteur and Robert G. Peck, jr.

183. ———. *Whippin' the Keys: A Classical Jazz.* Blackbird C12010. (Jazz from San Francisco Series, vol. 2.) [ca. 1976] Jacket notes by Hal Smith. Recorded June, 1971.

184. ———. *Revisited.** Stomp Off 1057. 1983. Jacket notes by Ed Sprankle. Note that a few rags Rose had recorded for Columbia were reissued in electronic stereo on Harmony KH 32421 (see 154). Of Rose's Columbia recordings, *Ragtime Piano Masterpieces* (Columbia CL 6260, 10" LP), probably contained the most ragtime.

185. ———, with Lu Watters and Yerba Buena Jazz Band. *Live from the Dawn Club.* Fairmont 102. 1973. Jacket notes by Dave Caughren. Piano with rhythm or jazz band accompaniment. Probably air shots from the 1940s. See also 298.

186. Schoenfield, Paul. *The Best of Scott Joplin.* Pro Arte Sinfonia SDS-613. 1983. Digital recordings of eight Joplin works—less than twenty-seven minutes of music.

187. Shields, Roger. *The Age of Ragtime.* Turnabout TVS 34579. (Americana, vol. IV.) 1974. Jacket notes by Roger Shields.

188. Singéry, Yannick. *Ragtime Piano Classics: The Scott Joplin Era.** Vogue [France] SLD 928. [OP?] 1975. Jacket notes by Jean-Christophe Averty.

189. Steinhardt, Victor et al. *American Sampler.* Two discs. Olympic OLY-104. 1975. Double-fold jacket notes by Naomi B. Pascal "in concert with the performers." Performers are Elizabeth Suderberg, vocals; Stuart Dempster, trombone and euphonium; Victor Steinhardt, piano; and Robert Suderberg, piano. Period songs; trombone and euphonium showpieces; and five rags—by Joplin, Lamb, Paul Pratt, and Will Held—performed by Steinhardt. Available from the University of Washington Press, Seattle, Washington 98105.

190. Sutton, Ralph. *Backroom Piano.* Verve MGV 1004. [OP+] [ca. 1956] Unsigned jacket notes. Sutton was one of the most respected

of the young jazz pianists active in the ragtime revival of the 1940s and 1950s. Of his albums, this contains more rags than most.

191. Swift, Duncan. *Piano Ragtime.* Black Lion BL-301. [American edition OP.] 1974. Jacket notes by Alun Morgan. Side One: mostly Jelly Roll Morton compositions; Side Two: mostly Scott Joplin rags.

192. Taylor, Keith. *Ragtime Piano.* Sami 1001. [ca. 1977] Brief, unsigned jacket notes. Recorded between September 1974 and October 1976. Available from: Sami Records, 915 La Alameda Ave., San Pedro, California 90731.

193. Tichenor, Trebor. *Mississippi Valley Ragtime.* Issued under the auspices of the Ragtime Society. Scroll LSCR-102. OP. 1966. Jacket notes by Trebor Tichenor. Tichenor also records with the St. Louis Ragtimers (see 249).

194. ———. *King of Folk Ragtime.* Dirty Shame 2001. 1973. Jacket notes by Trebor Tichenor.

195. ———. *Days Beyond Recall.** Folkways FS 3164. [1980?] Nine obscure country/folk rags, seven Tichenor originals.

196. Turner, Ray. *Kitten on the Keys.** Capitol H-306 (10-inch LP). [OP] [ca. 1950?] Turner is reputed to have been an experienced and highly skillful performer of novelty piano. A later Capitol recording (T-188) was called *Honky-Tonk Piano.*

197. Veri, Frances and Michael Jamanis. *Gershwin: The Complete Song Book; Joplin: The Entertainer.* Connoisseur Society CS 2073. [OP] 1975. Jacket notes by Edward Jablonski. Includes duo-piano performances of six Joplin compositions.

198. Waldo, Terry. *The Piano of Terry Waldo: Sounds of Ragtime and Vaudeville.* Fat Cat's Jazz FCJ-151. [Recorded January 1974] Jacket notes by Ray West. Piano solos, and vocals with piano accompaniment. All but two selections recorded in live performance with brief spoken introductions.

199. ———. *Snookums Rag: Ragtime Piano Solos by Terry Waldo.* Dirty Shame 1237. 1974. Jacket notes by Terry Waldo.

200. ———. *The Wizard of the Keyboard.** Stomp Off S.O.S. 1002. 1980. Piano accompanied on eight of the twelve pieces by Eddy Davis on banjo and Vince Giordano on tuba. Includes four vocals by Waldo, three classic rags, two "special rag arrangements," one Waldo original, one James P. Johnson piece, and one previously unrecorded work by Jelly Roll Morton. See also 297.

201. Weatherburn, Ron. *Ragtime Piano: Extemporizations & Innovations.* Rediffusion [U.K.] 0100170. [OP?] 1974. Jacket notes by Ron Weatherburn. Mostly piano accompanied by Sandy Sanders, drums.

202. Wellstood, Dick. *The Music of Scott Joplin.* Pickwick SPC 3575. [OP?] 1977. Jacket notes by Amanda Frances. Reissue of Pickwick SPC 3376, which had been issued, in 1974, with jacket notes by Wellstood, as a spinoff of the motion picture *The Sting.*

203. Werner, Ken. *Ken Werner Plays the Piano Music of Bix Beiderbecke, George Gershwin, James P. Johnson, and Duke Ellington.** Finnadar SR 9019. 1978. Jacket notes by Ilhan Mimaroglu. Includes rags composed by Gershwin, Johnson, and Ellington, as well as nonrags composed by Beiderbecke.

204. Wyndham, Tex. *He's a Rag Picker.* Fat Cat's Jazz FCJ 168. 1975. Jacket notes by Tex Wyndham and Johnson McRee, Jr. Piano solos, and period novelty songs with piano accompaniment. '

205. Zimmerman, Richard. *Scott Joplin: His Complete Works.* Five discs, boxed. Murray Hill 931079. 1974. Brochure notes by Ian Whitcomb, Richard Zimmerman, 16 pp., bibliog., illus. Contains piano compositions, the piano accompaniments of Joplin songs, the *School of Ragtime* exercises, and selections from the *Treemonisha* piano score. Selections from the set were issued on Olympic 7116 and 8139.

206. _____. *The Collector's History of Ragtime.** Five discs, boxed, Murray Hill M-60556/5. 1982. Brochure notes by Zimmerman, 8 pp., with twenty-one illustrations. A chronological survey, from 1899 to 1939, of piano rags from all parts of the United States. Includes both well-known rags (*Grace and Beauty, Temptation Rag, Pastime Rag No. 5*) and little-known rags (*A Dingy Slowdown, Bull Dog Rag, Whoa Nellie!*). The first disc in the set is also available as *The Roots of Ragtime,* Everest/Archives of Folk and Jazz Music FS 370.

OTHER KEYBOARD INSTRUMENTS: HARPSICHORD, PEDAL HARPSICHORD, ORGAN, AND SYNTHESIZER

207. Biggs, E. Power. *E. Power Biggs Plays Scott Joplin on the Pedal Harpsichord.* Columbia M 32495. 1973. Jacket notes by E. Power Biggs. Reissued in 1983 as CBS Records Masterworks MP 38782.

208. _____. *Scott Joplin on the Pedal Harpsichord, Volume No. Two.* Columbia M 33205. 1974. Jacket notes by E. Power Biggs.

209. Erwin, Lee. *Rosebud: Marches & Rags of Scott Joplin, & Kerry Mills, Eubie Blake, Harry Guy.* Angel S-36075. 1974. Jacket notes by Rory Guy. A veteran theatre organist playing the Fox-Capitol Theatre Wurlitzer pipe organ.

210. Roberts, Wm. Neil. *Great Scott! Ragtime on the Harpsichord.* Klavier KS-510. 1972. Jacket notes by Wm. Neil Roberts. Contains eleven rags by Joplin.

211. _____. *Scott Joplin: Ragtime Harpsichord,*

Vol. 2. Klavier KS 516. 1973. Jacket notes by Harold L. Powell and Wm. Neil Roberts.

212. Stone, Chris. *Gatsby's World: Turned-On Joplin; Chris Stone at the Moog.* ABC Records ABCX-823. [OP] 1974. Unsigned jacket notes. Joplin packaged with Gatsby/Sting anachronisms.

See also 106, 166–69, 258, and 303.

RAGTIME TRANSPOSED OR ARRANGED FOR DIVERSE INSTRUMENTS

Solo Performers

VIOLIN WITH PIANO

213. Perlman, Itzhak and Andre Previn. *The Easy Winners and Other Rag-time Music of Scott Joplin.* Arranged by Itzhak Perlman. Angel S-37113. 1975. Jacket notes by Itzhak Perlman and Rory Guy.

214. Zukofsky, Paul and Bob Dennis. *Classic Rags and other Novelties.* Arranged by Zukofsky or by Zukofsky and Dennis. Vanguard Everyman SRV 350 SD. 1975. Jacket notes by Robert Kimball.

GUITAR

215. *Advanced Fingerpicking Guitar Techniques; School of Ragtime: 10 Classic Rags for Guitar by Scott Joplin.* Produced by Stefan Grossman. Kicking Mule KM-147. [ca. 1979] Jacket notes by Stefan Grossman. Joplin rags arranged for guitar by Duck Baker, Lasse Johansson, Claes Palmqvist, Tom Engels, John James, and Tim Nicolai. Tablature books for Kicking Mule Records are usually available from the company at a modest price.

216. Barbosa-Lima, Carlos. *Carlos Barbosa-Lima Plays The Entertainer and Selected Works by Scott Joplin.* Concord Concerto CC-2006. 1983. Jacket notes by Jim Crockett. Arrangements for classical guitar by Barbosa-Lima.

217. *Contemporary Ragtime Guitar.* Produced by Stefan Grossman. Kicking Mule KM 107. [ca. 1974] Jacket notes by Stefan Grossman. Various artists. Mostly transcriptions of piano rags. Issued in the U.K. as Sonet SNKF 100.

218. Davis, Gary. *The Ragtime Guitar of Rev. Gary Davis.* Kicking Mule KM 106. [ca. 1973] Jacket notes by Stefan Grossman. Recorded 1962–70. Davis can also be heard on a dozen or more other albums, including *The Guitar and Banjo . . . ,* Prestige 7725, which also highlights his instrumental work.

219. *The Entertainer: The Classic Rags of Scott Joplin Arranged for the Six-String Guitar.* Produced by Stefan Grossman. Kicking Mule KM 122. [ca. 1976] Various guitarists performing arrangements of Joplin rags. Issued in the U.K. as Sonet SNKF 115.

220. Grossman, Stefan and Ton Van Ber-

geyk. *How to Play Ragtime Guitar.* Kicking Mule KM 115. [ca. 1974] Jacket notes by Stefan Grossman, including tuning and capo instructions. Folk rags, transcribed classic rags, and contemporary ragtime guitar solos. Grossman often includes rags on his other albums, issued mostly by Kicking Mule, Transatlantic [U.K.], and Sonet [U.K.]. See also 230 and 231.

221. Hancoff, Steve. *Classic Ragtime Guitar.* Dirty Shame 4553. [1978] Jacket notes by Al Mothershead and Eric Sager.

222. Johansson, Lasse and Claes Palmkvist. *Ragtime Guitar Duets: March and Two-Step.* Kicking Mule KM 130. [1977] Jacket notes by Lasse Johansson. Mostly arrangements of Joplin rags. Issued in the U.K. as Sonet SNKF 120. Originally issued in Sweden as Grammofonverket EFG 501 5001, in about 1975.

223. Laibman, David. *Classical Ragtime Guitar.** Rounder 3040. 1981.

224. _____ and Eric Schoenberg. *The New Ragtime Guitar.* (Folkways) Asch Records AHS 3528. 1971. Brochure notes by Sam Charters and David Laibman, 4 pp. A highly influential album. Issued in the U.K. as Transatlantic TRA 253.

225. Lolax, Paul. *Ragtime Guitar: Selected Works of Scott Joplin and Joseph Lamb Transcribed and Arranged by Paul Lolax.* Titantic Ti-13. [ca. 1976] Brief, incoherent jacket notes by Peter Kairo, Paul Lolax, and Lisa Raphals.

226. *Masters of the Ragtime Guitar: Echoes from the Snowball Club.* Kicking Mule KM 146. [1977] Jacket notes by Stefan Grossman. Arrangements for guitar by Duck Baker, Ton Van Bergeyk, Lasse Johansson, Claes Palmkvist, and Tim Nicolai. Released in the U.K. as Sonet SNKF 130.

227. *Novelty Guitar Instrumentals.* Produced by Stefan Grossman. Kicking Mule KM 127. [1977] Jacket notes by Stefan Grossman. Various American and European guitarists performing mostly rags and ragtime-derived compositions. Issued in the U.K. as Sonet SNKF 117.

228. *Picture Rags: A Selection of Ragtime Music on the Guitar.* Transatlantic [U.K.] TRA SAM 26. [ca. 1974] Jacket notes by Fred Dellar. A sampler of guitar ragtime from other Transatlantic albums by Stefan Grossman, John James, Rev. Gary Davis, *et al.*

229. Tryforos, Bob. *Scott Joplin, Composer; Bob Tryforos, Guitarist.* Puritan 5002. 1972. Brief, unsigned jacket notes.

230. Van Bergeyk, Ton. *Famous Ragtime Guitar Solos.* Kicking Mule KM 114. [ca. 1974] Jacket notes by Stefan Grossman, including interview with Van Bergeyk. Issued in the U.K. as Sonet SNKF 106.

231. _____. *Guitar Instrumentals to Tickle Your Fingers.* Kicking Mule KM 125. [ca. 1976] Jacket notes by Stefan Grossman. Transcriptions for guitar of rags and other pieces. Issued in the U.K. as Sonet SNKF 114. Van Bergeyk is also featured on several Kicking Mule anthologies. See also 220.

232. Wijnkamp, Leo, Jr. *Rags to Riches.* Kicking Mule KM 117. [1975] Jacket notes by Stefan Grossman. Released in the U.K. as Sonet SNKF 108.

BANJO

233. Ball, William J. *A Banjo Galaxy: The Classic Banjo of William J. Ball.* Rounder 3005. [ca. 1976] Jacket notes by Eli Kaufman. Accompaniment by Eileen Smith, piano. The majority of the works are compositions of British banjo virtuoso Joe Morley—a contemporary of Vess L. Ossman and Fred Van Eps. While most of the compositions are not rags they are of considerable interest as illustrations of possibilities inherent in the classic banjo style. See also 240.

234. Davis, Eddy. *Eddy Davis Plays Ragtime.* Pă Dă P 7401. 1974. Jacket notes by Eddy Davis. Features Buck Kelly on second banjo. May be available from Pă Da Publishing, P.O. Box 27083, Riverdale, Illinois 60627.

235. Erickson, Ed, Randy Morris, and W. C. Chester. *The Banjo Specialists.* House of Ragtime HR 1001. 1974. Jacket notes by Vikki Arneke. Vintage pop, originals, and some ragtime.

236. [Haworth, Bob.] *The Banjo King Plays Ragtime.* Piccadilly 3302. 1977. Brief jacket notes. Includes five rag standards, one march, six pop tunes.

237. Knopf, Bill. *Bill Knopf.** First Inversion Records FIR 001. [1982?] Four rags performed on the banjo with piano accompaniment by Kathy Craig and several nonrag pieces with varied accompaniment. Available from County Sales, P. O. Box 191, Floyd, Virginia 24091. See also 106.

238. Larson, Leroy. *Banjo Ragtime & Other Classics.* Banjar BR 1781. 1973. Jacket notes by Leroy Larson and Lowell Schreyer. Side One: banjo arrangements of classic rags; Side Two: mostly classical transcriptions. Banjo with piano and rhythm accompaniment.

239. _____. *Banjo Drifter: Ragtime to Recent.* Banjar BR 1784. 1977. Jacket notes by Leroy Larson and B. F. Woolfrey. Banjo with piano, rhythm, and occasional synthesizer accompaniment. Side One: classic and novelty rags; Side Two: mostly recent tunes, including two originals. Banjar 1782 also contains two rags.

240. Lillywhite, Derek. *Banjo Reminiscenses.** Rounder 0095. 1981. British classic style banjo. See also 233.

241. Sokolow, Fred. *Ragtime Banjo Bluegrass.** Kicking Mule KM 212. 1982. Banjo tablature

book also available.
See also 1, 15, 17, 43, 45–48, 78, 103, 152, 200, 245, and 247–49.

FLUTE

242. Rampal, Jean-Pierre. *Jean-Pierre Rampal Plays Scott Joplin.** CBS Masterworks FM 37818. 1983. With John Steele Ritter, pianos and harpsichord; Shelly Manne, drums; and Tommy Johnson, tuba.

Ensemble Performances

STRINGS, OR PIANO WITH STRINGS

243. Etcetera String Band, The. *The Harvest Hop: Old Rags, Cakewalks, and Marches from Missouri.* Moon 200. 1975. Brochure notes by Dennis Michael Pash with research assistance by Kevin Sanders, 8 pp., illus. Country dance music played by guitar, violin, and mandolin. Available from Moon Records, P.O. Box 4001, Kansas City, Kansas 66104.

244. Herouet, Marc *et al. Marc Herouet's Ragtime Cats.* Snow [Belgium] LN 1001. [ca. 1979] Piano with drums, bass, violin, and occasional vocals. Five Joplin works, three Herouet compositions, and four others (not all rags). See also 311.

245. Morath, Max, and the Ragtime Quintet. *The Ragtime Women.* Vanguard VSD 79402. 1977. Jacket notes by Max Morath. Morath on piano with cello, bass, guitar, and banjo/guitar/mandolin. See also 152–54, 272.

246. Philharmonische Cellisten Köln. *Ragtimes.** Werner Thomas, conductor and arranger. Wergo [East Germany] SM 1016. 1977. Jacket notes by K. Franke, with English translation by J. Hock. Arrangements of rags by Joplin, Lamb, and Scott. Also includes arrangements of works by Fats Waller, Dave Brubeck, and Heitor Villa-Lobos.

247. *Queen City Ragtime Ensemble, The.* Zeno HHZ-99. [ca. 1976] Jacket notes by Ray Leake, Bill Clark, and Duane Sutfin. Ray Leake, piano, with banjo, bass, and drums. Available from Zeno Productions, P.O. Box 1273, Littleton, Colorado 80120.

248. *Ragtime Banjo Commission, The.** GHB Records GHB-154. 1981. Jeff Frank, Cal Owen, and Maurie Walker, banjos, and Bill Clark, tuba. Mostly arrangements of classic rags.

249. St. Louis Ragtimers, The. *Theron C. Bennett Memorial Concert . . . 20th Anniversary Celebration. . . .* Ragophile Collectable Series TS81-359/360. 1981. "Vintage fidelity" recording of the Ragtimers' "first major appearance," at the National Guard Armory, Pierce City, Missouri, in 1961. The Ragtimers then comprised a trio including Trebor Tichenor, piano,

Al Stricker, banjo, and Don Franz, tuba. Though the sound is inferior, the material runs much more to rags than their later recordings which feature a more conventional jazz-band lineup. Available from Trebor Jay Tichenor, 3801 Federer Place, Saint Louis, Missouri 63116. See also 193–95.

250. *Zinn's Ragtime String Quintet.* Music Minus One CJ 13. 1974. Jacket notes by Rudi Blesh. Works arranged by William Zinn or Vincent Liota for two violins, viola, and cello.
See also 103, 152, 172, and 241.

PERCUSSION

251. Eastman Marimba Band. *Nola.* Mercury Golden Imports SRI 75108. [1977] Jacket notes by Francis Crociata. Five-piece marimba band performing compositions and arrangements from the golden age of the xylophone (1915–1935) by xylophone virtuosi George Hamilton Green, Harry Breuer, and Red Norvo.

252. Nexus. *Ragtime Concert.* Umbrella [Canada] UMB-DD2. [1977?] Jacket notes by Bob Becker, photos. Mostly compositions by xylophone virtuoso George Hamilton Green, performed by a six-piece percussion ensemble primarily employing xylophone, marimba, and toy piano. Most selections arranged by Bob Becker. Limited edition recorded direct to disc. Available in U.S. from Audio Technica U.S., Inc., 33 Shiawassee Avenue, Fairlawn, Ohio 44313.
See also 49 and 261.

BRASS

253. Canadian Brass. *Rag-Ma-Tazz.* Boot BMC 3004. 1975. Jacket notes by Richard Gale and Peter Gzowski. Side One: eight Joplin compositions. Side Two: various contemporary ragtime or ragtime-flavored works plus Henry Fillmore trombone showpieces. All works arranged for two trumpets, trombone, French horn, and tuba. Subsequently issued as Vanguard VSD 79420. Other albums by the Canadian Brass may occasionally contain rags.

254. Eastern Brass Quintet. *Rags and Other American Things.* Klavier KS-529. 1975. Jacket notes by Tupper L. Turner. Includes five classic rags arranged for horn, trombone, tuba, and two trumpets.
See also 94.

WOODWINDS

255. Amherst Saxophone Quartet, The. *An American Classic: Eubie Blake; The Amherst Saxophone Quartet Performs the Music of James Hubert Blake.* Musical Heritage Society MHS 4368. 1981. Jacket notes by Michael Nascimben and

Stephen Rosenthal. Fourteen Blake compositions arranged for soprano, alto, tenor, and baritone saxophone by group members Michael Nascimben, Stephen Rosenthal, and Salvatore Andolina. Also issued as Musicmasters 20013.

256. Brodie, Paul, Saxophone Quartet. *A Recital with the Paul Brodie Saxophone Quartet.** Golden Crest CRS 4143. 1975. Jacket notes by J. Stoltie. Mostly arrangements of classical (nonrag) piano works. Includes rags by Tom Turpin, Scott Joplin/Scott Hayden, and Robert Bauer.

257. Singulier Woodwind Trio. *Classical Ragtime.** Coronet 3047. 1978. Classic rags arranged for bassoon, clarinet, and oboe.
See also 179 and 242.

SYNTHESIZERS

258. Eden Electronic Ensemble, The. *Plugged in Joplin.* Produced by Peter Eden. Pye 12101. [OP] 1975. Four musicians playing Minimoog and EMS Synthi Aks. See also 212.

ORCHESTRAS AND JAZZ BANDS

259. Anderson, T. J., conductor. *Classic Rags and Ragtime Songs.* The Smithsonian Collection N 001. 1975. Notes, tipped in and on jacket, by T. J. Anderson, Thornton Hagert, and J. R. Taylor, 8 pp., illus. Available from Smithsonian Recordings, P.O. Box 10229, Des Moines, Iowa 50336.

260. Boston Pops, The. Arthur Fiedler, conductor. *Fiedler in Rags.* Polydor PD 6033 (2391 144). 1974. Side One: four Joplin rags, one by Eubie Blake. Side Two: *Tiger Rag, 12th Street Rag,* and three pop songs. Credited arrangements by Richard Hayman, Newton Wayland, and Jack Mason.

261. Breuer, Harry, and Orchestra. *Volume 3: The Happy Sound of Ragtime.** Audio Fidelity AFSD 5912. [OP?] 1969. Xylophone with orchestra. Breuer, a famous xylophone virtuoso and arranger/composer, also appears on *What This Country Needs . . .* (Audio Fidelity AFSD 6265) and *Percussive Vaudeville* (Audio Fidelity DFM 3001).

262. Chesapeake Minstrels, The. George Weigand, conductor. *Creole Belles: Music on the Mississippi from Stephen Foster to Scott Joplin.* Hyperion Records [U.K.] A66069. 1983. Jacket notes by George Weigand. Nine instrumentalists, most of whom double, playing period instruments, plus two singers. About half preragtime songs and instrumental pieces, half rags and ragtime songs.

263. Chrysanthemum Ragtime Band. *Bringin' 'Em Back Alive!* Stomp Off S.O.S. 1047. 1983. Jacket notes by Bruce Vermazen. Rags, novelty pieces, and a march by Fort T. Dabney,

Wilbur C. Sweatman, Thos. S. Allen, Charlotte Blake, and others. Period theater-orchestra arrangements adapted for ten-piece orchestra.

264. Dallwitz, Dave, Euphonic Sounds Ragtime Ensemble, The. *Ragtime.** Swaggie [Australia] 1393. 1979.

265. Dawn of the Century Ragtime Orchestra. David E. Bourne, conductor. *Professor David E. Bourne Presents the Dawn of the Century Ragtime Orchestra.* Arcane [601]. [ca. 1970] Jacket notes. Period orchestrations played by a nine-piece orchestra.

266. _____. *Silks and Rags.* Arcane AR 602. 1972. Jacket notes by David E. Bourne. Rags, cakewalks, marches, two-steps, etc.

267. _____. *This One's for Art.* Produced and conducted by David E. Bourne. Arcane AR 603. [1977] Jacket notes. Eight-piece orchestra playing mostly stock arrangements from 1895 to 1918.

268. Dukes of Dixieland, The. *Volume 11: Piano Ragtime with the Phenomenal Dukes of Dixieland.* Audio Fidelity AFSD 5928. 1960. Jacket notes. *Maple Leaf Rag, Johnson Rag, 12th Street Rag,* and other Dixieland standards performed by a seven-piece jazz band.

269. Glover, Joe, and his Cotton Pickers. *The Ragtime Sound.* Epic LN 3581. [OP+] [ca. 1960?] Jacket notes by Fred Danzig. Four selections by an eighteen-piece band; four selections performed by piano and rhythm section; and four selections by a seven-piece band. All-star studio musicians performing in postragtime styles.

270. Hamlisch, Marvin. *The Entertainer.* MCA-2115. [OP] 1974. Jacket notes by Susanella Rogers. Orchestrations, by Billy Byers, of classic rags, including those used in the soundtrack to *The Sting* (MCA-2040), with piano solos by Hamlisch featured on all but one track. See also 332.

271. Moonlight Ragtime Band, The. *Moonlight Ragtime.* National Geographic Society 07817. 1979. Notes, 6 pp., bound in, illus. Arranged and conducted by Dennis Burnside. Twenty-piece orchestra performing mostly Joplin rags. Available from: National Geographic Society, P.O. Box 1640, Washington, D.C. 20013.

272. Morath, Max. *Max Morath and his Ragtime Stompers.** Vanguard VSD 79440. 1981. Seven classic and folk rags and three pop/ singalong standards arranged for piano, guitar, banjo, harmonica, fiddle, washboard/drums, kazoo, and tuba. Morath combines bluegrass and traditional jazz sidemen to try to achieve a prosperous jug-band sound. See also 152–54 and 245.

273. Murphy, Turk, Jazz Band. *The Many Faces of Ragtime.* Atlantic SD 1613. 1972. Jacket

notes by Philip Elwood. Seven-piece jazz band.

274. New England Conservatory Ragtime Ensemble, The. Gunther Schuller, conductor. *Scott Joplin: The Red Back Book.* Angel S-36060. 1973. Jacket notes by Vera Brodsky Lawrence. "Red Back Book" orchestrations performed by a twelve-piece orchestra conducted by Gunther Schuller.

275. _____. *More Scott Joplin Rags.* Golden Crest CRS-31031. 1974. Jacket notes by Vera Brodsky Lawrence and Gunther Schuller. Period stock arrangements and new arrangements by Schuller for twelve- to fifteen-piece orchestra.

276. _____. *The Road from Rags to Jazz.* Two discs. Golden Crest CRS-31042. 1975. Jacket notes by Gunther Schuller. A sixteen-piece ensemble conducted by Gunther Schuller. Most selections arranged or edited by Schuller.

227. New Orleans Ragtime Orchestra. *Grace and Beauty.* Delmark DS 214. [ca. 1974] Jacket notes. Reissue of Pearl 7, released originally in about 1969.

278. _____. *Volume II.* Pearl 8. [ca. 1970] Jacket notes. Write regarding availability to Pearl Records, P.O. Box 1411, Salisbury, North Carolina 28144.

279. _____. *New Orleans Ragtime Orchestra.* Arhoolie 1058. 1971. Jacket notes provided by New Orleans Jazz Club, Tulane Jazz Archives, and by William Russell. Period orchestrations performed by a seven-piece orchestra of jazz musicians.

280. _____. *New Orleans Ragtime Orchestra, The.* Two discs. Vanguard VSD 69/70. 1974. Jacket notes by Sam Charters. Issued in the U.K. as Sonet SNTF 674 and SNTF 680.

281. _____. *A Recital at Old Fireman's Hall, Westwego, Louisiana.* Produced by Sam Charters. Sonet [U.K.] SNTF-709. 1976. Jacket notes by Sam Charters. Seven- or eight-piece ensemble playing period orchestrations or new orchestrations arranged in period style by Lars Edegran. Several selections performed by the New Orleans Ragtime Orchestra are included in the soundtrack to *Pretty Baby,* ABC AA 1076, 1978 [OP].

282. New Sunshine Jazz Band, The. *Old Rags.* (RCA) Flying Dutchman BDL 1-0549. [OP] 1974. Jacket notes by Nat Hentoff based on notes by Thornton Hagert. Eight-piece jazz band performing from, and improvising upon, period orchestrations.

283. Nichols, Keith, and his Ragtime Orchestra. *Ragtime Rules—O.K.* (EMI) One-Up [U.K.] OU 2135. 1976. Jacket notes by Chris Ellis. Ragtime, early jazz, and contemporary compositions performed by a seven- or eight-piece ensemble. Arrangements by Keith Nichols.

284. Parenti, Tony, and his Ragtime Gang.

Ragtime Jubilee. Jazzology J-21. [ca. 1967] Jacket notes by Rudi Blesh. Ten classic rags performed by a seven-piece jazz band.

285. Tony Parenti's Ragtimers, Tony Parenti's Ragpickers. *Ragtime.* Jazzology J-15. [ca. 1967] Jacket notes by Bob Aurthur and Harriet Janis. Reissue of Circle recordings made in 1947 and 1949, previously reissued on Riverside. Seven-piece jazz band (Ragtimers) and trio (Ragpickers) play classic rags.

286. Phoenix Symphony Ragtime Ensemble, The. World Jazz WJLP-S-12. [1977] Jacket notes by Leonard Feather and Barker Hickox. Rags performed by an eleven-piece orchestra.

287. *Ragtime.** Musica nova bohemica, Supraphon [Czechoslovakia] 1 15 1965. [1978?] Artists listed in Supraphon catalog as follows: Klusák/Pacák/Prague original Syncopation Orchestra/Classic Jazz Collegium/Ragtime Assotiation [sic] '76/Traditional Jazz Studio/Prague Television Orchestra/Zahradník.

288. Ragtime Society Frankfurt. *Pleasant Moments.** Joke JLP 205. [ca. 1978] Jacket notes by Klaus Pehl.

289. *Ragtime Special: Max Morath, Del Wood, The Ragtimers, Poppa John Gordy & Muggsy Spanier's Ragtime Band Play 24 Greats by Scott Joplin and others.** Reissue produced by Ethel Gabriel. Two discs. RCA Camden ADL 2-0778. 1974.

290. Ragtimers, The. *Scott Joplin's Ragtime Music by the Ragtimers.* Pye NSPL 41030. 1973. Jacket notes. One of many *Sting* spinoffs, but filled out with other Joplin compositions in arrangements "based on the original Scott Joplin orchestral line-up and sound." Subsequently repackaged, along with Max Harris's recordings of Jelly Roll Morton works, as (Pye) Golden Hour [U.K.] GH 651.

291. _____. *The Ragtimers Play Music from The Sting: "The Entertainer" and other hits by Scott Joplin.* RCA Camden ACL 1-0599. [OP?] 1974. Arranged and conducted by Al Caiola.

292. Red Wing Blackbirds Ragtime Band, The. Dick Roberts, leader; John Barath, co-leader. *Two-Step Ball.* Stomp Off S.O.S. 1018. 1982. Jacket notes by Dick Roberts. Period stock arrangements modified for ten-piece band (no strings).

293. Segal, George, and The Imperial Jazzband. *A Touch of Ragtime: Featuring the Music of Scott Joplin.* (RCA) Signature BSL 1-0654. [OP] 1974. Jacket notes by Nat Hentoff. Four Joplin rags played by a fourteen-piece band; two rag songs; and six period pop/vaudeville songs with ukulele and small band accompaniment.

294. Southland Stingers, The, with Ralph Grierson, piano. George Sponhaltz, conductor. *Scott Joplin: Palm Leaf Rag.* Angel S-36074. 1974. Jacket notes. "Red Back Book"-derived orchestrations by Sponhaltz.

295. _____. *Scott Joplin: Magnetic Rag.* Angel S-36078. 1974. Jacket notes. Arranged in the style of the "Red Back Book" by Sponhaltz.

296. *Tyler, James, and The New Excelsior Talking Machine.* Decca [U.K.] SKL 5266. 1977. Jacket notes by Joyce Tyler. Rags arranged for eight-piece ensemble. Tyler is the former banjoist with Max Morath's Original Rag Quartet. Record apparently issued in the U.S. in 1979 under the title *Ragtime* by Desto (DC 7181).

297. Waldo's Ragtime Orchestra. Terry Waldo, conductor. *Smiles and Chuckles.* Stomp Off S.O.S. 1007. 1981. Period orchestrations of rags, vaudeville novelties, and dance music (ca. 1898–1920) played by a twelve-piece orchestra. Also two piano solos by Waldo. See also 198–200.

298. Watters, Lu, Yerba Buena Jazz Band. *The San Francisco Style: Vol. 2, Watters Originals & Ragtime.* Good Time Jazz L-12002. (1946 Series, set A, vol. 2.) 1954. Jacket notes by Lester Koenig. Eight-piece jazz band featuring Wally Rose on piano. One of the first traditional jazz revival bands to regularly perform rags. See also 185.

299. White, Albert, and the Gaslight Orchestra. *Your Father's Moustache.* Barbary Coast SLP 33002. [ca. 1958?] Jacket notes by Shirley Bookie and Al Levitt. Twelve-piece orchestra playing original orchestrations of various turn-of-the-century pieces. One of the first LP recordings of period orchestrations.

300. _____. *Your Father's Moustache, Vol. 2.* Barbary Coast SLP 33008. [ca. 1958?] Jacket notes by Al Levitt. Volume 2 includes more ragtime tunes, but the first volume has a more convincingly period performance style. The two albums by White on the Fantasy label that bear titles similar to the Barbary Coast records are not the same albums. White also recorded albums of 19th century salon music, World War One tunes, and dance music of the 1920s, all in period style. See also 5, 326, 329, 331, and 332.

Contemporary Ragtime Compositions

301. Albright, William. *Albright Plays Albright.* Musical Heritage Society MHS 4253. 1980. Jacket notes by William Albright, dated 1973. Original rags composed between 1967 and 1970 including the *Grand Sonata in Rag,* the three *Dream Rags,* and five others. Recorded in 1973. See also 83, 90, and 316.

302. Ashwander, Donald. *Ragtime: A New View.* Jazzology JCE-71. (Jazz Piano Heritage Series, vol. 21.) [ca. 1970] Jacket notes by Rudi Blesh. Twelve original compositions.

303. _____. *Turnips: Pieces for Electric Harpsichord, Cordiana Rhythm Box and Piano.* Upstairs upst-1. 1973. Original, ragtime-influenced compositions.

304. _____. *Sunshine and Shadow.** Upstairs upst-2. [1979?] Jacket notes by Rudi Blesh. More rag-influenced originals.

305. Bolcom, William. *Bolcom Plays His Own Rags.* Jazzology JCE-72. (Jazz Piano Heritage Series, Vol. 22.) [ca. 1974] Jacket notes by Rudi Blesh. Eight rags, one four-part rag suite. See also 88–90 and 312.

306. Crozier, Hugh. *Ragtime 1970: A Programme of Original Compositions.* Stomp [U.K.] ROBB 002. [OP?] Jacket notes by Rex Harris. Twelve compositions by Crozier, two by Steve Lane.

307. Dykstra, Brian. *Something Like a Rag: Classic and Contemporary Piano Rags.* Advent Records 5021. 1976. Jacket notes by Brian Dykstra. Side One: Classic rags by Joplin and Lamb plus one original. Side Two: contemporary rags by Dykstra. See also 115–16.

308. Foehner, Gale. *Rhythms in Ragtime: The Music of Gale Foehner.* Stomp Off S.O.S. 1023. [1982] Jacket notes by George C. Willick. Includes ten selections, eight of which are Foehner originals.

309. Foley, George. *Cleveland Rag.* Century/Advent custom recording. Number GF-2-778. [1977] Jacket notes by George Foley. Side One: works by various composers. Side Two: original compositions. Obtainable from George Foley, College of Wooster, Box 1604, Wooster, Ohio 44691. An album by Foley with the same title (presumably this one reissued) was released in 1981 by Jazzology (JCE-85).

310. Gemsa, Eric. *Eric & Rags.* Cezame [France] CEZ 1002. [ca. 1975] Jacket notes, in French. Booklet enclosed, 12 pp., including brief analytic comments on ragtime style with many musical examples, plus sheet music for two of Gemsa's originals. Record includes eight Gemsa originals, one Joplin rag, and four period pop and jazz tunes.

311. Herouet, Marc, Alain Lesire, and Andre Van Lint. *Belgian Ragtime.* (EMI) Best Seller [Belgium] 4C054-96707. [ca. 1975] Unsigned jacket notes in French and, somewhat condensed, in Flemish. Eight original rags; six rags written by Belgian composers between 1909 and 1928. Recorded in December 1974. Obtainable from Marc Herouet, avenue Vandromme 9, 1160 Brussels, Belgium. See also 244.

312. Jacobs, Paul. *Blues, Ballads & Rags.** Nonesuch D 79006 (Digital). 1980. Includes William Bolcom's *Three Ghost Rags* as well as piano compositions by Copland and Rzewski.

313. Jasen, Dave. *Fingerbustin' Ragtime.* Blue Goose 3001. [ca. 1973] Jacket notes by Stephen Calt. Side One: Jasen originals. Side Two: Novelty, classic, and Tin Pan Alley rags. See also 126–28. The historian-collector-performer

Trebor Tichenor also includes many of his own rags in his performances. See, in particular, 195.

314. Johannesen, Grant. *Rags and Tangos.* Golden Crest CRS 4132. 1974. Jacket notes. Gathers together some of the best-known classical works influenced by ragtime or the tango. Ragtime-influenced works include: Igor Stravinsky, *Ragtime* (arranged for piano) and *Piano Rag Music;* Darius Milhaud, *Trois ragcaprices;* and Virgil Thomson, *Ragtime Bass.*

315. Lee, David R. *Original Rags: Composed and Played by David R. Lee.* Jazz Studies [Canada] JS-4. [1977] Jacket notes by David R. Lee and Ross H. Wilby. Eleven original compositions. Available from Jazz Studies, 186 Old Orchard Road, Burlington, Ontario L7T 2G1, Canada.

316. Mandel, Alan. *American Piano Music.* Grenadilla Records GS-1020. 1977. Jacket notes unsigned but apparently written in part by Albright and Starer. Includes William Albright's *Grand Sonata in Rag,* Siegmeister's *Theme and Variations No. 2,* and Starer's *Evanescents.* See also 149.

317. McDermott, Tom. *New Rags.* Stomp Off S.O.S. 1024. 1983. Jacket notes by Tom McDermott. Mostly McDermott originals in ragtime or stride style.

318. Milne, Bob. *Boogie, Blues & Rags.** Jim Taylor Presents JTP 113. [1980?] Twelve selections including six originals. Available from Jim Taylor Presents, 12311 Gratiot Avenue, Detroit, Michigan 43205.

319. Roberts, David Thomas. *Pinelands Memoir and Other Rags Composed and Played by David Thomas Roberts.** Euphonic ESR-1224. (Piano Series, Vol. 24.) 1983.

320. Shea, Tom. *Classic & Modern Rags by Tom Shea.* Ragtime Society Records RSR-1. [**OP**] [ca. 1963] Brochure notes by John A. Fisher, 2 pp. Seven original rags, six classic rags.

321. _____. *Prairie Ragtime.* Ragtime Society Records RSR-2. [**OP**] 1964. Jacket notes. Seven original rags, four classic rags.

322. _____. *Little Wabash Special.* Stomp Off S.O.S. 1022. 1982. Jacket notes by Mike Montgomery. Nine compositions by Shea, and eight pieces by Charles Hunter, Tom Turpin, J. Bodewalt Lampe, and others.

323. *They All Played Ragtime.* Jazzology JCE-52. (Jazz Piano Heritage Series, vol. 2.) [ca. 1968] Jacket notes by Rudi Blesh. Includes seven contemporary rags played by their composers, one late Joseph Lamb rag played by Lamb, and four classic rags played by contemporary composers.

324. Tilles, Nurit. *Ragtime Here and Now!.* Jazzology JCE-87. (Jazz Piano Heritage Series, vol. 37.) 1983. Jacket notes by Rudi Blesh and

George H. Buck, Jr. Rags by James Tenny, J. T. Thomas, Donald Ashwander, and others.

Joplin Curiosities

325. Houston Grand Opera, conducted by Gunther Schuller. *Scott Joplin, Treemonisha.* Two discs, boxed. Deutsche Grammophon 2707 083. 1976. Brochure notes by Schuller, Franco Colavecchia, Frank Corsaro, Louis Johnson, Robert Jones, Vera Brodsky Lawrence, libretto, photos, 30 pp. With Carmen Balthrop, Betty Allen, Curtis Rayam, *et al.* Arrangements, orchestration, and music supervision by Gunther Schuller.

326. London Festival Ballet Orchestra, conducted by Grant Hossack. *Scott Joplin: The Entertainer Ballet.* Columbia M 33185 [1975] Jacket notes by Grant Hossack. Originally performed and recorded in England as *The Prodigal Son.* Arranged and orchestrated by Grant Hossack; with Michael Bassett, piano.

327. Mimi and Russell. *Solace.** Mumpus [U.K.] MPS SLP 791. [1979?] Mimi [Daniel] on piano with Russell [Quaye] on washboard and vocal, and added accompaniment (arranged by Dave Watts) on most selections. Most of the selections are Joplin instrumentals for which Quaye has written lyrics. In a September 1979 *Rag Times* review, Dick Zimmerman finds the lyrics are "captivating" and "always fit the spirit of the music." Obtainable from Mumpus Records, 1/6 Underhill Road, London SE22 OAH, England.

328. Ragamuffins, The, and The Ragtimers. *Songs of Scott Joplin: Sung and Played by the Ragamuffins and the Ragtimers.* Pye [U.K.] NSPL 18445. 1974. Jacket notes. Despite the title, the record includes only one (*A Picture of Your Face*) of the works Joplin wrote primarily as a song, and its performance has an authenticity sadly lacking in the rest of the album. The remainder of the album consists of more or less reworked period lyrics or new lyrics written for Joplin's rags and performed in routine contemporary style.

329. Royal Ballet Orchestra, The. *Elite Syncopations: The Music of Scott Joplin and Others* [Lamb, Morath, Scott, Robert Hampton, Paul Pratt]. Performed by musicians from the Orchestra of the Royal Ballet conducted from the piano by Philip Gammon. Vanguard SRV 373. 1981. This is presumably the American issue of CRD [U.K.] 1029, *Elite Syncopations* (ca. 1978); however the *Gramophone Classical Catalog* listing for the earlier release identifies the performing group as the Covent Garden Orchestra. The *Gramophone* listing credits the arrangements to Schuller, Sponhaltz, Docker, and Gammon, so the work has evidently been cobbled together from New England Con-

servatory Ragtime Ensemble and Southland Stingers arrangements with added material by Docker and the conductor, Gammon.

330. *Scott Joplin, King of Ragtime: His Life and Music.* Written and directed by Ward Botsford; narrated by Gordon Gould. (Sine Qua Non) Meet the Classics MC 331. 1977. Jacket notes by Ward Botsford. Excerpts from eighteen Joplin rags drawn from piano rolls (mostly), from Roger Shields' album on Turnabout (TV 34579), and with selections by the New York Arts Ensemble, directed by Raymond Beegle, which have not been previously released to my knowledge. This record was also released as part of a four-disc, boxed set, *The Lives & Music of Foster, Joplin, Sousa & Gershwin,* Meet the Classics MC 3001/4 (1978), brochure notes, 4 pp.

331. *Scott Joplin: Music from the Original Motion Picture Soundtrack.* MCA 2098. 1977. Arranged and performed by Dick Hyman with orchestra and various featured performers, from Scott Joplin compositions. Also one Hyman original.

332. *The Sting* [soundtrack to the George Roy Hill film]. Music adapted [mostly from Joplin originals] by Marvin Hamlisch. Performed by Marvin Hamlisch, piano, and studio orchestra. MCA 2040. 1973. Jacket notes by George Roy Hill. Originally issued as MCA 390. Also available is the soundtrack to the 1982 film *The Sting II,* with music adapted, arranged, and conducted by Lalo Schifrin. MCA 6116. See also 270.

333. Swingle II. *Rags And All That Jazz.* Arranged by Ward Swingle. Columbia PC 34194. [OP] 1975. Five Joplin compositions plus works by Morton, Beiderbecke, and Waller, set to words by Tony Vincent Isaacs and performed by vocal octet and instrumental trio. Swingle II is the successor to the Swingle Singers.

334. Wofford, Mike. *Scott Joplin: Interpretations '76.* (RCA) Flying Dutchman BDL 1-1372. [OP] 1976. Jacket notes by Nat Hentoff. Excerpts from the score to *Treemonisha,* interpreted by Wofford, jazz piano, with Chuck Domanico, bass, and Shelly Manne, drums. See also 91, 100, 124, 205, 212, and 258.

Ragtime Compositions by Women

Max Morath and John Edward Hasse

The study of women composers of ragtime has just begun. As a first step in this direction, however, we have compiled an incomplete list of ragtime compositions written before 1930 by American women. Included are piano rags, syncopated cakewalks, ragtime songs and "coon songs," syncopated waltzes, and "ragging" of classics.

A few pieces appear whose scores were unavailable for scrutiny, but which, judging from the titles, are probably ragtime. Unless otherwise indicated, all pieces are piano solos. We have made no attempt to identify issuance of these pieces in various media (sheet music, player piano roll, sound recording, etc.). Where individually issued scores were not available, we have drawn information from other sources, in the following order of priority: (1) score published in a magazine, (2) United States copyright information, (3) issuance as a piano roll, (4) mention in a magazine. A composition identified only by copyright data was either (1) registered for copyright but never actually published; (2) self-published by the composer; or (3) issued by an established publisher with the composer retaining the copyright.

Where names of publishing firms are not given in full, the following abbreviations are used:

C&L   Carlin & Lennox, Indianapolis
JHA   J. H. Aufderheide & Co., Indianapolis
JHR   Jerome H. Remick & Co., New York and Detroit
JWJ   J. W. Jenkins Sons Music Co., Kansas City, Missouri
JWS   Joseph W. Stern, New York
LF   Leo Feist, Inc., New York
WW   Whitney-Warner Publishing Co., Detroit

Allyn, Opal
   The Opalescent Rag. Modesto, Illinois: Opal A. Allyn.
Arens, Bulah
   Checker: Rag Two Step, arr. Julia Rosenbush. C&L, 1908.
Atterbery, Corriene
   The Darkies Serenade; or Under the Sycamore Tree (song), arr. Mary Jacque. © 1907 by C. Atterbery, Webb City, Missouri.
Aufderheide, Frieda
   The Flyer: Rag. C&L, 1908.
Aufderheide, May
   Blue Ribbon Rag. JHA, 1910.
   Buzzer Rag. JHA, 1909.
   Dusty Rag. Indianapolis: Duane Crabb Publishing Co., 1908.
   Dusty Rag Song (words by J. Will Callahan). JHA, 1912.
   Novelty Rag. JHA, 1911.
   The Richmond Rag. JHA, 1908.
   The Thriller Rag. JHA, 1909.
   A Totally Different Rag. JHA, 1910.
   A Totally Different Rag (words by Earl C. Jones). JHA, 1910.

   You and Me in the Summertime (words by Rudolph Aufderheide). JHA, 1911.
Bailey, Queenie
   El Cosmopolita Rag, transcribed by Clarence E. Wheeler. Mentioned in *Ragtime Review* 3, no. 4 (April 1917): 7.
Baker, Lula K.
   Jolly Club Two Step. Kansas City, Missouri: Baker Publishing Co., 1908.
Bartlett, Margaret
   Sorority Rag. Chicago: Thompson Music Co., 1909.
Beauchamp, Eleanora
   Brush Creek Rag. Cincinnati: Geo. B. Jennings, 1913.
Beaumont Sisters, The
   You're Talking Ragtime (song). New York: T. B. Harms, 1899.
Becker, Josephine
   Oh You Rag. [Cincinnati?]: [publisher unknown], [ca. 1910?].
   Walli-Ki-Ki: Jungle Two Step. Cincinnati: The Emerson Music Publishing Co., 1911.
Bell, Mae
   Merry Madcap: March Characteristique. New

York: Will Wood, 1908.

Berger, Minnie
One More Rag, arr. Arthur Campbell. Saint Louis: Stark Music Co., 1909.
St. Loui-Loui: March and Two Step. © 1909 by Mrs. J. L. Cuddy, Saint Louis.
St. Loui-Louis (words by J. L. Cuddy). © 1909 by Mrs. J. L. Cuddy, Saint Louis.

Best, Marvel Doris
Oak Leaf Shuffle. Des Moines: Koch Bros. Printing Co., 1912.

Bierman, Ida G.
Pike Pickers: A Rag. Chicago: W. C. Polla Co., 1904.

Bierbaum, Nancy
Yankee Breezes: National Rag Medley. Cincinnati: Groene Music Publishing Co., 1907.
Zinzinnati: German Rag. Cincinnati: Nancy Bierbaum, 1907.

Blake, Charlotte
Dainty Dames. JHR, 1905.
The Gravel Rag. JHR, 1908.
King Cupid: March Two-Step Characteristic. WW, 1903.
The Mascot: March–Two-Step. JHR, 1905.
The Missouri Mule March. WW, 1904.
Poker Rag. JHR, 1909.
That Tired Rag. JHR, 1911.
The Wish Bone: Ragtime Two-Step. JHR, 1909.

Bloom, Eveyln
One of the Boys: The Novelty Two-Step. New York: Sol Bloom, 1906.

Bolen, Grace L.
The Black Diamond. Kansas City, Missouri: Carl Hoffman, 1899.
The Smoky Topaz. Kansas City: Daniels & Russell, 1909.

Boniel, Bessie and J. Russel Robinson
Daphne: Two Step. New York: Chas. K. Harris, 1911.

Bouska, Emma A.
Kehama Rag. Chicago: Victor Kremer Co., 1909.

Boyer, Opal
Purdue Rag. Lafayette, Indiana: Opal Boyer, 1914.

Brown, Fleta Jan
I Wish I Was In Heaven Sittin' Down (song). New York: M. Witmark & Sons, 1908.
Tangle Foot Rag. JWS, 1907.

Brown, Mae
Highbrow Rag: Syncopated Operatic Melodies. Issued on piano roll: U.S. Music 6486.

Burgess, Mattie Harl
Rag Alley Dream. Chicago: Will Rossiter, 1902.
"Wiggy Waggy" Rag, arr. William H. Tyers. LF, 1910.

Burnett, Ada M.
The Nickelodeon Rag. Cincinnati: Ada M. Burnett, 1909.

Cady, Gertrude
Tar Baby: Ragtime Two-Step. New York: H. L. Walker, 1904.

Carew, Millie
I'll Take a Little Ragtime for Mine (song). Saint Louis and New York: Stark Music Co., 1908.

Carney, Mabelle M.
The Jolly Batchelor: Intermezzo-Two Step. JWS, 1909.

Carpenter, Anna Hughes
Glad Rags. © 1907 by Anna Hughes Carpenter, Brownwood, Texas.

Chapman, Lydia M.
Echoes of the Congo, arr. Carl Frolich. WW, 1903.

Clark, Sadie
H-A-S-H, Dat Am De Word I Love (song). New York: M. Witmark and Sons, 1908.

Cloud, Mollie F.
Coldwater Rag. Lincoln, Nebraska: G. L. Dearing Music Publisher, 1913.

Coffee, Lily
Coffee Rag. Houston: W. C. Munn Co., 1915.
Regal Rag, arr. M. Paul Jones. Houston: Lily Coffee, 1916.

Combs, Dora Belle
Sun Down Dance: Two-Step. South Whitley, Indiana: D. Bell Combs, 1903.

Comfort, Anita
Mopsy Massy of Tallahassee: Plantation Song and Rag Dance. Saint Louis: Shattinger Piano Co., 1898.

Cook, Sarah E.
Restless Rag: Two-Step. Chicago: Victor Kremer Co., 1908.

Cowan, Martha Hare
Mammy's Little Coal Black Dove: A Negro Lullabye (words by Annie Hare). Boston: Charles L. Homeyer and Co., 1908.

Cox, Frances
The Tickler: Rag and Two-Step. Kansas City: Charles L. Johnson & Co., 1908.

Cozad, Irene
Eatin' Time Rag. JWJ, 1913.

Cranston, Marietta, and Elijah W. Jimerson
Talk of the Town. Saint Louis: Syndicate Music Co., 1919.

Crump, Margaret E.
The Billie Ritchie Rag. [n.p.]: [n.p.], 1915.

Dahlman, Anna
Salted Peanuts: March and Two-Step. Milwaukee: Jos. Flanner, 1908.

Davis, Fleta Brownfield
Freckles: Rag. Indianapolis: Fleta Brownfield Davis, 1908.

Davis, Mae
The Virginia Creeper: Characteristic March. Boston: Walter Jacobs, 1907.

Davis, Marian I.
Fluffy Ruffle Girls Rag: Characteristic Two-Step.

Cleveland: Charles I. Davis Music Publisher, 1908.

Dawson, Irma V.
Cotton Belt Rag. Galveston: Thos. Goggan & Bro., 1916.

Day, Ella Hudson
Fried Chicken Rag. Galveston: Thos. Goggan & Bros., 1912.
Quality Rag. Dallas: J. P. Juckolls, 1909.

De Haven, Rose
Automobile Two-Step. JHR, 1907.

Dillingham, Mynnie
Echoes from Old Kentucky: March, Two-Step and Cake Walk. Chicago: Windsor Music Co., 1901.

Dobyns, Geraldine
Bull Dog Rag. Memphis: Anderson-Reinhardt Co., 1908.
Holly and Mistletoe. New Orleans: Philip Weinlein, 1909.
Possum Rag. Memphis: O. K. Houch Piano Co., 1907.

Duryee, Maud Clair
The Old Virginia Plantation. Boston: Oliver Ditson Co., 1900.

Eaton, Helen S.
Mop Rag. JHR, 1909.

Egan, Sara B.
Turkish Trophies: Two Step. Chicago: Will Rossiter, 1907.

Erickson, Libbie
Skip: Characteristic. Chicago: Arnett-Delonais Co., 1906.
Topsy Two Step, arr. William B. Fassbinder. Chicago: W. C. Polla Co., 1904.
Trixy Two Step, arr. William B. Fassbinder. Chicago: W. C. Polla Co., 1904.

Fitzgerald, Maie
The Missouri Rag. Sedalia, Missouri: A. W. Perry & Sons, 1900.

Flennard, Eva Note
Shifty Shuffles: Buck Dance. Philadelphia: Welch & Wilsky Music Publishers, 1897.

Ford, Abbie A.
A Happy Coon From Dixie. Chicago: McKinley Music Co., 1901.

Foster, Jessie E.
The Lallapoloosa: Cake Walk and Two-Step. Saint Louis: Balmer & Weber Music House, 1902.

Franklin, Irene, and Burt Green
Red Head Rag. LF, 1910.

Gehr, Nettie
De Rag Man's A Comin' (song). Saint Louis: Thiebes-Stierlin, 1898.

Gibbins, Eva
Idlewilde March Two-Step. Columbus, Ohio: W. H. Croner, 1905.

Giblin, Irene M.
The Aviator Rag: Two-Step. JHR, 1910.
Black Feather: Two Step (as Irene M. Giblin-

O'Brien). Chicago: Victor Music Co., 1908.
Chanticleer Cock-a-Doodle-Do: Rag. Issued on piano roll: Cable Piano Co. 3875B.
Chicken Chowder: Characteristic Two Step. JHR, 1905.
Columbia Rag. JHR, 1910.
The Dixie Rag. Boston: Jos. M. Daly, 1913.
Ketchup Rag. JHR, 1910.
Pickaninny Rag. Cleveland: Sam Fox Publishing Co., 1908.
Sleepy Lou. JHR, 1906.
Soap Suds: March Two Step Characteristic. JHR, 1906.

Gibson, Jenora
Strawberry Shortcake: March and Two-Step. Louisville: Jenora Gibson, 1907.

Giles, Imogene
Red Peppers: Two Step. Quincy, Illinois: Giles Bros., 1907.

Gilmore, Mary
Electric Rag. Kansas City: W. M. Bodine, 1914.

Gilmore, Maude
Peach Blossom Rag. Kansas City, Missouri: Chas. L. Johnson & Co., 1910.
Slivers: Two-Step. Kansas City, Missouri: Chas. L. Johnson & Co., 1909. Also published as *Splinters: Two-Step.* Kansas City, Missouri: Chas. L. Johnson & Co., 1909.

Goben, Hattie
The Teddy Bear Rag. © 1907 by Hattie Goben, Dallas.

Godinski, Sadie
Georgiana: Characteristic March–Two-Step. Chicago: Victor Kremer, 1907.

Goodfried, Gussie
The Peekaboo Peek: March. New York: F. A. Mills, 1911.

Gooding, Grace
The Fadettes Call: Rag One Step Trot. JHR, 1914.

Goodwin, Hassie
Dixie Doodle Dum: March Two-Step. Sedalia, Missouri: A. W. Perry & Sons, 1914.

Gould, Lena
Ragged Edge: Two Step. Brooklyn: Lena Gould, 1901.

Graham, Anna M.
Ujiji: Cake Walk. Toledo, Ohio: Hayes Music Co., 1902.

Gray, Winnie
Dandy Darktown Dinah (song). JWS, 1909.

Green, Evangeline
Green Rag, arr. Edmund Green. New York: Shapiro Music Publishing Co., 1913.

Grey, Vivian (pseud. of Mabel McKinley)
Anona: Intermezzo & Two-Step. LF, 1903.

Gunn, Mamie A.
El Merito Two Step. Saint Louis: Mamie A. Gunn, 1898.
The Nashville Rag & Two Step. Saint Louis: Mamie A. Gunn, 1899.

Silver King Polka-March. Saint Louis: Thiebes-Stierlin Music Co., 1897.

Gustin, Louise V.
The Daughter of the Regiment: March (as L. V. Gustin). WW, [ca. 1901].
The Flag of Freedom March. WW, 1898.
Lindy: A March Two-Step. WW, 1902.
An Old Virginia Cakewalk: Two Step. Detroit: Belcher and Davis, 1899.
Soldiers of Fortune: March Two-Step. WW, 1901.
Topsy Turvy Two-Step (as L. V. Gustin). WW, 1899.
X-N-Tric: Two-Step Characteristic. WW, 1900.

Haas, Jean J.
The Comet Rag Two-Step. Buffalo: Bixby & Castle, [19—].

Hamel, Kittie M.
White Seal Rag. JHR, 1907.

Hannah, Ethel
Sleepy Hollow: Two Step. Sedalia, Missouri: A. W. Perry and Sons' Music Co., 1907.

Hawes, Lenora Searls
Dark Town Coon Step. Fort Wayne, Indiana: C. C. Powell, [ca. 1903].
In the Heart of Dixie: Characteristic March and Two-Step. Fort Wayne, Indiana: C. C. Powell, 1903.
Keep a Comin' Ma Honey: A Rag-Time Specialty, arr. Louis F. Boos. Jackson, Michigan: Louis F. Boos, 1899.

Henry, Marcella A.
Broadway Rag. Published in *Ragtime Review* 3, no. 10 (October 1917): 9–10.
The Covent Garden: Rag-Time Waltz. Chicago: Christensen School of Popular Music, 1917.
Glittering Stars: Rag-Time Waltz. Published in *Ragtime Review* 2, no. 6 (May 1916): 5–8.
The Green Mill: Rag. Chicago: Christensen School of Popular Music, 1917.
Kentucky Rag. Published in *Ragtime Review* 3, no. 7 (July 1917): 10–11.
National Colors Rag. Published in *Ragtime Review* 3, no. 6 (June 1917): 10–11.
Player Piano Rag: Fox Trot. Issued on piano roll: Kimball 7582.
Who Got the Lemon: Buck Dance Rag. © 1909 by Marcella A. Henry, Peru, Illinois.

Hightower, Winifred
Hightower Rag. Fort Worth: Winifred Hightower, 1914.

Hillman, Dora Loucks
Moustache Johnson: A Glad Rag Two-Step. Chicago: Miller Music Publishing, 1909.

Hopkins, Bertha
Society Rag-Time Amanda (song). © 1906 by Bertha Hopkins.

Houston, Annie
Motor Bus: Two-Step, arr. W. L. Peacock. Dallas: Bush & Gerts Publishing Co., 1914.

Hoy, Myrtle
Chippewa Rag. JHR, 1911.

Hudson, Lora M.
Bittersweets Rag. © 1914 by Lora M. Hudson, Chicago.
Hudson Rag: Rag Two-Step. © 1914 by Lora M. Hudson, Chicago.
Irresistible Fox Trot Rag. Issued on piano roll: U.S. Music 7589.
Pomp and Pride: March and Two-Step. © 1914 by Lora M. Hudson, Chicago.
Woodland Pranks: March and Two-Step. © 1914 by Lora M. Hudson, Chicago.

Igelman, Clara Campbell
Solitaire: Rag Two-Step. Richmond, Indiana: Wilson Music Publisher, 1909.

Irwin, May
May Irwin's Rag Time Dance. Boston: G. W. Setchell, 1906.
May Irwin's Rag Time Dance (song). Boston: G. W. Setchell, 1906.

Janis, Elsie
Anti Ragtime Girl. JHR, 1913.

Jenkins, Claudia
Hoe-Cake Shuffle. Boston: B. F. Wood Music Co., 1903.

Kamman, Effie F.
Darkey Doings: A Blackville Frolic. New York: M. Witmark & Sons, 1899.

Karns, Verdi
Black Beauty: A Rag Two-Step. Bluffton, Indiana: Verdi Karns, [1898?].
The Bluffton Carnival Rag. Bluffton, Indiana: Verdi Karns, 1899.
Ragamuffin: Two-Step. Bluffton, Indiana: Verdi Karns, 1899.

Kaufman, Mabel R.
Sapphire: Two-Step. Baltimore: Harman's Publishing Co., 1906.

Kenny, Margaret
Loretta: March Two-Step. Detroit and New York: Shapiro-Remick & Co., 1903.

Klaphake, Lillian Rose
Improved Rapid System of Ragtime Piano Playing. Cincinnati: Cincinnati School of Popular Music, 1910.

Kohler, Nina B.
Bugs Rag. Sherman, Texas: Nina B. Kohler, 1913.

Koninsky, Sadie
Boardin' House Johnson: Cake Walk. JWS, 1899.
'Cause the Sandman's Comin' Around (song). Troy, New York: Koninsky Music Co., 1905.
Eli Green's Cakewalk: March & Two Step, arr. Charles E. Pratt. JWS, 1898.
Eli Green's Cakewalk (words by Dave Reed, Jr.). JWS, 1896.
I Wants a Man Who Ain't Afraid to Work (words by Harry E. Stanley). New York: Edward M. Koninsky & Bros., 1902.

Phoebe Thompson's Cake Walk. Troy, New York: Edward M. Koninsky & Bros., 1899.

When I Return We'll Be Wed (words by Stewart M. Washburn). Troy, New York: Edward M. Koninsky & Bros., 1899.

Kuykendall, Grace
Budweiser Rag. Morgantown, Kentucky: Grace Kuykendall, 1908.

Kyro, Kate
Watermelon Breezes: An African Characteristic; March and Two Step. Boston: Louis H. Ross & Co., 1904.

Lantz, Dena Merle
Sprint Splinter Rag. Chicago: Victor Kremer Co., 1908.

Lawnhurst, Vee
Twentieth Century Blues. New York: Jack Mills, Inc., 1923.

LeBoy, Grace
Everybody Rag with Me: One-Step. JHR, 1915.
Everybody Rag with Me (words by Gus Kahn). JHR, 1914.
Pass the Pickles: Tango. JHR, 1913.

Loeb-Evans, Matilee
The Savannah Side-Swing Rag Two-Step. Troy, New York: Koninsky Music Co., 1912.

Longino, Eva
Paramount Rag. © 1915 by Eva Longino.
Red Rooster Rag. © 1915 by Eva Longino.

Marshall, Grace
Fashionable Vaudeville: March Two Step. C&L, 1902.

Mast, Clare
The Kaiser's Rag. Edgerton, Ohio: Clare Mast, 1915.

Mattingly, Martina
Ragtime Rifles: Two Step. Philadelphia: M. D. Swisher, 1901.

McClure, Elma Ney
The Cutter: A Classy Rag. Memphis: O. K. Houck Piano Co., 1909.

McCoy, Mrs. William Neal
Ginger: A Negro Shuffle. New York: Globe Music Co., 1908.

McKray, Ethel M.
Dreamy Rag: Two-Step. New York: Globe Music Co., 1912.

McPherran, Florence
Dottie Dimple March and Two Step. Chicago: Sterling Music Co., 1907.
Fi-Fi: Novelette Two-Step. Chicago: Sterling Music Co., 1907.
I'se Got No Use Foh Show Folks (words by R. H. Hanch). Chicago: Ellis Music Co., 1901.
La Zurita: Intermezzo Two-Step. Chicago: Sterling Music Co., 1907.
Laughing Lucas: Characteristic March and Two Step. Chicago: Ellis Music Co., 1901.
Sunny Sue: A Coon Ditty (words by Arthur J. Lamb). Chicago: Ellis Music Co., 1900.
Under the Wire: March & Two Step. Chicago:

Ellis Music Co., 1903.

Melville, Agnes
The Darkies' Drill Cakewalk. New York: Avon Music Corp., 1902.

Merrill, Blanche
My Syncopated Melody Man (words by Eddie Cox). New York: Meyer Cohen Music Publishing Co., 1918.
The Tanguay Rag. New York: Chas. K. Harris, 1910.

Metcalf, Nellie Smith
Isadore Two Step. Toledo, Ohio: Nellie Smith Metcalf, 1908.

Miller, Lola
Uncle Joshe's Jubilee: Two-Step. Sedalia, Missouri: A. W. Perry's Sons, 1906.

Million, Hazel
Pudge Ragtime Reverie: March and Two Step. New York: North American Music Co., 1905.

Mitenius, Alma
Ma Sugar Babe. Brooklyn, New York: H. Franklin Jones, 1898.

Moore, Luella Lockwood
Paprika: "Hot Stuff"; March and Two Step. Detroit: Grinnell Brothers, 1909.

Morgan, Mrs. Merrill
Very Raggy. © 1907 by Mrs. Merrill Morgan, Rotan, Texas.

Morton, Kathryn Athol
Ragtime Showers: March and Two-Step. New York: Richard A. Sallfield, 1902

Mowen, Lizzie
Jim Crow Rag. Rochester, New York, and Fort Wayne, Indiana: C. C. Powell, 1910.

Mumford, Lina
Black Cat Rag, arr. Dan Ball. Grand Rapids, Michigan: Mumford & Co., 1901.

Murphey, Claribel
Hermosa: Two Step. Toledo: Claribel Murphey, 1904.

Musgrove, Mrs. Stuart
Mixed Rags. © 1907 by Mrs. Stewart Musgrove.

Nelson, Lydia
The Vendyke: March or Two-Step. Saint Paul, Minnesota: W. J. Dyer & Bro., 1901.

Nichols, Nellie V.
Pasha's Passion. New York: Ted Snyder Co., 1911.

Niebergall, Julia Lee
Hoosier Rag: March Two Step. JHR, 1907.
Horseshoe Rag. JHA, 1911.
Red Rambler Rag: Two Step. JHA, 1912.

Nieman, Eva
Broadway Rag. Cincinnati: Eva Nieman, 1910.

Nugent, Maude
Wake Up Malinda: March Two Step. JHR, 1905.

Orndorff, Ruth
That Captivating Rag. Kendallville, Indiana: Ruth Orndorff, 1912.

Ossusky, Hilda

Tattered Melody Rag. JHR, 1910.

Owen, Anita
Dance of the Collywobbles: Cake-Walk and Two-Step. Chicago: Wabash Music Co., 1899.
Fire Fly: Intermezzo. JHR, 1909.

Parker, Ethel P.
The Magical Coon: Cakewalk for Piano. [n.p.]: [n.p.], 1906.

Parker, Fay
That Irresistible Rag. Saint Louis: Syndicate Music Co., 1914.

Payne, Meryle
Raggety Rag. Los Angeles: Fordi Music Publishing Co., 1910.

Phillips, Ethel Stuart
A Classy Rag, arr. Clarence Woods. Fort Worth: Ethel Stuart Phillips, 1915.

Phillips, Lucy
That Irresistible Rag. Kansas City, Missouri: Chas. L. Johnson, 1912.

Pollock, Muriel
Barbecue Rhythm. New York: Triangle Music Publishing Co., 1928.
The Carnival: Trot and One-Step. New York: M. Witmark & Sons, 1914.
Rooster Rag. JWS, 1917.

Powell, Bessie
Buster Rag. Scranton, Pennsylvania: Whitmore Publishing Co., 1915.

Powell, Marie
Chicken Pickin': A Rag. © 1908 by Marie Powell, Corinth, Mississippi.

Powers, Reba
Domino Rag, arr. Rudolph Moehl. Nashville: Lew Roberts, 1909.

Price, Lilla
Cuffee at a Corn Shuckin': A Brand New Cake Walk. Boston: Evans Music Co., 1899.

Rabb, Leah M.
Volcanic Rag. New York: Gotham-Attucks Music Co., 1912.

Rafael, Elsie Grace
Spitfire: Rag. New York: Weller-Hartmann Music Publishing Co., 1909.

Rallya, Leila
Liza: March Two Step Characteristic. Cincinnati: John Arnold, 1906.

Ralya, Edna
Sounds from Coontown. [Cincinnati: Philip Kussel, ca. 1903?].
Winnie's Arrival: A New Rag. Cincinnati: Philip Kussel, 1903.

Randale, Zema
Mutilation Rag, arr. Burell Van Buren. Chicago: The Cable Co., 1915.

Ransom, Nellie Brooks
The Climax Two Step. Toledo, Ohio: McCormick Music Co., 1900.

Ray, Marguerite
Copper King Rag. Los Angeles: Hatch & Loveland, 1912.

Reese, Mary Adelaide
The Louisiana Shuffle. New Orleans: Philip Werlein, 1904; and Kansas City, Missouri: M. A. Reese.

Reeves, Commie
Commiezell Cake Walk and Two Step. Asherville, Kansas: Commie Reeves, 1900.

Remeau, Jean
The Meadow Lark Rag. Ely, Nevada: Jean Remeau, 1910.

Richmond, Dolly
Sunflower Tickle. Chicago: McKinley Music Co., 1908.

Rion, Hanna
Audacious Arabella: Cake-Walk March. New York: F. A. Mills, 1900.

Rippy, Lottie McD.
American Rag (song). Birmingham, Alabama: L. McD. Rippy, 1913.

Rodwell, Ethel
Gem City Jubilee. [n.p.]: [n.p.]: 1901.

Rogers, Maude L.
Mickey Finn: Characteristic Two-Step. JHR, 1906.

Rossiter, Madeline
Douglas Cake Walk. [city, publisher, and year unknown].

Rudisill, Bess E.
Ain't I Lucky: March Two Step. JHR, 1905.
Bright Eyes: Characteristic March Two-Step. Saint Louis: S. Simon, 1903.
Burning Rags: Two Step. Saint Louis: S. Simon, 1904.
The Eight O'Clock Rush Rag, arr. Don Bestor. Chicago: Sear-Wilson Music Publishing Co., 1911.
Polka Dot: March and Two Step Characteristic. Chicago: Harold Rossiter Music Co., 1912.
Way Down East (Two Step). Saint Louis: Simon Publishing Co., 1900.

Saile, Clara
The Yellow Moccasin: March & Two Step. Cincinnati: The Razall Co., 1904.

Salisbury, Cora
Lemons and Limes: A Sour Rag. Chicago: Will Rossiter, 1909.

Sanders, Zellah Edith
Manilla Rag. Chicago: Lyon & Healy, 1898.

Sankey, Emma Laurence
Missouri Girl: March & Two Step. Saint Louis: Shattinger Piano & Music Co., 1904.

Scales, Mrs. J. M.
Coon Time Rag. Galveston: Thos. Goggan & Bro., 1903.

Senter, Abbie A.
Stuttering Sam. Passaic, New Jersey: Adams Music Co., 1900.

Serviss, M. Mae
Rising Moon: Rag Time Two Step. © 1912 by Miss M. Mae Serviss.

Shackford, Lillian W.
Radio Rag. Boston: C. I. Hicks Music Co.,

1927.

Shaul, Minnie
You'll Have to Hurry: Cake-Walk & Two-Step.
Lake Mills, Iowa: A. M. Farmer & Son,
1900.

Shaw, Grace
Claudia Rag. [Joplin, Missouri]: Gotfried &
McMillan, 1910.

Shepherd, Adaline
Live Wires Rag. Chicago: Adelphi Publishing
Co., 1909.
Pickles and Peppers: A Ragtime Oddity. Mil-
waukee: Joseph Flanner, 1906.
Wireless Rag. Chicago: Standard Music Pub-
lishing Co., 1909.

Simonson, Florence E.
The Jolly Little Coon: March and Two-Step. © 1907
by Florence E. Simonson, Philadelphia.

Slaughter, Nell Wright
Bronco Billy Rag. Dallas: Bush & Gerts, 1914.

Smith, Alma, and Lilburn Kingsbury
Razzle Dazzle: Two Step. [n.p.]: [n.p.], 1905.

Smith, Ethyl B.
Fontella Rag: Two-Step. Saint Louis: Thiebes-
Stierlin Music Co., 1907.

Smith, Ethyl B. and Frank Wooster
Black Cat Rag. Saint Louis: Frank Wooster
Co., 1905.

Smith, Hattie Leonore, and E. C. Barroll
Twinkle-Dimples: Rag. Saint Louis: Mid-West
Music Co., 1914.

Smith, Wynona
Alabama Rag, arr. James S. White. Boston:
James S. White Co., 1918.

Smythe, Alice R.
The Darktown Grenadiers: Ragtime Two Step, arr.
Charles Gluck. Chicago: Albright Music
Co., 1899.
Pensacola Pickaninnies: For Banjo—Crown Piano.
Issued on piano roll: Wilcox & White
X2323.

Spencer, Lera.
That Ticklish Rag. [n.p.]: [n.p.], 1913.

Starr, Hattie
Where the Cotton Grows: Cake Walk. New York:
Richard A. Saalfield, 1899.

Stevenson, Gwendolyn
Smash-Up Rag. JHR, 1914.

Stith, Kate Myers
Frizzles: March and Two-Step. Kansas City,
Missouri: Chas. L. Johnson, 1907.

Stokes, Nellie M.
Checkers: March Two Step Characteristic (as N. M.
Stokes). WW, 1903.
Hey Rube: Characteristic March & Two Step. JHR,
1906.
Razzle Dazzle: Rag. JHR, 1909.
Snowball: Rag (as Nellie W. Stokes). JHR,
1906.

Stone, Annette
The Discord Rag. New York: Popular Music

Co., 1914.

Story, Pauline B
Keep a Shufflin': Ragtime Dance. New York:
Hamilton S. Gordon, 1905.

Strain, Mrs. T. Fletcher
That Two-Step Strain. Louisville, Kentucky:
Strain Music Co., 1913.

Talbot, Billie
Imperial Rag: An Easy Riding Rag. Dallas: Bush
& Gerts, 1914.

Taylor, Billie
Dogzigity Rag. New York: Ted Snyder, 1910.

Thiele, Camilla
Ripples Rag. Janesville, Wisconsin: Peerless
Music Publishing Co., 1912.

Thomas, Lucy
'Lasses: A Negro Oddity for Piano. Cincinnati:
The Groene Music Publishing Co., 1904.

Thompson, Bertha Merritt
Hinky Dinky. C&L, 1903.

Thompson, Mattie Claire
Pickaninnies Parade. New York: M. Witmark &
Sons, 1912.

Thurston, Maude M.
Frankfort Rag, arr. Harry L. Alford. Chicago:
Maude M. Thurston, 1909.

Tice, Blanche M.
That Enticing Two-Step. Sioux City, Iowa:
Blanche M. Tice, 1915.

Tilton, Mabel
That Sentimental Rag. LF, 1913.

Trueblood, Edith
Camel Trot. Published in Popular Songs Monthly
1, no. 1 (April 1920).

Uhrig-Cummins, Ella
Kentucky Walk Away: Two Step. Saint Louis:
John Stark & Son, 1904.

Wahl, Dorothy Ingersol
The Diablo Rag: A Rag Fantasie Two-Step. Chicago: Victor Kremer Co., 1908.

Warner, Elva B.
Imagination: March and Two Step. Terre Haute,
Indiana: Indiana Music Co., 1907.

Watson, Nell Wright
That Texas Rag, arr. Phil Epstein. Fort Worth,
Texas: Philip Epstein, 1913.

Weaver, Lula
Sunflower Girls: March Two Step and Two Step.
Hiawatha, Kansas: Lula Weaver, 1903.

Wells, Susie
The Rattler Rag. Henrietta, Texas: Susie Wells,
1912.

Wertheim, Helena
Carolina's March, Two Step and Cake Walk.
Fremont, Ohio: Helena Wertheim, 1901.

Wheeler, Grace D.
Howdy Si Hopscotch: Two-Step. C&L, 1908.

White, Margaret Agnew
Ragged Terry. Dallas: Bush & Gerts, 1913.

White, Marie A.
Promenade Rag. © 1911 by Marie A. White,

Chicago.

Ragged Terry: Rag. Issued on piano roll: U. S. Music 6901.

University Rag: Two-Step. © 1911 by Marie A. White, Chicago.

Widmer, Kathryn L.

Notoriety Rag: Two-Step. JHR, 1913.

Williams, Edna

That Epidemic Rag (words by Billy Foran). JWS, 1911.

Williams, Mamie E.

Cold Feet Rag. JWJ, 1907.

Happy Hopper: Two Step. Kansas City, Missouri: Carl Hoffman Music Co., 1906.

The Honey Bee: March Two Step. JWJ, 1902.

Pig Ankles Rag. JWJ, 1907.

Snipes: Two-Step Characteristic. Kansas City, Missouri: Carl Hoffman Music Co., 1909.

Williamson, Carlotta

Go To Sleep My Little Creole Babe (words by William H. Gardner). Boston: The Colonial Music Publishing Co., 1902.

Mistah Johnson (words by George E. Schultz). Boston: The Colonial Music Publishing Co., 1902.

Osceola: March Two Step. Boston: The Colonial Music Publishing Co., 1906.

The Pickaninny Cake Walk: Two-Step. Boston: The Colonial Music Publishing Co., 1901.

Shiftless Sam: March Two-Step. Boston: The Colonial Music Publishing Co., 1904.

Smiling Susan: Characteristic March–Two-Step. Boston: The Colonial Music Publishing Co., 1906.

Wild Flower Rag. Boston: The Colonial Music Publishing Co., 1910.

Wilson, Florence

Fiddle Sticks: Rag–Two-Step. Milwaukee: Joseph Flanner, 1910.

Wood, Florence

Black Cinderella: Cake Walk. Toledo, Ohio: McCormick Music Co., 1900.

Yelvington, Gladys

Piffle Rag. JHA, 1911.

Young, Erma

De Winin' Coon. Cincinnati: The Groene Music Publishing Co., 1901.

Zeman, Carrie E.

Kinky: A Ragtime Two Step. Davenport, Iowa: Andreas Music Publishing Co., 1906.

Ragtime Organizations

To those who wish to keep abreast of ragtime activities and meet other ragtime aficionados, I recommend joining one or more of the five ragtime organizations. In addition, ragtime is a part of a number of societies devoted to traditional jazz.

The Hoosier Ragtime Society, 1527 Rogers Road, Indianapolis, Indiana 46227. Dues $5 per year. Founded in 1979, the Society has quickly grown to include members across Indiana and the Midwest, and as far away as New York and California. It issues *The Hoosier Rag* six times per year and holds bimonthly meetings. It sponsors an annual "Hoosier Ragtime Festival."

The Maple Leaf Club, 5560 West 62nd Street, Los Angeles, California 90056. Dues $7 per year. Founded in 1967, this organization now has members across the United States, in Canada, and in Europe. It issues a fine bimonthly magazine, *The Rag Times,* under the able editorship of Dick Zimmerman. The *Times* carries all sorts of ragtime news, record and book reviews, and historical articles. Bimonthly meetings attract pianists and listeners from throughout southern California.

Northern Virginia Ragtime Society, P.O. Box 494, Downtown Station, Manassas, Virginia 22110. Dues $6 per year. Founded in 1979, this organization grew rapidly and now has more than 100 members. Programs, held monthly except in January and August, feature members and local artists as well as professional ragtime performers. Members receive a quarterly newsletter, *The Nova Rag.* The Society maintains a library of music from the Ragtime Era and the 1920s.

The Ragtime Society, P.O. Box 520, Station A, Weston, Ontario M9N 3N3, Canada. Dues $10 per year. The Society was founded in 1962. It has reissued several hundred hard-to-find vintage piano rags and publishes a bimonthly newsletter, *The Ragtimer.* Each fall, the Society also hosts a "bash" in Toronto, which has featured pianists ranging from students and housewives to Eubie Blake.

Sacramento Ragtime Society, c/o Doug Parker, 10458 Joel Lane, Rancho Cordova, California 95670. No dues. This loosely structured organization was founded in 1982. Monthly meetings feature members who take turns at the piano, with each usually playing three to five selections. There is no newsletter, but *All That Jazz,* the newsletter of the Sacramento Traditional Jazz Society, carries detailed summaries of the meetings.

Contributors

Edward A. Berlin, born in 1936, holds an M.A. from Hunter College and a Ph.D. in musicology from The City University of New York. His major contribution to ragtime studies is *Ragtime: A Musical and Cultural History* (1980), a critically acclaimed book that demonstrates methodical approaches to the examination of popular music. He has published articles on ragtime and other subjects in journals and encyclopedias, including the forthcoming *New Grove Dictionary of Music in the United States*, for which he is also an area consultant. Among his academic teaching positions was an appointment, in 1982, as Senior Research Fellow at Brooklyn College's Institute for Studies in American Music. He has recently added computer courses to his teaching repertory, and is engaged in developing computer applications for ragtime and other musicological research.

Sanford Brunson Campbell, born in Oberlin, Kansas, in 1884, met Scott Joplin in about 1899 and reportedly became Joplin's only white pupil. Campbell became a professional pianist and traveled throughout the Midwest and South, playing venues ranging from lowly honky-tonks to high-class hotels. In 1908, he became a barber and gave up professional performing. In the mid-1940s, ragtime began to be revived, and Campbell was discovered. He was persuaded to make recordings, which documented his untutored, folksy style of ragtime composing and performing. In subsequent years, he wrote a number of articles on ragtime for *Record Changer* and *Jazz Journal*. Campbell died in Venice, California, in 1952.

David Cohen, born in 1942, was cofounder and codirector of the School of Traditional Folk Music at the Ash Grove in Los Angeles, where he taught finger picking and blues guitar styles for many years. He has also taught advanced guitar classes for the Extension Division of the University of California at Los Angeles. Cohen served as music editor for *Songs of the Gold Rush* (1964) and *Songs of the American West* (1968), both published by the University of California Press, and for *Long Steel Rail* (1981, University of Illinois Press). From 1966 to 1978 he worked as a studio guitar player, and currently he works as a computer programmer.

Norm Cohen, born in 1936, served for many years as Executive Secretary of the John Edwards Memorial Foundation at UCLA and Editor of the *JEMF Quarterly*. His acclaimed book *Long Steel Rail: The Railroad in American Folksong* (1981) won several noted awards including an ASCAP Deems Taylor Award, and a recording he edited, *Minstrels and Tunesmiths: The Commercial Roots of Early Country Music*, was nominated for a Grammy Award. He is author of numerous articles and reviews on American folk and early hillbilly music in *Journal of American Folklore, Western Folklore, New York Folklore Quarterly, JEMF Quarterly*, and other journals. Trained in chemistry and mathematics at Reed College (B.A.) and the University of California at Berkeley (M.A., Ph.D.), Cohen is head of the Chemical Kinetics Department at the Aerospace Corporation in El Segundo, California.

James Dapogny, born in Chicago in 1940, earned his B.M., M.M., and D.M.A. degrees in composition from the University of Illinois. He is associate professor of music theory at the University of Michigan, where he directs and plays piano for the Jazz Repertory Ensemble. A leading authority on Jelly Roll Morton, he is the editor-compiler of *Ferdinand "Jelly Roll" Morton: The Collected Piano Music* (1982), a critical edition published jointly by the Smithsonian Institution Press and G. Schirmer. The leader-pianist of Jim Dapogny's Chicago Jazz Band, he can be heard on records issued by the Smithsonian Collection, the University of Michigan School of Music, and Stomp Off Records.

Thomas J. Davin, born in about 1903, graduated from New York University. During the 1930s he was a press agent for several New York City night clubs, including the Silver Slipper, Connie's Inn, and the Cotton Club. Davin was the first serious chronicler of jazz pianist-composer James P. Johnson. During the 1950s Davin held a series of interviews with James P. Johnson, and portions of these interviews were published in installments in *The Jazz Review*. Davin had been business manager for *Creative Art* magazine during the late 1920s and associate editor of *Cosmopolitan* in the early 1930s. He also held public relations posts for the American

Museum of Natural History and several foreign governments. At the time of his death in 1961, he was director of Boating Information, Inc., a research and marketing company.

Frank J. Gillis, born in 1914, earned a B.A. with Honors from Wayne State University, and pursued graduate studies in musicology and library science at Columbia University and the University of Minnesota. An authority on jazz and phonoarchiving, he coedited *Oh, Didn't He Ramble, African Music and Oral Data, Indiana Ragtime: A Documentary Album*, and *Ethnomusicology and Folk Music*, and has written articles and reviews for a number of journals. Past president of the Society for Ethnomusicology and past editor of its journal *Ethnomusicology*, he is Director Emeritus of the Indiana University Archives of Traditional Music. A professional jazz pianist since 1935, Gillis has made several recordings and performs regularly in his retirement area of Grand Marais, Minnesota.

Thornton Hagert, born in 1930, is a collector and researcher of American vernacular musics and dance, with a special interest in changes in performance and compositional practice. For RCA, New World Records, and the Smithsonian Institution, he has produced, programmed, and annotated historical record albums, among which are *An Experiment in Modern Music: Paul Whiteman at Aeolian Hall, Classic Rags and Ragtime Songs* (both Smithsonian) and *Come and Trip It: Instrumental Dance Music, 1780s–1920s* (New World). Hagert is trumpeter in and leader of the New Sunshine Jazz Band in Washington, D.C., a group which specializes in dance music from the 1890s through the 1930s.

John Edward Hasse, born in 1948, earned a B.A. Cum Laude from Carleton College, an M.A. and Ph.D. with concentration in American music from Indiana University, where he was a Danforth Fellow, and a Certificate in Business Administration from The Wharton School. He is Curator, specializing in American popular music, at the Smithsonian Institution's National Museum of American History, in Washington, D.C. With Lilly Endowment funding, he coproduced *Indiana Ragtime: A Documentary Album* (1981), whose notes won an ASCAP Deems Taylor Award, and is completing a companion book. Hasse has published in *Down Beat, The Mississippi Rag, Annual Review of Jazz Studies, Ethnomusicology, Journal of American Folklore*, and other periodicals. He has presented illustrated lecture-concerts on ragtime at numerous colleges and has performed at the National Ragtime Festival.

Neil Leonard, born in 1927, earned his A.B. at Colby College and his Ph.D. in American Civilization at Harvard University. He has taught English at Northwestern University and American Studies at the University of Pennsylvania, where he is now Associate Professor. He is the author of *Jazz and the White Americans* (1962), and of articles on jazz, literature, and the other arts published in *The New Republic, American Quarterly, Film Heritage, Jazz Monthly*, and *Journal of Jazz Studies*. Leonard serves on the editorial board of the *Annual Review of Jazz Studies*. He is writing a book on religion and jazz.

Philip J. Moe, born in 1937 in Long Prairie, Minnesota, was educated at the University of Minnesota. He has operated Pyramid Record Sales, a specialty record store in Minneapolis, since 1971. He has been collecting ragtime recordings for a number of years and has previously published ragtime discographies in *The Mississippi Rag*.

R. Michael Montgomery, born in 1934, is a leading authority and collector of player piano rolls. For Biograph Records, he has produced and annotated a significant series of recordings of vintage jazz, ragtime, and popular music piano rolls. He has published articles in *Record Research, The Ragtimer*, and *American Life*, and contributed piano rollographies to a number of books. Montgomery performs blues and jazz paino, and has a substantial collection of American popular sheet music. He holds a B.A. in English from the University of Michigan and lives in Southfield, Michigan.

Max Morath, born in 1926, is a well-known entertainer and ragtime pianist, composer, and historian. He has recorded over a dozen albums for Epic, RCA, Vanguard, and New World Records, and is the editor-compiler of *One Hundred Ragtime Classics* (1963), *Guide to Ragtime* (1964), *Songs of the Early 20th Century Entertainers* (1977), *The Mississippi Valley Rags* (1975), and *Scott Joplin: The Missouri Rags* (1975). He has contributed articles to *Contemporary Keyboard, American Heritage*, and *Music Journal*. He appears frequently on American concert stages and television. Morath holds a B.A. in English from Colorado College.

Roland Nadeau, born in 1928, received B.M. and M.M. degrees from the New England Conservatory of Music, where he then taught piano and music theory for ten years before joining the faculty of Northeastern University in 1962. From 1964 to 1978 he served as chairman of the Department of Music and was Distinguished University Professor from 1978 to 1980. Nadeau is the author of eight books, including *The Symphony: Structure and Style*, and *Listen: A Guide to the Pleasures of Music*. He was a music critic for the *Christian Science Monitor* and has hosted more than three hundred educational television programs on local stations. In 1981, he became the host of "A Note to You," a public radio series broadcast in eighty-five cities, including New York, Boston, Pittsburgh, New Orleans, Cincinnati, and on Australian public radio.

Addison W. Reed, born in 1929, earned A.B., B.S., and M.A. degrees from Kent State University and a Ph.D. in music from the University of North Carolina with the dissertation "The Life and Works of Scott Joplin." He is chairman of the Division of Humanities and the Music Department at Saint Augustine's College in Raleigh, North Carolina. His publications include articles in *The New Grove's Dictionary of Music and Musicians, Piano Quarterly*, and *The Black Perspective in Music*. He was also a contributor to *Black Journals in the United States* (1981). Reed was chosen as a Fulbright-Hays lecturer in Liberia and has performed as a baritone soloist and choral conductor.

Ronald Riddle, born in 1934, holds an A.B. in Music from Antioch College, an M.A. from San Francisco State University, and a Ph.D. in Musicology from the University of Illinois. He also pursued graduate work in composition at Yale University. Riddle has taught at the University of Illinois, New College, and UCLA. He has contributed to the *Encyclopaedia Britannica* and is the author of *Flying Dragons, Flowing Streams: Music in the Life of San Francisco's Chinese* (1983), and articles and papers on Asian and Afro-American music. From 1977 to 1980 he was Editor of the *Society for Ethnomusicology Newsletter*. He has been a professional jazz and popular pianist since 1950.

Lowell H. Schreyer, born in 1929, is Director of the News Bureau at Mankato State University, Mankato, Minnesota, where he earned a B.S. in music. He has been a contributor on banjo and ragtime music to *BMG, FIGA News*, and *The Mississippi Rag*. He is researching a book on the history of the banjo. A performer of the plectrum, tenor, and five-stringed banjos, Schreyer has performed at the Sedalia Ragtime Festival, on the riverboat *Delta Queen*, on educational and commercial television, and with the Rochester (Minnesota) Symphony and the Minnesota Orchestra. He also recorded a banjo selection for *Indiana Ragtime: A Documentary Album* (1981).

Gunther Schuller, born in 1925, is an eminent American composer who has been active as a performer, conductor, educator, jazz scholar, and champion of ragtime, jazz, and new music. He is the author of the acclaimed *Early Jazz* (1968), and was one of the leading figures in the 1970s ragtime revival. Schuller organized and conducts the New England Ragtime Ensemble; arranged most of the Scott Joplin music used in *The Sting* (1974); and arranged, orchestrated, and conducted the Houston Grand Opera production of Joplin's opera *Treemonisha*. President of the New England Conservatory of Music from 1966 to 1977, Schuller now heads the Boston publishing firm of Margun/GunMar Music. He is Artistic Director of the Berkshire Music Center at Tanglewood, and conducts orchestras throughout the United States and Europe while continuing to compose numerous works.

Joseph R. Scotti, born in 1936, earned his B.A. from Depaul University and graduate degrees in musicology from the University of Illinois (M.M.) and the University of Cincinnati College-Conservatory of Music (Ph.D.). His Ph.D. dissertation was on Joseph Lamb. Scotti also has a background in the music industry. He has served as a staff organist for the Wurlitzer Piano and Organ Company, and as an education consultant and staff arranger for the Baldwin Piano and Organ Company. He currently is an assistant professor of music and coordinator of the business music program at Fontbonne College in Saint Louis. He has contributed articles and reviews to *Perspectives of New Music, America*, and other journals.

Trebor Jay Tichenor, born in Saint Louis in 1940, was educated at Washington University (A.B.), where he teaches ragtime history. A leading expert on ragtime, Tichenor coauthored *Rags and Ragtime* (with David A. Jasen, 1978) and compiled two rag folios, *Ragtime Rarities* (1975) and *Ragtime Rediscoveries* (1979). In the 1960s, he coedited *The Ragtime Review*. He owns the world's largest ragtime piano roll collection and a respected cumulation of rag sheet music. He has fifteen records to his name as pianist or producer, and performs regularly with the Saint Louis Ragtimers on the showboat *Goldenrod*, a National Registered Historic Landmark and home of the National Ragtime and Traditional Jazz Festival. Tichenor also hosts a weekly radio program on ragtime.

Marvin L. VanGilder, born in 1926, received a Bachelor of Music degree from Drury College, Springfield, Missouri. During the 1940s he performed as a professional saxophonist with USO troupes and with several regional dance bands. He also has worked as a radio musician, piano teacher, music sales representative, and public school music supervisor. From 1960 to 1979 he was historian and music columnist for the *Carthage* (Missouri) *Press*. He is currently News Director at radio stations KDMO and KRGK in Carthage. VanGilder is the author of numerous newspaper and magazine articles on historical and biographical subjects, as well as two books on local history in Missouri.

Guy Waterman, born in 1932, first learned the ragtime piano repertoire in the late 1940s, with the help and encouragement of Roy Carew. From 1950 to 1953 Waterman performed in Washington, D.C., nightclubs while earning a B.A. in economics at George Washington University. During the 1950s he contributed several essays on the music of ragtime to the magazine *The Record Changer* and to the book *Jazz* (edited by Nat Hentoff and Albert McCarthy). From 1953 to 1970 Waterman worked as an economist and speechwriter, and he currently lives near East Corinth, Vermont.

Index

Index

This index includes subjects, persons, places, and publications mentioned in the text of the book. Illustrations and musical examples are also included. As is customary, the index excludes the material in the bibliography and the other lists in the back of the book. Notes are abbreviated as "n.," so that "68 (n. 29)" refers to note 29 on page 68. Italicized page numbers refer to the main discussion of the entry. Many thanks to Ronald Riddle for compiling the index.

Toad Stool Rag (Lamb), 251
Too Much Mustard, (Macklin), 65, 96
Top Liner Rag (Lamb) 52, 245, 246;
    quoted, 249; syncopation in, 211
Topsy Turvy (Gustin), 163
Totally Different Rag, A (Aufderheide),
    160
Toye, Francis (1883-1964): quoted, 107,
    109
Travis, Merle, 303; quoted, 296-97
Treemonisha (Joplin), 51, 121, 152, 237,
    253; produced, 132-34; recorded,
    202; wins Pulitzer Prize, 134
Trés Moutarde (Too Much Mustard) (Mack-
    lin), 65, 96
Troubadour Rag (Scott), 142; as piano roll,
    98
Troublesome Ivories (Blake), 176
Try and Play It (Ohman), 288
Tucker, Sophie (1884-1966), 23
Turkey in the Straw (Zip Coon) (Dixon?
    Farrell? Nichols?), 222
Turkey in the Straw: A Rag Time Fantasy
    (Bonnell), 96
Turkey trot (dance step), 272
Turn of the Century (TV series), 187
Turpin, Charlie (ca. 1867-1935), 122,
    123
Turpin, Dick, 171
Turpin, "Honest" John, 122, 123
Turpin, Tom (1873-1922), 7, 23, 44, 49,
    84, 122, 123, 126, 150, 232; and
    Morton, 260; and Rosebud Bar, 7,
    21
Tutor for the Banjo (Langey), 61
12th Street Rag (Bowman), 229, 273; as
    country music, 297, 303; as piano
    roll, 96; quoted, cover illus., 230;
    recordings, 28
Twilight Rag (Johnson), 176
Two-step: popularity of, 272
Tyers, William (1876-1924), 151, 172

Ulanov, Barry, A History of Jazz in Amer-
    ica: quoted, 241
Uncle Joe's Cake Dance (Stewart), 60
Under the Anheuser Bush (Sterling and
    Von Tilzer), 74
Under the Bamboo Tree (Cole & Johnson
    Bros.), 74; quoted, 75

Under the Jungle Moon (Madden and Hoff-
    man), 74
Under the Matzos Tree (Fischer), 74
Under the Silv'ry Congo Moon (O'Connor),
    74
Under the Yum Yum Tree (Sterling and
    Von Tilzer), 74
United States Music Co., 95, 97

Valse Parisienne (Roberts), 94
Van Alstyne, Egbert, 23, 148
Van Eps, Fred, 294; comeback (1950s),
    66; as performer, 64-65; photo, 65
VanGilder, Marvin L.: biographical
    note, 380
Veit, Mrs. Russell, 157; quoted, 160
Victory March (Shepherd), 162
Victory Rag (Scott), 142
Votey, Edwin S. (1856-1931), 91

Waiting for the Robert E. Lee (Gilbert and
    Muir), 70, 77
Waldo, Terry (Ralph Emerson Waldo
    III) (b. 1944): biographical note,
    203-04; quoted, 34
Walker, George (1873-1911), 23, 132,
    172
Waller, Thomas "Fats" (1904-43), 80,
    96, 171, 264, 290; and James P.
    Johnson, 166, 167
Wall Street Rag (Joplin): quoted, 234
Walton, William, 81
Waltz. See Ragtime
Warm Reception, A (Anthony), 64; orches-
    tration quoted, 277-79
Washington, Mag, 120
Waterman, Guy: biographical note, 380
Waterman, Richard A., 220; and "hot"
    rhythm, 230-31
Waters, Ethel, 167
Watkins, Phil, 174
Watters, Lu, 202; and ragtime revival
    (1940s), 34
Weary Blues (Matthews), 49, 85
Weber, Max (1864-1920), 112; quoted,
    111
Webern, Anton, 196
Wednesday Night Waltz (Dunn), 296
Wednesday Rag (Dunn), 296
Weeping Willow Rag (Joplin), 46, 50;
    quoted, 224